ADVERTISING

Prentice Hall, Englewood Cliffs, New Jersey 07632

ADVERTISING

Principles
and
Practice

William Wells · John Burnett · Sandra Moriarty

DDB Needham Worldwide   Texas A&M University   University of Colorado

Library of Congress Cataloging-in-Publication Data

Wells, William
   Advertising, principles and practice.

   Bibliography
   Includes index.
      1. Advertising.   I. Burnett, John.
   II. Moriarty, Sandra E. (Sandra Ernst)   III. Title.
   HF5823.W455 1988   659.1   88-25369
   ISBN 0-13-014549-1

Editorial/production supervision: Cheryl Lynn Smith
Interior design: Suzanne Behnke
Development editor: Robert Weiss
Cover design: Lundgren Graphics, Ltd.
Manufacturing buyer: Margaret Rizzi
Page layout: A Good Thing
Photo research: Teri Stratford
Photo editor: Lorinda Morris-Nantz
Ad permission researchers: Hillary Blake and Susan Carter
Chapter opening photos: Chapter 1: Culver Pictures, Inc.   Chapter 2: Marmel Studios/The Stock
Market   Chapter 3: © Teri Stratford, 1988   Chapter 4: Jim Retzer   Chapter 5: FPG
International   Chapter 6: Hewlett Packard   Chapter 7: Craig Hammel/The Stock Market
Chapter 8: The Bettman Archive   Chapters 9, 10, and 11: Prentice Hall   Chapter 12: Alfred
Gescheidt/The Image Bank   Chapter 13: Brownie Harris/The Stock Market   Chapter 14: Jerry
Hummer   Chapter 15: Prentice Hall   Chapter 16: The World of Interiors, Orvis, Harry and
David, The Renovator's Supply, Spiegel, Tiffany & Co., and Bullocks Wilshire   Chapter 17: © Teri
Stratford, 1988   Chapter 18: L'eggs Products, Inc.   Chapter 19: Sailer Ltd.   Chapter 20: ©
Teri Stratford, 1988   Chapter 21: E. Gerhardt/FPG International   Chapter 22: Contel and The
Vertical Club, New York, New York   Chapter 23: The Coca-Cola Company.

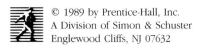

© 1989 by Prentice-Hall, Inc.
A Division of Simon & Schuster
Englewood Cliffs, NJ 07632

Printed in the United States of America

10 9 8 7 6 5 4 3 2 1

ISBN   0-13-014549-1

Prentice-Hall International (UK) Limited, *London*
Prentice-Hall of Australia Pty. Limited, *Sydney*
Prentice-Hall Canada Inc., *Toronto*
Prentice-Hall Hispanoamericana, S.A., *Mexico*
Prentice-Hall of India Private Limited, *New Delhi*
Prentice-Hall of Japan, Inc., *Tokyo*
Prentice-Hall of Southeast Asia Pte. Ltd., *Singapore*
Editora Prentice-Hall do Brasil, Ltda., *Rio de Janeiro*

Overview

Contents

PART ONE

ADVERTISING FOUNDATIONS AND ENVIRONMENT

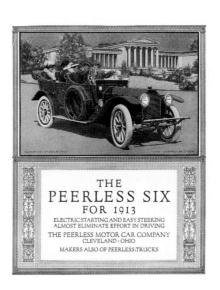

1 Introduction to Advertising 1

PART TWO

ADVERTISING BACKGROUND, PLANNING, AND STRATEGY

5 The Consumer Audience   115

PART THREE

ADVERTISING MEDIA

9 *Media Strategy and Planning* 215

10 *Broadcast Media* 243

11 Print and Other Media   271

12 Media Buying   293

PART FOUR
CREATING ADVERTISING

13   The Creative Process   315

17 *Creating Yellow Pages and Out-of-home Advertising*   433

PART FIVE

ADVERTISING OPERATIONS

PART SIX

MISCELLANEOUS ADVERTISING

22 Corporate, Business-to-Business, and Retail Advertising 535

Preface

ADVERTISING AND THE REAL WORLD

Advertising professionals often question whether this field can be taught from a book. Although nothing compares with the experience of "being there," it is obvious that all college students who want an introduction to advertising cannot work in an advertising agency. The solution, then, is to create a textbook and a teaching package that will bring the real-world experience of advertising alive using paper, ink, pictures, slides, overheads, audiotapes, and videotapes. That is the goal of this textbook.

A World of Experience

The secret to capturing the real world of advertising does not lie in a book or any of the other media involved in this project, but rather in *people and their experiences*—a wide variety of people representing all the different aspects of the diverse field of advertising. In order to provide a real-life view of advertising for a student who wants an introduction to the field, it is necessary to consult and involve specialists from all the different areas, to bring their stories to life, and to record their insight and wisdom. That's what this book attempts to do.

A World of Diversity

Another secret to capturing the real world of advertising is to present the breadth as well as depth of the field. An introductory textbook has an obligation to cover the field as accurately as possible. That does not mean writing about advertising from a business viewpoint, from a marketing viewpoint, or from a creative viewpoint, but instead writing about advertising from an *advertising* viewpoint.

Advertising includes *a variety of disciplines and specialties*. For example, advertising is a major element in a company's marketing plan, so it must dovetail with corporate marketing practices. Furthermore, the field of advertising itself contains such specialties as research, media buying and planning, copywriting, art direction, print and broadcast production, media sales, sales promotion and product publicity, strategic planning, personnel management, budgeting, scheduling, negotiating, and even business presentations. This book will introduce the advertising student to the richness and the variety of the real world of advertising.

The Focus

In the field of advertising you find writers, artists, producers, performers, composers and arrangers, researchers, accountants, salespeople, and managers, to name a few—and all of them are important. The focus of all their efforts, regardless of their professional area of expertise, is on the most effective way to present a sales message to a potential consumer. This is the focus of advertising departments and advertising agencies, of media sales departments and consumer behavior researchers, of national brand advertising managers as well as local entrepreneurs and retailers, of huge global mega-agencies and small creative boutiques. All of these activities are ultimately directed at producing *a message that sells something to someone,* and that, too, is the focus of this book.

Science and Art

No single area in the real world is called "advertising." Instead, advertising is an amalgamation of specialized skills and professions that utilize a number of approaches and philosophies, including scientific, or numbers-oriented; strategic, or problem/solution-oriented; and artistic, or aesthetically-oriented. An introduction to advertising is an introduction to all sides of the advertising field and to the processes—quantitative, strategic, and aesthetic—by which the sales message is planned and produced. This book will attempt to present both *the science and the art* of advertising.

Real World Insights

This book is built upon the work and insights of the stars and giants in the world of advertising. It reflects *advertising as professionals see it*—their theories, their styles and approaches, their rules of thumb, their hindsights and foresights, and their visions. Of course, because not everyone agrees with everyone else in the field, this book presents a variety of approaches, styles, and theories.

An approach upon which advertising professionals seem to agree is presented in this book as *a principle.* Advertising is still a young field, so these principles are evolving and changing as the field develops. The principles, do, however, reflect the current wisdom.

Professionals and Basic Philosophies

Some basic philosophies guide the direction of this book. For example, *the bottom line of advertising,* according to Lou Hagopian, chairman of the N.W. Ayer agency, is to sell more of something. Furthermore, advertising, and the diversity and variety of products that it supports, is an important part of a free-market economy. According to John O'Toole, the American Association of Advertising Agency's representative in Washington, advertising is an important factor in our economic freedom of choice. This book realizes, therefore, that advertising is not only a business itself, but it is an important aspect of business in general.

But advertising is more than just a sales pitch. Bill Bernbach, one of the founders of Doyle, Dane and Bernbach (now DDB Needham Worldwide), brought style and flair to advertising when he insisted that *what* is said is only the beginning: "*How* you say it makes people look and listen." Advertising is an art form because it is able to motivate people and move them emotionally. When it is done well—and admittedly not all advertising is done well—it touches common chords in all of us with carefully composed messages. So an important premise of this book is that *although what is said is important, how it is said is equally as important.*

Advertising professionals can create and deliver sales messages that touch us because they are students of human behavior, the most complicated and fascinating area of study in the world. *Insights into human behavior and respect for people* are absolutely fundamental to good advertising. Unfortunately, not all advertising is good, and not all advertising respects the people it tries to reach, but that is still the goal of the true professionals in the business—and another premise of this book.

John O'Toole explains it best in his book, *The Trouble with Advertising . . . ,* when he says you have to respect the critical faculties of the contemporary consumer. He points to the fact that 66 percent of new products do not make it. They are purchased and evaluated by the public and not bought again, no matter how powerful the advertising might be. He calls the public "these formidable folks whose wrath is so fearful." He describes the implicit contract, or at least understanding, between the advertiser and the public that makes advertising work in a free-market economy:

> I promise you this. My advertising won't lie to you, and it will not deliberately try to mislead you. It won't bore the hell out of you or treat you as though you were a fool or embarrass you or your family. But remember, it's a salesman. It's purpose is to persuade you to trade your hard-earned cash for my product or service.

This then is the purpose of this book—to introduce the real world of advertising—its diversity, its processes and principles, its people, and their professional experiences and ways of thinking.

*L*EARNING AIDS

Many aids are provided within this book to help students learn about advertising. The main ones are:

- *Chapter Objectives.* Each chapter begins with objectives that prepare the student for the chapter material and point out learning goals.
- *Chapter Outline.* A chapter outline is included at the beginning of each chapter.
- *Opening Examples.* Most of the chapters start with a dramatic advertising story that introduces the chapter material and arouses student interest.
- *Full-Color Advertisements, Photographs, and Illustrations.* Throughout the text, key concepts and applications are illustrated with strong, full-color visuals, including over 200 full-color advertisements and 100 color photographs.
- *Principles.* Throughout the text, principles are presented that reflect the current wisdom in the industry, giving students some memorable thoughts about advertising.
- *Inside the Advertising World.* These boxed materials reflect the thoughts and day-to-day activities of advertising professionals in "real-world" terms.
- *Concepts and Controversies.* Throughout the text, controversial issues in advertising are presented in a boxed format.
- *Lifestyle.* Based upon studies conducted by DDB Needham, short profiles of typical consumers are presented throughout the text.
- *Case Studies.* Case studies are presented at the end of each section of the text, illustrating the concepts in preceding chapters.
- *Margin Definitions.* Definitions of key terms are presented in the margins where these terms appear.

*S*UPPLEMENTS

A successful advertising course involves more than a well-written, well-illustrated book. It requires a dedicated teacher and a complete set of supplemental learning and teaching aids. The supplementary materials that have been developed to accompany *ADVERTISING: PRINCIPLES AND PRACTICE* are designed to enhance the classroom experience and to reflect the "real world" of advertising.

- **Annotated Instructor's Edition:** The entire text is annotated with additional examples, suggested activities, lecture outlines, and recommended applications of audio-visual materials. In addition, the front matter of the AIE contains a comprehensive teaching manual with complete lectures, answers to discussion questions and case questions, further suggestions for the use of audio- visual materials, and teaching suggestions for each chapter.
- **Test Item File:** The test item file contains about 2,500 multiple-choice, true-false, and essay questions. These questions are available on floppy disks and through the Prentice Hall Telephone Testing Service.
- **Prentice Hall Videos for Advertising:** A dynamic video program is available to adopters, featuring both exciting vignettes from *Adweek* and a full complement of broadcast commercials from the 1980s.
- **AMTRAK Case Study:** To each copy of the student text is shrinkwrapped a comprehensive case study prepared by AMTRAK and DDB Needham Worldwide. This study illustrates all of the major concepts presented in the text and includes questions for discussion.
- **THE MAKING OF AN ADVERTISING CAMPAIGN:** This book/video package brings to life a complete campaign prepared by Bozell, Jacobs, Kenyon & Eckhardt. Based upon an actual presentation to industry and government leaders in China, the text illustrates the development of the advertising strategy for an image campaign for China and Chinese silk. A video of portions of the original presentation and the broadcast commercials is also provided.

*A*CKNOWLEDGMENTS

ADVERTISING: PRINCIPLES AND PRACTICE has benefitted from an outstanding team of authors and contributors. We wish to acknowledge the assistance of many academics and professionals in bringing the real world of advertising into the text.

Various experts in the industry contributed to the development of parts of the text. We are indebted to Peter Turk of the University of Oklahoma for lending his expertise to the media sections of the text. We would also like to thank Mike White and Kevin Killian of DDB Needham for their assistance with the media chapters and Kris Hartzell and Susan Fignar of DDB Needham for their help in obtaining artwork and photographs.

William Novelli of Doremus Porter Novelli provided material and expertise for the public relations chapter. We would like to thank Ellen Eisner of this agency for her assistance as well.

Tom Duncan of Ball State University and Betty Reeder provided assistance with the chapter on retail and business-to-business advertising. Edward Forrest and C. Edward Wotring contributed to advertising research, Denise Smart of Texas A&M University assisted with ethics and regulation, and Norval Stephens of the Norval Stephens Company provided a wealth of experience in the areas of advertising agencies and international advertising. Jerry Johnson of Hill, Holliday, Connors, Cosmopulos and Victoria Winston of WANG were instrumental in supplying materials for the campaigns chapter. Stan Rapp of Rapp & Collins, Lee

Mathews of Bernard Hodes, and Michael James Smith of Lands' End contributed to the direct-response chapter.

Numerous people assisted in the preparation of the case studies. The Honda case was provided by Gerry Rubin of Rubin and Postaer. The Hamburger Helper case was provided by Jack Stratton of General Mills. The Clorox case was provided by Bob Johnson of Clorox. The Chester Cheetah case was provided by Frito Lay. The Blood Center case was provided by Ronald Franzmeier of the Blood Center of Southeastern Wisconsin. The Xerox case was supplied by Michael E. G. Kirby of Xerox.

Many thanks to Bill Norman of AMTRAK and Roy Lancaster of DDB Needham for preparing the AMTRAK Case Study that accompanies this text.

No text can be successfully developed without a supportive publisher. The team at Prentice Hall helped to develop both the text and the supplementary package. We express our gratitude to Robert Weiss, for his unfailing dedication to development; Deborah Garvin, for insightful market research; Whitney Blake, for putting the team together and overseeing the project; Cheryl Smith, for patience during a hectic production process; Hillary Blake and Susan Carter, for help with the endless permission requests and art program; Irwin Zucker and Ann Torbert, for aiding in the development of different parts of the text; Sue Behnke, for design; Lorinda Morris-Nantz and Teri Stratford, for photo research; and Jim Edwards and Lori Drazien, for developing the promotional program.

Many reviewers provided helpful comments on three drafts of the manuscript and attended focus groups. Their time and thoughtful comments are appreciated.

Edd Applegate
Middle Tennessee State University

Linda Baker
Highline Community College

Ann Marie Barry
Boston College

Tim Bengston
University of Kansas

Lucia Blinn
DDB Needham Worldwide

Larry Bowen
University of Washington

Thomas Bowers
University of North Carolina

Hugh Daubek
Central Michigan University

Michael Dotson
Appalachian State University

Nathan Himelstein
Essex County College

Darwin Krumrey
Kirkwood Community College

Priscilla LaBarbera
New York University

Harry Marsh
Kansas State University

H. Neal
County College of Morris

Charles Pearce
Kansas State University

Kathy Smith
Towson State University

Margery Steinberg
University of Hartford

James Taylor
California State University—Fullerton

Donald Vance
University of Miami

Joan Weiss
Bucks County Community College

Gary Wilcox
University of Texas—Austin

Anthony Zahorik
Vanderbilt University

About the Authors

William Wells

William Wells—Bill Wells, Executive Vice President and Director of Marketing Services at DDB Needham Chicago, is one of the industry's leading market and research authorities. He is, in fact, the only representative of the advertising business elected to the Attitude Research Hall of Fame. He earned a Ph.D. from Stanford University and was formerly Professor of Psychology and Marketing at the University of Chicago. He then joined Needham, Harper, Chicago as Director of Corporate Research. He is author of the Needham Harper Lifestyle Study as well as author of over sixty books and articles. In addition to *Advertising: Principles and Practice,* he will also publish *Planning for R.O.I.: Effective Advertising Strategy* (Prentice Hall) in 1989. ▪

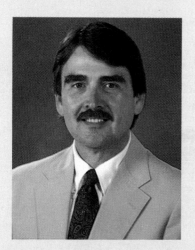

John Burnett

John Burnett—John Burnett is an Associate Professor of Marketing at Texas A&M University. He holds a D.B.A. Degree in Marketing from the University of Kentucky. He is author of *Promotion Management,* now in its second edition. In addition, he has authored numerous articles and papers in a wide variety of professional and academic journals. In particular, his research has examined the effectiveness of emotional appeals in advertising and how various segments respond to such strategies. He is an active consultant in marketing and advertising and has served as a consulting professor for AT&T, The Dallas Mart, and the AAFES organization. He has won several teaching awards and serves as faculty advisor for student chapters of the American Marketing Association. ▪

Sandra Moriarty

Sandra Moriarty—Formerly a copywriter, and then owner of her own agency, Sandra has been teaching at the university level since 1968. A journalism major at the University of Missouri, she worked in advertising and public relations before moving into academics. She started teaching part time while directing a program in university relations at Kansas State University, then moved to full-time teaching after completing her Ph.D. in educational communication. Before moving to the University of Colorado, she taught at the University of Kansas and Michigan State University. She is author of five books, including *Creative Advertising* (1986), and many professional articles in such areas as typography, the creative side of advertising, advertising presentations, agency approaches to effective advertising, and advertising management. She also has published numerous scholarly research reports in such areas as creative thinking, cognitive theory and communication, typography, graphic design, and visual communication. ▪

The Team

Thomas R. Duncan

Dr. Duncan provided expertise in the area of retail advertising. He is head of the advertising sequence at Ball State University. He has also held positions with Jeno's, as Vice President of Marketing, with Peter Eckrich as General Manager of Marketing Services, and with Leo Burnett as Account Executive.

Edward Forrest

Professor Forrest provided assistance with the material on advertising research. He currently teaches in the advertising sequence at Florida State University, Tallahassee.

William D. Novelli

Bill Novelli provided assistance with the material on public relations. He is president of Doremus Porter Novelli, one of the largest public relations agencies worldwide and the lead agency of the Omnicom PR Network. He regularly teaches courses at the University of Maryland. Bill holds undergraduate and graduate degrees from the University of Pennsylvania and did postgraduate work at New York University.

R. Charles Pearce

Dr. Pearce acted as supplements coordinator, responsible for the development of the Annotated Instructor's Edition and the entire ancillary package. Dr. Pearce obtained his Ph.D in Advertising from the University of Tennessee-Knoxville and has taught at several colleges, including his current position at Kansas State University.

Elizabeth Reeder

Dr. Reeder provided expertise in the area of business-to-business advertising. She received an M.S. degree from the University of Arizona and teaches advertising and marketing courses at Cameron University. She is an author of *Industrial Marketing: Analysis, Planning, and Control,* Prentice Hall, 1987.

Denise T. Smart

Professor Smart provided assistance with the material on advertising ethics and regulation. She is currently visiting assistant professor at Texas A&M University. She received her Ph.D from Texas A&M University and teaches in advertising and marketing.

Norval B. Stephens, Jr.

Norval Stephens provided assistance with the material on advertising agencies and international advertising. He has spent over 35 years in marketing, including his most recent position as chief operating officer of the International Division of DDB Needham Worldwide.

Peter B. Turk

Dr. Turk is an associate professor at the University of Oklahoma, and he is currently visiting at the University of Akron. He received his Ph.D in Mass Communication Law from the University of Wisconsin. He is the author of numerous articles and books, including *Advertising Media Research Sourcebook,* National Textbook Company, Fall 1988.

C. Edward Wotring

Professor Wotring provided assistance with the material on advertising research. He currently teaches in the advertising sequence at Florida State University, Tallahassee.

ALBRIGHT ART GALLERY, BUFFALO   "38-SIX" FIVE-PASSENGER TOURING

THE
PEERLESS SIX
FOR 1913

ELECTRIC STARTING AND EASY STEERING
ALMOST ELIMINATE EFFORT IN DRIVING

THE PEERLESS MOTOR CAR COMPANY
CLEVELAND · OHIO

MAKERS ALSO OF PEERLESS TRUCKS

1

Introduction to Advertising

Chapter Outline

Chapter Objectives

When you have completed this chapter you should be able to:

- Define advertising and discuss its component parts
- Identify the five types of advertising
- Explain the four roles of advertising
- Identify the three key players in the advertising world
- Explain the impact on advertising of the invention of new media forms such as print, radio, and television
- Relate key figures in the history of advertising to their contributions to the field
- Understand the difference between "hard-sell" and "soft-sell" advertising messages

*W*HAT MAKES AN AD GREAT?

You have been looking at ads in newspapers and magazines since you learned to read. You have been watching television commercials ever since you can remember. What ads do you recall best? Think about it. Get out a piece of paper and start a list. Which ones have caught your attention? Which are your favorites?

Several companies ask people questions just like these. *Advertising Age,* working with the SRI Research Center, conducts a monthly "AdWatch" survey of advertising awareness. Video Storyboard Tests asks consumers to list the most outstanding print advertisements and television commercials. *Advertising Age* also interviews top creative people regularly to identify ads professionals think are the most effective. The advertising industry evaluates its work through such programs as the Clios, Effies, and Addy Awards.

Classics

Your favorite ads are often the same as those named by consumers and professionals. Certain ads are simply outstanding; they are classics in their time. Some are from campaigns that have been running for a long time. Others are single ads or campaigns that have been around for only a short time. You might be surprised to learn that your favorites are, in many cases, also the ads that produce the highest level of sales response for the advertiser. Good ads work on two levels: They entertain while they deliver a selling message.

The California Raisins "I Heard It Through the Grapevine" commercials, for example, dominated the AdWatch awareness studies in 1986, 1987, and 1988 (see Ad 1.1). The catchy music and the parody of a rhythm-and-blues singing group performing a 1960s hit have made this campaign a favorite of consumers and professionals alike.

AD 1.1
This popular commercial for California raisins was created through a process called claymation.
(Courtesy of THE CALIFORNIA RAISINS™, © 1987 CalRab. Licensed by Applause Licensing.)

AD 1.2
Bud Light has developed a series of humorous ads built around the phrase "Give me a light."
(Courtesy of Anheuser-Busch, Inc.)

Two beer campaigns have topped the AdWatch charts for years. The Bud Light commercials have been using a series of humorous and inventive visual puns on the word "light" since 1983. While they are entertaining, they also hammer home a strong message of brand identity. Since 1975 Bud's chief competitor, Miller Lite, has exposed us to the funny, even crazy, side of "tough-guy" sports heros and show business personalities to position a low-calorie beer as acceptable for the macho drinker.

Spokespersons and celebrities have been an important part of many classic ads. Bill Cosby is a successful presenter for a number of companies, and his long-standing relationship with Jell-O has produced a number of winning ads. The use of "Mean Joe Greene," a tough football player who gets soft-hearted when a young fan offers him a Coke, produced a commercial that received some of the highest recall scores ever recorded.

Ed and Frank, two invented but believable characters for Bartles and Jaymes Wine Coolers, have become well-loved stars in their own continuing miniseries. Their "Baseball Tips" commercial, which ran for 2 weeks around the time of the World Series, reached and affected three times as many people as the average commercial.

AD 1.3
The fast-talking executive provides humor in this Federal Express ad.

(© 1981 Federal Express Corporation.)

These campaigns are widely remembered, not only because they are entertaining, but also because they involve viewers and make them wonder what the campaigns' creators will come up with next. The campaigns also use humor, ranging from soft and gentle to outrageous. Humor is an important part of some of the other all-time great ads, such as the Federal Express ad featuring the fast-talking executive (see Ad 1.3). Underneath the funny characterizations, however, the Federal Express ads carry a hard-hitting message of dependability: "When it absolutely, positively has to be there overnight."

Great ads often touch emotions other than humor. The AT&T/Long Distance Service, "Reach Out and Touch Someone" campaign has been touching emotions since 1979. The messages are warm and sentimental, but, more than that, they communicate the idea that it's easy and rewarding to call friends and family at any time.

Other outstanding ads have created memorable characters. Inspector 12 has been holding up the standards for Hanes underwear since 1980. Mikey, the finicky little boy who doesn't like anything, made viewers like Life cereal. The original commercial first ran in 1971 and was brought back in 1981. Even though the original Mikey is now grown, the commercial has maintained its appeal for several generations of Life consumers.

Children, cats, and puppy dogs are lovable and give a product warm associations. The Oscar Mayer kids have been singing the product's theme song since 1973. The sing-along music contributes to the Oscar Mayer success story.

Often the characters are fictional, like Ed and Frank and Inspector 12. Some of them, like Charlie the Tuna and the Jolly Green Giant, are total fantasy. But all these characters capture the "inherent drama" of the product. Imagine yourself an advertiser who wants to position vegetables to make them acceptable to children. Why not use a cartoon character like a giant to promote them? But giants are fearsome, you think, so how do I make this character appealing to kids? Make him "Jolly." This way a complex message is built into a single cartoon character.

Drama is often an important aspect of successful advertising. One of the most dramatic advertisements ever produced was a commercial for the launch of the Apple MacIntosh computer that took on Apple's most serious competitor, IBM. The stark images of the classic George Orwell novel *1984* (Ad 1.4) came alive in this commercial, which only ran once, on the Super Bowl before 100 million viewers. Not only was this ad a captivating drama, it also demonstrated the power of an effective media buy.

Significant images—that's another important part of advertising. The Mountain Dew campaign (Ad 1.5) has used a stream of successful commercials that depict the lifestyle of the intended audience, teenagers. Since 1980 these commercials have been showing active, lively, appealing teens having fun. But more than that, the water-oriented recreation scenes also say "refreshing," and the imagery is heightened by excellent photography and slow-motion shots of attractive young people in water. An even more effective visual was the Nestea "plunge" that overwhelmed the viewer with the feeling of refreshment.

Perhaps the most successful image advertising of all time, however, is the Marlboro campaign, which has been running since 1955. With overwhelming single-mindedness the campaign has focused on western imagery with cowboys, horses, and ranching. The cowboy myth is a strong and compelling image. This

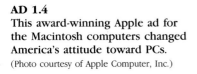

AD 1.4
This award-winning Apple ad for the Macintosh computers changed America's attitude toward PCs.
(Photo courtesy of Apple Computer, Inc.)

AD 1.5
One of a series of Mountain Dew ads that were directed toward a teenage audience.
(Courtesy of Pepsi Cola Company.)

campaign has been successful both as communication and as a marketing effort. It has helped to make Marlboro the best-selling cigarette in the world.

Characteristics of Great Ads

So what do you think makes an ad great? And what turns great ads into classics? What makes certain ads stand out in people's minds? And why do some ads continue to run for years, sometimes even for decades? From this discussion it should be clear that great advertising employs a variety of techniques: celebrities and spokespersons, fantasy characters, children and puppies, music, drama, significant imagery, and creative media buying. Advertising is complicated, and the rest of this book will try to explain how all of these factors are interwoven to create great advertising. The premise of this book, however, is that three broad dimensions characterize great advertising: strategy, creativity, and execution. This book is built around these three dimensions.

Strategy Every great ad has to be strategically sound. In other words, it is carefully directed to a certain audience, it is driven by specific objectives, its message is crafted to speak to that audience's most important concerns, and it is run in media that will most effectively reach that audience. The measure of an ad's success is how well it achieves its goals, whether they be increased sales, memorability, attitude change, or brand awareness.

The Mountain Dew commercials, for example, are perfectly on target for the teenage audience. The crazy characters and situations in the Federal Express ads bring to life a very important selling premise about the essence of dependability. Miller Lite ads assure men that it is acceptable to drink a low-calorie beer. Mikey likes Life, so it must be good.

Creativity The *creative concept* is a central idea that gets your attention and sticks in your memory. Every one of the ads we've discussed has a "Big Idea" that is creative and original. The Bud Light visual play on the word "light" is a captivating idea. Frank and Ed are totally unique characters, as is the Jolly Green Giant.

A concern for creative thinking drives the entire field of advertising. Planning the strategy calls for creative problem solving; the research efforts are creative; the buying and placing of ads in the media are creative. Advertising is an exciting field because of the constant demand for creative solutions to media and message problems.

Execution Finally every great ad is well executed. That means the craftsmanship is impressive. The details, the techniques, and the production values have all been fine-tuned. Many of these techniques are experimental, such as the dancing claymation raisins and the electronic effects used in the Bud Light "lights." But there is more to execution than technology. The warm touch in the AT&T commercials is a delicate emotional effect. It is sensitive without being overly sentimental or manipulative.

Good advertisers know that how you say it is just as important as what you say. *What you say* comes from strategy, while *how you say it* is a product of creativity and execution. The great ads, then, are ads that (1) are strategically sound, (2) have an original creative concept, and (3) use exactly the right execution for the message. Strategy, creativity, and execution—these are the qualities that turn great ads into classics.

*T*HE WORLD OF ADVERTISING

Reaching the Consumer

In an ideal world every manufacturer would be able to talk one-on-one with every consumer about the product or service being offered for sale. Personal selling approaches that idea, but it is very expensive. Calls made by salespeople can cost well in excess of $150.

Marketers who have products and services for sale get around the cost of personal contact by using mass media to convey their messages. There the costs,

AD 1.6
A classic "Mikey" ad for life cereal.
(Courtesy of The Quaker Oats Company.)

for *time* in broadcast media and for *space* in print media, are spread over the tremendous number of people that these media reach. For example, $650,000 may sound like a lot of money for one ad on the Super Bowl, but when you consider that the advertisers are reaching over 100 million people, the cost is not extreme.

Defining Advertising

So what is advertising? What are its important dimensions? From this discussion it should be obvious that advertising is a *paid form of communication,* although some forms of advertising, such as public service, use donated space and time. Not only is the message paid for, but the *sponsor is identified.* In some cases the point of the message is simply to make consumers aware of a product or company, although most advertising tries *to persuade or influence* the consumer to do something. The message is conveyed through many different kinds of *mass media* reaching a large *audience* of potential consumers. Because advertising is a form of mass communication, it is also *nonpersonal.* A definition of **advertising,** then, would include all five of those features:

> Advertising is *paid nonpersonal communication* from an identified *sponsor* using *mass media* to persuade or influence an *audience.*

advertising *Paid communication from an identified sponsor using mass media to persuade or influence an audience.*

Types of Advertising

Advertising is complex because so many diverse advertisers try to reach so many different types of audiences.

Brand Advertising   The most visible type of advertising is *national consumer advertising.* Another name for this is *brand advertising.* The message focuses on a product that is manufactured and distributed nationally. It concentrates on developing a distinctive brand image for that product.

Retail Advertising   In contrast, *retail advertising* is local and focuses on the store where a variety of products can be purchased or where a service is offered.

AD 1.7
Bill Cosby has become a popular spokesperson for Jell-O.
(© 1988 General Foods Corporation.)

The message announces products that are available locally, stimulates store traffic, and tries to create a distinctive image for the store. Retail advertising emphasizes price, availability, location, and hours of operation.

Direct-Response Advertising   Direct-response advertising can use any advertising medium, including direct mail, but the message is different from that of national and retail advertising in that it tries to stimulate a sale directly. The consumer can respond by telephone or mail, and the product is delivered directly to the consumer by mail or some other carrier.

Business-to-Business Advertising   Business-to-business advertising includes messages directed at retailers, wholesalers, and distributors, as well as industrial purchasers and professionals such as lawyers and physicians.

Institutional Advertising   Institutional advertising is also called corporate advertising. The focus of these messages is on establishing a corporate identity or on winning the public over to the company or organization's point of view.

Public Service Advertising   Public service advertising communicates a message on behalf of some good cause, such as a drug-free America or preventing child abuse. These advertisements are created for free by advertising professionals, and the space and time are donated by the media.

As you can see, there isn't just one kind of advertising; in fact, advertising is a large and varied industry. All of these areas demand creative, original messages that are strategically sound and well executed. In the chapters to come all of these types of advertising will be discussed in more depth.

Roles of Advertising

Advertising can also be explained in terms of the functions it has in business and in society. Four different roles have been identified for advertising:

1. Marketing role
2. Communication role
3. Economic role
4. Societal role

The Marketing Role   Along with sales promotion, public relations, and personal selling, advertising is one of the vehicles employed by a business or an organization to communicate to its customers. Although advertising is only one element in a company's overall promotional program, it is the most visible. The marketing role will be discussed in depth in Chapter 3.

The Communication Role   Advertising is a form of mass communication. It transmits different types of market information to match buyers and sellers in the marketplace. Advertising both informs and transforms the product by creating an image that goes beyond straightforward facts. Specific suggestions about how to accomplish these tasks will be discussed in later chapters on creating messages.

The Economic Role   The two major schools of thought concerning the effects of advertising on the economy are the market power school and the market competition school.*

*John M. Vernon, "Concentration, Promoting, and Market Share Stability in the Pharmaceutical Industry," *Journal of Industrial Economics,* July 1971, pp. 146–266.

TABLE 1.1
The Market Power and Market Competition Schools

	Advertising = Market Power		Advertising = Market Competition
Advertising affects consumer preferences and tastes, changes product attributes, and differentiates the product from competitive offerings.	**Advertising**		Advertising informs consumers about product attributes and does not change the way they value these attributes.
Consumers become brand loyal and less price sensitive, and perceive fewer substitutes for advertised brands.	**Consumer Buying Behavior**		Consumers become more price sensitive and buy best "value." Only the relationship between price and quality affects elasticity for a given product.
Potential entrants must overcome established brand loyalty and spend relatively more on advertising.	**Barriers to Entry**		Advertising makes entry possible for new brands because it can communicate product attributes to consumers.
Firms are insulated from market competition and potential rivals; concentration increases, leaving firms with more discretionary power.	**Industry Structure and Market Power**		Consumers can compare competitive offerings easily and competitive rivalry is increased. Efficient firms remain, and as the inefficient leave and new entrants appear, the effect on concentration is ambiguous.
Firms can charge higher prices and are not as likely to compete on quality or price dimensions. Innovation may be reduced.	**Market Conduct**		More informed consumers put pressure on firms to lower prices and improve quality. Innovation is facilitated via new entrants.
High prices and excessive profits accrue to advertisers and give them even more incentive to advertise their products. Output is restricted compared to conditions of perfect competition.	**Market Performance**		Industry prices are decreased. The effect on profits from increased competition and increased efficiency is ambiguous.

Reprinted with permission of the publisher from Mark S. Albion, *Advertising's Hidden Effects: Manufacturers Advertising and Retail Pricing,* Dover, MA, Auburn House, 1983, p. 18.

market power school *The view of advertising as a persuasive communications tool that marketers use to distract the consumer's attention away from price.*

THE MARKET POWER SCHOOL   The **market power school** views advertising as a persuasive communication tool that marketers use to reduce consumer concern about price. This distraction enables marketers to gain market power. How is it done?

The market power school believes that advertising is able to differentiate similar products on characteristics other than price. By changing consumer tastes, marketers can encourage brand loyalty and reduce consumer sensitivity to price differences. Eventually, according to this model, expenditures on advertising will be profitable as consumers are convinced to remain loyal to a particular brand, even when it is offered at a higher price. Moreover, the advertising expenses necessary to enter the field will discourage competitors.

market competition school *The view of advertising as an information source that increases consumers' price sensitivity and stimulates competition among firms.*

THE MARKET COMPETITION SCHOOL   The second model, known as the **market competition school,** takes a very different approach. This model regards advertising primarily as an information source that increases consumers' price sensitivity and stimulates competition among firms. By increasing competition, advertising lowers prices and reduces the likelihood of monopolistic market conditions. The more information consumers have, the more likely they are to explore options and find a lower price.* These two perspectives are summarized in Table 1.1.

*Stanley I. Ornstein, *Industrial Concentration and Advertising Intensity* (Washington, DC: American Enterprise Institute, 1977), pp. 2–3.

INFORMED CONSUMERS   Actually, little is known about the true nature of advertising in the economy. Charles Sandage, an advertising professor, provides a different perspective. He sees the economic role of advertising as "helping society to achieve abundance by informing and persuading members of society with respect to products, services, and ideals.* In addition, he argues that advertising assists in "the development of judgment on the part of consumers in their purchase practices."

The Societal Role

Advertising has a number of social roles. It informs us about new and improved products and teaches us how to use these innovations. It helps us compare products and features and make informed consumer decisions. It mirrors fashion and design trends and contributes to our aesthetic sense.

Advertising tends to flourish in societies that enjoy some level of economic abundance, that is, in which supply exceeds demand. It is at this point that advertising also moves from being a simple informational service (telling consumers where they can find the product) to being a message designed to create a demand for a particular brand.

The question is: Does advertising follow trends or lead them? At what point does advertising cross the line between *reflecting* social values and *creating* social values? Critics argue that advertising has repeatedly crossed this line and has evolved into an instrument of social control. Although these concerns are not new, the increasing power of advertising, both in terms of money (we spend more annually educating consumers than we spend educating our children) and in terms of communication dominance (the mass media can no longer survive without advertising support), has made these concerns more prominent than ever.

Economic and Social Issues

A number of questions about advertising's effect on the economy and the society are highly debatable and can best be answered with, "It depends."

ADVERTISING AND PRICES   Does advertising raise or lower prices? The answer varies according to the type of advertising and the product being marketed. Some studies have found that national advertising raises the price of goods, whereas retail advertising does the opposite.† But this generalization does not always hold true. For certain product categories such as gasoline, drugs, and soap, high levels of advertising can lower consumer brand prices.

Does advertising lower costs for large companies through economies of scale, and, if so, how does that affect price? Simply stated, **economies of scale** suggests that firms producing large quantities of goods gain substantial cost savings that create a much lower dollar cost per unit produced. To the extent that advertising increases the demand for a product, it enables a company to save money by maintaining a high level of production.

Advertising also has the potential to reduce marketing costs. For example, several insurance companies have replaced more costly salespeople with less expensive mass advertising. Likewise products can be distributed less expensively when consumers have been presold through advertising. In the case of products such as VCRs, computers, and televisions, production and marketing cost savings have been passed on to the consumer in the form of lower prices.

economies of scale *A system in which firms are able to create a lower dollar cost per unit by producing larger quantities of goods.*

*Charles H. Sandage, "Some Institutional Aspects of Advertising," *Journal of Advertising,* Vol. 1, No. 1 (1973), p. 9.

†Vincent P. Norris, "The Economic Effects of Advertising: A Review of Literature," in *Current Issues and Research in Advertising,* James H. Leigh and Claude Martin, Jr., eds. (Ann Arbor: Graduate School of Business Administration, University of Michigan, 1984), p. 93.

economic concentration *The relative size and strength of firms within a given industry.*

demand *The quantity of goods or services that consumers are willing and able to buy at various prices.*

ADVERTISING AND ECONOMIC CONCENTRATION   Does advertising affect economic concentration? **Economic concentration** refers to the relative size and strength of firms within a given industry. High economic concentration means that a few large firms dominate a market. Some critics have claimed that advertising causes high concentration levels and that advertising inequalities explain the largest differences in market concentration. The evidence for this conclusion is mixed.* There are probably specific industries and situations where advertising leads to higher levels of concentration, but we do not have evidence that this is the case in all, or even many, industries.

ADVERTISING AND DEMAND   Demand is not the same as sales, which are measured in physical units or dollars of revenue. **Demand** is a schedule of the various quantities of a good or service that consumers are willing and able to buy at various prices. Many people believe that advertising influences demand in two ways: (1) it increases consumption; and (2) it creates false demands.

The idea that advertising increases consumption and, consequently, employment, national income, and the standard of living has been debated for over 50 years. Again, evidence to support this claim is inconclusive.

Does advertising create false demands? Both economists and social critics have expressed concern about the possibility that advertising can persuade people to purchase products or services that they neither need nor want. Examples range from novelty items such as Pet Rocks and T-shirts to sports cars. Although advertising can help to convince people to try a new product, other factors influence purchases, including word of mouth, product performance, and price. Peter Kyle, economist at Cambridge, studied the demand for food, tobacco,

TABLE 1.2
A List of the Top 25 U.S.
Advertisers for 1986

Rank	Company	Ad Spending
1	Procter & Gamble Co.	$1,435,454
2	Philip Morris Cos.	1,364,472
3	Sears, Roebuck & Co.	1,004,708
4	RJR Nabisco	935,036
5	General Motors Corp.	839,000
6	Ford Motor Co.	648,500
7	Anheuser-Busch Cos.	643,522
8	McDonald's Corp.	592,000
9	K mart Corp.	590,350
10	PepsiCo Inc.	581,309
11	General Mills	551,561
12	Warner-Lambert Co.	548,726
13	BCI Holdings	535,852
14	Unilever N.V.	517,746
15	J.C. Penney Co.	496,241
16	Pillsbury Co.	494,877
17	Ralston Purina Co.	478,031
18	American Telephone & Telegraph	439,919
19	Kraft Inc.	437,952
20	Chrysler Corp.	426,000
21	Johnson & Johnson	410,672
22	American Home Products Corp.	395,718
23	Kellogg Co.	374,142
24	Coca-Cola Co.	370,379
25	General Electric Co.	354,250

Source: "Ad Growth Edges Up," *Advertising Age,* September 24, 1987, p. 1. Reprinted with permission from *Advertising Age.* Copyright Crain Communications, Inc. All rights reserved.

*David A. Aaker and John G. Meyers, *Advertising Management* (Englewood Cliffs, NJ: Prentice Hall, 1975), pp. 559–60; Ornstein, *Industrial Concentration and Advertising,* pp. 5–10; Lester G. Telser, "Advertising and Competition," *Journal of Political Economy,* December 1964, pp. 537–62; Jules Backman, *Advertising and Competition* (New York: New York University Press, 1967), pp. 40–45, 155–67.

clothing, automobiles, and alcohol in the United Kingdom and concluded, "No market showed advertising to have any effect upon its size."*

ADVERTISING AND MANIPULATION   Can advertising manipulate people? Some critics argue that advertising has the power to dictate how people behave. They believe that, even if an individual ad cannot control our behavior, the cumulative effects of nonstop television, radio, print, and outdoor ads can be overwhelming.

Although certain groups of people, such as young children, the less educated, and the elderly, might be more susceptible to certain kinds of advertising, it is hard to conclude that a particular ad or series of ads caused, tricked, or coerced anyone into making a particular buying decision. There is no solid evidence for the manipulative power of advertising because so many other factors contribute to the choices we make.

Although advertising does attempt to persuade, most people are aware that advertisers are biased in favor of their own products and learn how to handle persuasive advertising in their daily lives. Manipulation and other ethical issues will be discussed in more detail in Chapter 2.

*T*HE THREE PLAYERS

In addition to the types of advertising and advertising's various roles, advertising can be defined in terms of those who play important roles in bringing ads to you. The three primary players in the advertising world are:

1. The advertiser
2. The advertising agency
3. The media

The Advertiser

advertiser *The individual or organization that initiates the advertising process.*

PRINCIPLE
The advertiser makes the final decisions.

Advertising begins with the **advertiser.** This individual or organization usually initiates the advertising process. Likewise this individual or organization makes the final decisions as to the audience to whom the advertising will be directed, the media in which it will appear, the size of the advertising budget, and the duration of the campaign.

No one knows exactly how much money is spent annually by advertisers. In 1987 U.S. advertising expenditures exceeded $109 billion and were expected to increase to almost $120 billion in 1988, partly because of the Olympics and the presidential elections.† This figure includes all components of advertising: media costs, production, talent, and so forth.

Table 1.2 lists the major advertisers in the United States. Procter & Gamble was the leader with over $1.4 billion, followed by Philip Morris. Sears was the leading retailer, spending over $1 billion. Even the U.S. government, because of ads for its various military branches and certain government agencies, was a major advertiser with expenditures of over $300 million.‡

Types of Advertisers   There are a number of different types of advertisers. Some manufacture the product or service; others sell manufacturers' products to the ultimate consumer; some use advertising to represent themselves and the services they provide; and others provide a service to the public. The various

*Peter Kyle, "The Impact of Advertising on Markets," *International Journal of Advertising Research* 1 (October–December 1982), pp. 345–59.
†"Ad Spending Expected to Increase 9% in 1988," *Marketing News,* January 18, 1988, pp. 1–20.
‡C. Craig Endicott, "Ad Growth Edges Up," *Advertising Age,* September 24, 1987, p. 1.

PAT CAFFERATA, PRESIDENT AND CEO
YOUNG & RUBICAM, CHICAGO

As chief executive officer of the advertising firm of Young & Rubicam, Chicago, Pat Cafferata becomes involved in various advertising activities with clients throughout the country. Below Pat describes a typically hectic day in the world of advertising.

5:30 A.M.   Arose.

              Stopped at 7-Eleven on way to work to pick up *Chicago Tribune* and peruse the business section, especially George Lazarus's column on up-to-the-minute changes and happenings in advertising and marketing.

8:00 A.M.   Attended breakfast meeting of the Chicago Advertising Club. Agreed to chair the Chicago Advertising Person of the Year Event, a black-tie affair for 500 advertising, marketing, and media executives.

9:15 A.M.   Arrived at my office and quickly made calls to Y&R corporate offices in New York regarding administrative and financial issues.

9:30 A.M.   Held strategy review meeting for new Montgomery Ward creative. Meeting revealed that more research was needed to arrive at good strategy.

10:15 A.M.   Looked at rough cuts of new Garcia y Vega television commercials. Discussed what revisions were needed before presenting rough cuts to client the next day in New York.

11:00 A.M.   Went over activities of the day and week with secretary: decided on location for office Christmas party; discussed new decor for office lobby; discussed secretarial problems; called in office manager to help solve secretarial issues; finalized travel arrangements for new business trip to Phoenix day after tomorrow.

12:00 P.M.   Reviewed materials to be presented to Heileman client at 1 P.M. Helped creatives rehearse their presentation of storyboards. Helped account management people organize agenda for meeting. (Suggested that the Conference Room be tidied up prior to client's arrival.)

1:00 P.M.   Had luncheon meeting with Heileman client to review storyboards, production costs, and schedule for television production.

2:30 P.M.   Returned phone calls (one client, two employees, New York office training person,

president of Frankfurt office, headhunter, *AdWeek* reporter. Only reached two of seven people called. Left messages for them to call me back.) Signed two letters to new business prospects.

3:15 P.M.   Had meeting to review new business presentation to be made next week. Listened to research and media reviews and discussed alternative strategies for presentation.

5:30 P.M.   Attended cocktail party with The Chicago Network, a group of Chicago women in management positions.

6:45 P.M.   Drove home. Prepared dinner quickly so I could watch *Cheers* and *Night Court* on television.

(Courtesy of Pat Cafferata.)

businesses that perform these tasks fall into four categories: manufacturers; resellers; individuals; and institutions. These will all be discussed in Chapter 3.

How Advertisers Manage Advertising   Large advertisers, either companies or organizations, are involved in the advertising process in one of two ways: (1) through their advertising department, or (2) through their in-house agency.

THE ADVERTISING DEPARTMENT   The most common organizational arrangement in a large business is the *advertising department*. The primary corporate responsibility for advertising lies with the *advertising manager,* or *advertising director,* who usually reports to the *director of marketing.* In the typical multiple-brand, consumer-products company, responsibility is divided by brand, with each brand managed by a *brand manager.* The brand manager is the business leader for the brand and has the ultimate responsibility for sales, product development, budget, and profits, as well as for advertising and other promotions. The brand manager, or advertising director, along with the advertising agency, develops the advertising strategy.

The advertising is usually presented by the agency to the brand manager and the director of advertising. The director of advertising, a specialist in recognizing and supporting effective advertising, advises the brand manager. Frequently the advertising director is responsible for approving advertising before it undergoes preliminary testing with real consumers.

The advertising manager organizes and staffs the advertising department, selects the advertising agency, and coordinates efforts with other departments within the company and businesses outside the organization. The advertising manager is also in charge of advertising control, which involves checking on such things as: Have the ads been run? At the right time? Right size? Right place? Was the ad produced exactly the way the company wanted? Was the work done within the budget? And, most importantly, did the advertisement reach its objectives?

Who performs these tasks varies with the industry and the size of the business. The small retailer, for example, might have one person (often the owner) laying out the ad, writing the copy, and selecting the media. Physical production of the ad may be farmed out to free-lancers or to the local media. Large retailers have more complete advertising departments and may have specialists on staff to do much of the work in house. Manufacturers tend to rely more on ad agencies to perform these tasks, with the advertising manager acting as a liaison between the company and the agency.

THE IN-HOUSE AGENCY   Companies that need closer control over the advertising have their own in-house agencies. Large retailers, for example, find that doing their own advertising provides cost savings as well as the ability to make fast-breaking local deadlines. An **in-house agency** performs most, and sometimes all, of the functions of an outside advertising agency. The American Association of Advertising Agencies (AAAA) reports that the percentage of total business handled by in-house agencies remains fairly constant at about 5 percent.*

Most in-house agencies are found in retailing, for several reasons. First, retailers tend to operate under small profit margins and find they can save money by doing their own advertising. Second, retailers often receive a great many advertising materials either free or at a reduced cost from manufacturers and trade associations. Local media, for example, will provide creative and production assistance for free. Third, the timetable for retailing tends to be much tighter than that for national advertising. Retailers often create complete campaigns in hours, whereas advertising agencies may take weeks or months.

PRINCIPLE ——————————

The advertiser's ad manager is in charge of the total advertising program.

in-house agency *An advertising department on the advertiser's staff that handles most, if not all, of the functions of an outside agency.*

PRINCIPLE ——————————

An in-house agency provides more control for the advertiser over the costs and the time schedule.

---

*C. Craig Endicott, "Sales Surge 11% for Media Giants," *Advertising Age,* June 29, 1987, p. S-1.

Madison Avenue in New York City, where some of the nation's largest advertising agencies have their headquarters.
(Courtesy of Winstead/Monkmeyer Press.)

TABLE 1.3
The Ten Largest Advertising Agencies, 1987

Rank	Agency	Worldwide Billings (In millions)
1	Young & Rubicam	$4,905.7
2	Saatchi & Saatchi Advertising Worldwide	4,609.4
3	Backer Spielvogel Bates Worldwide	4,068.7
4	BBDO Worldwide	3,664.5
5	Ogilvy & Mather Worldwide	3,663.8
6	McCann-Erickson Worldwide	3,418.5
7	J. Walter Thompson Company	3,221.8
8	Lintas: Worldwide	2,787.2
9	D'Arcy Masius Benton & Bowles	2,494.3
10	Leo Burnett Co.	2,461.8

Source: Advertising Age, March 30, 1988, p. 6. Reprinted with permission from *Advertising Age.* Copyright Crain Communications Inc. All rights reserved.

The Advertising Agency

PRINCIPLE
The agency-client partnership is the dominant organizational arrangement in advertising.

The second key player in the advertising world is the advertising agency. Advertisers hire independent agencies to plan and implement part or all of their advertising effort. The agency-client partnership is the dominant organizational arrangement in advertising.

There are approximately 10,000 advertising agencies in the United States. One recent report indicated that less than 12 percent of these agencies accounted for over 84 percent of agency gross income.* Although on-going mergers and acquisitions continually change the rankings, Young & Rubicam is currently the largest agency with some 9,000 employees worldwide and nearly $5 billion in billings† (see Table 1.3).

In fact, the top 16 worldwide agencies each had annual billings exceeding $1 billion.

Rankings change when you look at agency megagroups, as listed in Table 1.4, Saatchi & Saatchi Co. becomes the industry leader with billings of over $11 billion.‡ The complexity of these super-groups can be seen in the Saatchi & Saatchi organizational chart (Figure 1.1), which includes a number of formerly independent agencies, such as McCaffrey & McCall; DFS (Dance, Fitzgerald, Sample) Dorland; Compton; Backer & Spielvogel; William Esty; Ted Bates; Conill; Campbell-Mithun; Rumrill-Hoyt; and Cochrane Chase and Livingston.

An advertiser that uses an outside advertising agency believes that it will be more effective and efficient in creating an individual commercial or a complete campaign. The strength of an agency is its resources, primarily the creative expertise, media knowledge, and advertising strategy that it brings to the problem at hand. Chapter 4 will discuss agencies in more detail.

The Media

media *The channels of communication used by advertisers.*

The third player in the advertising world is the set of media used by advertisers. The **media** are the channels of communication that carry the messages from the advertiser to the audience. The most frequently used advertising media are newspapers, television, radio, magazines, out-of-home media such as outdoor and transit, and direct response. The primary media used in advertising are listed on the bottom of page 19.

Advertising Age, March 26, 1987, p. 1.
†"Top 100 Agencies by Gross Income," *Advertising Age,* March 30, 1988, p. 6.
‡"Saatchi Widens Group Lead," *Advertising Age,* March 30, 1988, p. 92.

FIGURE 1.1

This organization chart for Saatchi & Saatchi illustrates the size and complexity of one super-agency.

Source: Advertising Age, March 26, 1987, p. 137. Reprinted with permission from Advertising Age. Copyright Crain Communications Inc. All rights reserved.

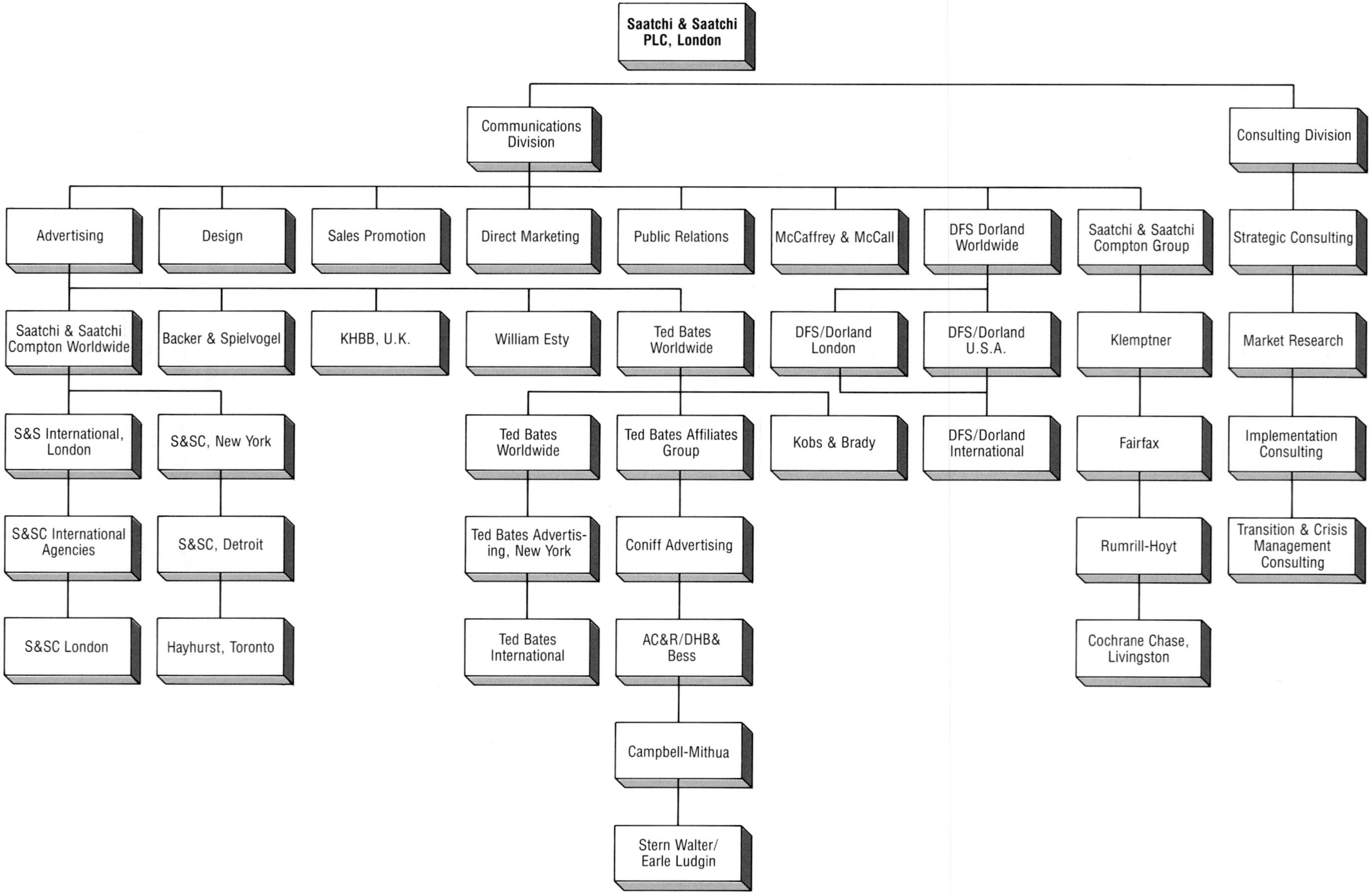

Rank	Group	Worldwide Billings, 1987 (In millions)
1	Saatchi & Saatchi: PLC	$11,357.0
2	Interpublic Group of Cos.	6,622.7
3	Omnicom Group	6,267.6
4	WPP Group PLC	5,952.9
5	Ogilvy Group	5,041.2
6	WCRS/Belier	1,633.7

Source: Advertising Age, March 30, 1988, p. 92. Reprinted with permission from *Advertising Age.* Copyright Crain Communications Inc. All rights reserved.

FIGURE 1.2
U.S. 1986 media advertising breakdown.

Source: Reprinted with permission from *Advertising Age.* Copyright Crain Communications Inc. All rights reserved.

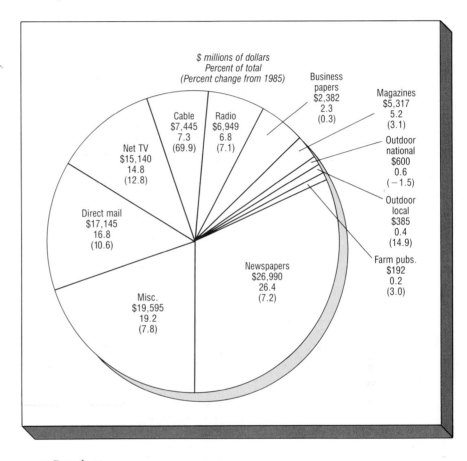

- *Broadcast*

  Television:
  - —network
  - —national spot
  - —local spot

  Radio:
  - —network
  - —national spot
  - —local spot

- *Print*

  Newspaper:
  - —daily (morning/evening)
  - —Sunday

  Magazines:
  - —consumer
  - —business/trade
  - —farm
  - —service/professional

TABLE 1.5
The 20 Leading Media Companies in 1986

Rank	Company	Media Revenues	Rank	Company	Media Revenues
1	Capital Cities/ABC	$4,124.4	11	New York Times Co.	1,564.7
2	CBS Inc.	3,224.0	12	Hearst Corp.	1,529.0
3	Time Inc.	3,099.0	13	Cox Communications	1,465.3
4	General Electric Co.	2,965.0	14	Washington Post Co.	1,162.0
5	Gannett Co.	2,727.0	15	McGraw-Hill	1,089.1
6	Times Mirror Co.	2,245.0	16	Dow Jones & Co.	1,078.0
7	Advance Publications	2,200.0	17	Scripps Howard	1,062.0
8	Dun & Bradstreet Corp.	1,932.0	18	Viacom International	855.0
9	Knight-Ridder Newspapers	1,879.6	19	News Corp. Ltd.	841.3
10	Tribune Co.	1,775.7	20	Westinghouse Electric Corp.	839.0

Source: Advertising Age, June 29, 1987, p. S-3. Reprinted with permission from *Advertising Age.* Copyright Crain Communications Inc. All rights reserved.

- *Other*

  Direct Mail
  Out-of-Home
  —outdoor (billboards/signs)
  —transit
  Motion pictures
  Point-of-purchase
  Specialty
  Directories
  Packaging

Media generated approximately $102 billion in advertising revenues in 1986, with newspapers representing approximately one-fourth of this total. As indicated in Table 1.5, Capital Cities/ABC was the top media company, with sales of nearly $4 billion.*

Media must deliver advertising messages in a way that is consistent with the creative effort. Media staff gather relevant information about their audiences so the message can be matched with the medium. Media also need to sell the product to prospective advertisers. Media representatives negotiate directly with the advertiser or work through the agency and its media department. They usually initiate the selling effort and make personal calls on the decision makers.

PRINCIPLE

Media provide information necessary to match the medium with the message.

*T*HE EVOLUTION OF ADVERTISING

OmIT pgs. 20-23

We've discussed the factors of great advertising. You've been introduced to the roles of advertising. You understand the basic roles of advertisers, agencies, and the media, and you are familiar with advertising's marketing and communication roles. Now let's look at how these roles and players developed historically.†

*"U.S. 1986 Media Advertising Breakdown," *Advertising Age.*

†Much of this historical review was adapted from Stephen Fox, *The Mirror Makers* (New York: Vintage Books, 1985).

The Ancient Period

Persuasive communication has been around since early times. Inscriptions on tablets, walls, and papyrus from ancient Babylonia, Egypt, and Greece carry messages listing available products and upcoming events.

Because of widespread illiteracy before the age of print, most messages were actually delivered by criers who stood on street corners shouting the wares of the sponsor. Stores, and the merchandise they carried, were identified by signs. Information rather than persuasion was the objective of the early commercial messages.

The Age of Print

The invention of movable type by Johannes Gutenberg around 1440 moved society toward a new level of communication—mass communication. No longer restricted by the time required by a scribe to hand-letter a single message, advertising could now be mass-produced. The availability of printed media to a greater number of people increased the level of literacy, which, in turn, encouraged more businesses to advertise. In terms of media, the early printed advertisements included posters, handbills, and classified advertisements in newspapers.

The Concept of Advertising   The word *advertisement* first appeared around 1655. It was used in the Bible to indicate notification or warning. Book publishers, for example, headed most of their announcements with the term, and by 1660 it was generally used as a heading for commercial information, primarily by store owners. The messages continued to be simple and informative through the 1700s and into the 1800s.

The Formative Years

The mid-1800s marked the beginning of the development of the advertising industry in the United States. The emerging importance and growth of advertising during this period resulted from a number of social and technological developments associated with the Industrial Revolution.

AD 1.8
An early English ad written by William Caxton in 1477.
Source: Alex Groner, *The American Heritage History of American Business and Industry* (New York: American Heritage Publishing Co., 1972), p. 19. (Courtesy of Bodleian Library, Oxford, U.K.)

FIGURE 1.3
The evolution of advertising in the United States.

PERIOD	PEOPLE	TIME	EVENTS
ANCIENT PERIOD			SIGNS
ANCIENT PERIOD			CRIERS
ANCIENT PERIOD			SEQUIS
ANCIENT PERIOD	JOHANNES GUTENBERG	1441	MOVABLE TYPE
ANCIENT PERIOD	WM. CLAXTON	1477	FIRST AD IN ENGLISH
ANCIENT PERIOD		1625	FIRST AD IN ENGLISH NEWSPAPER
ANCIENT PERIOD		1655	TERM ADVERTISING INTRODUCED
ANCIENT PERIOD		1704	FIRST U.S. NEWSPAPER TO CARRY ADS.
FORMATIVE PERIOD	VOLNEY PALMER	1841	FIRST AD SALES AGENT
FORMATIVE PERIOD	GEORGE ROWELL	1850	FIRST AD W/S
FORMATIVE PERIOD	CHARLES BATES	1871	FIRST FORMAL AGENCY
FORMATIVE PERIOD	FRANCIS AYER	1875	FIXED COMMISSION
FORMATIVE PERIOD	JOHN POWERS	1880	FIRST GREAT COPYWRITER
FORMATIVE PERIOD	E.C. ALLEN	1887	MAGAZINE ADVERTISING
FORMATIVE PERIOD	J. WALTER THOMPSON	1891	FIRST ACCOUNT EXECUTIVE

PERIOD	PEOPLE	TIME	EVENTS
MODERN PERIOD	E.E. CALKINS	1895	IMAGE COPY
MODERN PERIOD	JOHN B. KENNEDY	1904	HARD-SELL COPY
MODERN PERIOD	CLAUDE HOPKINS	1910	REASON-WHY COPY
MODERN PERIOD	ALBERT LASKER	1904 to 1944	GREAT ADVERTISING EXECUTIVE
MODERN PERIOD	THEODORE MacMANUS	1910	ATMOSPHERE ADVERTISING
MODERN PERIOD		1914	FTC ACT PASSED
MODERN PERIOD		1917	AM. ASSOC. OF ADVT. FORMED
MODERN PERIOD	STANLEY/HELEN RESOR	1920	INTRO. PSYCH./RES.
MODERN PERIOD	RAYMOND RUBICAM	1923	Y&R FORMED
MODERN PERIOD		1926	COMMERCIAL RADIO
MODERN PERIOD		1940	SELLING STRATEGEMS
MODERN PERIOD		1947	COMMERCIAL TELEVISION
MODERN PERIOD	ROSSER REEVES, MARION HARPER	1950s	MERGERS, RESEARCH AND HARD SELL
MODERN PERIOD	LEO BURNETT, DAVID OGILVY, WILLIAM BERNBACH	1960s	HIGH CREATIVITY
MODERN PERIOD		1970s	BACK TO THE 50s
MODERN PERIOD		1980s	MERGERS AND CREATIVITY

GEORGIA.

SHIPS or VESSELS, of *any* Bur-then, may be laden at the *firſt* Bluff, on the *North* Side of St. *Mary's River*, with LUMBER and SCANTLING for *London*, the *Weſt-Indies* or elſewhere, with Diſpatch, at reaſonable Rates for Money, or in Exchange for any Kind of Merchandize.   For further Particulars enquire at Mr. WRIGHT's Plantation, within a Mile of the ſaid Bluff.

The Inlet lieth between *Cumberland* and *Amelia* Iſlands, is a ſafe Navigation, being an eaſy ſhort Bar to paſs over, with ſufficient Depth of Water for large Ships ; it is about thirty Leagues to the Northward of *St. Auguſtine* Inlet. The River is bold, the Bluff in ſight of *Cumberland Iſland*, about five Miles up the River, where Ships may in Safety load in all Sea-ſons of the Year.

AD 1.9
It appears that coastal property in Georgia was just as valuable in 1700 as it is today.
Source: Alex Groner, *The American Heritage History of American Business and Industry* (New York: American Heritage Publishing Co., 1972), p. 19. (Courtesy of American Antiquarian Society.)

The Age of Mass Marketing   Because of inventions that increased productivity, such as the internal combustion engine and the cotton gin, manufacturers were able to mass-produce goods of uniform quality. The resulting excess production, however, could be profitable only if it attracted customers living beyond the local markets. Fortunately the long-distance transportation network of rivers and canals was being replaced in midcentury by a much speedier system of roads and railroads.

MEDIA BROKERS   All that remained for modern advertising to do was to devise an effective and efficient communication system that could reach a widely dispersed marketplace. National media developed as the country's transportation system grew. The early advertising experts, such as Volney Palmer, the first "adman," functioned strictly as *media brokers*. Thoroughly familiar with all the periodicals and their rates, they had a keen ability to negotiate. They received their commissions out of the fees paid by publishers. The messages were prepared primarily by the advertisers or writers they hired directly and often featured exaggerated and outrageous claims.

By the late nineteenth century the advertising profession was more fully developed. Agencies had taken on the role of convincing manufacturers to advertise their products. Ads had assumed a more complete informational and educational role. Copywriting had become a polished and reputable craft.

The Growth of the Retailer   In the late 1800s John Wanamaker revolutionized retailing. Prior to the Civil War there were no set prices for merchandise sold in retail outlets. As a result, store owners bartered and changed prices depending on the perceived wealth of the customer being served or on their own need for cash that day. Wanamaker, who owned a dry-goods store in Philadelphia, changed this tradition by standardizing the prices on all the merchandise he sold. Furthermore, he established even greater credibility by offering a money-back guarantee. This strategy of honest dealings and straight talk was so successful that Wanamaker built two more outlets and the huge Philadelphia Grand Depot department store.

POWERS AND NEWS   Wanamaker also hired the first great copywriter, John E. Powers. In 1880 Powers was hired to communicate Wanamaker's philosophy to the public. Powers "journalized" advertising by writing ads that were newsy and informationally accurate. He also made the ad more up-to-date with new copy every day. "My discovery," as Powers explained it, was to "print the news of the store."* With Powers's assistance, the sales volume in Wanamaker's stores doubled in just a few years.

The Advent of Magazines   During the 1800s most advertising was placed in newspapers or appeared on posters and handbills. Until the late 1880s magazines were strictly a medium for the wealthy and well-educated, containing political commentaries, short stories, and discussions of art and fashion. This changed with the introduction of the *People's Literary Companion* by E. C. Allen, which appealed to a large group of general readers. Also, about this time Congress approved low postage rates for periodicals, which allowed magazines to be distributed economically by mail.

Magazines offered a medium for longer, more complex messages. They also had enough lead time for the production of art such as engravings to illustrate articles and ads. As the production processes improved, photographs were introduced, and magazine advertisements became highly visual.

Modern Advertising

By the beginning of the twentieth century the total volume of advertising had increased to $500 million from $50 million in 1870. The industry had become a major force in marketing, and had achieved a significant level of respect and esteem.†

The Era of Professionalism   CALKENS AND GRAPHICS   The twentieth century also witnessed a revolution in advertising. Earnest Elmo Calkens of the Bates agency created a style of advertising that resembled original art and adapted

*Printer's Ink, October 23, 1895.
†Printer's Ink, October 23, 1953.

Claude Hopkins, considered by some people to be the greatest copywriter of all times.
(Courtesy of FCB/Leber Katz Partners.)

Copywriter John E. Kennedy explained that "Advertising is salesmanship in print."
(Courtesy of FCB/Leber Katz Partners.)

beautifully to the medium of magazines. Calkens's ads not only attracted the viewer's attention but also increased the status and image of the advertiser. His work represented the first venture into image advertising.

LORD & THOMAS SALESMANSHIP   The direction of advertising took a dramatic detour when John E. Kennedy and Albert Lasker formed their historic partnership in 1905 at the powerful Lord & Thomas agency. Lasker was a partner in the firm and the managerial genius who made Lord & Thomas such a force in the advertising industry. Ads that sold the product were all that mattered to him. Because of Lasker's philosophy, the agency was able to make a profit when others were losing money.

In 1905 Lasker was pondering the question: What is advertising? Like Powers he had been approaching advertising as news. John E. Kennedy, who had worked for a variety of retailers and patent-medicine clients, responded with a note that said: "I can tell you what advertising is." When the two met, Kennedy explained, "Advertising is salesmanship in print."*

Thus was born the "sales" approach to advertising copy. Kennedy's style was simple and straightforward, based on the belief that advertising should present the same arguments a salesman would use in person. This "reason-why" copy style became the hallmark of Lord & Thomas ads. Lasker, referring to his meeting with Kennedy in 1905, said, "The whole complexion of advertising for all America was changed from that day on."

HOPKINS AND TESTING   At the height of his career in the early 1930s Claude Hopkins was Lord & Thomas's best-known copywriter and made the unheard-of salary of $185,000. Sometimes called "the greatest copywriter of all time," he was also the most analytical.

*Merrill DeVoe, *Effective Advertising Copy* (New York: Macmillan Co., 1956), p. 21.

Hopkins worked with direct mail and used that medium to test and refine his techniques. In his 1923 book *Scientific Advertising,* he discussed the principles and laws he had discovered as a result of his constant copytesting: "One ad is compared with another, one method with another. . . . No guesswork is permitted. One must know what is best. Thus mail-order advertising first established many of our basic laws."*

MacManus and Soft-Sell   Theodore F. MacManus was a copywriter for the young General Motors company, where he produced an image style of advertising resembling that of Calkens. He felt that a "soft-sell" rather than a "hard-sell" copy style would better create the long-term relationship considered necessary between a car manufacturer and its customers. Image was everything. The only way to penetrate the subconscious of the reader was through a slow accumulation of positive images.† The positive illusions created by MacManus for Cadillac and Buick had much to do with their early successes.

PRINCIPLE ———————
Soft-sell advertising creates images through a slow accumulation of positive messages.

AD 1.10
A typical ad supporting the war effort in World War I.
Source: Alex Groner, *The American Heritage History of American Business and Industry* (New York: American Heritage Publishing Co., 1972), p. 222. (Courtesy of The New Jersey Historical Society.)

Ibid., p. 22.
†*Printer's Ink,* January 31, 1918.

Helen and Stanley Resor.

War and Prosperity   With the outbreak of World War I, the advertising industry offered its services to the Council of National Defense. The Division of Advertising of the Committee of Public Information was formed. This volunteer agency created advertising to attract military recruits, sell Liberty Bonds, and support the Red Cross and the war effort in general. Thus was born public service advertising that relied on volunteer professionals and donated time and space.

JWT AND THE POSTWAR BOOM   Following the war consumers were desperate for goods and services. New products were emerging constantly. A great boom in advertising was led by the J. Walter Thompson agency through the innovative copy and management style of the husband-and-wife team Stanley and Helen Resor. Stanley administered the agency and developed the concept of account services.

The JWT agency, under the Resors, was known for many innovations in advertising. The Resors coined the concept of *brand names* to associate a unique identity with a particular product. They also developed the status appeal by which they persuaded nonwealthy people to imitate the habits of richer people. JWT advertising introduced modern marketing research to advertising. Stanley Resor also built a network of agencies, including some outside the United States.

Dealing with the Depression   Advertising diminished drastically after the onset of the Great Depression in 1929. Clients demanded more service and special deals. The Depression brought back the hard-sell, reason-why copy approach of Lasker and Hopkins.

RUBICAM AND ORIGINALITY   During and after the Depression Raymond Rubicam emerged as one of the giants of advertising. In the spring of 1923 he

AD 1.11
This ad, written in 1919, shows the
copy style of Raymond Rubicam.
(Courtesy of Historical Pictures Service, Inc.)

STEINWAY

THE INSTRUMENT OF THE IMMORTALS

UPON hearing a Steinway for the first time, Richard Wagner wrote: "Our early tone masters, in writing the grandest of their creations for the pianoforte, seem to have had a presentiment of this, the ideal piano." Happily, the Steinway was born in time to inspire the immortal Richard, and to be divinely played and truly loved by Franz Liszt. Happily, too, it was here to voice the art of that most gifted and brilliant of pianists, Paderewski. And happily again, it is still here to bless the playing of Rachmaninoff and Hofmann, and to minister to all people who love great music.

STEINWAY & SONS, Steinway Hall, 107-109 East Fourteenth Street, New York

PRINCIPLE

The value of an idea is measured by its originality.

launched his own agency with John Orr Young, a Lord & Thomas copywriter. Young & Rubicam created unique ads with intriguing headlines. Rubicam emphasized fresh, original ideas. He also hired the researcher George Gallup and made research an essential part of the creative process.

CAPLES AND HEADLINES John Caples, a vice president of Batten, Barton, Durstine and Osborn (BBDO), made a major contribution to the field in 1932 when he published *Tested Advertising Methods*. His theories about the "pulling power" of headlines were based on extensive mail-order and inquiry testing. Caples was also known for changing the style of advertising writing, which had been wordy and full of exaggerations. He used short words, short sentences, and short paragraphs.*

*DeVoe, *Advertising Copy,* pp. 25–26.

The Advent of Radio   Radio offered the Depression-weary consumer an inexpensive form of entertainment. The tremendous potential of radio created two serious problems for advertising. First, it meant that advertising agencies had to find or train staff who could write copy for the ear. The second problem was financial. In the early days of radio sponsors underwrote the programming, which involved a much greater financial commitment than a single ad. The growth of radio, however, was phenomenal. Twelve years after its first commercial broadcast, radio surpassed magazines as the leading advertising medium.

World War II   During World War II the advertising industry once again served as mass communicator for America. The War Advertising Council (WAC) used advertising to enlist recruits, sell war bonds, and encourage the planting of victory gardens and the sending of V-mail letters. Over $1 billion was spent on the most extensive advertising campaign ever created. The effort was so successful that after the war, instead of disbanding, the WAC simply changed its name to the Advertising Council and has remained a very effective public service effort to this day.

PRINCIPLE ——————
For many products differentiation is created by advertising.

© 1945 The Studebaker Corporat

"To the few to whom so many owe so much!"

Back the attack
on all fronts with

WAR BONDS

Maybe you can't man
a Studebak r Weasel
but you can help our
fighting forces by
purchasing more and
more U.S. War Bonds.

*Awarded To All
Studebaker Plants*

THIS paraphrase of Winston Churchill's famous tribute to the Royal Air Force deservedly applies to all the men and women who wear our country's uniform.

A civilian grateful to all who have contributed to the success of the Flying Fortress addressed the sentiment to Studebaker some months ago. But it was really meant as an unreserved salute to every American fighting man on land, at sea and in the air.

Studebaker and its employees obviously

are proud to have been called upon by our government to build the Cyclone engines that power the Boeing Flying Fortress—to produce huge quantities of Studebaker military trucks—to design and manufacture the versatile Studebaker Weasel personnel and cargo carrier.

But they are prouder still that they have been privileged throughout the war to put their willing hands to work in support of the efforts of the men and women in all branches of our nation's armed services.

Studebaker *PEACETIME BUILDER OF FINE CARS AND TRUCKS*
WARTIME BUILDER OF WRIGHT CYCLONE ENGINES FOR BOEING FLYING FORTRESS

Also producing heavy-duty Studebaker military trucks and Weasel personnel and cargo carriers

AD 1.12
Many companies openly supported the World War II effort through their advertisements.
Source: Bryan Holmes, *Advertising: Reflections of a Century* (New York: The Viking Press, 1982), p. 159.

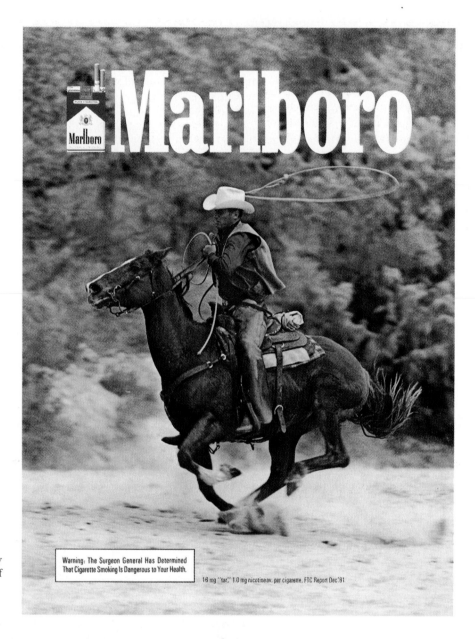

AD 1.13

The Marlboro campaign, created by the Leo Burnett agency, was one of the most successful campaigns of all times.

(Courtesy of Philip Morris Incorporated.)

Warning: The Surgeon General Has Determined That Cigarette Smoking Is Dangerous to Your Health.

16 mg "tar," 1.0 mg nicotine av. per cigarette, FTC Report Dec. '81

PEACE AND PRODUCTS　　During the 1950s markets were inundated with "me too" products with similar features. The primary difference between many of these products was the image created by the advertising.

ROSSER REEVES AND THE USP　　One person who was able to cut through this clutter of products was Rosser Reeves of the Ted Bates agency. Reeves proposed that an effective ad had to offer a "unique selling proposition" (USP) containing a benefit that was important to consumers and that no other competitor offered. "M&M's melt in your mouth, not in your hands" and "Double your pleasure, double your fun" are two USPs made famous by Reeves.

BEDELL AND SELLING STRATAGEMS　　Like Caples, Clyde Bedell was a student and a master of mail-order copy. In a 1940 book *How to Write Advertising That Sells* he expressed his philosophy of advertising, which focused on the selling aspects. He developed a set of "31 Proved Selling Stratagems" that defined the relationship between product features and selling points.*

*Ibid., p. 27.

OGILVY VERSUS BERNBACH

It's doubtful whether any two people in modern advertising had more impact on the creative product than David Ogilvy and the late Bill Bernbach. Curiously, to judge from their writings, it's also doubtful whether any two people could have disagreed more sharply on how to create it. On point after point, they're as dissimilar as the left brain and the right.

In a house ad that's since become a classic, Ogilvy wrote that "what you say is more important than how you say it." He ranked this as the No. 1 ingredient in his recipe for successful advertising.

For Bernbach, Ogilvy's No. 1 point is only the jumping-off point: "Finding out what to say is the beginning of the communication process. How you say it makes people look and listen and believe."

Ogilvy exalts research. Beneath his dozens and dozens of admaking rules lie dozens of research findings. He unabashedly calls research his strong suit, and plays it continually.

Bernbach, on the other hand, was relentlessly suspicious of research. It made him wary, and he took it with several grains of salt. In the most famous example, he overruled research findings that would have aborted Avis' "We try harder" campaign. One big problem with research, he said, is that "it tends to keep you from thinking. It tends to make you feel you have the answer. You don't have the answer until you sweat over research and use your own judgment."

Bernbach was equally skeptical of rules. He took the archetypal creative position that rules "are what the artist breaks; the memorable never emerged from a formula." He believed that advertising "is fundamentally persuasion and persuasion happens to be not a science but an art."

Whereas rules are a large and inseparable part of the Ogilvy persona. Ogilvy himself says that he hates rules, and means only to give hints. He should know—but for many, his "hints" have always sounded and felt like marching orders.

To answer creatives who chafed at rules, Ogilvy summoned up two masters: "Shakespeare wrote his sonnets within a strict discipline, fourteen lines of iambic pentameter, rhyming in three quatrains and a couplet. Were his sonnets dull? Mozart wrote his sonatas within an equally rigid discipline . . . were *they* dull?" To Ogilvy, rules only testify to "the importance of discipline in art."

And so it goes. Where Bernbach stands foursquare for one point of view, you can make a fortune by giving odds that Ogilvy says the opposite. They seem always to be crossing swords—and because both are giants, the air rings with a mighty din.

Source: Gerry Scorse, *Advertising Age,* October 26, 1987.

The Advent of Television   In 1939 NBC became the first television network to initiate regular broadcasting. Not until the 1950's, however, did television become a major player. By the end of that decade television was the dominant advertising medium. Its total advertising revenues grew from $12.3 million in 1949 to $128 million in 1951.*

The Era of Creativity   The 1960s brought a resurgence of art, inspiration, and intuition. This revolution was inspired by three creative geniuses: Leo Burnett, David Ogilvy, and William Bernbach.

BURNETT AND MIDDLE AMERICA   Leo Burnett was the leader of the "Chicago School" of advertising. He believed in finding the "inherent drama" in every product and then presenting it as believably as possible. The Leo Burnett agency created mythical characters who represented American values such as the Jolly Green Giant, Tony the Tiger, Charlie the Tuna, and Morris the Cat. The most famous campaign, one that was discussed in the introduction to this chapter, is the "Marlboro Man," which has built the American cowboy into the symbol of the best-selling cigarette in the world (see Ad 1.13). Burnett never apologized

*Stephen Fox, *The Mirror Makers: A History of American Advertising and Its Creators* (New York: Vintage Books, 1985), p. 211.

The Rolls-Royce Silver Cloud II — $15,655 P.O.E.

"At 60 miles an hour the loudest noise in this new Rolls-Royce comes from the electric clock"

*What __makes__ Rolls-Royce the best car in the world? "There is really no magic about it —
it is merely patient attention to detail," says an eminent Rolls-Royce engineer.*

1. "At 60 miles an hour the loudest noise comes from the electric clock," reports the Technical Editor of THE MOTOR. The silence of the engine is uncanny. Three mufflers tune out sound frequencies—acoustically.

2. Every Rolls-Royce engine is run for seven hours at full throttle before installation, and each car is test-driven for hundreds of miles over varying road surfaces.

3. The Rolls-Royce Silver Cloud II is designed as an *owner-driven* car. It is eighteen inches shorter than the largest domestic cars.

4. The car has power steering, power brakes and automatic gear-shift. It is very easy to drive and to park. No chauffeur required.

5. There is no metal-to-metal contact between the body of the car and the chassis frame—except for the speedometer drive. The entire body is insulated and under-sealed.

6. The finished car spends a week in the final test-shop, being fine-tuned.

Here it is subjected to ninety-eight separate ordeals. For example, the engineers use a *stethoscope* to listen for axle-whine.

7. The new eight-cylinder aluminium engine is even more *powerful* than the previous six-cylinder unit, *yet it weighs ten pounds less.*

8. The famous Rolls-Royce radiator has never been changed, except that when Sir Henry Royce died in 1933 the monogram RR was changed from red to black.

9. The coachwork is given five coats of primer paint, and hand rubbed between each coat, before *nine* coats of finishing paint go on.

10. By moving a switch on the steering column, you can adjust the shock-absorbers to suit road conditions. (The lack of fatigue in driving this car is remarkable.)

11. Another switch defrosts the rear window, by heating a network of 1360 invisible wires in the glass. The ventilating system is so efficient that you

can ride in comfort with all the windows closed. Air conditioning is optional.

12. The seats are upholstered with eight hides of English leather—enough to make 128 pairs of soft shoes.

13. A picnic table, veneered in French walnut, slides out from under the dash. Two more swing out behind the front seats.

14. You can get such optional extras as an Espresso coffee-making machine, a dictating machine, a bed, hot and cold water for washing, an electric razor.

15. The cooling fan is *lopsided*. Its five blades are unequally spaced and pitched to take thick and thin slices of air. Thus it does its work in a *whisper.* The company goes to fantastic lengths to ensure the peace and quiet of the occupants of the car.

16. There are *three* independent brake linkages. The Rolls-Royce is a very *safe* car—and also a very *lively* car. It cruises serenely at eighty-five. Top speed is in excess of 100 m.p.h.

17. Rolls-Royce engineers make periodic visits to inspect owners' motor cars and advise on service.

18. The Bentley is made by Rolls-Royce. Except for the radiators, they are identical motor cars, manufactured by the same engineers in the same works. The Bentley costs $300 less, because its radiator is simpler to make. People who feel diffident about driving a Rolls-Royce can buy a Bentley.

ROLLS-ROYCE AND BENTLEY

PRICE. The car illustrated in this advertisement — f.o.b. principal port of entry—costs **$15,655.**

If you would like the rewarding experience of driving a Rolls-Royce or Bentley, write or telephone dealer listed below. Rolls-Royce Inc., 45 Rockefeller Plaza, New York 20, N.Y.

AD 1.14
One of the most famous David Ogilvy ads.
(Courtesy of Ogilvy, Benson & Mather, Inc.)

for his common-touch approach. He took pride in his ability to reach the average consumer.

OGILVY: DISCIPLINE AND STYLE   David Ogilvy, founder of the Ogilvy & Mather agency, is a paradox because he represents both the "image" school of MacManus and Rubicam and the "claim" school of Lasker and Hopkins. Although he believed in research and mail-order copy with all of its testing, he had a tremendous sense of image and story appeal. He created enduring brands with

AD 1.15
This Coke commercial with football star "Mean Joe" Greene received some of the
highest recall scores ever recorded.

(Courtesy of Joe Greene and Coca-Cola USA.)

campaign symbols like the eyepatch on the Hathaway man. Among the other products he handled were Rolls-Royce, Pepperidge Farm, and Guinness.

THE ART OF BERNBACH Doyle, Dane, and Bernbach opened in 1949. From the beginning, William Bernbach was the catalyst for the agency's success. A copywriter with an acute sense of design, he was considered by many to be the most innovative advertiser of his time. His advertising touched people by focusing on feelings and emotions. He explained: "There are a lot of great technicians in advertising. However, they forget that advertising is persuasion, and persuasion is not a science, but an art. Advertising is the art of persuasion."*

The Era of Accountability The Vietnam War and the economic downturn of the 1970s led to a reemphasis on hard-sell advertising. Clients wanted results, and agencies hired marketing MBAs who understood strategic planning and the elements of marketing. Advertising increasingly reflected the safe 1950s "formula" ads—vignettes and slice-of-life commercials showing people enjoying the product. Despite the lack of fresh approaches, but bolstered by runaway inflation, 11 agencies—led by Y&R at $2.3 billion—had reached the billion-dollar mark by the end of the decade, compared to none in 1970.†

SALES PROMOTION In response to the intense emphasis on performance and profit in the 1970s and 1980s, many consumer-product companies shifted their budgets from traditional media to *sales promotion,* which uses strategies such as coupons, rebates, and sweepstakes to generate short-term sales gains. Agencies either learned to create sales promotions or acquired firms that specialized in doing so.

Mergers Another trend of the 1980s was mergers—both on the client side and among advertising agencies. In order to serve the global needs of major clients, agencies embarked on a spree of national and international mergers. The new super agencies, which are basically holding companies for a group of merged agencies, are promising more efficiency, more specialization, and better global service. Many of the old agencies, and the names of the giants who built them, are now buried in these conglomerates.

THE 1980s AND BEYOND As we approach the twenty-first century, advertising is in a state of tremendous flux and is seeking new directions that will enhance both creativity and profitability. Advertising continues to search for the appropriate balance between information and persuasion. The key players continue to grow and adapt to new markets, while advertising continues to serve its two masters—marketing and communication.

Printer's Ink, January 2, 1953.
†Fox, *Mirror Makers,* p. 262.

■ SUMMARY

- Great advertisements have (1) a strong, original creative concept that (2) is strategically sound and (3) has exactly the right execution for the message and audience.
- The definition of advertising has five elements: (1) paid communication (2) from an identified sponsor (3) using mass media (4) to persuade and influence (5) an audience.
- Advertising fulfills (1) a marketing role, (2) a communication role, (3) an economic role, and (4) a societal role.

- The three key players in the advertising industry are (1) advertisers, (2) advertising agencies, and (3) media.
- Advertising is handled either internally by an in-house agency or externally by an advertising agency.
- The development of each of the major media—print, radio, and television—has transformed advertising.
- Advertising styles have alternated between periods of hard sell (information and salesmanship) and periods of soft sell (image and emotion).

■ QUESTIONS

1. What are the four major roles of advertising?

2. What are the major theories concerning the effects of advertising on prices? Which theory sounds the most plausible? Why?

3. Critics charge that advertising seeks to manipulate its audience, whereas its supporters claim that it merely seeks to persuade. Which interpretation do you agree with? Why?

4. Describe the two tasks of media in advertising.

5. Identify five major figures in the history of advertising and explain their contributions to the field.

6. How did the advertising field change after the invention of movable type, radio, and television?

7. Analyze how advertising has developed in terms of hard-sell and soft-sell messages.

■ FURTHER READINGS

AAKER, DAVID A., and JOHN G. MEYERS. *Advertising Management.* Englewood Cliffs, NJ: Prentice Hall, 1975.

FOX, STEPHEN. *The Mirror Makers: A History of American Advertising and Its Creators.* New York: Vintage Books, 1985.

"How Advertising Is Reshaping Madison Avenue." *Business Week,* September 15, 1986, p. 147.

JAFFE, ANDREW. "Entrepreneurs Fashion Lean, Mean Shops." *Adweek,* January 19, 1987, p. 34.

OGILVY, DAVID. *Ogilvy on Advertising.* New York: Vintage Books, 1985.

ORNSTEIN, STANLEY I. *Industrial Concentration and Advertising.* Washington, DC: American Enterprise Institute, 1977.

ROTZELL, KIM B., and JAMES E. HAEFNER. *Advertising in Contemporary Society,* Cincinnati, OH: South-Western Publishing Co., 1986.

2

The Advertising Environment: Ethics and Regulation

Chapter Outline

Chapter Objectives

When you have completed this chapter you should be able to:

- Explain the current judicial position concerning the First Amendment rights of advertisers
- List the major federal agencies that regulate advertising
- Define the concept of self-regulation as it applies to advertising
- Discuss the major ethical issues that advertisers and government regulatory agencies must address
- Explain the remedies available to different groups when an ad is judged deceptive or offensive

GETTING THE FACTS STRAIGHT?

According to the *Wall Street Journal,* a 1987 television advertising campaign sponsored by Drexel Burnham Lambert, Inc. is a bit short on accuracy. The ad goes like this: "In 1983," the ad explains, "over 16 percent of the population of Vidalia, La., were unemployed. . . . In December 1986, the Catalyst Energy Corp. began construction on the Vidalia, La. hydroelectric plant, financed with the help of high-yield bonds provided by Drexel Burnham. . . . Today, this project has helped reduce unemployment by over 20 percent—proof that high-yield bonds are not just good for business, but for everyone."

Never mind that unemployment statistics specifically for Vidalia don't exist. Or that construction of the hydroelectric plant began in December 1985, not 1986. And what about the quaint little town shown with its pool hall, its Dixie Theatre, and the man playing solitaire on the sidewalk? This isn't Vidalia at all; it's Fort Smith, Ark., more than 300 miles away.

Drexel dismisses any mention of the flaws as merely "nitpicking." What really matters, according to the New York–based investment banking firm, is the message: Drexel and its high-yield bonds—often used to finance hostile takeovers—have gotten a bad rap.

"There aren't any misrepresentations in the ad," says Steven Anreder, a Drexel spokesman. "The only thing I can't quarrel with is that it was not shot in Vidalia. The other stuff is all minor stuff."

Some of the residents of Vidalia, however, don't agree. For example, Sidney Murray Jr., a former Vidalia mayor who is general manager of hydropower operations is concerned about the image of the town that emerges: "They wanted to design an ad that would nail home the point, 'Here we are, and here comes Drexel to save the day.' They couldn't have made us look any worse." What's worse, says Sam Randazzo, current mayor, is the portrayal of the town as a "destitute little city with a high unemployment rate." The figure used in the ad was for Concordia Parish, not Vidalia. Finally, most of the people who work at the hydroplant aren't even from Vidalia.*

Chapter 1 discussed some of the major social criticisms of advertising. Because advertising is so visible it receives a great deal of attention from citizens and the government. This chapter will examine the ethical questions faced by advertisers as well as the regulation imposed by government and by the industry itself.

ADVERTISING ETHICS

Advertising is a dynamic field where business interests, creativity, consumer needs, and government regulation meet in a public forum. Advertising's high visibility makes it particularly vulnerable to criticism. For example, in 1982 an Opinion Research media survey found that approximately two-thirds of the respondents felt television ads were misleading or exaggerated.† A Gallup Poll survey found that advertising people rate only slightly higher in perceived honesty and ethical standards than used-car salespeople, and they rate below insurance salespeople, local and state officeholders, members of Congress, and labor

*Laurie P. Cohen, "Drexel's New Television Ad Tugs at the Heart but Fudges the Facts," *The Wall Street Journal,* December 8, 1987, 29. Reprinted by permission of *The Wall Street Journal,* © Dow Jones & Company, Inc., 1987. All rights reserved.

†"The Image of Advertising," *Editor and Publisher,* February 9, 1985, pp. 15, 32.

union leaders.* Although negative attitudes toward advertising probably will never disappear, it is worthwhile to be aware of the social issues facing advertisers. Each of these issues is complex; each is surrounded by concern for public welfare along with concern for freedom of speech. The collective advertising industry, including agencies, advertisers, and the media, has an important stake in how these social issues are viewed both by the public and by those in a position to pass legislation to regulate the industry.

Ethical Criteria

Although advertisers face extensive regulation, every issue is not covered by a clear, written rule. Many advertising-related issues, such as those raised by the Drexel Burnham ad that introduced this chapter, are left to the discretion of the advertiser. Decisions may be based on a variety of considerations, including the objective of the advertising campaign, the attitudes of the target audience, the philosophies of the agency and the advertiser, and legal precedent. Many decisions are based on ethical concerns. Three issues are central to an ethical discussion of advertising: advocacy, accuracy, and acquisitiveness.†

Advocacy The first issue is *advocacy*. Advertising, by its very nature, tries to persuade the audience to do something. In doing this, it is not objective or neutral. This fact disturbs critics who think that advertising should be objective, informative, and neutral. They want advertising to provide information and to stop there. Most people, however, are aware that advertising tries to sell us something, whether it be a product, a service, or an idea.

Accuracy The second issue is *accuracy*. Beyond the easily ascertainable claims in an advertising message (for example, does the advertised automobile have a sun roof and a AM/FM radio, and is it available in different colors?) are matters of perception. Will buying the automobile make me the envy of my neighbors? Will it make me more attractive to the opposite sex? Such messages

---

"ADVERTISING PRINCIPLES OF AMERICAN BUSINESS" OF THE AMERICAN ADVERTISING FEDERATION (AAF)

1. Truth—Advertising shall reveal the truth, and shall reveal significant facts, the omission of which would mislead the public.
2. Substantiation—Advertising claims shall be substantiated by evidence in possession of the advertiser and the advertising agency prior to making such claims.
3. Comparisons—Advertising shall refrain from making false, misleading, or unsubstantiated statements or claims about a competitor or his products or services.
4. Bait Advertising—Advertising shall not offer products or services for sale unless such offer constitutes a bona fide effort to sell the advertised products or services and is not a device to switch consumers to other goods or services, usually higher priced.
5. Guarantees and Warranties—Advertising of guarantees and warranties shall be explicit, with sufficient information to apprise consumers of their principal terms and limitations or, when space or time restrictions preclude such disclosures, the advertisement shall clearly reveal where the full text of the guarantee or warranty can be examined before purchase.
6. Price Claims—Advertising shall avoid price claims which are false or misleading, or savings claims which do not offer provable savings.
7. Testimonials—Advertising containing testimonials shall be limited to those of competent witnesses who are reflecting a real and honest opinion or experience.
8. Taste and Decency—Advertising shall be free of statements, illustrations, or implications which are offensive to good taste or public decency.

Source: Courtesy of the American Advertising Federation.

The Gallup Poll, 1983, pp. 143–45.

†John Crichton, "Morals and Ethics in Advertising," in *Ethics, Morality & the Media,* Lee Thayer, ed. (New York: Hastings House, 1980), pp. 105–15.

may be implied by the situations pictured in the advertisements. Most of us are realistic enough to know that buying a car won't make anyone a new person, but innuendos in the messages we see cause concern among advertising critics. The subtle messages coming across are of special concern when they are aimed at particular groups, such as children and teenagers, with limited experiences.

Acquisitiveness   The third issue is *acquisitiveness*. Some critics maintain that advertising is a symbol of our society's preoccupation with accumulating material objects. Because we are continually exposed to an array of changing, newer-and-better products, critics claim we are "corrupted" into thinking that we must have these products. The rebuttal of this criticism is that advertising allows a progressive society to see and choose among different products. Advertising gives us choices and incentives for which we continue to strive.

Ultimately the consumer makes the final decision. If advertising for a product is perceived as violating ethical standards, consumers can exert pressure by refusing to buy the product. They can also complain to the company and to a variety of other regulatory bodies. However, decisions about advertising campaigns start with the advertiser.

The Problem of Being Ethical

Although advertisers can seek help in making decisions about questionable advertising situations from sources such as codes of ethics (see the box entitled "Advertising Principles"), these codes provide very general guidance. Sometimes when advertising decisions are not clearly covered by a code, a rule, or a regulation, an individual must make an ethical decision. The individual must weigh the pros and cons, the good and the bad, the healthy and harmful effects, and make a value judgment about an unfamiliar situation. These decisions are complex because there is no clear consensus about what constitutes ethical behavior. There is also a potential conflict between personal ethics and what might be good for the business. Even though it might increase sales of your product, do you use copy that has an offensive double meaning? Do you use illustrations that portray people in stereotypical situations? Do you stretch the truth when making a claim about the product? Do you malign the competitor's product even though you know it is basically the same as your own?

The complexity of ethical issues requires us to make a conscious effort to deal with each situation. We should develop personal standards of what is right or wrong. That way we will be less likely to behave unethically. Remember, it is people who make up the ethical atmosphere of the organization. Advertising people in particular must address the following questions:

- Who should, and should not, be advertised to?
- What should, and should not, be advertised?
- What should, and should not, be the content of the advertising message?
- What should, and should not, be the symbolic tone of the advertising message?
- What should, and should not, be the relationship between advertising and the mass media?
- What should, and should not, be advertising's conscious obligation to society?*

Unfortunately, answers to these questions are not always clear or straightforward. Rather, the advertiser must consider a number of related factors, such as the company mission, marketing objectives, reputation, available resources, competition, and so forth.

*Kim B. Rotzoll and James G. Haefner, "Advertising and Its Ethical Dimensions," in *Advertising in Contemporary Society* (Cincinnati, OH: South-Western Publishing Company, 1986), pp. 137–49.

ETHICAL ISSUES IN ADVERTISING

Puffery

Because the federal government does not pursue cases involving obviously exaggerated, or "puffing," claims, this question has become an ethical issue. The following familiar slogans are examples of puffery:

- Bayer works wonders.
- When you say Budweiser, you've said it all.
- Nestlé's makes the very best chocolate.
- If it's Borden's, it's got to be good.
- Keebler—uncommonly good.
- You can be sure if it's Westinghouse.
- Things go better with Coke.*

puffery *Advertising or other sales representation that praises the item to be sold using subjective opinions, superlatives, and similar mechanisms that are not based on specific fact.*

Puffery is defined as "advertising or other sales representations which praise the item to be sold with subjective opinions, superlatives, or exaggerations, vaguely and generally, stating no specific facts."† Critics contend that puffery is misleading and should be regulated by the FTC. Defenders suggest that

---

GOOD HUMOR OR BAD TASTE?

At first glance, it seemed that the punk movement had finally hit American farmers. Why else would one of them be sporting that very stylish Mohawk haircut?

Actually, it was part of a campaign for Commence, a new herbicide by FMC Corp., Chicago. The ads were originally intended as a humorous look at what happens when two farmers make a friendly wager. Some viewers, however, found the ad's portrayal of farmers objectionable, according to Brad Chalk, the company's communications manager.

The campaign was stopped in mid-February.

In the controversial series of ads created by The Martin Agency, Richmond, Va., a farmer bets a few of his friends that Commence can get rid of three types of troublesome weeds.

When the herbicide really works, the farmer forces his doubting friends to pay up. Or as in the case of the most recent ad, to paint up. One friend is forced to change the color of his $80,000 John Deere tractor to a charming shade of pink—not a very pretty sight, according to Cabell Harris, the agency's art director.

Another farmer has to eat his hat, literally, when he loses the bet.

FMC was hoping the ads would set it apart in the crowded soybean herbicide category. The company wanted a campaign that stood apart from the traditionally bland advertising in the field, Chalk said.

The ads have been successful in their bid for attention. Not all of it, however, has been favorable. Some farmers are finding the ads inconsistent with the image they are trying to project to the general public, Chalk said. Because it's a joint project with Elanco, the agricultural division of Eli Lilly & Co., FMC was especially sensitive to the criticism.

FMC has received 10 negative letters to which it has responded with an apology. The ads were not meant to be abusive, according to Chalk. The company just wanted to break through the clutter.

"We felt we really needed to create impact for this product because it's new and there are so many other herbicides," he said.

The company recognized the risks when it made the ads and had an alternative commercial waiting in the wings. Chalk is promising something a little less controversial this time around.

Questions

Do you feel that these ads were offensive? Were the farmers justified in complaining? Why or why not? Should the company have cancelled the campaign? Who should decide whether an ad is acceptable? Who should have the authority to remove an ad from the media?

Source: Cyndee Miller, "Humor in Herbicide Ad Campaign Is Not A Big Joke to Some Farmers," *Marketing News,* February 29, 1988, p. 6.

---

*Ivan L. Preston, *The Great American Blow-up* (Madison: The University of Wisconsin Press, 1975).
†"The Image of Advertising," *Editor and Publisher,* February 9, 1985.

reasonable people know that puffery is just a way to show enthusiasm for a product and that consumers understand this aspect of selling. Nobody really believes that Exxon will "put a tiger in your tank." One study lent support for that position. A test of 50 automobile advertisements, some using puffery and others not, found no difference in readership between the two types of ads. The researchers concluded that puffery did not enhance the attention-getting ability of the magazine message.*

Taste and Advertising

We all have our own ideas as to what constitutes good taste. Unfortunately, because these ideas vary so much, creating general guidelines for good taste in advertising is difficult. Different things offend different people. What is in good taste to some people is objectionable to others. Although Mel Tillis, a country and western singer who stutters, did not object to saying, "They're my kind of f-f-folks at Fina," the American Speech Language Hearing Association did.† They urged their members to complain about American Petrofina's gasoline advertising campaign, including accompanying billboards that read, "Ffffillerup," and bumper stickers with the message, "H-honk if you're f-folks." Some people felt the campaign exploited Mr. Tillis's handicap and thus was not in good taste. That possibility probably did not occur to many others who saw the campaign.

Product Categories and Taste   One dimension of the taste issue focuses on the product itself. Television advertising for certain products such as designer jeans, panty hose, bras and girdles, laxatives, and feminine-hygiene products produces higher levels of distaste than other product categories.‡ These products, combined with the ability of television to allow a spokesperson to come into our living rooms and "talk" to us about "unmentionables," probably embarrass many people, who then complain that the advertisements are distasteful. Although certain ads might be in bad taste, viewer reactions to commercials are also affected by such factors as sensitivity to the product category, when the message is received (for example, in the middle of dinner), and whether the person is alone or with others when the message is seen.

Tastes change over time. What is considered offensive today may be not offensive in the future. In 1919 a *Ladies' Home Journal* deodorant advertisement that asked the question, "Are you one of the many women who are troubled with excessive perspiration?" was so controversial that 200 readers immediately canceled their subscriptions.§ By today's standards that advertisement seems pretty tame.

Current Issues   Today questions of taste center around the use of sexual innuendo, nudity, and violence. Although the use of sex in advertising is not revolutionary, the blatancy of its use is more pronounced than in earlier years. The fashion industry has often been the focus of criticism for its liberal use of sex in advertising. Calvin Klein was one of the first to employ sexual innuendo in his advertising messages for designer jeans. His 1980 advertisement featured model Brooke Shields coyly asking, "Do you want to know what comes between me and my Calvins? Nothing." More recently Guess jeans created a stir with a

*Bruce G. Vanden Bergh and Leonard N. Reid, "Puffery and Magazine Ad Readership," *Journal of Marketing,* Spring 1980, pp. 78–81.

†Neil Maxwell, "Fina's New Ads Are Criticized for Making Use of a Stutterer," *The Wall Street Journal,* July 29, 1982, p. 21.

‡Bill Abrams, "Poll Suggests TV Advertisers Can't Ignore Matters of Taste," *The Wall Street Journal,* July 23, 1981, p. 25.

§Julian Lewis Watkins, *100 Greatest Advertisements, Who Wrote Them and What They Did* (New York: Moore Publishing Company, 1949).

series of black-and-white ads featuring a variety of scenes. The ads contained virtually no copy, which left them open to individual interpretation. Some of the ads contained a view of two girls in a field in an embrace that many found disconcerting, while another showed a sinister-looking man dressed in black kissing one woman while another watched.

It is to the advantage of the advertiser to be aware of current standards of taste. The safest way to make sure that the advertiser is not overlooking some part of the message that could be offensive is to pretest the advertisement. Pretest feedback should minimize the chances of producing distasteful advertising.

Stereotyping in Advertising

Stereotyping involves presenting a group of people in an unvarying pattern, one that lacks individuality. Critics claim that many advertisements stereotype large segments of our population, particularly women, minorities, and the elderly. The issue of stereotyping is connected to the debate about whether advertising shapes society's values or simply mirrors them. Either way the issue is very important. If you believe that advertising has the ability to shape our values and our view of the world, you will believe it essential that advertisers become aware of how they portray different groups. Conversely, if you believe that advertising mirrors society, you will think that advertisers have a responsibility to ensure that what is portrayed is accurate and representative. Advertisers struggle with this issue every time they use people in an ad.

Women in Advertisements The portrayal of women in advertisements has received much attention over the years. Initially critics complained that ads portrayed women as preoccupied with beauty, household duties, and motherhood. Advertising executives were accused of viewing women as zealous homemakers who were

> in endless pursuit of antiseptic cleanliness. Television ads for Lysol, Spic and Span, and Lemon Pledge, for example, show these ladies frantically spraying and polishing everything in sight—from refrigerator doors to dining-room tables to kitchen floors.*

Although there is still some concern about this stereotype, more advertisers are recognizing the diversity of women's roles. However, with the effort to portray women as more than obsessive housewives came a different problem. Suddenly advertisements focused on briefcase-toting professional women. Consider the commercial where a woman discusses the benefits of serving her children a powdered breakfast drink. She is a NASA engineer. The image of "Supermom" was displaced by the image of "Superwoman."† The challenge facing advertisers today is to portray women realistically, in diverse roles, without alienating any segment of women. Experts agree that today's woman wants to see women portrayed with a new freedom, but also as mature, intelligent people with varied interests and abilities.‡

Racial and Ethnic Stereotypes Racial and ethnic groups also complain of stereotyping in advertising. The root of most complaints is that certain groups are shown in subservient, unflattering ways. Many times minorities are the basis of a joke or, alternatively, consigned to a spot in the background. Other critics

*William Meyers, *The Image Makers* (William Meyers, 1984).

†Jim Auchmutey, "Graphic Changes Charted in the Middle Class," Special Report: Marketing to Women, *Advertising Age,* September 12, 1985, pp. 15–17.

‡Lynn Folse, "Workers Labor to Raise Women's Status," Special Report: Marketing to Women, *Advertising Age,* September 12, 1985, pp. 36–38.

Is your face paying the price of success?

You work hard at work, you work hard at home. You're under a lot of pressure.

You skip a meal here and there.

You're getting less sleep than maybe you should.

Eventually, of course, it begins to show on your face: a little less resilience, a few more lines.

Now, from Europe's leading skin care experts, there's new Nivea® Visàge.

Nivea Visàge is a non-greasy, fast-absorbing moisturizer, created especially for your face.

Enriched with Aloe and Vitamin E, it's specifically designed to fight the signs of pre-mature aging and other effects of stress.

It helps replenish and nourish your skin by reducing moisture loss.

It also actually assists your skin's natural ability to renew itself.

Keeping it looking firmer, healthier and younger, longer.

For over seventy years, at Nivea, our concern has been the care of your skin.

And it's still all we care about today.

New Nivea Visàge, in lotion or creme, is available at your favorite drug store.

It's the moisturizer that's made to help you live with success.

From Nivea. Europe's Number One Moisturizer.

AD 2.2
Advertising agencies are recognizing the importance of the minority market.
(Courtesy of EPC International.)

complain about underrepresentation of minorities in advertisements. A review of magazine and television advertising determined that Blacks account for between 2 and 6 percent of models in print ads and about 13 percent in television advertisements. (Blacks constitute about 12 percent of the total U.S. population.) The same study found that Blacks are overrepresented in advertising for certain product categories such as telephones (26.6 percent), liquor/wine (22.8 percent), beer (42.8 percent), and hair products (45.7 percent); and underrepresented in two other categories, tobacco (5.5 percent) and clothing (2.9 percent).*

Senior Citizens   Another group frequently mentioned with regard to stereotyping is senior citizens, a growing segment of the population with increasing disposable income (see Chapter 5). Critics often object to the use of older people in roles that portray them as slow, senile, and full of afflictions. Although Clara Peller achieved success in the Wendy's hamburger commercials, some critics charged that these ads were too cutesy.† Others were offended by the shrill "Where's the beef?" and felt that the tone of the commercial portrayed older people as hard to get along with, obstinate, and unattractive.

Advertising to Children

Advertising to children was one of the most controversial topics of the 1970s. In 1977 experts estimated that the average child watched more than 1,300 hours of television annually, which resulted in exposure to over 20,000 commercials.‡ Proponents of regulating children's advertising were concerned that children did not possess the skills necessary to evaluate advertising messages and to make purchase decisions. There was concern that certain advertising techniques and strategies appropriate for adults would be confusing or misleading to chil-

*Lynette Unger and James M. Stearns, "The Frequency of Blacks in Magazine and Television Advertising: A Review and Additional Evidence," *Southern Marketing Association Proceedings,* Robert L. King, ed., 1986, pp. 9–13.

†Laurie Freeman and Nancy Giges, "Ads Giving Older Consumers Short Shrift," *Advertising Age,* November 3, 1986, p. 92.

‡National Science Foundation, *Research on the Effects of Television Advertising on Children,* 1977.

dren. Two groups in particular, Action for Children's Television (ACT) and the Center for Science in the Public Interest (CSPI), petitioned the FTC to evaluate the situation.

In 1978 the FTC initiated proceedings to study possible rule making for children's television. Several regulations were suggested, including banning some types of advertising directed at children. Opponents of the proposed regulations argued that there were many self-regulatory mechanisms in place and that, ultimately, the proper place for restricting advertising to children was in the home.* This issue is addressed more closely in the Concepts and Controversies box on page 50.

AD 2.3
Advertisers have changed their portrayal of the elderly during the last 5 years.
(Courtesy of WATS Marketing of America, Inc.)

We turned seniors into jet setters for United Airlines.

Kathleen Malow
Fulfillment Manager
United Airlines

"Last February we rolled out our Silver Wings Plus program — a new promotion directed to seniors. To handle the volume of calls we knew we'd get, we turned to WATS Marketing of America.

"We had heard good comments about WATS Marketing of America and we felt they could give us the type of customer service we demand at United. We also wanted to work with a company that could tailor a program to our changing needs.

"I'd definitely use WATS Marketing of America again. They helped turn a new promotion into an extremely successful program."

Helping clients reach marketing objectives. That's our goal at WATS Marketing of America. No one has more experience and no one gets results like we do.

For information on how WATS Marketing of America can help you achieve your marketing goals, give us a call. We'll get your next promotion off the ground.

Call our President, Tony Holzapfel
1-800-351-1000

 WATS MARKETING of America, Inc.
Omaha, Nebraska 68134
402-572-5512
Full Range of Inbound and Outbound Services Available.

An American Express company

---

* "The Positive Case for Marketing Children's Products to Children," Comments by the Association of National Advertisers, Inc., American Association of Advertising Agencies and the American Advertising Federation before the Federal Trade Commission, November 24, 1978.

"I CAN'T COME RIGHT NOW, MOM ...
I'M WATCHING A COMMERCIAL
SPECIFICALLY TARGETED AT MY
DEMOGRAPHIC SEGMENT OF
THE POPULATION."

(Courtesy of Bill Whitehead.)

After years of debate over the issue, the proposed regulations by the FTC were abandoned. This does not mean, however, that advertisers to children have unlimited freedom. Advertising to children is carefully monitored by self-regulation. The National Advertising Division (NAD) of the Council of Better Business Bureaus, Inc. has a group charged with helping advertisers deal with children's advertising in a manner sensitive to children's special needs. The Children's Advertising Review Unit (CARU) was established in 1974 to review and evaluate advertising directed at children under the age of 12.

Advertising Controversial Products

One of the most heated advertising issues of the 1980s has been proposed restrictions on advertising such product categories as alcohol and tobacco. Restrictions on products thought to be unhealthy or unsafe are not new. Cigarette advertising on television and radio has been banned since January 1, 1971. In 1987 the issue was the advisability of a total ban of any form of media advertising of tobacco and alcohol products. A 1986 Tobacco-Free Young American Project poll of 1,025 Americans, 70 percent nonsmokers and 30 percent smokers, found that most respondents favored tougher restrictions on public smoking and tobacco-related promotional activities.*

Proponents of such a ban argued that advertising tobacco or alcohol products might result in sickness, injury, or death for the user and possibly others. Restricting advertising of those products would result in fewer sales of the products and consequently would reduce their unhealthy effects.

*Joe Agnew, "Trade Groups Align to Counter Public, Government Ban Efforts," *Marketing News,* January 30, 1987, pp. 1, 18.

Opponents of an advertising ban counterargued that such restrictions are in direct conflict with the First Amendment right to free speech. Critics contended that banning truthful, nondeceptive advertising for a legal product is itself illegal under the Constitution. As attorney and First Amendment authority Floyd Abrams pointed out, "Censorship is contagious and habit-forming . . . even for commercial speech. . . . What we need is more speech, not less. There would be a precedential effect for all other lawful products . . . that are said to do harm." Opponents also cited statistics demonstrating that similar bans in other countries had proved unsuccessful.*

AGAINST

The tobacco and alcohol industries maintained that their intent is to advertise only to those who have already decided to use their products and not to persuade nonusers to try the questionable products. R. J. Reynolds defends its position by messages explaining that they do not advertise to children (see Ad 2.4). Adolph Coors Company sponsored a "Gimme the Keys" television commercial intended to remind people to be responsible drinkers. They also developed a public service campaign using the movie character "E.T." to deliver the message, "If you go beyond your limit, please don't drive. Phone home." The outcome of the proposed advertising bans has far-reaching implications for advertisers, advertising agencies, and the general public. Stay tuned for further developments.

Condoms   Another topic of controversy is whether condoms should be advertised and, if so, in what media. Magazines have been more receptive to con-

AD 2.4
R. J. Reynolds used a series of ads to try to offset the negative publicity that the tobacco industry had been receiving.
(Courtesy of R. J. Reynolds Tobacco Co.)

We don't advertise to children.

Who are you kidding?
The newspapers and magazines and billboards are filled with cigarette ads. Kids can't help but see them.
How can you expect us to believe you're not trying to reach and influence our children?

We're not surprised if many people feel this way—especially when years of negative publicity have made them totally cynical about our industry.

Nevertheless, we'd like to set the record straight.

First of all, we don't want young people to smoke. And we're running ads aimed specifically at young people advising them that we think smoking is strictly for adults.

Second, research shows that among all the factors that can influence a young person to start smoking, advertising is insignificant. Kids just don't pay attention to cigarette ads, and that's exactly as it should be.

Finally—and this is sometimes hard for people outside the marketing field to understand—all of our cigarette ads are what we call "brand advertising." Its purpose is to get smokers of competitive products to switch to one of our brands, and to build the loyalty of those who already smoke one of our brands.

At the present there are some 200 different cigarette brands for sale in the U.S. Many of them have only a very small fraction of the total cigarette market. Getting smokers to switch is virtually the only way a cigarette brand can meaningfully increase its business.

That's why we don't advertise to young people.

Of course, if you'd like to share *this* ad with your children, that would be just fine with us.

R.J. Reynolds Tobacco Company

© 1984 R. J. REYNOLDS TOBACCO CO.

*Steven W. Colford, "Tobacco Ad Foes Press Fight," *Advertising Age,* February 23, 1987, p. 12; and "Strict Ad Bans Not Effective," *Advertising Age,* August 18, 1986.

THE PROS AND CONS OF TOY ADVERTISING DIRECTED AT CHILDREN

Against Viewpoint: National Coalition on Television Violence

Thanks to the toy industry's use of children's programming as 30-minute commercials to sell a variety of war toys, sales of war toys have soared by 700 percent since 1982. At the same time, the number of hours of war cartoons in national distribution has increased from 1½ hours a week to 43 today. Since each of these cartoons is nothing more than a 30-minute advertisement for war toys, it is no wonder that 11 of the 20 best-selling toys in the U.S. now have violent themes.

Now, with the approval of the Federal Communications Commission, the toy industry has begun a campaign to promote expensive, high-tech war toys through interactive children's cartoon programming—a future escalation of violent children's programming to reap huge profits through sales of war toys.

NCTV has found 43 studies looking at the impact of cartoon violence and/or violent toy play on children 3 to 11 years old. Forty of these studies have reported at least some harmful effects, including increases in loss of temper, fighting, kicking, choking, selfishness, cruelty to animals and disrespect for others, as well as decreases in sharing, imagination and school performance.

NCTV opposes any attempts to ban the toys themselves. However, NCTV is working with U.S. senators and representatives to get legislation introduced that would prohibit the use of children's programming by toy companies as a way of selling toys with violent themes.

For Viewpoint: Toy Manufacturers of America

Clearly, children's television, the burgeoning toy industry, and where they overlap have become increasingly volatile issues. Broadcasting and the toy business each have their share of critics, yet when the two intersect the uproar increases exponentially.

Let's examine the issues separately. Toy-based programming is not "30- (or 60) minute commercials." It is entertainment featuring characters that children know and love and it is not a new concept. Was anyone concerned in the '50s that "The Mickey Mouse Club" was a 60-minute promotion? Of course not.

Few, if any, of the toys, programs or story lines are "pro-war"; rather, they are 1980s versions of the ageless, cross-cultural good vs evil theme. It is the most enduring and important one we can teach our children. There is no evidence that playing with action figures or toy guns, or watching adventure programming on television, leads to violent behavior. Although many children spend too much time in front of the set, the influence of parents, siblings, school, peers and community, not to mention the differences in personality between individual youngsters, makes such generalizations about the impact of toy ads on behavior absurd.

The toy industry is a responsive one. In short, it doesn't set trends, but fulfills a perceived demand in the marketplace. Which is where parents come in, because—need it be said—4-year-olds don't have much purchasing power. If parents don't approve of a toy, they shouldn't buy it or allow it into their home. Adults ought to control the dial and on/off button of the television set, too.

It's getting into dangerous territory when somebody decides what is good for all 44.3 million American children.

Source: "Viewpoint: Forum," *Advertising Age,* September 21, 1987, p. 18.

---

dom ads than television even though the National Association of Broadcasters repealed its ban on the broadcast of contraceptive ads in 1982. The major networks have been hesitant to accept condom ads because of the sensitive nature of the product. Supporters of such advertising contend that the growing number of sexually transmitted diseases, including AIDS, makes such advertising necessary. They further argue that such messages can be done in good taste and at appropriate times, so that few groups would be offended. This issue raises difficult questions that will not be easily resolved.

Subliminal Advertising

Generally when we think of messages we consider symbols that are consciously seen and heard. However, it is possible to transmit symbols in a manner that

subliminal message *A message transmitted below the threshold of normal perception so that the receiver is not consciously aware of having viewed it.*

puts them below the threshold of normal perception. When this happens, the message is termed "subliminal." A **subliminal message** is one that is transmitted in such a way that the receiver is not consciously aware of it. This usually means that the symbols are too faint or too brief to be clearly recognized.

The Movie-Theater Controversy The furor over subliminal perception began with a 1958 study by James Vicary in a movie theater in Fort Lee, New Jersey. The words "Drink Coke" and "Eat Popcorn" were presented briefly on the movie screen. Allegedly the sale of popcorn went up almost 60 percent, and the sale of Coke increased 18 percent. Mr. Vicary was asked to repeat the test under controlled conditions that were supervised by The Psychological Corporation, a major research company. The second test produced no changes in purchases of either Coke or popcorn, and Mr. Vicary admitted that he had fabricated the results of the first experiment in hope of reviving his failing business.*

Packard and Key The phenomenon was further publicized by Vance Packard in his book *The Hidden Persuaders,* which has had a lingering effect in the minds of many people. The issue was revived in the 1970s with the publication of the books *Subliminal Seduction* and *Media Sexploitation* by Wilson Bryan Key. Key maintained that subliminal "embeds" are placed in ads to manipulate

---

GUIDELINES FOR CHILDREN'S ADVERTISING

The controversy surrounding the issue of children's advertising has encouraged the advertising industry to regulate this practice carefully. In the 1970s the industry issued written guidelines for children's advertising and established the Children's Advertising Review Unit within the Council of Better Business Bureaus to oversee the self-regulatory process. The Unit revised the written guidelines in 1977 and again in 1983. The following are the five basic principles on which guidelines for advertising directed at children are based.

(Courtesy of Elizabeth Hathon/The Stock Market.)

1. Advertisers should always take into account the level of knowledge, sophistication and maturity of the audience to which their message is primarily directed. Younger children have a limited capability for evaluating the credibility of what they watch. Advertisers, therefore, have a special responsibility to protect children from their own susceptibilities.

2. Realizing that children are imaginative and that make-believe play constitutes an important part of the growing up process, advertisers should exercise care not to exploit that imaginative quality of children. Unreasonable expectations of product quality or performance should not be stimulated either directly or indirectly by advertising.

3. Recognizing that advertising may play an important part in educating the child, information should be communicated in a truthful and accurate manner with full recognition by the advertiser that the child may learn practices from advertising which can affect his or her health and well-being.

4. Advertisers are urged to capitalize on the potential of advertising to influence social behavior by developing advertising that, wherever possible, addresses itself to social standards generally regarded as positive and beneficial, such as friendship, kindness, honesty, justice, generosity and respect for others.

5. Although many influences affect a child's personal and social development, it remains the prime responsibility of the parents to provide guidance for children. Advertisers should contribute to this parent-child relationship in a constructive manner.

Source: "Self-Regulatory Guidelines for Children's Advertising," 3rd ed., Children's Advertising Review Unit, National Advertising Division, Council of Better Business Bureaus, Inc., 1983, pp. 4–5.

---

*Walter Weir, "Another Look at Subliminal Facts," *Advertising Age,* October 15, 1984, p. 46.

purchase behavior, most frequently through appeals to sexuality. For example, he suggests that 99 percent of alcoholic beverage ads employ subliminal embeds. He finds the letters "S-E-X" embedded in ads for drinks, Ritz crackers, and pictures of political candidates. He also finds images of death and violence. A prime example is an April 1986 cover of *Time* magazine that Mr. Key claims contains the letters "K-I-L-L" on the right cheek of Moammar Gadhafi. Mr. Key contends that the messages are buried so skillfully that the average person does not notice them unless they are pointed out. He believes the subliminal embeds are the work of airbrush retouch artists.*

Whether or not subliminal stimuli can cause some types of minor reactions has never been the advertising issue. In tightly controlled laboratory settings subliminal stimuli have been shown to produce some reactions, such as a "like/dislike" response. The advertising issue is whether a subliminal message is capable of affecting the public's *buying behavior.*

Research in this field has uncovered several practical difficulties with the theory that subliminal embeds can be used to influence buying behavior. To begin with, perceptual thresholds vary from person to person and from moment to moment. Symbols that are subliminal to one person might be consciously perceived by another. A message guaranteed to be subliminal to an entire audience would probably be so weak that any effect would be limited. Another problem is the lack of control that the advertiser would have over the distance and position of the message receiver from the message. Differences in distances and position could affect when the stimulus is subliminal and when it is recognizable. The third problem comes from the effect of recognizable (supraliminal) material, such as the movie or commercial, used in conjunction with the subliminal message. The supraliminal stimulus might overpower the subliminal material.

Many people still believe subliminal advertising is used frequently, widely, and successfully. However, little evidence exists to support this belief. A survey of advertising agency art directors found that over 90 percent claimed no personal knowledge of it. Timothy Moore concluded after his overview of the subliminal area: "In general, the literature on subliminal perception shows that the most clearly documented effects are obtained in only highly contrived and artificial situations. These effects, when present, are brief and of small magnitude. . . . These processes have no apparent relevance to the goals of advertising."†

*A*DVERTISING AND THE LAW

Few elements of business have been more heavily legislated than advertising. This section discusses the most important federal legislation as well as attempts at self-regulation.

Advertising and the First Amendment

Freedom of expression in the United States is protected from government control by the Bill of Rights to the Constitution. In particular the First Amendment states that Congress shall make no law "abridging the freedom of speech, or of the press; or the right of people peaceably to assemble, and to petition the Government for a redress of grievances." Although Congress adopted the amendment in 1791, the Supreme Court continues to interpret it as it applies to different situations. Initially the Court ruled that freedom of expression is not absolute, although only the most compelling circumstances justify prior restraint

*Daniel A. LaBry, "Subliminals Draw Large Crowd," *The Battalion,* October 2, 1986, p. 1.
†Timothy Moore, "Subliminal Advertising: What You See Is What You Get," *Journal of Marketing,* Spring 1982, pp. 38–47.

PEOPLE HAVE BEEN TRYING TO FIND THE BREASTS IN THESE ICE CUBES SINCE 1957.

The advertising industry is sometimes charged with sneaking seductive little pictures into ads.

Supposedly, these pictures can get you to buy a product without your even seeing them.

Consider the photograph above. According to some people, there's a pair of female breasts hidden in the patterns of light refracted by the ice cubes.

Well, if you really searched you probably *could* see the breasts. For that matter, you could also see Millard Fillmore, a stuffed pork chop and a 1946 Dodge.

The point is that so-called "subliminal advertising" simply doesn't exist. Overactive imaginations, however, most certainly do.

So if anyone claims to see breasts in that drink up there, they aren't in the ice cubes.

They're in the eye of the beholder.

ADVERTISING
ANOTHER WORD FOR FREEDOM OF CHOICE.
American Association of Advertising Agencies

on the spread of information. Specifically the Court held that the First Amendment applied to most media, including newspapers, books, magazines, broadcasting, and film. However, in 1942 the Supreme Court ruled in *Valentine v. Christensen* that the First Amendment does *not* protect "purely commercial advertising."* The Court reasoned that commercial advertising does not serve the historic First Amendment interest of protecting free discussion that contributes to decision making in a democracy.

By 1976 the Supreme Court had reconsidered this position. In the case of *Virginia State Board of Pharmacy v. Virginia Citizen's Consumer Council* it ruled that the First Amendment barred a state from prohibiting pharmacists from advertising the prices of prescription drugs. In his opinion for the Court Justice Blackmun came close to equating the traditionally protected marketplace of ideas with the more regulated commercial marketplace. "Advertising," Blackmun said,

> however tasteless and excessive it sometimes may seem, is nonetheless dissemination of information as to who is producing and selling what product, for what reason, and at what price. So long as we preserve a predominantly free enterprise economy, the allocation of our resources in large measure will be made through numerous private economic decisions. It is a matter of public interest that those decisions, in the aggregate, be intelligent and well informed. To this end, the free flow of commercial information is indispensable.†

Valentine v. Christensen, 316 U.S. 52, 54 (1942).
† *Virginia State Board of Pharmacy v. Virginia Citizen's Consumer Council,* 425 U.S. 748, 765 (1976).

Since *Virginia Pharmacy* the Court has struck down other statutes prohibiting commercial expression. As a result, states no longer can bar attorneys from advertising the prices of "routine" legal services, home owners from advertising their houses by placing "For Sale" signs in their yards, drugstores from advertising contraceptives, or utilities from promoting the use of electricity.*

Can advertisers assume they are now free from government regulation? Hardly. Although the Supreme Court has ruled that some very limited forms of advertising content merit First Amendment protection, it has not said that a business has the same First Amendment right of expression as a private individual or a newspaper. Nor has the Court accorded the same degree of protection to commercial advertising that it insists upon for other protected content.

Perhaps the best illustration of current Supreme Court views concerning the Constitutional protection of advertising was expressed in the *Central Hudson Gas & Electric Corporation v. Public Service Commission of New York* case of 1980. To encourage energy conservation the PSC prohibited all promotional advertising by utilities. The Court ruled the state's prohibition to be overly broad and therefore unconstitutional. The decision placed limitations on government regulation of lawful, nondeceptive advertising.

In a 1986 case, *Posadas de Puerto Rico Associates v. Tourism Company of Puerto Rico,* the Court upheld a Puerto Rican law banning advertising of gambling casinos to residents of Puerto Rico. The majority opinion argued that the prohibition directly advanced a government interest and was no more extensive than was necessary. Although the Court's interpretation of constitutional protection for advertising remains unsettled, it does appear to be moving in a direction that favors advertising.

PRINCIPLE

Recent interpretations of the First Amendment find that commercial information should not be prohibited, but the "right" of expression for advertisers is still being defined.

GOVERNMENT REGULATORY AGENCIES

Federal Trade Commission

Federal Trade Commission (FTC) *A federal agency responsible for interpreting deceptive advertising and regulating unfair methods of competition.*

The **Federal Trade Commission** (FTC) is the government agency responsible for regulating much of American business. It was established in 1914 to prevent business activities that were unfair or anticompetitive. Its original mission was to protect business rather than the consumer, and its enabling act contained no statement about advertising. In 1922 a Supreme Court ruling placed deceptive advertising within the scope of the FTC's authority, giving the agency the right to regulate false labeling and advertising as unfair methods of competition.

The Wheeler-Lea Amendment that was passed in 1938 extended the FTC's powers, and the agency became more consumer oriented. This amendment added "deceptive acts and practices" to the list of "unfair methods of competition." In addition, the Wheeler-Lea Amendment gave the FTC authority to: (1) initiate investigations against companies without waiting for complaints; (2) issue cease-and-desist orders; and (3) fine companies for not complying with cease-and-desist orders. The FTC was also given jurisdiction over false advertising of foods, drugs, cosmetics, and therapeutic devices. False advertising was defined as "any false representation, including failure to reveal material facts".†

The FTC acquired increased authority during the late 1960s and mid-1970s through a series of improvement acts. One, a two-section act, had the greatest impact. The first section, The Magnusson-Moss Warranty Section of 1975, dealt

---

*Ivan L. Preston, "A Review of the Literature on Advertising Regulation," in *Current Issues and Research in Advertising, 1983,* James H. Leigh and Claude L. Martin, eds. (Ann Arbor: University of Michigan, 1983), pp. 2–37.

†*Bates v. State Bar of Arizona,* 433 U.S. 350 (1977). *Linmark Associates, Inc. v. Township of Willingboro,* 431 U.S. 85 (1977); *Carey v. Population Services International,* 431 U.S. 678 (1977); *Central Hudson v. Public Services Commission,* 6 Med. L. Reptr. 1497 (U.S. 1980).

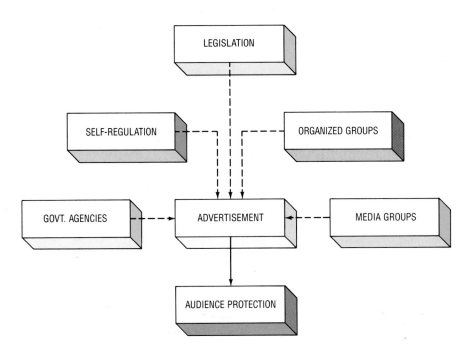

FIGURE 2.1
Regulatory factors affecting advertising.

with protecting consumers' rights in respect to product warranties. It facilitated consumers' ability to compare warranties for similar products, and it allowed the FTC to require restitution for deceptively written warranties costing the consumer more than $5.

The second section, the FTC Improvements Section of the act, allowed the FTC to establish Trade Regulation Rules—industry-wide rules that defined unfair practices before they occurred. Prior to this act, the Commission could prosecute improper practices only on a case-by-case basis, which had proven to be costly and time-consuming. By expanding FTC regulation to "unfair" as well as "deceptive" practices, the act created a great deal of controversy. Critics of the act argued that "unfair" was an extremely vague concept and difficult to prove or disprove. Perhaps most controversial was the trade regulation rule that limited children's television advertising because it tended to be "unfair."

By 1980, however, Congress had come to believe that the use of the "unfairness" criteria had been too broadly interpreted by the FTC. Thus, the 1980 FTC Improvements Act included a provision prohibiting the use of unfairness as a basis for designing any trade regulation rules on advertising. At the present time, Congress is debating the concepts of "deception" and "unfairness" in order to come up with an acceptable FTC Reauthorization Bill. In the meantime the power of the FTC has been diminished, and deception is again appraised on a case-by-case basis.

In addition, the political climate in the 1980s has resulted in new appointees to the FTC who have been less aggressive in regulating advertising. The Reagan administration's position was that regulation is justifiable only if it produces benefits that outweigh the costs.

The FTC and Advertisers Regardless of the philosophy of a given administration, the very existence of a regulatory agency like the FTC can influence the behavior of advertisers.

Although most cases never reach the FTC, advertisers prefer not to run the risk of a long legal involvement with the agency. Advertisers are also conscious of the reaction of competitors who, with a lot of consumer dollars at stake, may be quick to complain to an appropriate agency about a questionable advertisement. As was suggested in an editorial in *Advertising Age:*

We've long since agreed that lies, deception, and fraud are beyond debate. No, ethics in advertising goes far beyond that. To the study of fine-lines-manship of what constitutes "weasel-wording" and what constitutes the whole truth. . . . if the copy stretches the truth even by a hair, or can be misinterpreted by anyone exposed to it, find another way. Chances are you'll end up with a stronger, more believable, more persuasive product presentations. And isn't that what good advertising is all about anyway?*

Ultimately most advertisers want their customers to remain happy and pleased with their products and advertising, so they take every precaution to make sure their messages are not deceptive.

Food and Drug Administration

Food and Drug Administration (FDA) *A federal regulatory agency that oversees package labeling and ingredient listings for food and drugs.*

Federal Communications Commission (FCC) *A federal agency that regulates broadcast media and has the power to eliminate messages, including ads, that are deceptive or in poor taste.*

Two other major government agencies deal with advertising-related concerns: the **Food and Drug Administration** (FDA) and the **Federal Communications Commission** (FCC). The FDA is the regulatory division of the Department of Health and Human Services. It oversees package labeling and ingredient listings for food and drugs and determines the safety and purity of foods and cosmetics. Although not directly involved with advertising, the FDA provides advice to the FTC and has a major impact on the overall marketing of food, cosmetics, and drugs.

Federal Communications Commission

The FCC was formed in 1934 to protect the public interest with regard to broadcast communication. It has limited control over broadcast advertising through its authority to issue and revoke licenses to broadcasting stations. The FCC is concerned with radio and television stations and networks, and it has the power to eliminate messages, including ads, that are deceptive or in poor taste. The agency monitors only those advertisements that have been the subject of complaints and works closely with the FTC with regard to false and deceptive advertising. The FCC takes action against the media, whereas the FTC is concerned with advertisers and agencies.

Other Federal Agencies

Other federal agencies are involved in the regulation of advertising, although most are limited by the type of advertising, product, or medium. For example, the Postal Service regulates direct-mail and magazine advertising and has control over the areas of obscenity, lottery, and fraud. Consumers who receive advertisements in the mail that they consider sexually offensive can request that no more mail be delivered from that sender. The postmaster general also has the power to withhold mail that promotes a lottery. Fraud can include any number of activities that are questionable, such as implausible get-rich-quick schemes.

The Bureau of Alcohol, Tobacco, and Firearms within the Treasury Department both regulates deception in advertising and establishes labeling requirements for the liquor industry. This agency's power comes from its authority to issue and revoke annual operating permits for distillers, wine merchants, and brewers. Because there is a danger that public pressure could result in banning all advertisements for alcoholic beverages, the liquor industry strives to maintain relatively tight control on its advertising.

The Patent Office, under the Lanham Trade-Mark Act of 1947, oversees registration of trademarks, which include both brand names and corporate or

*Win Roll, "A Valuable Lesson in Integrity," *Advertising Age,* May 25, 1987, p. 18.

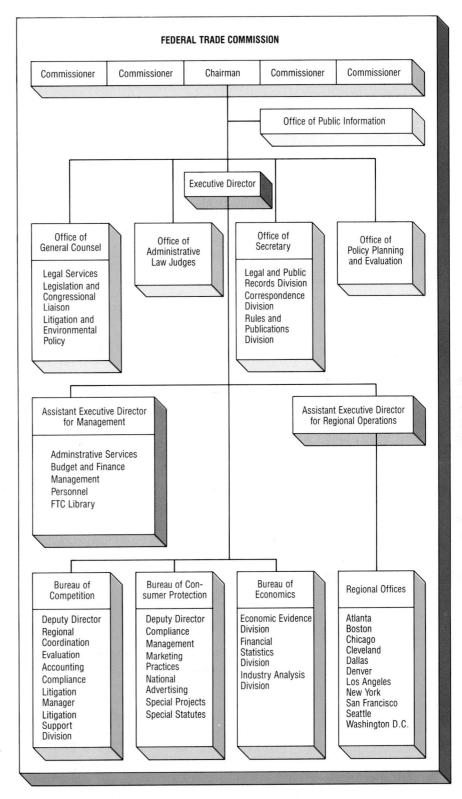

FIGURE 2.2
The Federal Trade Commission.

Source: Your Federal Trade Commission: What It Is and What It Does (Washington, DC: Federal Trade Commission, Government Printing Office, 1977).

store names as well as their identifying symbols. This registration process protects unique trademarks from infringement by competitors. Because trademarks are critical communication devices for products and services, they are important in advertising.

Finally the Library of Congress provides controls for copyright protection. Legal copyrights give creators a monopoly on their creations for a certain time.

TABLE 2.1
Important Advertising
Legislation

Pure Food and Drug Act (1906)
  Forbids the manufacture, sale, or transport of adulterated or fraudulently labeled foods and drugs in interstate commerce. Supplanted by the Food, Drug, and Cosmetic Act of 1938; amended by Food Additives Amendment in 1958 and Kefauver-Harris Amendment in 1962.

Federal Trade Commission Act (1914)
  Establishes the commission, a body of specialists with broad powers to investigate and to issue cease and desist orders to enforce Section 5, which declares that "unfair methods of competition in commerce are unlawful."

Wheeler-Lea Amendment (1938)
  Prohibits unfair and deceptive acts and practices regardless of whether competition is injured; places advertising of foods and drugs under FTC jurisdiction.

Lanham Act (1947)
  Provides protection for trademarks (slogans and brand names) from competitors and also encompasses false advertising.

Magnuson-Moss Warranty/FTC Improvement Act (1975)
  Authorizes the FTC to determine rules concerning consumer warranties and provides for consumer access to means of redress, such as the "class action" suit. Also expands FTC regulatory powers over unfair or deceptive acts or practices.

FTC Improvement Act (1980)
  Provides the House of Representatives and Senate jointly with veto power over FTC regulation rules. Enacted to limit FTC's powers to regulate "unfairness" issues. A reauthorization bill is currently being considered at the writing of this book.

(handwritten: Summary of previous info)

Advertising is a competitive business where "me too" ads abound. Copyrighting of coined words, illustrations, characters, and photographs can offer some measure of protection from advertisers who borrow too heavily from their competitors.

Certain state laws also regulate unfair and deceptive business practices. These laws are important supplements to federal laws because of the sometimes limited resources and jurisdiction of the FTC and the Justice Department. Because these laws are so numerous and diverse, we cannot begin to examine them in this chapter.

Because the bulk of advertising-related regulation is handled by the FTC, the focus of this section will be on that agency's policies. Also covered will be the FTC's remedies for deceptive or unfair advertising practices.

*F*TC CONCERNS WITH ADVERTISING

Deception

Deceptive advertising is a major focus of the FTC. Some of the activities that the commission has identified as deceptive are deceptive pricing, false criticisms of competing products, deceptive guarantees, ambiguous statements, and false testimonials. Until recently the legal standard of deceptiveness involved judging only that an advertisement had the capacity to deceive consumers, not that it had actually done so. In 1983 the FTC changed the standard used to determine deception. The current policy contains three basic elements:

PRINCIPLE _____
Data must be on file to substantiate claims made by advertisers.

(handwritten: Current Policy)

1. Where there is a representation, omission, or practice, there must be a high probability that it will mislead the consumer.
2. The perspective of the "reasonable consumer" is used to judge deception. The FTC tests "reasonableness" by looking at whether the consumer's interpretation or reaction to an advertisement is reasonable.
3. The deception must lead to material injury. In other words, the deception must influence consumers' decision making about products and services.*

*"Letter to Congress Explaining FTC's New Deception Policy," Advertising Compliance Service, Westport, CN: Meckler Publishing, November 21, 1983; and Preston, "A Review of the Literature," pp. 2–37.

This new policy makes deception more difficult to prove. It also creates uncertainty for advertisers, who must wait for congressional hearings and court cases to discover what the FTC will permit.

Reasonable Basis for Making a Claim

The advertiser should have a reasonable basis for making a claim about product performance. This involves having data on file to substantiate any claims made in the advertising.

Determining the reasonableness of a claim is done on a case-by-case basis. The FTC has suggested that the following factors should be examined:

1. Type and specificity of claim made
2. Type of product
3. Possible consequences of the false claim
4. Degree of reliance by consumers on the claims
5. The type and accessibility of evidence available for making the claim*

Reinforcement of False Beliefs

One focus of deception has been advertisements that create and reinforce false beliefs. This perspective is not as concerned with the truthfulness of the actual message as it is with how consumers perceive the ad and how it affects their opinions and beliefs about the advertised product or service. Thus an ad would be judged deceptive when consumer perception of truthfulness and actual truthfulness of a particular claim are inconsistent. For example, if a consumer perceives an over-the-counter drug to have certain healing capabilities, that's all that matters. Complicating the issue is the fact that deception can sometimes occur at a more subtle level. It has been proposed that consumers may internalize preexisting or advertised benefits about an advertised product that are not necessarily true.† For example, consumers may perceive that colored crystals in laundry detergent are cleaning agents. Because this perception exists, consumers can be deceived by copy that simply mentions the crystals are present, even though nothing is specifically said about the cleaning capacity of the crystals.

Comparative Advertising

The FTC supports comparative advertising as a way of providing more information to consumers. A substantial percentage of all television commercials use a comparative strategy. The commission requires that comparative claims be substantiated by the advertiser, just as any other claim. Comparative advertising is considered deceptive unless its comparisons are based on fact; the differences advertised are statistically significant; the comparisons involve meaningful issues; and the comparisons involve meaningful competitors.

Endorsements

A popular advertising strategy involves the use of a spokesperson (see Chapter 8) who endorses the brand. Because consumers often rely on these endorsements when making purchase decisions, the FTC has concentrated on commercials that use this approach. Endorsers must be qualified by experience

---

Federal Trade Commission v. Raladam Company, 283 U.S. 643 (1931).

†Dorothy Cohen, "The FTC's Advertising Substantiation Program," *Journal of Marketing,* Vol. 44, Winter 1980, pp. 26–35.

or training to make judgments, and they must actually use the product. If endorsers are comparing competing brands, they must have tried those brands as well. Those who endorse a product improperly may be liable if the FTC determines there is a deception.

Demonstrations

Product demonstrations in television advertising must not mislead consumers. A claim that is demonstrated must be accurately shown. This mandate is especially difficult for advertisements containing food products because such factors as hot studio lights or the length of time needed to shoot the commercial can cause an unappealing portrayal of the product. For example, because milk looks gray on television, advertisers often substitute a mixture of glue and water. The question is whether or not the demonstration falsely upgrades the consumer's perception of the advertised brand. The FTC evaluates this kind of deception on a case-by-case basis.

Bait Advertising

Bait advertising is an attractive but insincere offer to sell something that the advertiser does not really intend to sell. The FTC prohibits advertising that does not represent a bona fide offer to sell the advertised product. In addition, advertisements should not misrepresent factors such as the actual price, quality, or salability of the product in a way that would pressure consumers into buying a different, and usually more expensive, product.*

*F*TC REMEDIES FOR DECEPTIVE AND UNFAIR ADVERTISING

The most common sources of complaints concerning deceptive or unfair advertising practices are competitors, the public, and the FTC's own monitors. If a complaint is found to be justified, the Commission can follow several courses of action. Prior to 1970 cease-and-desist orders and fines were the FTC's major weapons against deception. However, the Commission has developed alternative remedies over the years.

Corrective Advertising

corrective advertising *A remedy required by the FTC in which an advertiser who produced misleading messages is required to issue factual information to offset these messages.*

PRINCIPLE
Corrective advertising is required when the FTC determines that an ad has created lasting false impressions.

Corrective advertising is required by the FTC in cases where consumer research determines that lasting false beliefs have been perpetuated by an advertising campaign. With this remedy, the offending firm is ordered to produce messages that correct any deceptive impressions created in the consumer's mind. The purpose of corrective advertising is not to punish a firm but to prevent that firm from continuing to deceive consumers. The FTC may require a firm to run corrective advertising even if the campaign in question has been discontinued.

The landmark case involving corrective advertising was *Warner-Lambert v. FTC* in 1977. According to the FTC, Warner-Lambert's 50-year-old campaign for Listerine mouthwash had been deceiving customers into thinking that Listerine was able to prevent sore throats and colds or to lessen their severity. The company was ordered to run a corrective advertising campaign, mostly on television, for 16 months at a cost of $10 million. Interestingly, after the corrective campaign was run, 42 percent of Listerine users still believed the mouthwash was being advertised as a remedy for sore throats and colds, and 57 percent of users

*John F. Cady, "Advertising Restrictions and Retail Prices," *Journal of Advertising Research,* October 1976, p. 29.

rated cold and sore throat effectiveness as a key attribute in purchasing the brand.* The results raised questions concerning the effectiveness of corrective advertising. However, the *Warner-Lambert* case remains significant because for the first time the FTC was given the power to apply retrospective remedies and to attempt to restrict future deceptions. In addition, the Supreme Court rejected the argument that corrective advertising violates the advertiser's First Amendment rights.

Substantiating Advertising Claims

In 1971 the FTC initiated a policy that required advertisers to validate any claims when requested by the Commission. Advertisers must have a "reasonable basis" for making a claim. It is the responsibility of the advertiser to show the reasonableness of a claim; it is *not* up to the FTC to disprove a claim's validity. Documentation may be based on a variety of sources, including scientific research and the opinions of experts.

Consumer Redress

The Magnuson-Moss Warranty–FTC Improvement Act of 1975 empowers the FTC to obtain consumer redress in cases where an individual or a firm engages in deceptive practices. The Commission can order any of the following: cancellation or reformation of contracts; refund of money or return of property; payment of damages; and public notification.

SELF-REGULATION

In addition to governmental controls, the advertising industry has created a self-regulating mechanism in an attempt to control such issues as deception. The rationale is that if the industry can police itself better, it can avoid confrontations with the government.

National Agencies

In the case of both advertisers and advertising agencies, the most effective attempts at self-regulation have come through the Advertising Review Council and the Better Business Bureau. In 1971 the National Advertising Review Council was established by several professional advertising associations in conjunction with the Council of Better Business Bureaus. The main purpose of the Council is to negotiate voluntary withdrawal of national advertising that professionals consider to be deceptive. The National Advertising Division (NAD) of the Council of Better Business Bureaus and the National Advertising Review Board (NARB) are the two operating arms of the National Advertising Review Council.

NAD The NAD is a full-time agency made up of people from the field of advertising. It evaluates complaints that are submitted by consumers, consumer groups, industrial organizations, or advertising firms. The NAD also does its own monitoring. After a complaint is received, the NAD may ask the advertiser in question to substantiate claims made in the advertisement. If such substantiation is deemed inadequate, the advertiser is requested either to change or to withdraw the offending ad. When a satisfactory resolution cannot be found, the case is referred to the NARB.

*William Wilke, Dennis L. McNeil, and Michael B. Mazis, "Marketing's 'Scarlett Letter': The Theory and Practice of Corrective Advertising," *Journal of Marketing,* Spring 1984, p. 26.

NARB The NARB is a 50-member regulatory group that represents national advertisers, advertising agencies, and other professional fields. When a case is appealed to the NARB, a five-person panel is formed that consists of three advertisers, one agency person, and one public representative. This panel reviews the complaint and the NAD staff findings and holds hearings to let the advertiser present its case. If the case remains unresolved after this process, the NARB can: (1) publicly identify the advertiser and the facts about the case; and (2) refer the complaint to the appropriate government agency, which is usually the FTC. Although neither the NAD nor the NARB has any real power other than threatening to invite governmental intervention, these groups have been relatively effective in controlling cases of deception and misleading advertising.

Local Regulation: BBB

At the local level self-regulation has been supported by the Better Business Bureau (BBB). The BBB functions much like the national agencies, and in addition provides local businesses with advice concerning the legal aspects of advertising. The origin of the Bureau can be traced to the "truth in advertising campaign" sponsored by the American Advertising Federation in 1911. Since that time more than 240 local and national bureaus, made up of advertisers, agencies, and media, have screened hundreds of thousands of advertisements for possible violation of truth and accuracy. Although the BBB has no legal power, it does receive and investigate complaints and maintain files of violators. It also assists local law enforcement officials in prosecuting potential violators.

Media Regulation of Advertising

PRINCIPLE
Media can refuse to accept advertising that violates standards of truth or good taste.

The media attempt to regulate advertising by screening and rejecting ads that violate their standards of truth and good taste. For example, *Reader's Digest* doesn't accept tobacco and liquor ads, and many magazines and television stations will not show condom ads. Each individual medium has discretion to accept or reject a particular ad. In the case of the major television networks, the ABC's advertising standards and guidelines serve as the primary standard.

A FINAL THOUGHT

Although the negative aspects of advertising will continue to be with the industry in one form or another, thought should be given to what role a person can play in promoting quality, inoffensive, nondeceptive, nonstereotypical advertising messages.

From the viewpoint of an advertising practitioner, the first step is establishing individual ethical parameters. Setting personal standards and evaluating how they relate to advertising issues prepares the individual to deal with a number of questionable situations. Prior preparation helps prevent being caught off guard and being swayed by arguments contrary to solid ethical beliefs. Naturally there is some concern about whether ethical behavior in an extremely competitive environment will allow a company to survive and prosper. Although empirical evidence is not conclusive, there is an encouraging amount of material about companies that accept social responsibility and promote ethical behavior and how they not only prosper but excel. Ultimately we hope the consumer will recognize and reward those companies that respect standards of taste and social responsibility.

When in doubt, you might want to follow the advice given by David Ogilvy: Never run an advertisement you wouldn't want your family to see.

SUMMARY

- Federal courts have ruled that advertising is protected under the First Amendment.
- The primary regulatory agencies governing advertising are the Federal Trade Commission, the Food and Drug Administration, and the Federal Communications Commission. They are concerned with the following advertising issues: deception, reasonable basis for making a claim, reinforcement of false beliefs, comparative advertising, endorsements, demonstrations, bait advertising, and children's advertising.

- Regulatory agencies have a variety of remedies for deception and unfair advertising practices.
- Because of legislative pressure and costs, advertising and media have set up a variety of institutions for self-regulation.
- A number of ethical issues in advertising are not governed through specific legislation. Advertisers have been very active in addressing these ethical issues.

QUESTIONS

1. According to the federal courts, how does the First Amendment relate to advertising?
2. Discuss the primary tasks of the FTC, the FDA, and the FCC. What types of remedies can they order?
3. What is deception in advertising? What standards are used to determine whether an ad is deceptive?
4. What are advertising's primary means for self-regulation?
5. What are the central issues in ethical decision making?

6. What is puffery? Stereotyping? Subliminal advertising? How do you think the advertising industry should address these issues?
7. Think of an ad you have found deceptive or offensive. What bothered you about the ad? Should the media have carried the ad? Is it proper for the government or the advertising industry to act in cases like this? Why or why not?

FURTHER READINGS

ALEXANDER, GEORGE A. *Honesty and Competition: False Advertising Law and Policy under FTC Administration.* Syracuse University Press, 1967.

DALY, JOHN CHARLES. *Advertising and the Public Interest.* Washington, DC: American Enterprise Institute for Public Policy Research, 1976.

LICHTENBERGER, JOHN. *Advertising Compliance Law: Handbook for Marketing Professionals.* New York: Quorum Books, 1986.

National Science Foundation. *Research on the Effects of Television Advertising on Children.* 1977.

PRESTON, IVAN L. *The Great American Blow-Up: Puffery in Advertising and Selling.* Madison: The University of Wisconsin Press, 1975.

ROM, EDWIN P., and WILLIAM H. ROBERTS. *Corporate and Commercial Free Speech: First Amendment Protection of Expression in Business.* Westport, CN: Quorum Books, 1985.

3

Advertising and the Marketing Process

Chapter Outline

Remaining the Top Dog
The Marketplace
The Concept of Marketing
Marketing Elements
The 4Ps of Marketing
The Marketing Mix

Chapter Objectives

When you have completed this chapter, you should be able to:

- Understand the marketing concept and how it differs from production-oriented marketing
- Explain how a company's market philosophy is expressed
- Identify four types of markets
- Define and explain the 4Ps of the marketing mix
- Explain the four stages in a product's life cycle
- Identify the key elements involved in establishing a brand

REMAINING THE TOP DOG

In 1987 Ralston Purina put Quaker Oats on notice that it intended to keep its leadership in the $3.4 billion dog-food market. In 1986 Quaker had purchased the Gaines dog-food line and subsequently launched a major advertising campaign to displace Purina as the market leader. Purina responded by doubling its own product introductions and reformulations. Purina also tried innovative advertising when it reintroduced its 8-year-old Butcher's Blend dry dog food with a bacon-scented "scratch 'n sniff" newspaper insert—a first in the dog-food industry.

In reaction to Quaker's aggressive spending, Purina also restaged its 9-year-old Moist 'n Chunky line, which had declined in sales from $40 million to $27 million since the early 1980s. The soft dry food now carries the name Benji's Moist 'n Chunky and features movie star Benji as its celebrity spokesdog.

Purina also introduced Grrravy dry dog food with television spots showing animated dog firefighters adding water to the product to make gravy. This move was a direct assault on Gravy Train, which Quaker had picked up with its Gaines acquisition.

Purina is trying to win consumers by pricing its 40-pound bag of Grrravy at $10, compared to $16 for Gravy Train. Purina also is offering coupons for up to $1.50 off any bag 20 pounds or larger. Purina has introduced other brands into specialized niches, including Smaller Dog Chow with smaller chunks; Purina One, a superpremium dry dog food; Hearty Chews dog treats; and Purina Pro Plan, a superpremium dry food sold through nongrocery outlets.[*]

The marketing battles between Purina and Quaker Oats will continue, with each company challenging its competitor with new product lines, pricing strategies, innovative sales promotions, and advertising breakthroughs. Undoubtedly the winner in this intensely competitive market will be the one that best applies its various marketing weapons.

THE MARKETPLACE

A market is a place where goods are bought and sold—a shop, a store, a bazaar, a fair. That is the source of the term *marketing,* which is used in business to refer to the process of selling merchandise to people who want to buy. In marketing literature buying and selling is referred to as "an exchange." The buyer gets a product or a service by exchanging something of equal value, usually money, although for some products and in some cultures *bartering,* or negotiating a price, is still acceptable.

Advertising is used to communicate information about the product and to persuade consumers to buy it. This communication occurs before consumers even go to the market. Along with their money, consumers take some fragments of the advertising message with them.

THE CONCEPT OF MARKETING

marketing *Business activities that direct the exchange of goods and services between producers and consumers.*

The American Marketing Association defines **marketing** as "the process of planning and executing the conception, pricing, promotion, and distribution of ideas, goods, and services to create exchanges that satisfy individual (customer)

[*]Beth Austin, "Dog Days of Summer," *Advertising Age,* August 31, 1987, p. 5.

and organizational objectives."* Although the exchange is the focus of the effort, marketing is a complex process operating in a complex business environment.

Marketing is an important business function because its purpose is to find, to satisfy, and to retain customers. It differs from the other functional areas of business, such as manufacturing and finance, in that its primary concern is with exchanges that take place *in markets* outside the organization.

PRINCIPLE ————————
Advertising is a component of marketing.

Marketing influences all aspects of making the product or service available *for sale,* including such activities as product development, distribution, packaging, pricing, personal selling, and promotional activities, including advertising. Thus, advertising is a subset of marketing. Without a basic understanding of marketing, it is virtually impossible to comprehend how advertising works.

Leo Bogart, formerly an advertising strategist with McCann-Erickson, Exxon, and Revlon and now general manager of the Newspaper Advertising Bureau, described the contemporary business climate as "increasingly competitive" with "more new products than ever." He observed that in this highly competitive environment advertising is at "the white-hot center of marketing competition."†

The Idea of a Market

market *An area of the country, a group of people, or the overall demand for a product.*

The word *market* originally meant the place where the "exchange" between seller and buyer took place. The term now has taken on several new meanings. Today we speak of a **market** as either a region where goods are sold and bought or a particular type of buyer. In other words, a market can be an *area of the country* or a *group of people.* In a more general sense, we also use the word to refer to the *demand for a product.*

Types of Markets

When marketing strategists speak of markets they are generally referring to groups of people. The four primary types of markets are: (1) consumer; (2) industrial; (3) institutional; and (4) reseller.

Consumer Consumer markets consist of individuals who buy products and services for their own personal use or for the use of others in the household. As a student you are considered a member of the market for companies that sell jeans, sweatshirts, pizza, textbooks, backpacks, and bicycles, among a multitude of products.

Industrial Industrial markets consist of companies that buy products or services to use in their own businesses or in making other products. General Electric, for example, buys computers to use in billing and inventory control, steel and wiring to use in the manufacture of its products, and cleaning supplies to use in maintaining its buildings.

Institutional Institutional markets include a wide variety of profit and non-profit organizations, such as hospitals, government agencies, and schools, that provide goods and services for the benefit of society at large. Universities, for example, are in the market for furniture, cleaning supplies, computers, office supplies, groceries and food products, audio-visual materials, and tissue and toilet paper, to name just a few.

* "AMA Board Approves New Marketing Definition," *Marketing News,* March 1, 1985, p. 1.
† Leo Bogart, *Strategy in Advertising,* 2nd ed. (Chicago: Crain Books, 1984), p. 2.

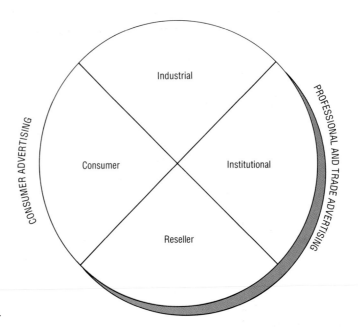

FIGURE 3.1
The four principal types of markets.

Reseller   The reseller market includes what we often call "the middlemen." These are wholesalers, retailers, and distributors who buy finished or semifinished products and resell them for a profit. Resellers are considered a market by companies that sell such products and services as trucks, cartons, crates, and transportation services.

Of the four markets the consumer market is probably the largest in terms of dollars spent on advertising. Marketing to this group is generally done through mass media such as radio, television, newspapers, general consumer magazines, and direct-response advertising media. The other three markets—industrial, institutional, and reseller—are reached through trade and professional advertising using specialized media such as trade journals, professional magazines, and direct mail.

The Marketing Concept

The post-1950 "Marketing Era" is considered to be the true beginning of contemporary marketing. Technology could produce more products than the market demanded. In addition to necessities, people could choose among a number of "luxury" items. Therefore it became necessary to *appeal* to consumers in areas other than basic needs in order to stimulate demand. It wasn't enough to produce a product efficiently and offer it for sale. In a competitive situation it became necessary to identify consumers' needs and preferences. This approach, which emphasized consumers' needs and attitudes, is now called *the marketing concept*.

Marketing Approaches

The Complex Model   More recent scholars have criticized this traditional idea that marketing developed sequentially. Ronald Fullerton, in a *Journal of Marketing* article, traced the growth of production, sales, and consumer-oriented marketing and found that all three have been developing simultaneously since the beginnings of commerce in the 1500s in Britain and Germany and the 1600s in North America.*

*Ronald A. Fullerton, "How Modern Is Modern Marketing? Marketing's Evolution and the Myth of the 'Production Era,'" *Journal of Marketing*, January 1988, pp. 108–25.

CONSUMER INFLUENTIALS: WORD-OF-MOUTH MARKETING?

When advertisers discuss the major approaches to marketing a product, one option often escapes their consideration: the advice of friends, family, and colleagues. A recent marketing survey suggests that this omission could be a mistake.

The survey asked a group of consumers to list their most reliable sources of information for nine different product categories, including movies, food, clothes, and restaurants. Among the possible information sources were newspaper, television, and magazine ads. For seven of the nine categories, consumers listed personal recommendations as their best source. For certain categories, such as restaurants to try (63 percent), places to visit (50 percent), and books to read (45 percent), no other source even came close.

What are the implications of this survey for advertising? If word of mouth is as important as the survey indicates, then advertisers can reach large numbers of consumers by targeting those people to whom these consumers turn for advice. The survey used the term "consumer influentials" to describe those consumers whose advice is most frequently sought. It concluded that consumer influentials are more likely to belong to upscale, educated groups and to live in major metropolitan areas. Thus, advertising directed at these groups could have a "pass-along" effect on other groups. Another important element is gender: Men are more likely to be consulted for advice on sports activities, investments, and automobiles, whereas women are approached concerning personal-appearance products, decorating, and health.

If word of mouth is the most effective sales technique, does it follow that advertising plays little, if any, role in promoting goods and services? No. On the contrary, the survey results also emphasize a second—and sometimes overlooked—function of advertising: *reinforcing* consumer perceptions. After consumers have been "sold" on a product by friends or family, advertising can help maintain the product's positive image in the mind of these consumers.

Source: "Targeting Consumer Influentials," *Public Pulse,* March 1988, pp. 1–3.

PRINCIPLE _____

The "marketing concept" turns the focus from the seller's product to the buyer's needs.

Consumer-Centered Marketing   The marketing concept changes the focus in commerce from the seller's product to the buyer's needs. It recognizes that in times of scarcity people buy what is available; in times of plenty buyers have choices, and the seller has to make special efforts to provide what buyers want and need.

This concept was explained by Philip Kotler in *Principles of Marketing*. He said that the "marketing concept starts with the needs and wants of the company's targeted customers." In addition to focusing exclusively on more efficient manufacturing processes, companies should focus on consumer problems and try to develop products to solve them. In Kotler's view, "The marketing concept expresses the company's commitment to *consumer sovereignty*."[*]

That is exactly the philosophy that has made Honda, for example, so successful in the American market. When consumers wanted fuel efficiency, Honda brought out the Civic. When they wanted roominess, comfort, and performance, Honda brought out the Accord.

Because Honda has consistently listened to its customers, its overall rating is very high on the industry's Customer Satisfaction Index (C.S.I.). In 1986 Honda outscored Mercedes-Benz to become number one in providing overall satisfaction. And when it comes to owner loyalty, R. L. Polk & Company has named Honda the leading import for 10 consecutive years.[†]

market philosophy *The general attitude of the marketer toward the customer.*

Market Philosophies   A market philosophy is the general perspective or attitude the marketer has toward the customer. Successful companies seem to have an explicit philosophy that is communicated clearly to employees and customers alike. This philosophy is developed by paying careful attention to the customer. Companies following this philosophy know more about their custom-

[*]Philip Kotler, *Principles of Marketing*, 3rd ed. (Englewood Cliffs: Prentice Hall, 1986), pp. 15–16.
[†]"The Honda Way: The Marketing of Honda Automobiles in America," unpublished case study by Rubin Postaer and Associates, 1987.

AD 3.1
Honda has become successful by following the basic principle of marketing: supply-
ing the needs and wants of its customers.
(Courtesy of American Honda Motor Company, Inc.)

ers and tend to produce more successful advertising. The L. L. Bean ad (Ad 3.2)
demonstrates the company's market philosophy in a manner that is clear to
anyone who reads it.

$\mathcal{M}$ARKETING ELEMENTS

With the refocusing of commerce from product-centered to consumer-centered
strategies, the revolution in marketing brought together a group of activities that
had been existing on the fringe of the manufacturing process. Bogart explains
that "when American business was reorganized in the postwar years, marketing
emerged as a major function" that coordinated previously separate specialties—
such as product development, sales promotion, merchandising, advertising, and
market research; "great emphasis was placed on the integrated marketing
plan."*

The idea of coordination suggests that there are a number of elements
involved in the marketing process, including the product, the distribution channel, the sales force, and the marketing communication program. These elements
can also be viewed as *activities,* such as product design and development, branding, packaging, pricing, distribution, personal selling, advertising, sales promotion, and public relations.

*Bogart, *Strategy in Advertising,* p. 3.

Product Qualities

There are a number of ways to categorize all these various elements and activities. One way is to divide them into two categories based on their relationship to the product. For example, some of these elements are based on the product itself, whereas others are external to the product.

"THE GOLDEN RULE OF L.L.BEAN"

"Sell good merchandise at a reasonable profit, treat your customers like human beings and they'll always come back for more."

Leon Leonwood Bean started a company 75 years ago based on this simply stated business philosophy. We call it L.L.'s Golden Rule and today we still practice it.

Everything we sell is backed by a 100% unconditional guarantee. We do not want you to have anything from L. L. Bean that is not completely satisfactory. Return anything you buy from us at any time for any reason if it proves otherwise.

L. L. Bean pays all regular postage and handling charges on orders shipped within the United States. This means that the price listed is the only amount that you pay. There are no additional costs.

Send for our FREE 1987 Christmas Catalog. It features quality products for men and women who enjoy the outdoors. Rugged footwear and clothing for active outdoor use, as well as attractive and well-made weekend wear. Winter sporting equipment and furnishings for relaxing at home or camp. All 100% guaranteed and honestly described.

Order anytime 24 hours a day, 365 days a year by mail or with our convenient TOLL FREE phone number. Our Customer Service and Telephone Representatives are always here to serve you. We maintain large inventories and ship promptly.

☐ **Please send FREE 1987 Christmas Catalog.**
or call 1-800-548-4306

Name_____
Address_____
City_____
State_____ Zip_____

L. L. Bean, Inc., 5661 Alder St., Freeport, ME 04033

L.L.Bean®

Those elements that are inherent in the product itself include product design and development, packaging, distribution channels, product service, handling and storage, branding, pricing, and product display. Those marketing elements that are removed from the product include advertising, sales promotion, personal selling, and product publicity.

Marketing communication, particularly advertising, is therefore separate in concept and function from the product-based marketing elements such as packaging. In a sense, advertising is removed from the product because it can deliver a message and have an impact on the consumer even if the product isn't physically present (unlike packaging, for example).*

Internal and External Environment

Another way to analyze the elements of marketing is to look at the overall marketing environment. The *environment* includes all factors, both internal and external to the company, that affect the marketing effort. Some are controllable and can be managed; some are uncontrollable and simply have to be handled.

Internal The *internal marketing environment* includes activities, situations, and people that tend to be under the control of the business. The most important internal environmental factors are the firm's organizational structure, its financial situation, its technological capabilities, and the expertise and availability of its personnel. These affect the everyday activities of the business, especially decision making and resource allocation.

External The *external marketing environment* encompasses factors that are much more difficult to control and have a long-term impact on the business. The external environment includes economic conditions (interest rates, inflation), politics (party and people in office), legal issues (regulation and deregulation), social and cultural patterns and values (working mothers, disease, birth rates, aging), the emerging technology (lasers, satellites, fiber optics), and physical conditions (floods, droughts, heat waves).

Automotive marketing in the 1970s, for example, had to deal with a number of external factors that affected its marketing program. The OPEC embargo worked to the advantage of small, gas-efficient cars, many of them imported, that were in a position to take advantage of rising gas prices as well as the new federal fuel-efficiency regulations.

FIGURE 3.2
The 4Ps of marketing.

Product	Place
• Design and Development • Branding • Packaging • Features	• Distribution Channels • Inventory • Transportation
Price	Promotion
• List Price • Sale Pricing • Trade Allowances • Price/Quality Relationship	• Personal Selling • Advertising • Sale Promotion • Public Relations and Publicity

*William M. Weilbacher, *Advertising* (New York: Macmillan Publishing Co., 1979), pp. 84–87.

Companies must monitor both the internal and external environments if they are to compete effectively. This is particularly true for advertising. Because of its size and visibility, advertising seems to be particularly susceptible to changes in the internal and external environments.

THE 4PS OF MARKETING

Jerome McCarthy, in *Basic Marketing*, popularized the classification of the various marketing elements into four categories that have since been known in the marketing industry as "the 4 Ps."* They are:

1. *Product:* Includes product design and development, branding, and packaging.
2. *Place* (or Distribution): Includes the channels used in moving the product from the manufacturer to the buyer.
3. *Price:* Includes the price at which the product or service is offered for sale and establishes the level of profitability.
4. *Promotion:* Includes personal selling, advertising, public relations, and sales promotion.

Product

PRINCIPLE
Without a competitive product, all other marketing efforts are irrelevant.

The product is both the reason for marketing and the object of the advertising. There is little doubt that without a competitive product, everything else would be irrelevant.

Product Characteristics The simplest way to analyze the product is to look at its **features.** How do you describe the product in terms of size, color, styles, and the materials that it is made from? Is the product covered by service programs, warranties, and guarantees? Feature analysis will be discussed in more detail in Chapter 7, where this activity becomes an important part of advertising strategy.

features *Attributes of a product such as size, color, and style.*

Products can also be analyzed in terms of tangible and intangible attributes. The tangible features are usually physical, such as size and color, and the intangible ones are nonphysical, such as style and warranties. These features are planned by the seller but must also be perceived by the audience. Advertising's role is to see that the product's features, both tangible and intangible, are communicated to consumers and understood by them.

durable goods *A classification of products that are expected to last for an extended time period.*

Product Classifications In marketing, most products can be classified as (1) durable goods; (2) nondurable goods; or (3) services (see Figure 3.3). **Durable goods** are major products, often high-ticket items, that are expected to last for an extended period of time, such as appliances and automobiles. **Nondurable goods** are frequently purchased and consumed in a relatively short period of time; for example, cereals, soft drinks, soap, and light bulbs. **Services** are not products, but rather are time or activities that you purchase from another person. Activities such as hair styling, medical care, real estate, and banking are services.

nondurable goods *A product category that includes items that are frequently purchased and consumed in a relatively short time period.*

services *Time or activities that are purchased from another person.*

product life cycle *The history of the product from its introduction to its eventual decline and withdrawal.*

Product Life Cycle The concept of **product life cycle** was introduced by Theodore Levitt in an article in the *Harvard Business Review*.† It is based on a metaphor. It treats products as people and assumes that they are born (or introduced), develop, grow old, and die.

The product life cycle is broken into four stages: (1) introduction; (2) growth; (3) maturity; and (4) decline. These four stages can vary from several

*E. Jerome McCarthy and William D. Perreault, Jr., *Basic Marketing,* 9th ed. (Homewood, IL: Irwin, 1987).
†Theodore Levitt, "Exploit the Product Life Cycle," *Harvard Business Review,* November–December 1965, pp. 81–94.

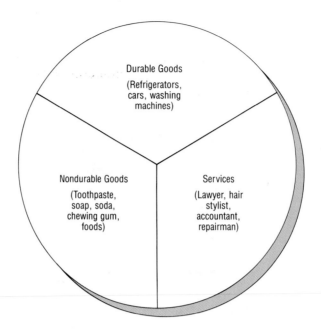

Durable Goods
(Refrigerators, cars, washing machines)

Nondurable Goods
(Toothpaste, soap, soda, chewing gum, foods)

Services
(Lawyer, hair stylist, accountant, repairman)

FIGURE 3.3
Products generally are classified as durable goods, nondurable goods, and services.

_____
line extensions *New products introduced under existing brand names.*
_____

days to many years, depending on the product. The point that the product occupies in its life cycle has a major effect upon the advertising strategy for that product. The messages for new products are considerably different from those for products that have been around for many years.

INTRODUCTION   During the introductory stage a newly developed product is introduced to its market. These products can represent new categories or improvements on old products. Both consumers and the trade must be educated about the new product, and product trial is very important. This level of awareness is costly to create. In fact, during a new-product startup costs frequently exceed sales.

GROWTH   During the growth stage it is hoped that the consumers who tried the product in its introductory stage will become repeat customers. But success attracts competition, and the number of brands competing in the same market will likely increase. Then advertising must carve out a distinctive position for the product in a cluttered market.

MATURITY   During the maturity stage the company shares the market with successful and vigorous competitors. Sales increase more slowly and eventually level off. Advertising attempts to create strong brand loyalty. **Line extensions,** which are new products or reformulated products that carry existing brand names, are introduced. They attempt to skip some of the introductory stage by trading on a brand's already established reputation.

The market leaders fight to maintain their market share while eliminating minor players and new challenges. This can be an extremely competitive period with comparisons, challenges, and counterchallenges. The taste-test battle between Pepsi and Coca-Cola demonstrate how intense this competitiveness can become.

DECLINE   Many products face a period of obsolesence when, for various reasons, the product no longer sells as well as it previously did. In such cases advertising might be reduced to a level that will maintain market share, or it might be eliminated if the product is to be phased out. Not all products have to decline. It often happens that a product is reformulated or turned around, and the product life cycle begins again.

Branding   When you think of bread, what product name comes to mind? When you think of facial tissues, what product name do you think of? What name comes to mind when you think of a copy machine? Do you think of a product name when you think of salt?

Wonder Bread, Kleenex, Xerox, and Morton's have been extensively advertised over many years. **Branding** makes a product distinctive in the marketplace. Bogart explained: "Where products are very similar, brand identity—based on the name, packaging, or advertising themes and techniques—produces the illusion of difference that is vital to competitive selling."*

Some 29,000 different brands are advertised nationally in the United States, according to Bogart. Although none of us knows all of them, most of us have a large and varied group of brand names anchored in our memories. One study asked 400 housewives to recall as many brand names as they could in a 4-minute period; the average response was 28 brand names. When the responses were grouped into product categories, food products accounted for over one-half; 16 percent were soaps, detergents, and household supplies; 11 percent were toiletries, cosmetics, and pharmaceutical products; and 9 percent were big-ticket items such as appliances and household furnishings.

The study also found that branding is a long-term development. Of the 106 brands named by at least 5 percent of the respondents, none had been introduced within the previous 5 years. Although brand names continue to be powerful, the introduction of **generic products** in the 1970s has made them somewhat less attractive. A 1975 study by Needham, Harper, and Steers (now DDB Needham Worldwide) reported that 80 percent of the women and 72 percent of the men surveyed agreed with the statement, "I try to stick with well-known brand names." By 1980 the agreement level had dropped to 64 percent and 56 percent, respectively.†

branding *The process of creating an identity for a product using a distinctive name or symbol.*

PRINCIPLE
Branding makes a product distinctive in the marketplace.

generic products *Products that are marketed without any identifying brand; they are usually less expensive than branded products.*

FIGURE 3.4
The product life cycle.

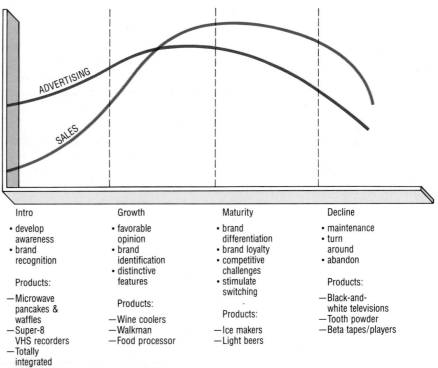

*Bogart, *Strategy in Advertising*, pp. 26–27.
†*Ibid.*, pp. 93–96.

Generic products cost less than brand names but lack a brand identity.
(Courtesy of Charles Gupton/Stock, Boston.)

The FAMOUS CHICK with THE FRENCH NAME

Believes that a cleanser doesn't have to be tough on America, to be tough on dirt.

Take home a can of Bon Ami– it'll take you back to the good old days. 98 years old – and "hasn't scratched yet."* Say goodbye to abrasive cleans- ers that harm your lovely things. Say good- bye to chlorine that smells up your fin- gers and gets up your nose. Say goodbye to noxious gases that foul the indoor air you breathe. A cleanser doesn't have to be tough on America to be tough on dirt. Bon Ami cleans clean. It keeps new things looking new. It restores lustre to old things. No won- der so many great American com- panies recommend Bon Ami. Amana.® Corelle.® Corning.® Cuisinarts.® Farber- ware.® Melitta.® Mirro.® Pyrex.® Rival.® West Bend.® They all know that Bon Ami is committed to loving care for the people who care about the nice things they own. Bon Ami, your good friend.

AD 3.3
In this ad Bon Ami emphasizes its distinctive product name.
(Courtesy of Faultless Starch/Bon Ami Company.)

Bon Ami, a cleanser that has been marketed since the turn of the century, is an example of a distinctive product name. Ad 3.3 focuses on the name to reinforce the product identity.

BRAND IMAGES   Branding uses symbols that stand for a product and also communicate our images and feelings about that product. These symbols help establish relationships with customers, relationships built on experience and reputation. A *brand image* summarizes the bundle of impressions that make up a long-term product personality. Whirlpool (Ad 3.4) uses its brand advertising to spell out the product's image as well as the company's *reputation platform*.

BRAND NAMES   Brand names are developed by the manufacturer. Some-times the advertising agency helps, but the trend recently is to hire a consulting firm that specializes in researching and advising companies on new product names.

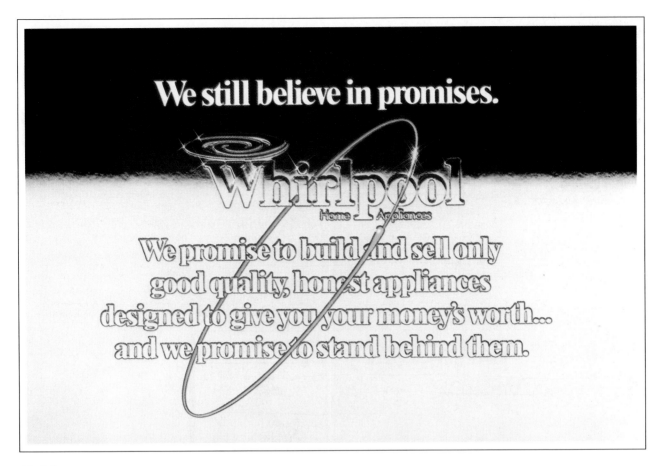

AD 3.4
This Whirlpool ad is designed to convey a brand image.
(Courtesy of Whirlpool Corporation.)

Research into names considers linguistics as well as associations. How does the name sound? What does it sound like, and what does it remind you of? Manufacturers must also be certain that the name does not convey any unintended meanings. When Esso renamed itself Exxon, it sponsored years of study to find a distinctive name that did not have any unwanted meanings. Major companies such as Procter & Gamble and General Motors have name banks with lists of names that have been copyrighted by the company for future product use.

One problem with successful brand names is that they can become generic names for the category and thus lose their copyright. That has happened to refrigerator and thermos. Kleenex and Xerox are currently fighting to maintain their distinctive names; the public uses these names to refer to the product category. Obviously that means tremendous public acceptance, but the loss of exclusive use of a well-known brand name is a corporate disaster.

TRADEMARKS   A **trademark** is a distinctive visual brand that identifies a company's products. For example, distinctive detailing easily separates the bucking bronco used by Ford's Bronco from the running horse used by the Mustang and the prancing horse used by Ferrari (see Ad 3.5). Trademarks are an important part of brand image and reminder advertising programs.

TRADE CHARACTERS   Created characters humanize a product and link the personality of the brand with well-loved images and personality characteristics. The little chick in the Bon Ami ad, for example, is used to depict the gentleness of the cleaning product.

trademark *Sign or design, often with distinctive lettering, that symbolizes the brand.*

A tough team to beat! Bronco II has the most powerful V-6 engine — more horsepower and torque than Chevy S-10 Blazer.

Perfect size for 4-wheeling! Turns in less space than S-10 Blazer or Jeep CJ's.

"Set-up" for action with Tested Twin-Traction Beam

suspension, for a controlled ride. Plus, proven manual locking hubs. At Ford, Quality is Job 1.

Let the sun in with new flip-out removable rear quarter windows and sun roof options. Seats four with split fold-down rear seats.

Flip to 4-wheel drive from driver's seat,

with auto-lock hub option. In town or off road it's a beautiful way to go 4-wheeling.

IT'S A
BRAND NEW KICK.

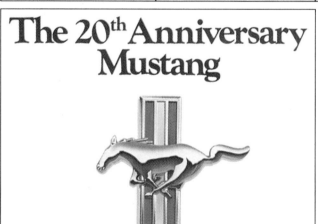

AD 3.5
All of these automobiles use a variation on one symbol—the horse.
(Courtesy of Ford Motor Company and Ferrari North America.)

Betty Crocker (a fictional character) made her advertising debut in 1936 as a symbol of General Mills. She has been through five face-lifts as her character has been updated to appeal to changing audiences. The sixth version was introduced in 1986 (see Ad 3.6).* The most recent change in the Betty Crocker character is discussed in more detail in Chapter 21.

Packaging   The package is another important communication device. In today's marketing environment a package is much more than a container. The self-service retailing phenomenon means that the consumer in the typical grocery store or drugstore is faced with an endless array of products. In such a situation the package is the message. When the package works in tandem with consumer advertising, it catches attention, presents a familiar brand image, and

*"Betty Crocker Goes Yuppie," *Time,* June 2, 1986, p. 63.

AD 3.6
The familiar face of Betty Crocker
has actually changed several times
since the 1930s.
(Courtesy of General Mills, Inc.)

The package helps a brand to stand out from the competition.
(Courtesy of Erich Hartmann/Magnum Photos.)

communicates critical information. Many purchase decisions are made on the basis of how the product looks on the shelf.

An article in *Advertising Age* explained the importance of the package as a communication medium: "Even if you can't afford a big advertising budget, you've got a fighting chance if your product projects a compelling image from the shelf."*

For products that are advertised nationally, the package reflects the brand image developed in the advertising. It serves as a very important reminder at that critical moment when the consumer is choosing among several competing brands.

PACKAGE DESIGN   As an advertising medium, the package has to be an eye-catcher as well as an identifier. Most of us carry around in our minds some kind of visual image of our most familiar products. That image is usually the package.

Packaging is one of the most innovative areas in modern marketing. Inventions are continuous, and one reason packaging is such a big industry is that marketers have to keep up with the competition in new packaging ideas. The package itself becomes a selling point.

*Lori Kesler, "Shopping Around for a Design," *Advertising Age,* December 28, 1981, pp. 2-1, 2-8.

Whenever we start to show our age, we do a little face lifting. Isn't that just like a woman?

No salt salts like Morton Salt salts.

AD 3.7
One major role of the package is to help consumers identify the product. Although the box for Morton Salt has changed over the years, the basic design has remained similar so that customers will not become confused.

(Courtesy of Morton Salt Division of Morton Thiokol, Inc.)

Some recent ideas are plastic squeeze bottles, cans with pull tabs, aerosol containers, boil-in-bags, crushproof bags for fragile things like potato chips, ziplock bags, unbreakable bottles like those used with shampoos, shrink wrapping, and vacuum-seal plastic lids and bags. "Blister cards" seal the product under a clear plastic bubble.

There are packages with windows, like the back of a bacon package, because some products are bought only after the consumer has had an opportunity to inspect them visually. Ornamental packages are being used for commonplace household items like facial tissue. Reusable packages include jelly sold in glasses and teabags sold in decorative tins. Liquor at holiday time is packaged in fancy bottles that serve as decanters.

Package design is very important to advertisers because it is such an important part of brand image and product identity. For this reason the design needs to be coordinated with the overall advertising program. Leo Bogart expressed the importance of packaging: "The main source of messages to the consumer is not within advertising mass media at all, but at the point of sale. We are subjected to more product ideas and impressions from packages and store window displays than we get from television commercials or magazine ads."*

Physical Distribution (Place)

The *distribution channel* can be short or long depending upon how many resellers are involved and what their relationship is to the manufacturer. Some companies, such as Hallmark Cards and Goodyear Tires, control the entire distribution channel. Other distribution channels are more complicated. Computer software, for example, may be distributed by a manufacturer to its own stores, it may go directly from the manufacturer to a separate chain of retail stores, or it may go through a series of distributors who eventually deliver the product to various types of retailers. The type of distribution channel determines how much advertising is directed to the reseller and how much to the consumer.

Automobiles, for example, have a very complex and well-developed distribution channel with a network of dealers all over the country. The attitudes of the dealers are a very important part of the manufacturer's success.

Pricing

The pricing of a product seems a simple concept, yet it is more complex than it first appears. The price a seller sets for a product is based not only on the cost of making and marketing the product but also on the seller's level of profit. Certain psychological factors also affect the price. Consumers often view the price as a measure of status and quality. Thus the price delivers a message about the brand.

Value is the term used to describe how the consumer looks at the price. What do you get for your money? A product that is priced less than others in the category is considered a bargain, but it may also be lower in quality. A high-priced product may suggest higher-quality production as well as prestige and status. Most consumers understand this price-quality trade-off and are able to make decisions based on their own sense of values.

$$\text{Value} = \frac{\text{Benefit}}{\text{Price}}$$

Information about price is one of the most important messages that advertising can convey, especially in retail advertising. It is so important that the term

*Bogart, *Strategy in Advertising*, p. 2.

Packaging is a key component of a successful marketing strategy.
(Courtesy of Peter Arnold, Inc.)

PRINCIPLE ——————————
Advertising helps establish the price-quality relationship.

price copy has been coined to designate message copy devoted principally to this information.

Advertising plays a role in helping customers to gauge the price-quality relationship. Ads for upscale retail stores look classy and expensive, whereas ads for discount stores look busy and inexpensive. Advertising should clearly and consistently reflect the product's pricing strategy.

Promotion

promotion *The element in the marketing mix that encourages the purchase of a product or service.*

Promotion is that part of the marketing effort that encourages the purchase of a particular product or service. Promotion, in the marketing sense, is a broad term that includes a number of different activities. According to the book *Promotional Strategy:* "Advertising, sales promotion, personal selling, direct marketing, public relations and publicity, and corporate advertising are all component parts of *one integrated promotional mix*." It continues: "There is no way that an individual activity, say advertising, can be managed without fully considering these strategic interrelationships."*

*James F. Engle, Martin R. Warshaw, and Thomas C. Kinnear, *Promotional Strategy,* 6th ed. (Homewood IL: Irwin, 1987), p. vii.

The Promotion Mix The four basic promotional elements identified in most marketing plans are:

1. Personal selling
2. Advertising
3. Sales promotion
4. Public relations and publicity

These elements are combined under the heading of *promotion mix*. These four areas differ in terms of their intended effect, the type of customer contact, and the time element.

PERSONAL SELLING **Personal selling** is face-to-face contact between the marketer and a prospective customer. The intention is to create both immediate sales and repeat sales.

There are several different types of personal selling, including sales calls at the place of business by a field representative (field sales), assistance at an outlet by a sales clerk (retail selling), and calls by a representative who goes to consumers' homes (door-to-door selling). Personal selling is most important for companies that sell products requiring explanation, demonstration, and service. Such products tend to be higher priced.

ADVERTISING Advertising can help the salesperson by laying the groundwork and preselling the product. Products that are sold door to door might not use much advertising. If advertising is utilized, its function is to introduce and support the personal sales effort. Shaklee, Amway, and Tupperware all rely on door-to-door and personal sales with little or no advertising support. Avon only recently began national advertising. In industrial sales, advertising plays a critical role. An industrial salesperson will have a much better chance of success if potential customers are aware of the company and its reputation. Advertising is one of the most effective means of accomplishing this.

SALES PROMOTION *Sales promotion* includes a number of communication devices offered for a limited period of time in order to generate immediate sales. Simply stated, sales promotion is an extra incentive to buy *now*. Examples are price discounts, coupons, product sampling, contests or sweepstakes, and rebates. Sales promotion will be discussed in greater detail in Chapter 18.

Advertising is used to promote sales promotion activities such as sweepstakes and contests. Likewise sales promotions can be used in support of advertising campaigns. Advertising and sales promotion can work together to create a *synergy* in which each makes the other more effective.

PUBLIC RELATIONS *Public relations* encompasses a set of activities intended to enhance the image of the marketer in order to create good will. Public relations includes publicity (stories in the mass media with significant news value), news conferences, company-sponsored events, open houses, plant tours, donations, and other special events.

personal selling *Face-to-face contact between a salesperson and a potential customer.*

PRINCIPLE
Advertising helps the salesperson by laying the groundwork and preselling the product.

PRINCIPLE
Sales promotion activities are used to generate immediate sales.

FIGURE 3.5
Promotional-mix comparison.

Promotion Type	Intended Effect	Customer Contact	Timing
Personal Selling	Sales	Direct	Short
Advertising	Attitude Change Behavior Change	Indirect	Moderate-Low
Sales Promotion	Sales	Semidirect	Short
Public Relations	Attitude Change	Semidirect	Long

Personal selling can create immediate sales, but it can also be costly.
(Courtesy of Gregg Mancuso/Stock, Boston.)

Rather than attempt to sell the product, public relations seeks to influence people's attitudes about the company or product. In most cases the lag effect associated with public relations tends to be quite long, making any relationship between promotion and sales difficult to determine.

Advertising interacts with public relations in several ways. A public relations event or message can serve as part of an advertising campaign. Product publicity can also be used in support of an advertising campaign. For example, Kingsford charcoal sponsors a Ribfest in Chicago that includes free charcoal to all contestants. This event reinforces the association between Kingsford and outdoor activities. Public relations is discussed in greater detail in Chapter 19.

Marketing Communications Contemporary trends in marketing find planners looking at the promotional segment of the marketing program in a different way—as part of an integrated program rather than as separate elements.

Under the traditional promotion-mix approach, the various promotional activities were planned separately, and the workers who carried out these activities may even have reported to different managers within a company. The **integrated marketing communications** (IMC) concept brings all these areas together and attempts to integrate their programs and activities.

integrated marketing communications *Promotional planning that focuses on integrated communication based on an analysis of consumer behavior.*

Tom Duncan, a marketing manager who is now an advertising professor, explains that the integrated marketing communications concept is an umbrella that includes the traditional promotional areas and a lot of other things as well.

VICTORIA M. AMON, SENIOR VICE PRESIDENT, MANAGEMENT SUPERVISOR, DDB NEEDHAM WORLDWIDE

Victoria Amon is responsible for advertising several Campbell's food products and also helps to train new employees. Below is a brief description of her daily activities.

Time/Place	Attendees	Issues
8:00–9:00 Office	—	Prepare for day, open door for group, finish letters written on train; place early calls
9:00–10:30 10th Floor Conference Room	—Task Force (Account Management, Research, Creative & Media Groups)	Planning session for Retail Deli Foods Project; agreement to strategic and research needs for Test Market
10:30–10:45 Accounting Dept.	—Billings & Estimate Supervisor	Chanel Billings Review
10:45–11:00 Accounting Dept.	—Billings & Estimate Supervisor —Assistant Account Executive	Campbell's Estimate and Budget Summary
11:00–11:30 ACD's Office	—SVP Associate Creative Director (ACD) Team —Account Supervisor	Review and approve strategy developed for special promotion radio flight (Hearty)
11:30–12:00 AMD's Office	—Associate Media Director (AMD) —Senior Planner	Update on media plans in development (Hearty)

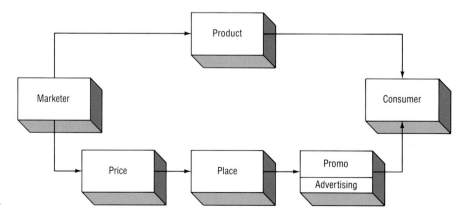

FIGURE 3.6
Marketing as a communication model.
Source: Charles Pearce, Kansas State University.

Time/Place	Attendees	Issues
12:00–12:30 Office	—	Return phone calls, place calls for PM, proof and sign letters typed in AM
12:30–2:00 Local Restaurant	—Lunch with colleague (former Client, VP, New Product Director)	Input for Agency's New Business Procedures and Processes Project
2:00–2:30 Office	—President & AE for Promotion Dynamics (supplier) —Account supervisor	Supplier presentation of resources and service capabilities; brief for spec assignment
2:30–3:00 Office	—SVP, Strategic Planning Director	Review and agree upon revisions to Agency's New Business Positioning & Procedures Recommendation
3:00–4:00 10th Floor Conference Room	—Task Force (see above)	Brainstorming session for New Product ideas for Franco-American line
4:00–4:30 Office	—Account Group	Follow-up to AM Retail Deli Foods Planning Session; review/coordinate responsibilities, next steps and meeting timetable
4:30–4:45 Office	—	Return phone calls
4:45–5:15 Office	—Personnel Manager	Agreement to objectives, needs for training seminar I will present to AAE's
5:15–5:45 Office	—Recent graduate job seeker (referred to me by a friend)	Interview candidate as to job objectives/ talent; if strong, I will send through my contacts network
5:45–6:35 Office	—	Time to read, think, plan, write (to be continued on train ride home)

(Courtesy of Victoria Amon.)

"Everything the consumer sees that has your brand on it communicates— everything from trucks and shopping carts to packages and shopping bags."* Terence Shimp and M. Wayne DeLozier make the same point in their book on promotion management: "All marketing mix variables, not just the promotional variable alone, communicate with customers."†

Philip Kotler points out that marketing communications recognizes that a concept such as corporate identity is an important factor in developing consumer confidence in products. He explains:

> Communication goes beyond specific communication/promotion tools. The product's styling, its price, the package's shape and color, the salesperson's manner and dress—all communicate something to the buyers. The whole

*Thomas R. Duncan, personal communication, January 19, 1988.

†Terence A. Shimp and M. Wayne DeLozier, *Promotion Management and Marketing Communications* (Chicago: Dryden, 1986), p. 4.

PRINCIPLE
Marketing communications integrates all communication activities for a brand or company under a coordinated plan.

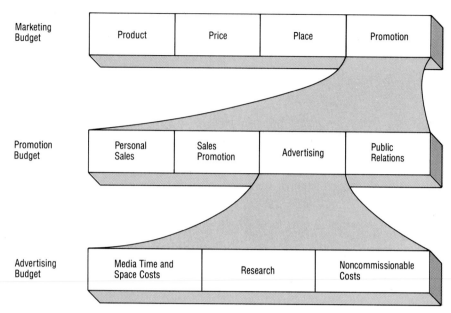

| Marketing Budget | Product | Price | Place | Promotion |

| Promotion Budget | Personal Sales | Sales Promotion | Advertising | Public Relations |

| Advertising Budget | Media Time and Space Costs | Research | Noncommissionable Costs |

FIGURE 3.7
Advertising budget decision making.

marketing mix, not just the promotional mix, must be orchestrated for maximum communication impact.*

*T*HE MARKETING MIX

How does a marketing manager know what combination of elements should be used? How much emphasis should be placed on these various elements? Is personal selling more important than advertising, or equal in importance? How do pricing and distribution affect the advertising and sales promotion programs? How much attention should be paid to sales promotion? The manner in which the four primary marketing areas are strategically combined is called the **marketing mix.** Advertising, of course, is only one part of the marketing mix. That is why advertisers must understand how advertising can function effectively within the mix.

marketing mix *A plan that identifies the most effective combination of promotional activities.*

The concept of marketing mix was developed by Harvard Professor Neil Borden to explain the decision making behind a marketing plan. Borden explained it this way:

> What combination of marketing procedures and policies has been or might be adopted to bring about desired behavior of trade and consumers at costs that will permit a profit? Specifically, how can advertising, personal selling, pricing, packaging, channels, warehousing, and the other elements of a marketing program be manipulated and fitted together in a way that will give a profitable operation?†

The concept of marketing mix means that all the elements are evaluated to decide how much emphasis should be placed on each one. This is an interactive problem. Advertising is only one element in this mix, and it does not operate in a vacuum. It will be affected by the level of sales promotion or publicity activity.

The effectiveness of each activity determines its level, or share of the budget. When we talk about "levels of emphasis," what we are really discussing is setting objectives and allocating the budget. The marketing mix and the promotion mix are both expressed in terms of percentage of the budget. Of the marketing communications activities, advertising might receive 60 percent of the budget, while sales promotion receives 30 percent and public relations 10 percent.

PRINCIPLE
The emphasis given to each promotional element in the marketing mix determines its budget level.

*Philip Kotler, *Marketing Management,* 4th ed. (Englewood Cliffs, NJ: Prentice Hall, 1980), p. 588.
†Neil H. Borden, "The Concept of the Marketing Mix," *Journal of Advertising Research,* June 1964.

There are no hard-and-fast rules for determining the appropriate mix. Most marketing strategists say that the mix is determined by the situation, and each situation demands a different type of mix. Although case studies provide some guidance, the marketing-mix question is one of the most difficult problems that advertisers face.

■ SUMMARY

- The marketing concept focuses on the needs of the consumer rather than on the marketer's production capabilities.
- Advertising is a category within the promotion mix and promotion is a category within the marketing mix.
- The marketing mix identifies the most effective combination of four variables: product, price, place (distribution), and promotion.
- The typical product moves through the following stages in its life cycle: introduction, growth, maturity, and decline.

- The package is the last chance to affect consumer choice.
- The promotion mix identifies the optimum level of sales promotion, personal selling, public relations, and advertising.
- The amount of emphasis given to each promotional element in the marketing mix determines its budget level.

■ QUESTIONS

1. How would advertising for hand soap differ for the four types of markets?
2. How would you go about marketing an automobile under a production-oriented approach and a consumer-oriented approach?
3. How would you advertise a toothpaste at the four different stages in its life cycle?
4. Imagine you are starting a company to manufacture fudge. Consider the following questions:

a. What internal and external elements in the environment will affect your marketing and advertising program?
b. Describe the marketing mix that you think would be most effective for this company.
c. Describe the promotion mix you would recommend for this company.
d. How would you determine the advertising budget for your new fudge company?
e. Develop a plan for a brand image for this fudge.

■ FURTHER READINGS

AAKER, DAVID A., and JOHN G. MYERS. *Advertising Management.* 3rd ed. Englewood Cliffs, NJ: Prentice Hall, 1987.

BURNETT, JOHN J. *Promotion Management,* 2nd ed. St. Paul, MN: West Publishing, 1988.

ENGEL, JAMES F., MARTIN R. WARSHAW, and THOMAS C. KINNEAR. *Promotional Strategy: Managing the Marketing Communications Process.* 6th ed. Homewood, IL: Irwin, 1987.

KOTLER, PHILIP. *Marketing Management: Analysis, Planning, and Control.* 4th ed. Englewood Cliffs, NJ: Prentice Hall, 1980.

KOTLER, PHILIP. *Principles of Marketing.* 4th ed. Englewood Cliffs, NJ: Prentice Hall, 1989.

McCARTHY, E. JEROME, and WILLIAM D. PERREAULT, JR. *Basic Marketing: A Managerial Approach.* 9th ed. Homewood, IL: Irwin, 1987.

RAY, MICHAEL L. *Advertising & Communication Management.* Englewood Cliffs, N.J.: Prentice Hall, 1982.

SHIMP, TERENCE A., and M. WAYNE DELOZIER, *Promotion Management and Marketing Communications.* Chicago: Dryden, 1986.

4 Advertising Agencies

Chapter Outline

The Perils of a New Ad Agency
The Agency World
How Agencies Are Paid
Why Hire an Agency?
Changes in the Agency World

Chapter Objectives

When you have completed this chapter you should be able to:

- Explain the four primary functions in an agency: account management, creative services, media services, and research
- Explain which support services are provided by departments such as traffic, print production, accounting, and personnel
- Explain the difference between the commission and the fee system
- Explain why advertisers hire agencies rather than do the work themselves
- Analyze the pros and cons of the trend toward megamergers
- Analyze the impact of high productivity on agencies

THE PERILS OF A NEW AD AGENCY

Most people in advertising dream of starting and owning their own agency. But what is it really like? Angotti Thomas Hedge (known as ATH) opened for business in 1985 in closetlike premises—sandwiched between a jewelry manufacturer underneath and a pastry brush maker above on East 21st Street in New York. The agency's billings are too small to be officially quantified, but it aims to be at least a $20-million agency by Year Two. Let's look in on ATH at the end of its first year.*

We are in Hawthorne, New York, a small town in Westchester County, shooting a TV spot for *Barron's,* its first with ATH. It is also ATH's first television spot, and its principals look like expectant fathers in a maternity waiting room. While Thomas nervously chain-smokes Marlboros through a cigaret holder, Angotti paces around the studio.

To a new agency with high hopes of growing older, this is a crucial time. And *Barron's* represents a crucial direct-response campaign. In the past the agency's partners have been more accustomed to working on $40 million accounts and buying big chunks of television time.

They may be spending less, but this is ATH's first campaign running on stations across the country, and they are aware that an important target audience will be watching. The spot is designed to appeal to an upscale audience that might conceivably not only want to subscribe to the publication but—who knows?—also hire the agency.

"Everything we do is important because we don't do a lot of it," says Angotti. "If we do a clunker, it could be really devastating."

This emphasis on value and clients with luxury products is what ATH is all about. Thomas explains, "We've seen so many mediocre ads for really good products, we decided to focus on an upmarket area because we believe that's where advertising can make the most difference."

Angotti and Thomas are former Ammirati and Puris associate creative directors who established a reputation for stylish and witty work for BMW and Club Med, unmistakably upmarket clients. With just four employees, the three principals are trying to make it in a land bottle-fed on "Big is beautiful." What gives them the audacity to think they *can* is their unshakable belief that a gap exists between upmarket advertisers and creative talent that understands these markets.

"We're trying to do what we've always done—find a niche and fill it," says Thomas. "When you do something that's hard to do and there aren't a lot of people doing it, you become a commodity that's worth more." ATH is struggling to establish itself as a small agency with a unique vision. Is there a place for ATH in the agency world? Let's look at the way the agency world is shaping up, and then you decide if the gamble is worth it.

THE AGENCY WORLD

Advertising agencies range in size from one-person shops to giants that employ thousands. The smallest agencies usually have up to a dozen employees. In small markets they tend to offer a range of services. In larger markets these small shops usually specialize either in a type of service, such as media buying or

*"Upscale Niche," *Advertising Age,* February 16, 1986, pp. 4–5.

creative work, or in a particular type of market, such as health care, agribusiness, or the upscale market (as ATH is trying to do).

As the agency grows larger, a division of labor occurs. Most full-service agencies offer certain functions handled by many specialists. Smaller agencies offer the same basic functions, but they employ a smaller number of people who are less specialized and usually perform more than one function. For the purpose of giving a full explanation, the following description of agency organization is based on larger agencies.

How Agencies Are Organized

business units *Organizational units in a company that are focused around product lines, brands, or specific services.*

Major corporations are focused on one or a cluster of product lines, brands, or services called **business units.** Advertising agencies use a similar structure but have a variety of clients and product lines. The agency's product, however, is not manufactured goods but ideas, and these ideas are apparent in advertisements and plans for campaigns and media programs.

Rather than organizing around a business unit, an agency organizes around a client's account. Because clients come and go and account needs change, agencies must be adaptable. An agency's product is an idea. It must encourage new ideas and protect them as they are refined. Openness and flexibility are more important than organizational structure in most agencies.

Unlike corporations, agencies often change structure to accommodate the needs of new clients or the talents of their people. There are, however, standard functions around which most agencies, large and small, organize. The following are the four primary functions of most agencies:

PRINCIPLE

Openness and flexibility are more important than organizational structure in most agencies.

1. Account management
2. Creative services
3. Media services
4. Research

In addition to these functional areas, most agencies offer support services, such as traffic, print production, accounting, and personnel. Figure 4.1 illustrates the organization of a large advertising agency.

Account Management

account management *The function in an agency that serves as a liaison between the agency and the client.*

CLIENT LIAISON FUNCTION   The role of **account management** is to serve as a liaison between the client and the agency. The account management function ensures that the agency focuses its resources on the needs of the client and develops its own point of view, which is presented to the client. Once the client (or the client and the agency together) establishes the general guidelines for the advertising, the account management department supervises the day-to-day development of the account within these guidelines.

The original title for this function, "account service," has been changed in most agencies because it suggests that the agency should be subservient to the client, rather than providing an independent professional viewpoint. "Account management" suggests initiative and responsibility by the agency.

PRINCIPLE

The account management role focuses on agency initiative and responsibility, rather than subservience to the client.

This can be a difficult role to handle. Paul Harper, chairman emeritus of DDB Needham, put it this way in a *Memorandum to All Our Account Executives:*

> Most good clients have strong views of their own. You will win client respect for yourself and the agency mainly for two things: (1) for forthrightness and thoroughness in presenting the agency's views, and (2) for respectful knowledge of the problems the client faces as he makes his own often difficult decisions. When his answer is "No," as it will sometimes be, this may be a professional defeat. But it will never be a moral defeat if the agency's position has been well presented and stoutly defended.

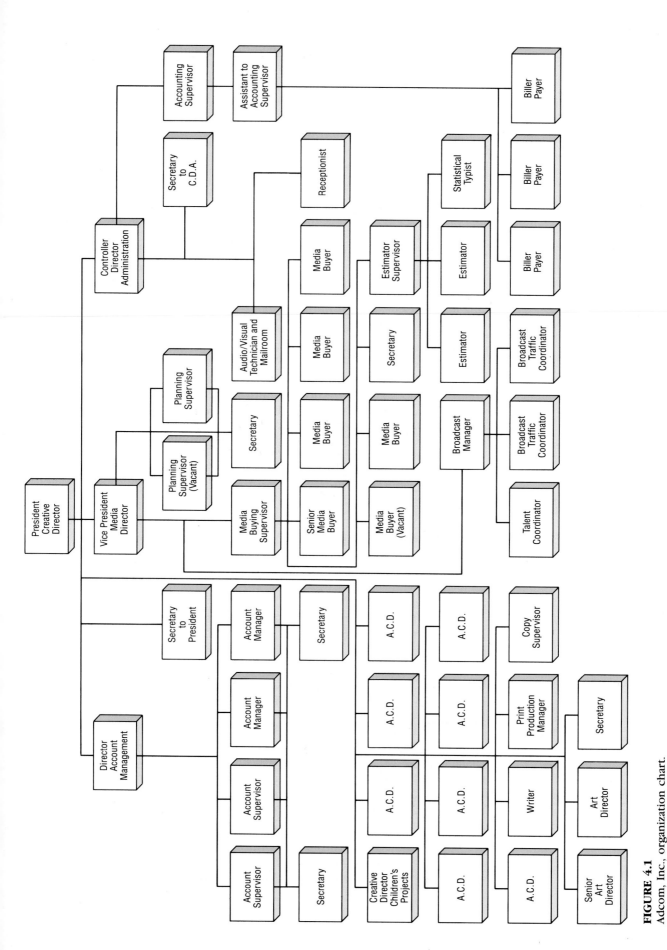

FIGURE 4.1
Adcom, Inc., organization chart.

Note: Due to space limitations, no significance should be attached to vertical positioning below V. P. level

Source: Courtesy of Bayer Bess Vanderwarker & Flynn.

RICK SINGER, ACCOUNT EXECUTIVE
KINGSFORD CHARCOAL, DDB NEEDHAM/CHICAGO

An account executive's job involves a variety of tasks, all focused on one key goal—finding creative ways to move the business forward. That creativity comes into play in two specific areas. The first is in the development of new marketing and advertising ideas. Secondly, and equally important, is finding creative ways to motivate all who work on your business. Throughout the day, both areas are constantly tested, and my response to those challenges can very well determine DDB Needham's success on the Kingsford charcoal business.

Here's one typical day.

- 8:15—This is the time I usually arrive at the agency. It gives me time to relax, collect my thoughts, check last night's baseball scores, etc., prior to diving into the day's work. This morning I have a meeting scheduled for 9:00 with Media to discuss our Agency's position on the appropriateness of 15-second television commercials for Kingsford. In preparation I review our past media plans and agency position papers on variable-length commercials.
- 9:00—My assistant account executive and I travel three floors down for the meeting with our media team. Since it's my meeting, I lay out the issues. Are 15's appropriate for Kingsford? Is our message simple enough? Do the networks have enough 15's available to satisfy our requirements? The media supervisor has definite opinions on the subject. She feels Kingsford is a known brand with clearly apparent features. The message is simple, and the use of 15's would double our weight. We all agree, though, that such a decision is contingent on the input of our creative director. I agree to talk with him after lunch.
- 9:45–11:40—Meetings and memos.

- 11:40—Back once more to my office. As I arrive, the phone is ringing. It's my client, the product manager on Kingsford Charcoal. It is practically a miracle that we talk on the first attempt of the day. After some good-natured kidding about the recent failures of my beloved Yankees, he drops a huge piece of news. A small company in the Midwest has begun marketing a new charcoal briquet. It's rare that Kingsford receives a threat from a new product. This one is especially unusual since it is a briquet that claims a clear point of difference. He's clearly concerned that this entry could steal a significant share and usurp our leadership image. We discuss strategic changes to our advertising, as well as new product ideas as ways to protect the Kingsford franchise. Suddenly, my "Things to Do" list has changed. This issue becomes #1.
- 12:15—I'm starving! There's a great fast-food Chinese restaurant downstairs. I run downstairs, take out "Today's Special," run back upstairs, and eat a quick, delicious lunch.
- 1:00–3:00—More meetings and sessions.
- 3:00—I phone my client once again. The division manager is looking for our response to the new competitor. That includes a complete marketing analysis with thorough recommendations in all areas. And he wants it in 2 days. I agree to fly out to Oakland tomorrow. It'll be a long few days, but I appreciate his request for my help.
- 3:30—In the final moments before I leave for the airport, I write two quick memos. One to the media supervisor, outlining key next steps prior to media plan development, and one to my boss, explaining the status of our various projects.
- 4:15—Off to the airport. Find a newspaper. Who's pitching for the Yanks tonight?

Source: DDB Needham Worldwide.

Account management in a major agency typically has four, and sometimes five, levels: management representative or supervisor, account supervisor, account executive, and assistant account executives. A smaller agency may combine some of these levels.

MANAGEMENT SUPERVISOR   The *management supervisor* reports to the upper management of the agency. This person provides leadership on strategic issues, looks for new business opportunities, helps develop personnel growth and development within the account team, keeps agency management informed, and ensures that the agency is making a realistic profit on the account. The position normally carries the title of senior vice president and is offered to someone who has been working in account management for 10 to 15 years.

ACCOUNT SUPERVISOR   The *account supervisor* is usually the key working executive on the client's business and the primary liaison between the client and the agency. This person writes the strategic plans, assigns priorities, reviews and approves all recommendations before they are taken to the client, supervises the presentation of annual plans and other major recommendations to the client,

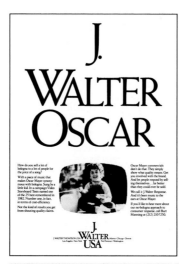

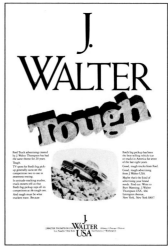

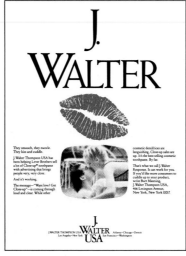

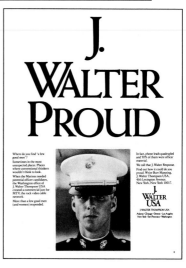

AD 4.1
This campaign for the J. Walter Thompson agency focuses on successful ads for its best-known clients.
(Courtesy of J. Walter Thompson.)

and ensures agency adherence to plans and schedules. Account supervisors usually carry the title of vice president.

ACCOUNT EXECUTIVE   The *account executive* is responsible for day-to-day activities that include keeping the agency team on schedule and delivering the services as promised to the client. Other functions are seeing that all assignments are completed on time and within budget, maintaining the operating records of the account, preparing status and progress reports, supervising the production of materials, and securing legal or network approval of all advertising before production begins.

ASSISTANT ACCOUNT EXECUTIVE   This is normally the entry-level position in the agency's account management department. The focus is on learning the business and helping the account executive with records and schedules.

Creative Development and Production   To some people "creative organization" is a self-contradiction. Many people believe that creativity can only occur in an unstructured environment. However, in an agency, management must take into consideration how people work together and what assignments are flowing through the agency. The wisest agency managers are flexible in terms of organization but strict in terms of quality and deadline control.

CREATIVE DIRECTOR   Most agencies have one senior executive called a *creative director,* or executive creative director, who serves as the keeper of the agency's creative conscience. Other titles include executive creative director or director of creative services. This person stimulates the department to do better creative work and approves all ideas before they are presented outside the department.

CREATIVE DEPARTMENT MANAGER   There may also be a person who oversees the internal management process, the administrative activities needed to keep the department running. Referred to as the *creative department manager,* this person handles budgeting, salary administration, office assignments, hiring and supervising secretarial and support staff, recruiting professional staff, and internal accounting. Practitioners add such terms as "house mother," "warden," "priest, rabbi, confessor," "crying towel," and "punching bag." Creative directors can survive the loss of a senior staff member more easily than the loss of the creative department manager.

PERSONALITIES   Within the creative department two types of people are generally found. One is the brilliant, and sometimes eccentric, creator who conceives, writes, and produces pattern-breaking advertising. Staff is often built around this person as an extension of his or her skills.

The second type is the coach, the one who delegates assignments, works with the staff to find an idea, and then molds, improves, nurtures, and inspires the staff. Agencies organize teams around these people, who may be called creative group heads, associate creative directors, or creative directors (if the senior title is executive creative director). Both types can exist within a department. In fact, many people possess some characteristics of both types.

THE CREATIVE GROUP   A creative group includes people who write, people who draw ideas for print ads or television commercials, and people who translate these ideas into television or radio commercials. The titles are *copywriter, art director,* or *producer*. In many agencies an art director and copywriter who work well together are teamed up, and a support group is built around them. (This is discussed in more depth in Chapter 13.)

BROADCAST PRODUCTION   In some cases the broadcast production department is a separate department (as the print production department usually is), but it may be a part of the creative department. Because executing the tone and action of broadcast advertising is so central to its success, the creative team usually includes a broadcast producer. This person, and often the whole creative team, will be directly involved in the filming and editing of the commercial.

THE BULLPEN   An art studio, often called the *bullpen,* is another part of the creative departments. The bullpen includes artists who specialize in doing presentation pieces called comprehensives, lettering, and paste-up. This is where beginning art directors often start in an agency.

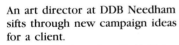

An art director at DDB Needham sifts through new campaign ideas for a client.

(Courtesy of DDB Needham Worldwide.)

Media Planning and Buying   The media department performs one of the most complex functions in an advertising agency. This department must recommend the most efficient means of delivering the message to the target audience. Media work is divided among planning, buying, and research. Most media departments basically break down into those three functions. These functions will be outlined here and discussed in more detail in Chapters 9 and 12.

THE MEDIA PLANNER   Planning involves determining which medium or media to use, when, for what length of time, and at what cost. Developing a media plan is a creative skill. The *media planner* must be involved in the overall strategy and creative development. Most media and creative plans are prepared concurrently so the message and the medium will work together.

THE MEDIA BUYER   The media buyer determines what media coverage is likely to be available at what costs. Buying is ordering media, on behalf of the client, according to the plan approved by the client. Once the plan is approved by the client, the media buyer acts quickly to place orders. There is no point in recommending a plan calling for network television on specific programs if those programs are already sold.

MEDIA RESEARCH   In addition to planning and buying, most media departments have a research section that gathers and evaluates media data. The department's forecasts of future prices, ratings of television programs, and audience composition are prepared by the media research manager. Media research often provides entry-level positions.

Research Department   The emphasis in agency research is on assisting the development of the advertising message. Most major agencies do research before the advertising is prepared to make the advertising more focused and appropriate to the target audience. They also purchase research from companies that specialize in this area.

Whether composed of a single person in a small agency or teams of professionals in a large agency, the research department has a number of duties besides helping the creative side. It ensures that the agency has reliable information; screens all new research findings to determine if they change the body of

AD 4.2
Agency clients come from all different fields. This public service ad was produced by Chiat/Day, which also produced the widely recognized Nike billboards.
(Courtesy of Chiat/Day inc.)

NOT EVERYONE WHO DRIVES DRUNK DIES.

Before you drive drunk or get into a car with someone who's been drinking, remember this. You could live to regret it.

Members of the print services department check proofs of print ads returned from the printer for color and accuracy.
(Courtesy of DDB Needham Worldwide.)

information about a brand, company, industry, or market; and provides the agency with accurate information about consumer behavior. The agency, when it does original research, almost always concentrates on consumer attitudes and behavior. Advertising research will be discussed in more detail in Chapters 6 and 21.

Traffic Department   The traffic department is responsible for internal control and tracking of projects to meet deadlines. The account executive works closely with the assigned traffic coordinator or traffic manager to review deadlines and monitor progress. The traffic department is the bloodstream of the agency, and its personnel keep track of everything that is happening in the agency.

PRINCIPLE —————————————
The traffic department is the bloodstream of the agency.

Traffic requires diligence, tact, and great attention to detail. Although computers now can help trace and program projects, nothing replaces the persistent traffic coordinator who has heard every excuse for delay.

Print Production   Taking a layout, a photograph, or an illustration, and a page of copy, and turning these elements into a four-color magazine page in a magazine or a full-page newspaper advertisement is the work of the print production department.

Because of the technical nature of making the printing plates, adjusting and matching color, and achieving reproduction, this task is not done within the creative department, as opposed to television or radio production. The art director on the account will normally supervise the illustrator or photographer and will approve the work, but will not supervise the production of the material sent to the publication.

Internal Services

ACCOUNTING   Whether large or small, the agency must get its invoices out on time, pay its bills on time, control its costs, ensure that expenses incurred on

AD 4.3
This ad stresses the advantages of a small agency.
(Courtesy of John Noble Advertising, Inc.)

behalf of a client are properly invoiced to that client, meet its payroll, pay its taxes, and make a profit within its budget. This function is managed by the chief financial officer. In a large agency the treasurer is responsible for cash management and the controller or comptroller for internal procedures.

PERSONNEL   An operation of any size requires keeping personnel files and records. The larger the agency, the more likely it will have a professional personnel staff. These people handle the hiring and, at times, the firing of clerical, secretarial, and support staff. Recruitment of professional staff, although conducted by the head of the department in which the person will work, is normally coordinated by the personnel department.

*H*OW AGENCIES ARE PAID

agent *Someone who acts on behalf of someone else, usually for a fee.*

Agencies derive their revenues and profits from two main systems—commissions and fees. To understand these processes, we must first understand the word **agent.** An agent is one who acts for another. Thus, an advertising agency acts for another, the advertiser, in creating the advertising.

The Development of Media Commissions

commission *A form of payment in which an agent or agency receives a certain percentage (often 15 percent) of media charges.*

Early advertising agents acted not on behalf of the client, but on behalf of the medium. Well into the nineteenth century advertising agents acted as representatives for newspapers, magazines, and handbill printers. If the agent brought advertising to the publisher, the publisher paid the agent a **commission.** Custom and practice have standardized that commission at 15 percent of the price charged by the medium.

The commission was justified by the work the agent did in bringing the publisher the business and preparing the advertisement for publication. The agent might write the copy, prepare the layout, set the type, and arrange for any drawings or plates that were part of the advertisement. These efforts saved the publisher time and work.

As advertising grew in importance, advertisers began to work with fewer and fewer agents and eventually signed with one agent exclusively. That practice changed the entire advertising industry. Instead of representing one medium to many advertisers, the agent now acted on behalf of one client and placed ads with many media. The commission system remains, however, as a legacy of the early years of advertising.

The Commission System   The standard agency commission around the world is still 15 percent of the negotiated price of the media. If a television commercial costs $100,000 for its time, the agency is charged $85,000 and charges the client $100,000. The difference of $15,000 is the agency's commission. The agency will also add on a rate for media or services that do not include commissions.

"Standard" does not mean universal. The standard commission in New Zealand, for example, is 20 percent. The argument is that New Zealand is a small country and the agency has to do as much work preparing a campaign to reach 3.5 million New Zealanders as does an agency in Australia, which is five times as populous. The Australians have a 16 percent standard commission. On large campaigns some English companies have negotiated rates below 15 percent.

Very large clients sometimes negotiate sliding scales on commission: 15 percent up to $10 million, 10 percent above that. Seldom does the commission go below 10 percent. Some clients place their own media but buy all other services from an advertising agency. These clients might pay a commission of 11 to 13.5 percent. Even when 15 percent is the agreed-upon rate, part is often rebated to the client. A full 15 percent commission is now rare and may be on its way out, as is indicated in Figure 4.2.

Another factor is that agencies have expenses above and beyond the actual billable client work. Because the agency also works on new products or con-

FIGURE 4.2
Fewer industry clients are paying a full 15 percent commission, as indicated by this chart.
Source: DDB Needham Worldwide. 1986.

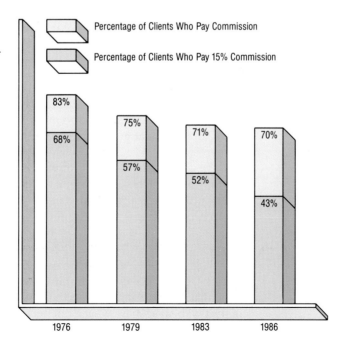

David Ogilvy. As indicated in Table 4.1, the Ogilvy Group is among the largest agency holding companies. (Courtesy of Ogilvy & Mather, New York.)

ducts other projects it is not compensated for, even when a client pays 15 percent, the effect is that the true commission on work done for that client is much lower.

fee *A mode of payment in which an agency charges a client on the basis of the agency's hourly costs.*

The Fee System   The second form of compensation is the fee system. It is comparable to the means by which advertisers pay their lawyers and accountants. The client and agency agree on an hourly **fee** or charge. This fee can vary according to department or levels of salary within a department. In other cases a flat hourly fee for all work is agreed upon regardless of the salary level of the person doing the work. Charges are also included for direct expenses.

Trust is the critical element in a fee system. The client must believe that each individual in the agency is keeping track of his or her time accurately and charging that time correctly to a particular brand or project. In addition, the client must believe that the agency's hourly charge for salary, overhead, and profit is fair.

How is the agency fee calculated? The agency assigns costs for salary, rent, telephone, postage, internal operations, equipment rental, taxes, and other expenses, and then determines what hourly charge will recover all of these costs and also provide the agency with a profit. A common rule of thumb in setting the fee for an individual is to charge three times the annual salary divided by the number of hours that person worked.

The fee system has many supporters within the field. People who favor it over the commission system do not believe that an agency's payments should be based on the price a medium charges. The commission system has survived, however, because it is simple and easy to understand.

WHY HIRE AN AGENCY?

Chapter 1 briefly discussed why advertisers hire agencies. This section will examine that question in more depth. Why should an advertiser sign a long-term contract with an agency? What extra benefit comes from hiring an agency? Does it cost more or less to use an agency?

The answers vary from client to client and from agency to agency, but generally the agency-client relationship is carefully established and carefully maintained. Although the trade press reports the comings and goings of notable clients, the fact is that the average tenure of a client with an agency is 12 years. Many have lasted 50 years.

These are the reasons why advertisers set up long-term relationships with agencies.

Expertise and Objectivity

Professional Expertise   An agency has experience across a *variety* of clients and can apply lessons learned with one client to another. In-house agencies and departments lack this broader perspective, which is often the key to solving difficult advertising problems. Just as a company may hire an outside law firm even if it has an attorney on staff, so will a company hire an agency.

Objectivity   Clients expect an agency to tell them when they are misreading the situation or are out of step with consumers. Agency objectivity is a necessary part of the relationship. Someone from outside is more likely to speak up. Agencies pride themselves on their independent and detached view of the marketplace and the consumer. Advertising people are experts in their field, and few clients feel competent to judge, as well as create, advertisements. They depend on the agency for professional judgment.

Dedication and Commitment   Clients, especially the good ones, receive dedication and commitment from their agencies. The agency becomes very much a team player. This relationship produces an extra effort, an interest in every aspect of the client's business, and a drive never to be satisfied with "good enough."

AD 4.4
Young & Rubicam used this "house ad" to highlight its philosophy of service and creative strategy.
(Courtesy of Young & Rubicam Inc.)

You can really fly
once you know where you're going.

We believe the sharpest advertising strategies provide the greatest creative freedom. Only when you know exactly where you're going can the imagination soar free, without fear or formulas.
YOUNG&RUBICAM INC.

CONFLICTS AND LOYALTY

The standard industry contract has wording in which the agency agrees not to handle products or companies in the same category or industry. In contrast to lawyers or accountants, who may specialize in a sector or an industry and handle a number of clients in the same field, advertising agencies agree not to work for a competing product or company because this would cause a conflict of interest. ("How can you work for a competitor and assure me I'm getting your best ideas and the best media buys?") In concept, the conflict clause is simple. In practice, it has become one of the major controversies in the industry for several reasons: mergers of clients, internationalization of agencies, and the mega-mergers of agencies.

As clients merged, agencies and clients were confronted with new complexities. A client might acquire a new division and want the agency to take on the new assignment—but the agency might already have the leading product in the category from another very important client. Either way, the agency would risk offending one client. The worst case would have both clients insisting that the agency resign the other company because only one of the company's many divisions competed with the client. Usually goodwill and loyalty resolved these conflict-interpretation problems, with clients agreeing that the agency could handle divisions of competing companies as long as the agency kept the people working for one multidivision client from working on any division of another multidivision client. For example, the 1987 merger of Doyle Dane Bernbach, the agency for Weight Watchers International, with Needham Harper Worldwide, the agency for the Mrs. Paul product line, created a potential conflict because both companies produced frozen fish. However, the Campbell Soup Company, which produces the Mrs. Paul line, did not ask the new agency to drop either product.

Loyalty helped. Agencies develop loyalties to clients and vice versa. The conflicting policies of each client are subject to interpretation. Client nationalities even come into play. One case involved a Japanese client's U.S. division and a U.S. company. Inquiring about the Japanese client's reaction to soliciting the U.S. company would be taken as a lack of loyalty—even though the U.S. company was comfortable that the inquiry be made. But out of loyalty to a client, an agency might keep itself free of direct conflicts (product-to-product) anywhere in the world and avoid indirect conflicts (where two companies had similar divisions but the agency would avoid the second company altogether). In the late 1980s companies rewarded this loyalty by concentrating their assignments with agencies that avoided their competitors altogether. This was especially true in soaps and detergents (Procter & Gamble, Colgate, Lever, and Henkel), automobiles (General Motors, Ford, Chrysler, Toyota, and Nissan), and beer (Anheuser-Busch, Miller, and Stroh's).

Internationalization created a second problem. Suppose a client has no European distribution or plans to enter Europe. Could its U.S. agency safely take a competitive product in its client's category in Germany? Usually it could, but in one recent instance the U.S. client was bought by a European company, and the agency found itself with an unanticipated conflict problem in Europe. Mergers in the United States and continuing acquisition of companies by the large global corporations have created a need for agencies and clients to maintain communication on what the policy is and how it will be interpreted. This requires a central learning mechanism at agency headquarters which includes new-product assignments. These are particularly nettlesome problems: What if two clients which the agency has successfully kept separated decide the same week to ask the agency to begin work in the same new-product area? The agency is suddenly in possession of a valuable piece of competitive intelligence. (Best answer: Keep the decision at the highest level and make an informed judgment quickly.)

Staffing and Management

Specialists Even the largest clients might have need for a statistician, a network negotiator, and television producer, or a special events coordinator only once a year. Only large agencies can afford to employ these specialists full time because they have multiple accounts needing this kind of service.

Managing Creatives The people who work for advertising agencies may not be at all like the employees of a corporation. Artists, writers, and television producers might not fit easily into the culture of the corporate environment. Rigid work hours, dress codes, and limitations on overtime would be difficult to enforce among the "free spirits" who tend to work in advertising.

Incorporating creative people into a corporation might be clumsy or upsetting. It might be difficult to explain why a brilliant writer who just seems to sit around is paid more than a division or department head. Advertising agencies provide a different environment. They can organize creative skills, maintain morale, and build spirit more effectively than corporations can.

Flexibility in Staffing Advertising budgets go up and down, and as the budget level goes, so goes the employment level. Because agencies handle a number of clients, they are better able to handle the comings and goings of clients. Clients would have a hard time adjusting to the marketplace impact on an advertising budget. A company with a lifetime employment policy (or a very liberal termination policy for redundant employees) might find it difficult to deal with hiring and firing employees whose positions depended on the advertising budget. It is better to let the agency deal with the staffing problem, spread the effects among a roster of clients, and build personnel policies that adjust to, and compensate for, these risks.

CHANGES IN THE AGENCY WORLD

OMSTPg 105 - 108

Megamergers

In April 1987 three agencies merged in what was called the "Big Bang." Batten, Barton, Durstine, and Osborne (BBDO), Doyle Dane Bernbach, and Needham Harper Worldwide formed Omnicom Inc, a $5-billion giant. The three agencies

AD 4.5
This ad was specially prepared to announce the formation of DDB Needham Worldwide.
(Courtesy of DDB Needham Worldwide.)

Fasten your seatbelts.

TABLE 4.1
Top Ten Agency Holding Companies

Agency	Gross Income	Billings
1. Saatchi & Saatchi PLC	$1.21 bill.	$8.26 bill.
2. Interpublic Group of Cos.	822.4	5.55 bill.
3. Omnicom Group	820.1	5.82 bill.
4. JWT Group	644.8	4.30 bill.
5. Ogilvy Group	548.7	3.80 bill.
6. Eurocom	216.4	1.46 bill.
7. Lowe Howard-Spink & Bell PLC	111.3	759.8
8. WCRS Group PLC	86.2	660.3
9. Alliance International	66.7	437.8
10. Mojo-MDA International	42.4	282.8

Source: Reprinted with permission from *Advertising Age,* May 11, 1987, copyright Crain Communications Inc. All rights reserved.

realigned into two international agencies, BBDO and DDB Needham, and placed most of their specialist agencies into a third group, Diversified Agency Services, which included public relations, direct response, several midsized agencies, recruitment, and medical. Bringing these functions together helped the firm to implement the integrated marketing communications (IMC) philosophy discussed in Chapter 3. Shortly after this merger Saatchi & Saatchi acquired the Ted Bates agency, which owned, among others, the William Esty agency. The new Saatchi giant was even larger than Omnicom.

megamergers *Combinations of large international agencies under a central holding company.*

Megamergers among agencies have produced *holding companies,* that is, companies that own the stocks of other corporations. At least two of these companies have global agencies. One objective of keeping the agencies separate and competitive in the holding company is to avoid client conflicts by steering one client to one subsidiary and a competing client to the second. The ten largest holding companies are listed in Table 4.1.

FIGURE 4.3
As in other industries, the number of acquisitions and mergers within the advertising industry has increased during the 1980s.
Source: DDB Needham Worldwide.

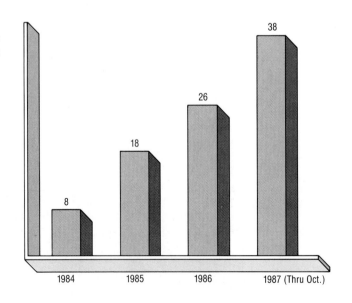

An agency audio-visual technician at the controls of sophisticated videotape editing equipment.
(Courtesy of DDB Needham Worldwide.)

The detergent, automotive, and beer giants have made some agency realignments within the mega-agencies but have frowned on or avoided placing assignments within the mega-agencies that handle a competitor anywhere in the holding company. Over $700 million in billings have switched or had to be resigned because of conflicts.

Agencies have defended the mergers by saying they were forced to merge to match the scope and geographic reach of the new global megacorporation.

Some clients agree, others don't. Roger Smith of General Motors voiced the opinion that stronger, more global agencies would be better able to invest in support of client worldwide marketing plans. The late Robert Goldstein of Procter & Gamble argued that the agencies didn't merge to benefit clients but to benefit their stockholder-managers.

Even though some of the stockholder-managers made a great deal of money on the deals, the surviving agencies proved their point by emerging as stronger and more valuable resources for their clients. Although the argument may never be settled, the megamerger has changed the nature of the advertising business.

High-Productivity Agencies

high-productivity agencies *Advertising agencies with a low staff-to-billings ratio.*

"High productivity" applies to agencies with a low staff-to-billing ratio. By the late 1980s most American agencies had roughly two staff members per million dollars of billing. Some agencies were able to get that ratio down to one staff member per million dollars. These so-called **high-productivity agencies** typically hired fewer, more highly qualified people and paid them above-market salaries. In addition, they reduced or eliminated staff.

These agencies attracted clients who were also slimming down as part of the general restructuring of industry that occurred in the late 1980s. Just as companies were utilizing consultants to increase their capabilities, these agen-

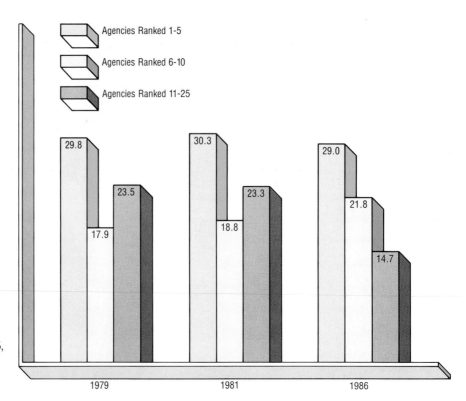

FIGURE 4.4
Most of the growth in the advertising industry has occurred among the largest agencies. The 25 largest agencies, which accounted for 65 percent of industry growth in 1986, represent only a small fraction of all advertising agencies.
Source: DDB Needham Worldwide.

cies were using free-lance professionals as they needed them. This trend seems likely to continue as a survival technique, especially for smaller and middle-sized agencies.

Squeezing the Middle

High productivity has hurt the middle-sized agencies. Growth in the advertising world has occurred among the largest and smallest agencies (see Figure 4.4). For this analysis, "large" means the top 20 agencies. "Small" means agencies under $50 million in New York and Chicago and under $25 million elsewhere.

The agencies in the middle ranks are being squeezed. They are not large enough to compete for the major accounts, and they may be too large to grow by adding small accounts. Furthermore, they are not big enough to be able to squeeze productivity by reducing staff sizes while still meeting the demands of a "full-service" shop.

Many of the medium-sized agencies have merged with other agencies to vault into the top rank, as in the Saatchi mergers. Others have been acquired by larger agencies. Some have specialized in sections of the business as a survival technique. This trend has been occurring for 30 years and will continue into the future.

■ SUMMARY

Agencies usually have four basic functions: account management, creative development and production, media planning and buying, and research.

Support departments include traffic, print production, accounting, and personnel.

The account management function is the primary liaison between the agency and the client.

Agencies typically receive a 15-percent commission from media placed, although this rate is increasingly being negotiated.

Under the fee system agencies' charges are computed on the basis of actual time and services provided.

The pressure toward high productivity means fewer, but more qualified, staff.

QUESTIONS

1. Why does the organizational chart for an agency remain flexible?
2. Why do many agencies prefer the fee system to the commission system? Why is the commission system still so widely used?
3. What are the entry-level jobs in a typical agency?
4. How do agencies separate the internal management function from the creative process in the creative department?
5. What are megamergers, and how are they changing the character of advertising in the United States?

FURTHER READINGS

DUBOFF, ROBERT S. "Can Research and Creative Co-exist?" *Advertising Age,* March 17, 1986, pp. 18, 22.

"U.S. Advertising Agency Profiles: 1988 Edition." *Advertising Age,* March 30, 1988. (Special edition.)

The Honda Way

In the fall of 1969 Honda produced the top-selling motorcycle in America. Honda automobiles, however, had not yet appeared in this country. Over 7,000 miles away at Honda corporate headquarters in Tokyo, plans were being made to change that.

The plans were successful. By the 1980s Honda was manufacturing some of the best-selling cars in the United States. What took the company from zero to 738,000 cars a year in record time? It was a combination of innovation, commitment, and good timing, all driven by a company philosophy known as "The Honda Way." This philosophy included a consistent, yet flexible, marketing and advertising strategy.

From the beginning, Honda's marketing philosophy had stressed supplying high-efficiency products at a reasonable price. The company has continually emphasized customer satisfaction. Honda Associates were encouraged to be ambitious and daring, to develop fresh ideas, to embrace challenges, and to respond quickly to unforeseen changes and opportunities. In 1969 Honda engineers set the ambitious goal of developing a "world car." This project took them to the center of a profoundly changing automotive marketplace.

At that time over 88 percent of all automobiles sold in the United States came from Detroit. Moreover, the majority of imported cars were European, not Japanese. Toyota was the leading Japanese import, followed by Datsun (now Nissan). Mazda and Subaru were just making plans to enter the U.S. market.

The popularity of the Volkswagen Beetle convinced Honda executives that a market for a quality small car existed in the United States. In 1970 Honda introduced its first car to America—the N600. Sales were modest. Only a few thousand were sold.

Then, in 1973, the company introduced its "world car," the innovative Honda Civic. The Civic was nearly 8 inches longer than the 600 model, and it featured an advanced 4-cylinder engine and front-wheel drive. Available in both a 2-door sedan and a 3-door hatchback, it was priced at only $2,150.

Although the Civic was well received by the automotive press and the American public, it was still considered too small. At that point, however, international politics intervened. In October 1973 the Arab oil-producing countries banned oil imports to the West. As gasoline lines grew and prices skyrocketed, Detroit's large engines—some delivering under 12 miles per gallon—began to lose their appeal. Sales of small, fuel-efficient automobiles like the Honda Civic grew rapidly. By the end of 1974 Civic sales had climbed to over 43,000.

Meanwhile the OPEC embargo produced tough new federal fuel economy regulations. The Environmental Protection Agency (EPA) issued strict new emissions standards. As Detroit car makers scrambled to meet the new regulations,

Honda engineers had already developed their next big idea: the 1975 Civic CVCC. With its fuel-efficient new engine, the Civic not only met the EPA clean air standards, it also ran on any grade of fuel. At 42 miles per gallon, the Civic was promoted as both the most fuel-efficient and lowest-priced car in America. The advertising campaign for the Civic positioned the car in the forefront of the move toward economical transportation. The Honda advertising slogan, "What the World Is Coming To," stressed the innovative philosophy behind the Civic (see Exhibit A). More than 100,000 Civics were sold.

But Honda's research indicated that the market was about to change once again. As both fuel shortages and gasoline prices eased somewhat, car buyers began to favor values like quality, roominess, performance, and comfort. Honda developed a car to meet this need and in June 1976 launched what would become its most popular model—the Accord (see Exhibit B).

Honda advertising emphasized the roominess and lively performance of the Accord. The automotive press praised its clean design and advanced engineering. And its public reception was remarkable: by the end of 1978, Honda sales had climbed to over 274,000 cars.

During this time, car buying had become more complex. There was a growing number of manufacturers and car models. Financing was becoming more complicated. And Detroit was offering an expanding array of optional equipment. Amid this confusion, Honda's marketing approach was clear and simple: Honda builds quality cars that are simple to drive, simple to park, simple to understand, and simple to own. The message was summed up in Honda's slogan, used in print ads, brochures, on television, and even on shopping bags, "We Make It Simple." It was The Honda way—and it worked.

By the end of 1978 Honda was number three in car import sales, behind Toyota and Nissan. Over the next few years, the company increased its momentum by refining and expanding its product line. 1979 saw the addition of Honda's third series—the Prelude. In 1980 the second-generation Civic was named Motor Trend magazine's "Import Car of the Year." Annual sales were now well over 375,000. In 1984 Honda launched its newest idea—the CRX. Conceived as a sporty commuter car with high gas mileage, it too was named "Import Car of the Year."

Honda was now selling 12 different models in the United States, at a rate of over half a million cars a year. For the first time, Honda advertising began to focus on the particular personality of each model instead of using a unifying corporate slogan. Honda portrayed its luxury Accord as the benchmark in its class and the Prelude Sport Coupe as "a sports car for adults." Its second-generation Civics were marketed as being larger and more stylish than their predecessors while still keeping earlier fuel economy and value. Ironically, "We

Honda Civic. What the world is coming to.

The Honda Civic was designed from scratch for today's person to drive in today's world. It is a brilliant invention.

Most brilliant of all is the new Advanced Stratified Charge Engine available in the 1975 Civic CVCC. The Civic CVCC burns its fuel mixture so efficiently that it meets all 1975 emissions requirements without a catalytic converter. And it runs brilliantly on regular, low-lead, or no-lead gas.

You get all this without giving up remarkable gas mileage. The Civic CVCC 4-speed sedan got about 28 miles to the gallon around town, about 38 for highway driving in EPA tests.

But if you want performance instead of great gas mileage, it can do 86 miles an hour.

The Honda Civic is also remarkable for its brilliant use of space. One look at the inside of other leading subcompact imports should convince you.

The Honda Civic has a short hood — made possible by mounting the engine sideways — and a short rear deck. Its compactness makes it ideal for today's crowded cities.

See your local Honda Civic dealer for details and date of 1975 availability.

When you get the full story, plus a test drive, we think you'll like what the world is coming to.

HONDA CIVIC

Exhibit A

A little more car from Honda.

The Accord.

We ask you to compare our imposing list of standard features with any other car in the world today. Then compare our price. $3,995.*

CVCC® Advanced Stratified Charge Engine, Honda mileage (44 mpg hwy/31 city in EPA mileage estimates),† deluxe interior, electronic warning system, 5-speed transmission, tachometer, radial tires, big rear tailgate with remote release, automatic maintenance reminders, AM/FM radio, rack and pinion steering, rear window wiper and washer, four wheel independent MacPherson strut suspension, side and rear window defrosters, flow-thru ventilation system, tinted glass all-around, power-assisted front disc brakes, reclining front bucket seats, wall-to-wall color coordinated carpeting, low fuel warning light, protective side mouldings, day/night mirror, locking fuel filler door, trip odometer, even a coin box. All standard.

HONDA ACCORD CVCC

Exhibit B

Make It Simple" was no longer the simplest way to advertise an increasingly sophisticated product line, which now appealed to a wider variety of buyers.

Honda has always emphasized customer satisfaction. In 1986 Honda outscored Mercedes-Benz to become number one in overall customer satisfaction, based on how owners rate the quality of their cars and the quality of the dealerships that service them. Honda spotlighted this success with the advertising slogan, "We're Happy You're Happy."

One reason for Honda's consistently strong performance in customer satisfaction is its dealer network. Honda works closely with its dealers to ensure that their operations—sales, service, parts, and accessories—reflect the quality of the cars themselves. Honda provides its dealers with support materials, from sales training and service manuals to full-line product brochures and videos.

Part of Honda's corporate philosophy is to be a good corporate citizen. In this spirit, Honda also began another important campaign: saving lives. For 3 consecutive years Honda sponsored a multimillion-dollar advertising effort to persuade drivers to use their seat belts (see Exhibit C). The company placed ads on television and in print media that were designed to convince drivers of the importance of seat belts in saving lives.

Responsible corporate citizenship took another form as well. With the desire to manufacture products in the market in which they are sold, by 1980 Honda began work on a new automobile plant in Marysville, Ohio (see Exhibit D). The decision posed certain problems and opportunities. Research indicated that prospective buyers might perceive an Ohio-built Honda as inferior to one made in Japan. However, many Americans who felt uncomfortable buying an imported car would now consider an Accord built in the United States.

Honda decided to use advertising and marketing campaigns to help sell the idea of its Ohio-made cars. These campaigns described the contribution that Honda was making to the U.S. economy. The company also ran a series of ads in key business publications such as the *Wall Street Journal* emphasizing the quality of Ohio-built Accords.

When the Marysville plant opened in November 1982, the Honda state of mind had been successfully imported to Ohio. Impartial road tests gave the American-built Accord and the imported Accord equal marks on fit, finish, and quality. By 1988 the Marysville Plant produced over 360,000 cars—55 percent of all Hondas sold in America. Moreover, Honda began to implement a new five-part strategy for the future of Honda's operations in the United States. The plan calls for Honda's total manufacturing involvement in this country to

Exhibit C

Exhibit D

Then. It was the wide paisley tie, Woodstock, mankind taking a giant leap on the moon and the Honda Civic. And while you may think you know all about the Civic, times have changed. Now. It's the new Civic.

The new Civic is bigger than the old Civic ever dreamed of being. It has a sleek aerodynamic shape that's as now as a miniskirt.

Outside, it has more doors. Count 'em. Inside, it has more room. From just a year ago, interior space has been increased by a full four cubic feet. New bigger windows all around provide the room with a view.

The new Civic is innovative. It's full of high-tech engineering.

A 16-valve, fuel-injected engine will get you where you're going faster than a power tie. With no compromise in operating efficiency.

A four-wheel double wishbone suspension gives you a ride as comfortable as, well, earth shoes. Handling is crisp. Responsive.

The Civic LX 4-Door shown here comes with even more sophisticated equipment. Like power steering, power windows, power door locks and power-

operated mirrors. All standard. And to think the world was once content with mere flower power.

But the real beauty of all this advanced engineering? The new Civic is more efficient and practical than ever before. And still remarkably affordable.

Now there's an idea that always seems right for the times.

HONDA
The New Civic

That was then. This is now.

Exhibit E

reach $1.7 billion, including the construction of a second U.S. auto plant, the increase of U.S. research and development activities, the expansion of production engineering, the increase of domestic content in American-made Hondas to 75 percent by 1991, and the export of U.S.-built Honda products.

The Accord Coupe is the first Honda to be manufactured exclusively in the United States. A special edition of this Accord became the first Japanese nameplate ever exported to Japan. Approximately 4,000 Coupes made their way to Japan in 1988. By 1991 Honda plans to export 70,000 automobiles to Japan and other countries.

From the beginning, perhaps the key factor in Honda's success has been consistency. Honda products have consistently been of the highest quality and value. And they have consistently evolved in terms of engineering innovations, performance, styling, and comfort.

Throughout the years, Honda also has maintained a consistent image through its advertising and marketing (see Exhibit E). Honda advertising has continuously appealed to the intelligence and common sense of its customers. Often

lighthearted and whimsical but always honest and confident, Honda's advertising, created by Rubin Postaer & Associates, Los Angeles, has been praised and awarded. In a recent issue of *Adweek* automotive journalist Chris Cedergren said: "Honda's strength is in its greater U.S. production capacity, and the fact that they don't radically change their advertising every six months like the others do. Honda definitely won't tamper with success."

Source: Adapted from "The Honda Way: The Marketing of Honda Automobiles in America." (Courtesy of Gerry Rubin, Rubin Postaer and Associates.)

Questions for Discussion

1. What themes in Honda's advertising and marketing reflect what you know of social needs and issues in the 1970s and 1980s?

2. What advertising strategy could be used to position Honda cars in a more competitive market during the 1990s? How can Honda reach the desired audience for these cars?

5 The Consumer Audience

DON'T READ THIS CHAPTER!

Chapter Outline

Lessons from a Shopping List
Consumer Behavior
Influences on You as a Consumer
Audience Descriptors
Understanding the Consumer Audience

Chapter Objectives

When you have completed this chapter you should be able to:

- Understand the different factors that affect the responses of consumers to advertisements
- Define the concept of culture as it applies to advertising and consumers
- Distinguish between psychographics and demographics and explain how advertisers use each one
- Relate such concepts as family, reference groups, and VALS to the practice of advertising

*L*ESSONS FROM A SHOPPING LIST

It is Thursday afternoon, and Joan is leaving work a little early to run some errands. She has a few items she has to pick up at the grocery store, and both bathrooms are totally out of toilet paper, which has created a minor emergency. She also wants to look around for a little portable television for John's birthday present.

At the grocery store she pulls out her list—bread, milk, breakfast cereal, eggs. The eggs are a simple matter; she only has to choose between sizes, and she always buys the large ones. Milk is easy, too. She worries about her weight and her family's health, so she always buys lowfat 2 percent milk—in gallons, of course. She does have a favorite brand, Viva. She bought another brand one time and the milk soured in a couple of days. The kids were furious. So she always gets a brand that has never caused her any problems, and she checks the date to make certain that it is the freshest on the shelf.

She stops at the bread section and thinks for a minute. The kids need sandwich bread, but she would also like something special for toast in the morning. The last time she tried the store's brand of raisin-nut bread. It was the cheapest in the raisin category, and it was great. As she walks up and down the shelf looking for it she realizes how many different varieties of bread the store is now stocking—different grains and flours, sourdough, and all those different sizes. She finds the raisin bread and then turns to the sandwich problem. She probably ought to get the store's biggest loaf of white bread for sandwiches; it's the cheapest and goes the furthest. However, she has heard that the nutritional value of white bread is very low. Now that the kids are a little older they are beginning to eat bread with more texture, so she decides to get a wheatberry. It's a lot more expensive than the basic white bread but, after all, nutrition is important.

Turning back toward the checkout counter, she heads for the cereal aisle. This is the biggest decision—no one in the family likes the same brand. One kid likes Life; the other likes Cheerios. John likes Shredded Wheat, and she likes Grape-Nuts. Well, there is one they all like—it's that Quaker 100% Natural Raisin and Date cereal, but it's so expensive. She knows the kids are almost out so she picks up Life and Cheerios.

Standing in line to pay, she picks up a Butterfinger. It's been a long day and she has a lot to do, so a little quick energy is probably worth the calories.

She hurries next door to K-Mart, intending to pick up a big six-roll pack of toilet paper. She thinks to herself that she could have bought it at the grocery store but it is so much cheaper at a discount store. Of course there's a trade-off: she has to stand in another line, and the lines are so long at this store. But even the brand names are cheaper. Refusing to buy Charmin because she hates Mr. Whipple, she looks for the softest of the other brands. She never knows what she is getting with toilet paper. She wants something soft, and a lot of the textured brands that look soft feel like cardboard. She notices that the store is having a sale on Northern, and because it is reliable, she gets two four-roll packs. This way she can get yellow for the downstairs bathroom and blue for upstairs.

Now the television—she knows what John wants, but she can't find it. He wants a little portable television that is easy to carry, but not one of those tiny ones with a miniature screen. He wants to be able to see it from across the room. She saw a 13-inch television advertised at the new "home entertainment store" that just opened, but the price was over $300. She checks K-Mart and finds something like what he wants, only it's clearly designed for teens and comes in crazy colors. Next she stops at a discount appliance store—nothing. She has time for one more store so she stops at Ward's. Success! She finds a 13-inch model in a contemporary white design and it's only $199—plus she can use her credit card.

CONSUMER BEHAVIOR

What does this little scenario tell us about consumers and how they behave? It points out that many factors affect consumers' purchasing decisions. Sometimes brands are important; sometimes they aren't. Sometimes price is important; other times features like size or color make a difference. Some purchases are made on impulse; some are made after a lot of searching and comparative shopping. In order to develop advertising that makes sense, it is necessary for advertisers to understand consumers and how they behave in the marketplace.

The Consumer Audience

consumers *People who buy or use products.*

Consumers are people who buy or use products. There are actually two types of consumers: those who shop for and purchase the product, and those who actually use the product. This distinction is important because the two groups can have different needs and wants. In the case of children's cereals, for example, parents (the purchasers) look for nutritional value, whereas children (the users) look for a sweet taste and a game on the back of the package. As a result of the consumer orientation in marketing, consumer behavior has become a very important field. Companies need to understand how consumers think and make decisions about products. In order to do this they undertake sophisticated research efforts into consumer behavior. Who are the consumers, why are they buying what they buy, and how do they go about buying things? (Research will be discussed in Chapter 6.)

PRINCIPLE
Marketers look at people as consumers who buy products; advertisers look at people as an audience for messages.

Consumers not only purchase goods, they are also an audience for advertising. Advertising messages are designed to reach **prospects,** consumers who might be in the market for a given product. To help them speak to this audience, advertisers conduct research into consumers as listeners, readers, and viewers. Who are these people and what do they want to hear? What moves them?

prospects *Consumers who are potential purchasers or users of a given product or service.*

INFLUENCES ON YOU AS A CONSUMER

Many things affect your responses to an advertising message. Study yourself. You are going to be the subject of our field research for this chapter. You are a product of the culture and the society in which you were raised. Many of your values and opinions were shaped by your social environment. Likewise you are a product of the family in which you were raised, and many of your habits and biases were developed within the family environment.

But you are also an individual. As you matured and began to think for yourself, you developed your own individual way of looking at the world, based on such factors as your age, income, sex, education, occupation, and race. Deep within you are factors that influence every decision you make—such things as how you perceive events and other people, how you learn from experience, your basic set of attitudes and opinions, your internal drive and motivation, and the whole bundle of characteristics called your "personality." These factors are illustrated in Figure 5.1.

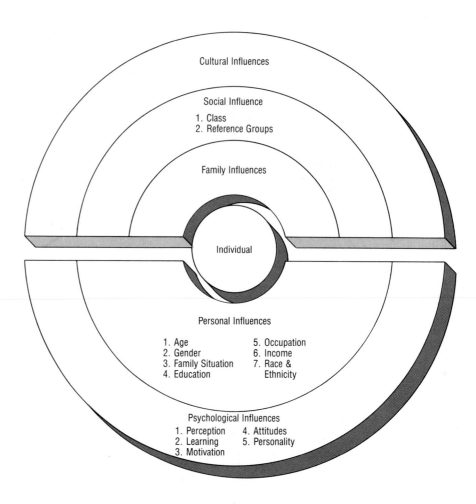

FIGURE 5.1
Circle of influences.

Social and Cultural Influences

The forces that other people exert on your behavior are called **social influences.** They can be grouped into four major areas: (1) culture, (2) social class, (3) reference groups, and (4) family.

Culture **Culture** is defined as a complex of tangible items (art, literature, buildings, furniture, clothing, and music) plus intangible concepts (knowledge, laws, morals, and customs) that define a group of people or a way of life. The concepts, values, and behavior that make up a culture are learned and passed down from one generation to the next. The boundaries that culture establishes for behavior are called *norms.* Norms are simple rules that we know intuitively and that specify or prohibit certain behaviors.

Cultural influences have broad effects on buying behavior. For example, the busy working mother of today is not as devoted to meal preparation and household cleaning as was the full-time homemaker of the past. Thus food marketers have changed their promotional strategies to reach these women. We see more advertising now for fast foods, convenience foods, and restaurants.

How does culture affect you as a consumer? Can you think of any cultural factors that affect your behavior? How about patriotism and sacrificing for the good of others? Can you see yourself signing up for the Peace Corps? How about materialism? How do you feel about acquiring things and making money?

Subcultures A culture can be divided into *subcultures* on the basis of geographic regions or human characteristics such as age, values, or ethnic background. In the United States, for example, we have many different subcultures: teenagers, college students, retirees, Southerners, Texans, Blacks, Hispanics, athletes, musicians, and working single mothers, to list just a few. Within subcultures there are similarities in people's attitudes.

What subcultures do you belong to? Look at your activities. Do you do anything on a regular basis that might identify you as a member of a distinctive subculture?

social class *A way to categorize people on the basis of their values, attitudes, lifestyles, and behavior.*

Social Class A **social class** is the position that you and your family occupy within your society. Social class is determined by such things as income, wealth, education, occupation, family prestige, value of home, and neighborhood.

Every society has some social class structure. In a rigid society you are not allowed to move from the class into which you were born. In the United States we like to think we have a classless society because it is possible for us to move into a different class regardless of what social class our parents belonged to. However, even in the United States we speak of an upper class, a middle class, and a lower class.

Marketers assume that people in one class buy different goods from different outlets and for different reasons than people in other classes (see Table 5.1). Advertisers can get a feel for the social class of a target market by using marketing research or available census data.

The proliferation of fast-food restaurants is an example of the influence of culture on consumer behaviors.
(Courtesy of Dennie Cody/FPG.)

TABLE 5.1
A Summary of Social Classes and Related Behavior

Class (percentage of population)	Characteristics
Upper 2%	Inherited wealth; high-level professionals; live in exclusive neighborhoods; purchase expensive and prestigious products and avoid mass merchandisers.
Upper-middle (10–15%)	Well-educated; top management or professional; socially involved; purchase expensive, conspicuous products; seek security.
Lower-middle (35–40%)	Achieve respectability through careful acquisitions; live for children; own small businesses or have white-collar occupations; are price-conscious.
Upper-lower (35–40%)	Blue-collar; want security; earn good incomes but live modestly; use credit; shop at discount stores; tend to be brand-loyal.
Lower-lower (15–20%)	Poorly educated; pessimistic about future; buy products to improve appearance; seek easy credit; shop impulsively.

Sources: James F. Engel and Roger D. Blackwell, *Consumer Behavior* (Hinsdale, IL: Dryden Press, 1986), pp. 348–58; "What Is Happening to the Middle Class?" *American Demographics,* January 1985, pp. 18–25; and Richard P. Coleman, "The Continuing Significance of Social Class to Marketing," *Journal of Consumer Research,* December 1983, pp. 265–80.

In what class do you see yourself? Does social class affect what you buy and how you respond to advertising? Do you know people you would consider to be upper- or lower-class? Do they buy different products than you do? Do they look at products differently in terms of price or quality?

Reference Groups

reference group *A group of people that an individual uses as a guide for behavior in specific situations.*

A **reference group** is a collection of people that you use as a guide for behavior in specific situations. General examples of reference groups are political parties, religious groups, racial or ethnic organizations, clubs based on hobbies, and informal affiliations such as fellow workers or students.

For consumers, reference groups have three functions: (1) they provide information; (2) they serve as a means of comparison; and (3) they furnish guidance. Sometimes the group norms have the *power* to require the purchase or use of certain products (uniforms, safety equipment). The reference group members may be so *similar* to you that you believe that any product or service the group members use is right for you too. Ads that feature typical users in fun or pleasant surroundings are using a reference-group strategy. You also may be *attracted* to a particular reference group and wish to be like them out of respect or admiration. Advertisers use celebrity endorsements to tap into this desire.

Think about all the groups you belong to, both formal and informal. Why do you belong to those groups? How do other members influence you or keep you informed? Have you ever bought anything specifically because it was required by a group you belonged to?

family *Two or more people who are related by blood, marriage, or adoption.*

household *All those people who occupy one living unit, whether or not they are related.*

lifestyle *The pattern of living that reflects how people allocate their time, energy, and money.*

Family   A **family** consists of two or more people who are related by blood, marriage, or adoption living in the same household. It differs from a **household,** which consists of all those who occupy a living unit, whether related or not.

Your family is critical to how you develop as an individual. It provides two kinds of resources for members: *economic,* such as money and possessions; and *emotional,* such as empathy, love, and companionship. The family is also responsible for raising and training children and establishing a lifestyle for family members. Your **lifestyle** determines how you spend your time and money and the kinds of activities you value.

How has your family influenced you in your choice of schooling, lifestyle, and the way you spend your time and money? Now think about your best friend. Are the two of you different in any ways that can be traced to family differences?

Personal Influences

A consumer is a product of culture and society, social class, and family. Ultimately, however, a consumer is an individual. Individual characteristics say a lot about the way you think, decide, and behave as a consumer. The following personal characteristics influence how you behave as an individual consumer.

Age People in different stages of life have different needs. In turn, advertising for products and services must use a message approach and a medium that are appropriate to each age group.

How old are you? What products did you use 5 or 10 years ago that you don't use now? Look ahead 5 years—what products will you be in the market for then? What products do your parents buy that you don't? Do you read different publications and watch different programs than your parents do? If you were in the market for a car, would you look at the same features that your parents look at? Can you see how age is a critical factor in the marketing of products and development of message strategies?

Reference groups exert a major influence over our behavior.
(Courtesy of Comstock.)

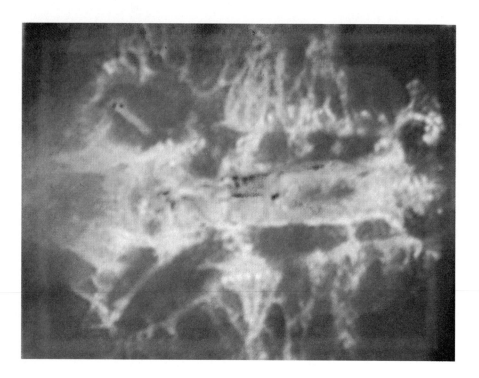

AD 5.1
This ad for the "Nestea plunge" is targeted toward a young audience.
(Courtesy of J. Walter Thompson.)

Gender Gender, or sex, is an obvious basis for differences in marketing and advertising. The primary physical characteristics of men and women create different demands for products and services. Certain brands and product categories are characterized as masculine or feminine. It is unlikely that men will ever use White Shoulders after-shave. Marketers of products formerly associated with one sex who want to sell them to both sexes usually find it necessary to offer "his and hers" brands or even different product names for the same basic goods. There are, of course, "crossover" products like T-shirts and sunglasses. What products do you buy that are unisex?

Family Status Your purchasing patterns are affected by your family situation. People living alone buy different products, and in different sizes, than people living in families. The stage in the family cycle is an important factor in advertising strategy.

Education The level of education you have attained also influences your behavior as a consumer. Advertisers know they must market products differently to better-educated consumers. Such consumers are often more responsive to technical-scientific appeals, prefer informative ads, and are better able to judge the relationship between the price and the quality of a product. Ad 5.2 is targeted to a better-educated audience.

Occupation Most people identify themselves by what they do. Even homemakers and students who may not be earning significant salaries identify themselves this way. And what you do with this very important part of your life affects your self-concept as well as your behavior as a consumer.

If you are a student, you belong to that occupational category, but you are also in training for some other profession. Why did you choose that career objective? Obviously your decision to go to college was affected by occupational considerations, and also by the geographical area in which you live. What other decisions have you made on the basis of your occupation or profession—either past, present, or intended?

Income   You are only meaningful to a marketer if you have the resources to buy the product. That means money and credit. Income is generally related to occupation and education, and it is a major indicator of whether you are in the market for the product. Most college students, for example, aren't looking at Ferrari Testarossas that can cost as much as $125,000. If the money isn't there, you are simply *not in the market.*

Can you think of any product that you wanted to buy recently but couldn't afford? Do you have a "wish list" of products that you would like to be able to buy "someday"?

Race and Ethnicity   The United States has long been considered the "melting pot" of the world. This image implies that the diverse peoples who settled here adopted the same basic values and norms. Although that may be true to an extent, it is probably less true than most people imagine. For the majority of white Anglo-Saxon Americans race and ethnic background might not be much of a factor in consumer behavior because such considerations simply are not very important in their daily lives.

For nonwhites and people with strong ethnic backgrounds, however, racial and ethnic identities affect both self-image and consumer behavior. This is a complex area because race and ethnicity are difficult to separate from such factors as family and reference groups.

AD 5.2
BMW is an example of a company that directs its advertising toward a well-educated audience.
(Courtesy of BMW of North America, Inc.)

Psychological Influences

We have analyzed you as a member of social and reference groups and have looked at your personal characteristics. Now let's look at the internal elements that make you an individual. The variables that shape your inner self are referred to as your *psychological makeup*. Although a number of internal psychological factors affect your behavior, the following have been shown to exert especially strong influence on your response to advertising: perception, learning, motives, attitudes, and personality.

Perception   Each day you are bombarded by stimuli—faces, conversations, products, buildings, advertisements, news announcements—yet you actually see or hear only a small fraction. Why? The answer is perception. **Perception** is the process by which we receive information through our five senses and assign meaning to it. We *select* some bits of information and ignore others because we do not have the ability to be conscious of all incoming information at one time. The process of screening out information that does not interest us and retaining information that does is called **selective perception.**

Advertisers are interested in these selective processes because they affect whether you will perceive an ad and, if so, whether you will remember it. Advertisers want you to remember the brand name so you will recall it when you are deciding which product to choose.

The next time you watch television, study yourself as you watch the ads. What do you select to pay attention to? Why? When do you "tune out?" Why? Did you find yourself disagreeing with a message or arguing with it? Can you see how your own selection processes influence your attention and response to advertising?

Learning   Perception leads to learning. That is, we cannot learn something unless we have accurately perceived the information and attached some meaning to it. Advertisers must understand this learning process if they are to be successful.

Educational psychologists tell us that the learning process is sequential. In other words, it begins with something that stimulates or encourages action, such as hunger. Advertisers call this a *need*. Next a *cue* addresses that particular need, such as a fast-food ad with a coupon. Let's say you respond to this cue in a positive way because you have had pleasant experiences with this restaurant in the past. Finally *reinforcement* of learning occurs when the response is followed by satisfaction.

Positive reinforcement strengthens the relationship between the cue and the response and therefore increases the probability that the response will be repeated. When we have repeated this process enough times we reach a point called *habit*, where we no longer put much thought into the decision.

Advertisers use a number of techniques to improve learning. Music and jingles improve learning because they intensify the repetition. Also, creating positive associations with a brand enhances learning. Testimonials by well-liked celebrities and scenes of attractive people in attractive settings are used to intensify positive associations. Humor is used because it gives the audience some reward for paying attention.

Motivation   A **motive** is an internal force that stimulates us to behave in a particular manner. At any given point in time you are probably being affected by a number of different motives, some of which may be contradictory. Some motives are stronger than others, but even this pattern changes from time to time. For example, your motivation to buy a new suit will be much higher when you start going out on job interviews.

---

perception *The process by which we receive information through our five senses and acknowledge and assign meaning to this information.*

selective perception *The process of screening out information that does not interest us and retaining the information that does.*

PRINCIPLE
Selective perception means we screen out information that does not interest us.

PRINCIPLE
An ad will be perceived only if it is relevant to the consumer.

PRINCIPLE
An advertisement acts as a cue to trigger some kind of response in the consumer.

PRINCIPLE
Ad messages will be learned best if positive reinforcement follows.

motive *An unobservable inner force that stimulates and compels a behavioral response.*

If you love your husband, give him a pat.

The natural goodness of butter enhances the flavor of everything it touches. And, it has no more calories than margarine. So when you cook for the people you love, do something special. Give them all a pat. And cook with butter.

REAL BUTTER

AD 5.3
The "Pat of Butter" campaign speaks to a mother's love for her family, a very strong motivation.
(Courtesy of California Milk Advisory Board.)

needs *Basic forces that motivate you to do or to want something.*

PRINCIPLE _____
Advertising tries to address consumers' buying motives.

This desire to impress was discussed earlier as a need. **Needs** are the basic forces that motivate you to do something. Some needs are concerned with your physical well-being, others with your psychological well-being. Among the major consumer needs are achievement, independence, recognition, and dominance.

Advertisers are interested in the buying motives that determine (1) what consumers want to do, and (2) how much they want to do it. Advertisements try to speak to these two motivational factors by identifying buying motives and giving reasons to buy.

What are your buying motives? Think back over all your purchases during the past week. Did you have a reason for buying it that you might tell your mother or an interviewer, but also a hidden reason that you will keep to yourself? You can see how important the concept of buying motives is to an understanding of consumer behavior.

Attitudes An **attitude** is a learned predisposition, a feeling that you hold toward an object, a person, or an idea that leads to a particular behavior. An attitude focuses on some topic, something that provides a focal point for your beliefs and feelings. Attitudes also tend to be enduring. You can hold an attitude for months or even years.

We develop and learn attitudes, we are not born with them. Because they are learned, we can also change them, unlearn them, or replace them with new ones. Attitudes also vary in direction and in strength. That is, an attitude can be *positive* or *negative,* reflecting like or dislike.

Attitudes are important to advertisers because they influence how you evaluate products. A strong positive attitude might be turned into brand preference and loyalty. A weak attitude, even if it is positive, might not be strong enough to convince you to act. Changing an attitude is not impossible, but it is difficult.

AD 5.4
The nation's pork producers are trying to change consumers' attitudes and behaviors concerning food and nutrition.
(Courtesy of National Pork Producers Council.)

AD 5.5
The cosmetic surgery industry is speaking to our self-image in this ad.
(Courtesy of Northside Hospital, Atlanta.)

personality *Relatively long-lasting personal qualities that allow us to cope with, and respond to, the world around us.*

Personality All of these personal and psychological factors interact to create your own unique personality. A **personality** is a collection of traits that makes a person distinctive. How you look at the world, how you perceive and interpret what is happening around you, how you respond intellectually and emotionally, and how you form your opinions and attitudes are all reflected in your personality. Your personality is what makes you an individual.

SELF-CONCEPT Self-concept refers to how we look at ourselves. Our self-image reflects how we see our own personality and our individual pattern of strengths and weaknesses. Take a minute to think of the traits that best describe you. What do they tell you about your own self-concept? Are they basically positive or negative? Do you have high or low self-esteem? What image of yourself do you see?

Now consider yourself as a consumer. Explain how these same characteristics affect your response to different products, to advertising, and to your behavior as a consumer. Can you see how understanding personality is important in developing a relevant message?

*A*UDIENCE DESCRIPTORS

PRINCIPLE
Advertisers try to identify consumers in terms of what makes prospects similar as a group and different from other groups.

So far we have been talking about cultural, social, personal, and psychological influences on your behavior as a consumer. Now let's look at how this knowledge is applied by advertisers. The advertiser's goal is to be able to draw a complete picture of the consumer or prospect for a product or service. Advertisers use two types of descriptors to sketch in the features of these consumers and make them come to life as people: demographics and psychographics. Both help to explain what makes prospects *similar* to one another and, furthermore, what makes these people *different* from others who aren't in the group.

Demographics

demographics *The vital statistics about the human population, its distribution, and its characteristics.*

Demographics are the statistical representation of social and economic characteristics about people, including age, sex, income, occupation, and family size. Demographics are the common characteristics of all people that allow for counting and meaningful comparisons. We can count how many people are between the ages of 18 and 24, and we can compare that with the number of people between 25 and 31.

In our discussion of personal characteristics of you as a consumer, we were talking about demographics. As Table 5.2 indicates, age, income, gender, education, family situation, occupation, location or geography, racial or ethnic group, and religion are all examples of demographic categories. Now we will look at what advertisers know about these categories and how they use this information.

Population In developing marketing and advertising goals, as well as in media planning, it is important to know the number of people in different groups. Population is an important concept to advertisers. People are grouped in some fairly standard geographic categories.

A number of population trends affect advertising. Significant shifts are occurring in both regional and urban-rural patterns. For example, the biggest markets remain in the East North Central (Illinois, Ohio, Pennsylvania), the South Atlantic (Georgia, Florida, Virginia), and the Middle Atlantic (Maryland, New Jersey, New York) Census regions. However, the greatest rate of population growth is occurring in the southern and western regions. By the year 2000 the three most populous states will be California, Texas, and Florida, in that order.*

The movement from the farm to the city is another trend that is expected to continue. Demographers point out that in 1950 about 1 out of 6 people lived on a farm; in 1980 it was about 1 out of 40.† Where are these farm people moving? Statistics indicate that they are *not* moving to central cities. In fact, the older established parts of some cities are losing population. The real growth is occurring in the fringe areas of the central cities and in the suburbs outside these cities.

Age The Census gives us standard categories to use in counting age groups (see Table 5.2). Definite trends are occurring with respect to age groups, particularly those associated with the "Baby Boom" and seniors.

THE "BABY BOOM" The "Baby Boom" includes all of the 76.4 million people born between 1946 and 1964. These people make up almost one-third of the U.S. population. A great deal of marketing and advertising planning revolves around the current and projected needs of this enormous market.‡

Baby boomers now are getting older, and many are reaching their high-earning years. Despite better education, higher-paying jobs, and two-salary families, the older Baby Boomers (later 30s to early 40s) are experiencing a crisis of expectations because of increasing costs and excessive competition for high-paying jobs. Many are unable to achieve their goal of attaining a more affluent lifestyle than their parents enjoyed.

The younger Baby Boomer group (23–28) is somewhat smaller and has found career opportunities and job advancement to be easier because the older Boomers expanded the size of the job market. It is this group that has popularized Audis, BMWs, and Porsches.

Statistical Abstract of the United States (Washington, DC: Bureau of the Census, 1985), p. 839.
†*Ibid.*
‡"Growing Pains at 40," *Time*, May 19, 1986, pp. 22–41.

TABLE 5.2
Examples of the Major Demographic Categories Used by Marketers

Gender:
Female
Male

Region:

New England	Northeast	New England
Middle Atlantic	North Central	Mid-Atlantic
East Central	South	East North Central
West Central	Midwest	West North Central
Southeast	West	South Atlantic
Southwest		East South Central
Pacific		West South Central
		Mountain
		Pacific

Community Size:
4,000,000 and over
1,000,000–3,999,999
500,000–999,999
250,000–499,999
100,000–249,999
50,000–99,999
10,000–49,999
2,500–9,999
Below 2,500

Urbanized Area:
Central city
Urban fringe
Surburban

Household Unit:
Single-family home
Multiple-family home
Apartment
Mobile home

Ownership:
Own home
Cooperative
Condominium
Rent

Age:
17 and younger
18–24
25–34
35–44
45–54
55–64
65 and older

Marital Status:
Married
Widowed
Divorced or separated
Single (never married)
Roommates/living together

Education:
Grade school or less
Some high school
High school graduate
Some college
College graduate
Postgraduate

Occupation:
Managerial
Professional
Technical
Administrative support (includes clerical)
Sales
Operatives, nonfarm laborers
Service workers, household workers
Farmers, farm managers, farm laborers
Craftsmen
Others

Income:
Under $10,000
$10,000–$14,999
$15,000–$19,999
$20,000–$24,999
$25,000–$29,999
$30,000–$39,999
$40,000–$49,999
$50,000–$74,999
$75,000 and above

Religion:
Protestant
Catholic
Jewish
Other
None

Race and Ethnic Background:
White
Black
Hispanic
Oriental
Other

Not all "Baby Boomers" exhibit the upscale purchasing behaviors that are associated with this group.
(Courtesy of John T. Turner/FPG.)

Because Baby Boomers are having fewer children, the youth market is shrinking. The relative size of the youth market decreased by about 20 percent during the 1980s, although this is still an important group to marketers.*

YUPPIES   One group that is frequently confused with Baby Boomers is the "Yuppie," or Young Urban Professional. Few market segments have drawn greater attention and inspired more ideas from marketing executives and advertising planners than this group. Unlike "Baby Boomer," however, "Yuppie" refers to more than just an age group. The most commonly accepted description of a Yuppie is a person with a college education, an income over $30,000, age between 25 and 44, white-collar or professional occupation, and urban residence.†

SENIORS   Along with the Baby Boomers, the elderly market is growing in size and importance. By the turn of the century, one person in eight will be at least 65 years old. The number of people between 75 and 84 will double. Of greater significance for marketers is the fact that the 65-and-over group is quite affluent, with about half the discretionary buying power of the nation and over three-quarters of the country's personal financial assets. An *Advertising Age* article claimed: "People over age 50 own 80 percent of all money in savings and loans, 77 percent of the country's financial assets, or, taken altogether, 70 percent of the total net worth of U.S. households—nearly $7 trillion."‡

*"Ten Forces Reshaping America," *U.S. News and World Report,* March 19, 1984, pp. 40–52.
†John J. Burnett and Alan J. Bush, "Profiling the Yuppies," *Journal of Advertising Research*, April/May 1986, pp. 27–34.
‡Lenore Skenzay, "These Days, It's Hip to Be Old," *Advertising Age*, February 15, 1988, p. 81.

THE YUPPIE: REALITY OR MYTH?

Imagine millions of young people with lots of money to spend who define themselves by what they own. It is no wonder that a whole range of companies, from Ford and American Express to Campbell and Michelob, have introduced new advertising campaigns or designed new products to court them. But what is a Yuppie? For the most part marketers see Yuppies as the largest, richest, best-educated generation ever born. We are told that Yuppies worship quality in their furniture, automobiles, clothes, grooming products, and entertainment. They prefer townhouses and condominiums, foreign cars, and gadgets. They buy the best brands: BMW, Rolex, and Ralph Lauren.

Critics of this theory contend that Yuppies are essentially a "marketing figmentation." They might, in fact, be correct. But the questions remain: Do Yuppies exist, what are they really like, and has their time passed? In a 1986 study researchers surveyed several people who fit the Yuppie definition. The study found that:

1. Although Yuppies tend to hang around health facilities, they are not all that concerned with maintaining their health.

2. Yuppies are heavy users of products and services that enhance convenience.

3. Yuppies tend to be optimistic and exhibit leadership, self-confidence, and adventuresomeness.

4. Yuppies are not more mobile than the rest of the population.

5. Yuppies are more interested than other Americans in income management, investing, expensive cameras, ice cream, chocolate, Japanese cars and sports cars, and being successful.

6. Yuppies dislike advertising and do not use it as a source for decision making.

The authors concluded that Yuppies (approximately 8 to 9 percent of the population) do exist. Advertisers, however, had better be careful about how they approach this group.*

A more recent article in *Esquire,* however, described the Yuppie concept as something undesirable. It pointed out that the word "is now understood almost universally as a term of abuse." The author suggests you try it out on the person next to you in exercise class—or in an MBA program. The reason that people are so defensive about being labeled a Yuppie is that the term is taken to mean not "you're a young urban professional," but rather "you have lousy values"—you're self-centered, greedy, and consumed by materialism.

The *Esquire* article further concludes that the end is near for Yuppiedom. Part of the reason is demographic—the current Yuppies are getting older and will soon be middle-aged. Furthermore, the 1987 stock market crash "wiped the condescending smile off many a smooth Yuppie mug." According to the article, much of the American population is getting poorer, not richer, so the Yuppie promise is no longer coming true. "The vast majority of those tagged Yuppies by the media have been heading down, down, down for more than a decade, and the worst is yet to come. The very word *Yuppie* is a taunt, a lie, a fraud: insult added to injury."

What do you think? Is the Yuppie dead, is the Yuppie a myth, or is this still a healthy category? Should advertisers continue to target a group called Yuppies?

*John J. Burnett and Alan J. Bush, "Profiling the Yuppies," *Journal of Advertising Research,* April/May 1986, pp. 27–34 and Hendrik Hertzberg, "The Short Happy Life of the American Yuppie," *Esquire,* February 1988, pp. 100–6.

In the same article Ken Dychtwald, president of a company specializing in "senior boom" marketing, said: "The era of America as a youth culture is coming to an end, and it will not reappear in our lifetime." He explained that whereas 200 years ago the median age was 17, it is now 31—and still climbing. Babies born in the year 2000 routinely will live into their 90s, according to Dychtwald's projections.

Although Dychtwald's predictions might be exaggerated, marketers have responded to this new-found market with new products that appeal to affluent, healthy older people who have leisure time. Advertisers have changed their portrayals of the elderly from sedentary and passive to attractive and active, as is shown in Ad 5.6. New media are emerging that are directed at this age group.

Gender As previously discussed, a person's sex is an obvious basis for consumer market analysis.

AD 5.6
This Piedmont ad is an example of the changing portrayal of the elderly in recent ads.
(Courtesy of Piedmont Aviation, Inc.)

GENDER-BASED PRODUCTS In the past the marketing of some gender-related products was highly restricted. For example, advertising of tampons or sanitary pads was restricted to media devoted strictly to women, and condoms, purchased at one time almost exclusively by men, were behind-the-counter or under-the-counter items. Today those barriers have all but vanished.

Marketing products related to gender-based characteristics is still complicated. For years skin-care products were the exclusive domain of women, and erotic magazines were restricted to men. Now skin-care products for men represent a $40 million market, and *Playgirl* magazine grows in popularity with women.

WOMEN IN THE WORK FORCE The major trend related to gender is the increasing number of women in the work force and the influence of female employment on family patterns. By the mid-1980s about 40 percent of American families had two wage earners. The women in these familes are better educated and have greater professional skills and goals than their mothers had. The wage-earning wife has caused a substantial realignment of family spending and roles. Families with two wage earners eat out more often, own more (and more expensive) cars, take more vacations, and dress more expensively. Husbands in many of these families participate more in child care, housecleaning, laundry, and food shopping and preparation.

Career women often postpone marriage, and if they do marry, they are likely to have fewer children than noncareer women. From 1970 to 1984 the proportion of American families with no children increased by about a third, while the proportion with only one or two children increased by about 18 percent.*

Education   People are categorized in terms of their educational level. Those who are currently in school are usually classified as full-time or part-time students.

Since the end of World War II higher education has become more common in the United States. In 1985 almost 20 percent of people 25 years of age and over had graduated from college, up 10 percentage points from 1965. Although some discrepancy between the sexes still exists, it is gradually disappearing, and by the end of this century as many women as men will have college degrees.

At the same time that educational levels are going up, the illiteracy rate of certain parts of the U.S. population is increasing dramatically. According to a 1987 Department of Education study, almost one in six adults in California is "functionally illiterate," and most of these people are native English speakers who went to school in the United States. Those judged "illiterate" can't read well enough to understand newspaper ads, simple recipes, or job applications. Nationally 15 percent of young adults are "semiliterate," defined as reading below an eighth-grade level.† The United States is becoming a country with both a large number of people who are highly educated and a large number of people who can barely read.

Family Situation   Advertisers have to understand the structure of contemporary families. For example, what is the impact on advertising messages of changing family patterns—more divorces, working single mothers, two-parent–two-family households, and later marriages?

INFLUENCERS   Advertisers also have to understand how a family affects purchase and consumption patterns. For example, certain family members screen and evaluate product information. Other members strongly influence which product or brand is purchased, and this varies according to the product category. These people may or may not be the actual decision makers.

PURCHASING ROLES   Purchasing patterns vary with the composition of the household. Singles have to make all of their purchases, whereas families can practice a division of labor and influence. The male is likely to be involved in the purchase of products like cars, tires, and liquor. Although female roles are changing, research shows that women still make many of the buying decisions related to household items such as health-care products, laundry supplies, and food.‡ Teenagers are becoming important shoppers for household products.

FAMILY PATTERNS   The family with two parents and children is still the most common arrangement among U.S. households. Within this traditional model are families in which either or both parents work outside the home. Families vary from those with infants and small children to those with teenage

---

*"The Last Yuppie Story You Will Ever Have to Read," *Forbes*, February 25, 1985, pp. 134–35.
†Robert B. Settle and Pamela L. Alreck, *Why They Buy: American Consumers Inside and Out* (New York: John Wiley and Sons, 1986), p. 293.
‡*Purchase Influence: Measures of Husband/Wife Influence on Buying Decisions* (New Canaan, CN: Haley, Overholser, and Associates, 1975), pp. 13–22.

U.S. Families: 1965 to 1985

	1965	1980	1985
Marriage rate (number of marriages per 1000 population)[1]	9.3	10.6	10.2**
Median age at first marriage [1] Men Women	22.5 20.4	23.6 21.8	25.0* 22.9*
Divorce rate (number of couples divorcing per 1000 population)[1]	2.5	5.2	5.0**
Single-parent families (percentage of all families with children under age 18 having one parent)[2]	10.1	19.5	22.2
Births to Unmarried Women (percentage of all births)[1]	7.7	18.4	21.7*
Living alone (percentage of all households occupied by a single person)[2]	15.0	22.7	23.7

Sources:
1 National Center for Health Statistics   2 Bureau of the Census
* Psychology Today projection   **Provisional data

NINA WALLACE

FIGURE 5.2
Trends in U.S. families, 1965–1985.
Source: PSYCHOLOGY TODAY, MAY 1987, p. 64.
Copyright © 1987 American Psychological Association.)

children. There is a big difference in consumer patterns and buying decisions between homes with young children and those with teenagers. Sometimes the children make the actual purchase, but more often they influence the purchases that are made by the parents.

Alternatives to this traditional model are becoming more common. The prevalence of divorce—the number of divorces granted each year doubled between 1977 and 1987—has contributed to alternative family situations. These include families with a single parent—either mother or father and "his, hers, and ours" families with children from different marriages living together in the same home with remarried parents.*

*"Portrait of Divorce in America," *Newsweek*, February 2, 1986, p. 87.

NONMARRIED ADULTS   An important trend in the United States is the increase in nonmarried adults. It is estimated that there are approximately 58 million single adults in the United States. More specifically, 37 percent of women and 32 percent of men aged 18 and over have never been married. When you combine that with divorced and widowed people, experts predict that by 1990 one-half of all U.S. households will consist of singles living alone.*

AD 5.7
Families with young children have a different set of needs from those with teenagers or no children.
(Courtesy of DuPont Company.)

* "Singles Surge," *American Demographics*, January 1986, p. 26.

Generalizing about singles would be a mistake because they are a diverse group who display a wide range of economic well-being and spending patterns. Never-married people, for example, have a great deal of personal freedom and spend heavily on themselves. In contrast, divorced women with children often struggle financially and represent a new poverty group.

Unmarried couples who share a household represent another growing group. This group, although estimated to be only 2 percent of the population, exhibits some interesting purchasing patterns. Uncertain how long their relationship will last, they are reluctant to buy items to be shared and, instead, keep duplicates of many household products, for example, stereos, furniture, and appliances.*

Occupations   Employment categories include full-time employed, part-time employed, or unemployed. Self-employed is often a separate category. Occupational descriptions are based on categories supplied by the U.S. Census or the Department of Labor.

As the American public has become better educated and more familiar with advanced technologies, there has been a gradual shift from blue-collar to white-collar occupations. Moreover, there have been shifts within the white-collar category, from sales to other areas. Also, the number of jobs offered in the service sector is expected to increase, especially in health care, education, law, and business.

Much of this transition is a direct result of computer technology, which has eliminated many labor-intensive blue- and pink-collar occupations. This shift has affected advertising in a number of ways. Blue-collar jobs are portrayed less often in advertising, which now stresses managerial and service occupations. Women are also being seen in professional roles.

New Collars and Bright Collars   Ralph Whitehead of the University of Massachusetts argues that the Baby-Boom generation is far too varied to be discussed as a single category.† In particular, their occupational patterns and resulting lifestyles cannot be lumped into a single category. He points out that there are as many as 25 million Baby Boomers struggling along on family incomes between $20,000 and $40,000. He describes them as "a postindustrial working class whose members do the kinds of jobs that fall somewhere between physical labor and middle-management pencil pushing." He calls this group the New Collars.

He also identifies a new class of 19 million knowledge workers, whom he calls the Bright Collars, in such occupations as middle management, social work, teaching, bureaucracy, law, and software engineering.

Income and Spending Power   In general, the average family income in the United States has been increasing (even after adjustment for inflation) throughout the 1980s, and some experts expect it to continue to rise. By 1995, 20 percent of U.S. families will earn over $50,000. If these figures hold up, marketers can look forward to an increasingly affluent American consumer population.

An interesting corollary is that the majority of consumer spending power and discretionary spending power is in the hands of only a minority of the most affluent American families. That is, although only 10 percent of all American households have incomes exceeding $50,000, this 10 percent owns 40 percent of America's net worth.‡

---

*"Y&R Study: New Life to Singles," *Advertising Age*, October 1982, p. 14; and Jacqueline Simenaiver and David Carrse, *Singles: The New Americans* (New York: Simon & Schuster, 1982).

†Hendrik Hertzberg, "The Short Happy Life of the American Yuppie," *Esquire*, February 1988, pp. 100–6.

‡*Sales Management 1985 Survey of Buying Power*, July 22, 1985, p. C-3.

Marketers are becoming increasingly aware of the growing numbers of Hispanic consumers.
(Courtesy of Rhoda Sidney/Monkmeyer Press.)

discretionary income *The money available to a household after taxes and spending on basic necessities are removed.*

Discretionary income is the money available to a household after taxes and spending on basic necessities such as food and shelter are removed. As total income increases, the proportion considered discretionary income grows at a much faster rate. This is one reason for the rapid growth in the demand for luxury items during the last decade. More and more people have more discretionary income.

Race and Ethnicity

Racial and ethnic identification are important to advertisers because they are basic to individual identification and self-concept. The general Census categories include white, Black, and other. The Census also asks about other languages spoken at home and includes the categories of "English," "Spanish," and "Other."

More than one out of ten families speaks a language other than English at home. In some areas of the country the rate is much higher. For example, in Miami and San Antonio, about one out of three households speaks Spanish. In fact, the market of Hispanic consumers almost doubled from 9 million consumers in 1970 to 17 million in 1986.*

Race and ethnicity have to be approached with caution. Advertising appeals directed at such groups can be seen as patronizing, if not naive. There is a tendency to fall into easy stereotypes. Some advertisers have treated all 28 million Black consumers as the "Black market," ignoring other relevant dimensions. For example, young middle-income Black working couples are a distinctive, but almost ignored, $25-billion-a-year market. These working couples have the same values as the rest of middle America—although they may have different ways of thinking, live in different areas, and respond to different media.† The issue of stereotyping is addressed in more detail in Chapter 2.

Psychographics

psychographics *All the psychological variables that combine to shape our inner selves, including activities, interests, opinions, needs, values, attitudes, personality traits, decision processes, and buying behavior.*

Advertisers use the term **psychographics** to refer to all the psychological variables that combine to shape our inner selves. Psychographics goes beyond demo-

*"Special Report: Hispanic Marketing," *Advertising Age*, February 27, 1986, pp. 11–12.
†"Segmenting the Black Market," *Marketing Communications*, July 1985, pp. 17ff.

graphics in attempting to explain complex behavior patterns. For example, why does one mother with a newborn infant choose disposable diapers while other mothers still use reusable cloth diapers? And why does she use Pampers while others use generic brands or the brand for which they have a coupon? Why does one person drive a brand-new BMW while a neighbor in the identical condo next door drives an old Volvo?

To explain these "true" motivations for behavior, advertisers look at a variety of dimensions including activities, interests and hobbies, opinions, needs, values, attitudes, and personality traits. Taken together, these elements give a much broader picture of a person than do demographic data.

Although hundreds of different dimensions are encompassed under psychographics, the areas with the most relevance to advertising are *attitudes, lifestyles,* and *buying behavior.*

Attitudes Attitudes and opinions are important elements of psychographics. Opinion research is used to check how people feel about other people, products and brands, appeals, and contemporary trends. Attitudes reflect consumers' values. They tell the world what we stand for and identify the things and ideas we consider important. They also track our positive and negative reactions to things in our life. One of the most important areas for opinion research in advertising is product and brand perception. It is important to know how the consumer sees the product before developing an advertising strategy. Furthermore, what is the product associated with in the consumer's mind?

Lifestyles Lifestyle factors are often considered the mainstay of psychographic research. Essentially lifestyle research looks at the ways people allocate time, energy, and money. Marketers conduct research to measure and compare people's activities, interests, and opinions; in other words, what they usually do or how they behave, what intrigues or fascinates them, and what they believe or assume about the world around them. Table 5.3 lists some of the categories identified in lifestyle research.

VALS In 1980 the firm of SRI International began a major lifestyle research project. The result was a new conceptual model known as *VALS,* an acronym for "Values and Lifestyles"*

The VALS model describes three types of individuals: need-driven, outer-directed, and inner-directed. The *need-driven* include "survivors" and "sustainers." They are often poor and dependent, such as elderly widows and single mothers. The second category, the *outer-directed,* includes "belongers," "emulators," and "achievers." The *inner-directed* category includes the "I-am-mes," "experimentals," and "societally conscious." These people are young and inno-

TABLE 5.3
Typical Psychographic Variables

Activities	Interests	Opinions
Work	Family	Themselves
Hobbies	Home	Social issues
Social events	Job	Politics
Vacation	Community	Business
Entertainment	Recreation	Economics
Club membership	Fashion	Education
Community	Food	Products
Shopping	Media	Future
Sports	Achievements	Culture

Source: Reprinted from Joseph T. Plumber, "The Concept and Application of Life Style Segmentation," *Journal of Marketing,* published by the American Marketing Association, January 1974, pp. 33–37.

*Philip H. Dougherty, "New Way to Classify Consumers," *The New York Times,* February 25, 1981.

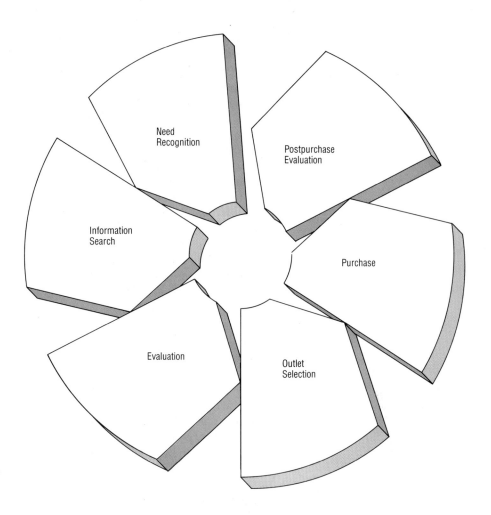

FIGURE 5.3
The major stages of the consumer purchase process.

vative. They are involved with inner growth and have a high sense of social responsibility. The fourth category identified by VALS is a small group called the *integrateds*. These are the rare people who combine the power of the outer-directed with the sensitivity of the inner-directed.

Using these categories, SRI is able to track groups of people and suggest to clients how these groups are changing and how that change will affect the client's advertising strategy.

Buying Behavior INFORMATION NEEDS Consumer decision making is an important area of information. How does the consumer go about buying the product? Is it an impulse buy, or is it a purchase that involves a lot of deliberation and searching for information? Some products, like Joan's candy bar, are often bought on the spur of the moment. Other purchases are carefully considered and thoroughly researched in advance. Products that are purchased without much consideration are called **low-involvement products;** those that demand some deliberation are called **high-involvement products.**

Decision Process The process that consumers go through in making a purchase varies considerably between low-involvement and high-involvement situations. There are some generally recognized stages, however, that are highlighted in Figure 5.3.

NEED RECOGNITION The first stage, *need recognition,* occurs when the consumer recognizes a need for a product. This need can vary in terms of seriousness or importance. Advertising interacts with this stage by activating or

low-involvement products *Products that require limited deliberation; sometimes purchases are even made on impulse.*

high-involvement products
Products that require an involved purchase process with information search and product comparison.

stimulating this need. For example, the Burger King "Aren't you hungry?" campaign appeals to people's appetites and nutritional needs.

INFORMATION SEARCH   The second stage is the *information search.* This search can be casual, such as reading ads and articles that happen to catch your attention, or it may be formal, such as searching for information in publications like *Consumer Reports.* Another type of informal search is recalling information you have seen previously. Advertising helps the search process by providing information in the advertisement itself.

EVALUATION AND COMPARISON   The third stage is *evaluation and comparison.* Here we begin to compare various products and features and reduce the list of options to a manageable number. We select certain features that are important and use them to judge our alternatives. Advertising is important in this evaluation process because it helps sort out products on the basis of features.

OUTLET SELECTION AND PURCHASE DECISION.   The fourth stage is *outlet selection.* Is this product available at a grocery store, a discount store, a hardware store, a boutique, a department store, or a specialty store? Will the consumer select the brand first and then try to find a store that carries it, or will he or she select a store first and then consider the available brands? In-store promotions such as packaging, point-of-purchase displays, price reductions, banners and signs, and coupon displays affect these choices. This is also the site of the fifth stage, which is the actual *purchase.*

POSTPURCHASE EVALUATION.   The last step in the process is the point where we begin to reconsider and justify our purchase to ourselves. As soon as we purchase a product, particularly a major one, we begin to engage in postpurchase evaluation. Is the product acceptable? Is its performance satisfactory? Does it live up to our expectations? This experience determines whether we will repurchase the product.

Even before you open the package or use the product, you may experience doubt or worry about the wisdom of the purchase. This doubt is called *postpurchase dissonance.* Many consumers continue to read information even after the purchase in order to justify their decision to themselves. Advertising helps reduce postpurchase dissonance by restating the features and confirming the popularity of the brand or product.

UNDERSTANDING THE CONSUMER AUDIENCE

Although advertisers cannot know everything about the people with whom they communicate, the more they know, the more effective their message will be. Creative and strategic advertising requires a basic familiarity with the audience. Advertisers use extensive research to find out this information, a subject this is discussed in more detail in the next chapter.

■ SUMMARY

- The social and cultural influences on consumers include society and subcultures, social class, reference groups, and family.
- Personal influences on consumers include age, gender, family status, education, occupation, income, and race.
- Psychological influences on the individual as a consumer include perception, learning, motivation, attitudes, personality, and self-concept.

- Advertisers identify audiences in terms of demographics and psychographics.
- Demographic profiles of consumers include information on population size, age, gender, education, family situation, occupation, income, and race.
- Psychographic profiles of consumers include information on attitudes, lifestyles, buying behavior, and decision processes.

■ QUESTIONS

1. The influence of reference groups on consumer decision making is an important factor for advertisers. Why? How do reference groups influence your consumer behavior?

2. Define "motivation" and explain the factors that motivate a consumer to resolve a problem. What role does advertising play in motivating consumers?

3. What are the major demographic variables, and why are they of interest to advertisers?

4. Explain the term *psychographics*. How can knowledge of a target market's psychographic characteristics help in creating advertisements?

5. Choose four VALS categories and find one or more print advertisements that appear to be targeted toward individuals in each category. Explain why you think the ad addresses that audience.

6. Define "attitudes." Why are they important to advertisers?

7. What are the six stages in the consumer decision process? Give examples of how advertising can influence each stage. Find an ad that addresses the concerns of consumers in each stage.

■ FURTHER READINGS

BARD, BILL. "The Eighties Are Over," *Newsweek,* January 4, 1988, pp. 40–45.

BARTOS, RENA. *The Moving Target.* New York: The Free Press, 1982.

KAHLE, LYNN. "The Nine Nations of North America and the Value Basis of Geographic Segmentation," *Journal of Marketing,* Vol. 50, No. 2, 1986, pp. 37–47.

ROGERS, EVERETT. *Diffusion of Innovations.* New York: Free Press, 1962.

RUBENSTEIN, CARIN. "Women in the Driver's Seat," *Across the Board,* April 1986, pp. 40–45.

WEIN, BIBI. "Psychographics," *Omni,* July 1980.

WELLS, WILLIAM D., and DOUGLAS J. TIGERT. "Activities, Interests, and Opinions," *Journal of Marketing Research,* August 1971, pp. 27–35.

6

Strategic Research

Chapter Outline

A Research Odyssey
Research: The Quest for Intelligence
Marketing and Advertising Research
Message Development Research

Chapter Objectives

When you have completed this chapter you should be able to:

- Explain the difference between qualitative and quantitative research
- Develop a research program using all four types of fact finding: marketplace, consumer, corporate, and product
- Distinguish between primary and secondary research
- Understand how and when to use the six basic research methods: surveys, experiments, observation, content analysis, in-depth interviews, and focus groups
- Develop an outline of the steps in the research process
- Understand how research is used in the development of the creative message

A RESEARCH ODYSSEY

In June 1986 a motor home loaded with a video recorder, a VCR monitor, two computers, an audiotape recorder, two cameras, a refrigerator full of film, and four professors took off from Santa Monica, California. The professors intended to wind up in Boston by the end of August. In the meantime they planned stops at swap meets in Los Angeles; a casino in Las Vegas; Zion National Park; an arts festival in the Rockies; a Fourth of July celebration in Clinton, Iowa; a shelter for the homeless in Milwaukee; the Kane County Fair near Chicago; Amish and Mennonite communities in Indiana and Pennsylvania; and New York's Central Park.*

Does it sound like your typical summer vacation? Not exactly. The trip was dubbed the "Consumer Behavior Odyssey"; the researchers' goal was to experience and record consumer behavior in many different settings. The original four travelers were joined at various points along the way by some 24 other researchers who spent 2 to 4 weeks working on the project.

Their goal was to use naturalistic inquiry to study consumer behavior first-hand where and as it happened. The team used photographs, video and sound recordings, and detailed written accounts in two forms—field notes and personal journals. In the course of the Odyssey they generated more than 800 single-spaced pages of field notes, journals, and logs; more than 60 hours of videotape recordings; dozens of audiotapes; and 3,000 photographs.

The technique of *direct observation* was used instead of more focused research techniques like surveys because the team felt that trained observers would notice things that a casual observer would not. Furthermore, when you ask people about their past behavior, they usually don't recall everything they thought or did at the time. Sometimes the things consumers don't consider significant are actually very important to a researcher.

The data from this massive effort are still being analyzed, but already the team has developed some important themes such as the effect of role transitions on consumers, women as entrepreneurs, and the carving out of private space in a home.

RESEARCH: THE QUEST FOR INTELLIGENCE

Research is the backbone of advertising and marketing. It provides the factual foundation for making intelligent marketing and advertising plans. We have some general theories of how consumers behave and how they respond to advertising, but every product evokes a different set of decision processes and consumer attitudes.

Strategy and Testing

People who develop advertising strategies, as well as those who create the advertisements—concepts, headlines and slogans, layouts, and logos—use a variety of research techniques to prepare themselves for their tasks. They also use research to test strategies and different versions of a concept or approach. After the advertising campaign has run, research is used to evaluate its success. Research is the thread that ties all the decision making together throughout the development of the marketing plan, advertising plan, campaign, and individual ad.

*Mary Connors, "A Research Odyssey," *Adweek,* December 1, 1986, pp. F.K. 4–6.

Intuition The intelligent strategy decision in advertising is based on both knowledge and understanding of the marketing situation. Understanding can come in a variety of forms. A manager who has worked in an industry for 25 years may have an intuitive understanding of how the business operates plus a headful of facts about the field. Past experience provides expertise. Someone who has tried various techniques knows from experience what works and what doesn't.

This intuitive understanding and experience-based wisdom are the basis for many strategy decisions. In fact, some corporate executives believe that experience is the best basis for a decision. But even people who have been intimately involved in a business for years sometimes fail to understand what is happening with consumers or why their product's market share is eroding.

Systematic Research Research is a more systematic way to acquire information and to gain an intelligent viewpoint. Although it is particularly useful for people who do not have 25 years' experience, it can also provide surprising information to experienced advertisers. Many corporate executives have discovered they were "running blind" before a systematic research effort was undertaken to answer a question or investigate a problem.

Qualitative and Quantitative Research

Intelligence about consumers is derived from two different types of research. **Qualitative studies,** like the Consumer Odyssey, try to understand how and why people think and behave as they do. Usually the results are conveyed in words. **Quantitative studies,** on the other hand, amass great amounts of numerical data, such as exposures to ads, purchases, and other marketing-related events. The results are expressed in numbers.

Dr. Simon Broadbent, director of brand economics at Leo Burnett, is a self-professed "data jock," and his work typifies quantitative research. He is immersed in the statistical analysis of marketing and advertising data—"number crunching," as it is sometimes called. Broadbent receives data from computer scanning services such as Scan America, Scan Track, and BehaviorScan. This information tells him where, when, and how much a given product sold, as well as what sort of ad, coupon, or display support the product received. Broadbent considers his method to be the wave of the future because it provides "information that was rarely available before." He uses this information to help understand what is driving sales and how ads work. His work addresses such questions as should the ad budget be cut or increased, should the product price be increased, and what is the real benefit of promotions?*

There is much debate between the two types of researchers. Those who believe strongly in one approach are likely to criticize the limitations of the other. Most advertising planners, however, use both qualitative and quantitative information because they feel it is important to understand consumer behavior as well as to describe it.

*M*ARKETING AND ADVERTISING RESEARCH

Marketing and advertising plans are based on information, and information is gathered through research. **Marketing research** is used to identify consumer needs, develop new products, evaluate pricing levels, assess distribution methods, and test the effectiveness of various promotional strategies. One type of marketing research, called **market research,** is much more specific and is used to gather information about a specific market. **Consumer research** is another important type of marketing research. It focuses on how consumers think, feel, decide, and behave.

*Ibid.

HELP PREVENT UNWANTED PRODUCTS.

There's nothing sadder than a product that hasn't found a home in the marketplace.

Nothing more disappointing than an idea that's ill conceived, badly delivered and poorly evaluated.

But saddest of all is the fact that most unwanted products need never happen.

At Yankelovich Clancy Shulman, we know how to prevent those big marketing mistakes.

Our "state-of-the-science" models are designed to do just that. To give you the kind of information you need for successful marketing action.

At every stage of product development—from target selection to product positioning and configuration all the way to actual test market—our Litmus™ and strategic models work to put you in touch with the answers critical to the decisions you have to make.

And because they're geared toward product success, the answers they provide are the *optimal* ones for your product and marketing plan. The kind of answers no one else can give.

So before you go too far in product development, talk to our Senior Vice President for Marketing, Mr. Watts Wacker, at (203) 227-2700.

He'll show you how we can help turn the arrival of your next new product into a truly joyous event.

Yankelovich Clancy Shulman
Marketing Intelligence℠

Eight Wright Street Westport Connecticut 06880

AD 6.1
An ad for a marketing research company.
(Courtesy of Yankelovich Clancy Shulman.)

Exploratory Research

Exploratory research is informal intelligence gathering. When advertising people get a new account or a new assignment, they start by reading everything that is available on the product, company, and industry: sales reports, annual reports, complaint letters, and trade articles about the industry.

What you are looking for with exploratory research is the problem—a problem that ultimately might demand more formal research and, perhaps, the development of a new strategy. This is what we mean by *strategic research,* a form of intelligence gathering that identifies the problem to be solved by the advertising. Jerry Della Femina, chairman of Della Femina, Travisano & Partners, called this type of research "pre-search."*

Exploratory research is very important to creatives. Shepard Kurnit, chairman of the board of DKG Advertising, interviewed a number of agency execu-

*Shepard Kurnit, "The Impact of Creative Research on Creativity," speech given to 25th Annual Conference of the Advertising Research Foundation, New York, October 22–23, 1979.

JACK STRATTON, MARKETING RESEARCH DIRECTOR
BETTY CROCKER DIVISION, GENERAL MILLS, INC.

8:20 A.M.   I arrive at the R&D Labs. Nineteen people are crowded into a kitchen for our monthly lab review on desserts. We talk about the Twins winning the AL Championship.

8:30   The labs present a progress report on new cake flavors. The general manager wants to know what "conceptual underpinnings" support this effort. Jane, an assistant marketing research manager, presents a very brief summary of sensory profiles on ten flavors of layer cakes. We discuss how to link this data to consumer preference data.

9:30   The Frostings brand group joins the meeting. Discussion on whether we should add new flavors to our line. Several people express concern on the effort devoted to new flavors and argue for a major product improvement across the entire line. An assistant marketing research manager leads the meeting as she presents the results of three product tests that have recently been completed. We are eating samples of the test frostings. When the meeting breaks up, the kitchen is littered with plates, spoons, and frosted cake rounds.

10:15   I give the general manager a lift to the main office when his car won't start. We continue to talk about frosting.

10:30   Miscellaneous.

11:00   We join Marketing in the Betty Crocker Kitchens to look at a new Tuna Helper product. The labs have reformulated the product and everyone is pleased with the taste and appearance of the latest version. A marketing research assistant presents a recommendation for an expensive form of in-home product testing. She expects resistance from the marketing director. However, he nods approval and the meeting is over.

12:00   I meet a friend for lunch in the company cafeteria. He works in the Corporate Planning Department and I pump him for information on possible acquisitions. He asks me about the likely success of several new Betty Crocker products.

1:00   Afternoon presentations.

3:00   Return phone calls. I get a viewing of a rough commercial for a project I approved this morning. I listen carefully to make sure the singing can be understood and that the degree of finish is comparable to the alternative roughs we will test.

3:30   Meeting with Information Systems Manager.

4:30   I start reading through my in-basket. Check with other department heads on the likelihood of getting World Series tickets through the company.

5:45   Leave for home.

(Courtesy of General Mills, Inc.)

tives about the impact of creative research on creativity. Most of them acknowledged the need for background fact finding. Tom Dillon, then chairman of the board of BBDO, explained the need for what he calls "upfront" research: "Upfront research is very important because all too often what you think is perfectly clear, is *perfectly mud!*"*

In addition to exploratory research used for problem definition and idea development, four other areas are commonly addressed in strategic research: marketplace, consumer, corporate, and product research. The following discussion reviews these areas and the kinds of questions advertising planners try to answer using exploratory research.

Ibid.

People involved in creating advertising should collect as much background information as possible.
(Courtesy of Rion Rizzo, Creative Sources/ FPG.)

Marketplace Fact Finding   Market research attempts to create a picture of the marketplace. Ultimately you will want to identify holes and opportunities in the market—those are strategy decisions—but first you have to understand the size, composition, and structure of the marketplace. Initial information includes a profile of the category, the competitors, their market shares, and their *share of voice,* an index comparing market share with advertising expenditure (see Chapter 9).

CATEGORY INFORMATION   What business are you in? What service does the company or product provide? That seems like a silly question, but many consultants have found otherwise sophisticated CEOs focusing on the wrong function. For example, the market leader in its category, Windex, lost market share to a newcomer, Glass Plus, because Windex was presented only as a window cleaner. The research for Glass Plus found that Windex was used for cleaning all kinds of surfaces in addition to windows. The name of the product, Glass Plus, as well as its advertising reflected this finding. Arm and Hammer saw sales increases when baking soda moved from being a seldom-used baking ingredient to a refrigerator deodorizer and tooth cleanser.

After you identify the category, look at its health and growth. Look at the industry sales figures for the current year as well as for the last 10 years. What are the trends? Analyze the category lifecycle. Is this an old, worn-out category, a new one, or a redefined one? Are sales declining or growing? What are the opportunities for category expansion? Could other product categories provide indirect competition?

COMPETITIVE ANALYSIS   Now look at the direct competition. Who else competes for the same customers? Who offers similar products or services? Analyze the structure of the competitive environment: Who are the leaders, the challengers, the followers, the fall-behinds, and the also-rans? Who is strong and who is vulnerable? Compare the sales records for each competitor, current as well as past. Finally, develop the market share picture for the industry. Do a trend analysis to see if share of market has changed over the past 5 years, 10 years, or longer.

Analyze the competitive advertising situation. What themes does the competition use? What media vehicles are used? How much is everyone spending on advertising? What are the trends over time in advertising expenditures?

Consumer Fact Finding Consumer research leads directly to the targeting decision, and targeting is the heart of advertising strategy. How consumers think, feel, act, and make a decision is very important to strategic planning.

These are the kinds of questions you might want to ask:

- Who are these people?
- What are they like?
- What do they think?
- What do they want?
- What moves them?
- Which media do they read or watch?
- Where do they live?
- How much money do they have to spend?

In order to make the strategy decision on how to target your message, you first need to obtain a big picture of the entire consumer population for your product. Then you need to know what separates the prospects from the more general population of consumers. And finally you need to know everything you can find out about these prospects, as individuals and as a group.

DESCRIPTIONS You should remember from Chapter 5 that information about people is collected in two big categories: demographics and psychographics. Both are necessary to target the best audience.

AD 6.2
This Lotus ad incorporates the results of a research study.
(Courtesy of Lotus Publishing Corporation.)

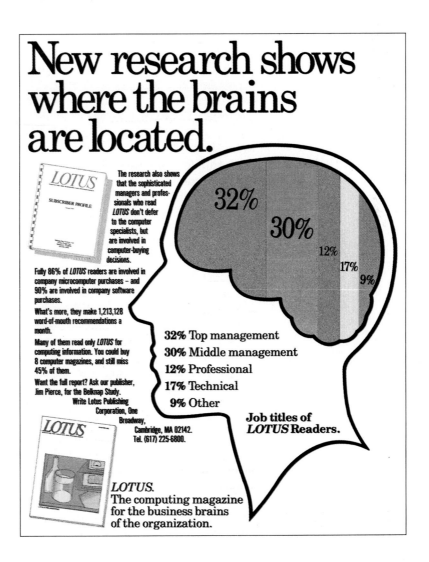

A critical concept that is emerging here is the number of different ways to describe groups of people. This initial consumer research tries to identify the major groups of potential prospects, their most prominent characteristics, and where they are located.

BEHAVIOR   Because targeting is sometimes based on groups with similar purchase patterns, consumer intelligence is used to draw a picture of consumer purchasing patterns and decision making. (Targeting is discussed in more detail in Chapter 7.)

This is the kind of information being compiled in the Consumer Odyssey study described at the beginning of the chapter. Such research explores how consumers go about buying a product or service. It tries to find out if they plan purchases in advance, or if they buy things spontaneously. The scale of the purchase is important. Does it involve a risk? Is it a major purchase? Finally, look at the customers and sales staff. Do consumers rely on their own judgment, or does a sales clerk provide information and demonstrate product use?

For a given group of prospects, you need to know the alternative products, categories, or brands they consider. Identify the features that make a difference in the decision. How important is quality? Price? Style? Because buying behavior is important, you might want to find out who actually does the shopping. There may be some surprises here. For example, grocery stores have found that teenagers now do much of the family shopping.

Product usage is another important area of consumer behavior. Who uses the product? When? Where? How does product usage change with time and circumstances?

PRODUCT PERCEPTION   The customer's perception of the product or service is another important part of consumer research. This area of research investigates the interaction between product and consumer. Because most products are created to serve a consumer need, the consumer's perception of the product is more important than the manufacturer's. As the authors of the book *Advertising Theory and Practice* explain, "The product is what the consumer perceives it to be."*

An interesting study of consumer perceptions of beef has revolutionized the beef industry. H. Russell Cross, a Texas A&M professor, conducted a 5-year study to explain a decade of declining sales. He discovered that one of the consumers' main objections to beef was the high fat content. A second concern was chemical additives. As a result of this research, the industry is now marketing new *light-beef* brands and *natural* beef from cows raised without antibiotics or steroids.†

Fact finding about perceptions of products asks such questions as: What is the image of the product or brand? Is it seen as expensive or cheap? High- or low-quality? Stylish or stodgy? What kind of personality does the product or brand project? How important to consumers are various features? How well do these features rate for this product?

Corporate Fact Finding   An advertising plan begins with research to discover everything that relates to product development and marketing. Corporate research involves exploring internal records and conducting interviews, as well as investigating the personality of the company. Determine whether the company takes risks or is conservative. Does it have a set way of doing things, a corporate method or philosophy? Evaluate the firm's financial picture. Does the company have resources to invest in advertising? What is its credit rating? How does the company look at advertising, as an investment or an expense? In other

*C. H. Sandage, Vernon Fryburger, and Kim Rotzoll, *Advertising Theory and Practice,* 10th ed. (Homewood, IL: Richard D. Irwin, 1979).

†Roy Furchgott, "What's Your Beef?" *Adweek,* December 1, 1986, p. F.K. 22.

PRINCIPLE _____

Know everything you can about how consumers think, feel, decide, and act.

words, does the firm expect the benefits from advertising to accrue over time, or will it want to see an immediate return?

Power and decision making are important. You must learn who the influencers and decision makers are and whether there is a behind-the-scenes power figure. Analyze how power is spread throughout the company. Does the advertising manager make decisions or just carry reports? Do the decision makers understand and appreciate advertising? In many cases advertising proposals are designed specifically to address the attitudes and concerns of key decision makers.

Product Fact Finding   Next the fact-finding effort turns to the product itself. Advertising professionals are very loyal to the products they serve because they have spent so much time with them. The parking lot of Campbell-Ewald, a Detroit agency, is filled with Chevrolets, its major client. Leo Burnett ate Nestlé's chocolate; David Ogilvy wore Hathaway shirts. Although this commitment does reflect loyalty to a client, it also grows out of the need to be familiar with the company's product. The first step in fact finding is to buy, wear, use, break, tear, taste, test, and compare the product or service. Product intelligence demands intimate experience.

Analysis comes next. Why does this product or service exist? Who developed it? When? Why? What problem was it created to solve? How is it made? What are its components? How do you use it? What are the attributes of this product or service? Which features are important? Who thinks so? Does the product have an established brand image, an identity?

The Research Springboard

Background research into the corporation, the product, the marketplace, and consumer behavior is essential for strategic decision making. Kurnit's interviews with agency leaders supported this need. Jerry J. Siano, executive vice president and corporate creative director for N. W. Ayer, explained, "The amount of time getting basic background is the most important part of the process of making advertising." That view was echoed by Amil Gargano, president and CEO of Ally & Gargano, Inc., who said, "I want to be as knowledgeable as I can. . . . Research can help you break new ground. . . . It can be the springboard to doing something innovative and great."*

The Research Process

problem definition *The use of research questions to identify a key problem that needs to be solved by the advertising.*

Identifying the Questions   Intelligence always begins with a question, or list of questions. In research this is called **problem definition.** What is it you want to find out? What is the problem? These problem-definition questions develop as you begin exploratory fact finding. In other words, you might not know what questions to ask until you start doing some backgrounding. For example, in the airline industry there may be a question about which service features are most highly valued by business travelers. This question might lead to a research study that identifies the important service features in addition to assessing the kinds of trade-offs that business travelers are willing to make among these service features.

research design *The structure of the research project.*

The Research Design   These research questions act as a blueprint to guide the design of the research, the collection of data, and the writing of the research report. A **research design** specifies how the research project will be handled. It anticipates what needs to be done, exactly how and when it is to be accom-

*Kurnit, "Creativity."

secondary data *Information that has been compiled and published.*

primary data *Information that is collected from original sources.*

verbatims *Spontaneous comments by people who are being surveyed.*

survey research *Research using structured interview forms that ask large numbers of people exactly the same questions.*

population *Everyone included in a designated group.*

sample *A selection of people who are identified as representative of the larger population.*

experiments *A research method that manipulates a set of variables to test hypotheses.*

plished, and what it will cost. Three basic areas need design decisions: the type of data to collect, the collection techniques, and the method of analysis.

SECONDARY AND PRIMARY DATA   **Secondary data** have already been compiled and are usually available in some kind of report. *Internal secondary data* are produced within the organization and include such information as accounting reports, sales figures, profit-and-loss statements, inventory levels and shipment figures, billings, sales expenses, and advertising and other promotional expenditures. *External secondary data* are collected by outside organizations for their own use or for public use. Examples are U.S. government documents and commercial data such as The Gallup Poll and the *Advertising Age* lists of top 100 agencies and advertisers. **Primary data** are collected from original sources. When you interview someone, for example, you are conducting primary research.

CONTACT METHODS   There are a number of ways to collect data from people. The contact can be in person, by telephone, or by mail. In a personal interview, the researcher asks questions of the respondent in person. The questions can be either tightly structured in a questionnaire or they can be open-ended. Advertisers use *intercept surveys* to get a quick response on a strategy or creative idea. These interviews are often conducted in malls or downtown areas.

A telephone survey is used when the questions are relatively simple and the questionnaire is short. It is efficient and, depending upon the number of interviewers, can reach many people quickly and easily. A mail survey can be longer and more in-depth than a telephone survey; however, it has to be absolutely clear because there is no interviewer to explain procedure or ambiguous questions.

Research Methods   Primary research data can be collected through a number of research methods. For example, you might conduct a survey to find out how many people prefer two-ply toilet paper. The results would be expressed *quantitatively* as a number and as a percentage of the total. If you also reported the spontaneous comments, or **verbatims,** given to explain the preference, then you would be reporting *qualitative* data.

SURVEY RESEARCH   Several types of quantitative research are important in marketing and advertising. **Survey research** uses structured interview forms to ask large numbers of people the same questions. The questions can deal with personal characteristics, such as age, income, behavior, or attitudes. The people can be from an entire group, or **population,** or they can be a representative **sample** of a much larger group. Sampling uses a smaller number of people to represent the entire population.

EXPERIMENTAL RESEARCH   In **experiments,** researchers attempt to manipulate one (and sometimes more than one) important variable while controlling all the other variables that might affect the outcome. For example, an agency might want to know which of two commercials works better for a particular audience. People who represent that audience would be divided into equivalent groups, and the first group would be shown one commercial while the second group would be shown the other. Both groups would then be questioned about whether they understood, liked, or were moved by the message. If the only important difference between the groups was the commercial, differences in response could be used to estimate which of the two commercials was more effective.

DIRECT OBSERVATION   Direct observation is a type of field research that takes researchers into a natural setting where they record the behavior of consumers. This is how the Consumer Odyssey study was conducted. You might, for example, be asked to do an *aisle study* in a supermarket. Your assignment would be to note how people buy a particular product or brand. Do they deliberate or

FREQUENT USERS OF FAST FOOD RESTAURANTS: A RESEARCH PROFILE

In order to find out more about their potential market, advertisers use many research techniques. Advertisers must collect both qualitative and quantitative information to develop advertising campaigns. From a market research study of fast-food users, we can see the value of data collected in a large-scale survey of consumers' activities, interests, and opinions.

The Study

The study defined a frequent fast-food user as someone who eats a meal at a fast-food restaurant at least once a week. The results indicate that frequent fast-food users are more likely than other Americans to be single and in their twenties. They tend to be blue-collar workers who live in the South or Midwest. Their income and levels of education are similar to the rest of the population.

The study further tried to identify the users' political and social attitudes. Many of these questions asked participants whether or not they agreed with certain statements; for example: "Couples should live together before getting married"; "There is too much sex on prime-time television"; and "My opinions on things don't count very much." These responses portrayed frequent fast-food users as more liberal but "somewhat more politically alienated" than Americans in general.

Another set of questions focused on which products, including food, frequent fast-food users purchased. The study asked participants whether they consumed certain snack foods such as soft drinks, packaged snack cakes, and potato chips. It also asked about use of convenience foods, such as frozen dinners, Mexi-can dinner mixes, and instant mashed potatoes. In addition to food purchases, the study also dealt with future purchases of high-tech items such as VCRs, personal computers, and cellular phones. The results showed that frequent fast-food users were more likely than Americans in general to eat snacks between meals, to use convenience foods, and to purchase high-tech electronic products.

Media habits were another topic of questions. The study asked participants which special-interest magazines they read, what types of television programs they watch, and what types of music they listen to on the radio. The study also asked whether they watched specific television programs. The results show that frequent fast-food users read certain magazines (including *Working Women, Glamour,* and *Penthouse*) more frequently and watch more television both during the day and the evening than do Americans in general. They also listen to more rock and soul music and less classical music on the radio than do Americans in general.

Closely related to media habits are people's attitudes toward advertising. Again using responses to specific statements, the study asked participants whether they agree or disagree that advertising insults their intelligence and that ads directed toward children should be removed from television. According to the results, users are less concerned about these issues and have a somewhat more positive view of advertising than do Americans in general.

Source: DDB Needham Worldwide, *Life Style Profile of Frequent Users of Fast Food,* December 1986.

just grab a product and run? Do they compare prices? Do they read the labels? How long do they spend making the decision?

A pioneering study of the direct-observation technique concluded that "direct observation has the advantage of revealing what people actually do, as distinguished from what people say. It can yield the correct answer when faulty memory, desire to impress the interviewer, or simple inattention to details would cause an interview answer to be wrong."[*] The biggest drawback to direct observation is that it shows *what* is happening, but not *why.* It is not very effective for evaluating attitudes and motives.

CONTENT ANALYSIS   Content analysis is a type of research that analyzes various dimensions of a message. In preparation for the development of a new advertising campaign, for example, the agency people might browse through magazines or listen to radio or television programming and code every advertisement by the competition. The print categories include such factors as size,

[*]William D. Wells and Leonard A. Lo Sciuto, "Direct Observation of Purchasing Behavior," *Journal of Marketing Research,* August 1966, pp. 227–33.

use of color, type of layout, and type of headline. Television categories include length, number of scenes, use of music, types of shots, actors, characters, and product visuals. Content analysis can be used by advertising planners to suggest which message approaches have been most effective.

IN-DEPTH INTERVIEW A common type of qualitative research is the in-depth, one-on-one interview. This technique is used to probe feelings, attitudes, and behaviors such as decision making. Because such interviews are not quantitative, the responses can't be projected to a large group of people. The insights, however, can be instructive about how a typical member of the target audience views some research question.

FOCUS GROUPS A **focus group** is another method used to structure qualitative research. This is like an in-depth interview, except that it involves a group rather than an individual. The objective is to stimulate people to talk candidly about some topic with one another. The interviewer sets up a general topic and then lets conversation develop as group interaction takes over.

focus group *A group interview that tries to stimulate people to talk candidly about some topics or products.*

Conducting Research

Students of marketing and advertising often conduct research projects as part of their studies. If you are in such a position, then you will have to make several decisions. In addition to identifying the key question you want answered, choos-

Focus groups have become increasingly important within the creative process.
(© 1987 by Prentice-Hall, Inc.)

FOCUS GROUPS

In a typical focus group members of the target audience are invited to attend a group discussion at a central interviewing location.

When the group has been assembled and seated around a conference table, the "moderator" introduces the group members to each other and tries to make them feel at home. The moderator then leads the group through a preset list of topics, encouraging responses and attempting to make sure that all members of the group have opportunities to express what they think and how they feel.

Most focus group facilities provide a viewing room where observers can watch and listen to the discussion from behind a "one-way" mirror. Although respondents are told that the observers are present, they soon forget that they are there.

Focus groups are valuable because they bring decision makers into direct contact with consumers. Most marketing executives, and most members of advertising agency creative departments, live so differently from their customers that they have little direct day-to-day contact with how consumers think.

The outcome of a focus group depends heavily upon the skill of the moderator. The moderator's responsibilities are to make sure that the most significant points are adequately covered and to follow up the most potentially useful ideas by asking insightful, probing questions. That task requires the ability to think quickly in a complex and rapidly changing interview. It requires sensitivity and good judgment. And it demands an understanding of what the client needs to know. Moderators with those skills are scarce and are therefore in constant demand.

After the interview the moderator usually meets with the observers to discuss and evaluate what has gone on. In this discussion the moderator might contribute observations derived from other interviews or from other research in which the problem was somewhat the same.

The moderator may prepare a report that summarizes and evaluates the results obtained from a series of groups. Often such reports contain extensive quotations from the group interactions so that readers who were not in attendance can get some feel for how consumers react and for the language they use to express their thoughts. Such information can prove extremely helpful to writers who must understand the thoughts and feelings of their audience.

Focus groups provide direct contact with consumers. Compared with many other research methods, they are more intimate and more personal, and they can be fast and cheap. Although focus groups have many obvious limitations, they are becoming more and more popular.

ing the right research method, and identifying the right audience, designing a research effort involves developing the research materials, analyzing the data, and explaining your findings.

Measurement   Choosing a data-collection technique for quantitative research is an important step in designing the research effort. First the method of measurement must be determined. What are you comparing—the number of responses, the intensity of the response, the frequency, height, amount, column inches, or seconds? The nature of the comparison determines the type of measurement to be used and the type of information you will be recording.

The method of measurement is how you assign some value to the responses. With a questionnaire, for example, the responses are usually structured so that the respondents indicate which category of response is appropriate. You might use categories like a frequency (2, 3, or 4 times), a level (from $20,000 to $30,000), or a rating (high, low). In observational research you count the number of people contemplating or choosing the product. These categories are carefully pretested to make sure they include the answers you are most likely to receive.

Analysis   After the data have been collected, researchers must determine what the information tells us. What do all the numbers mean? The numbers are added up, or *tabulated,* and then compared. *Statistical analysis* is used to decide how important the differences between the groups really are. Interpreting the meaning involves reducing this data and its statistical "significance" to meaningful conclusions.

Reporting the Findings   The final step in research is to produce a report of the findings and present it to a client. Research reports, whether written or verbal, summarize and analyze the tabulations and comparisons and then make some concluding statements about the importance of the findings. These reports also identify the limitations of the research effort and specify new questions and areas for further research.

MESSAGE DEVELOPMENT RESEARCH

Research is fundamental to the development of marketing and advertising strategies, but it is also important in the development of the actual advertising message. We are now going to look more closely at how research influences the work of those who create the advertising. This section will focus on the two types of research used in the development of the message strategy: preparation and diagnosis.

Preparation

Most of the fact finding necessary for the development of the advertising plan will also be useful to the creatives who must know the basic facts about the product, the consumer, and the competitive environment. Writers also need a general knowledge of society and of human behavior.

Most of the larger advertising agencies maintain information centers that provide opportunities to browse. In addition to general-interest books and periodicals, these centers usually maintain subject files, picture files, and standard reference books such as atlases, encyclopedias, and textbooks. The library staff are also excellent at chasing down the answers for the most obscure questions.

As ideas begin to take shape, browsing becomes more specific. If a campaign is to feature Sumo wrestlers, for example, writers will browse through articles and books on Sumo wrestling.

Empathy   Writers must gain an intimate understanding of the prospects' feelings concerning the product, brand, and category. Writers must be able to think as the prospects think, to see things as they see them, and to empathize with their concerns. This depth of understanding is important because an advertisement is fundamentally a message from one person to another. The more the sender knows about the audience, the better the chance the advertisement will have its intended effect.

To gain that first-hand information, writers talk to people in the target audience. Informal, first-hand research, conducted independently or with the assistance of the research department, gives writers a "feel" for the attitudes and motives that influence the target audience. Writers might also watch or even participate in focus-group interviews with prospects.

They might also browse through stores or showrooms where the product is being purchased and talk with salespersons about how customers react while making purchasing decisions. Some writers become consumers by purchasing the product and going through all the steps of using it. Without this first-hand feel, the writer's message can become distant and mechanical because it does not speak truly to the consumer's needs.

Diagnosis

diagnostic research *Research used to identify the best approach from among a set of alternatives.*

PRINCIPLE
Concept testing helps creatives decide which ideas are worth pursuing and which are not.

Early Diagnostic Research **Diagnostic research** is used to choose the best approach from among a set of alternatives. As the creative people get down to work, they continually entertain and reject ideas about how the message might be executed. At this stage the creative people want to know as much as they can about how consumers might react to various concepts. In short, they need an early diagnosis of alternative concepts. The creatives usually have a large number of ideas at this stage, and they cannot possibly pursue all of them. They must decide which ideas are worth pursuing and which are not.

To help the creatives make this decision, rough concepts can be tried out on members of the target audience. That enterprise—*early diagnostic research*—is difficult and risky. It is difficult because the ideas are still half-formed. It is risky because a negative reaction might kill a concept that contained the seeds of a brilliant campaign.

Qualitative Interviews Early diagnostic research is almost always qualitative. Instead of following an established list of questions, the researcher discusses ideas with respondents, forms further probing questions in response to their comments, listens, thinks—and probes some more. The process is like trying to find out what a friend is thinking. Qualitative interviews can be one-on-one, or they can be conducted in a focus group. The creative people can participate and ask questions, or they can merely watch the interaction. The whole process is uncertain, unsystematic, and highly tentative.

Later Diagnostic Research When advertising has begun to approach a more finished form, diagnostic research can become more clearly defined. Creative concepts have been translated into rough "comps" and storyboards. Ideas have begun to look more like print ads and television commercials. Consumers now have something specific to look at, and their reactions and evaluations can therefore be taken more literally.

Consumers aren't the only source of reactions at this stage. Writers have supervisors who react favorably or unfavorably to early versions. Creative directors—executives who are ultimately responsible for the agency's creative product—exercise editorial direction. Creative review boards—groups of senior executives—might have the final word concerning what can and cannot be submitted to the client.

In most cases the client also will make contributions. Brand managers or their assistants review and comment on rough advertisements. They might request major changes. They also might pass the advertisement up the line where higher-level executives can insert their own ideas.

Whether on the agency or on the client side, these evaluations are all based upon guesses about how consumers will ultimately react to the advertising. This is where diagnostic research can make a valuable contribution. Instead of guessing how prospects will react to the advertisement, the creative people and the advertiser can get feedback from real consumers.

Using Focus Groups for Diagnosis We have already described focus groups, but it is important to understand the critical role this research method plays in testing ideas as they evolve. Focus groups used to assess early advertising ideas are a type of *concept test*. Later, focus groups can be used to evaluate rough executions.

When the focus group is conducted in a central location, those who are responsible for the advertising often attend and observe, thus bringing the people who most need the information into direct contact with real consumers and their reactions. The potential danger is that every observer will pick out the reactions that support the views he or she wants to hear.

Another problem with group interviews is that assertive and articulate respondents sometimes dominate the coversation, swaying others' opinions and decreasing the likelihood that others will express their true feelings. Sometimes a focus group discussion represents only the opinions of the one or two most aggressive members of the group.

Using Communication Tests for Diagnosis   The drawbacks of focus groups have led many advertisers to use *communication tests* instead. These are one-on-one interviews, usually in shopping malls that supply central interviewing facilities. Respondents are recruited from shoppers to fill age, sex, income, and product-use quotas. They are asked to participate in a "study of consumers' opinions," and they are sometimes offered a small fee for their cooperation.

In the interviewing room respondents are shown advertisements one at a time and asked a standard list of questions such as:

- As you looked at the commercial, what thoughts or ideas went through your mind and what feelings did you have?
- In your own words, please describe *what went on* and *what was said* in the commercial.
- Besides trying to sell the product, what was the *main* point of the commercial?
- What was the name of the product advertised?
- Was there anything in this commercial that you found confusing or hard to understand?
- What, if anything, did you *like* or *dislike* about this commercial?

As the respondent answers the questions, the interviewer writes the answers down verbatim. These responses are analyzed to determine how well respondents understood the message and how they reacted to the way the message was presented.

Ratings   Many communication tests also include a set of scales intended to capture a wide range of reactions. The scales, designed to include most of the ways consumers would respond to the advertisement, supplement the answers to the open-ended questions. They also help less articulate respondents express their opinions, and they sometimes suggest ideas that respondents have not thought to mention.

Even though the communications test has some obvious limitations, it can usually provide answers to three fundamental questions:

1. Did the advertisement convey the message it was intended to convey?
2. Did the advertisement convey any messages it was not intended to convey?
3. How did consumers react to the characters, the setting, the message, and the tone of the advertising?

The answers to these questions are valuable because they come at a time when it is still relatively easy to make changes. Later in the advertising development process changes will be much more difficult and expensive to make.

Problems with Diagnostic Research   All diagnostic methods share some major problems. Because the advertising is still in a preliminary form, it might fail to portray important details that will contribute greatly to the impact of the finished executions. If the rough advertisements do not truly represent the final campaign, reactions to them will usually be misleading.

Accurate diagnosis also requires that the research subjects represent the target audience. Finding the group of people can be difficult. Busy executives and professionals, the prime customers for many important products, are hard to reach and impatient with detailed interviews. Even when the target audience is easy to reach, the sample may not truly represent the actual population. Those people who agree to participate and those who are available at a central location, such as a mall, may not be representative.

Another problem with diagnostic research is that the research setting is different from the setting in which the advertisement will ultimately be introduced. In the research setting the respondent will pay close attention and will try to portray himself or herself as a rational shopper. When the advertisement is received in a natural setting, the whole environment is different, and so may be the responses of the reader or viewer.

Despite all these problems, diagnostic research can still be very helpful. The respondents are, after all, real consumers. And they will say things that advertisers can't find out any other way. The feedback, particularly about communication problems, is very important at this stage.

■ SUMMARY

- Advertising uses quantitative research to describe consumers and qualitative research to understand them.
- Marketplace research focuses on the category and the competition.
- Advertising planners should learn everything they can about how consumers think, feel, decide, and act.
- Advertising planners must know their product intimately.
- Research always begins with a question.

- Advertising uses secondary research, which has already been compiled and published, and primary research, which is information you find out yourself from original sources.
- Exploratory research uses six tools: surveys, experiments, observations, content analysis, in-depth interviews, and focus groups.
- Creatives use research to collect background information and to test alternative ideas, approaches, and concepts.

■ QUESTIONS

1. What is the difference between qualitative and quantitative research?
2. What are the four areas of fact finding used in exploratory research?
3. What is the difference between primary and secondary research?
4. What are the six research methods and when would you use each?
5. If you were setting up a focus group to investigate consumer perceptions of local banks, what topics would you have on your list for discussion by the group?

6. A new radio station is moving into your community. The management is not sure how to position the station in this market and has asked you to develop a study to help with this decision.
   a. What are the key research questions that need to be asked?
   b. Outline a research program to answer those questions that uses as many of the research methods as you can incorporate.

■ FURTHER READINGS

EMORY, C. WILLIAM. *Business Research Methods,* rev. ed. Homewood, IL: Irwin, 1980.

FLETCHER, ALAN, and THOMAS BOWERS. *Fundamentals of Advertising Research,* 2nd ed. Columbus, OH: Grid, 1983.

GREEN, PAUL E., DONALD S. TULL, and GERALD ALBAUM. *Research for Marketing Decisions,* 5th ed. Englewood Cliffs, NJ: Prentice Hall, 1988.

KRESS, GEORGE. *Marketing Research,* 3rd ed. Englewood Cliffs, NJ: Prentice Hall, 1988.

WEIERS, RONALD M. *Marketing Research,* 2nd ed. Englewood Cliffs, NJ: Prentice Hall, 1988.

WIMMER, ROGER D., and JOSEPH R. DOMINICK. *Mass Media Research.* Belmont, CA: Wadsworth, 1987.

7

Strategy and Planning

Chapter Outline

The International Coffee War
Strategy and Planning
The Marketing Plan
The Advertising Plan
The Advertising Budget
An Advertising Campaign Plan
Creative Platforms

Chapter Objectives

When you have completed this chapter you should be able to:

- Identify the key elements of a marketing plan and an advertising plan
- Understand how marketers allocate funds among advertising and other marketing functions
- Explain the difference between product-centered and prospect-centered strategies
- List the key elements of a creative platform

THE INTERNATIONAL COFFEE WAR

When you think of coffee, what country do you think of? When researchers asked that question in the 1960s, most U.S. consumers replied, "Brazil." The National Federation of Coffee Growers of Colombia found to their dismay that the country of Colombia received almost no mentions.

Obviously the Colombian coffee growers felt a major awareness campaign was needed. They also wanted U.S. consumers to identify brands with 100% Colombian coffee as quality or premium. This might sound like an impossible mission. Who, after all, cares which country grows the coffee beans?

The Colombian coffee growers federation accepted the challenge. It developed the slogan "Richest Coffee in the World" and the character of Juan Valdez as a spokesperson who taught consumers how to identify brands that contain 100% Colombian coffee. The Valdez character also explained the unique properties of Colombia that enabled it to grow the best coffee in the world.

AD 7.1
Ads such as these, featuring the Juan Valdez logo and the campaign slogan, helped 100% Colombian coffee to compete effectively with Brazilian coffee in the U.S. market.
(Courtesy of The National Federaton of Coffee Growers of Colombia.)

Needham ads established the premium image by featuring upscale settings with discriminating consumers enjoying 100% Colombian coffee. For example, one ad featured a businessman sitting in a lush grand parlor in front of a fireplace reading *The Wall Street Journal* and drinking a cup of Colombian coffee. The copy featured only the headline: "50% Tax Bracket, 100% Colombian Coffee," the Juan Valdez logo, and the campaign slogan.

By the mid-1980s unaided awareness of Colombia as a coffee-producing country reached an all-time high of 48 percent compared to Brazil's 45 percent. Additionally, 58 percent of consumers believed that Colombia grows the best coffee, compared to 29 percent for Brazil. In the great coffee war Colombia took the offensive away from Brazil. In 1983 only 35 coffee brands featured the Colombia logo. Today 320 brands are in the program.*

STRATEGY AND PLANNING

Advertising is both an art and a science. The art comes from writing, designing, and producing exciting messages. The science, however, comes from strategic thinking. Advertising is a disciplined art, and the messages are developed to accomplish specific objectives. Strategy begins with information, with background research, and with as much intelligence about the situation as possible.

Strategy: Making Intelligent Decisions

The word *strategy* is a military term. It means the art and science of planning and conducting a combat operation. The word also means *the plan of action* used to direct a military operation. In many respects marketing resembles a war, and the marketplace is a battleground. Major corporations invest millions of dollars in the introducton and support of products in highly competitive situations. The combatants assault each other's positions and attempt to wrest market share from one another. Attacks and counterattacks are frequent, all to the beat of music and the battle cry of slogans.

Marketing and advertising strategies are chosen from an array of possible alternatives. Intelligent decision making means weighing the alternatives and sorting out the best approach. Often there is no *right* way, but there may be a *best* way.

marketing plan *A document that proposes strategies for employing the marketing elements to achieve a marketing goal.*

advertising plan *A document that matches the right audience to the right message and presents it in the right media.*

advertising strategy *The development of a plan for persuasive communications in a competitive marketing situation.*

Strategy in Marketing and Advertising   Major combatants in the marketing war operate with a carefully developed strategy, a plan that directs all phases of the effort, particularly the advertising and promotional activities. A **marketing plan** describes how all the elements—product, pricing, distribution (place), and promotion—should be employed to maximize the impact of the total effort.

An **advertising plan** matches the right audience to the right message and presents it in the right medium to reach that audience. An **advertising strategy** refers to the development of a plan for persuasive communication. There are many possible audiences for the advertising message, numerous ways to express the message, and a multitude of media vehicles available to carry the message.

Strategic planning occurs on three levels in advertising. The *corporate advertising plan* is developed annually and may be a part of the overall marketing plan. An *advertising campaign* can be directed by a written campaign plan that summarizes the underlying strategy for this major effort. A *creative platform* or work plan also may be developed on a one-time basis for an individual ad.

Many of the decisions for all three types of plans are similar; the difference lies more in the time frame and scale of the advertising effort. All three will be

*"Richest Coffee in the World," DDB Needham Case Study, unpublished document.

discussed in more detail in this chapter. The entire process begins, however, with the marketing plan.

THE MARKETING PLAN

A marketing plan is a written document that analyzes the marketing situation, identifies the problems, outlines the opportunities, sets the objectives, and proposes strategies to solve the problems and meet the objectives. A marketing plan is developed and evaluated annually, although certain sections dealing with long-run objectives might extend for a number of years. Some companies are finding that the marketplace changes so rapidly that plans have to be updated even more frequently—perhaps even quarterly. The following is an outline for a typical marketing plan:

- Situation Analysis:
  1. Product
  2. Marketplace
  3. Distribution
  4. Pricing
  5. Promotion
  6. Consumer behavior
- Problems and Opportunities
- Objectives:
  1. Sales
  2. Dollars
  3. Share of market
- Strategies (will vary with the situation but include such areas as the following):
  1. Target markets
  2. Branding
  3. Geographical emphasis: CDI/BDI
  4. Channel: push or pull
  5. Cooperative promotions
- Implementation and Evaluation
  1. Schedule
  2. Budget
  3. Follow-up research

Situation Analysis

situation analysis *The section of the marketing plan that analyzes the research findings.*

The **situation analysis** is a standard section in most marketing plans. It summarizes relevant information about the product, marketplace, competition, demand, consumer behavior, distribution channels, costs, and environmental factors. This section will seek to answer questions like the following:

- *Product:* What are the product's features? Are any distinctive? What is the competitive advantage? Any new developments? What is the product's life-cycle stage?
- *Marketplace:* What are total sales (in units and dollars) for the product, the competition, and the category? What is the projected size of the market and the level of demand? What are the current market shares?
- *Promotion:* What is the advertising and promotion history for the firm and its competitors? What are the current advertising expenditures?
- *Distribution:* How do products get to the purchase location? Where do people buy the product—number and type of stores, locations?
- *Pricing:* What is the pricing picture? History?
- *Consumers:* Who buys the product? How do they make the purchase decision? Do they seek information? How do they perceive the brand? The competition?

Problems and Opportunities

Analysis is the heart of strategic planning. It is the process of figuring out what all the information means. After you have studied all the information, then the

TABLE 7.1
Setting Marketing Objectives

I. Assumes the price and the total category sales remain the same:			
	Units	**Dollars**	**Share of Market (%)** **(Market = 12.5 million units)**
This year:	500,000	$1.0 million	4.0
Next year:	600,000	$1.2 million	4.8
Net difference:	100,000	$200,000	0.8
% Increase:	(20%)	(20%)	(20%)

II. Assumes price increases as well as increases in total category sales:				
	Units	**Price**	**Dollars**	**Share of Market (%)***
This year:	500,000	$2.00	$1.0 million	4.0
Next year:	600,000	$2.10	$1.26 million	4.6
Net difference:	100,000	$ .10	$260,000	0.6
% Increase:	(20%)	(5%)	(26%)	(15%)

*This year's category sales = 12.5 million units; next year's estimated category sales = 13 million units.

problems and opportunities should begin to emerge. Spotting the key problems is often very difficult. It takes experience, marketing sophistication, and an analytical mind. Problems and opportunities are the positive and negative implications of your findings. Some of the problems that you identify in a situation analysis can be solved or overcome. Others have to be circumvented. Any problem that isn't addressed can become a potential advantage for a competitor. An opportunity comes from a problem that can be reversed or from a situation where your product has an advantage.

In the Colombian coffee story one of the problems was how to become a bigger presence in the market. That was accomplished by using a strong umbrella campaign. The "Juan Valdez" campaign was so successful that the number of brands identified as Colombian coffee increased from 35 to 320.

Marketing Objectives

The primary objective, of course, for most marketing efforts is sales, or profit. In the marketing arena objectives are usually stated in terms of sales and market share, and both should be specific and measurable. The objectives may also be given as short-term (annual) and long-term goals (up to 5 years).

Sales-volume objectives are specified in both units and dollars. Share of market describes how much of the market your product has garnered; it is expressed as a percentage.

share of market *The percentage of the total category sales owned by one brand.*

For example, let's say the marketing manager predicts a sales increase of 20 percent from 500,000 units this year to 600,000 units next year. If the units sold for $2 each, then the dollar volume would increase from $1 million to $1.2 million, also an increase of 20 percent. If the new sales level raised the products' share of market from 4 to 4.8 percent, that would also represent an increase of 20 percent. These numbers are explained in Table 7.1.

PRINCIPLE
Marketing objectives are given in terms of sales and share of market.

Secondary objectives might focus on such areas as distribution levels and store traffic, or on actions that need to be taken to solve specific problems. The success or failure of the marketing plan will be evaluated on the basis of how well these objectives are met, so they need to be realistic.

Marketing Strategies

Key strategy decisions found in a marketing plan include the identification of target markets, branding, and channel decisions such as the push-pull emphasis, pricing, and the use of cooperative promotional efforts. These strategic decisions are particularly relevant to advertising.

target market *A section of the country or a group of consumers who are potential users of the product or service.*

prospects *People who might buy the product or service.*

target audience *People who can be reached with a certain advertising medium and a particular message.*

market segmentation *The process of identifying segments by demographic or psychographic characteristics.*

segmentation *The process of identifying subgroups within a targeted population.*

brand development index (BDI) *An index that identifies the demand for the brand within a region.*

category development index (CDI) *An index that identifies the demand for the category within a region.*

Target Markets   A very important strategic decision in marketing planning is the identification of the target market. The **target market** is a section of the country or a group of consumers who are potential users of the product or service. Targeting is an outgrowth of the marketing concept with its consumer-oriented focus. In contrast, production-oriented strategies just produce a product and consider all consumers to be in the market.

Several related terms here might be confusing. Marketing uses the term *target market* to identify **prospects** who might buy the product or service; advertising identifies a **target audience** who can be reached with a certain advertising medium and a particular message. The target audience can be equivalent to the target market, but it often includes groups of people other than consumers, such as people who influence the product purchase. For example, the target audience for an over-the-counter diet program might include customers as well as doctors, pharmacists, dietitians, and government agencies.

THE CONCEPT OF TARGETING   A target is something you aim at. The implication is that if you hit the target, your message will have a better chance of being understood and accepted than if it falls among random groups of consumers who are less likely to be interested. If you miss the target, the odds are high that you have wasted the effort.

MARKET SEGMENTATION   The identification of markets that deserve special emphasis is based on the concept of **market segmentation,** which breaks down the overall market into smaller groups. **Segmentation** lets the seller speak more directly to the needs and wants of a certain type of buyer.

Markets can be segmented on the basis of demographic factors, such as geography. For example, iced tea is easier to sell during the winter in southern states than in northern ones. Chapstick, on the other hand, has a larger market in northern and mountain states.

UNDIFFERENTIATED MARKETS   An *undifferentiated* strategy is used for nationally marketed products that appeal to broad groups of people and ignore individual differences. In general, this strategy works for Coca-Cola, McDonald's, and Kodak, but not for many other products. Even mass-marketed products like Coke will occasionally target markets by age, season, and region. The undifferentiated strategy works best for products that have a universal appeal and are bought by large numbers of people. The advertiser must have sufficient resources to support a massive marketing program.

Branding   Branding was discussed in a previous chapter as an important part of the product concept. The decision to develop a strong brand image, however, is a strategic one. Manufacturers can sell products under store names, as generic products, as local brands, or as national brands. The approach taken will obviously affect the scale of the advertising effort.

GEOGRAPHICAL EMPHASIS   On another level marketing strategy combines a brand's market position with market segmentation using a type of opportunity analysis. Two terms are important for understanding this strategic decision. The **brand development index** (BDI) and the **category development index** (CDI) are measures of sales potential by brand and by region. These are compared to actual category sales to determine where the opportunities lie to increase sales.

An area with a high CDI has a strong demand for the category; an area with a high BDI has a strong demand for the brand. The ideal strategy is to find an area that has a high CDI and a low BDI. This information is used by advertising planners to target certain geographical areas for special emphasis in the advertising plan.

Distribution   PUSH-PULL STRATEGIES   Another strategic decision that affects advertising is the orientation to the reseller market. Promotion that is directed to

push strategy *A promotional strategy that is directed to the trade in an attempt to move the product through the distribution channel.*

pull strategy *A promotional strategy that is designed to encourage consumers to ask for the product.*

the trade in an attempt to move the product through the distribution channel is said to use a **push strategy.** Promotion that is directed to consumers, who then go to retailers and ask for the product, is said to use a **pull strategy.** Advertising for new and largely unknown products might rely more on push strategy to get the product into the stores where the sales staff can *push* the product. Advertising for major national brands uses a *pull* strategy. It is important for the marketing advertising planner to understand the push-pull strategy in order to determine how much emphasis should go to trade promotion and how much to consumer promotion.

PRICING   Although the price charged for a product appears obvious and easy to understand, it is a complex factor in marketing strategy. First of all, it is the prime determinant of profit. The price not only reflects the cost of making and marketing the product, but also considers the profit level, the competitive situation, the reseller's profit, and the willingness of customers to pay that price.

A *customary pricing strategy* uses a single, well-known price for a long period of time. Movie theaters and candy manufacturers use this strategy, in which the customer supposedly becomes insensitive to the price. With *prestige pricing* the price is set at a high level in the hope that buyers will see the product as unique or special or as a status symbol. A *price-reduction* strategy reduces the price temporarily to encourage consumers to purchase the product. This strategy includes "sales," "specials," and other forms of discount pricing. Some stores will use *loss leaders*—products priced below cost—to generate store traffic.

Information about price is probably the most important message content that advertising can transmit. The term *price copy* has been coined to designate a message strategy that is devoted primarily to announcing price information.

CO-OP PROMOTIONS   With cooperative promotions the manufacturer agrees to help the local retailer with the advertising and promotion costs. The strategic decision involves how much of the effort should be on building national brand identity and how much on stimulating store traffic on the local level. This strategic decision has major budget and advertising implications. Co-op ads are discussed in more detail in Chapter 22.

All advertising is directed toward a particular audience.
(Courtesy of Owen Franken/Stock, Boston.)

Implementation and Evaluation

The implementation sections deal with two critical aspects of planning: scheduling and budgeting. The various elements in the plan are analyzed in terms of both time and money. Evaluation is an important part of any marketing effort, and a marketing plan will also end with a section that details how the plan is to be evaluated to see if it was successful in meeting its objectives. Both the implementation and evaluation sections in a marketing plan can include advertising.

THE ADVERTISING PLAN

An advertising plan uses many of the same terms and concepts as the marketing plan. However, the focus is on the advertising message and what it can be expected to accomplish. Marketing plans focus on sales; advertising plans focus on communication.

Advertising Strategy Decisions

The following seven strategic decisions are particularly important to advertising, because they guide the development of both the creative and the media plans:

1. The problem to be solved by the advertising message
2. The communication opportunities available to turn the problem around
3. The communication objectives to be accomplished
4. The audience group to be targeted
5. The competitive product advantage
6. The product's personality
7. The available position in the marketplace

The Advertising Problem Advertising is developed for strategic reasons: to deliver a message, to create some kind of effect on the consumer, and, ultimately, to solve some communication problem that affects the successful marketing of the product. Analyzing the situation and identifying the problem that can be solved with an advertising message is the heart of strategic planning.

Different agencies employ different strategies. BBDO uses a process called "Problem Detection" as the basis of its strategy building.* Problem Detection takes the question directly to consumers to find out what bothers them about the product or product category. Often the problems are not what the manufacturer expected to hear. A classic example involved the BBDO client Burger King. A Problem Detection study had revealed that customers of fast-food hamburger restaurants objected to the fact that the hamburgers were all prepared the same way and then prepackaged. Thus, a consumer with a particular preference—for example, no pickle or no onions—would have to wait while a special order was cooked. Burger King responded to this survey with its "Have It Your Way" campaign, in which the food was not packaged until the customer placed an order. Under this system, consumers could order hamburgers prepared specially for them without having to wait.

DDB Needham searches for "Barriers to Purchase."† These barriers are reasons why people are not buying or are not buying enough of a product. The American Dairy Association asked DDB Needham to find out why the consumption of cheese was declining. A study identified the major barriers to increased consumption and eventually directed the agency toward the *one* barrier that was most easily correctable through advertising: the absence of *simple* cheese reci-

---

*E. E. Norris, "Seek Out the Consumer's Problem," *Advertising Age,* March 17, 1975, pp. 43–44.
†*Research for R.O.I.: 1987 Communications Workshop,* DDB Needham, Chicago, April 10, 1987.

pes for homemakers. The previous advertising used a campaign that focused on *elaborate* uses of cheese with *complicated* recipes.*

Advertising can only solve message-related problems such as image, attitude, perception, and knowledge or information. It cannot solve problems related to the price of the product or its availability. A message can speak, however, to the perception of the price as too high. It can also portray a product with limited distribution as exclusive. In other words, although advertising does not determine the actual price or availability of a product, it can affect the way price and availability are perceived by consumers.

Advertising Opportunities Advertising planners are adept at spotting problems and turning them into opportunities. For example, a high price can be turned into a status symbol. Likewise, limited distribution can be considered a sign of an exclusive product. Traditionally in advertising planning problem identification is followed by a statement describing the opportunity. In other words, how can you turn this problem into an opportunity?

For example, a DDB Needham strategy called the "Opportunity Quotient" tries to structure this process of identifying opportunities.† The Opportunity Quotient combines acceptability and primary choice. For example, a major department store wanted to know which types of apparel from its diverse line of apparel items would offer the best advertising opportunity. After surveying the store's customers DDB Needham constructed the Opportunity Quotient for the various apparel lines by dividing the percentage of people who would consider the store for that item by the percentage who already bought the item most frequently there. Those apparel items with higher Opportunity Quotients represent the best advertising opportunities.

Advertising Objectives Closely related to the identification of an advertising problem is the statement of the **advertising objectives.** Objectives are goal statements; they identify the effect the message is intended to have on the audience within a specified time frame. They are logically derived from the problem analysis. Ideally, if the advertising accomplishes its objectives, then the problem will have been solved.

MESSAGE EFFECTS   What can advertising do? No simple answer to this question exists. Different forms of advertising have different objectives. Direct-response advertising can directly generate sales. Newspaper advertising can build store traffic. These are action responses indicating some kind of behavioral impact. Coupon return also indicates an action response.

Most advertising, however, creates delayed action or indirect responses. Basically advertising seeks to establish, modify, or reinforce attitudes. Brand advertising, for example, seeks to create an image or carve out a unique position for a product. Other advertisements try to call attention to a product feature or to associate a product with a certain lifestyle or typical user. The Colombian coffee campaign, for example, resulted in an attitude change, with 58 percent of the audience coming to believe that Colombia grows the best coffee as opposed to 29 percent for Brazil.

Some advertisements attempt to stimulate an emotional response, such as the AT&T "reach out and touch someone" campaign. The Dreyer's ice cream commercials about good things that happen when you eat ice cream try to create warm feelings for the product.

MODELS FOR OBJECTIVES   A number of models help advertisers analyze the effectiveness of their messages. Most of these models organize message effects

---

PRINCIPLE _____
Advertising turns problems into opportunities.

---

advertising objectives *Statements of the effect of the advertising message on the audience.*

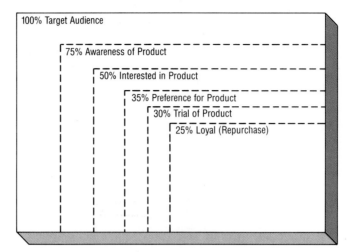

100% Target Audience

75% Awareness of Product

50% Interested in Product

35% Preference for Product

30% Trial of Product

25% Loyal (Repurchase)

FIGURE 7.1
Setting objectives using a hierarchy-of-effects model.

hierarchy of effects *A set of consumer responses that moves from the least serious, involved, or complex up through the most serious, involved, or complex.*

from the simplest kind of impact to the most complex. Some of them present these effects as a series of steps in the process of moving consumers from initial awareness to final action. This series of steps is called a **hierarchy of effects.** [*]

One of the oldest advertising models is called the *AIDA* formula. It describes the process as beginning with *Attention*, then moving to *Interest*, then *Desire*, and finally *Action*.

Attention → Interest → Desire → Action

A similar four-step model was developed by the advertising theorist Russell H. Colley in his book *Defining Advertising Goals for Measured Advertising Results.*[†] This *DAGMAR* model begins with awareness, then moves to comprehension, then conviction, and ends with action.

Awareness → Comprehension → Conviction → Action

A model by Robert C. Lavidge and Gary A. Steiner approaches the analysis of message effects in a different way.[‡] It identifies three categories of effects called *cognitive* (mental or rational), *affective* (emotional), and *conative* (deciding or action). This model is referred to as the "think/feel/do" model. The three categories are associated with the following steps in the process:

cognitive   awareness
↓   knowledge
↓
affective   liking
↓   preference
↓
conative   conviction
    purchase

Simpler responses, such as awareness, which are relatively easy to create, get higher levels of response. The more complex the response, the lower the level of response. In other words, a lot of people may be aware of the product, but far fewer will actually try it. The hierarchy model in Figure 7.1 illustrates the relative

[*]John D. Leckenby, "Conceptual Foundations for Copytesting Research," *Advertising Working Papers,* No. 2, February 1976.

[†]Russell Colley, *Defining Advertising Goals for Measured Advertising Results* (New York: Association of National Advertisers, 1961).

[‡]Robert C. Lavidge and Gary A. Steiner, "A Model for Predictive Measurements of Advertising Effectiveness," *Journal of Marketing 25* (October 1961): 59–62.

impact of these various effects with the simplest, but broadest, response at the bottom and the most complex, but smallest, response at the top.*

An example of an advertising campaign that is designed to stimulate action is one used by the California Almond Growers. Each ad ends with the suggestion to "Eat a can a week."

Some examples of a set of advertising objectives structured in a hierarchy are listed below. These objectives would all be established within a given time frame.

- To create an 80 percent *awareness* of the slogan (package, logo)
- To establish *knowledge* of the product's unique construction feature among 60 percent of the audience
- To create a positive *liking* among 50 percent of the targeted audience
- To create a *preference* for the brand among 30 percent of the targeted audience
- To *convince* 30 percent of the audience that this product is the best in its category
- To elicit a 10 percent *response* to a coupon

Targeting the Audience The purpose of targeting in advertising is to identify the group, or groups, that will provide the highest level of response to an advertising message. It is not an attempt to leave anyone out, but rather to

AD 7.2
Who is the target audience for this ad?
(Courtesy of MasterCard International, Inc.)

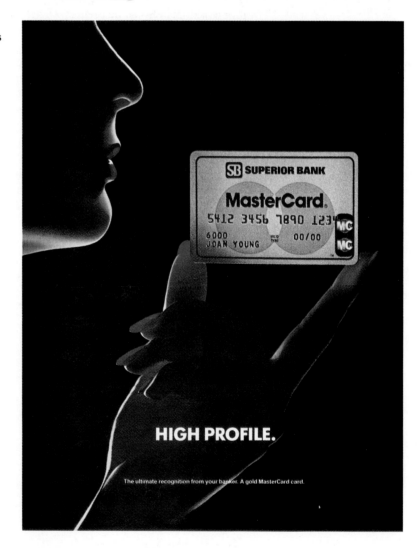

*DDB Needham, *Research for R.O.I.*

concentrate and direct the message for maximum impact. The 80:20 rule helps explain how and why planners target their market as tightly as possible. In many product categories 20 percent of the consumers buy 80 percent of the product. The goal of targeting is to zero in on that 20 percent. The MasterCard ad in Ad 7.2 tries to do just that.

In targeting audiences demographic categories often overlap psychographic categories. In other words, you might target women 25 to 35 and also target suburban shoppers. Those two categories would overlap because a certain percentage of women 25 to 35 are also in the suburban shopper category.

Targeting looks at those characteristics that best define groups of prospects, compares the descriptors, and then overlaps the groups to find the best combination of descriptors. This kind of analysis lets the advertising planner pinpoint the target and zero in on the most responsive audience. Figure 7.2 illustrates how these descriptors are used to zero in on a target.

TARGETED SEGMENTS   One approach to targeting that was discussed earlier is segmentation, which identifies subgroups within the overall market. Marketing planners identify a *target market* and *market segments.* Advertising operates in a similar way, although it segments *audiences* rather than markets in order to direct appropriate messages at the various types of people. Levi's, for example, sells jeans to a variety of segments, including young boys, teenagers, farmers and other working men, young adults who are active and interested in the outdoors, and to a fashion-oriented segment of teenage women. The messages for each targeted audience must use different appeals.

Benefit segmentation marries the targeting decision to the product analysis. It is an approach that identifies segments of the audience in terms of the specific appeals used to motivate them. Toothpaste advertisers, for example, know that different people buy different brands of toothpaste for different reasons. Some people buy a brand of toothpaste because it whitens their teeth, others buy a brand because it cleans their breath. Some buy a toothpaste to protect against cavities, others buy a different brand of toothpaste to fight plaque, and still others buy a brand because it tastes good. Different brands are segmented to appeal to these different audiences who want different things from a basic product like toothpaste.

benefit segmentation *Segments identified by the appeal of the product to their personal interests.*

FIGURE 7.2
Targeting involves the use of overlapping descriptors to identify the most receptive audience.

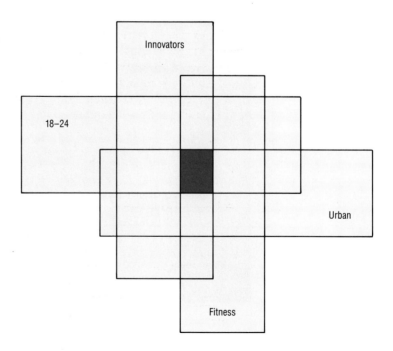

172 ■ PART TWO: ADVERTISING BACKGROUND, PLANNING, AND STRATEGY

Don't waste your military experience. Guard it.

It took you years of study and plain, hard work to master a military skill. So why throw that experience away just because you're a civilian now?

With a part-time job in the Army National Guard, you could be earning good extra income and adding some excitement to your life, while you keep up on the latest military skills and regain some of your best military benefits.

It won't take much of your time—two days a month and two weeks annual training. And you'll be serving close to home, helping people in your community and state when natural disaster and other emergencies strike. Good pay. Good benefits. That's a smart-time job in the Army National Guard.

For more information on how you can Guard your military experience, contact your local Army Guard recruiter, or call toll-free 800-638-7600.*

*In Hawaii: 737-5255; Puerto Rico: 723-4550; Virgin Islands (St. Croix): 773-6438; Maryland: 728-3388; In Alaska, consult your local phone directory.

The Guard is America at its best.

ARMY NATIONAL GUARD

AD 7.3
This ad illustrates the National Guard's strategy of appealing to the "Stable" group.
(Courtesy of National Guard Bureau.)

An example of identifying segments in order to make the most strategic targeting decision is illustrated in a consumer study conducted for the Army National Guard. The Guard wanted to identify those groups that would be the most desirable to recruit and retain. Knowing more about the audience would enable the Guard to communicate better to these people. A study of 1,671 enlisted men in the Guard found four broad clusters of individuals:

- *The "Stable" group* (20 percent): Active, optimistic, content, politically active, open-minded, 26–45, some college, higher-than-average income. More likely than other groups to be married, to have prior service, and to want to stay in the Guard.
- *The "Misfits"* (26 percent): Pessimistic, fearful, angry, not ambitious or motivated, financially insecure, possess few educational or traditional values, lack self-confidence, have the least respect for the military, 18–25, single, minorities, high-school drop-outs. Less likely to remain in the Guard.
- *The "Conservatives"* (28 percent): Homebodies, traditional, religious, not adventurous, don't like change, oldest group, been in the Guard longer, more likely to be in higher ranks, most likely to be married and have children, go out and entertain less, read less.
- *The "Swaggerers"* (25 percent): Active, optimistic, liberal, outgoing, adventurous, partiers and swingers, confident, lowest ranks, in the Guard the least amount of time, single, no prior service, enrolled in college, youngest (18–21), lowest income, read the most.

These results indicated that the "Stable" group were the most content in the Guard and the "Misfits" were the least happy. The "Swaggerers" were more likely to be attracted by the Guard's college benefits.

This analysis brought about a complete change in the Guard's advertising strategy. The agency recommended changing the Guard's priority target from young men right out of high school to an older group of men, especially those with prior service who have some college background and are active in their communities. It also suggested a change in media placement to more upscale, middle-of-the-road and news-oriented publications. Another recommendation was to focus on young men in college or with college aptitude who would be interested in the tuition benefits. Ad 7.3 offers an example of this new strategy.

PROFILES   Marketing planners and media buyers may look at the target as groups of numbers, but the creative people need to see a target as an individual—a warm, living, breathing person, preferably someone they know. For this reason, advertising research usually redefines the target as a **profile** of a typical prospect. This individual, the typical prospect, is given a name and a whole set of personality and lifestyle characteristics.

profile *A personality sketch of a typical prospect in the targeted audience.*

Competitive Advantage   If marketing is war, then there must be an enemy. If a product category has room for expansion, then everyone can grow and competition is often less intense. If, however, a particular category is static, then growth must come at someone else's expense and competition can be intense. Identification of the competition is a way of targeting the vulnerable opposition.

IDENTIFYING THE COMPETITION   Advertisers analyze data on direct and indirect competition to shed light on consumer behavior. **Direct competition** includes all other brands in the category. **Indirect competition** includes other options, perhaps outside the category. American Greetings, for example, is Hallmark's direct competition, but the telephone company is an indirect competitor. Both Hallmark and the telephone company are after the consumer's "sentiment message." When an advertiser dominates its category, as Hallmark does, an indirect competitor can be more formidable than a direct competitor.

A knowledge of the consumer and his or her purchasing decisions identifies these alternative choices. As mentioned earlier, the competition is identified by the pattern of consumer alternatives rather than simply by listing the other brands and companies in the same category.

A basic principle to remember is that even when you and your competition can grow in a growth market, you still might not be increasing market share. Because market share is a percentage of the whole market, you can't increase your own market share unless someone else's shrinks.

The problem is to identify which competitors are most vulnerable and on what basis. Does your product have an advantage over any of these competitors? Detecting a clear product advantage will give direction to the advertising message. If, for example you find a distribution advantage, then geographical targeting might give you a competitive advantage.

What you are trying to decide with this strategy decision is where your **competitive product advantage** lies. The analysis of the product, the competition, and the target all happen simultaneously. These factors are interdependent because the concept of product advantage involves identifying what the consumer wants and comparing that with the competition's strengths and weaknesses as well as those of your product.

FEATURE ANALYSIS   **Feature analysis** is an easy way to structure the competitive process. If you are trying to puzzle out competitive advertising, first make a chart for your product and the competitor's products. Underneath each product list its features or attributes. The relevant features will vary for every product. Taste, for example, is important for sodas, horsepower and mileage are important for cars, and trendiness is important for fashion watches.

direct competition *A product in the same category.*

indirect competition *A product that is in a different category but functions as an alternative purchase choice.*

PRINCIPLE
The indirect competition may be more important than the direct competition.

PRINCIPLE
Your share of market can't increase unless a competitor's share shrinks.

competitive product advantage *The identification of a feature that is important to the consumer where your product is strong and the competition is vulnerable.*

feature analysis *A comparison of your product's features against the features of competing products.*

AD 7.4
An example of competitive advertising.
(Courtesy of *Business Week* and McGraw-Hill, Inc.)

PRINCIPLE

Competitive advantage means you are strong in some area that matters to the target where your competitors are weak.

Next evaluate these lists on two dimensions. First rate how important each feature is to the target audience. (This requires primary research.) Then evaluate how well all the products perform on that feature. Your competitive advantage lies in that area where you have a strong feature that is important to the target and your competition is weak. Table 7.2 illustrates a sample analysis using a common set of hypothetical features. With parity, or undifferentiated products, the competitive advantage might lie with the image created by the advertising rather than with any specific feature.

		Product		
TABLE 7.2 **Feature Analysis**	Importance to Prospect	Performance		
Feature		Yours	X	Y	Z

Feature	Importance to Prospect	Yours	X	Y	Z
Price	1	+	−	−	+
Quality	4	−	+	−	+
Style	2	+	−	+	−
Availability	3	−	+	−	−
Durability	5	−	+	+	+

INSIDE THE ADVERTISING WORLD

KEITH REINHARD, CHIEF EXECUTIVE OFFICER, DDB NEEDHAM WORLDWIDE

When we speak of personality in human terms, we refer to the collection of traits that define an individual beyond physical qualities. When we say a person is "witty," "well organized," or "well groomed," we refer to characteristics of intelligence and style that separate one person from another. We admire people who are "smart," we're attracted to people who are "young at heart" or "vivacious," and we appreciate people who are "warm and caring." The combination of traits we call personality can be an individual's most important asset. It can also be a person's most important liability. We all know people who have met with added success in life because of their winning personalities. And we can probably name a few otherwise capable people whose lives or careers suffer from "personality problems."

In the same way, marketers of products and services must be concerned about a brand's personality. State Farm's neighborliness, Michelin's concern for your family's safety, Betty Crocker's trustworthiness, and Chivas Regal's specialness all result from advertising that consistently highlights those brands' best features. Wheaties' all-American sports-mindedness is a personality trait created entirely by advertising.

For a dramatic reminder of how important brand personalities really are, you need only stroll through a supermarket's generic food section. The disorientation you feel is real and immediate. There are no familiar symbols to signal how products will taste or to predict how they will perform. Generics will never succeed in any important way because, like faceless people, they rob products of their identities and thus rob consumers of real values like trust and predictability. It is hard to like a product with no personality. More important, it is impossible to trust a manufacturer who keeps his name and reputation a secret.

Indeed, as advanced technology makes it nearly impossible for any brand to maintain a product-related competitive edge, the need to differentiate brands by personality becomes even greater. This is especially true in those categories where the product and its user appear together in public. In these cases, the brand's personality is frequently its *most important* attribute. The label on the seat of the jeans or the side of the bottle represents values important to the customer. Those values are willingly paid for because they help the user define his or her own personality. Just as size and shape help define the *appearance* of a product, the image and associations created by advertising define the *experience* of using a product. When a customer identifies with the personality of a product and finds its values and behavior attractive, he or she transfers that personality to himself or herself by buying and using the product. It's like putting on a badge and wearing it proudly. What a product stands for is a very real part of what a product *is*. Thus, investing brands with winning personalities is one of advertising's most important jobs.

Source: Keith Reinhard, DDB Needham Worldwide, 1988.

INTRODUCING A WAGON LIKE THERE'S NEVER BEEN BEFORE.

NISSAN INNOVATION STRIKES AGAIN.

It took Nissan to come up with a way of getting you around, designed for how you live today. The 1986 Nissan Stanza Wagon. From how you get in it, to what you get out of it, this wagon is unlike any you've ever experienced before.

It's the only wagon with sliding doors on both sides. Which not only makes the Stanza a cinch to get in and out of in a tight parking space...it also makes it a cinch to get to its 80 cu. ft. of cargo space. And to the extra seating provided by its optional jump seats. It's powered by a 2.0 liter fuel-injected engine. And, with front-wheel drive, it handles as crisply as any car you've ever driven. It comes to you with a full array of standard equipment. From a state-of-the-art tilt steering column to an electronically-tuned AM/FM stereo. It's aerodynamically stylish. Technologically modern. And logically right on the money.

The 1986 Nissan Stanza Wagon opens up a whole new side to family transportation. Your Nissan/Datsun dealer can show it to you today. If you're looking for innovation... The Name is Nissan.

BELT YOURSELF

NEW 1986 STANZA WAGON. THE FIRST AND ONLY WAGON WITH DUAL SLIDING DOORS.

THE NAME IS
NISSAN

NISSAN

AD 7.5
An example of a positioning ad. Given the number of automobiles available to the consumer, what unique position is the Nissan company trying to establish for its station wagon?
(Courtesy of Nissan Motor Corporation.)

positioning *The way in which a product is perceived in the marketplace by the consumers.*

PRINCIPLE
A product's position is located in the minds of the consumers.

Positioning

Positioning refers to the way in which a product is perceived by consumers in the marketplace relative to the competition. A position is a "niche" in the marketplace. A lot of strategic planning is directed at finding that "hole" or "home" in the market where a product can be positioned. The coffee campaign, for example, was able to position Colombian coffee as the richest in the world.

The concept of positioning was developed by Jack Trout and Al Ries in a 1972 article that appeared in *Advertising Age.** They pointed to an advertising classic, the "We try harder" campaign for Avis. It positioned the car rental company as one that would serve its customers better because it had to work harder to compete with the number-one company, Hertz. Ad 7.5 tries to position the Nissan Stanza in the automobile market.

*Jack Trout and Al Ries, "The Positioning Era," *Advertising Age,* April 24, May 1, 8, 1972.

AD 7.6
Budget Gourmet's unusual marketing strategy has helped to make the product a success.
(Courtesy of Kraft, Inc.)

An example of a positioning problem was one faced by a frozen food that is both gourmet and inexpensive (see Ad 7.6). The product, Budget Gourmet, features gourmet meals at an inexpensive price. A unique low-cost package makes it possible to keep the price down. Focus groups conducted by Silverman Advertising, however, revealed that people had a problem with the name and image. Labeling a product as both "budget" and "gourmet" seemed contradictory and unrealistic. The solution was to avoid the downscale stigma by printing the word "Gourmet" in bold type with the word "Budget" in a small script that appeared to be penciled in. The company's rapid growth to 13.4 percent of the $2.5 billion frozen-entree category attests to the strength of this unusual positioning strategy.*

Positioning research begins with the feature analysis described previously. From this research you should be able to describe the most relevant attributes of your product. You can then create *a map of the marketplace* that locates the position of your product relative to the positions of all the competitors. A sample two-dimensional (using two attributes) **perceptual map** based on the preceding feature analysis appears in Figure 7.3.

Strategically the first step is to identify the current position of the product, if one exists. For a new product, and for some established ones, a position has to be established. For ongoing product lines, the decision is either to reinforce a current position or to move it. In Figure 7.4 General Motors presents perceptual maps outlining past, present, and future positions for several of its models.

Establishing and moving positions requires a tremendous advertising effort. Both Marlboro cigarettes and Miller beer were originally sold to women at a time when market opportunities for cigarettes and beer for women were limited. Both were repositioned as "macho" products through extensive and costly advertising campaigns. Ad 7.7 illustrates a case in which an advertiser had to **reposition** a traditionally feminine product for a male audience.

perceptual map *A map that shows where consumers locate various products in the category in terms of several important features.*

reposition *Changing the consumer's perception of a product.*

*"Budget Gourmet's Downscale Look (and Its Upscale Taste) Whetted Consumers' Appetites," *Adweek,* August 3, 1987, p. M.R.C. 30.

THE ADVERTISING BUDGET

The advertising budget comes from the advertiser. A certain percentage of the advertiser's overall marketing budget is allocated to the promotion mix. Within the promotion mix a certain percentage is allocated to advertising. These decisions on the budget allocation are based on the level of emphasis given to promotion within the marketing mix and to advertising within the promotion mix.

The advertising budget may be spent by the advertising department within the company if advertising is an in-house function, or it may be assigned to the company's advertising agency. Most agencies receive commissions from the media with whom they have placed the advertising, although other reimbursement systems are becoming more popular. (Agency compensation is discussed in more detail in Chapter 4.) A typical advertising budget, then, is primarily for media expenses.

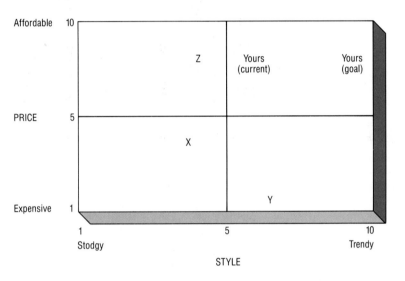

FIGURE 7.3
A two-dimensional perceptual map that examines two product attributes, price and style.

FIGURE 7.4
Four perceptual maps that involve the positioning of General Motors automobiles.
Source: Jesse Snyder, "4 GM Car Divisions Are Repositioned in Effort to Help Sales," *Automotive News,* September 15, 1986. (Reprinted with permission from *Automotive News.* Copyright 1988.)

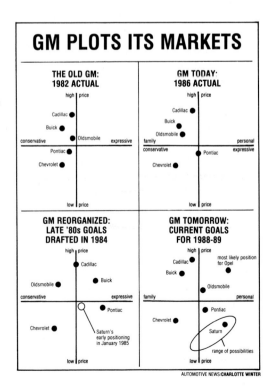

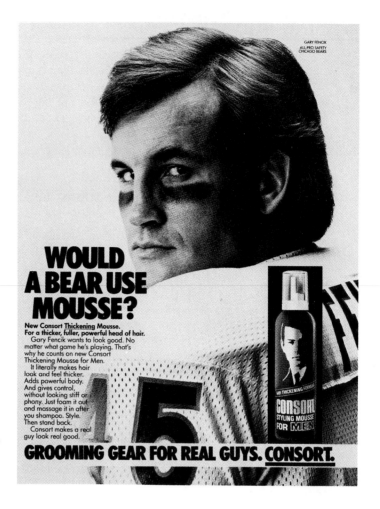

AD 7.7
This ad uses Gary Fencik of the Chicago Bears to reposition a traditionally feminine product for a male audience.

(Courtesy of Alberto Culver Company.)

Setting the Budget Level

forecasting *Estimating sales levels and the impact of various budget decisions on sales.*

The big question at each of these levels (marketing mix, promotion mix) is: How much to spend? Budgeting for the advertiser is essentially a **forecasting** operation. In other words, the advertiser is trying to figure out what level of sales will be generated by various levels of promotion budgeting.

Budget Approaches Advertising planners use two primary approaches to establish the advertising budget. One is to work from the *top down,* in other words, set a figure and then allocate it among the various activities. The other way is to *build up* the budget by estimating how much each of the activities will cost and adding them up. Within these two general approaches are a number of specific procedures, some more formal than others.

task-objective method *A budgeting method that builds a budget by asking what it will cost to achieve the stated objectives.*

TASK-OBJECTIVE METHOD The build-up approach is more commonly called the **task-objective method,** and this is probably the most common method for determining the budget level. This method looks at the objectives set for each activity and determines the cost of accomplishing each objective. In other words, what will it cost to make 50 percent of the people in your market aware of this product? How many people do you have to reach and how many times? What would be the necessary media levels and expenses?

HISTORICAL METHOD History is the source for a very common top-down budgeting method. For example, a budget may simply be based on last year's budget with a percentage increase for inflation or some other marketplace factor.

percent-of-sales method *A technique for computing the budget level that is based on the relationship between cost of advertising and total sales.*

PERCENT-OF-SALES METHOD   The **percent-of-sales method** is another type of top-down method. It compares the total sales with the total advertising (or promotion) budget during the previous year or the average of several years to compute a percentage. This technique can also be used across an industry to compare the expenditures of different product categories on advertising.

For example, if a company had sales figures of $5 million last year and an advertising budget of $1 million, then the ratio of advertising to sales would be 20 percent. If the marketing manager predicts sales of $6 million for next year, then the ad budget would be $1.2 million. The following explains how the percent-of-sales is computed.

$$\text{Step 1:} \quad \frac{\text{Past advertising dollars}}{\text{Past sales}} = \% \text{ of sales}$$

$$\text{Step 2:} \quad \% \text{ of sales} \times \begin{array}{c}\text{Next years}\\ \text{projected}\\ \text{budget}\end{array} = \begin{array}{c}\text{New}\\ \text{advertising}\\ \text{budget}\end{array}$$

Some categories spend a much higher percentage on promotion than others. And within the promotion budget some companies may spend more on one type of promotion and less on others—even within the same product category. For example, in the cosmetics industry Noxell, whose brands include Cover Girl and Noxzema, spends over 20 percent of its sales on advertising, whereas Avon spends only 1 percent on advertising. Avon has a much higher emphasis on personal sales in its promotional mix than does Noxell.

COMPETITIVE PARITY METHOD   Other top-down methods are used to determine whether the budget is adequate. *Competitive parity,* also called *share-of-voice* budgeting, relates the amount invested in advertising to the share of market. The share of advertising done by an advertiser can be related to the share of attention the brand will receive, which relates to the share of market that can be obtained.* The relationship can be depicted as follows:

$$\frac{\text{Share of}}{\text{media voice}} = \frac{\text{Share of}}{\text{consumer mind}} = \frac{\text{Share of}}{\text{market}}$$

Some marketing and advertising planners use sophisticated computer models.

COMBINATION OF METHODS   In practice many companies use a number of budget approaches in combination to determine a realistic budget level, comparing one benchmark or estimated budget level against another obtained from a different method.

Three marketing professors have developed a budgeting-decision game that uses different factors and modifies the level according to the product's situation.† The underlying philosophy is to develop a base budget level using the percentage-of-sales method and then modify it for various situations. A limit is set keeping in mind the advertising budgets of key competitors. The base budget is modified to increase or decrease the level after considering such factors as market share, product life cycle, market growth rate, product quality, and pricing strategy.

The important thing to understand about budgeting is that it reflects the marketing-mix and promotion-mix decisions. The level of the budget is determined by the emphasis that the company has decided to give to a certain area such as advertising.

---

*John J. Burnett, *Promotion Management,* 2nd ed. (St. Paul, MN: West Publishing, 1988).

†Amir Rashid, Hugh M. Cannon, and Edward A. Riordan, "Toward a Rule-Based Knowledge System for Making Advertising Budget Decisions in the Context of a Marketing Simulation Game," Annual Conference of the American Academy of Advertising, Chicago, April 11, 1988.

AN ADVERTISING CAMPAIGN PLAN

The advertising plan that guides the development of a campaign is similar in some ways to a marketing plan. Some of the sections, such as situation analysis, budget, and evaluation, are also in a campaign plan. The most important difference, however, is found in the sections that focus on message and media strategy. Because these areas are so central to advertising, both will be discussed in much greater depth in following chapters. A typical campaign plan is outlined below.

An Advertising Campaign Plan

- Situation Analysis:
    The advertising problem
    Advertising opportunities
- Key Strategy Decisions:
    Advertising objectives
    Target audience
    Competitive product advantage
    Product personality
    Product position
- The Creative Plan
- The Media Plan
- The Promotion Plan:
    Sales promotion
    Public relations
- Budget
- Evaluation

CREATIVE PLATFORMS

In addition to annual advertising plans and campaign plans, a plan also can be developed for an individual advertisement. This kind of plan goes by a number of different names—creative or copy platform, creative work plan, creative blueprint. Not all agencies use such a document, but those that do, use it as a guide to develop their message strategy and consider it an important part of advertising. The creative people, along with the account executive, are responsible for developing this **creative platform.** Most combine basic advertising decisons—such as problem, objective, and targeting—with a sales strategy to create a creative platform. The sales strategy in the message focuses on three additional factors: (1) the appeal, (2) the association, and (3) the selling premise.

creative platform *A document that summarizes the message strategy decisions behind an individual ad.*

Appeals

Persuasion in advertising rests on the psychological appeal to the consumer. An **appeal** is something that makes the product particularly attractive or interesting to the consumer. Common appeals are security, esteem, fear, sex, and sensory pleasure. Appeals generally pinpoint the anticipated response of the prospect to the product and message.

appeal *Something that moves people.*

Advertisers also use the word *appeal* to describe a general creative strategy. For example, if the price is emphasized in the ad, the appeal is then value, economy, or savings. If the product saves time or effort, then the appeal is convenience. A message that focuses on a mother or father making something for a child—like cookies or a rocker—might elicit an appeal of family love and concern. A *status appeal* is used to establish something as a quality, expensive product. *Appetite appeal* using mouth-watering visuals, as in Ad 7.8, is used in food advertising.

And you thought Bisquick only made pancakes.

Impossible Pizza Pie

The pie that's impossibly easy because it makes its own crust. Topped with Hormel Pepperoni, it's also impossibly delicious.

⅔ cup chopped onion
⅓ cup grated Parmesan cheese
3 eggs
1½ cups milk
¾ cup Bisquick® baking mix
Sauce (below)

¼ cup grated Parmesan cheese
3½ ounces Hormel Pepperoni, sliced
½ cup chopped onion
½ cup chopped green pepper
1 to 1½ cups shredded mozzarella cheese

Heat oven to 425°. Grease pie plate, 10 x 1½ inches. Sprinkle ⅔ cup onion and ⅓ cup Parmesan cheese in plate. Beat eggs, milk and baking mix until smooth, 15 seconds in blender on high or 1 minute with hand beater. Pour into plate. Bake 20 minutes. Spread Sauce over top. Layer remaining ingredients on Sauce. Bake until cheese is light brown, 15 to 20 minutes. Cool 5 minutes. 6 to 8 servings.

Sauce: Mix 1 can (6 ounces) tomato paste, ¼ cup water, 1 teaspoon dried oregano leaves, ½ teaspoon garlic salt, ½ teaspoon dried basil leaves and ¼ teaspoon pepper.

High Altitude: No adjustments.

®Reg. TM of General Mills, Inc.   © General Mills, Inc., 1983

AD 7.8
This Bisquick ad is an example of appetite appeal. Is it effective?
(Courtesy of DDB Needham Worldwide.)

Associations

association *A link or connection between two ideas.*

Association strategies are used to build images. An **association** is a link or connection between two ideas. Advertisements that use association try to link the product with a lifestyle, mood, setting, or type of personality. The links are usually established visually by showing the product being used by the right people or in the desired setting. This is a favorite technique of cosmetics, perfume, fashion-oriented products, cigarettes, and beverages. For example, the Rolex campaign has been using associations to signal the lifestyle of the rich and famous, as pictured in Ad 7.9.

Selling Premises

selling premises *The sales logic behind an advertising message.*

The various approaches to the sales message are called **selling premises.** A selling premise states the logic of the "sales pitch" in the message, in contrast to an appeal, which states the psychological attraction to the consumer. The most common premises are categorized as either product-centered or prospect-centered.

Seve Ballesteros takes the rough with the smooth. Just like his Rolex.

In 1980 America was introduced to a new golfing sensation who seemed to delight in hitting drives far off the fairway, then recovering with a beautiful approach shot to record a birdie.

His style allowed Seve Ballesteros that year to become the youngest player ever to win the Masters. In 1983 he repeated—in characteristic fashion. One stroke behind going into the final round, he shot a birdie, eagle, par and birdie on the first four holes, and breezed to his second title.

His go-for-broke approach to golf has won Seve numerous major tournaments on five continents—including the prestigious British Open.

While he is a natural athlete with enor-mous physical strength, his early introduction to the game in Pedreña, Spain, a tiny fishing village, is also a factor in his success. Seve grew up learning golf with a single iron and frequently played in semidarkness. Such conditions require inventiveness, and that is precisely what makes Ballesteros such a remarkable player today.

While his golf seems to thrive on adversity, his watch is known for its reliability and consistently excellent performance: the Rolex Oyster Day-Date.

"I may have good days and bad days," he says, "but this watch only has good days."

The unpredictable Seve Ballesteros. And his entirely predictable Rolex.

ROLEX

© 1983 Rolex Watch, U.S.A., Inc.

Pictured: The Rolex Day-Date Chronometer. Available in 18 kt. gold, with matching bracelet.

Write for brochure. Rolex Watch, U.S.A., Inc., Dept. 000, Rolex Building, 665 Fifth Avenue, New York, NY 10022-5383. World headquarters in Geneva. Other offices in Canada and major countries around the world.

AD 7.9
This Rolex ad associates the product with a highly successful golfer.
(Courtesy of Rolex Watch U.S.A.)

claim *A statement about the product's performance.*

Product-Centered Strategies Product-centered strategies refer to advertisements that focus on the product itself. These ads look at the attributes of the product and build a selling message on them. The following are two of the most common product-centered strategies.

CLAIMS A feature can be transformed into a selling point by stating what the product can do or has done. The **claim** is based on performance: how long the product lasts, how much it cleans, how little energy it uses. Torture tests, competitive tests, and before-and-after demonstrations can generate particularly strong claims. Often some scientifically conducted performance test supports such a claim.

BRAG AND BOAST Probably the least effective message strategy is one that focuses on the company. It emphasizes the company's point of view, goals, and pronouncements with an overuse of the pronoun *we*. This kind of copy is boastful and egotistical. When you see copy with pompous headlines like "We're #1," "We've been in business for 50 years," or "We're reaching out in new directions," you know you are reading brag-and-boast advertising.

Prospect-Centered Strategies The development of the marketing concept has led to a major increase in prospect-centered advertising strategies. Along with the change in marketing came a parallel switch in advertising, as message strategies focused on consumer needs rather than on product attributes. A number of message strategies use prospect-centered messages. They include

(1) benefits, (2) reasons why, (3) promises, and (4) unique selling propositions (USPs).

BENEFITS **Benefits** are at the heart of consumer-centered messages. In benefit strategies the product is promoted on the basis of what it can do for the consumer. Copywriters put themselves in the shoes of the prospect and ask themselves: "What does this mean to me? What can it do for me?" Is the product a bargain? Will it make the prospect healthier, happier, more prosperous, more comfortable, more important, more secure, more attractive? Will it make work easier for the prospect? Will it save the consumer time or money?

To develop a benefit strategy, you must be able to turn an attribute into a benefit. Take a common product, like the shoe you're wearing. Ask yourself what each feature of that shoe does. Look at the sole—besides keeping your feet off the ground, what else does it do for you? Composition leather, for example, means it is durable and long-wearing; textured rubber may mean nonslip; different types of soles have shock-absorption features built in to help diminish the punishment of jogging or aerobics.

To develop a benefit, use the following formula to guide your analysis. First specify how you use the product, then follow with a statement of what it will do for you. Fill in the blanks and you will have developed a benefit statement:

When I use __(product)__, I will get __(what benefit)__

Note that the benefit is strictly in the mind of the consumer, not in the product; it is a subjective experience. Some sample benefit statements are:

- When I take Amtrak, I will be more comfortable, better treated, and more valued (than when I take a plane).
- When I take Excedrin for my headache, I will be better able to cope with the stresses of my life.
- When I stay at Ramada, I will have fewer hassles than when I stay at other hotels.*

PROMISES A **promise** is a benefit statement that looks to the future. It says something will happen if you use a given product. For example, if you use a certain type of toothpaste, then your breath will smell better, or your teeth will be whiter, or you will have extra cavity protection.

You can promise a benefit, so the two are interrelated. What makes a promise distinct is the idea of a future reward, an assurance or pledge that something will happen in the future as a result of product use. An example of a promise is taken from the strategy statement for Dial soap:†

> *Promise:* When you use Dial deodorant soap, you will feel more confident than when you use other brands.

REASON WHY A **reason why** you should buy something is another form of a benefit statement. It differs from a promise in that it clearly states a reason for the benefit gained. In many benefit strategies this reason is unstated or assumed. The reason why you buy and use something is to get a certain benefit. A reason-why statement is based on logic and reasoning. The development of this form is highly rational. A reason-why statement usually begins with a benefit statement, then follows with a "because" statement that provides the "proof" or "support."

For example: This shoe is comfortable *because* it has a unique padded interior. Or: This shoe is good for my foot *because* it has a special arch support. The padded interior and the arch support are both features. They are translated into benefits by the use of a reason-why statement that describes why the feature

*William D. Wells, *Planning for R.O.I.* (Chicago: DDB Needham Worldwide, 1987).
†*Ibid.*

is important. The following are some sample reason-why statements. Notice how the "because" statement is used to give support to the argument in the examples:*

- When I take Amtrak from New York to Washington, I will feel more comfortable, better treated, and more valued than when I take a plane *because* Amtrak is a more civilized and less dehumanizing way to travel.
- When I use Dial deodorant soap, I will be more confident than when I use another brand *because* Dial has twice as much deodorant ingredient as the next-best-selling brand.

UNIQUE SELLING PROPOSITION   The final consumer-oriented selling premise is the most complicated because it includes pieces of other premises such as claims, promises, and benefits. The concept of a **unique selling proposition**, or USP, was developed by Rosser Reeves, the head of the Ted Bates advertising agency.†

The heart of a USP is the *proposition,* a promise that states a specific benefit you will get from buying and using this product. This proposition must, however, be *unique.* If your product has a special formula, design, or feature protected by a patent or copyright, then you are assured that it is truly unique. In addition, the proposition has to be something that, in Reeves's words, will "move the mass millions." In other words, it has to be *relevant* to the prospect.

A USP, then, is a promise of a benefit that is both unique to the product and important to the prospect. A USP is frequently marked by the use of an "only" statement. This can be an outright statement or just implied. For example, the following is a USP taken from the copy for a camera:

> *USP:* This camera is the only one that lets you automatically zoom in and out to follow the action of the central figure.

Using Selling Premises

All of these message strategies are currently used by the industry. Different agencies favor different versions of these premises, but most of them use some structured approach to guide the development of the logic of the sales message.

Support   Regardless of which selling premise an advertiser uses, you should be able to analyze the logic behind the premise. Most selling premises demand facts, proof, or explanations to support the claim, benefit, reason, or promise. A reason why includes the support in the "because" part of the statement. The rest of the selling premises are usually followed by copy that elaborates on the point. A claim, for example, demands some sort of proof or it won't be believed.

An example of a USP and its support is this excerpt from the strategy statement for Hubba Bubba bubble gum:‡

> *USP:* Hubba Bubba is the only chewing gum that lets you blow great big bubbles that won't stick to your face.
> *Proof:* Hubba Bubba uses a unique and exclusive nonstick formula.

Support may be more important than any other part of the message strategy. Remember, support refers to everything in the message that lends credibility to the promise. If the message is to be believable or have impact, it must have support.

Ibid.

†Rosser Reeves, *Reality in Advertising* (New York: Knopf, 1963).

‡Wells, *Planning for R.O.I.*

---

unique selling proposition *A benefit statement about a feature that is both unique to the product and important to the user.*

PRINCIPLE
Support makes the selling premise believable.

The Creative Platform

Copy or creative platforms vary from agency to agency. Some of them are elaborate, but most are simple. The model used here is complex because we are trying to explain all of the concepts that you might encounter at various agencies. Our elaborate platform, then, includes all seven of the basic advertising strategy decisions plus the three message strategy decisions. A complete copy platform follows.

Creative Platform

- Advertising Strategy:
  1. Problem and opportunity
  2. Objectives
  3. Target audience
  4. Competitive product advantage
  5. Product or brand personality
  6. Position in the marketplace

- Message Strategy:
  1. Appeal
  2. Associations
  3. Selling premise (claim, benefit, promise, reason why, or USP)

SUMMARY

- Strategy involves choosing the best approach for many alternatives.

- A marketing plan analyzes the situation, identifies the problems and opportunities, sets objectives, and proposes strategies.

- Advertising objectives focus on communication, or message-related, effects. Marketing objectives focus on sales.

- Advertising tries to turn problems into opportunities.

- Competitive advantage identifies those product features where you are strong and your competitors are vulnerable.

- Product personalities affect how consumers feel about products and brands.

- A position is where the consumer locates the product relative to the competition.

- An appeal is something that moves people.

- The selling premise states the logic of the sales message.

- A benefit states what the product will do for the user.

QUESTIONS

1. What do advertisers mean by "strategy?" What are the key considerations in an advertising strategy?

2. What is targeting? Why is it important to advertisers?

3. What is a creative platform, and what is its strategic function?

4. Think of a product you have purchased recently. How was it advertised? Which strategies can you discern in the advertising? Did the advertising help to convince you to purchase the product? Why or why not?

FURTHER READINGS

AAKER, DAVID, and JOHN G. MYERS. *Advertising Management,* 3rd ed. Englewood Cliffs, NJ: Prentice Hall, 1987.

ANDERSON, ROBERT L., and THOMAS E. BARRY. *Advertising Management: Text and Cases.* Columbus, OH: Charles E. Merrill Publishing, 1979.

ENGEL, JAMES F., MARTIN R. WARSHAW, and THOMAS C. KINNEAR. *Promotional Strategy,* 6th ed. Homewood, IL: Irwin, 1987.

GREYSER, STEPHEN. *Advertising and Communications Management,* 2nd ed. Englewood Cliffs, NJ: Prentice Hall, 1981.

RAY, MICHAEL. *Advertising and Communication Management.* Englewood Cliffs, NJ: Prentice Hall, 1982.

SACHS, WILLIAM S. *Advertising Management: Its Role in Marketing.* Tulsa, OK: PennWell Books, 1983.

SHIMP, TERENCE A., and M. WAYNE DELOZIER. *Promotion Management and Marketing Communications.* Chicago: The Dryden Press, 1986.

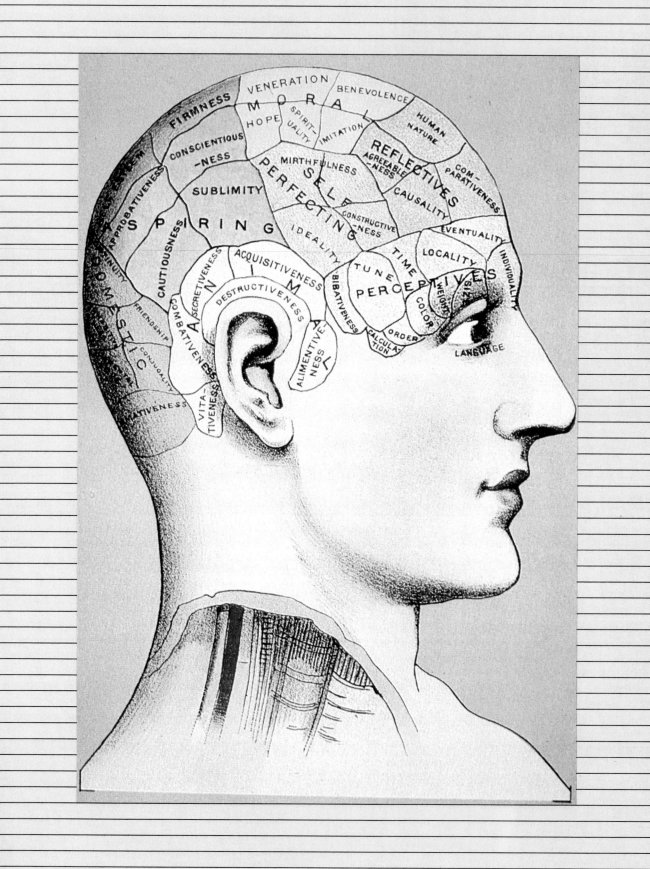

8

How Advertising Works

Chapter Outline

Lessons from Real Life
How Ads Really Work
The Psychology of How an Ad Works
How Brand Images Work

Chapter Objectives

When you have completed this chapter you should be able to:

- Understand the barriers that an effective advertisement must overcome
- Be familiar with the different levels on which a viewer or reader will react to an ad
- Explain the different functions of an ad
- Explain what "breakthrough advertising" is and how it works

LESSONS FROM REAL LIFE

John, a 39-year-old father of two girls, has just arrived home from work. He is sitting in front of the television watching the news. At the same time he is working his way through the newspaper that he didn't have time to read before work.

As he pages through the newspaper, he is scanning the headlines and looking at the photos with one eye and watching the television set with the other. Actually his attention is moving back and forth between the set and the paper. Occasionally a newspaper headline catches his attention and he stops and reads a little bit of the story. Then he hears something interesting on television and looks up to watch it for a while.

Right now he is looking at a story on a problem one of the major automakers is having with a new model. He reads the first couple of paragraphs, gets the gist of the story, finds he is not all that interested, and goes back to scanning. He probably spent 5 seconds on the auto story.

All of a sudden the news on television moves to a chase scene involving a couple of teenagers who stole a car. Attracted by the action and noise, he lets the paper drop while he watches the chase. As the police walk up to the crashed car, his attention shifts back to the paper. He probably spent 25 seconds following the chase.

Then the girls come in from playing with friends. When they leave, he looks back to the television just in time for a commercial break. He starts to get up to go to the refrigerator to get a beer, but the first commercial is for tortilla chips and the scenes are all from the Southwest. That reminds him of an upcoming sales meeting that he has to attend in Albuquerque. He watches the spot all the way through its 30 seconds. The next spot is for a toilet bowl cleaner, so he heads to the kitchen and returns with his beer.

The last commercial is playing out, so he picks up the newspaper and sees an ad for a new income tax guide. Ugh! He still hasn't put his records in order and the deadline is approaching, so he tears out the ad. That took about 5 seconds; he can't force himself to spend a lot of time thinking about taxes.

He hears a distinctive piece of music and looks up to see that one of his favorite commercials is on. He watches it for its full 30 seconds. The next commercial, however, is for a feminine-hygiene product. He changes the channel to see what is on another station.

John finds nothing but ads on the other channels, so he changes the channel back to the original station and turns to the next section of the paper, which is the sports section. For the next 5 minutes he carefully reads the main stories. Nothing that happens on television can get through to him. At the bottom of the last story is an ad for tires, and he checks the prices because he needs new tires for the van. He tears the ad out and thinks he had better start looking for other ads to see how these prices compare.

The girls come in and ask if they can change the channel to MTV. He looks up and notices that the newscaster is just signing off. He starts to hand them the remote control but just then one of those beer commercials comes on that he thinks is really funny. He yells for his wife to come watch. When the commercial is over, he gives the girls the remote control and goes to the kitchen to see what he can do to help with dinner.

Competition

This little scenario isn't necessarily typical of how everyone watches television and reads the newspaper, but it does represent a lot of the behaviors that advertisers know must be accommodated when they plan an advertising message.

For example, there is a lot of *competition* for people's attention. Other media, other ads, news stories, family, and random thoughts get in the way of very expensive and carefully constructed commercial messages.

Inattention

In addition, most people only give advertising their *divided attention*. A few ads may break through and receive some kind of concentration, but that is very rare. At best an ad gets half the mind and one eye.

Advertisers are also up against a *short attention span*. Human concentration happens in quick bursts. A compelling story may get a minute or two of concentrated time, but most media messages can only count on a few seconds. The actual information that gets attended to, then, is nothing more than a quick impression or a **message fragment.**

message fragment *A quick impression that gets filed away in the memory; highlights, but not details.*

Information Processing

Besides problems with attention, there are problems sorting out the information. Media messages become entangled in what cognitive psychologists call our *information processing*.

Our minds are not tidy. For example, most people reading a newspaper or magazine don't see much difference between editorial information and advertisements. They browse, scan, jump back and forth, and find snippets of useful information in both categories. In newspapers and magazines ads are often welcomed—ads are news, too. Furthermore, print ads are not forced on people. They can be scanned or ignored, but the decision to follow through and read or to jump to another message is the reader's.

Every time John watches a commercial, he has to make a similar decision whether to attend to it. The decision is always there, even though he may not be aware of it. If he makes a commitment, it lasts only as long as his interest is maintained by the message. When he loses interest, his attention shifts, and he moves on to some other message.

Avoidance

Bombarded with a huge number of commercials on television, John has become very good at avoidance. When watching television he doesn't even scan the ads that don't interest him. He leaves the room, changes channels, or turns his attention elsewhere. He probably avoids at least half of the commercials. Typically he notes the first one in a cluster; then, depending upon whether it catches his attention, he may or may not be around for the remaining messages. He probably pays full attention only to very few commercials.

Scorn

Furthermore many consumers are scornful of advertising. A recent national survey found that 60 percent of consumers agreed that "advertising insults my

Dramatic, colorful, and unusual events can capture and maintain interest.

(Courtesy of J. J. Clark/The Stock Market.)

intelligence" and over 70 percent agreed that they "don't believe a company's ad when it claims test results show its product to be better than competitive products."* Disbelief and dislike are very important parts of the consumer response to advertising.

Breakthrough Advertising

Finally, this little story dramatizes how few advertisements actually get read or watched. John may scan most of the stories and ads in the newspaper, but with limited concentration. Maybe only half of the ads actually get noticed on a "thinking" level. Perhaps only 20 percent get read a little, and very few are read thoroughly.

Advertising that makes any impact at all has to break through the inattention and the mindless scanning; it has to help consumers sort out and remember what they see and hear; and it has to overcome the patterns of avoidance and scorn. Such advertising is called *breakthrough advertising*. It is novel, compelling, and interesting. It speaks to the concerns of its audience on a personal level without being patronizing or phony.

*T*HE PSYCHOLOGY OF HOW AN AD WORKS

How does advertising work? This is a very complex question. One thing we know is that advertising may be communicating a number of messages in a number of areas simultaneously. For example, at the same time you are trying to understand a copy point, you may also be forming a favorable or an unfavorable opinion of the product. The message's impact on both knowledge and liking can happen simultaneously.†

For that reason the following discussion will analyze how advertising works in terms of three basic psychological categories. One of the categories, *perception,* is a foundation for the other two, *cognition* and *persuasion.*

*Stephen J. Hoch and Young-Won Ha, "Consumer Learning: Advertising and the Ambiguity of Product Experience," *Journal of Consumer Research,* September 1986, pp. 221–33.

†Sandra E. Moriarty, "Beyond the Hierarchy of Effects: A Conceptual Model," in *Current Issues and Research in Advertising,* James H. Leigh and Claude R. Martin, Jr., eds. (Ann Arbor: University of Michigan Graduate School of Business, 1983), pp. 45–56.

Perception

When something has been perceived, it has been noted; the message has registered. If you are an advertiser trying to reach our friend John with either a newspaper or a television message, one of your biggest problems is simply to get him to notice it. As you can tell from our opening story, this is a little harder than it first appears. John probably misses half the messages directed at him. And what about all those commercials that are on other channels that he is not watching and in other newspapers that he is not reading? Simple *exposure* is the first step in perception.

Exposure Exposure is primarily a media-buying problem. First the message has to be in a medium that John sees, reads, watches, or listens to. In addition, the message must survive the initial scan-and-avoidance decision. In other words, exposure is also dependent upon whether the message is attractive enough to keep the viewer or reader from changing the channel or turning the page. Exposure is therefore the minimum requirement for perception. If John has switched the channel, then no matter how great the message is, it will *not* be perceived.

Attention Attention means the mind is engaged, that it is focusing on something. Attention is aroused by a **trigger,** something that "catches" attention. It can be something in the message or something within the reader or viewer that makes him or her "lock onto" a particular message.

Attention is triggered by something. In print it may be a sale price, a startling illustration, or a strong headline. On television the trigger may be sound effects, music, a scene that is action-oriented or visually interesting, or a captivating phrase or thought. For an example of an attention-grabbing ad see Ad 8.1 (p. 196).

Getting attention, however, involves more than just attracting the notice of the viewer or reader. When John is in the scanning mode, his attention is wandering. To nail it down to one story or ad requires some kind of **stopping power.**

Once John's attention has shifted to the ad or article, he has to decide whether or not it interests him. Interest is usually based on something personal

trigger *Something that catches attention and sets off a complex set of consumer responses.*

stopping power *The ability of an ad to capture and maintain audience interest.*

Exposure to a message does not guarantee that the audience is paying attention.

(Courtesy of Barbara Kirk/The Stock Market.)

TRAIN TRAVELERS: WHO ARE THEY?

Appealing to the emotions, attitudes, and convictions of a particular audience is a major challenge in advertising. An advertisement is not only a statement of information about a product or service. It must also grab the viewer's attention, entice the viewer to continue paying attention, and, hopefully, persuade the viewer to purchase that product. To create an effective campaign, advertisers need to know more about what attracts potential customers. To learn more about their audience, Amtrak made use of a lifestyle study of train travelers.

Profile

In the study, train travelers are defined as people who have taken at least one train trip of over 100 miles within 12 months. The study found this group to be well educated and more likely than non-train travelers to have graduated from college and to have managerial and professional jobs.

Train travelers are very sociable and take part in many activities. They are more likely than non-train travelers to take part in exercise and sports activities, including exercise classes. They enjoy cultural and educational activities such as visiting art galleries and museums, attending lectures and concerts, and going to movies and rock concerts.

The media habits of train travelers differ from those of non-train travelers. Train travelers are less likely to consider television to be their "primary form of entertainment" and often find magazines more interesting. They have a positive attitude toward advertising, which they consider to be a source of consumer information. They are also more likely to buy products of companies that support educational television. As consumers, train travelers are more careful and demand more information before making purchases. For example, they are more likely to shop for specials, check prices on smaller items, and consult *Consumer Reports* on the purchase of larger items. They also make greater use of toll-free numbers to get information about products and services.

Marketing and Promotion Recommendations

The study included several recommendations for increasing the effectiveness of Amtrak's advertising programs. Below is a summary of these suggestions.

Advertising Themes The report offered several messages that could be used in advertising. For example, it suggested highlighting the "adventurous spirit" of train travel as well as the "heritage of railroads." Another approach was to differentiate train travel from air travel by showing how scenery "unfolds before the traveler's eyes." Because many train travelers enjoy foreign travel, an "exotic, foreign, or far-away flavor" was proposed as a theme. Other approaches were to emphasize the sensations of speed and motion and to stress the opportunity to meet new people on a train trip.

Amenities The report suggested that train travelers might like different types of entertainment and a more "cosmopolitan" atmosphere. Some of the amenities suggested included: music programming, free literature about sites on the train's route, movies, videotaped television shows (such as "60 Minutes" or PBS shows), an exercise car, and special Amtrak greeting cards and postcards featuring destinations, sites, or the train itself.

Packages and Promotions The study also suggested that Amtrak should strengthen its ties to travel agencies for both booking reservations and arranging package tours and vacation getaways. Suggestions included "frequent rider" programs, joint train tours of the United States and Canada, package tours of theme parks, and gift certificates to major department stores or restaurants in a destination city. The report also suggested continuing Amtrak's toll-free reservations number.

Source: DDB Needham Worldwide, Life-Style Profile of Train Travelers, August 1986.

or something intriguing. John has some predispositions that affect what interests him: a deck that he wants to build, the dread of income tax, a trip to the Southwest, a car that needs tires. If a message applies to his life, if it affects him personally, then he will have an interest. He may also respond to general "human interest"—in other words, a topic that strikes some universal chord in all of us, such as babies, kittens, and puppies.

Different topics, different product categories, and different products have different levels of *built-in interest*. Some products are just inherently more interesting than others—food and vacations, for example, are more interesting than toilet cleaners. Some products are of interest to specific groups of people. John would look at an ad for tires but avoid an ad for a feminine-hygiene product.

Awareness Awareness can be achieved only if there is some measure of attention. Awareness implies that the message has made an impression on the viewer or reader, who can subsequently identify the advertiser or product. Awareness is a low-level form of impact, but it is the goal of a great many ads. A simple recognition test can determine whether an ad has created product awareness.

Attention and awareness are message-design problems. The advertising message can, and must, compete with other messages in the same medium. Within a news medium, the advertising has to be able to compete with the intrinsically interesting nature of news. In an entertainment medium like television, the advertising has to compete with the mesmerizing entertainment values of programming. Radio is almost always a background medium, and outdoor advertising is directed toward an audience whose attention, by definition, is directed elsewhere. Not only does outdoor advertising have to compete for attention, it has to be able to win out over distractions such as other signs along the road, the car radio or tape deck, and conversations with passengers.

Relatively low levels of attention can create a minimal level of awareness for low-interest products. If the objective is simply brand or product reminder, then the attention level doesn't need to be as high as it does when the objective calls for the understanding of a copy point.

selective perception *The tendency in most people to see or hear only information they agree with.*

Selection Attention to an advertising message is complicated by a process psychologists call **selective perception.** People hear what they want to hear and remember information that agrees with their personal views. We all have our own predispositions and preconceptions. If we hear something we don't agree with, we will either turn it off, tune it out, or manipulate the message in our minds so it sounds like something we can agree with. In advertising people tend to listen to messages about products they like. This is a real problem for a new product or for a product in an unpopular category like laxatives.

Advertisers who realize this design the ad so that the message will grab audience attention in spite of disinterest. One way to accomplish this is to begin with a related concept or association that is acceptable and then make a transition to the difficult information after you have the audience's attention. Of course, some material is selected out because it is simply inappropriate. For example, when John saw the beginning of a commercial for a feminine-hygiene product, he wasn't in the target, so he selected himself out.

PRINCIPLE _____
Impact means the message must be strong enough to break through the indifference, stop the scanning, arouse attention, and make an impression on the prospect.

Impact The term *impact* refers to an advertisement's ability to overcome audience indifference and focus sharp attention on the message. We already know that most advertisements just "wash over" their audiences without any effect. However, effective advertisements with impact strike a responsive chord. They are intrusive without being obnoxious, and they seize attention while they penetrate the mind.

Intrusive Although impact is always desirable, it is especially important for products that have a small "share of mind." In other words, the actual products are not very involving or interesting, or there is little difference between competing brands. When there is little product interest, the impact has to be created solely by the advertising message.

intrusive *A message that is not wanted by the audience; it uses techniques to force attention.*

Television commercials are **intrusive,** and viewers often resent the intrusion because they feel captive to the television set. Like John, they have a

THE IRRITATION FACTOR

Everyone loves to hate the "ring around your collar" commercials, and more people make fun of Mr. Whipple than any other television celebrity. Why do advertisers use these techniques when viewers find them so irritating? Why do people like some commercials and despise others? Irritating ads are defined as those that cause displeasure and momentary impatience. The response is more negative than simply *dislike*.

Research has found that disliked advertising might still work because it generates high levels of attention and recall. Everyone does remember Mr. Whipple, after all. Even if consumers dislike these commercials, when they get to the store they remember the product name and forget their irritation at the ad. It does seem to make sense, though, that viewer's negative perceptions of the message would carry over to the product itself. One might wonder if those irritating commercials are successful in spite of the message strategy rather than because of it.

Research into irritating advertising has found that a major source of irritation is the product itself; for ex-ample, feminine-hygiene products, underwear, laxatives, and hemorrhoid treatments. Regarding message strategy, irritation levels are higher when the situation is contrived, phony, unbelievable, or overdramatized. In the case of a sensitive product, the ads are more irritating when the product and its use are emphasized; indirect approaches seem to work better. Viewers also don't like to see people "put down" or forced into stereotypical roles. Neither do they like to see important relationships threatened, such as mother-daughter or husband-wife.

What do you think about the irritation factor in advertising? Can you remember any ads that you particularly disliked? Can you remember some that you liked? Why did you react that way? Are there products and situations where it isn't important for the commercial to be liked? If a particular commercial is irritating and unpopular but the product sells well, should that commercial be considered a success? Why or why not?

Source: David A. Aaker and Donald E. Bruzzone, "Causes of Irritation in Advertising," *Journal of Marketing,* Spring 1985, pp. 47–57.

AD 8.1
This ad for Busch Gardens amusement park uses bold graphics to attract viewer attention.
(Courtesy of DDB Needham Worldwide.)

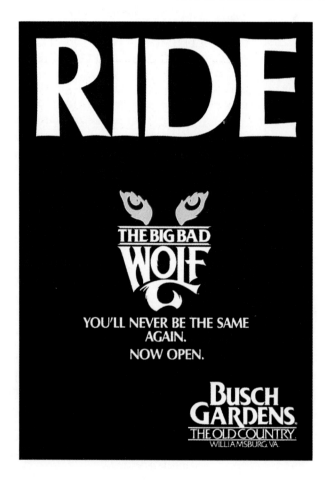

well-developed habit of leaving the room or changing the channel when ads come on. There is no guaranteed audience for any advertisement.

If you are designing an advertisement, what can you do to create impact? Obvious shouting is one common technique. Many ads use loud, bold effects to attract viewer attention. This is typical of a hard-sell approach to advertising. Bold, startling graphics also create impact, as is illustrated by Ad 8.1 for Busch Gardens.

For print ads, research has found that *contrast* can attract viewer attention. If every other ad in the medium is big and bold, then be small, quiet, and simple—use a lot of white space. If everything is tiny and gray (like type), then be bold and black—or use color. If everything is colorful, then use black and white. Identify the characteristics of the medium environment and then do something different.

Originality   Another important factor in creating impact is *originality*. Originality means the advertising message is fresh, novel, and unusual. It breaks through all the old patterns without being irrelevant or bizarre. The unexpectedness of the idea or thought is what creates stopping power.

Outrageous effects can also create impact. An article in *The New York Times* described an effort at the Young & Rubicam (Y&R) agency to push its creative people to take more risks to make their ads more distinctive. For an Irish Spring ad the agency used a fully clothed man with a bar of soap in his hand. By all appearances, he is about to launch into a standard pitch. Suddenly the ad turns slapstick. He loses control of the soap. It squirts him in the face and lathers up in his pocket. Such unorthodox ideas are being used successfully by Y&R to sell things like toothpaste, coffee, and ice cream.

To encourage this kind of freewheeling thinking Y&R set up a program called The Risk Lab that allowed copywriters and art directors to have their ideas informally tested by researchers in the early stages of concept development. The director of creative research, Dr. Stephanie Kugelman, took the title "Dr. Risk" and moved to the creative floors to work closely with the creative people.

As an example of daring to do something different, Y&R used a set of teeth 17 feet tall as an attention-getting device in a tartar-control ad for Colgate. A consumer during a research session described tartar as a "wall" and that image became the creative concept. The action showed a construction crew inside the "mouth" painting tartar on the teeth. The commercial was used first in England, and people were so intrigued they even asked to see it again. It also contributed to a huge increase in Colgate's share of the toothpaste market.[*]

Personal Interest   Another important stopper is *personal interest*. People want to hear or read about themselves and the things they care about. They want to know how to improve certain skills, look better, make more money, or save themselves time and expense. Remember John: He's sitting there saying, "What's in it for me? Make it worth my time and I'll pay attention to your message." Advertisers make sure the target gets something worthwhile from the product.

Cognition

Cognition refers to a conscious mental effort to understand the information being presented. Attention can be a relatively passive response, but cognition of any kind involves an active response from the audience. The cognitive effects of a message lie in interest, knowledge, and memory. First we find ourselves inter-

[*] Eileen Prescott, "An Agency's Turn to Madcap Ads," *The New York Times,* June 7, 1987, pp. 1, 8–9.

AD 8.2

The stopping power for this ad comes from the combination of a popular celebrity and an opening question. The viewer must follow the entire commercial to discover what makes John Madden mad.

(Courtesy of Ramada Inc.)

ested in some piece of information, then we learn something about it, then we file it away in our memory.

Interest   Interest is generated by curiosity—you want to know more. It can be accompanied by disbelief, doubt, or puzzlement. Whatever the stimulus, curiosity provides the "cognitive nudge" that engages a person's mind. Whenever you are confronted with something new, there is a period of curiosity, usually caused by doubt or some kind of questioning. New information is often greeted by phrases like "I don't believe it" or "Can you believe it?" This confrontation means you have now entered the *interested* state.

If you are trying to develop a message that stimulates interest, then you will probably do something to elicit curiosity, to make your target want to know more. Ads that open with questions or dubious statements are high in stopping power. For a colorful example see the John Madden ad for Ramada Inns.

Ambiguity   A message that can be interpreted several ways is described as *ambiguous*. Ambiguity can be used to stimulate interest. It asks the readers or viewers to construct their own version of the story. The advertiser is willing to trade off directness for the engaging power of curiosity.

Ambiguity can be a gamble. Challenges and other approaches that are thought-provoking are good at engaging interest. However, recent research suggests that ambiguity should be avoided for everyday products. It is probably more effective for messages that involve fantasy and out-of-the-ordinary situations.*

Maintaining Interest   Interest is a momentary thing, and it dies easily as attention shifts. A major problem in advertising is to maintain interest long enough to get to the point of the message. Because of the scanning and browsing behavior of many readers and viewers, maintaining interest is more difficult than developing it initially.

If you are worried about maintaining interest in an advertisement, then you must consider the *pulling power* of your message. This is primarily a sequencing problem: Does your copy pull the reader or viewer through to the end? How does the message develop? For example, if you start with a question, then the reader has to continue through the ad to find the answer. Storytelling is a good technique to keep the audience with you. Most people want to know how a story comes out. Suspense, drama, and narrative are good literary tools for maintaining interest.

PRINCIPLE

Have something interesting to say, something that has stopping power and pulling power.

Effective ads must attract the viewer's attention and convey the desired information.

(Courtesy of Bob Shaw/The Stock Market.)

*Hoch and Young-Won Ha, "Consumer Learning," pp. 221–33.

THE MOST POWERFUL EFFICIENT ENGINE EVER BUILT OR SOLD IN AMERICA.

It's GM's Quad 4 engine, an achievement of GM people, developed by Oldsmobile, and called by Business Week, "the little engine that could."

This new world-class powerplant will be available this fall from Oldsmobile, Pontiac, and Buick. The Quad 4 has its heritage in such milestone GM engines as the Cadillac V-16, the Chevrolet Straight 6, and the Oldsmobile Rocket V-8. Yet, it is unlike anything GM has ever produced before.

The Quad 4 has the horsepower of an 8-cylinder and, for the power it delivers over its rpm range, it's the most fuel-efficient, normally aspirated gasoline engine ever mass produced. Its many advanced features make the Quad 4 so clean-burning that it doesn't need the usual complex emission controls. It is designed for reliability as well as easy servicing and maintenance. The high precision of its componentry has set new standards for the entire industry.

To develop the Quad 4—the only state-of-the-art, 16-valve,

4-cylinder engine made in America—we literally started from scratch, reworking nothing and rebuilding nothing. Together with the United Auto Workers, we pioneered new production methods in one of the world's most modern plants in Lansing, Michigan.

Our engineers put prototypes of the Quad 4 through 6.7 million miles of testing, including the most rigorous test they ever ran on a single engine: on a test stand the Quad 4 ran at 100 mph for 100,000 miles. That's like running wide open for 40 days and 40 nights. Then, last month, on the road, a modified version set a world closed-course speed record of better than 257 mph. In its combination of power and efficiency, there's never been anything like it.

The Quad 4 is still another tangible payoff to our customers on GM's investments in technology and people. We have a vision and a commitment to the future, to an American industrial renaissance. And GM is leading the way.

GM

THE VISION IS PAYING OFF.

AD 8.3
An example of an ad using a straightforward, educational approach.
(Reproduced courtesy of General Motors Corporation.)

Television has built-in sequencing with the moving image. If skillfully used, the motion and action of a video message are very hard to ignore. A layout in a print ad can do the same thing. A layout can be designed with strong direction or movement cues that keep the eye of the reader engaged.

Knowledge   Another part of the cognitive problem is knowledge and learning. Teaching is a very important element of advertising, though it is not often appreciated. In the case of new products, ads must bridge the gap in people's experience by teaching them how to recognize and use the product. Some brand advertising is primarily designed to teach people how to say the name and recognize the package. This may be simple identification, but it is learning nonetheless.

Understanding   A more complicated form of learning involves the *understanding* of copy points. Understanding means that the reader or viewer is able to follow the logic, make discriminations, compare and contrast points of view, comprehend reasons and arguments, synthesize and organize facts, and, in general, make sense of things. If you are designing an advertising message where understanding is an objective, then you are probably dealing with factually based information, and you will be testing the effectiveness of your message by recall methods. Knowledge means the facts have been acquired through experience or study. Your ad must present the facts in a way that makes it easy for people to assimilate the information. Clarity is important.

An example of an educational approach was found in a recent automotive ad by General Motors that focused on a new engine called the "Quad 4." This ad was not for any particular auto, it simply explained the features of the engine (see Ad 8.3).

The literary tools of a message designed to stimulate understanding include definition, explanation, demonstration, comparison, and contrast. Definition and explanation are primarily verbal concepts, but demonstration, comparison, and contrast are often communicated in visuals. Any visual, whether print or video, can be used to compare two products or show before-and-after scenarios. Television is particularly good for demonstration because it can show a sequence of operations.

Memory   One of the most important aspects of cognition is memory. It is very important to advertisers that their messages get locked into people's minds. If John can't remember seeing the ad, then he might as well have not seen it at all. When John goes to the discount store, it is important that he remember that soft drinks are on sale, as he noted in the paper, and that the brand he saw advertised on television is popular with his daughter's friends. How does that happen?

Our memories are like filing cabinets. John watches a message, extracts parts of it that interest him, and then finds a category in his mental filing cabinet where he can store that little fragment of information. The fragment, incidentally, may not look much like the original information as it was presented because John's mind will operate on it to make it fit into his own system of concerns and preconceptions.

A week later he may not remember that he has a fragment labeled "soft drink" filed away, or he may not be able to find it in the file. Most of us have messy filing systems. You have probably found yourself trying to remember something that you know. You can concentrate until your head hurts and the thought just won't come to the surface.

Memorability   If you are designing a message and want to ensure its memorability, there are several things you can do. One technique is *repetition*. Psychologists maintain that you need to hear something three times before it crosses the threshold of perception and enters into memory. **Jingles** are valuable memorability devices because the music makes it possible to repeat a phrase or product name without boring the audience. The Energizer® battery commercial pictured in Ad 8.4 uses repetition to hammer home a claim as well as the product identity. The claim "lasts longer" is repeated three times, and the product name is repeated four times, twice in a clever phrase, "The extraordinary Energizer."

Clever phrases and riveting visuals also contribute to memorability. Advertisements use **slogans** for brands and campaigns (a series of ads run under some kind of thematic umbrella). Slogans are written so that they are highly memorable. **Taglines** are clever phrases that are used at the end to summarize the point of the ad's message in a highly memorable way.

In addition to jingles and slogans, most television commercials utilize a **key visual.** This is a dominant visual that the advertiser hopes will be left in the mind of the viewer. Remember that the memory's filing system usually stores fragments of information. Television is primarily a visual medium, and an effective commercial is built on some dominant scene or piece of action that conveys the essence of the message and can be easily remembered.

There is also a structural dimension to memorability. Just as the beginning of an advertising message is the most important part for attracting attention, the end or closing of a message is the most important part for memorability. If you want someone to remember the product name, repeat it at the end of the commercial. Most print ads end with a **logo** (a distinctive mark that identifies the product or company) or a **signature** (the name of the company or brand written in a distinctive type style). Television commercials will **superimpose** the product name on the last visual, accompanied by the announcer repeating the name.

jingles *Commercials with a message that is presented musically.*

slogans *Frequently repeated phrases that provide continuity to an advertising campaign.*

taglines *Clever phrases used at the end of an advertisement to summarize the ad's message.*

key visual *A dominant image around which the commercial's message is planned.*

logo *Logotype; a distinctive mark that identifies the product, company, or brand.*

signature *The name of the company or product written in a distinctive type style.*

superimpose *A television technique where one image is added to another that is already on the screen.*

ENERGIZER®

EVEREADY BATTERY COMPANY, INC.
30 Second Television Commercial

Commercial No.: RPEN3230
Commercial Title: "Train"

(OPEN WITH DRIVING MUSIC TRACK)

JACKO: OY!

(MUSIC)

All aboard.

I'm gonna

surprise ya.

Here's what ya need --

the Energizer.

CHORUS: TOO RIGHT. THE EXTRAORDINARY ENERGIZER.

(MUSIC)

JACKO: It took the test.

It settled

the score.

This battery's best. It gives you more.

CHORUS: TOO RIGHT. THE EXTRAORDINARY ENERGIZER.

ANNCR (VO): Laboratory tests prove in most devices

Energizer lasts longer than any other battery.

CONDUCTOR: End-a-the-line.

JACKO: Not for me Energizer. Get Energizer.

CHORUS: OY!

AD 8.4

This ad for Energizer batteries, starring former Australian football player Jacko Jackson, uses repetition to make its point. How many times are the product name and claim used in this one ad? Within 2 months this campaign had increased consumer awareness of the product by almost 30 percent.

(Courtesy of Ralston Purina Company.)

SLOGAN TEST

The following is a list of famous slogans. How many can you identify? What does this test tell you about the role of slogans in establishing product memorability?

_____	1. Like a good neighbor	a.	Prell
_____	2. Head for the mountains	b.	Secret
_I_	3. Thank you for your support	c.	Kodak
_____	4. If you care enough to send the very best	d.	General Electric
_I_	5. Own a piece of the rock	e.	Wheaties
_u_	6. Be all you can be	f.	Master Charge
_____	7. Taste as good as they crunch	g.	Merrill Lynch
_T_	8. Carry the big fresh flavor	h.	Doritos
_____	9. A breed apart	i.	Prudential
_____	10. Let the good times roll	j.	Bartles & Jaymes
_F_	11. We circle the world	k.	State Farm
_R_	12. You deserve a break today	l.	Chevrolet
_E_	13. Breakfast of champions	m.	Visine
_____	14. Gets the red out	n.	Johnson's Baby Shampoo
_b_	15. Strong enough for a man, but made for a woman	o.	Polaroid
_N_	16. Gentle enough to use every day	p.	*Wall Street Journal*
		q.	Ford
_C_	17. America's storyteller	r.	McDonald's
_____	18. Today is the first day of the rest of your life	s.	Kawasaki
_D_	19. We bring good things to life	t.	Wrigley Spearmint
_Q_	20. Quality is Job 1	u.	Army
		v.	Hallmark
		w.	Busch
		x.	Pringles

(Answers: 1-k, 2-w, 3-j, 4-v, 5-i, 6-u, 7-h, 8-t, 9-s, 10-s, 11-f, 12-r, 13-e, 14-m, 15-b, 16-n, 17-c, 18-p, 19-d, 20-q)

One of the greatest challenges in the advertising world is to create memorability. It is easier to create a memorable advertisement than it is to create an advertisement that makes the product memorable. Testing has proved time and again that people often remember the commercial but not the product. This problem, called **vampire creativity,** occurs primarily with advertisements that are too original, too entertaining, or too involving. The story of the commercial can be so mesmerizing that it gets in the way of the product. It is essential that the commercial establish a strong link between the message and the product so that remembering the story also means remembering the product.

Persuasion

In addition to providing information, advertisements must persuade people to believe or do something. A persuasive message will try to establish, reinforce, or change an attitude, build an argument, touch an emotion, or anchor a conviction firmly in the prospect's belief structure. How do people feel about the product—do they like it or hate it? How do they feel about the ad?

Attitudes and Opinions Beliefs, attitudes, and values structure our opinions, which in turn reflect how negatively or positively we feel about something.

This is how we *evaluate* the information we receive.

People's opinions are built on a complex structure of attitudes. Every person has a different attitude structure based on individual experiences. Advertising that seeks to affect this complex structure of attitudes will usually attempt to accomplish one of three things:

1. Establish a new opinion where none has existed before
2. Reinforce an existing opinion
3. Change an existing opinion

New opinions need to be created when a new product is introduced. If this is your goal, then you can assume the slate is clean, and your advertising will be a primary force in the development of the target audience's initial opinion about your product. Consumer opinion concerning the product or service, of course, will be modified or confirmed as the product is used. No matter how strong your advertising, a bad experience with a new product will negate all of the positive attitudes your message has implanted.

brand loyalty *Existing positive opinions held by consumers about the product or service.*

Likability   Likability is an important indicator of positive attitudes toward a product or a message. An advertiser will try to build positive attitudes for new products and maintain existing positive attitudes for successful mature products. When a product is liked well enough by consumers to generate repeat sales, that is called **brand loyalty.**

It is more unusual, and much harder, to try to change attitudes. If your product has a negative image—perhaps because the initial product or marketing strategy was faulty—then a major objective is to turn that consumer attitude around. This is very difficult and requires both a big budget and a major media blitz.

Miller beer, for example, was originally seen as a woman's beer. Its slogan, "The champagne of bottled beer," spoke to that audience but turned off the male audience, which, in the 1950s and 1960s, consumed more beer than women did. After the Philip Morris Company bought Miller, the beer was repositioned as a man's product, and the subsequent advertising campaigns ignored that original slogan and, instead, used scenes of "macho" males in "tough guy" roles.

Twizzlers, a licorice candy, had a category problem. It had to compete against such big names as Tootsie Roll in the "chewy candy" subcategory of the candy market. The target for these candies is generally teens and children. Although most people like candy, licorice is not as well accepted. DDB Needham took on the challenge and created a strikingly visual campaign based on "singing mouths." (see Ad 8.5). Sales increased by 30 percent during the first year of the campaign. While all its competitors lost share, Twizzler increased nearly 10 percent to 37 percent. Despite the limited growth by Twizzler's competition, the category grew at a rate of 7 percent, most of which represented Twizzler's growth.*

Arguments   Persuasive messages deal with more than just basic attitude structure. People are persuaded by argument or reasoning. Reasons are based on logic and the development of an argument. Argument in this sense refers, not to a disagreement, but to a line of reasoning where one point follows from another, leading up to a conclusion. Your ad must focus on logic and proof when you are dealing with reasons. That is why the "reason-why" selling premise is a very common message strategy used in advertising.

Emotions   Persuasion is also concerned with emotions. How someone "feels" about your product, service, brand, or company is just as important as what that person knows about it. *Feeling* in this sense refers to an attitude, but it

*"Twizzler Case Study," unpublished document by DDB Needham, Chicago, 1986.

AD 8.5
An example of the types of colorful ads that enabled Twizzlers to grow at a much faster rate than the competition.
(Courtesy of DDB Needham Worldwide and Hershey Foods Corporation.)

is an attitude surrounded by emotions. The intensity of the response comes from the emotions. If you touch someone's emotions with your message, he or she is more likely to remember the message.

Many of our buying decisions are emotional ones. We buy shoes because we don't want to go barefoot, but we buy a closetful of shoes for reasons other than necessity. different styles for different occasions and different moods. We often use "logical" surface reasons to justify emotional decisions that we seldom acknowledge.

Convictions Attitudes, reasons, logic, and emotion are all part of the persuasive package. What they lead to is belief. We believe something about every product we purchase; if we didn't, we wouldn't buy it. We believe it is good for us, it will make us look better or live better, or it will make us richer or healthier. Even low-involvement products like chewing gum involve some belief system. I buy this brand of gum rather than another one because I believe this gum will taste better, freshen my breath, or do less damage to my teeth.

A conviction is a particularly strong belief that has been anchored firmly in the attitude structure. It is built of strong rational arguments that use such techniques as test results, before-and-after visuals, and demonstrations to prove something. Opinions based on convictions are very hard to change. Changing such a belief may mean completely rebuilding our entire attitude structure, which is a difficult and painful process. However, an advertiser who can build conviction in the target audience about a product or service achieves a virtually unassailable position.

AD 8.6
Ads such as these are designed to appeal to emotions rather than logic. Who is the target audience for this ad? What are they supposed to feel when they see the ad?
(Courtesy of AT&T.)

Believability is an extremely important concept in advertising. Do consumers believe ads? Are the claims believable? Do spokespersons, particularly authority figures, have credibility? Consumers say they do not believe advertising claims, but at the same time they find advertising helpful in making better decisions. Recent research has found that although consumers want proof of the validity of advertisers' claims, they do not require very convincing evidence to accept these claims.*

Support may be more important than any other part of the message strategy. Remember, support refers to everything in the message that lends credibility to the promise. If you want your message to be believable or to have impact, it must have support.

HOW BRAND IMAGES WORK

Many products are what marketers call "parity products"; that is, there are few, if any, major differences in their features. The products are "undifferentiated" in the marketplace. Products and services such as soap and gasoline are relatively

*Hoch and Young-Won Ha, "Consumer Learning," pp. 221–33.

indistinguishable. What makes the difference between products is advertising. In such cases the distinctions may be unreal, but the difference is not—and the difference lies in the perceived image and personality of the product. Product personalities were discussed in Chapter 7. Personality is important both in positioning a brand and in developing a brand image.

One of advertising's most fundamental roles is to provide information: the name of the product, where it can be purchased, the price, the size or sizes, and similar facts. In those cases where product differences exist, the features and how they translate into selling points are also important pieces of information. If the difference is something unique, something that is protected by a patent, copyright, or secret process, then the difference may even be a unique selling proposition.

One requirement of informational advertising is that the product attribute be immediately and obviously important to the consumer. If the attribute isn't relevant to the prospect, then it isn't a selling point. In addition, an informative ad should be clear. Consumers have little patience with ads that are confusing, vague, or unfocused. Finally, the claims presented in informative advertising must be technically verifiable.

PRINCIPLE _____
Give enough information to fill in the blanks in the prospect's knowledge.

Transformation Advertising

There's a lot of difference between a pair of K-Mart jeans and a pair of Levi's 501s. Advertising has transformed Levi's 501s beyond the basic requirements of the category. Levi's has been endowed by advertising with the capacity to provide an experience different from the experience that comes from wearing any old pair of jeans. This concept of transformation was developed by Bill Wells of DDB Needham to explain how advertising, particularly brand-image advertising, works.*

The distinctions are very real because the experience of using the product is truly different. The experience of smoking a Marlboro is different from the experience of smoking a Pall Mall. The experience of using Coast is different from the experience of using Irish Spring or a generic bar of soap. If you doubt the reality of such differences, try giving your mother a watch for her birthday in a box that comes from K-Mart, as opposed to giving the same watch in a box that comes from Tiffany. No doubt, you'll find the experiences of buying, giving, and wearing the watch are quite different.

PRINCIPLE _____
Good advertising transforms mundane products into magical brand images.

transformation advertising
Image advertising that changes the experience of buying and using a product.

Advertising provides information and, at the same time, transforms the experience of buying and using the product. Transformation is the secret to building a product personality and image. It is an expensive objective. One of the requirements for **transformation advertising,** or image advertising, is a big budget. Frequent exposure is the price of success. Furthermore, the process takes time because the effect is cumulative. It is a form of indirect advertising as opposed to direct-action advertising.

Because the effects of image advertising build up over time, consistency is critical to this process. You can't say one thing today and something different tomorrow. David Ogilvy, founder of Ogilvy and Mather, believed strongly in brand-image advertising. He said that every ad contributes to the image. The message must focus on what that image is supposed to be, and should be consistent over a long time.†

For transformation advertising to be effective in selling a product it should be *positive.* Its function is to make the experience richer, warmer, and more

---

*William D. Wells, "How Advertising Works," a speech presented to St. Louis AMA, September 17, 1986.
†David Ogilvy, *Confessions of an Advertising Man* (New York: Dell, 1964).

AD 8.7
The Marlboro cigarette ads are among the most well-known examples of transformation advertising. What others can you think of?

(Reprinted by permission of Philip Morris, Incorporated.)

AD 8.8
By portraying themselves as a "good neighbor," State Farm hopes to overcome the
negative attitudes that many people hold toward insurance companies.

(Courtesy of DDB Needham Worldwide.)

enjoyable. For this reason, transformation may not be appropriate for certain products. Upbeat advertising messages might not work for products related to drudgery or unpleasant experiences. The message will sound phony. It may not be realistic to turn cleaning the oven, scrubbing the floor, or taking a laxative into a joyous occasion. Although some advertisements try to do this, they stretch believability.

It is possible to use transformation advertising, or image advertising, to turn around perceived negatives. For example, the campaigns for the financial company HFC—"Never Borrow Money Needlessly" and "People Use Our Money to Make the Most Out of Life"—have taken some of the threat out of applying for a loan. The State Farm "agent" series, pictured in Ad 8.8, has helped generate trust in a potentially brittle relationship. Transformation advertising for airlines has probably taken some of the anxiety out of flying.

Another requirement for transformation advertising is that it "ring true." Because it deals with images, it may not be technically verifiable in a literal sense, but it must feel true. The characters must act as the characters would really act. And they must use the product as they would use it in real life.

A final requirement for transformation advertising is that it link the brand so tightly to the experience that people cannot remember one without remembering the other. One example where this did *not* occur involved a series of ads for a soap company that said:

"New blouse?"	"No, new bleach."
"New dress?"	"No, new bleach."
"New shirt?"	"No, new bleach."

That campaign created a strong link between the experience and the product category, but not the actual product. Almost everyone remembered the line. Almost no one remembered the advertiser.*

*Wells, *Planning for R.O.I.*

■ SUMMARY

To be effective an ad must be able to penetrate the inattentiveness of the audience.

Advertising works on several levels: perception, cognition, and persuasion.

Effective advertising can make a product or brand stand out from the competition.

Although an ad ideally should be informative and entertaining, advertisers sometimes must choose between the two.

■ QUESTIONS

1. What is meant by breakthrough advertising? How is this accomplished?

2. How does the construct of perception-cognition-persuasion relate to advertising? What types of ads are appropriate at each level?

3. What is a unique selling proposition? What are some prominent examples?

4. What do advertisers mean by "arguments"? How are they used in advertising?

5. What is transformation advertising? When is it used?

6. What are some common methods of attracting and maintaining consumer interest?

■ FURTHER READINGS

HOCH, STEPHEN J., and YOUNG-WON HA. "Consumer Learning: Advertising and the Ambiguity of Product Experience." *Journal of Consumer Research,* September 1986, pp. 221–33.

OGILVY, DAVID. *Confessions of an Advertising Man.* New York: Atheneum, 1980.

REEVES, ROSSER. *Reality in Advertising.* New York: Alfred A. Knopf, 1963.

WELLS, WILLIAM D. *Planning for R.O.I.* Chicago: DDB Needham Worldwide, 1987.

Hamburger Helper: Changing Advertising Strategies

Hamburger Helper is a dry-mix casserole product from General Mills, Inc. (GMI), developed and introduced to the marketplace in the early 1970s. Dry-mix casseroles had become popular among consumers in the 1960s. They were convenient, easy-to-make pasta or rice side dishes that could be kept in the consumer's cupboard until needed. General Mills's first dry-mix casserole, Noodles Romanoff, was introduced in 1962. It was soon followed by other flavors as well as by similar products from other companies. Besides convenience, economic factors—higher disposable family income and more women entering the work force—contributed to the popularity of these products. For several years demand for dry-mix casseroles grew. As the market for these products became more crowded and competitive, however, sales of General Mills noodles-and-sauce products began to decline.

In response to this trend General Mills decided to try a new marketing strategy by developing a dry-mix product that would be a *main dish* rather than a side dish. It also reasoned that building the new product around *hamburger* would broaden its consumer appeal. Market research had revealed that 80 percent of all U.S. households served hamburger at least once every 2 weeks. Moreover, consumers always seemed to be looking for new hamburger recipes. With this information, the company felt it had identified a basic consumer need—more ways to serve hamburger. It set about trying to develop a product to fill this need.

In 1968 General Mills introduced its first add-to-meat products. Advertised as the "new dinners for eating out *in*," they did not do very well. The company decided that they were too foreign-sounding. No one knew what a Monte Bello dinner was, for example. Nor did advertising stress the *convenience* of the products, which was one of the appeals of dry-mix casseroles.

However, General Mills felt that having a successful entry was still a desirable goal. The market for dry-mix casseroles had grown 45 percent since 1964; there were over 160 dry-mix products on the market in 1969. Meanwhile the art director at Knox Reeves, General Mills' local Minneapolis ad agency, was still mulling over the basic consumer need of more ways to serve hamburger. He decided that consumers needed "help"—and thus the idea of Hamburger Helper was born.

General Mills undertook consumer interviews in 1969 to test the concept of Hamburger Helper. Of those interviewed, 48 percent were interested in purchasing the product; another 48 percent were somewhat interested. Respondents felt that the product would provide a convenient, one-pot meal that the entire family would enjoy. General Mills was impressed with these results, which were well above the average for new products. On the negative side, some of those interviewed felt that a meal made from Hamburger Helper would be more expensive than cooking a casserole from scratch and that it would not taste as good. After considering both the favorable and unfavorable reactions, General Mills decided to focus on *convenience* in Hamburger Helper's advertising.

In the meantime, Hunt began test-marketing its new Skillet Dinners, which were very similar to Hamburger Helper. General Mills tested Hamburger Helper versus Hunt's dinners in consumer homes. Consumers were asked to try both products; they then were asked if they would buy them again, and if not, why not. The results were disappointing: Consumers liked the taste and texture of Hunt's dinners better than meals made with Hamburger Helper. The convenience of Hamburger Helper was what consumers liked best about it.

In response to the consumer test results, General Mills changed the ingredients in Hamburger Helper and conducted a second in-home test. This time the results were better: Hamburger Helper's taste was strongly preferred over that of Hunt's dinners.

General Mills now was ready to test-market the new product. In December 1970 it shipped Hamburger Helper to several West Coast markets. The basic advertising strategy, used on television and in magazine print ads, was *convenience*—"one pan, one pound, one package." Advertising and packaging also mentioned secondary features that General Mills had found important: economy (25 cents per serving), variety (five flavors), and size (five servings, "enough for the whole family").

Hamburger Helper's closest competitor—the only other add-to-meat packaged dinner on the market—was Hunt's, which was now selling nationally. Hunt's was priced at 89 cents, Hamburger Helper at 59 cents. Usage studies found that although many people tried Hunt's, only an average number of people bought it a second time.

The success of Hamburger Helper in the test market was phenomenal. It was accepted by every grocery account. After a trial period of 3 months, sales volume was 230 percent ahead of company projections. In August 1971 GMI began national distribution of Hamburger Helper.

Sales volume far exceeded the company's projections. In its first year Hamburger Helper became the leading product in the new add-to-meat category. The company sold more than 6 million cases and garnered a market share of 80 percent. In that year 27 percent of all U.S. families purchased Hamburger Helper. By July 1972 GMI was second in the whole packaged dinner market, behind long-time market leader Kraft.

Going into Hamburger Helper's second year, GMI's long-range goals for the product were (1) to maintain its leadership position; (2) to extend Helper to new product lines such as turkey, ham, or tuna; and (3) to introduce new flavors. Sales doubled in the second year. However, because they were relatively easy to produce and potentially profitable,

add-to-meat products became an attractive business opportunity for other companies. Between 1971 and 1973 14 products similar to Hamburger Helper were introduced to the market.

There was real panic at General Mills in 1973 when sales volume of Hamburger Helper began to decline. Market share was down 15 percent; profit was down 68 percent. GMI's response was to conduct more consumer research. It found that the primary reason for use of Hamburger Helper still was convenience; secondary reasons were variety, taste, and economy. The drop in usage was explained by boredom with Hamburger Helper's taste, the perception that the product was expensive, and a trend in making more casseroles from scratch.

General Mills tried several new strategies. It developed and introduced new flavors and a tuna helper. It shifted a greater portion of its budget from advertising to promotions, such as coupons, designed to build sales volume. And in 1974 it changed ad agencies. The new agency suggested changing the advertising strategy from convenience to flavor, which GMI agreed to do. However sales volume continued to slide drastically. Some people suggested that Hamburger Helper was at the end of its natural life cycle and that not much could be done to turn sales around.

Hamburger Helper was not alone in its sales decline. Sales volume of add-to-meat products in general was falling off. Five major brands and nine private-label brands dropped out of the market. Part of the reason for the general decline was the U.S. economy. The country was experiencing a recession, with inflation, and food prices were rising at a fast pace. Consumers evidently saw convenience products as an expendable item in the family budget, and the trend toward making casseroles from scratch continued. Accordingly, GMI changed its advertising theme to focus on economy first and variety second. Sales, however, continued to slide.

In 1975–76 GMI once again changed its advertising strategy. Because more people were making casseroles from scratch, GMI tried to convince consumers that Hamburger Helper could be used as an oven, rather than just a stovetop, casserole.

In the course of 5 years, GMI had used convenience, flavor, economy, and use as an oven casserole as primary advertising themes, but nothing seemed to do much good. Sales were down to 6 million cases a year. General Mills again turned to a new ad agency and more research. The new agency conducted a product personality study that found that consumers regarded Hamburger Helper as *easy, helpful, versatile,* and *male.* It also found that Hamburger Helper was used primarily in large, busy, blue-collar families, who frequently used convenience foods. With this specific type of user in mind, the ad agency suggested something surprising—a return to the original advertising strategy of *convenience.* They produced six sample commercials, which they then tested.

The biggest winner among the commercials was one that used a little talking hand. The hand embodied some of the qualities discovered in the product personality study: easy (a clean, simple design), helpful, and male. Research revealed that both children and adults liked the "little guy." They saw him as a thinking, active, entertaining creature with a human personality. The commercial sold convenience only and was one of the most effective commercials General Mills had ever used.

Adopting a "now or never" attitude, General Mills also made other changes in the promotion plan. It increased the total promotion budget for Hamburger Helper as well as advertising's share of that budget. The company hoped to get the attention of infrequent users of Hamburger Helper with more advertising. The results were immediate and gratifying. As soon as the talking hand commercial went on the air, sales picked up. After 4 years of decline, sales increased 5 percent. General Mills management was very pleased. The talking hand truly turned out to be a helper, not only to the harried housewife who he promised to help with meals, but also to the Hamburger Helper product and its parent company as well.

Discussion Questions

1. Which was more important in turning around the sales pattern of Hamburger Helper—knowledge of the consumer or the advertising gimmick of the talking hand? Explain why you think so.

2. What other advertising characters for different products can you think of that seem central to the product and its message?

3. If you were a manager at General Mills, would you have persisted as long as GMI in fact did in trying to find a way to improve Hamburger Helper sales? If not, at what point would you have abandoned the effort?

(Courtesy of General Mills, Inc.)

9

Media Strategy and Planning

Chapter Objectives

When you have completed this chapter you should be able to:

- Explain how planners use communication aperture to give direction to media planning strategy
- Understand the central position of media planning in campaign development and how this function utilizes information from numerous sources, including product sales performance, competitor surveillance, and message creative strategy, to form the campaign design
- Explain how the media's qualitative features (atmosphere and environment) are blended with their quantitative dimensions (reach, frequency, and efficiency) to provide the needed profile for selection
- Understand the organization and purpose of the media plan, and see how each decision on selection and scheduling is coordinated with the client's sales objectives

THE CASE OF THE DISAPPEARING CAPTAIN

A few years ago Quaker Oats faced a challenge that is typical in the industry—how to inject some fresh consumer interest into a brand, Cap'N Crunch®, that had been seen on store shelves for some time. What Cap'N Crunch® needed was to create some excitement to keep its consumer awareness at a time when new brands were trying to erode that position. Maintaining identity is particularly difficult in the children's cereal market where the target audience is split between users (children) and purchasers (adults).

Quaker wanted an imaginative promotion that would quickly capture public attention. Working with its advertising agency, Backer & Spielvogel, Quaker conceived a contest with an unusual and mysterious angle. Suppose the cartoon likeness of Cap'N Crunch® were to disappear from his prominent position on the front of the package and be replaced with an outline of his former self and a large question mark? Under the theme "Where's the Cap'N?" the national audience of children and teens would be asked to use the package clues and enclosed detective kit to locate the missing character. To add some excitement, rewards totaling $1 million were to be offered.

It was an ingenious concept that needed some very special media attention because the child and teen audiences are not easy to reach. Limited time–frame promotions must generate fast awareness without using up the brand's yearly advertising budget. Quaker sought an innovative solution to its media problem. The media planner in charge of the Cap'N Crunch® brand, Mary Struble, knew she would have to come up with something out of the ordinary. She did. Mary recommended what the media business calls a "blitz" (an intense pattern of multimedia activity). Her plan included a Saturday morning "roadblock" purchase of commercial time on three networks simultaneously and advertisements in the comics section of the Sunday newspaper. For the teenagers she recommended MTV and announcements on the top teen radio stations across the country. To top off the plan, Mary proposed that skywriting and airplane-towed banners be used to attract attention in major markets.

The search for Cap'N Crunch® was an unqualified success. The advertising agency reported that not only did the campaign create comment and excitement, but sales of the brand *doubled* during the 5-month campaign. Mary Struble was rewarded by sharing first place in a national competition for Creative Media Awards in 1986.*

THE FUNCTION OF MEDIA PLANNING IN ADVERTISING

media planning *A decision process leading to the use of advertising time and space to assist in the achievement of marketing objectives.*

Media planning is the process of designing a strategic course of action that shows how advertising space and time can be used to present the message in order to achieve the advertiser's goals. Planning is not an isolated specialty performed in a vacuum. It is an integrated component of the marketing decision process, combining data from the marketplace with mass communication inputs.

Media planning was not always the sophisticated process it is today. In fact, it has undergone a substantial evolution in the last 20 years. What was once a clerical function of choosing outlets and contracting is now a central element in

*Adapted from Marianne Paskowski, "The Winners Are . . . ," *Marketing & Media Decisions,* January 4, 1987, p. 4.

The "Where's the Cap'N?" campaign for Cap'N Crunch® was a major marketing success for Quaker Oats. (Courtesy of The Quaker Oats Company.)

marketing strategy. Media department employees who once toiled in "backroom" obscurity are now in the forefront of directing marketing strategy.

This chapter will introduce you to the operation of media planning with particular emphasis on its integral role in joining the science of marketing to the art of advertising. In this way you will see the planner's role as a marketing analyst and an expert in appraisal of media channel effectiveness.

Aperture in Media Planning

Each customer or prospect for a product or service has an ideal point in time and place at which he or she can be reached with an advertising message. This point can be when the consumer is in the "search corridor"—the purchasing mode. It can also occur when the consumer is seeking more information prior to entering the corridor. The goal of the media planner is to expose consumer prospects to the advertiser's message at these critical points.

This ideal opening is called an *aperture*. The effective advertisement must expose the product to the consumer when interest and attention are high. Aperture is like the home-run swing in baseball: The ball meets the bat at the right spot and at the precise instant for maximum distance.

Locating the aperture opportunity is a major responsibility of the media planner. The planner must study the marketing position of the advertiser to determine which media opportunities will do the best job of message placement. This is a complex and difficult assignment. Success depends on accurate marketing research, appreciation of the message concept, and a sensitive understanding of the channels of mass communication.

The search for aperture involves a series of strategic decisions. Some of the major elements are discussed in the following paragraphs.

Target Audience

Who are the best customers or prospects for a product or service? How can we identify them? The advertiser seldom knows them by name or address. Just the same, to avoid wasting advertising dollars these people must be identified in some way. Finding their common consumer traits or characteristics is a very important initial step in the aperture process.

Marketing research describes the economic, social, and psychological characteristics of customers and noncustomers. From this marketplace research,

AD 9.1
Cable television uses the advertiser's audience as evidence of a popular demographic profile.
(Courtesy of Stouffer Foods Corporation.)

MAMA NEVER SAID THERE'D BE DAYS LIKE THIS.

Today, mama's got a lot more cooking than dinner.
That's why she reads Family Circle.® The magazine that's not written for old fashioned
housewives, it's written for the newest, hottest mamas ever. Or at least 23,000,000 of them.

FamilyCircle

FOR THE WOMEN OF TODAY RAISING THE GENERATION OF TOMORROW.

AD 9.2
This advertisement for *Family Circle* magazine emphasizes the nontraditional life-style of its female readers.
(Courtesy of *Family Circle*.)

the media planner must translate and match the characteristics with media audience characteristics. As a detective looks at clues, the planner looks at the consumer profile for information that will locate the prospect in a media audience. Because the sources of the profiles are different, that is, the advertiser's research and the media research are done independently, the matching of characteristics can be a challenge. The most common ways that consumers and audiences are characterized are described below.

Demographics   Demographics represents the most common "name tags" given to people. People are described by age, income (personal and household), education, occupation, marital status, family size, and many others. Ad 9.1 illustrates the use of demographic data in an ad for cable television.

Psychographics   A second form of classification looks for more sensitive measures of motivation and behavior. It attempts to classify people according to how they feel and act. For example, the lifestyle profile, one form of psychographic research, describes people by the way they view their careers and leisure/recreation pursuits (see Ad 9.2). A lifestyle profile provides perspective on the *chosen* social and cultural environment. From these consumer self-evaluations preferences for products, services, and entertainment are defined.

Product-Use Segmentation   Audiences can also be classified according to their consumption habits (usage). Media planners then have information on

Perception.

what readers, viewers or listeners buy and how often it is used or consumed. The *Rolling Stone* advertisement (Ad 9.3) incorporates this type of information on the consumption habits of its readers.

Even with all this information, finding the best audience is still difficult. Some syndicated research is not focused on the company or brand in question. Sometimes the advertiser's own studies describe consumers in ways that are incompatible with other studies of media audiences. The matching of a prospect profile to a medium's audience measurement can also be a frustrating task when two different studies do not use compatible data. Planners may use less guesswork today than they did years ago, but planning is still often intuitive.

Finding the Best Time to Advertise

Timing is crucial to successful advertising. As previously stated, an advertising message has maximum effect when it reaches the target audience at the point

Reality.

If you think a plate of homemade brownies can satisfy the munchies of a Rolling Stone reader, here's the scoop on what else it takes. Last week, Rolling Stone readers spent 320 million dollars in grocery stores, drank 51 million glasses of soda, ate 2 million cups of yogurt and polished off 5 million candy bars. And they're still hungry.

Source: Simmons 1986

**AD 9.3
(CONTINUED)**

when they are most receptive. Although most advertisers recognize the value of timing, locating the optimal position is not easy. Ask a planner when the best time to advertise is and you will likely hear, "It depends." A number of variables affect a timing strategy: consumer needs, the use cycle of the product, and the degree of usage and competitive actions. The strategy employed will often reflect the particular circumstances of the product. The following examples illustrate how various factors can influence the timing of a campaign.

Seasonal Considerations The demand of many goods and services is directly tied to changes in weather. Obvious examples are snow tires and other winter-oriented automotive products, recreation equipment (golf or skiing), and tourism and travel. Although purchasing is not exclusive to the appropriate season, sales curves show a significant change when the weather is "right."

The strategic challenge for media planners is to schedule advertising when most consumers are preparing to make the purchase decision. Scheduling too

The demand for certain goods will vary greatly from season to season. (Courtesy of Hub Willson/The Stock Option.)

early misses aperture because the consumer is not ready to buy. Waiting too long is worse; delay misses those who have been anxious to buy a fishing reel or suntan lotion. A good example of aperture timing involves the Standard Oil Company of Ohio (SOHIO). Some years ago, SOHIO introduced a special gasoline additive designed to resist ice formations in the fuel systems of automobiles. The additive was exclusive in the SOHIO marketing area. Consumer research, however, cautioned that a significant proportion of gasoline buyers were not at all interested in the chemistry of additives and that the additive feature became important only when consumers were faced with the threat of a frozen fuel system.

SOHIO rejected a season-long campaign for two reasons. First, Ohio traditionally has uneven winters with as many thaws as freezes and at least three distinct bands of temperature from north to south. Second, a long campaign would absorb funds intended for other SOHIO products. The obvious solution was a series of short campaigns during cold spells. But, how could anyone know when temperatures would fall?

The problem was solved by the media planner for the SOHIO advertising agency. He recommended that prearranged radio station schedules be set up to use SOHIO "Freeze Alert" commercials *automatically* whenever the local weather bureau forecast below-freezing temperatures for a 24-hour period. The weather forecast was the "trigger" for the schedule. That winter, every time the mercury dipped, SOHIO was promoting its additive. Just when the consumer's need for protection opened the customer's aperture for the SOHIO message, SOHIO was on the air.

Holiday Timing The timing of advertising schedules can also be coordinated with holiday and other national promotional celebrations. However, just as with seasonal planning, media planners must use careful judgment on when the advertising can take advantage of the consumer's interest. Nowhere is this more critical than in children's toys and gifts.

Although toys and gifts are bought some time before they are given, the best aperture is difficult to determine. At what point does the child's interest coincide with the parents' decision to do the shopping? Media planning based on the child's aperture may be wasteful in that it is too early. Planning based on the purchaser's action may be too late. Finding the most appropriate point requires a delicate balance.

Furthermore, even the effect of a perfectly timed brand message can be seriously reduced by the advertising actions of rival firms. Consider the circumstances faced by a famous manufacturer of men's watches (Corum) some years ago.

A CASE IN POINT   Market research for Corum had indicated that the man about to receive a watch as a Christmas gift was often consulted beforehand for his preferences. On the basis of this information, the firm wanted to schedule advertising in a pre-Christmas issue of a male-oriented magazine. The media plan recommended the December issue of *Esquire* as a particularly appropriate vehicle, because that issue would be distributed in mid-November. The four-color page Corum advertisement featured several attractive gold watches. It seemed like perfect strategy. However, delight turned to dismay when the advertising agency discovered that *Esquire's* December issue contained no less than 12 other men's gold watch advertisements! How would the readers be able to recall one watch from another?

How Long to Advertise

continuity *The strategy and tactics used to schedule advertising over the time span of the advertising campaign.*

In advertising, the term **continuity** refers to the length of the campaign. Although dictionaries define continuity as uninterrupted activity, advertisers define it as any pattern that spreads the message through time.

The three most popular patterns used in continuity scheduling are continuous, pulsing and flighting. These patterns are illustrated in Figure 9.1. Each strategy has strengths and weaknesses that must be balanced against the brand's situation. Some advertiser's will rely on one of these patterns for a campaign, whereas others prefer to mix the patterns within the same campaign.

continuous pattern (scheduling) *Advertising spending that remains relatively constant during the campaign period.*

Continuous Patterns   In **continuous patterns** advertising spending stays relatively constant and runs throughout the campaign period. Campaigns need not be year-long to be considered continuous. A heavy continuous pattern might bankrupt the firm, whereas a light continuous pattern might reduce the level of advertising to a point where it would receive no notice. The cost of steady advertising is always an important consideration.

Another factor in the scheduling decision is the consumer's purchase or consumption cycle. Some products are quickly consumed in daily use (soft drinks, toothpaste, candy and gum). Most stores also need daily traffic. Because an important proportion of the prospect audience makes buying decisions nearly each day in these short-cycle situations, advertisers often spread advertising to cover as much of the year as possible. Failure to use continuous advertising might allow competitors to make inroads on brand or company loyalty.

pulsing *An advertising pattern in which time and space are scheduled on a continuous but uneven pattern; lower levels are followed by bursts or peak periods of intensified activity.*

Pulsing   **Pulsing** is a popular alternative to continuous advertising. It is designed to intensify advertising prior to an open aperture and then to reduce advertising to much lighter levels until the aperture opens again. The pulse pattern has peaks and valleys and often resembles the silhouette of a city skyline.

Fast-food companies like McDonald's and Burger King use pulsing patterns. Although their contest for daily customers demands continuous advertising, they will greatly intensify activity to accommodate special events such as new menu items ("Chicken McNuggets"), merchandise premiums ("Smurf Glasses"), and contests ("McDonald's Monopoly Game"). Pulsed schedules cover most of the year and still provide periodic intensity.

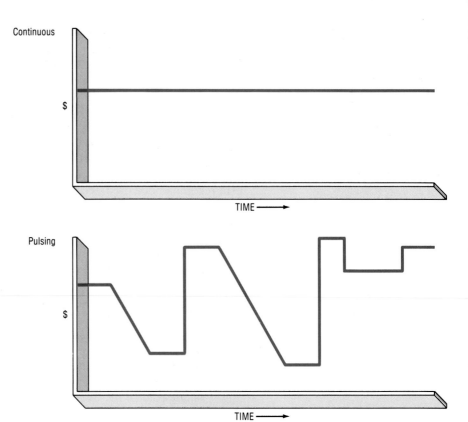

Continuous

$

TIME ⟶

Pulsing

$

TIME ⟶

Flighting

$

TIME ⟶

FIGURE 9.1
This diagram illustrates the three
continuity tactics. In each case the
line reflects the dollar level of ad
spending.

FIGURE 9.2
Flighting tactics are supported by
awareness research that proves recall does not disappear once advertising stops. Awareness is shown by
the single line.

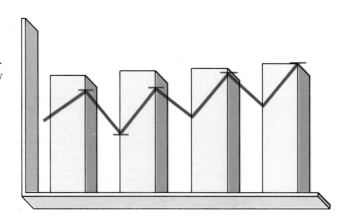

flighting *An advertising pattern characterized by a period of intensified activity, called a flight, followed by periods of no advertising, called a hiatus.*

carry-over effect *A measure of residual effect (awareness or recall) of the advertising message some time after the advertising period has ended.*

Flighting **Flighting** involves a period of scheduling called a *flight,* followed by a period of no advertising called a *hiatus.* Because no advertising is scheduled between flights, the intensity of the flight period can be higher than it would be for the pulse technique. The risk of flighting is that awareness levels can erode during the hiatus. Figure 9.2 illustrates how this pattern might affect awareness. Note that the line representing awareness drops after advertising ceases but does not disappear. This is what is meant by the **carry-over effect.** Some of the advertising remains in the consumer's mind, and awareness will increase once the next flight is underway. The shape of this "wave" is determined by the length of the hiatus between flights.

Impact-Stimulating Aperture

Thus far the discussion of media planning has concerned the natural aperture opportunities based upon normal consumer behavior patterns. Suppose, however, the normal patterns are not there. Perhaps an advertiser has a new product ready for the marketplace. The question then becomes, can aperture be induced or created? The answer is a qualified yes.

Apertures have been widened by a number of marketing techniques, including price strategy (low "APR" financing for cars), dramatic creative devices (Spuds MacKenzie or the dancing raisins), and new positioning for a brand (Arm & Hammer Baking Soda).

Fast-food restaurants use a pulsing scheduling pattern for their advertising.
(Courtesy of Billy E. Barnes/Stock, Boston.)

9.5
9.5
9.5
9.5
10.0

How
does
it
feel?

**Sports
Illustrated**
Get the feeling.

---

impact *A value of media influence
on the audience that is expected to
produce higher-than-normal awareness of the advertiser's message.*

Apertures have also been widened by dramatic use of media environments
to capture attention. One famous example of media **impact** was the use of
gigantic wall paintings for Nike athletic equipment during the 1984 Summer
Olympics. For an example of an advertisement with impact see Ad 9.4.

Another good example of media impact was the gamble taken by the J. R.
Williams Company for a hand lotion called Rose Milk. Though Rose Milk was
comparable to its competitors Jergins and Vaseline, it had nearly no consumer
awareness and, even worse, poor distribution in drug and department stores. In
1975 Williams learned that the telecast of the Tournament of Roses Parade on
January 1, 1976, was available for sponsorship from both the NBC and CBS
television networks. There was a risk involved: sponsorship would require com-
mitting nearly half of the year's advertising budget to a single day! Despite the
risks, Rose Milk flooded New Year's Day with commercials, stressing the connection between Tournament of Roses and Rose Milk. The impact was immediate,
and Rose Milk went from an also-ran competitor to a category leader. Rose Milk
created aperture instead of finding one.*

*Stephen A. Greyser, *Cases in Advertising and Communication Management,* 2nd ed. (Englewood
Cliffs, NJ: Prentice Hall, 1981).

Any candid evaluation of persuasive communication would admit that in most media channels the advertiser's message is an intrusion. At best, the public tolerates advertising in its daily life in return for free or low-cost information and entertainment. However, because some media environments are more appropriate than others, part of the aperture concept in media planning is to seek out the most conducive atmospheres. The following are illustrations of each strategy.

Media Content and Product Compatibility

Media content is said to be compatible with the product when the advertiser can find programming or editorial material that complements the message. For an example of compatibility between product and content see Ad 9.5.

AD 9.5
One of a series of "leadership" themes that *Esquire* uses to demonstrate its reader status.
(Courtesy of *Esquire*. Photography by Jean Moss/Chicago.)

Ralph Lauren. Chairman Polo/Ralph Lauren Corporation/Esquire reader since 1960.

Ralph Lauren on Leadership.

A leader has the vision and conviction that a dream can be achieved. He inspires the power and energy to get it done.

Ralph Lauren

Leadership attracts leadership. Leaders are the difference between success and mediocrity. Where do you find them? In the one place where style and substance meet. In Esquire. **Esquire** Man At His Best

© 1987 Esquire Associates. An affiliate of the Hearst Corporation.

We move more Amer

cans to communicate.

Reader's Digest articles on how to talk—and how to listen—to friends and family encourage more people to make the effort. More people read us, believe us and act because of us.

Reader's Digest

We make a difference in 50 million lives.

Think of the sport and recreation magazines that are filled with advertisements for clothing and equipment. Think of televised golf and tennis matches, financial reports, hunting and fishing shows, cartoon adventures, and cooking shows. All offer advertisers a ready-made focus. One attraction of these opportunities is simply audience characteristics. The other attraction is a special communication between the customer and the content. When this environment is right, advertising becomes an enjoyment and not an intrusion.

Mood and Product Compatibility

Mood refers to the intangible feeling that surrounds audience participation in a media activity. Many advertisers believe that this emotional context is extremely important. In Ad 9.6, *Reader's Digest* emphasizes the emotional features of its content.

One of the major reasons the Hallmark Corporation underwrites the high cost of its long-running series, *Hallmark Hall of Fame,* is the atmosphere that program provides for greeting-card advertising. A card is a personal and often sentimental purchase. The wrong program atmosphere could ruin the aperture. Can you imagine a Hallmark commercial within *Miami Vice* or *Wrestlemania?*

Media Clutter: A Negative Atmosphere

PRINCIPLE
Media clutter is not beneficial to anyone—the audience, the advertiser, or the media.

Today most of the mass media allow too many promotional messages to compete for audience attention. Media planners cannot avoid all cluttered conditions, but they can reduce or limit the effect by isolating messages from those of competitors and by advising against the use of the most cluttered media.

ADVERTISING MESSAGES AND APERTURE

An important part of the success in aperture strategy is the planner's sensitivity to the kind of message to be used. This understanding concerns all dimensions of the message: the consumer benefit employed, the informational support for the benefit, and the tone of the presentation. The planner's job is to match these dimensions with the media that will best complement the message content.

MEDIA PLANNING: COORDINATING INFORMATION

Successful media planning requires incorporating a great deal of information and data into media decision making. Figure 9.3 provides a descriptive model of the sources and types of information used in the planning decisions for a major consumer product.

Company or Brand Sources

Consumer Profiles   Consumer profiles are crucial for assisting the planner in locating the best media vehicles for the brand. Planners need current descriptions and value priorities of each target audience. The profiles are of most use when the advertiser's consumer target is described in the same way as a media audience.

Seasonal and Use Cycles   The media planner must consider seasonal and use cycles when selecting appropriate continuity patterns. Data on the sales pattern (days or weeks) between purchases help to arrange the correct scheduling tactics (continuous, pulsing, or flights).

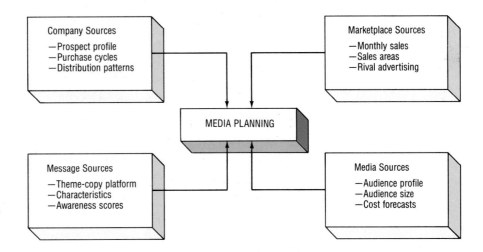

FIGURE 9.3
Media planning is an information hub. Note the diverse types of information a media planner must use.

Distribution Patterns   Distribution patterns tell the planner the proportion of retail outlets carrying the brand on an area-by-area basis. Poor distribution in a market can indicate a need to reduce advertising. There isn't much sense in promoting a band that is not widely available for sale. Advertising *follows* distribution; it does not create it.

Marketplace Sources

Monthly Sales Patterns   Monthly sales patterns can dictate the timing of advertising. In the ideal situation the planner knows both brand and competitor patterns before deciding on month-by-month media budget allocations.

Area Sales Patterns   Area sales patterns are necessary for effective media planning. Even the best-selling brands in the United States are not "Number 1" everywhere in the country. Uneven geographic sales patterns prompt many advertisers to use media plans that vary the amount of advertising pressure according to local conditions.

Rival Advertising Patterns   Rival advertising patterns tell the planner where competitors are advertising and how much effort they are expending. In crowded product segments the brand's **share of voice** (SOV) can have a powerful influence on aperture opportunity. Share-of-voice strategies can shift timing and even media selection.

Message Sources

Theme and Copy Platforms   Theme and copy platforms for some products might suggest the need for television demonstrations. Technical or extended copy indicates the use of print rather than television or outdoor advertising. Media decisions cannot be isolated from techniques of what to say and how to say it. Media choices may either improve or limit message effectiveness. Similarly, message characteristics such as a testimonial or use of humor can influence the selection of media vehicles.

Awareness and Recognition Research   Awareness and recognition research can assist the planner in judging how long the hiatus can be sustained before the carry-over effect is severely diminished. In the same way, planners can also judge the effect of intense advertising pressure in the pulse or flight* patterns.

share of voice *The percentage of advertising messages in a medium or vehicles owned by one brand among all messages for that product or service.*

Media Sources

Audience Profiles Audience profiles are the essence of media selection. Few brands are of such a general nature that they can appeal to any audience. Today's marketing demands a very careful segmentation of media audiences. As discussed in Chapter 6, an enormous effort is expended to provide advertisers with the research measurements needed for selection.

Forecasting Forecasting media costs is as much an art as it is a science. Because media plans are developed before the campaign begins, a careful and accurate estimate of what the advertiser will pay for space and time is vital to successful planning. Media planning is a customized effort. Each situation dictates its distinctive use and application of sources.

*E*VALUATING MEDIA OPPORTUNITIES

Considerations of aperture give the media plan direction and focus but do not give the planner all that is needed for evaluating media alternatives. Other performance measures are needed to gauge the power of the campaign. These "yardsticks" concern the number of different people exposed to the message (reach), the degree of exposure repetition (frequency), and the efficiency (CPM) of the selected vehicles. Each of these major dimensions of media planning will be examined in detail. But in order to understand their contribution, you must be familiar with basic audience terms that planners use to measure media impact.

Basic Measures Used in Media Planning

In the same way a carpenter uses feet and inches and a printer uses points and picas, the media planner uses some special terms to evaluate a media plan.

Gross Impressions Each impression represents one person having the opportunity to be exposed to a program, newspaper, magazine, or outdoor location. Impressions, then, measure the size of the audience either for one media

A media supervisor presents a prospective media plan to a client.
(Courtesy of Diane Niederman.)

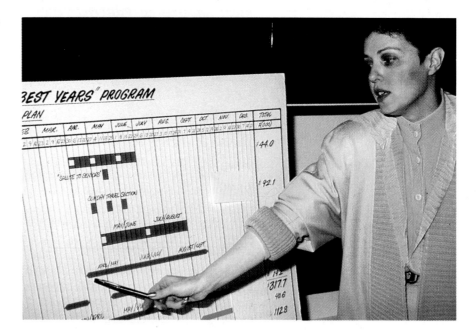

TABLE 9.1
Acme Company
Gross Audience Impressions,
October 1989

Vehicle	Audience	Message Opportunities	Total Impressions
Daily newspaper	278,000	7	1,946,000
"Wheel of Fortune"	312,000	4	1,248,000
Metro magazine	170,000	1	170,000
Total gross impressions			3,364,000

vehicle (one announcement or one insertion) or a combination of vehicles as estimated by media research.

If television program "A" has an audience of 100,000 viewers, then each time the advertiser uses that program the value in impressions is 100,000. If the advertiser used an announcement in each of four consecutive broadcasts, the total viewer impressions would be 100,000 times 4, or 400,000. In practice, planners discuss **gross impressions** when dealing with multiple vehicles in a schedule. The summary figure is called *gross* because the planner has made no attempt to calculate how many *different* people viewed the show. Gross values simply refer to the number of people viewing, regardless of whether each viewer saw one, two, or all of the shows.

gross impressions *The sum of the audiences of all media vehicles used within a designated time span.*

Impressions are often totaled for a "boxcar" figure, one that represents the maximum exposure for all or part of the campaign. All the planner needs to do is to find the audience figure for each vehicle used and multiply that figure by the times the vehicle was used. After that it is merely necessary to add the vehicle figures for the sum of "gross impressions." Table 9.1 demonstrates the arrangement of data to calculate the monthly impressions for a fictional company.

Gross Rating Points   As you might imagine, gross impression figures tend to become very large and difficult to remember. The rating (percentage of exposure) is an easier method of measuring the intensity of schedules because it converts the raw figure to a percentage. When this is summarized for a media schedule, the summary is called **gross rating points.**

gross rating points (GRP) *The sum of the total exposure potential of a series of media vehicles expressed as a percentage of the audience population.*

To demonstrate, the previous example of program A had 100,000 viewer impressions. Suppose there was a total of 500,000 possible viewers. The 100,000 of the possible 500,000 would represent 20 percent of viewers, or a 20.0 rating. The gross rating point total on four telecasts would be 80 (20 rating × 4 telecasts).

Rating values are summed just as impressions are. By using the sum of rating points, planners can calculate the total of gross rating points for any schedule, whether actual or proposed. In Table 9.2 the schedule for our ficticious company is recalculated to reflect gross rating points. For ease in showing the relationships, the total possible audience has been estimated as 1 million adults.

Although gross rating points originated with broadcast audience measurement, GRP is now used to represent print and out-of-home audiences as well.

TABLE 9.2
Acme Company
Gross Rating Points, October
1989

Vehicle	Audience Rating	Message Opportunities	Total Ratings
Daily newspaper	27.8	7	195
"Wheel of Fortune"	31.2	4	125
Metro magazine	17.0	1	17
Total gross rating points			337

TABLE 9.3

Week Number	Home Number 1	2	3	4	5	6	7	8	9	10	Total
One	X		X					X	X		4
Two		X		X	X			X			4
Three	X				X		X	X			4
Four	X	X		X	X						4
Viewing/Home	3	2	1	2	3	0	1	3	1	0	16

Reach and Media Planning

An important aspect of an advertising campaign is how many *different members of the target audience* can be exposed to the message in a particular time frame. Different, or unduplicated, audiences are those that have at least *one* chance for message exposure. Most advertisers realize a campaign's success is due, in part, to its ability to cover as many prospects as possible.

reach *The percentage of different homes or persons exposed to a media vehicle or vehicles at least once during a specific period of time. It is the percentage of unduplicated audience.*

Reach, then, is the percentage of the target population exposed at least once to the advertiser's message within a predetermined time frame. The reach of a schedule is produced by research estimates that forecast the unduplicated opportunity. Most of the mass media are measured in this way, although for some media the estimate is only a statistical probability. This means the reach is not based on *observation* but is calculated from the laws of chance.

To see how the reach calculation could work in television activity, we will use a very simplified situation. Our fictional television market of Hometown has a total of ten television households. Table 9.3 is a television survey that shows home viewing for program "X." The viewing survey is for 4 weeks during which "X" ran once each week.

Each week 4 homes viewed "X." Because there are 10 homes in Hometown, the program rating per week was 4 of 10 or 40.0. This viewing was done by all homes except home 6 and home 10. To be counted as "reached" the household only has to view one episode, and 8 of the 10 homes did that. The reach is then 8 of 10, or 80 percent.

Reach can also be demonstrated in print advertising. Bushville has a population of 10,000 households. It has two newspapers servicing the population. The *Advocate* has a circulation of 5,000 and the *Bugle* has a circulation of 3,000. If a media plan called for using both papers, the combined circulation would be 8,000. However, the reach of the two newspapers is not 80 percent (8,000/10,000) because readership surveys show that some of the households subscribe to both papers. Table 9.4 illustrates the reach as estimated from survey research.

Reach can only be calculated when the planner has access to media audience research or projections from statistical models. It is not guesswork.

frequency *The number of times an audience has an opportunity to be exposed to a media vehicle or vehicles in a specified time span.*

effective frequency *A recent concept in planning that determines a range (minimum and maximum) of repeat exposure for a message.*

Effective Frequency as a Media Planning Dimension

Many planning experts now believe that repetition is the most important dimension of media strategy. Reach is the exposure dimension, but repetition or **frequency** is how many times the exposure could take place. When frequency of exposure is used strategically it is known as **effective frequency.** It is a "bottom line" proposition. What is the minimum number of times the prospect should come in contact with the message? And what is the maximum number of times necessary for message effectiveness? The answers are, as planners term it, a "judgment call."

TABLE 9.4

Newspaper	Circulation	Homes Reading Both	Unduplicated Homes
Advocate	5,000	2,000	3,000
Bugle	3,000	1,000	2,000
Reach = 5,000 unduplicated homes or 50 percent.			

Why is there no absolute answer? To prove that an effective frequency range is ideal, all of the central communication facts would have to be known: the aperture, the persuasiveness of the message, the consumers' involvement, and the anticipated intensity of competing messages.

Even without all the answers, planners can use their knowledge and experience to determine a probable range of effective frequency. The theory and technique behind these determinations is complex. Although the understanding of these questions is not complete, many planners are convinced that effective frequency is the essential planning dimension.

Frequency Calculation To measure the frequency of a schedule, planners use two methods, either a "shorthand" summary called *average frequency* or the preferred message distribution method that forecasts the anticipated reach at each level of repetition. Both methods are illustrated below.

AVERAGE FREQUENCY To figure the "average" frequency you need only two numbers: the gross rating points (GRP) of a schedule and the reach estimate. The average frequency can also be determined from the gross impressions and the unduplicated impressions if ratings are not available. Table 9.5 illustrates a situation involving a purchase of space in three magazines. For demonstration, the schedule is summarized in rating and impression values. The formulas for calculation are as follows:

$$\text{Average frequency} = \frac{\text{Gross rating points}}{\text{Reach (\%)}}$$

OR

$$\text{Average frequency} = \frac{\text{Gross audience impressions}}{\text{Unduplicated impressions}}$$

FREQUENCY DISTRIBUTION Averages can give the planner a distorted idea of the plan performance. Suppose you had a schedule that could be seen a maximum of 20 times. If we figured the average from one person who saw 18 and another who saw 2 exposures, the average would be 10. But 10 exposures isn't close to the experience of either member. Planners who consider frequency in a functional way will not accept average frequency if a *frequency distribution* is available. The distribution will show the number of target audience members

TABLE 9.5
Magazine Exposure

Magazine	Reader/Issue	Rating (GRP)	Unduplicated Readers
A	20,000	20.0	10,000
B	15,000	15.0	4,000
C	12,000	12.0	5,000
	47,000	47.0	19,000
Total gross impressions = 47,000 (20K + 15K + 12K)			
Gross rating points = 47.0 (20 + 15 + 12)			
Unduplicated impressions = 19,000 (10K + 4K + 5K)			
Reach = 19.0 (10.0 + 4.0 + 5.0)			
47,000/19,000 = 2.47 or 2.5 average frequency.			

TABLE 9.6
Television Message Distribution

Programs Seen	Potential Audience	Per Cent
0	40,000	40.0
1	30,000	30.0
2	15,000	15.0
3	10,000	10.0
4	5,000	5.0
	100,000	100.0

exposed *at each level of frequency.* Table 9.6 illustrates the message distribution idea based on a schedule of two television programs each used twice in a month. The minimum exposure was once and the maximum was four times.

A planner examining these data may decide to use an alternate schedule because nearly one-third of the possible audience would see only one of the four programs. Planners can examine alternative schedules until they find one that best matches the desired frequency distribution.

The frequency distribution method is more revealing and thus more valuable than average frequency method of reporting repetition. Frequency distribution data are only available from special research tabulations or from sophisticated math models. Special research is expensive, and planners often have to settle for the average frequency method.

Balancing: Reach-Frequency-Continuity

The goal of a media plan can be to have a special reach, effective frequency range, and schedule length, but that might not be possible within a given budget. The reality of planning is that each of these dimensions cannot be used to the maximum without sacrifice of one or more of the other dimensions. The dollars available for media are never adequate to maximize all dimensions. Without the luxury of unlimited budgets, planners must work out carefully organized compromises. If they extend one of the plan dimensions, another dimension must be reduced. Figure 9.4 illustrates how the compromise works. The triangle on the left (A) represents the elements in balance. But if the planner needs more reach with the same schedule length, triangle B shows how the frequency would be sacrificed. Triangle C represents the effect if schedules had to be extended, with an equal sacrifice of reach and frequency.

PRINCIPLE

Media are compared on the basis of their relative efficiency, which means cost and audience size.

Aperture and the objectives of the advertiser form the reference points for the balance design. The shape of the triangle expresses symbolically the strategic solution to the brand's situation. Although triangle A appears as the most balanced, it is not necessarily the best arrangement for all campaign situations.

Efficiency as a Planning Dimension

cost per thousand (CPM) *The cost of exposing each 1,000 members of the target audience to the advertising message.*

cost per rating point (CPRP) *A method of comparing media vehicles by relating the cost of the message unit to the audience rating.*

The cost of time and space not only determines the number of message units that can be placed, it also influences the selection of media or of media vehicles. Inherent in media planning is the notion that media should be selected according to their ability to expose the largest target audience for the lowest possible cost. The key is *target* because the advertiser wants prospects and not just readers, viewers, or listeners. *Target audience* is that proportion of a media audience that best fits the desired aperture situation. Therefore, each media vehicle proposed should be evaluated on its cost in relation to its delivered target audience. In planning the process of measuring the target audience size against the cost of that audience is called efficiency, or as it is popularly known, **cost per thousand** (CPM) and **cost per rating point** (CPRP).

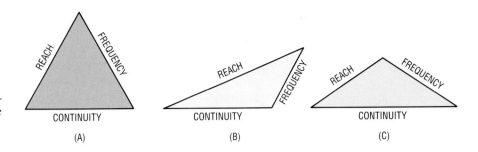

FIGURE 9.4
The reach-frequency-continuity triangle. It is impossible to maximize one dimension without sacrificing another.

(A)   (B)   (C)

Cost per Thousand   The CPM analysis allows the planner to compare vehicles within a medium (one magazine with another or one program with another) or to compare vehicles across media (the CPM of radio compared with that of a newspaper). Although the analysis can be done for the total audience, it is more valuable to base it only on the portion that have the target characteristics. To calculate the CPM you only need two figures, the cost of the unit (page or 30 seconds) and the estimated audience to be reached. The target audience (gross impressions) is divided into the cost to determine the advertising dollars needed to expose 1,000 members of the target.

$$CPM = \frac{\text{Cost of message unit}}{\text{Gross impressions}} \times 1,000$$

Here are examples from print and broadcast media to illustrate the formulas used in CPM analysis.

MAGAZINES   For illustration, magazine A has 10,460,000 readers who could be considered a target audience. The advertising unit is a page (color) and its rate is $42,000. The CPM is:

$$CPM = \frac{\text{Cost of page or fractional page unit}}{\text{Target audience readers}} \times 1,000$$

$$\frac{\$42,000 \times 1000}{10,460,000} = 4.015 \ (\$4.02)$$

TELEVISION   Program E has 92,000 target viewers. The cost of a 30-second announcement during the show is $850.

$$CPM = \frac{\$850.00}{92,000} \times 1,000 = \$9.24$$

Cost per Rating Point   Some planners prefer to compare on the basis of rating points (ratings) instead of impressions. The calculation is parallel. The exception is that the divisor in CPRP is the rating percentage rather than the total impressions used in CPM.

$$CPRP = \frac{\text{Cost of message unit}}{\text{Program or issue rating}}$$

Note: Because this is not on a per thousand basis, the multiplication by 1,000 is not necessary.

If the target audience rating for the program above were a 12.0 and the cost were still $850, the CPRP would be 850/12 or $70.83.

Although both efficiency calculations are used, in recent years the CPRP has been favored by planners for its simplicity. Both the CPM and the CPRP are relative values. The absolute numbers mean very little unless there are similar values to compare. As a planner, I would not know if *Newsweek's* CPM of $27.89

for my target audience was good or bad unless I had comparable figures for *Time* and *U.S. News & World Report.*

One final point concerning efficiency analysis. Although these analyses can be used across media (comparing one medium to another), this should be done with caution. When, for example, you compare the CPMs for radio and television, you are comparing very different audience experiences. If the experience is totally different it is difficult to say that one is more efficient than the other. CPM and CPRP are more valid when used to compare alternatives *within* a medium.

OPERATIONAL STAGES WITHIN A MEDIA PLAN

PRINCIPLE

Media plans are interwoven with all other areas of advertising: the budget, the target audience, the advertising objectives, and the message demands.

To control this information loading and to assure that each component makes a logical contribution to strategy, the planner must use a sequence of decision stages to form the media plan. The plan is a written document that summarizes the recommended objectives, strategies, and tactics pertinent to the placement of a company's advertising messages. Plans do not have a universal form, but there is a similar (and logical) pattern to the decision stages. To illustrate a style of presentation in a real-life setting, an actual media plan (excerpted) from a major consumer product marketer is used. The advertiser is the Frigidaire Company*, makers of high-quality kitchen and laundry appliances. The plan shown is from a recent year.

If there is a systematic direction of media plans, it would begin with the general and work down to the more specific questions. Similarly, it would begin with the most important decisions and work down to those of lesser priority. The following section offers a brief description of each stage.

Background/Situation Analysis

This is the marketing aperture perspective discussed in the beginning of the chapter. The Frigidaire summarized overview includes: consumer target profiles, geographic emphasis, and seasonality (see Figure 9.5).

FIGURE 9.5
Frigidaire Company
fiscal year 1987

BRAND: Frigidaire	**MEDIA BUDGET:** $5,300 K

DEMOGRAPHIC TARGET: Adults 25–54 (60% female/40% Male Skew) Married, Living in A Counties, 3+ Households $40,000+ Household Income

TARGET UNIVERSE: 10,234.0 (6% of total Adults)

PSYCHOGRAPHICS: Upscale

OVERALL BRAND MARKETING OBJECTIVE: Short-Term
— % volume increase vs. 1986
Long-Term
—Establish Frigidaire as a premium quality demand brand

GEOGRAPHIC SKEW: Improved distribution has flattened the geographic skew

SEASONALITY: Refrigerator   —Sales skew June–October
Total Appliances—Flat, with a dip November–February

CREATIVE EXECUTIONS: Television: 30's
(Creative executions focus on refrigerators and laundry)

PROMOTIONAL ACTIVITY: June—National Frigidaire Week (Paper promotion)

*(Courtesy of WCI Appliance Group.)

FIGURE 9.6

MEDIA OBJECTIVES:
> Target advertising to active and inactive appliance purchasers,
> demographically defined as:
>> Married Adults 25–54
>> Homeowners, 3+ Household Size
>> $40,000+ Household Income
>> 500,000+ Geographic Areas
> Concentrate advertising during the summer months, with some exposure
> during the Fall
>> Refrigerator sales are greatest
>> Supports introduction of new refrigerator line
> Provide key market advertising to support improved distribution and support
> the entire retailer organization
>
> **Aperture being sought, reach & frequency time frames used, adjusted numbers
> used:**
> Aperture
>> Weekend focus
>> Programming which is visible to the Trade

Media Objectives/Aperture Opportunities

A media objective is a goal or task to be accomplished by the plan. Objectives are pertinent to the brand's strategy, specifically detailed, and capable of being measured within a given time frame. The objectives listed in the media portion (see Figure 9.6) should be limited to goals that can be accomplished specifically from media directions. Similarly, aperture guidance (though less specific) details the best opportunities for exposing the Frigidaire message. Observe that the objectives concentrate on target profile, concentration periods, and geographic strategy. Note the aperture importance that Frigidaire advertising be seen by the dealer group.

Strategy: Selection of Media

This section of the media plan explains why a single medium or set of media are appropriate for the campaign objectives. A sound strategy should be able to

FIGURE 9.7

Audience Delivery (BROADCAST):

# Weeks	22
Geography	Key Markets/50% US
Daypart Mix	25% Early Fringe
	25% Early Day
	25% Late Fringe
	25% Late News
Commercial Length	100%: 30's
A25-54 GRP's	
Weekly	120-139
Total	2811
Weekly Aud. Delivery	
Reach/Avg. Freq.	58/2.1 (Key Market HH/50% US)
Reach at 2+	31%

MEDIA STRATEGIES/TACTICS:

> Spot TV
>> Scheduled for 22 weeks at weight levels
>> comparable to test efforts
>> Daypart expansion for upscale adults
> Continuity over peak sales period

TABLE 9.7

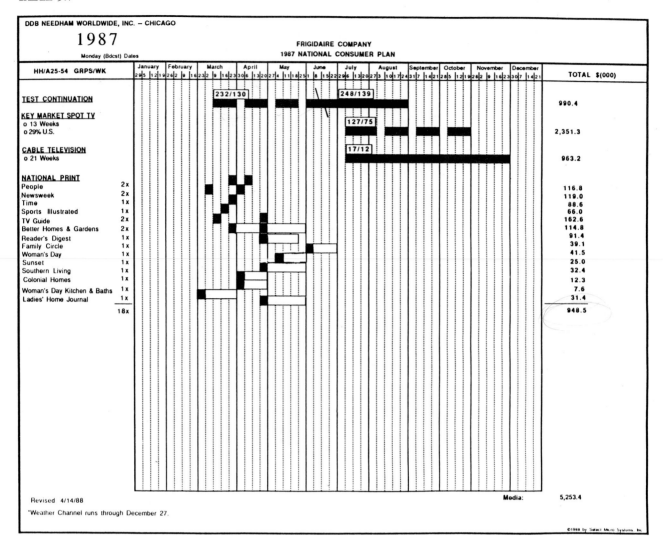

anchor each dimension to the recommendation. Because planning occurs usually months before the campaign actually begins, some detail is omitted. For the television portion of the Frigidaire campaign (Figure 9.7), the planner cannot be assured of the program availability or specific pricing in television. In such situations the recommendation must deal with the overall characteristics without identifying specific locations. This isn't guesswork, as the anticipated performance of the television activity is shown in detail.

The Flow Sheet: Scheduling and Budget Allocation

The graphic document depicted in Table 9.7 is designed to illustrate most of the media recommendations. It shows the month-by-month placement of messages, details the anticipated impact through forecasted levels of GRP, and illustrates how the campaign budget is allocated by medium and by month. In a concise fashion, a flow sheet is the "blueprint" of the recommended media plan.

SUMMARY

- Media planning involves the strategic use of marketing information to create an advertising schedule for a campaign.
- The ideal time to communicate with target prospects is called *aperture*.
- Media continuity refers to the scheduling of a campaign over a period of time. It does not mean that the ads run continuously or evenly.
- Impressions measure the total audience exposure to an advertising message but do not take duplication into account.

- Reach is more specific than impressions in that it measures the ability of a medium to attract different members of the target audience.
- Frequency refers to the potential of the media schedule to generate repeat exposure to the advertising message.
- Media expenses are usually analyzed on a cost-per-thousand basis. These costs can be compared within the same medium, but comparisons between different media are usually not valid.

QUESTIONS

1. Why is the media planning function considered the "bridge" between sales marketing and the creative function of advertising?

2. In what ways does the aperture concept influence the strategic decisions in media planning?

3. Contrast the continuity tactics of these scheduling patterns: continuous, pulsing, and flighting.

4. Why is the dimension of effective frequency so important to media planners?

5. Explain why media planners try to *balance* the reach, frequency, and continuity of proposed media schedules. What considerations go into this decision?

FURTHER READINGS

BARBAN, ARNOLD M., STEVEN M. CRISTOL, and FRANK J. KOPECK. *Essentials of Media Planning: A Marketing Approach,* 2nd ed. Lincolnwood, IL: NTC Business Books, 1987.

JUGENHEIMER, DONALD W., and PETER B. TURK. *Advertising Media.* Columbus, OH: Grid Publishing, Inc., 1980.

SISSORS, JACK, and JAMES SURMANEK. *Advertising Media Planning,* 2nd ed. Chicago: Crain Books, 1985.

10 *Broadcast Media*

Chapter Outline

Image Transfer
The Television Audience
The Structure of Television
Television Advertising
Advantages and Disadvantages of Television
The Radio Audience
The Structure of Radio
Radio Advertising
Advantages and Disadvantages of Radio

Chapter Objectives

When you have completed this chapter you should be able to:

- Understand the basic nature of both radio and television
- Describe the audience for each medium and explain how that audience is measured
- List the advantages and disadvantages of using radio and television commercials

IMAGE TRANSFER

Ever since the emergence of commercial television, radio has been given less importance by large advertisers. Recently Jess Korman at Benton & Bowles, New York, devised a technique that combines radio and television. The technique, called *image transfer,* involves implanting the images of the television ad into the radio spot. If you can see a hamburger sizzle on the screen, you can hear it sizzle on the radio. "One objective is to recreate exactly what you've got on television," says Korman. "Some spots are so successful on television that if you run the radio track (the spoken words), the listener will automatically make the closure between the two."

"Image transfer is a long overdue mini-revolution because, as television becomes more expensive to do and more zap-prone, radio has an opportunity to do something to make TV work harder," says Lou Di Joseph, a group creative director at Young & Rubicam, New York.

Image transfer isn't necessarily confined to recasting pictures in sound, according to Charlie Trubia, a media expert with Ted Bates, New York. He argues that for a radio spot to be effective, the jingle on the television ad must run on radio as well. The sound of the radio ad, however, has to fit the format of the station. "The radio sound is a departure [from the TV sound track]," Trubia says, "but not a huge one. The idea is simply to make TV and radio compatible."

General Foods has been very successful using image transfer. Their research had shown that most families had a box of Jell-O pudding somewhere on the shelf gathering dust. Research also showed that the "identifiability" of their spokesperson, Bill Cosby, was so strong that listeners and viewers instantly made the connection between the two. Young & Rubicam, which handles the Jell-O account, decided to experiment with an intensive reminder campaign on the radio. Nearly 30 radio spots were produced. The ads were warm and pithy. Cosby engages in a dialogue with a youngster, and he probes the child's love for

Jess Korman of Benton & Bowles, New York, is a pioneer in the area of image transfer.

Jell-O. They end with the tag line: "It's probably on your shelf. Why not put it on your table?" The ads pleased General Foods, and the company ordered a television execution as well. In this instance the image transfer was from a television personality to a radio message.

Image transfer appears to be one approach that is finally uniting radio and television in a way that supports the notion of broadcast media.*

Broadcast media, the process of transmitting sounds or images, includes radio and television. Experts on advertising contend that creating commercials for broadcast media is quite different from creating advertisements for print media. Certainly broadcast media tap into different human senses: sight (through movement and imagery) and sound.

Print is a space medium that allows the reader to digest information and images at his or her own speed. Broadcast is a time medium that affects the viewer's emotions for a few seconds and then disappears.

This chapter is about broadcast media. Chapter 11 deals with print media. The overview contained in these chapters will provide the necessary background for Chapter 12, "Media Buying."

THE TELEVISION AUDIENCE

With an estimated $24.4 billion in advertising revenues in 1987, television is big business. Television has become a mainstay of American society. Almost every home has at least one television set. Nearly six out of ten homes have two or more sets. Over 90 percent have a color set.† People gather around the set day after day, night after night, to find a source of entertainment, an escape from reality. This dependency explains why a great number of advertisers view television as their primary medium. What do we really know about how audiences watch television? Are we a generation of zombielike television addicts?

A great deal of information describing the characteristics of television viewers has been gathered. For example, average household viewing time was approximately 50 hours per week in 1987. This number represents an increase of about 10 hours per week since the mid-1960s. Women were the heaviest daytime viewers, averaging over 6 hours per weekday. Nonworking women spent more than twice as much time viewing daytime television as working women. Women were also the heaviest prime-time viewers, averaging over 10 hours per week. Young children (ages 2 through 5) spent over an hour more time viewing television than did older children (ages 6 through 11). Teenagers watched the least amount. Older people (over 55) watched more television, as did middle-income and less-educated people.‡

How People Watch Television

Further insights into this question were provided by a 5-month study by Peter Collett, research psychologist at the University of Oxford in England. Collett used a video camera to examine the viewing behavior of 20 families. After studying 400 hours of videotape, Collett concluded that viewers often do anything but view. They read, talk, knit, vacuum, blow-dry their hair, and sometimes fight over the remote control. The study found two major responses to commercials:

---

*Adapted from Verne Gay, "Image Transfer: Radio Ads Make Aural History," *Advertising Age,* January 24, 1985, p. 1. Copyright 1985 by Crain Communications, Inc. All rights reserved.

†*Media Trends,* DDB Needham Worldwide, 1987, p. 11.

‡*Ibid.,* pp. 25–30.

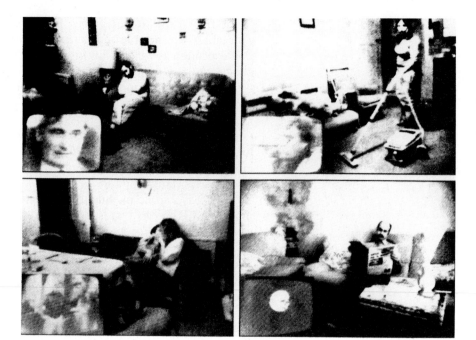

Collett's research indicated that people do other things while they are watching television.

Source: Mary Connors, "Catching TV Viewers in the Act of Being Themselves," *Adweek,* March 9, 1987. Reprinted with permission of *Adweek.*

A large segment watched less than 10 percent of a given commercial, and another segment watched more than 90 percent of a spot. Why this disparity? Collett believes it has to do with:

- The nature of the commercial, the way in which it is structured, or the nature of the product advertised.
- The makeup of the audience. Some viewers tend not to watch commercials at all; others are "commercial consumers."
- The positioning of commercials: what time of day they run, where spots fall in the commercial break.
- Viewer attention, perhaps related to the presence of others in the room. For example, the more people present, the fewer the commercials that are watched.
- The programming environment. If a break follows a popular, engaging program, viewers spend more time watching the commercial messages.

This study suggests that people are not just television addicts. Actually they seldom give their full attention to the set. These facts must be kept in mind when considering television as an advertising medium.*

THE STRUCTURE OF TELEVISION

A great deal of change has taken place in the technical aspects of delivering the television picture to audiences. As a result, several different types of television systems are now available to advertisers. Nevertheless, as noted in Figure 10.1, network television still dominates.

Wired Network Television

Whenever two or more stations are able to broadcast the same program, which originates from a single source, a network exists. Networks can be "over-the-air" or cable.

Currently there are four national over-the-air television networks—the American Broadcasting Company (ABC), the Columbia Broadcasting System

*Mary Connors, "Catching TV Viewers in the Act of Being Themselves," *Adweek,* March 9, 1987, p. 30.

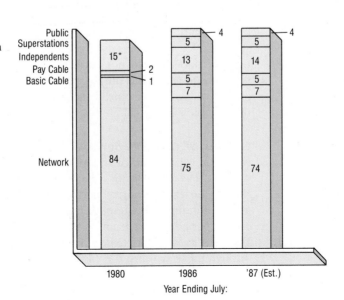

BARTLES & JAYMES
PREMIUM RED
"FIRST FLIGHT"
:30 Commercial

Frank: Well, Ed is finally ready to make his first solo flight,

and will soon be skywriting the name of our new wine cooler above your home or workplace.

Camera Follows Ed On Takeoff

So keep an eye on your sky. But do not expect to see the whole name, as we are reducing our skywriting costs by just calling it "Ed's Red".

We hope you enjoy our new Bartles and Jaymes Premium Red Wine Cooler, and thank you for your support.

Bartles & Jaymes Co., Modesto, Calif. 704BJC-001-5786

AD 10.1
The characters Frank and Ed have been featured in a continuing series of humorous ads for Bartles and Jaymes Wine Coolers.
(Copyright Gallo Winery 1985.)

FIGURE 10.1
A summary of the various television systems: percentage of advertising expenditures.
Source: Media Trends, DDB Needham Worldwide, 1987, p. 13.

Public
Superstations
Independents
Pay Cable
Basic Cable

Network

	1980	1986	'87 (Est.)
Public		4	4
Superstations		5	5
Independents	15*	13	14
Pay Cable	2	5	5
Basic Cable	1	7	7
Network	84	75	74

Year Ending July:

(CBS), the National Broadcasting Company (NBC), and Fox Broadcasting Company. The first three own 15 regional stations, and the remaining 600 regional stations are privately owned affiliates (each network has about 200 affiliates). An affiliate station signs a contract with the national network (ABC, CBS, NBC, or Fox) whereby it agrees to carry network-originated programming during a certain part of its schedule. These major networks originate their own programs and are compensated at a rate of 30 percent of the rate charged for programs in a local market. In turn, affiliates receive a percentage of the advertising revenue (12 to 25 percent) paid to the national network and have the option to sell some advertising time during network programs and between programs. This is the primary source of affiliate revenues.

Public Television

Although many people still consider public television to be "commercial-free," the Public Broadcasting Service (PBS) has engaged in advertising for several years. Public television turned to advertising to compensate for a cutback in federal funding and to compete more effectively with cable television. It is an attractive medium for advertisers because it attracts a large audience and because PBS has adopted a much more consistent programming schedule in the 1980s. Since 1979 PBS and its member stations have spent more than $8 million on advertising and promotions, including $2.5 million for ads in *TV Guide*.

Cable and Subscription Television

cable television *A form of subscription television in which the signals are carried to households by a cable.*

The initial purpose of **cable television** was to improve reception in certain areas of the country, particularly mountainous regions and large cities. However, alternate programming, with an emphasis on entertainment and information, has been primarily responsible for the rapid growth of cable systems. By 1990 it is estimated that over 50 percent of U.S. households will receive cable stations. Although cable still represents only 12 percent of all television advertising revenues, it is growing rapidly. In 1987 cable systems generated approximately $1.5 billion in advertising revenue.*

Some of these cable systems develop and air their own programs as well as pass along programs initiated by VHF stations, those 12 channels (2–13) located on the very high frequency band on the wavelength spectrum, or UHF stations (WTBS). "Pay programming" is an option available to subscribers for an additional monthly fee. Pay programming normally consists of movies, specials, and sports under such plans as Home Box Office, Showtime, and The Movie Channel. Pay networks do not currently sell advertising time. Homes that do not subscribe to cable may purchase "subscription television" that is broadcast over the air with an electronically scrambled signal. Subscribers own a device that unscrambles the signal.

Origins of Cable Programs   Most of the programming shown on cable television is provided by independent cable networks such as Cable News Network (CNN), the Disney Channel, the Nashville Network, Music Television (MTV), the Entertainment and Sports Programming Network (ESPN), and a group of independent superstations whose programs are carried by satellite to cable operators (for example, WTBS-ATLANTA, WGN-CHICAGO, WWOR-NEW YORK). Although approximately 80 percent of cable programming is provided through these systems, the cable operators themselves are originating more of their own programs.

*Media Trends, DDB Needham, p. 27.

RECENT PURCHASERS OF CABLE TELEVISION

Although cable television has greatly expanded programming choices for viewers, it has created some serious problems for advertisers. With more channels available in each market, advertisers are faced with a diluted audience and must target consumers more precisely. In a study, a major advertising agency developed a portrait of the cable purchaser that has important implications for television advertising in the future.

Profile

The study focuses on adults who purchased cable television within the past year. It identifies two types of recent cable purchasers, those who subscribe to basic cable service and those who subscribe to premium pay channels. (There is an overlap between the two groups.) Compared to adults in general, recent purchasers of cable television are younger and tend to have more children living at home. They are also more likely to have an education beyond high school and to have professional and managerial jobs.

Many recent cable purchasers are planning a variety of purchases, including personal computers, VCRs, and home video games. Because many of them have recently purchased homes or plan to in the near future, they are more likely than adults in general to have purchased such household items as microwave ovens, color televisions, and automatic dishwashers. Although they return unsatisfactory products more frequently than other people, they also try new products more often and consider themselves impulse buyers.

This group enjoys a higher standard of living and spends more money on entertainment than do adults in general. They go to more movies and amusement parks, travel more frequently, and purchase more records and cassette tapes. They also participate more frequently in sports activities, such as swimming and bicycling, and in educational activities, such as attending lectures and going to libraries. They are more mobile than adults in general, seeing themselves as likely to move within 5 years.

Recent cable purchasers have liberal attitudes toward television programming and advertising. For example, they are less likely than other adults to feel there is too much sex and violence on television, and they are less opposed to television advertising of alcoholic beverages. They are also more likely to believe advertising test results that compare competing products. Despite these differences, they tend to watch the same types of programs as other adults.

Exercise

Cable television subscribers are good potential customers for advertisers. They are inclined to spend money, and they expect to make more money in the future. They also have a more favorable attitude toward advertising than do adults in general. However, they watch a greater variety of television programs and networks. How could you target such an audience? What are the implications for television advertising as the number of cable subscribers increases?

Source: DDB Needham Worldwide, *Life Style Profile of Recent Purchasers of Cable TV (Basic Service or Premium Pay),* February 1985.

---

interconnects *A special cable technology that allows local advertisers to run their commercials in small geographical areas through the interconnection of a number of cable systems.*

Interconnects One recent development in the cable industry is the availability of **interconnects,** a special cable technology that allows local or regional advertisers to run their commercials in small geographical areas through the interconnection of a number of cable systems. Interconnects are either "hard," in which different ads are distributed electronically by cable or microwave, or "soft," in which the same commercials are simply scheduled at the same time. Either way, they offer small advertisers an affordable way to reach certain audiences through television. Interconnects generated $95 million in revenues in 1987.*

Local Television

Local television stations are both affiliated with a network and carry network programming and program their own shows. Costs for local advertising differ depending on the size of the market and the demand for the programs carried.

*John Motavalli, "And the Secret Word Is: Interconnect," *Adweek,* March 31, 1987, pp. 6–7.

The local television market is substantially more varied than the national market. Most advertisers are local retailers, primarily department stores or discount stores, financial institutions, automobile dealers, restaurants, and supermarkets.

Specialty Television

Several alternate delivery systems have appeared recently. These systems attempt to reach certain audiences with television messages in a way that is more effective or efficient than network, cable, or local television. For example, low-power television (LPTV) has a much smaller market coverage than conventional television, but it can reach local markets very inexpensively. Multipoint distribution systems (MDS) and subscription television (STV) both deliver limited programming without incurring the cost of cable installation. The former is used by hotels and restaurants in an attempt to give guests access to special movies and other entertainment. The latter offers one-channel capabilities of pay-cable-type programming transmitted to individual homes through a signal decoder. All these specialty systems can carry advertisements.

Television Syndication

syndication *Television or radio shows that are reruns or original programs purchased by local stations to fill in during open hours.*

The **syndication** boom has been fueled mainly by the growth of independent stations that required programming. Today both networks and independents have been forced to bid on syndicated shows to fill the many open hours in the morning, late afternoon, early evening, and late night. Every winter hundreds of station directors attend the National Association of Television Program Executives (NATPE) meeting in order to bid on the many shows available for syndication. The top syndicated shows in 1986, along with their ratings and numbers of markets, are shown in Table 10.1. Although *The Cosby Show* did not appear in syndication until the fall of 1988, it was expected to generate over $600 million in revenue during its first 5 years.*

Off-Network Syndication There are two primary types of syndicated programming. The first is *off-network syndication*, which includes reruns of network shows. Examples are *M*A*S*H, The Bob Newhart Show, Star Trek,* and *Remington Steele.* The FCC imposes several restrictions on such shows. Most important, a network show must produce 65 episodes before it can be syndicated. The prime-time access rule prohibits large network affiliates from using

TABLE 10.1
The Top Ten
Syndicated Television
Shows for 1986

	Rating	Markets
1. Wheel of Fortune	18.4	205
2. Jeopardy	13.8	206
3. Wheel of Fortune	12.2	154
4. New Newlywed Game	9.8	182
5. People's Court	8.9	184
6. World Wrestling Federation	8.7	178
7. Hollywood Squares	7.3	142
Jeopardy	7.3	114
9. Entertainment Tonight	7.2	140
10. Liberty Bowl	6.8	141

Source: Nielsen Fast Weekly Syndication and Occasional Network Report for the week ending January 4, 1987. Shows listed twice ran in other time slots during that week. Courtesy of Nielsen Newscast.

*Wayne Walley, "First-Run Comedies at Stake in NATPE Action," *Advertising Age,* January 19, 1987, pp. S-1, S-2.

these shows from 7:30 to 8:00 P.M. Eastern time. These shows are often used as lead-ins to the local or network news.

First-Run Syndication   Sometimes network shows that did not meet the minimal number of episodes, such as *Too Close for Comfort, It's a Living,* and *What's Happening!!,* are purchased away from the networks and moved into syndication even as they continue to produce new episodes. This is referred to as "first-run" syndication. Such shows are now produced strictly for syndication, an arrangement that allows them to avoid the FCC's prime-access rule.

Both network syndication and first-run syndication programs are purchased by barter, cash, or some combination of the two. With *barter programming,* the show is provided free to the station in exchange for commercial time. About half of the commercial time is presold to national spots, and half is available to be sold by the local station. This approach is popular because new independent stations have available commercial time but little cash. Sometimes, as was the case when *The Cosby Show* went into syndication, the independents wanted the show so desperately that they were willing to pay *cash.* Finally, a show like *The New Gidget Show* is sold under a *barter/cash* arrangement.*

Television Information Services   Television information systems deliver product information to viewers without accompanying programming. The two basic systems of information delivery are *teletext* and *videotex.* Rather than carrying a picture, these two systems carry alphanumerics (characters using letters and numbers) and graphics. Teletext transmits to the vertical blanking interval (the unused black lines) of the television set. A converter supplies pages, or screens, of information to the receiver. Videotex is linked to a computer system that allows viewers to see specific information and to order desired merchandise.

TELEVISION ADVERTISING

Like television programming, television ads can be aired through a number of different arrangements. Television advertisers can run their commercials through over-the-air network scheduling, local scheduling, cable scheduling, or unwired networks.

AD 10.2
Former baseball player Bob Uecker has appeared in a number of radio and television ads for Miller Lite.
(Courtesy of Miller Brewing Company.)

*Alison Rogers, "What's New in Retro TV?," *Adweek,* January 20, 1987, pp. 26–27.

Rank	Advertiser	Network Television Ad Expenditures 1986
1	Procter & Gamble Co.	$456,324
2	Philip Morris Cos.	342,444
3	General Motors Corp.	233,786
4	Unilever NV	202,371
5	McDonald's Corp.	193,002
6	Ford Motor Co.	188,815
7	American Home Products Corp.	186,428
8	Anheuser-Busch Cos.	177,496
9	Kellogg Co.	166,261
10	Johnson & Johnson	164,322

Rank	Advertiser	Spot Television Ad Expenditures 1986
1	PepsiCo Inc.	$257,033
2	Procter & Gamble Co.	233,932
3	Philip Morris Cos.	134,725
4	McDonald's Corp.	128,180
5	General Mills	127,253
6	Pillsbury Co.	125,218
7	Anheuser-Busch Cos.	97,999
8	Toyota Motor Corp.	90,292
9	Coca-Cola Co.	82,993
10	Hasbro Inc.	72,281

Rank	Advertiser	Cable Network Ad Expenditures 1986
1	Procter & Gamble Co.	$27,673
2	Philip Morris Cos.	22,186
3	Anheuser-Busch Cos.	19,487
4	Mars Inc.	17,668
5	Time Inc.	16,037
6	General Mills	15,538
7	RJR Nabisco	10,455
8	Gillette Co.	7,738
9	General Motors Corp.	7,203
10	American Home Products Corp.	6,821

Source: Advertising Age, September 24, 1987, pp. 74, 78, 116. Reprinted with permission from Advertising Age, 1987. Copyright Crain Communications, Inc. All rights reserved.

Over-the-Air Network Scheduling

In over-the-air *network scheduling* the advertiser contracts with either a national or a regional network to show commercials on a minimal number of affiliated stations. Sometimes an advertiser purchases only a portion of the network coverage, known as a *regional leg*. This is common with sports programming where different games are shown in different parts of the country. The top network television advertisers are listed in Table 10.2.

Local Scheduling

Local scheduling means that the programming originates with the local television station. Therefore the advertiser must buy time on a station-by-station basis. Although this arrangement makes sense for a local retailer, it is not an efficient strategy for a national or regional advertiser, who would have to deal individually with a large number of stations.

Cable Scheduling

Cable scheduling is divided into two categories: network and local. The system is the same as for the noncable systems. Network cable systems show commercials across their entire subscriber group simultaneously. Through interconnects local advertisers are able to show their commercials to highly restricted geographic audiences.

Unwired Network Scheduling

In contrast to the wired networks like ABC, NBC, CBS, and Fox, which do business directly with their affiliates in terms of programming, the unwired network station has nothing to do with programming and everything to do with advertising sales. Unwired networks are basically sales representative organizations. They represent large market stations on a commission basis (15 percent). They simplify the buying process for the agency by providing one person at a network to handle the total buy. They also assist the client in media planning.*

Forms of Television Advertising

The actual form of a television commercial varies depending on whether a network, local, or cable schedule is employed (see Figure 10.2). Networks allow either *sponsorships* or *participations,* and local affiliates allow *spot announcements* and *local sponsorships.*

FIGURE 10.2
This figure illustrates the choices facing a television advertiser.

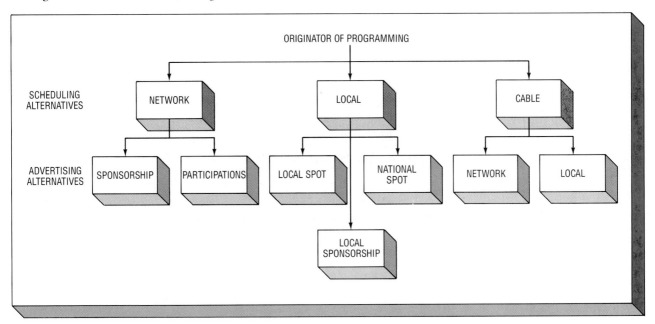

---

*Cara S. Trager, "Unwired Networks Work to Unplug Rivals' Shares," *Advertising Age,* April 14, 1986, p. S-8.

sponsorship *An arrangement in which the advertiser produces both a television program and the accompanying commercials.*

ADV.

DISADV.

participations *An arrangement in which a television advertiser buys commercial time from a network.*

ADV

DISADV

PRINCIPLE —————
Spot buys are dominated by local advertising.

Sponsorships   In **sponsorship,** which characterized most early television advertising, the advertiser assumes the total financial responsibility for producing the program and providing the accompanying commercials. Examples of early sponsored programs are *Bonanza* (sponsored by Chevrolet), *The Hallmark Hall of Fame,* and *The Kraft Music Hour.* Sponsorship has a powerful impact on the viewing public, especially because the advertiser can control the content and quality of the program as well as the placement and length of commercials. However, the costs of producing and sponsoring a 30- or 60-minute program make this option too expensive for most advertisers today. An alternative is for several advertisers to produce a program jointly. This plan is quite common with sporting events, where each sponsor receives a 15-minute segment.

Participations   Sponsorships represent less than 10 percent of network advertising. The rest is sold as **participations** in which advertisers pay for 15, 30, or 60 seconds of commercial time during one or more programs (spots). The advertiser can buy any time that is available on a regular or irregular basis. This approach not only reduces the risks and costs associated with sponsorships but also provides a great deal more flexibility in respect to market coverage, target audiences, scheduling, and budgeting. Conversely, participations do not create the same high impact as sponsorships, and the advertiser does not have any control over the content of the program. Finally, the "time avails" for the most popular programs are often bought up by the largest advertisers, leaving fewer good time slots for the small advertiser.

Spot Announcements   The third form a television commercial can take is called a *spot announcement.* (Note that the word *spot* is also used in conjunction with a time frame such as a "30-second spot," and this usage should not be confused with spot announcements). Spot announcements refer to the breaks between programs, which local affiliates sell to advertisers who want to show their ads locally. Commercials of 10, 20, 30, and 60 seconds are sold on a station-by-station basis to local, regional, and national advertisers. The local buyers clearly dominate spot television.

This art director at a television station is using graphics to create a commercial.

(© 1988 by Prentice Hall. All rights reserved.)

This is not always an optimal time slot for advertisers because there is a great deal of clutter from competing commercials, station breaks, public service announcements, and other distractions. Program breaks also tend to be times when viewers take a break from their television sets.

Measuring the Television Audience

Many of us have had our favorite television show taken off the air because of "poor ratings." Although we may have had some idea of how these ratings were derived, the "Nielsen family" and the rating process remain a mystery to most people.

Actually the derivation of television ratings is a relevantly simple process. Several independent rating firms periodically sample a portion of the television viewing audience, assess the size and characteristics of the audiences watching specific shows, and then make this data available to subscribing companies and agencies, which use it in their media planning. Two rating companies dominate this industry: Arbitron and A. C. Nielsen. Nielsen is the better known of the two, and through its Nielsen Ratings it provides the most frequently used measure of national television audiences.

Nielsen Indexes   Nielsen measures television audiences at two levels: network (Nielsen Television Index, NTI) and spot (Nielsen Station Index, NSI). In both cases, two measurement devices are used. The most famous is the Nielsen Storage Instantaneous Audimeter, or Audimeter for short. The Audimeter can record when the set is used and which station it is tuned to, but cannot identify who is watching the program. Data on who is watching are provided by diaries mailed once every 3 weeks to about 2,600 households, of which about 850 are returned every week. These periods, or "sweeps," are conducted three times a year. However, evidence of sloppy record keeping has diminished the credibility of the diary technique.

PEOPLE METERS   A. C. Nielsen, along with several other rating companies, has begun to measure not only what is being watched but who is watching. In the fall of 1987 Nielsen replaced their Audimeter and diary system with *people meters*. The people meter provides information on what television shows are being watched, the number of households that are watching, and which family members are viewing. The type of activity is recorded automatically; household members merely have to indicate their presence by pressing a button. People meters have become the primary method for measuring national television audiences. However they are quite controversial, as noted in the Concepts and Controversy box that follows. For an illustration of the people meter and the services it provides see Figure 10.3.

Arbitron   Arbitron audience measurement service covers every television market four times each year. These ratings periods, when all 214 markets are surveyed, are known as "sweeps." In 201 markets, Arbitron uses diaries exclusively to measure viewing. In 13 markets, the service uses both household meters and diaries to measure set usage and audience identity. These markets are: New York, Chicago, Cleveland, Detroit, Miami, Washington, D.C., Boston, Philadelphia, Atlanta, Dallas/Ft. Worth, Los Angeles, San Francisco, and Houston. In addition, Arbitron has a people meter service in Denver. The service is called ScanAmerica and also collects household product purchase data from households in the panel. Figure 10.4 illustrates a sample Arbitron page.

Both Nielsen and Arbitron publish their findings between four and seven times per year in a descriptive format called the *television market report*. A

TABLE 10.3   An Example of Summary Statistics Provided to Clients by A. C. Nielsen

Nielsen Television Index
Top 50 Programs
Ranked by Average Audience Estimates (%)

Rank	Program Name	Telecast Date	Net.	Duration Minutes	Avg. Aud. (%)	Share	Avg. Aud. (000)
1	M*A*S*H Special	Feb. 28, 1983	CBS	150	60.2	77	50,150
2	Dallas	Nov. 21, 1980	CBS	60	53.3	76	41,470
3	Roots Pt. VIII	Jan. 30, 1977	ABC	115	51.1	71	36,380
4	Super Bowl XVI Game	Jan. 24, 1982	CBS	213	49.1	73	40,020
5	Super Bowl XVII Game	Jan. 30, 1983	NBC	204	48.6	69	40,480
6	Super Bowl XX Game	Jan. 26, 1986	NBC	231	48.3	70	41,490
7	Gone With The Wind-Pt. 1 (Big Event-Pt. 1)	Nov. 7, 1976	NBC	179	47.7	65	33,960
8	Gone With The Wind-Pt. 2 (NBC Mon. Mov.)	Nov. 8, 1976	NBC	119	47.4	64	33,750
9	Super Bowl XII Game	Jan. 15, 1978	CBS	218	47.2	67	34,410
10	Super Bowl XIII Game	Jan. 21, 1979	NBC	230	47.1	74	35,090
11	Bob Hope Christmas Show	Jan. 15, 1970	NBC	90	46.6	64	27,260
12	Super Bowl XVIII Game	Jan. 22, 1984	CBS	218	46.4	71	38,800
12	Super Bowl XIX Game	Jan. 20, 1985	ABC	218	46.4	63	39,390
14	Super Bowl XIV Game	Jan. 20, 1980	CBS	178	46.3	67	35,330
15	ABC Theater (The Day After)	Nov. 20, 1983	ABC	144	46.0	62	38,550
16	Roots Pt. VI	Jan. 28, 1977	ABC	120	45.9	66	32,680
16	The Fugitive	Aug. 29, 1967	ABC	60	45.9	72	25,700
18	Super Bowl XXI	Jan. 25, 1987	CBS	206	45.8	66	40,030
19	Roots Pt. V	Jan. 27, 1977	ABC	60	45.7	71	32,540
20	Ed Sullivan	Feb. 9, 1964	CBS	60	45.3	60	23,240
21	Bob Hope Christmas Show	Jan. 14, 1971	NBC	90	45.0	61	27,050
22	Roots Pt. III	Jan. 25, 1977	ABC	60	44.8	68	31,900
23	Super Bowl XI	Jan. 9, 1977	NBC	204	44.4	73	31,610
23	Super Bowl XV	Jan. 25, 1981	NBC	220	44.4	63	34,540
25	Super Bowl VI	Jan. 16, 1972	CBS	170	44.2	74	27,450
26	Roots Pt. II	Jan. 24, 1977	ABC	120	44.1	62	31,400
27	Beverly Hillbillies	Jan. 8, 1964	CBS	30	44.0	65	22,570
28	Roots Pt. IV	Jan. 26, 1977	ABC	60	43.8	66	31,190
28	Ed Sullivan	Feb. 16, 1964	CBS	60	43.8	60	22,445
30	Academy Awards	Apr. 7, 1970	ABC	145	43.4	78	25,390
31	Thorn Birds Pt. III	Mar. 29, 1983	ABC	120	43.2	62	35,990
32	Thorn Birds Pt. IV	Mar. 30, 1983	ABC	180	43.1	62	35,900
33	CBS NFC Championship Game	Jan. 10, 1982	CBS	195	42.9	62	34,960
34	Beverly Hillbillies	Jan. 15, 1964	CBS	30	42.8	62	21,960
35	Super Bowl VII	Jan. 14, 1973	NBC	185	42.7	72	27,670
36	Thorn Birds Pt. II	Mar. 28, 1983	ABC	120	42.5	59	35,400
37	Super Bowl IX	Jan. 12, 1975	NBC	190	42.4	72	29,040
37	Beverly Hillbillies	Feb. 26, 1964	CBS	30	42.4	60	21,750
39	Super Bowl X	Jan. 18, 1976	CBS	200	42.3	78	29,440
39	Airport (Movie Special)	Nov. 11, 1973	ABC	170	42.3	63	28,000
39	Love Story (Sun. Night Mov.)	Oct. 1, 1972	ABC	120	42.3	62	27,410
39	Cinderella	Feb. 22, 1965	CBS	90	42.3	59	22,250
39	Roots Pt. VII	Jan. 29, 1977	ABC	60	42.3	65	30,120
44	Beverly Hillbillies	Mar. 25, 1964	CBS	30	42.2	59	21,650
45	Beverly Hillbillies	Feb. 5, 1964	CBS	30	42.0	61	21,550
46	Beverly Hillbillies	Jan. 29, 1964	CBS	30	41.9	62	21,490
47	Miss America Pageant	Sept. 9, 1961	CBS	150	41.8	75	19,600
47	Beverly Hillbillies	Jan. 1, 1964	CBS	30	41.8	59	21,440
49	Super Bowl VIII	Jan. 13, 1974	CBS	160	41.6	73	27,540
49	Bonanza	Mar. 8, 1964	NBC	60	41.6	62	21,340

PLEASE NOTE:
—Average Audience % Rankings based on Reports—July 1960 through January 25, 1987.
—Above data represent sponsored programs, telecast on individual networks, i.e., no unsponsored or joint network telecasts are reflected in the above listings.
—Programs under 30 minutes scheduled duration are excluded.

Source: "The Coming Revolution in Television Measurement Research," *Nielsen Newscast,* No. 1, 1987, p. 17. Courtesy of Nielsen Newscast.

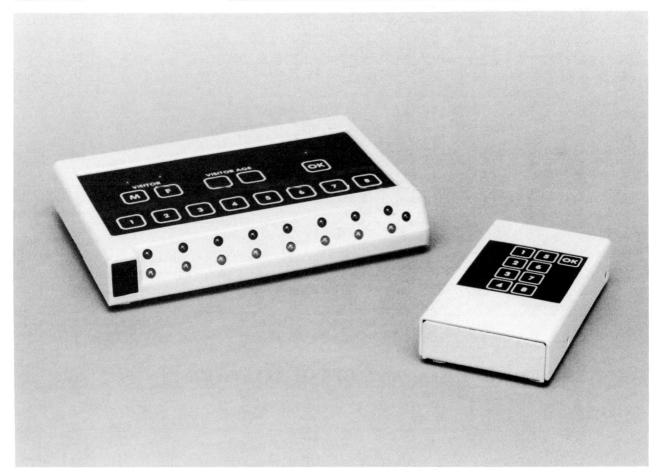

SAMPLE CHARACTERISTICS

Age of Head of House

	People Meter	Universe
55 +	36.6	36.5
35-54	34.2	34.5
Under 35	29.0	29.0

Education of Head of House

	People Meter	Universe
4 + Yrs. College	31.3	20.9
1 + Yrs. College	22.2	16.2
4 yrs. H.S.	30.9	36.0
1-3 Yrs. H.S.	8.8	12.2
0-8 Yrs. Grade S.	6.9	14.3

FIGURE 10.3

A picture of the people meter along with a description of the sample employed. The total sample size will be 4,000 in the fall of 1988.

Source: "Nielsen Putting It All Together," *Nielsen Newscast,* No. 4, 1985, p. 6. Courtesy of Nielsen Newscast.

FIGURE 10.4

A sample page from Arbitron, explaining how television markets are measured.

Source: "How to Read Your Arbitron Television Market Report," *Arbitron Ratings,* 1987, p. 4. Copyright 1988 Arbitron Ratings Company.

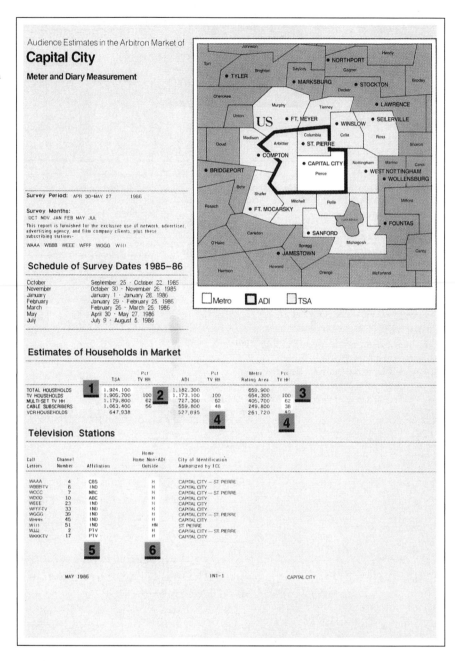

television market *An unduplicated geographical area to which a county is assigned on the basis of the highest share of the viewing of television stations.*

television market is an unduplicated geographical area to which a county is assigned on the basis of market size. One county is always placed in just one television market to avoid overlap. Arbitron refers to television markets as Areas of Dominant Influence (ADIs). Nielsen refers to comparable television markets as Designated Market Areas (DMAs). The industry refers to this information as simply "The Book."

ADVANTAGES AND DISADVANTAGES OF TELEVISION

Advantages

Advertisers would not invest large sums of money in television commercials unless these ads were effective. The major strengths of television as an advertising medium are discussed on the next page.

CONCEPTS AND CONTROVERSIES

PEOPLE METERS

People meters continue to stir controversy. An embattled A. C. Nielsen Co. has fired back at critics of the people meter system, insisting that its ratings are accurate and the company's detractors self-serving. "There is integrity in the people meter numbers," reports senior VP John Dimling, senior vice president Nielsen People Meter.

CBS, the most outspoken critic of the people meter system, saw a significant drop in its 1987–88 prime-time ratings from 1986 levels. "The shortcomings of the Nielsen people meter service has already had a disproportionate economic impact . . . and, if not corrected, will continue to cost the networks millions of dollars," argues Gene Jankowski, president of CBS/Broadcast Group. He has suggested that Nielsen conduct a validation study and overhaul the system. Sources say such a study would cost $1 million.

Some advertisers have been concerned about the drop in ratings for many prime-time and daytime shows, and want to see proof that the people meter is accurate.

People meters, however, do have supporters in industry. "We feel there is no question that Nielsen is doing its job properly," said Pearl Joseph, a senior Vice President in charge of media research at Young & Rubicam. "From a researcher's point of view, there is no question the current system is better [than the diary-based system]. We see no major problems."

While several specific problems are being discussed, it seems clear that some form of people meter will be used to measure TV audiences.

Source: Verne Gay, "Neilsen Strikes Back at CBS," *Advertising Age,* January 25, 1988, pp. 3, 76. Copyright 1988 by Crain Communications, Inc. All rights reserved.

PRINCIPLE
Television advertising reaches mass audiences and is very cost-efficient.

Cost Efficiency   Many advertisers view television as the most effective way to deliver a commercial message. The major advantage of television is its wide reach. Millions of people watch some television regularly. Television not only reaches a large percentage of the population, it also reaches people who are not effectively reached by print media. This mass coverage, in turn, creates excellent cost efficiencies. For an advertiser attempting to reach an undifferentiated market, a 30-second spot on a top-rated show may cost a penny or less for each person reached.

Impact   Another advantage of television is the strong impact created by the interaction of sight and sound. This feature creates a level of consumer involvement that often approximates the shopping experience, including interacting with a persuasive salesperson. Television also allows a great deal of creative flexibility because of the many possible combinations of sight, sound, color, motion, and drama. Television has tremendous dramatic capacity; it can make mundane products appear important, exciting, and interesting.

Influence   The final advantage of television is that it has become a primary facet of our culture. For most Americans television is a critical source of news, entertainment, and education. It is so much a part of us that we are more likely to believe companies that advertise on television, especially sponsors of drama and educational programs like IBM, Xerox, and Hallmark Cards, than we are to believe those that don't.

Disadvantages

Despite the effectiveness of television advertising, problems do exist.

Expense   The most serious limitation of television advertising is the extremely high absolute cost of producing and running commercials. Although the

AD 10.3
This Pepsi ad featuring Michael J. Fox shows the visual impact provided by television.
(Courtesy of Pepsi Cola Company.)

AD 10.4
The original Joe Isuzu television campaign has taken a serious cultural problem, lying, and turned it into a very effective attention-getting device.
(Courtesy of Della Femina Travisano & Partners and actor David Leisure.)

cost per person reached is low, the absolute cost can be restrictive. Production costs include filming the commercial (several hundred to several hundred thousand dollars) and the costs of talent. For celebrities such as Bill Cosby, George C. Scott, Michael Jackson, and Cybil Sheppard, the price tag can be millions of dollars. The prices charged for network time are simply a result of supply and demand. Programs that draw the largest audiences can charge more for their advertising space. A 30-second prime-time spot averages about $150,000, with *The Cosby Show* leading the market at $380,000.* Special shows, such as the Super Bowl, World Series, or Academy Awards, charge much more. Some experts estimate that only 50 U.S. companies can afford a comprehensive television media schedule at these costs. It has been said that television advertising is very cheap if you can afford it.

Clutter   Television suffers from a very high level of commercial clutter. Until recently the National Association of Broadcasters (NAB) restricted the amount of allowable commercial time per hour to approximately 6 minutes. In 1982 the Justice Department found this restriction illegal. Although the networks now continue to honor the NAB guidelines, this could change as their needs for revenue increase. The Justice Department ruling could eventually increase the number of 30-second commercials, station-break announcements, credits, and public service announcements, which in turn would diminish the visibility and persuasiveness of television advertisements. Further increasing the clutter and confusion is the growth of the 15-second spot. In 1986–87 all three networks accepted :15s in prime-time. The networks estimate that approximately 20 percent of all their commercials were 15 seconds in length, and that most of the spots air as "split :30s," that is, back-to-back :15s advertising different products from the same manufacturer. Finally much of the clutter is also a result of the many network and local stations promoting their own programming.

Nonselective Audience   Despite the introduction of various technologies that better target consumers, television remains nonselective. Network television still attracts about 75 percent of the U.S. audience. Although the networks attempt to profile viewers, their descriptions are quite general, offering the advertiser little assurance that appropriate people are viewing the message. Thus, television advertising includes a great deal of *waste coverage;* that is, communication directed at an unresponsive—and often uninterested—audience.

PRINCIPLE
Television should be used as a primary medium when the objective is to reach a mass audience simultaneously with a visual impact.

Inflexibility   Television also suffers from a lack of flexibility in scheduling. Most network television is bought in the spring and early summer for the next fall season. If an advertiser is unable to make this up-front buy, only limited time-slot alternatives will remain available. It is difficult to make last-minute adjustments in terms of scheduling, copy, or visuals.

THE RADIO AUDIENCE

PRINCIPLE
Radio is a highly segmented medium.

Radio is a highly segmented medium. Program formats offered in a typical market include hard rock, gospel, country and western, "Top 40" hits, and sex advice. Virtually every household in the United States has a radio set (507 million radios in total, with an average 5.4 sets per household), and most of these sets are tuned in to a vast array of programs.†

---

*"Media Outlook," *Advertising Age,* November 17, 1986, p. S-1.
†"Syndication Boosts Stations on a Budget," *Advertising Age,* August 31, 1987, p. S-2.

Radio usage has decreased slightly since 1980. In 1986 people 12 and older listened to the radio for an average of 21 hours and 21 minutes per week, down from 23 hours and 47 minutes in 1980. Listening has declined in all time slots and among all broad demographic groups: men, women, and teenagers.*

THE STRUCTURE OF RADIO

signals *A series of electrical impulses that compose radio and television broadcasting.*

frequency *The number of radio waves produced by a transmitter in one second.*

Radio can be classified according to transmission and power. The actual range of the station depends on the height of the antenna, the quality of the equipment, and so forth. Radio is a series of electrical impulses called **signals** that are transmitted by *electromagnetic waves.* Radio signals have a height (amplitude) and width. The width dictates the **frequency** of the radio signal. Simply, the wider the signal, the lower the frequency, and the narrower the wave, the higher the frequency. Frequency is measured in terms of thousands of cycles per second (kilohertz) or millions of cycles per second (megahertz). Thus a radio station assigned a frequency of 930,000 cycles per second would be found at 93 on your radio dial. The Federal Communication Commission (FCC) assigns these frequencies in order to ensure that station signals do not interfere with one another.

AM Radio

Radio stations are designated either AM or FM. An AM, or *amplitude modulation,* station has the flexibility to vary the height of its electromagnetic signal so that during the daytime it produces waves, called *ground waves,* that follow the contour of the earth. At night the station transmits waves into the sky, called *sky waves,* that bounce back to earth and are picked up by receivers far beyond the range of the station's ground waves.

The actual power or strength of an AM signal depends upon the power allowed by the FCC. Stations with a broadcast range of approximately 25 miles are considered *local stations.* Most local stations are allowed 100 to 250 watts of power. *Regional stations* may cover an entire state or several states. The most powerful stations are called *clear channel stations* and may use up to 50,000 watts. The relative power of each type of station will vary depending on the frequency assigned. Generally, the lower the frequency, the farther the signal will travel.

FM Radio

An FM, or *frequency modulation,* station differs from AM in that the band width (frequency) is adjusted rather than the amplitude, which remains constant. Because the signal put out by a FM station follows the line of sight, the distance of the signal depends on the height of the antenna. Typically, 50 miles is the maximum signal distance. However, the tonal quality of an FM signal is superior to that of AM.

Although AM radio revenue is growing at approximately 1 percent annually, the growth on FM stations exceeds 7 percent. As long as the economy remains in relatively good health, this trend is expected to continue. AM stations have responded with new and better formats and the development of AM stereo stations. Format changes include talk shows, all-news shows, expert-advice shows, and special music or discussion formats. There are approximately 8,800 commercial radio stations, of which 55 percent are AM.†

*Trager, "Unwired Networks," p. S-8.
†"Steady Revenue Rise Creates Confidence," *Advertising Age,* April 14, 1986, p. S-5.

TABLE 10.4
The Top Ten Network and Spot
Radio Advertisers, 1986

Rank	Advertiser	Expenditure (000's)
Network:		
1.	Sears, Roebuck & Co.	$47,658
2.	Warner-Lambert Co.	22,707
3.	American Telephone & Telegraph	22,552
4.	General Motors	22,212
5.	Anheuser-Busch Cos.	16,529
6.	Bayer AG	16,206
7.	Greyhound Corp.	15,545
8.	Ford Motor Co.	14,871
9.	Procter & Gamble	13,879
10.	Schering-Plough Corp.	11,442
Spot:		
1.	Anheuser-Busch Cos.	$50,400
2.	General Motors	35,200
3.	Miller Brewing Co.	28,700
4.	PepsiCo	22,300
5.	Sears, Roebuck & Co.	21,900
6.	Delta Airlines	21,700
7.	Chrysler Corp.	21,100
8.	Southland Corp.	20,000
9.	VanMunching & Co.	18,700
10.	Pillsbury Co.	

Sources: Broadcast Advertisers Reports, *Advertising Age,* September 24, 1987, p. 102; *Radio Advertising Bureau and Radio Expenditure Reports,* 1986. Reprinted with permission from *Advertising Age,* 1987. Copyright Crain Communications, Inc. All rights reserved.

*R*ADIO ADVERTISING

network radio *A group of local affiliates providing simultaneous programming via connection to one or more of the national networks through AT&T telephone wires.*

Radio advertising is available on national networks and on local markets. **Network radio** refers to a group of local affiliates connected to one or more of the national networks (ABC, CBS, NBC, Mutual) through AT&T telephone wires and satellites. The network provides simultaneous network programming, which is quite limited compared with network television programming. Therefore many local or regional stations belong to more than one network, with each network providing specialized programming to complete a station's schedule. Each station then sends out the network's signal through its own antenna. There are also regional networks (for example, Intermountain Network and the Groskin Group) that tend to serve a particular state or audience segment, such as farmers.

The top ten network radio advertisers are listed in Table 10.4.

Network Radio

Complete market coverage combined with quality programming has increased the popularity of network radio. Over 20 national radio networks program concerts, talk shows, sports events, and dramas. Satellite transmission has produced important technological improvements. Satellites not only provide a better sound but also allow the transmission of multiple programs with different formats. Network radio is viewed as a viable national advertising medium, especially for advertisers of food, automobiles, and drugs. Although network radio still represents only 5 percent of all dollars spent on radio advertising, it has been growing at an annual rate of 12 to 18 percent.*

Syndication As the number of affiliates has boomed, so has the number of new syndicated radio shows, creating more advertising opportunities for com-

Media Trends, DDB Needham, p. 42.

panies eager to reach new markets. In fact, syndication and network radio have practically become interchangeable terms. Syndication has been a boon to network radio because it offers advertisers a variety of high-quality specialized programs. Both networks and private firms offer syndication. Essentially a syndication offers a complete catalogue of programming to the local affiliate. For example, on February 7, 1987, WNDE-AM, Indianapolis, switched from live, local broadcasting to 24-hour syndication provided by Transtar Radio Network, which broadcasts live from Los Angeles. "What this means," says Ed Sanders, WNDE's general manager, "is that now we have at our disposal better disc jockeys, more music to choose from, and better sound quality for less money."* Transtar, located in Colorado Springs, claims about 600 affiliates. Its only direct competitor is Satellite Music Network, Dallas, which claims 800 affiliates. Both offer 24-hour programming daily, which could provide all a station's programming needs. With this kind of arrangement a broadcaster needs nothing but a satellite dish and a sales staff. The station remains, but much of the operating costs disappear.

Unwired Networks   The final reason for the growth of network radio is the emergence of unwired networks. Network radio has always been at a disadvantage because of the difficulty of dealing with the many stations and rate structures available in large markets. This system was discussed earlier in connection with unwired television networks.

Spot Radio

When an advertiser places an advertisement with an individual station rather than through a network, **spot radio advertising** is being employed. Although networks provide prerecorded national advertisements, they also allow local affiliates open time to sell spot advertisements. Spot-radio advertising represents nearly 80 percent of all radio advertising. Its popularity is a result of the flexibility it offers the advertiser. With over 8,000 stations available, messages can be tailored for particular audiences. In large cities such as New York, Chicago, or Los Angeles, 40 or more radio stations are available, most of which provide vertical programming. Local stations also offer flexibility through their willingness to run unusual ads, allow last-minute changes, and negotiate on rates. Buying spot radio and coping with its nonstandardized rate structures can be very cumbersome, however. *Vertical programming* means that a variety of programs are offered, each appealing to a different radio audience.

Radio advertising revenue is divided into three categories: network, spot, and local. A local station can sell spot advertising to either national advertisers or local advertisers. Network revenues are by far the smallest category, accounting for approximately 5 percent of total radio revenues.

Measuring the Radio Audience

Advertisers considering radio are most concerned with the number of people listening to a particular station at a given time. The radio industry and independent research firms provide several measures considered useful to the advertiser.

The most basic measure is the station's *coverage*. This is simply the geographical area (which includes a given number of homes) that can pick up the station clearly, whether or not they are actually tuned in. A better measure is

---

*Hortense Leon, "Syndication Boosts Stations on a Budget," *Advertising Age,* August 31, 1987, p. S-2.

circulation, which measures the number of homes that are actually tuned in to the particular station. This figure is influenced by such factors as the competing programs, the type of program, and the time of day or night.

Arbitron Several major audience rating services operate in the advertising industry. One, the Arbitron Ratings Company, estimates the size of radio audiences for over 250 markets in the United States. The primary method used by Arbitron is a 7-day, self-administered diary that the person returns to Arbitron at the end of the week.

Radar A second radio rating service is Radio's All-Dimension Audience Research, or RADAR. This service deals with local and network radio and is jointly sponsored by ABC, NBC, CBS, and the Mutual Broadcasting Company. Using a random dial system, respondents are contacted as many as nine times during a 7-day period in order to assess radio usage. Final reports are based on data collected over 48 weeks.

Birch BIRCH radio audience surveys measure station listenership in the 80 largest U.S. markets and in smaller markets when specifically requested. BIRCH uses telephone interviews to construct profiles of listener habits based on major demographic categories and selected product-usage categories. The frequency of these reports varies according to the size of the market.

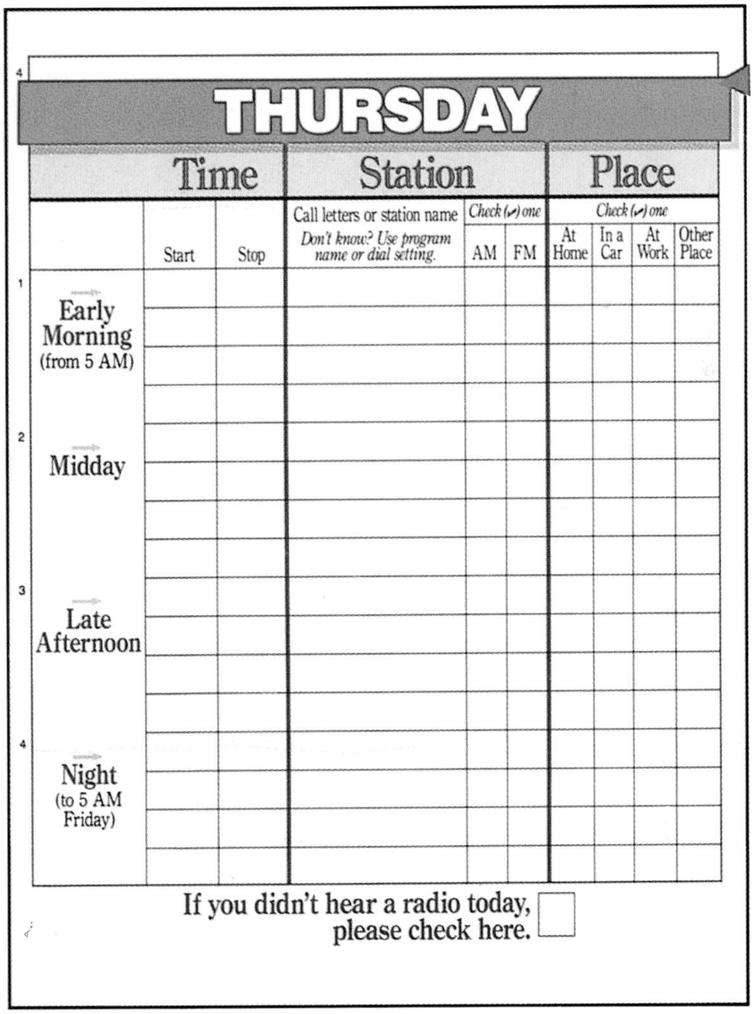
THURSDAY

	Time		Station			Place			
	Start	Stop	Call letters or station name *Don't know? Use program name or dial setting.*	Check (✓) one AM	FM	Check (✓) one At Home	In a Car	At Work	Other Place
Early Morning (from 5 AM)									
Midday									
Late Afternoon									
Night (to 5 AM Friday)									

If you didn't hear a radio today, please check here. ☐

FIGURE 10.5
Arbitron asks radio listeners to complete this survey daily.
(Copyright 1988 Arbitron Ratings Company.)

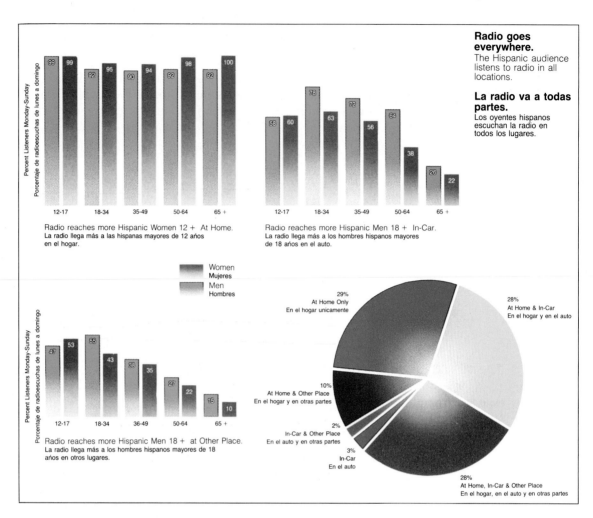

FIGURE 10.6
Arbitron provides subscribers with radio-usage data on special audiences such as Hispanics.

Source: "Radio Today: The Hispanic Listener," Arbitron Ratings Company, 1985, p. 6.
(Copyright 1985 Arbitron Ratings Company.)

*A*DVANTAGES AND DISADVANTAGES OF RADIO

Radio is not for every advertiser, and it is important to understand the relative strengths and weaknesses of this medium.

Advantages

Target Audiences The most important advantage offered by radio is that it reaches specific types of audiences by offering specialized programming. In addition it can be adapted to different parts of the country and can reach people at different times of the day. Radio, for example, is the ideal means of reaching people driving to and from work. The radio station in Ad 10.3 emphasizes the professional backgrounds and income levels of its listeners.

Speed and Flexibility The *speed and flexibility* of radio have already been noted. Of all the media, radio has the shortest *closing period,* in that copy can be submitted up to airtime. This allows advertisers to adjust to local market conditions, current news events, and even the weather. For example, a local hardware store can quickly implement a snow shovel promotion the morning after a snowstorm.

Costs   Radio may be the least expensive of all media. Because airtime costs are relatively low, extensive repetition is possible. In addition, the cost of producing a radio commercial can be low, particularly if the message is read by a local station announcer. Radio's low cost and high reach of selected target groups make it an excellent supporting medium. In fact, the most appropriate role for most radio advertising is a supportive one.

Mental Imagery   An important advantage of radio is its ability to allow listeners to use their imagination. Radio uses words, sound effects, music, and tonality so as to enable listeners to create their own picture of what is happening. For this reason, radio is sometimes referred to as the "theater of the mind."

AD 10.5
The Wall Street Radio Network reaches a very selective audience.
(Courtesy of The Wall Street Journal Radio Network.)

High Levels of Acceptance The final advantage of radio is its high acceptance at the local level. Partly because of its passive nature, radio is normally not perceived as an irritant. People have their favorite radio stations and radio personalities, which they listen to regularly. Messages delivered by these are more likely to be accepted and retained.

Disadvantages

Inattentiveness Radio is not without its drawbacks. Because radio is strictly a listening medium, radio messages are fleeting and commercials may be missed or forgotten. Many listeners perceive radio as pleasant background noise and do not listen to it carefully.

Lack of Visuals The restrictions of sound may also hamper the creative process. Clearly products that must be demonstrated or seen to be appreciated are inappropriate for radio. Creating radio ads that allow the listener to see the product is a difficult challenge. Experts believe that the use of humor may be the most effective way to create such imagery.

AD 10.6
Sometimes one radio network can claim to reach several audiences.
(Courtesy of Satellite Music Network.)

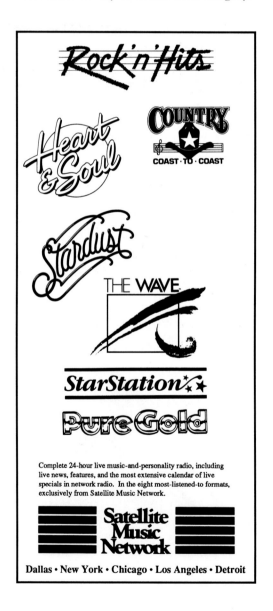

Clutter The proliferation of competing radio stations, combined with the opportunity to engage in heavy repetition, has created a tremendous level of clutter in radio advertising. Coupled with the fact that radio listeners tend to divide their attention among various activities, this clutter greatly reduces the likelihood that a message will be heard or understood.

Scheduling and Buying Difficulties The final disadvantage of radio is the complexity of scheduling and buying radio time. The need to buy time on several stations makes scheduling and following up on ads very complicated. The bookkeeping involved in checking nonstandardized rates, approving bills for payment, and billing clients can be a staggering task. Fortunately computers and large-station representatives have helped alleviate much of this chaos.

■ SUMMARY

- Broadcast media include both radio and television. Whereas print media are bound by space, broadcast media convey transient messages and are bound by time.

- Among the different television systems that an advertiser can use are network, cable, subscription, local, specialty, and public television. Network television is still the dominant form.

- The size of the television audience is measured in a number of ways, including the use of diaries and people meters.

- Advertisers have a choice of scheduling their commercials on a network, local, or cable scheduling basis.

- Television commercials can take the form of sponsorships, participations, or spot announcements.

- Radio can be used as a complement to television campaigns or as the primary advertising medium.

- Radio is classified as either AM or FM according to transmission and power.

- The audience for radio can be measured in terms of a stations's coverage, its circulation, the radio cume, or homes-using-radio (HUR).

■ QUESTIONS

1. What are the major differences between broadcast and print media? How are the two media similar?

2. Compare and contrast spot radio and local radio advertising.

3. List and discuss the advantages and disadvantages of radio as an advertising medium.

4. Describe television syndication. What are the two types of syndication? How does syndication affect the advertiser?

5. What are the three forms that television advertising can take? Which form is used the most, and why?

6. List and discuss the advantages and disadvantages of television as an advertising medium.

■ FURTHER READINGS

HEDGES, MICHAEL. "Radio Life Styles." *American Demographics,* February 1986, pp. 32–35.

JURGENHEIMER, DONALD W., and PETER B. TURK, *Advertising Media,* Columbus, OH; Grid, 1980, Chapter 6.

MARTIN, STEPHEN H. "Television: The Time for Alternatives." *Marketing and Media Decisions,* February 1986, pp. 129–31.

Nielsen Report on Television in 1986. Chicago: A. C. Nielsen, 1986.

ZEIGLER, SHERILYN K., and HERBERT H. HOWARD. *Broadcast Advertising,* 2nd ed. Columbus, OH; Grid Publishing Inc., 1984.

11 *Print and Other Media*

Chapter Outline

Deck the Halls
Print Media
Newspapers: A Local Phenomenon
Magazines
Specialty Advertising
Other Media

Chapter Objectives

When you have completed this chapter you should be able to:

- Understand the similarities and differences between newspapers and magazines
- Explain the advantages and disadvantages of newspaper, magazine, and other forms of media advertising
- Distinguish among direct mail, direct-response advertising, and mail-order catalogs
- Understand which forms of advertising would work best for different products
- Explain the major trends in print advertisements

"DECK THE HALLS"

Christmas of 1987 was a special time for print media. Magazines not only had a special smell, they also made noise. Taking their cue from song-filled greeting cards, Carillon Importers, Ltd., and Brown-Forman Beverage Co. ran a series of musical magazine ads on behalf of Absolut Vodka and Canadian Mist Whiskey. Via the magic of microchips, they played several carols, including "Deck the Halls".

But why have print ads gone to the extravagances of pop-up ads that stand at 3-D attention and musical microchips? The answer is simple—to create maximum impact. Says John B. Caldwell, Jr., senior vice-president for marketing development at the Magazine Publishers of America: "You not only want to get consumers' attention, but you want to get them involved in the ad."

Not only has this new technology nearly doubled magazine ad sales from 1986 to 1987, it has also added new excitement to the medium. "When you take a look at the cost of television advertising," observes Richard McEvoy, vice-president for sales at Carillon, "you can take the same money and stand out in print."

Liquor marketers aren't the only advertisers who are innovative in their magazine displays. Toyota Motor Sales USA Inc. unveiled its 1988 Corolla model with a pair of cardboard 3-D viewfinders inserted in *Time, People,* and *Cosmopolitan. Architectural Digest* readers got a whiff of a Rolls-Royce's leather interior, thanks to a special scent strip. Dodge trucks, Disney World, Chicago's Northern Trust Co., and Camel Agarettis have all used pop-ups.

Such ads present production problems and are expensive to produce. Yet, the costs seem worth it. A Transamerican Corp. pop-up appearing in *Time* in 1986 produced a recall of 97 percent. Jerry Della Femina, creator of the advertisement, states that such creations are not just ads but a "happening."*

PRINT MEDIA

Print is primarily a static, visual medium. It is a picture that consists of words, photographs, drawings, colors, and white space. Like television and radio, its primary functions are to inform and entertain. It differs from broadcast in its respectability and permanence. Print is a record of something that was said by someone. It is close to literature and art. People working in print media win prestigious awards for journalistic achievement. Print advertising has a history and credibility unmatched by broadcast advertising.

NEWSPAPERS: A LOCAL PHENOMENON

For centuries advertising appeared in three basic formats: handbills and circulars, outdoor signs, and newspapers. Whereas the first two have greatly diminished as important advertising media, newspapers remain the leading local medium. Yet maintaining this dominant position has not been easy. Competition began with magazines in the late 1800s, continued with radio in the 1920s, and reached its apex with commercial television in the 1950s.

PRINCIPLE
Newspapers serve the local market.

The initial response of the newspaper industry was to develop new technologies to alleviate the most glaring deficiencies of the medium. Examples are moving from hot metal to cold type, text editing, offset printing, on-line circulation information systems, electronic libraries, data-base publishing, and, most recently, satellite transmission and computerization. There have also been at-

*"Print Ads that Make You Stop, Look—and Listen," *Business Week,* November 23, 1987, p. 38.

TABLE 11.1
A Listing of the Top 25
Newspaper Advertisers in 1986

Rank	Advertiser	Newspaper Ad Expenditures 1986	As % of Co.'s 1986 Ad Total
1	General Motors Corp.	$146,430	17.5
2	Ford Motor Co.	76,136	11.7
3	Texas Air Corp.	63,417	47.9
4	Philip Morris Cos.	57,590	4.2
5	RJR Nabisco	50,347	5.4
6	Chrysler Corp.	42,203	9.9
7	American Telephone & Telegraph	31,106	7.1
8	Trans World Airlines	29,329	37.2
9	General Electric Co.	26,987	7.6
10	Allegis Corp.	26,900	15.7
11	AMR Corp.	25,194	22.3
12	Daimler-Benz AG	23,340	30.1
13	Toyota Motor Corp.	22,878	11.0
14	Delta Air Lines	22,309	21.3
15	NWA Inc.	22,219	42.0
16	Honda Motor Co. Ltd.	21,087	10.3
17	CBS Inc.	20,116	10.9
18	Pan-American World Airways	18,784	N/A
19	Nynex Corp.	18,614	16.6
20	GTE Corp.	18,140	15.7
21	Nissan Motor Co. Ltd.	17,627	9.8
22	International Business Machines Corp.	16,646	5.6
23	Volkswagen AG	15,914	10.5
24	Southwest Airlines Co.	14,153	N/A
25	Time Inc.	13,951	7.3

Note: Dollars are in thousands.

Source: Advertising Age, September 24, 1987, p. 36.

tempts to match the advantages offered by magazines and radio (market selectivity) and television (total market coverage). Examples of market selectivity are free-standing inserts and special-interest newspapers. The latter strategy is reflected in nationally distributed newspapers such as *The Wall Street Journal* and *USA Today.* Finally the high cost of competing, combined with the increased costs of producing newspapers, has resulted in a general consolidation in the newspaper industry. The major owners have become publishing empires, such as Gannett, Knight-Ridder, and Times-Mirror.

Statistics for 1986 indicated that total daily and Sunday circulation had increased to 63.3 million and 59.4 million, respectively. All national newspapers, as well as 19 of the top 25 daily newspapers and 17 of the top 25 Sunday newspapers, showed gains in 1986. Newspaper advertising revenue increased to over $26.8 billion in 1986, a growth of 6.6 percent above 1985. Local/retail advertising accounts for 87 percent of total newspaper advertising expenditures.* As shown in Table 11.1, the two top national newspaper advertisers are auto makers, General Motors and the Ford Motor Company.

The Structure of Newspapers

Newspapers can be classified by frequency of publication, size, and circulation.

Frequency of Publication   Newspapers are published either daily or weekly. There are approximately 1,700 dailies and 7,500 weeklies in the United States. Daily newspapers are usually found in cities and larger towns. *The Wall*

*Belinda Hulin-Salkin, ''Stretching to Deliver Readers' Needs,'' *Advertising Age,* July 20, 1987, p. S-2.

Street Journal is the nation's largest daily. Dailies have either morning editions, evening editions, or all-day editions. Daily papers printed in the morning deliver a relatively complete record of the previous day's events, including detailed reports on local and national news as well as business, financial, and sports happenings. Evening papers follow up the news of the day and provide early reports of the events of the following day. Evening papers also tend to depend more on entertainment and information features than do morning papers. Approximately 30 percent of the dailies and a few of the weeklies also publish a Sunday edition. Sunday newspapers are usually much thicker and contain a great deal of news, advertising, and special features. The circulation of Sunday papers is usually greater than that of dailies because they contain more information and because the reader spends more time with the paper.

Weekly papers appear in towns, suburbs, and smaller cities where the volume of hard news and advertising is not sufficient to support a daily newspaper. These papers emphasize the news of a relatively restricted area; they report local news in depth but tend to ignore national news, sports, and similar subjects. Weeklies are often shunned by national advertisers because they are relatively high in cost, duplicate the circulation of daily or Sunday papers, and generate an administrative headache because ads must be placed separately for each newspaper.

tabloid *A newspaper with a page size of 5 to 6 columns wide and 14 inches deep.*

Size   There are two common sizes of newspapers. The first, referred to as the **tabloid,** consists of five or six columns, each about 2 inches wide, and a total length of approximately 14 inches. This form makes tabloids look similar to an unbound magazine. The *Chicago Sun Times* employs this size, as does the New York *Daily News,* the *National Enquirer,* and *The Star.* The *standard size,* or **broadsheet,** newspaper is about twice as large as the tabloid size, usually eight columns wide and 300 lines deep, or 22 inches deep by 14 inches wide. However, for both pragmatic and aesthetic reasons, many standard-sized newspapers are reducing to layouts that are six columns wide. More than 90 percent of all newspapers use standard size.

broadsheet *A newspaper with a page size of 8 columns wide and 22 inches deep.*

circulation *A measure of the number of copies sold.*

Circulation   For the most part, newspapers are a mass medium, attempting to reach either a regional or a national audience. Industry people use the word **circulation** to refer to the number of newspapers sold. A few newspapers have a *national* circulation, such as the *London Times* and *U.S.A. Today,* and a far greater number are restricted to a *regional* circulation. Some newspapers, however, have attempted to reach certain target audiences in other ways. Most common among these are newspapers directed at specific ethnic or foreign-language groups. For example, over 200 newspapers in the United States are aimed primarily at Black Americans. In New York City alone papers are printed in Chinese, Spanish, Russian, Yiddish, German, and Vietnamese.

Special newspapers also exist for special-interest groups, religious denominations, political affiliations, labor unions, and professional and fraternal organizations. For example, *Stars and Stripes* is the newspaper read by millions of armed services personnel.

The Readers of Newspapers

Two-thirds of all American adults read a newspaper every weekday; 86 percent read a paper at least once a week. Newspapers are purchased regularly in 74 percent of all U.S. households.*

Newspaper readers encompass all income brackets, educational levels, age groups, and ethnic backgrounds. They live in cities, suburbs, towns, resorts, and

*Ibid., p. S-7.

rural areas. By all demographic standards, the newspaper is a solid mass-market medium. Admittedly there are a few general reader differences. For example, older, better-educated adults with higher incomes tend to read newspapers more often and more thoroughly than do other people.

The most useful way to assess newspaper readers is in terms of which sections they read. That is, do certain types of people read specific sections of the newspaper more than others? Reg Murphy, president and publisher of Times Mirror Company's *Baltimore Sun,* notes: "Think of each special interest as a 10 percent block of the paper: sports, comics, news, business, features . . . each of these is worth 10 percent. If a person is interested in only one 10 percent block of the paper, you have an occasional reader. With two 10 percent blocks, you get a regular reader. And with three blocks, you've got a subscriber."*

Advertising in Newspapers

Although newspapers are not formally classified by the type of advertising they carry, this is a useful way of thinking about newspapers. In this context there are three general types of newspaper advertising: classified, display, and supplements.

classified advertising *Commercial messages arranged in the newspaper according to the interests of readers.*

Classified Historically **classified advertising** was the first type of advertising found in newspapers. Classified ads generally consist of all types of commercial messages arranged according to their interest to readers, such as "Help

AD 11.1
The Westgate Center, St. Louis, provides a very colorful newspaper ad.
(Courtesy of Paragon Group, Inc. and Bartels & Carstens.)

Ibid., p. S-2.

Wanted," "Real Estate for Sale," and "Cars for Sale." Classified ads represent approximately 27 percent of total advertising revenue. *Regular classified* ads are usually listed under a major heading with little embellishment or white space. *Display classified* ads use borders, larger type, white space, photos, and, occasionally, color. Often newspapers will also include legal notices, political and government reports, and personals in the classified section.

display advertising *Sponsored messages that can be of any size and location within the newspaper, with the exception of the editorial page.*

Display   **Display advertising** is the dominant form of newspaper advertising. Display ads can be of any size and can be found anywhere within the newspaper, with the exception of the editorial page. Display advertising is further divided into two subcategories—local (retail) and national (general).

THE CHECKING ACCOUNT FOR ANYONE WHO THINKS IT'S SILLY TO PAY FOR THINGS THEY DON'T NEED.

Why pay for anything you don't need?

American Charter No-Frills Checking Account: Only What You Need. For Free.

If you don't need a lot of financial services, you need No-Frills Checking.

You get 50 free checks imprinted with your name and address, 10 free transactions per month (each additional withdrawal is only 25¢) and no minimum monthly balance or service charge.

Plus, you have the option of adding many other services, like Automated Teller Machine access, telephone bill paying and VISA card, for a modest charge.

American Charter Horizon Checking Account: How To Have It All For Just $3 Per Month.

Need a full range of financial services? Then check into Horizon Checking.

You get 40 free imprinted checks, 28 free transactions per month (each additional withdrawal is only 25¢), a discount on the VISA card, free VISA travelers checks, overdraft protection and much, much more.

American Charter Checking Accounts: They're Worth Checking Into.

Get the checking account that's just right for you. Quickly and easily.

American Charter has five different checking account plans. So call your American Charter branch today and say "I'm checking into checking."

You'll get just what you need.

AMERICAN CHARTER
Federal Savings and Loan Association
Member FSLIC

AD 11.2
American Charter Federal Savings and Loan reaches a regional audience with this humorous newspaper ad.
(Courtesy of American Charter Federal Savings and Loan.)

A comparison of the rough and final versions of a newspaper ad.
(© 1988 by Prentice-Hall, Inc.)

Local display advertising is placed by local businesses, organizations, or individuals who pay the lower, local advertising rate. Approximately 85 percent of all display advertising is local, with the great majority of it placed by local retailers. Such ads tend to follow a pattern and are replete with coupons and announcements of sales items.

National display advertising is run by national and international businesses, organizations, and celebrities in order to maintain brand recognition or to supplement the efforts of local retailers or other promotional efforts. National advertisers pay higher rates because newspapers argue that it costs more to serve national accounts.

supplements *Syndicated or local full-color advertising inserts that appear in newspapers throughout the week.*

Supplements Both national and local advertising can be carried in newspaper supplements. **Supplements** refer to syndicated or local full-color advertising inserts that appear throughout the week and especially in the Sunday edition. One very popular type of supplement is the magazine supplement, of which there are two types.

Syndicated supplements are published by independent publishers and distributed to newspapers throughout the country. The logo for the publisher and the local paper appear on the masthead. The best-known syndicated supplements are *Parade* and *USA Weekend.*

Local supplements are produced by either one newspaper or a group of newspapers in the same area. Whether syndicated or locally edited, in content and format magazine supplements resemble magazines more than newspapers.

free-standing insert advertisements *Preprinted advertisements that are placed loosely within the newspaper.*

Another type of newspaper supplement is the **free-standing insert advertisement** (FSIA), or "loose insert." These preprinted advertisements can range in size from a single page to over 30 pages and can be in black and white or full color. This material is printed elsewhere and then delivered to the newspaper. Newspapers charge the advertiser a fee for inserting the material plus a special rate for carrying the ad in a particular issue. This form of newspaper advertising now represents approximately 15 percent of daily display newspaper advertising.* It is growing in popularity with retail advertisers for two reasons: (1) It allows greater control over the reproduction quality of the advertisement;

*DDB Needham Worldwide, *Media Trends,* 1987 ed., p. 63.

and (2) the multipage FSI is an excellent coupon carrier. Newspapers are not necessarily happy about the growth of free-standing inserts. Not only do they make less revenue from this form of advertising, but they also have the problem of finding news and features to fill the physical space left when advertising is free-standing rather than display.

Measuring the Audience for Newspapers

Statements regarding newspaper circulation are verified by an independent auditing group, the Audit Bureau of Circulation (ABC), that represents the advertiser, the agency, and the publisher. ABC members include only paid-circulation newspapers and magazines. The ABC reports have nothing to do with the rates that a newspaper charges. They simply verify the newspaper's circulation statistics and provide a detailed analysis of the newspaper by states, towns, and counties.

Newspapers that do not belong to an auditing organization must provide either a "publisher's statement" or a "Post Office statement" to prospective advertisers. The former is a sworn affidavit, and the latter is an annual statement given to the Post Office.

Simmons-Scarborough The research firm Simmons-Scarborough provides a syndicated newspaper readership study that annually measures readership

AD 11.3
The Advertising Checking Bureau, Inc., is just one company seeking to provide newspaper research data.
(Courtesy of the Advertising Checking Bureau, Inc.)

profiles in approximately 70 of the nation's largest cities. The study covers readership of a single issue and the estimated unduplicated readers from a series of issues. Scarborough is the only consistent measurement of popular audiences in individual markets.

The Advantages of Newspapers

Market Coverage   There are numerous advantages to advertising in newspapers. Undoubtedly the most obvious is the extensive market coverage provided by newspapers. When an advertiser wishes to reach a local or regional market, newspapers offer an extremely cost-efficient alternative. Even special-interest groups and racial and ethnic groups can be reached through newspapers.

Comparison Shopping   The second advantage of newspapers is the attitude consumers hold toward them as shopping vehicles. Many consumers use newspapers for comparison shopping. Consumers can also control when and how they read the paper. As a result, newspaper ads are viewed very positively.

PRINCIPLE _____
Newspaper advertising is viewed positively by consumers who use it for a shopping reference.

Positive Consumer Attitudes   Closely related to this positive attitude toward newspaper advertising is consumers' positive attitudes toward newspapers in general. Readers generally perceive newspapers to be very immediate and current, including the advertisements.

KENNETH O. HUSTEL—VICE PRESIDENT—NEWSPAPER ADVERTISING BUREAU, INC.

Organizations such as the Newspaper Advertising Bureau are responsible for the economic health of the newspaper industry. As noted in this box, people like Kenn Hustel spend a very active life trying to make sure newspapers prosper.

A.M. The first order of business today is to solidify plans for the Chicago Advertising Club's December 17th program that will feature Creative Newspaper 12. [This is a multiprojector program featuring the best in creativity—award winners—in 1987 newspaper advertising. The Bureau produced the show, and they will provide the speaker, audio-visual equipment, and copies of the 48-page newspaper (all ads) for each of the 340 attendees.]

He advises his secretary of the need to complete the following:

1. Send to C.A.C. directors a checklist covering all specifics from seating arrangements on the dais to the menu.
2. A letter to the *Tribune* and *Sun-Times* advising them of the Ad Club plans.
3. Letters to newspaper-representative firms and other newspaper advertising people encouraging their attendance (at $20 a pop—payable to the Ad Club).
4. Letters to each of the creative people at agencies and advertisers who won awards to be guests of the Bureau. Will need 5 tables (10 people per table).

The first phone call is from a new member of the Bureau's New York sales team. He has been given the assignment to begin covering advertising personnel in Philip Morris in New York. Since Kenn has been covering Philip Morris's major ad agency—Leo Burnett in Chicago—for a number of years, the new man feels Kenn can provide him some background information. Names, billing, brands, etc. are given verbally over the phone. The follow-up letter that is sent repeats the transmitted information and includes reports published in well known periodicals—*Ad Age, Adweek,* etc.

Time to review and rehearse new Food Pages presentation—scheduled for 3:00 P.M. meeting tomorrow with the Foote, Cone & Belding Media Director.

Now it's time to turn attention to the planned visit to Minneapolis/St. Paul. The mission here is to schedule "Food Pages" presentation with the key players in the Twin Cities, 2 weeks down the road. Letters have been sent, and today is the day Kenn promised/threatened to call them back. Results are fairly good. Meetings set at Pillsbury, General Mills, The Haworth Group (agency on Pet Foods business), Campbell-Mithun (Land O' Lakes agency), and BBDO (Hormel's major agency). Conflicts have made it impossible to meet with Land O' Lakes and Hormel—so they will have to be visited on the next trip. (A 3- to 5-day trip to Minneapolis will run $800 to $1,000 including air fare, so these trips must be carefully scheduled.) Like most advertising sales people, Kenn has an annual travel budget that he must watch closely.

A major meeting is set with National Car Rental. And, meetings with the marketing director at the *Minneapolis Star Tribune* and *St. Paul Pioneer Press Dispatch* are added to the itinerary (both are dues-paying mem-

Flexibility   Flexibility is a major strength of newspapers. One type of flexibility is geographic. Advertisers can choose to advertise in some markets and not in others. Also newspapers are often flexible in the actual production of the ads. Unusual ad sizes, full-color ads, free-standing inserts, different prices to appear in different areas, and supplements are all options for a newspaper advertiser.

Interaction of National and Local   Finally newspapers provide an excellent bridge between the national advertiser and the local retailer. A local retailer can easily tie in with a national campaign by utilizing a similar advertisement in the local daily. In addition, quick-action programs, such as sales and coupons, are easily implemented through local newspapers.

The Disadvantages of Newspapers

As with any advertising medium, newspapers also have their disadvantages.

Short Life Span   Although a great many people do read newspapers, they read them quickly (the average time is 15 minutes) and they read them once. The life span of a daily newspaper is only 24 hours.

bers of the NAB) to review new programs produced or being prepared by the Bureau, Kenn's planned meetings in the Twin Cities, etc.

The National Car meeting will take time to prepare. Kenn has forwarded key objectives and strategy to the Bureau's marketing department in New York, and asked them to pull key auto rental and user data. Marketing will respond eventually, but the chances are strong that New York will not have time to prepare (write) the presentation. Kenn calls his favorite chartmaker—Doot-Russell—in Chicago to check timing. 24" × 36" easel charts are decided upon—and within 2 days or less, 25 to 35 charts can be prepared.

AFTERNOON (No lunch today)

The numerous letters pertaining to the C.A.C. luncheon have been written and are currently in the display writer.

Time to rereview the food show in preparation for tomorrow's meeting with FCB. Kenn wants to change the stated recommendation. It needs a touch of urgency—something to provoke a positive response—a quick response.

It's done. Now a call to the chartmaker will ensure that the chart is back tomorrow morning.

Final piece of business today is to solidify plans for the various advertising clubs that have invited Kenn to give the Creative Newspaper 12 audio-visual presentation. To date, commitments have been received from Black Hills Ad Fed (Rapid City, South Dakota); LaCrosse-Winona; Columbus, Ohio; South Bend; Massillon-

Canton. Dates for Fort Wayne (IN) and Madison have not been set.

Kenn will specify equipment needs and forward a photograph, biography, and brief description of the program. The ad clubs like to send out publicity notes to stimulate attendance.

(Courtesy of Kenneth O. Hustel.)

Clutter   High clutter is a serious problem with most newspapers. This is particularly true on supermarket advertising days and on Sundays, when information overload reduces the impact of any single advertisement.

Limited Coverage of Certain Groups   Although newspapers have wide market coverage, certain market groups are not frequent readers. For example, newspapers do not reach a large part of the under-20 age group. The same is true of the elderly and those speaking a foreign language who do not live in a large city.

Products That Don't Fit   Newspapers suffer the same limitations shared by all print media. Certain products should not advertise in newspapers. Products that require demonstration or need to create a high level of emotional involvement would have a difficult time in the newspaper format. Similarly products that consumers do not expect to find advertised in newspapers might be easily overlooked.

Poor Reproduction   With the exception of special printing techniques and preprinted inserts, the reproduction quality of newspapers is comparatively poor and limiting, especially for color advertisements, although color reproduction has improved thanks to the popularity of *USA Today*. In addition, the speed necessary to compose a daily newspaper prevents the detailed preparation and care in production that is possible when time pressures are not so great.

MAGAZINES

History may remember the 1980s as a time of paradox for magazine publishing. In spite of intense competition and sluggish ad sales, new magazines have been appearing at an astonishing rate—362 in 1986 alone* (see Figure 11.1). In addition, publishers are investing more money than ever in existing titles. Individual magazines have become bigger and brighter. Heavier paper stocks, lush photography, and sophisticated graphics are used to create beautiful, eye-catching editorial environments that entice both readers and advertisers.

The magazine industry has entered the "age of skimming" when 80 percent of the information comes from the story titles, the subheadings, the captions, and the pictures. Although magazine advertising revenue increased 41 percent between 1985 and 1986 to a total of $5.6 billion, magazines are still unsure as to which format to adopt and which audiences to go after.† It is a medium that advertisers tend to view cautiously.

The Structure of Magazines

Magazines are commonly classified in terms of frequency of publication and audience by the *Standard Rate and Data Service*. On the basis of audiences served, there are three types of magazines. The first category, *consumer magazines,* is directed at consumers who buy products for their own consumption. These magazines are distributed through the mail, newsstands, or stores. The

FIGURE 11.1
The growth in the number of magazines published: 1956–1986.
(Courtesy of Magazine Publishers of America.)

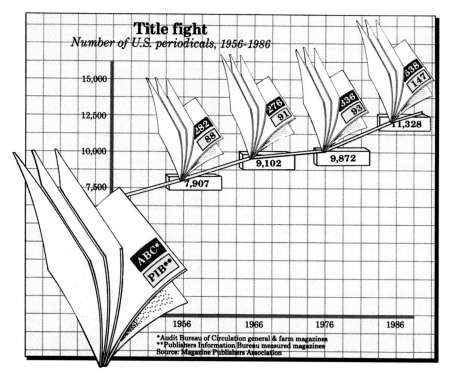

*Belinda Hulin-Salkin, "Style, Looks Enthrall Publishers," *Advertising Age,* September 14, 1987, p. S-2.
†DDB Needham, *Media Trends,* p. 55.

TABLE 11.2
A Listing of the Top 25 Magazine Advertisers: 1985–1986

Rank	Advertiser	Magazine Ad Expenditures 1986	As % of Co.'s 1986 Ad Total
1	Philip Morris Cos.	$230,130	16.9
2	RJR Nabisco	135,657	14.5
3	General Motors Corp.	129,408	15.4
4	Ford Motor Co.	125,071	19.2
5	Procter & Gamble Co.	86,506	0.6
6	Chrysler Corp.	78,905	18.5
7	American Telephone & Telegraph	74,014	16.8
8	CBS Inc.	58,871	31.8
9	Time Inc.	51,166	26.8
10	General Electric Co.	50,776	14.3
11	Unilever NV	49,815	9.6
12	Sears, Roebuck & Co.	42,933	4.2
13	U.S. Government	39,679	12.9
14	International Business Machines Corp.	39,007	13.2
15	Volkswagen AG	37,265	24.4
16	Loews Corp.	34,434	23.5
17	Kraft Inc.	33,823	7.7
18	Honda Motor Co. Ltd.	32,518	15.8
19	Revlon Group	31,935	21.4
20	E.I. du Pont de Nemours & Co.	31,613	28.0
21	American Express Co.	30,911	16.2
22	Capital Cities/ABC	30,555	48.4
23	Bristol-Myers Co.	30,248	9.1
24	American Brands	27,433	17.2
25	Grand Metropolitan PLC	25,163	16.4

Note: Dollars are in thousands.
Source: Advertising Age, September 24, 1987, p. 28.

The number of magazines available in the marketplace increased steadily during the 1980s.
(Courtesy of Brownie Harris/The Stock Market.)

second category is *business magazines*. These magazines are directed at business readers and are further divided into *trade papers* (read by retailers, wholesalers, and other distributors), *industrial magazines* (read by manufacturers), and *professional magazines* (read by physicians, lawyers, and others). *Farm magazines* represent the third category. Such magazines go to farmers and those engaged in farm-related activities.

The magazine industry also classifies magazines by *geographic coverage, demographics,* and *editorial diversity.*

Magazines generally cover certain sections or regions of the country. The area covered may be as small as a city *(Los Angeles Magazine* and *Boston Magazine)* or as large as several contiguous states (the southwestern edition of *Southern Living Magazine).* Geographic editions help encourage local retail support by listing the names of distributors in the advertisement.

Demographic editions group subscribers according to age, income, occupation, and other classifications. *McCall's* for example, publishes a ZIP edition to upper-income homes, *Newsweek* offers a college edition, and *Time* sends special editions to students, business executives, doctors, and business managers.

Various magazines emphasize certain types of editorial content. The most widely used categories are: general editorial *(Reader's Digest);* women's service *(Family Circle);* shelter *(House Beautiful);* business *(Forbes);* and special interest *(Ski).*

AD 11.5
Business Week ran this comparison ad to attract potential advertisers.
(Courtesy of Business Week.)

If you're angling for top management, you'll catch more with Business Week than with Forbes or Fortune.

Every issue of Business Week gives you 39% more top management coverage than Forbes at a 14% lower CPM. And 23% more than Fortune at a 10% lower CPM.

Break it down by IEI $50,000+. Purchase Decision-Makers, $50,000+. Or company size.

Forbes and Fortune seem to let the big ones get away.

So to fill your nets with top management, remember Business Week is the leader among business magazines. Every business week.

And that's no fish story.

COMPARISON CHART			
	BUSINESS WEEK	**FORBES**	**FORTUNE**
'87 NORTH AMERICA RATE BASE	✓ 810,000	720,000	650,000
TOTAL READERS	✓5,631,000	3,249,000	4,012,000
TARGET AUDIENCE COVERAGE			
Top Management:			
% Coverage	✓ 12.5%	9.0%	10.2%
4/C CPM	✓ $98.00	$114.47	$108.94
Top Management:			
IEI $50,000+ : % Coverage	✓ 15.0%	11.5%	12.9%
4/C CPM	✓ $166.10	$181.29	$174.30
Top Management:			
Co. Size 1,000+ % Coverage	✓ 24.7%*	17.3%*	10.8%*
Employees: 4/C CPM	✓ $564.75	$676.61	$1,170.29
Top Management:			
Co. Size Under % Coverage	✓ 11.5%	7.9%	9.8%
100 Employees: 4/C CPM	✓ $152.12	$186.65	$161.90
Top Management:†			
Purchase Decision-Makers			
$50,000+ : % Coverage	✓ 24.0%	10.1%	10.6%
4/C CPM	✓ $152.12	$303.12	$312.67

Audience Data: 1987 MRI Doublebase
*Projection Relatively Unstable Because of Small Base—
  Use With Caution
†1986 MRI Doublebase Business-to-Business

BusinessWeek
The leader among business magazines.

© 1987 McGRAW HILL, INC.

Physical Characteristics   The structure of the magazine industry is also reflected in the terminology used to describe the physical characteristics of a magazine. The most common magazine page sizes are 8½ × 11 inches and 6 × 9 inches.

Distribution   The method used to distribute a magazine partly reflects its structure. **Traditional delivery** is either through *newsstand purchase* or *home delivery* via the U.S. Postal System. **Nontraditional delivery** systems include the following: hanging bagged copies on doorknobs; delivery within newspapers; delivery through professionals, such as the *College Musician* distributed by music teachers to their students; and direct sales or special sales.* These unconventional distribution systems have made it easier for magazines to reach their target audiences.

The Readers of Magazines

Historically magazines have been read by upscale people. That is, people who read magazines tend to have above-average educations and incomes and to work in white-collar occupations. Although this generalization is still true today, the most meaningful way to appraise magazine readership is to look at the characteristics of people who read similar kinds of magazines. For example, the *Business Week* ad pictured in Ad 11.5 compares its readers with those of *Forbes* and *Fortune* in respect to several characteristics considered important by advertisers.

One magazine category that has taken special advantage of the idea of readership segmentation is children's magazines. Twenty years ago this category was limited to a handful of magazines. In 1986, 7 magazines were introduced just for preschoolers, while the Educational Press Association of America counted 92 magazines aimed at children aged 13 and under.† Advertisers of toys, clothing, educational games, tapes, and computers can easily reach prospective customers through these magazines.

Measuring Magazine Readership

Magazine rates are based on the number of readers, which correlates with the circulation that a publisher promises to provide, that is, the *guaranteed circulation*. As with newspapers, the ABC is responsible for collecting and evaluating this data to ensure that guaranteed circulation was obtained. The ABC audits subscriptions as well as newsstand sales. It also checks the number of delinquent subscribers and rates of renewal.

Magazine circulation refers to the number of copies of an issue, not the readership of the publication. A single copy of a magazine might be read by one person or several people, depending upon its content.

The SMRB goes one step further by relating readership patterns to purchasing habits. The Bureau provides data on who reads which magazines and which products these readers buy and consume. Most advertisers and agencies are very dependent on SMRB estimates of magazine audiences.

MAI   A company known as MediaMark provides a service called MAI that measures readership for most popular national and regional magazines (along with other media). Reports, issued twice annually, cover readership by demographics, psychographics, and product usage.

*Stuart J. Elliott, "Publishers Direct Sales Efforts at the Retail Level," *Advertising Age,* March 9, 1987, p. S-2.
†Joanne Cleaver, "Rise of the Dual Income Makes Kids a Hot Target," *Advertising Age,* November 10, 1986, p. S-4.

Advertising in Magazines

The actual selection and placement of advertising in magazines vary according to the specific magazine selected. For example, if we look at product classifications, the automotive industry places the most advertising in magazines, followed by business and consumer services and food and food products (see Figure 11.2).

Each magazine or magazine category has its own unique terminology to describe its format and rate structure. Nevertheless, all magazines share some characteristics. For example, the front cover of a magazine is called its first cover page. The inside of the front cover is called the second cover page, the inside of the back cover the third cover page, and the back cover the fourth cover page. Normally the double-page spread is the largest unit of space sold by magazines. The two pages usually face each other. When a double-page ad is designed, it is critical that the *gutter* (the white space between the pages running along the

FIGURE 11.2
A listing of the top 10 magazine advertising classifications.
Source: DDB Needham Media Trends, p. 57.

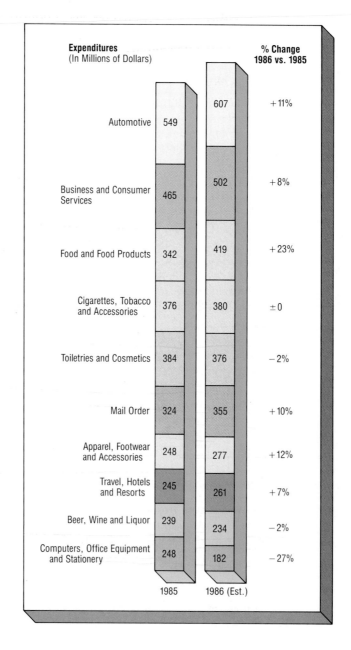

outside edge of the page) be bridged or jumped meaning that no headline words run through the gutter and that all body text be on one side or the other. A page without outside margins, in which the color extends to the edge of the page, is called a *bleed page.* Magazines sometimes can offer more than two connected pages (four is the most common number). This is referred to as a *gatefold.* Finally a single page or double page can be broken into a variety of units called *fractional page space* (for example, vertical half-page, horizontal half-page, double horizontal half-page, half-page double spread, and checkerboard).

The Advantages of Magazines

PRINCIPLE

Magazines are becoming more specialized.

Target Audiences The overriding advantage of magazines originally was their ability to reach a wide, general audience. Today this is no longer the case. As noted, the greatest areas of growth are expected to be in special-interest magazines and special editions of existing publications. The ability to reach specialized audiences has become a primary advantage.

Audience Receptivity The second advantage of magazines is the high level of audience receptivity. The editorial environment of a magazine lends authority and credibility to the advertising. Many magazines claim that advertising in their publication lends prestige to a product. Clearly an ad in *Fortune* would impress business audiences, just as an ad in *Seventeen* would impress teenagers.

Long Life Span Magazines have the longest life of all media. Some magazines, such as *National Geographic* or *Consumer Reports,* are used as ongoing references and might never be discarded. Other publications, such as *TV Guide,* are intended to be used frequently during a given period of time. In addition magazines have very high reach potential because of a large pass-along, or secondary, audience of family, friends, customers, and colleagues.

Magazines have the longest life span of all media.
(Courtesy of D. Aretz/The Stock Option.)

AD 11.6
This ad illustrates two primary advantages of magazines: the ability to reproduce color and the capacity to carry sales promotions.

(Courtesy of Campbell Soup Company.)

Finally, people tend to read a magazine at a relatively slow rate. Research indicates that the typical reader devotes 60 to 90 minutes to a magazine over 3 days. Therefore, magazines offer an opportunity to use long copy. The magazine format also allows more creative variety through multiple pages, inserts, and other design features.

Visual Quality   The visual quality of magazines tends to be excellent because they are printed on high-quality paper stock that provides superior photo reproduction in both black and white and color. This production quality often reflects the superior editorial content. Feature stories are frequently written by well-respected writers.

Sales Promotions   Magazines are an effective medium through which to distribute various sales promotion devices, such as coupons, product samples, and information cards. A 1987 Post Office ruling allowed magazines to carry loose editorial and advertising supplements as part of the publication provided the magazine is enclosed in an envelope or wrapper.* Ad 11.6 illustrates a magazine that carries a sales promotion.

*DDB Needham, *Media Trends,* p. 55.

The Disadvantages of Magazines

Limited Flexibility Although magazines offer many benefits to advertisers, long lead time and lack of flexibility and immediacy are two of their drawbacks. For example, ads must be submitted well in advance of the publication date, requiring advertisers to have engravings for full-color advertisements at the printer more than 2 months before the cover date of a monthly publication. Magazines are also inflexible in respect to available positions. Prime locations, such as the back cover or inside front cover, may be sold months in advance. Some readers do not look at an issue of a magazine until long after it has reached their homes, so impact builds slowly.

High Cost The second disadvantage associated with magazines is their relatively high cost. Cost per person reached can also be high for magazines designed for a broad, nonselective audience because such magazines produce a high level of waste circulation. However, magazines with carefully segmented audiences can be very cost-efficient.

Distribution The final disadvantage associated with magazines is the difficulty of distribution. Many magazines, such as *Woman's Day* and *People,* are purchased primarily through newsstands. Yet there is no way that 2,500 different magazines can all appear on store racks. Some magazines are simply not available to all possible target audiences.

AD 11.7
This ad sponsored by the International Catalog Media, Inc. offers over 1,500 American catalogs to Japanese consumers.

(Courtesy of *Direct Marketing* and Catalog International Inc.)

PRINCIPLE _____
Specialty advertising brings a long life to reminder messages.

An estimated 6,000 companies manufacture and sell specialties. In 1986 these companies gave away more than $3 billion of specialty items. Writing instruments accounted for 17.3 percent of sales, followed by clothing items (14.3 percent), calendars (14 percent), and leather/vinyl products (11.9 percent).* Items usually carry the name and address of the advertiser, along with a short sales message.

The Advantages and Disadvantages of Specialty Advertising

Thanks largely to improved printing processes, specialty items can be extremely inexpensive. An advertiser's message can be imprinted on 5-cent pencils and little packets of popping corn with a message thanking customers. But the trend is toward more expensive gifts. At the Specialty Advertising Association (SAA) annual meeting, advertisers can select Pierre Cardin calf-leather binders, silk jackets, and business cards in a bottle for the customers and prospects they really want to impress.

The most important advantage of specialty advertising is its long life. An SAA study showed that 60 to 80 percent of people who had received specialty items were using them 6 months later.† Another advantage is the positive attitude recipients have toward specialty items, especially if they are useful. For example, the *Vancouver Sun* newspaper rewarded new parents who ran birth announcements in its classified ads by mailing them replicas of the announcement encased in a lucite paperweight with the newspaper's name. So many additional requests were received that the *Sun* began offering the item for sale to parents who placed birth announcements for 2 days. The third advantage of specialty advertising is the ability to preselect the audience so that there is very little waste circulation. The final advantage is the flexibility found in this industry. Not only do specialty houses store thousands of existing items, but they will also design specific items on request.

On the negative side, specialty advertising tends to be quite expensive on a per-prospect basis. There is also the "junk" image associated with poor-quality specialty merchandise. Although better-quality items do get used, poor-quality merchandise is often quickly discarded.

Specialty items can be effective memory devices if they are useful and reasonably well made.
(Courtesy of Teri Stratford.)

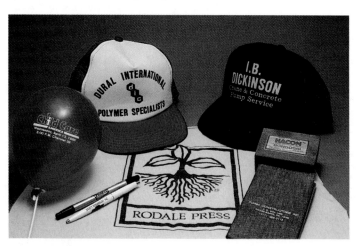

*Kevin T. Higgins, "Specialty Advertising Thrives—Even in Tough Times," *Marketing News,* October 11, 1985, pp. 18–20.
†*Ibid.,* p. 19.

OTHER MEDIA

Several other media types are given less consideration here, either because they do not play a prominent role in the typical media strategy or they are noncommissionable media. Nevertheless, they may play a prominent role for a given advertiser. They are listed in Table 11.3. A more complete discussion is provided in later chapters.

**TABLE 11.3
Summary Listing of Secondary Media**

Type	Description
Outdoor	Advertising messages delivered through billboards, painted bulletins, or spectaculars intended to reach people on the move in order to create brand association and/or impulse buying.
Transit Advertising	Advertising messages delivered through car cards, traveling displays, or station posters and displays to reach people traveling in order to create last-minute reminders.
Direct Mail	Advertising messages delivered through the mail service in order to deliver longer, more complex messages for products that are presold or low risk.
Directories	Advertising messages delivered through a book or catalog that lists advertisers by category in order to reach selective target audiences.
Films	Advertising messages delivered at movie theaters in order to reach selective target audiences.

SUMMARY

- Print media are static and visual. They differ from broadcast media in their respectability, permanence, and credibility.

- Newspapers are still the leading local medium, have improved technology owing to increased competition from broadcast and direct mail, and are diminishing in number.

- The structure of newspapers is determined by frequency of publication, size, and circulation.

- Magazines have the greatest ability to reach preselected audiences. This selectivity is exhibited through the elaborate structure found in the industry.

- The out-of-home media are outdoor advertising and transit advertising.

- Other advertising media include direct mail, directories, specialty advertising, exhibits and booths, film and audio-visual, and miscellaneous.

QUESTIONS

1. What are classified, display, and supplemental newspaper advertising? How are they similar? How are they different?

2. What are the advantages and disadvantages of advertising in newspapers?

3. How has the nature of magazines changed over the years?

4. What are the advantages and disadvantages of advertising in magazines?

FURTHER READINGS

CLARKE, GEORGE. *Transit Advertising.* New York: Transit Advertising Association, 1970.

GAW, WALTER A. *Specialty Advertising.* Chicago: Specialty Advertising Association International, 1972.

McGANN, ANTHONY F., and THOMAS RUSSELL. *Advertising Media.* Homewood, IL: Richard D. Irwin, 1981, Chapters 7–8.

RUTH, MARCIA. "Advertising in Unusual Places." *Presstime,* September 1986, pp. 20–21.

SANDAGE, C. H., VERNON FRYBURGER, and KIM ROTZOLL. *Advertising Theory and Practice,* 12th ed. Homewood, IL: Richard D. Irwin, 1986, Chapter 13.

STRAUSS, STEVE. *Moving Images: The Transportation Poster in America.* New York: Fullcourt Press, 1984.

12 Media Buying

DON'T READ THIS CHAPTER! (handwritten)

Chapter Outline

Media Buying: The First Time
Media Buying versus Media Planning
Media-Buying Functions
Special Skills: Expert Knowledge of Media Opportunities
Special Skills: Knowledge of Media Pricing
Special Skills: Media Vehicle Selection and Negotiation
Special Skills: Maintaining Plan Performance

Chapter Objectives

When you have completed this chapter you should be able to:

- Explain how media buying is different from media planning and how it complements media planning
- Understand the major duties of a media buyer: research analyst, expert evaluator, negotiator, and troubleshooter
- Explain how buyers translate media-plan objectives into target-directed advertising schedules
- Understand why media pricing and negotiating skills will have even greater roles in the advertising strategies of the 1990s

MEDIA BUYING: THE FIRST TIME

I was nervous. Only months out of college and only 2 weeks in my position as assistant media buyer on the Carling Brewing Company account, I was going to have the sole responsibility for negotiating the buys for all the Black Label radio spot schedules.

Gerry, my tough, cigar-chewing boss, was leaving on an emergency field trip that would mean 2 weeks away from the office. The brewing company media plan was finished, and the traffic department had to send the commercials to the stations soon. The buying had to be finished, as Gerry put it, "Yesterday!"

Gerry explained the radio schedules situation and briefed me on exactly what had to be accomplished. The media plan detailed the number of announcements expected and recommended the radio time periods to be used. The prices had been estimated from past schedules; all were *below* what the stations normally charged. "You tell the station our plans, but don't mention the price—let the station tell you," Gerry explained. He then told me that the prices were still too high for Carling. "I expect you to negotiate even lower rates," he said. "If you expect to be a professional buyer—you better be very good at negotiating . . . don't mess this up." With that cheery news, he grabbed his briefcase and left the office.

I had some retail selling experience, but I didn't feel at all prepared. "What will I do if the station's price is higher than the one in the plan?" No ready answer came to mind. With a feeling I did not belong in a pressure business, I placed my first call.

There was quiver in my voice as I explained to the station manager the brand's radio plans for the new campaign. "Now that is our schedule . . . what will the price be for the spot announcements?" I asked. The station manager paused. Then, after what seemed to be an hour, the manager said, "Well, let's see . . . we have had an increase in our prices . . . " I felt a tightening in my stomach. "Here it comes," I thought, "the very first call and I'm in big trouble." As the manager spoke, I checked the plan for the price. It was budgeted at $50 per announcement. The manager then replied, "Based on your frequency, we'll have to price these at $60 each." At that instant, I had reached for a pencil and knocked over the large coffee mug on my desk. Coffee ran everywhere; over the papers, the plans book, my notes, off desk, and onto my lap. I jumped back, dropped the phone and cursing loudly began frantically to move papers from the spreading pool. When I finally found some composure I picked up the phone to hear the manager say, "My gosh! . . . Settle down . . . OK . . . OK . . . we'll use the $50 rate from last year."

Since then, I have often recalled that lucky first buy. It was never that easy again, but it was invariably an interesting experience.

MEDIA BUYING VERSUS MEDIA PLANNING

Chapter 9 explained what media planning is and how media planners design objectives and strategies to reflect the advertiser's needs. Planning concentrates on the strategy of audience delivery and recommends an approach. Media buying involves the next series of decisions—the tactical execution of the media plan. If media planning is the *design,* buying is the *construction.*

Media buyers work with the boundaries of the media plan and translate recommendations and expectations into reality. The buyer is the person who makes the campaign plan happen; until the buyer sets up the schedules and the individual agreements with each of the media suppliers, the plan exists only on paper.

Even though the activities of planning are usually considered separate from buying functions, they can overlap. Although "buying" actually begins with the selection of campaign vehicles, this selection may have begun at the planning stage, because the media department desires to make the plan as complete as possible. Advertisers always want specific details. Planners want to comply, but they must be cautious about being too specific. Don't forget, the plan is developed well before the beginning of the campaign—months before in most cases. The greater the time before the starting date, the greater the chance for changes and shifts in media performance.

MEDIA-BUYING FUNCTIONS

Regardless of who performs the buying activities or when these activities are performed, the role of the media buyer includes a distinct set of operational duties. We will begin by describing the traditional tasks in the order in which they are completed. Later in this chapter we will examine some of these functions in greater detail.

Providing Support Data for the Media Planner

Buyers are close to the action. They have current experience with media performance and unit pricing that is vital to the planning design. Buyers provide this information to planners so that the planner's recommendations will be as accurate as possible.

Media Research Analysis

Media performance (audience reaction) is very changeable. In many advertising agencies, the media buyers are specialists who carefully monitor changes in audience patterns as reflected in field research. One of the more active media areas is in spot or market-by-market television (see Ad 12.1). Buyers who specialize in negotiation of spot schedules constantly check the rating reports from each television market. Time buyers also discuss programming changes with sales representatives in order to anticipate how the schedule shifts might affect current and future schedules.

Media Vehicle Selection

One essential part of buying is choosing the best media vehicles to fit the target audience's aperture. Planning lays out the direction, but much of the choosing process falls to the buyer. Armed with the media plan directives, the buyer seeks answers to a number of difficult questions. Does the vehicle have the right audience profile? Will the program's current popularity increase, stabilize, or decline? How well does the magazine's editorial format fit the brand? Does the radio station's choice of music offer the correct atmosphere for the creative theme? How well does the newspaper's circulation pattern fit the advertiser's distribution? The answers to those questions bear directly on the campaign's success.

AD 12.1
This ad for spot television is geared to an area with a Hispanic population.

(Courtesy of KXLN-TV, Pueblo Broadcasting Corporation, Houston, Texas.)

Negotiating for the Price

Buying takes place in a world of transaction. Currently, few arrangements for space and time are fixed. Each year advertisers are demanding more assurance that the rates paid for media are as low as possible. This pressure forces buyers to request prices below what media representatives expect to receive. Although most media are responsive to requests, price concessions are made only after serious bargaining between the buyer and the seller.

Monitoring Vehicle Performance

In an ideal world every vehicle on the campaign schedule would perform at or above expectations. Likewise, every advertisement, commercial, and posting would run exactly as planned. In reality, underperformance and schedule problems are facts of life. The buyer's response must be swift and decisive. Poorly performing vehicles must be replaced, or costs must be modified. Production and schedule difficulties must be rectified. Delayed response could hurt the brand's sales.

Postcampaign Analysis

Once a campaign is completed, the buyer's duty is to review the plan's expectations and forecasts against what actually happened. Did the plan actually achieve GRP, reach, frequency, and CPM objectives? Did the newspaper and magazine placements run in the positions expected? Such analysis is instrumental in providing the guidance for future media plans. For a full discussion of postcampaign research see Chapter 21.

These six tasks provide an overview of media buying. To get a better understanding of buying operations, however, we must examine some of the media buyer's duties in closer detail.

*S*PECIAL SKILLS: EXPERT KNOWLEDGE OF MEDIA OPPORTUNITIES

Because the operations of the mass media are so complicated and detailed, most large agencies want media buyers to concentrate upon a particular medium. Although planners, by necessity, are generalists, buyers must develop a much deeper knowledge of their assigned area.

The scope of this knowledge is quite broad. Ask buyers what they need to know about a medium and most will answer, "Everything I can." The following outline can only begin to explain the depth of the buyer's expertise.

AD 12.2
CNN Headline News portrays itself as a vehicle to reach an audience that network programming cannot.
(Courtesy of Turner Broadcasting System, Inc.)

Media Content

Buying isn't just choosing shows, stations, and publications by popularity. Buyers must develop instincts for the quality of media content. Knowledge of what audiences want to read and view allows buyers to appreciate programming and editorial qualities. Deeper understanding uncovers the special, the unusual opportunity for audience aperture.

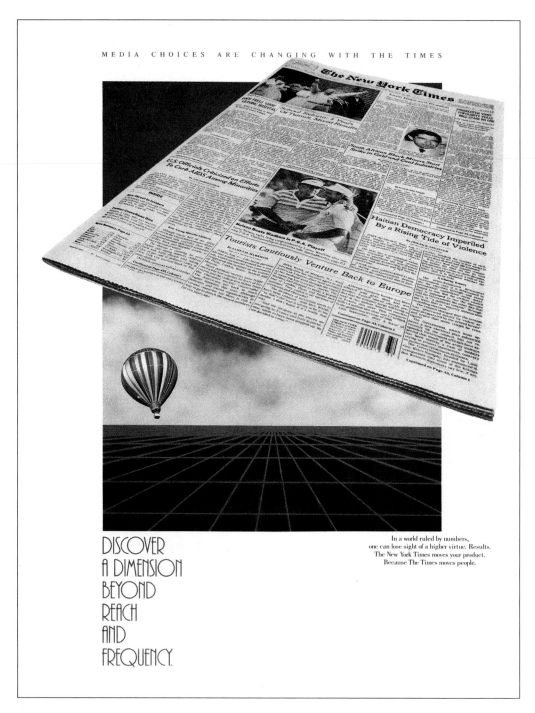

AD 12.3
The New York Times has a unique position as a local newspaper with national readership among upscale audiences.

(Copyright © 1987 by The New York Times Company. Reprinted by permission.)

The Seal that sells the seal.

Your ordinary run-of-the-sea seal doesn't have it. Only the Dakin seal carries the Good Housekeeping Seal. The Dakin seal earned it by conforming to the requirements of Good Housekeeping magazine. Now Dakin proudly displays our Seal on its seals and lions and tigers and giraffes and the rest of the kingdom.

A recent study by Simmons shows retailers and advertisers agree that the Good Housekeeping Seal helps sell their products. Consumers say it helps them decide which products to buy. Call it part of a label if you want. We like to think of it as a performing Seal. **Good Housekeeping**

Good Housekeeping is a publication of Hearst Magazines, a division of The Hearst Corporation. © 1987 The Hearst Corporation.

AD 12.4
In this ad *Good Housekeeping* emphasizes its ability to reach a particular audience. What images are being used here? What types of advertisers would want to appeal to this audience?
(Courtesy of *Good Housekeeping*.)

Audience Habits

Consumption of media is neither stable nor consistent. Audiences are fickle about how they spend their leisure time. Seasons change their interests. Viewers grow tired of one entertainment mode and quickly shift to another. Buyers cannot afford to wait until the shifts occur; they must sense the coming changes and select accordingly. Fresh and interesting media options have the best opportunity for aperture. Buyers who can judge where media audiences are headed will have their messages prepared.

Cost/Benefit Values

Much of the buyers' skill involves finding message opportunities that offer full communication value for the price paid. This is not simply getting the lowest price. A talented buyer can judge when the price is right. We will look at price judgments later in this chapter.

Research Evaluation

Skilled buyers seldom accept audience estimates without understanding what the numbers really say. To do this they must be able to evaluate the quality of the medium's research. How and when are the surveys taken? Has anything occurred since the survey that would make its estimates suspect? Buyers can only answer these questions if they are carefully trained in the strengths and weaknesses of audience research.

SPECIAL SKILLS: KNOWLEDGE OF MEDIA PRICING

Advertisers bear many costs in the advertising campaign. They must pay for the talent that develops the message, the production to create the message and, above all, the media costs to place the message before the target audience. With few exceptions, media costs are the largest area of advertising investment.

Because media costs are great, buyers must be experts in all aspects of media pricing. They must be knowledgeable of all the variables that influence the rate structure of the media.

A buyer's training begins with an understanding that where media costs are concerned, the advertiser and the media are adversaries. The advertisers want the lowest possible price, and the media want the highest possible prices. As a representative of the advertiser, the buyer is expected to use all available leverage to get the lowest possible price. At the same time, the buyer learns that selection based solely on price can compromise the quality of the advertising schedule. As has already been noted, the balance between efficiency (cost) and quality is often very delicate, and it takes a great deal of skill to maintain an effective equilibrium.

Media Cost Trends

The results of these "contests" between buyer and seller are found in the shifts of pricing for each media opportunity. These **media unit cost trends** are reflected in two ways: as the actual (unit) price and as the price paid relative to audience delivered (CPM).

media unit cost trends *A history of changes in the average unit (per message) prices for each medium that is used in cost forecasting.*

Unit Prices The general unit cost history (shown in Table 12.1) for most of the media shows an upward spiral, roughly parallel to other major economic indicators such as gross national product, rate of inflation, and consumer price index.

**TABLE 12.1
Media Unit Cost Trends,
1984–1988
(Expressed as % change from
previous year)**

Medium	1984	1985	1986	1987*	1988*
Television					
DayNet	+11.4	+10.5	+3.9	−7.7	+0.5
PrimeNet	+10.6	+7.9	+5.9	+3.2	+6.0
Spot	+9.8	+7.6	+5.8	+5.6	+8.4
Radio					
Net	+8.0	+7.9	+9.1	+5.7	+6.4
Spot	+8.7	+6.7	+5.6	+4.4	+6.0
Magazine	+9.1	+8.0	+7.0	+4.3	+5.6
Newspaper	+9.0	+8.0	+7.4	+6.5	+6.6
Outdoor	+8.0	+6.5	+5.7	+4.9	+5.3
Sunday Supplement	+9.1	+8.3	+2.9	+4.8	+5.6

*Estimated.

Source: Marketing & Media Decisions, August 1987, p. 34.

Media unit costs are increasing but at a slower rate.

Medium	1984	1985	1986*	1987*
Television				
DayNet	+9	+15	−2	−13
PrimeNet	+15	+10	0	+9
Spot	+11	+6	+5	+2
Radio				
Net	+10	+6	+6	+8
Spot	+7	+5	+5	+5
Magazines	+8	+8	+6	+6
Newspapers	+9	+7	+7	+7
Outdoor	+9	+6	+5	+5
Sunday Supplement	+6	+4	−11	+5

*Estimated.

Source: Backer Spielvogel Bates Worldwide.
Media efficiency levels continue to decrease at well beyond the rates of
inflation and the consumer price index.

CPM trend analysis *Longitudinal (long-term) history of average cost-per-thousand tendencies of advertising media that is used to assist in forecasting future CPM levels.*

Cost-per-Thousand Trends A more sensitive index of media costs is in the cost per thousand (CPM) for audiences delivered (shown in Table 12.2). Remember, CPM is the direct relation between the size of the media audience and the cost for a placement before that audience. There are many variables at work in a **CPM trend analysis.** Change reflects unit cost shifts, audience reactions to media quality, and the demand of advertisers.

SPECIAL SKILLS: MEDIA VEHICLE SELECTION AND NEGOTIATION

A buyer's knowledge and expert preparation are tested when the buyer represents the client in the media marketplace. It is here that execution of the plan takes place. The key questions are: Can the desired vehicles be located, and can a satisfactory schedule be negotiated?

These buying tasks are often anxiety-producing. In many circumstances media selection and negotiation is a high-stakes competition. The challenge is simple: Find the best possible audience vehicles and secure them for the lowest possible price. So easy to say—so hard to do.

The Boundaries: Working within Plan Requirements

The boundaries of media negotiation are set by the advertising plan (Chapter 7). How many dollars are available? Who is the target audience? When does the advertising run? What atmosphere is desired? What is the duration of scheduling? Question after question must be covered in the construction of the advertiser's schedule. The following paragraphs detail some of the critical considerations.

PRINCIPLE
Negotiation involves getting the best schedule at the best price.

allocations *Divisions or proportions of advertising dollars among the various media.*

Budget Allocations The budget is the amount of funds available to achieve the objectives, a limit that cannot be exceeded. These funds must be *allocated*, or divided among media. **Allocations** in the plan are expected to be closely followed.

If a company's campaign budget for the 1990 fiscal year is $100,000, the buyer cannot commit more than that; not $1,000 more, not $100 more. If the allocations are 50 percent for newspaper and 50 percent for television advertising, the buyer is expected to manage $50,000 for each medium. If the buyer can fulfill the objectives for less than $100,000 without sacrificing quality, then so much the better. Goals must be accomplished for less, if possible, but never for more.

One rate. No debate.

No matter how big your ad budget, how small your account, how fat your franchise, or how regional your retail, The Record, New Jersey's largest evening newspaper, guarantees one low rate for all advertisers whether national, retail, or co-op. This means you're able to reach a market whose impressive EBI places it 28th in the nation, for just the agency commission over local rates.

While many newspapers continue to charge national advertisers a premium of up to 150 percent above local rates, The Record eliminates the national and local rate differential and also offers you contract options at all levels. So now, your advertising message in The Record can reach an audience of fashionable and affluent big spenders for small change.

Reach across the Hudson River to a market whose residents wield a disposable income of $22.1 billion. Reach the super market of Bergen/Passaic.

You'll find this wealthy market reading The Record, the best media bargain in town. Call Jonathan Theophilakos, Director of Advertising, at (201) 646-4259.

The Record
We cover your world. All of it.

150 River Street, Hackensack, N.J. 07601-7172
1350 Route 23, Wayne, N.J. 07470-5839

Source: © S&MM Survey of Buying Power, 1987

AD 12.5
A New Jersey newspaper promotes the fact that, unlike many local papers, it charges national and local advertisers the same rates.
(Courtesy of *The Record*.)

Target Audiences The media plan will give the buyer a clear profile, with media-sensitive characteristics, of the target prospect. If multiple targets are specified by the plan, the plan should also specify a weighting or priority for each characteristic.

Airline advertising offers a good illustration. Some adults fly much more than others. Suppose an airline profiled a key prospect as an adult traveler, between 25 and 54 years old, with a sales/managerial occupation. This profile specifies two elements: age and occupation. But which dimension is more important?

MARIE NETOLICKY—DDB NEEDHAM/CHICAGO— MEDIA BUYER

I'm running late this morning—late enough so that I must phone in a "hold" to ABC before I leave home. A "hold" on two :30 units in *The American Comedy Awards* will reserve it at the negotiated price until I can get an order from the client. This was unexpected. We recommended a 2-night sponsorship in the miniseries *The Bourne Identity,* based on the Robert Ludlum novel. Can you believe it? The ratings projection is good, but the client will not purchase it because they "don't like the leading man and woman." When will professional people learn to keep their personal feelings out of a sound business decision? Anyway, the last thing the client said last night was they *definitely* wanted two :30's in the awards show.

With that phoned in, I proceed to the office. When I get in, there are already five messages waiting for me. As I grab a cup of tea and look through my morning mail, the network calls me back to inform me that only one :30 unit is left in the awards show. They are holding that one :30 for me, but this changes everything. I now must go back to the drawing board and reconstruct another recommendation, because one :30 will not achieve the media plan goals.

While I try to rethink and rework, my two associates—planners on our accounts—pop in and out of my office with questions, problems, solutions, and jokes for comic relief. I could use them! Meanwhile I try to reach the media supervisor to discuss the changes to the recommendation, and we keep playing phone tag. My boss steps into my office to tell me he would like to meet with me and a few other supervisors in our group to discuss Viacom's selling of the national syndication of *The Cosby Show.* They are offering the national media time on a closed-bid basis only. Nationally syndicated television time has never been negotiated this way before. We must meet to discuss the pros and cons and whether we are in the game or not.

I finally reach the media supervisor on the changes and we discuss the alternatives. She asks if I am available for a conference call with the client and, of course, I am. I wait until 12:40 P.M. to get a call back from her saying that I will not be needed for the conference call. Her boss is sending her over to the client to speak to them directly and to sell the new alternative recommendation.

By now it is 2:00 P.M. and I have to deal with the traffic problem. I speak to the associate media director on this account and we decide which of the other brands will cover the spots for the unfinished creative. I call a meeting with the broadcast traffic manager and the planner, and we agree on what is to be done. I really feel for the planner because his job is to change all the brand codes against the spots so that traffic can reschedule. Network and syndication are not bad, but the cable television changes involve several hundred units.

Finally, I receive the phone call I have been waiting for—the media supervisor calls and tells me that the alternative recommendation sold and that the client was happy. All that is left now is to get some promotional posters ordered with the client's logo imprinted on them.

It's getting near the end of the day, and I go through the rest of my mail. And the mail is endless . . . trade magazines to read, client correspondence which outlines new projects, contracts that must be checked and filed and inter-office memos that need to be acted upon. And it starts all over again tomorrow.

(Courtesy of Marie Netolicky.)

This account executive is selling television advertising time.

weighted audience values *Numerical values assigned to different audience characteristics that help advertisers assign priorities when devising media plans.*

Suppose that consumer research done for the airline indicates that occupation is twice as important as age. In such a situation the buyer would assign value weights to each feature. Occupation figures would be multiplied by 2 and age figures by 1. Then both figures would be added to give a *weighted value* to the medium's audience. These **weighted audience values** could be changed for each market segment. This formula is also applied to products with several different audience segments.

Timing and Continuity Many schedules must work within a tight time frame. Buyers are expected to follow any flight or pulse pattern required by the media plan (see Chapter 9). The buyer must adjust the number of message placements to reflect the desired campaign calendar. This may mean arranging an on-off schedule to reflect a flight pattern. The greater the changes in intensity and in advertising periods, the more difficult the scheduling is for the buyer.

Gross Rating Point Levels Many plans dictate the weighting of messages according to goals based on desired repetition (frequency) or exposure (reach). Often the rating point levels are primarily for budget guidance. These levels are then translated by the buyer into insertion frequencies (print) or into announcement frequencies (broadcast). The buyer's task is to use the GRP guides (with the dollar allocation) to develop schedules that can also match frequency and reach objectives.

For example, imagine this situation for a fast-food company. The plan calls for a special month-long schedule for October in selected markets. The buyer's instruction might look like this:

- Markets: As listed.
- Anticipated GRP Level: 400
- Medium: Spot Television
- Dayparts: 25 percent of GRP in Evening-Fringe (5–7:30 P.M. E.S.T.) and
- 75 percent in Prime Evening (8:00–11:00 P.M. E.S.T.)

Use maximum dispersion to achieve desired reach potential.

The buyer for each market would negotiate schedules for 4 weeks at a target GRP of 100 per week (4 weeks × 100GRP = 400). The placements must

dispersion *The use of as many different stations and programs as possible to avoid duplicating the message audience.*

follow the dayparts and the proportions. In fringe 100 (25 percent of 400) must be scheduled. Prime evening should have 300 (75 percent of 400 GRP).

Dispersion refers to a media policy that places the message in as many different programs and spots as possible to avoid duplicating the audience. The request for *maximum dispersion* means that reach is to have a priority over frequency. In this case the buyer should avoid duplicating programs as much as possible. Using different shows increases the opportunity for different or unduplicated audiences.

Negotiation: The Art of a Buyer

Just as a labor union transacts with management for pay raises, security, and work conditions, so does a media buyer pursue special advantages for clients. The following are some of the key areas of negotiation.

Vehicle Performance Selection through negotiation is especially important where the medium offers many options and where the buyers might need to use forecasted audience levels. One typical example is network television.

Nighttime programming is particularly fluid or changeable. As noted in Table 12.3, networks, because of the dollars at risk, are very quick to rearrange programs, to cancel them and replace them with new ones, and to make other sorts of shifts. Buyers of time in network situations are usually faced with selecting programs that (1) are new, (2) are not new but have been scheduled on a different night, or (3) have new lead-in programs. Selection must be made with little or no guarantee of audience popularity. Buyers deal with these uncertainties through careful research on the type of program (action, situation comedy), the rating history of the time slot, the audience flow patterns of competing programs, and a close examination of the content of the program itself, including scripts, talent, and all other elements. For all this research, buyers still need good "instincts" to make successful selections.

fixed pricing *A traditional method of media pricing where rates are published and are applied equally to all advertisers.*

open pricing *A method of media pricing in which prices are negotiated on a contract-by-contract basis for each unit of media space or time.*

Unit Costs It should come as no shock that buyers are under heavy pressure to secure the lowest possible prices for message placements. The rules are changing. Advertisers are now less inclined to accept the quoted or fixed price. **Fixed pricing** is a standard policy that treats all advertisers alike. Television decided that this price structure was too restrictive and limited profit potential. Network television shifted to **open pricing,** in which each buyer or buying group negotiates a separate price for each program. Spot television followed, and magazines might be leaning in this direction.

TABLE 12.3
Prime-Time Network—New Series Cancellations, 1980–1987 (Weekly Series)

Year	Number canceled	As percent of new shows
1979–80*	*	
1980–81	27	67.5
1981–82	38	64.4
1982–83	41	75.9
1983–84	42	71.2
1984–85	40	74.1
1985–86	34	64.2
1986–87	34	63.0

*Data unavailable.

Source: A. C. Nielsen, *Household Tracking Report.* (Courtesy of Nielsen Marketing Research.) In recent years over seven of every ten new nighttime network shows have been canceled.

Open pricing makes buyer negotiation both important and risky. Buyers fear that too much emphasis on negotiating a low price will diminish the effectiveness of the media campaign. The balance or trade-off between price and audience objectives must be fully understood before an all-out pursuit of open pricing is attempted. Some media experts believe that pricing will replace all other values, and media will eventually be treated like a bag of grain or a barrel of oil.

guarantees *Agreements in which the medium promises to compensate the advertiser should the audience fall below a specified level.*

Audience-Level Guarantees   To offset the risk of forecasted performance, buyers seek concessions from the media in the form of "insurance." **Guarantees** offer the buyer some sort of protection if media audiences fall below projected expectations.

In broadcasting, the arrangement might mean that the network or station will add free placements to the schedule to offset audience decline. In print, particularly magazines, the guarantee may mean returning some of the contract cost to the advertiser if the circulation falls below a certain level.

AD 12.6

In addition to providing advertising space and time, the media must offer merchandising and sales support to advertisers. What attraction would this ad hold for an advertiser?

(© Copyright by Meredith Corporation 1988. All rights reserved.)

A WORLD OF MEREDITH MERCHANDISING/SALES SUPPORT OPPORTUNITIES

We can also help create a customized merchandising/sales support program that maximizes the effectiveness of your advertising with your sales staff, distributors and dealers. Some of the many possibilities:

▲ Producing special videos for promotional use.
▲ Using consumer direct mail lists (35 million names in all) for specialized direct marketing.
▲ Creating special publications to maintain contact with your customers or with your distribution network.
▲ Using Meredith books as consumer premiums or in sales incentive programs.
▲ Conducting quantitative or attitudinal marketing research.
▲ Using our real estate network to reach homebuyers.

These and other programs can be used individually or in combination.

Preferred Positions In magazines there are assumed readership advantages in having the advertising message placed next to well-read pages or in special editorial sections. These placements are known as **preferred positions.** Imagine the value to a food advertiser of having its message located in a special receipe section that can be detached from the magazine for permanent use by the homemaker. How many additional exposures might that ad get? For newspapers an ideal position might be opposite the editorial page or a location in the food, financial, or sports section. With so many competing "voices" buyers are very anxious to find the most widely read sections.

Because they are so visible, preferred positions often carry a premium surcharge, usually 10 to 15 percent above standard space rates. In these days of negotiation, space buyers are not hesitant to request that such charges be waived. Buyers will offer publications a higher number of insertions if the special positions are guaranteed without extra cost.

Merchandising Support for Advertisers Most of the major media are willing to assist advertisers with additional sales support activities. In recent years this has become a major focus for negotiation, and the activities themselves have become more elaborate and costly. In Ad 12.6 the Meredith company lists the support activities it offers to advertisers.

Consider a promotion that buyers for a major soft-drink firm worked out in some major markets recently. Radio stations were offered substantial summer schedules. In return, the station had to agree to co-sponsor a season-long promotional contest. Each day the station would send out a van specially painted with the advertiser's colors and logo. The audience would be urged to find the van to receive prizes of cases of soft drinks and cash. The station was also obliged to promote the contest on the air with a specific number of announcements per week, each announcement to include the name of the advertiser. All of these extras were offered free to the advertiser.

The pressure on buyers to gain extra leverage ("more bang for the buck") has grown enormously. Agencies, which once felt it unprofessional to squeeze the media for special concessions, are now willing to press very hard for this special treatment. Media buying has become an unsettling process because there are so few standards to follow.

SPECIAL SKILLS: MAINTAINING PLAN PERFORMANCE

The buyer's responsibility for the plan schedule continues after the contract is signed. The buyer also must see that the campaign stays on schedule. As noted earlier, there are ample opportunities for planned media schedules to go off track. It is logical to give the buyer, the closest media contact, the task of surveillance. Any changes or adjustments should come through the buyer. The following section describes some of these responsibilities with various media vehicles.

Monitoring Audience Research

When campaigns begin, the forecasts in the media plan are checked against actual performance. Whenever possible, buyers check each incoming research report to determine whether the vehicle is performing as promised.

Network Television Network programming is under constant research scrutiny. Nielsen's National Television Index (NTI) reports are issued every 2 weeks. There are also "overnight" surveys that will give performance ratings in a day or two. The frequency of these reports encourages close scrutiny of client schedules.

Spot Radio/Television   Stations and programs are selected, in part, on the *past* rating reports. Whenever the rating report schedule cooperates, buyers will check on the spot schedule's current audiences. The sources are ARBITRON and Nielsen Station Index (NSI) for television and ARBITRON and BIRCH Reports for radio.

Outdoor Postings   Major users of billboards know from experience that it is prudent to check outdoor showings. This means sending buyers to at least the larger markets to *ride the showing*—that is, to check the condition of the billboards, the presence of obstructions (new buildings or trees), and any other situation that might impair traffic flow.

Magazines and Newspapers   Research reports on readership for magazines and newspapers are limited in frequency, but buyers also monitor issues to determine if advertisement positions are correctly placed.

Schedule and Technical Problems

There are all sorts of temporary snags in scheduling and in the reproduction of the advertising message. For positions missed or errors in handling the message presentation, buyers must be alert to make the needed changes to reconcile difficulties. Most adjustments involve either replacement positions at no cost or money refunds. This policy of various forms of substitution is called *making good on the contract.* The units are known as **makegoods.** Here are some examples.

Program Preemptions   Special programs or news events often interrupt regular programming. When this happens, the commercial schedule is also interrupted. **Program preemptions** occur nationally and locally. In the case of long-term interruptions—for example, congressional hearings—the disruption can be very serious. Buyers have difficulty finding suitable replacements before the schedule ends.

Message Preemptions   Message preemptions are unique to spot television and radio. Most stations offer a commercial position at a number of different rates reflecting degrees of protection from other advertisers who want the same position. Advertisers willing to risk being moved will pay a lower rate called a **preemptible rate.** Should the position be "bumped," the buyer will negotiate to find replacement positions. Because this is a common occurrence, it is not stressful for the experienced buyer.

Missed Closings   Magazines and newspapers have clearly set deadlines, called *closings,* for each issue. Sometimes the advertising materials do not arrive in time. If the publication is responsible, it will make some sort of restitution. If the fault lies with the client or the agency, there is no restitution by the publication.

Technical Problems   Technical difficulties are responsible for the numerous "goofs," "gliches," and "foul-ups" that haunt the advertiser's schedule. Years back, for example, the buyer for a major airline received a call from the sales representative of the *Washington News.* A very unfortunate thing had occurred, and the representative was most apologetic. It seemed the makeup staff at the

---

makegoods   *Compensation given by the media to advertisers in the form of additional message units that are commonly used in situations involving production errors by the media and preemption of the advertiser's programming.*

program preemptions   *Interruptions in local or network programming caused by special events.*

preemptible rate   *A form of open pricing in which spot television buyers purchase a spot position at a lower rate with the understanding that they might lose the position to an advertiser who is willing to pay a higher rate.*

newspaper had missed the intended position for the airlines ad and had run it instead on the *obituary page*. A makegood was forthcoming. In another case the buyer for a new consumer brand accidentally learned that someone in production at the television station had inserted a "super" (an optical phrase superimposed on the film or tape) informing viewers the product was only available in two small area towns. In truth those towns accounted for less than 10 percent of the brand's distribution. The damage was beyond calculation, and the station did more than make good. It settled out of court.

Most technical problems are not quite so disastrous. The "bleed-through" and out-of-register color for newspapers, the torn billboard poster, the broken film, and the tape out of alignment are more typical of the problems that plague media schedules.

■ SUMMARY

- Media buying involves a series of duties and functions that are separate from media planning.

- Media buyers are responsible for executing the media plan recommendations. To do this they must find and select the media vehicles that best fulfill the advertiser's needs.

- The media buyer must observe activity in the media marketplace, analyze audience research, negotiate for positions and price, and monitor schedule performance.

- Price negotiation has become more important as media have shifted from fixed to flexible pricing. Buyers are under strong pressure to get the lowest possible rates without sacrificing desired audience values.

- Buyers are also responsible for maintaining the performance standards established by the media plan throughout the campaign. Changes that lower the value of the message placements must be rectified quickly and efficiently.

■ QUESTIONS

1. Explain the job-related differences between media planning and media buying.

2. A major role for media buyers is negotiation. Using the magazine medium as your illustration, explain the buyer's activity in negotiation.

3. Discuss the difference between open and fixed pricing of the media. How does the use of these price policies affect the buying process?

4. What are makegoods? In what situations are they appropriate? Inappropriate?

■ FURTHER READINGS

Barban, Arnold M., Donald W. Jugenheimer, and Peter B. Turk. *Media Research Sourcebook and Workbook*. Lincolnwood, IL: NTC Business Books, 1989.

Wall, Robert W. *Media Math: Basic Techniques of Media Evaluation*. Lincolnwood, IL: NTC Business Books, 1987.

Soft Scrub Cleanser

Abrasive cleansers, such as Comet, Ajax, and Soft Scrub, are used by over 75 percent of the households in the United States for general-purpose cleaning, primarily in the bathroom and kitchen. Sales of abrasive cleansers in 1985 were estimated at $200 million, or about 14 million units. Unit sales of cleansers, however, have been declining, partly as a result of consumer trends away from general everyday household cleaning and a shift toward convenience products that perform specific cleaning tasks—such as bathrooms—quickly and effectively.

There are two segments of the abrasive cleanser market—powders and liquids. Powdered cleansers cost about half of what liquid cleansers do and thus have a significant pricing advantage. In general, powdered cleansers also provide better heavy-duty cleaning than liquids because they contain harsher abrasives and bleach. Liquid cleansers, however, offer better surface safety—less scratching—and a nice fragrance. Powdered cleansers represent about 85 percent of unit sales of abrasive cleansers. In recent years, however, both unit sales of powdered cleansers and their market share have declined. Comet (from Procter and Gamble) and Ajax (Colgate/Palmolive) dominate the powdered segment of the market, with 1984 market shares of 49.0 percent and 20.9 percent, respectively. Bon Ami comes in a distant third, with a 2.8 percent market share in 1984.

In 1977 Clorox introduced a liquid abrasive cleanser, Soft Scrub, in response to consumer dissatisfaction with the harshness and inconvenience of powdered abrasive cleansers. It was positioned as a safe, effective alternative to powdered cleansers. Soft Scrub showed consistent consumption and share growth. For years its only liquid competitor was Comet Liquid, which was introduced in 1978. By 1984 Soft Scrub dominated the liquid cleanser category. It had an 11.2 percent market share, whereas Comet Liquid had only a 1.6 percent share. However, Tough Act and Scrub Free, recently introduced bathroom cleansers, represent new, indirect competitors. Both are convenience products that compete for bathroom usage, part of the shifting consumer trend toward specialty products.

In September 1985 the brand manager of Soft Scrub heard from the Clorox sales force that Proctor and Gamble was planning to introduce Mr. Clean Soft Cleanser nationally at the end of the year. Clorox management felt the need to develop a comprehensive advertising plan to combat the Mr. Clean challenge to Clorox's dominant market position. The company gathered data on the abrasive cleanser market in order to reexamine the major aspects of its advertising campaign: product strategy, media plan, pricing strategy, and promotion plan.

Product Strategy Soft Scrub's current advertising emphasizes its safety advantages over powdered cleansers by comparing ingredients in the two forms of cleanser. Past market research studies found that consumers perceived Comet powder as an excellent cleanser but rated it low on safety and

noted that it left a "gritty residue." In May 1985, in an effort to eliminate these weaknesses, Procter and Gamble began testing a new "Safer for Surfaces" Comet containing the same mild abrasive as Soft Scrub. The success of "Safer for Surfaces" Comet could significantly dilute Soft Scrub's safety claim versus powdered cleansers. Initial test market results indicate that the reformulation has been successful in slowing Comet's long-term usage decline and in rebuilding market share.

Second-place powdered cleanser Ajax discontinued advertising in 1980 and now is promoted primarily through price reductions. Bon Ami, the third-place powdered cleanser, positions itself as the "powdered cleanser that doesn't scratch."

Comet Liquid, developed by Procter and Gamble in response to Soft Scrub, was positioned as the versatile cleanser that disinfects. During its introduction in 1978, Comet Liquid attracted consumer interest because of the strong Comet name and reputation, as well as the product's comprehensive advertising and promotion plan. But Comet Liquid's market share has steadily declined since its introduction. Consumers

TABLE 1 Abrasive Cleanser Retail Pricing, September 1985

| | Liquid Cleansers | |
	Soft Scrub	Mr. Clean
13 oz.	$1.19	$1.19
26 oz.	2.09	2.09
39 oz.	2.99	—

| | Powdered Cleansers | | |
	Comet	Ajax	Bon Ami
14 oz.	$.53	$.53	$.69
21 oz.	.78	.78	—

TABLE 2 Estimated 1984 Abrasive Cleanser Media Spending (in thousands of dollars)

| | | Comet | | | |
	Soft Scrub	Powder	Liquid	Ajax	Bon Ami
Network Television					
Day	$2,118	$1,776	—	—	—
Prime time	2,482	3,477	—	—	—
Total	4,600	5,253	—	—	—
Television					
syndication	47	—	—	—	154
Spot	515	1,138	—	11	94
Magazines	670	–	—	—	779
TOTAL	$5,832	$6,391	—	11	$1,027

found that Comet Liquid did not provide the same level of cleaning as Comet powder. In addition, the product separated in the bottle, thus reducing users' satisfaction with the product's aesthetics. Over the past several years, P&G has provided no advertising and only minimal promotional support for Comet Liquid.

Mr. Clean Soft Cleanser is a mild abrasive cleanser with a lemon fragrance. The brand is positioned as the superior cleaning soft abrasive cleanser. Advertising capitalizes on the reputation of Mr. Clean Dilutable Cleaner's shine while claiming surface safety and ease of rinsing. Market research shows a preference for Mr. Clean Soft Cleanser among current Soft Scrub users. This preference appears to be based primarily on fragrance, in which Mr. Clean achieved a strong preference

(61 percent versus 20 percent for Soft Scrub). Clorox research studies show that Soft Scrub users rate their brand very high for surface safety, versatility, and mildness. However, the studies found some consumer dissatisfaction with the brand's heavy-duty cleaning performance.

Pricing Strategy Another consideration for Clorox is pricing strategy. Table 1 shows retail prices for the major abrasive cleansers. Mr. Clean's sizing and pricing are similar to Soft Scrub's.

In January 1985 Ajax ran an economy positioning test with its four cleaning brands (powdered cleanser, dishwashing detergent, laundry detergent, and dilutable cleaner). In the test, Colgate/Palmolive reduced the price of all its cleaning brands by 20 percent. Initial results showed sales volume gains of 15 percent of Ajax powder.

Media Plan Soft Scrub put most of its media budget into television advertising. Table 2 summarizes 1984 media spending for existing abrasive cleansers. In 1985, in an effort to increase its advertising presence, Soft Scrub began using 20-second television commercials in its media plan; previously it had used only 30-second spots. Comet powder was the only other abrasive cleanser using television advertising. However, Mr. Clean's national introduction will be supported by heavy media advertising: Media spending is estimated to be $14 million, assuming use of a 30-second spot. With a 45-second ad, as was used in the test market, first-year media spending could reach $20 million.

Promotion Plan Soft Scrub's promotion plan for the year was to do five trade promotions on the different sizes and to offer two coupons during the year. The trade promotions primarily consist of an allowance given to retailers to offer the product to consumers at a reduced price. The year-one promotion plan for Mr. Clean Soft Cleanser includes a mail-in refund offer, a specially priced 6-ounce sample size at 49¢, and two coupons. Table 3 compares Soft Scrub's current promotion plan with Mr. Clean's projected plan. The total first-year promotion spending for Mr. Clean Soft Cleanser is estimated to be approximately $9 million.

Questions for Discussion

1. Should Clorox continue to pursue dissatisfied powdered-cleanser users, or should the company address Mr. Clean's competition head on? Should the company look at ways to compete with the new specific-task convenience products?
2. Should any changes be considered in the Soft Scrub product itself?
3. How can Clorox maintain Soft Scrub's strong shelf presence in stores and minimize that of Mr. Clean?
4. Should Clorox consider a change in pricing strategy in response to the introduction of Mr. Clean?
5. Does the Soft Scrub promotion plan need adjustment? If so, in what ways?
6. What changes should Clorox consider in its media plan?
7. Is further market research needed to answer any unsettled questions in regard to Mr. Clean's introduction? If so, what does the company need to find out?

Source: Courtesy of The Clorox Company.

TABLE 3 Promotion Plan Comparison

Jul '85	Aug	Sep	Oct	Nov	Dec	Jan '86	Feb	Mar	Apr	May	Jun '86
Mr. Clean Projected Plan											
						Intro. Allow.			Spring Trade Promotion		Bounce Back Coupon on Mr. Clean Liquid
						Buy 1 Get 1 Free 13 oz.			30¢ Coupon		
							6 oz. 49¢ Sample Size 49¢ Coupon				
Soft Scrub Current Plan											
13 oz. Trade Promotion	26 oz. Trade Promotion					13 oz. Trade Promotion		26 oz. Trade Promotion			39 oz. Trade Prom.
		25¢ Coupon						20¢ Coupon			

13

The Creative Process

Chapter Outline

The Tough and Tender Sides of Selling Chicken
Advertising: Strategy and Creativity
Creative Concept: The Big Idea
The Message Strategy
Images and Advertising
Words and Advertising

Chapter Objectives

When you have completed this chapter you should be able to:

- List various characteristics of creative people
- Explain what advertisers mean by a creative concept
- Describe the various stages involved in creating an advertisement
- Understand how the various elements in an advertisement work together to create impact
- Distinguish between effective copywriting and adese

THE TOUGH AND TENDER SIDES OF SELLING CHICKEN

It was 1971, and the young agency, Scali, McCabe, Sloves, had just been picked by Frank Perdue, who wanted to broaden the market for his chickens through television advertising. Perdue demanded that Ed McCabe, a partner and creative director in the agency, handle the account along with Alan Pesky, the agency's chief operating officer and head marketing man, and Sam Scali, the vice-president and creative director. Considering that Perdue, at $250,000, would be the agency's smallest account, that was a rather remarkable demand.

It was a rather remarkable demand in other ways, too. Perdue wanted some of the top creative talent in New York to help him sell chickens, a commodity that had never been advertised before as a brand. What would you have said to Frank Perdue, this rather unusual guy with balding head, beaked nose, thin neck, and gruff, squawky voice? Would you have told him to get lost?

McCabe, Scali, and Pesky agreed to handle the account on Perdue's terms and traveled to Salisbury, Maryland, to learn about chickens. The problem, as they saw it, was that consumers couldn't distinguish one chicken from another. McCabe, Scali, and Pesky had to figure out why consumers should buy a Perdue chicken rather than any others.

The first thing they noticed was that the Perdue chickens were markedly yellower than the chickens found in most stores. They were told this was due to their special diet, which included marigold-petal extracts among other things. In New York these yellow chickens were considered to be premium.

Another impression they received was that Perdue was very involved in every aspect of the business. Not only were the chickens fed marigold and fresh corn, there was even music playing in the chicken houses. The advertising executives realized that chickens were not a manufactured product and that Perdue was growing, nurturing, his product. Pesky explained, "We realized that what really set Perdue chickens apart from other chickens was Frank Perdue."

McCabe explained that yellow chickens were not enough to build a campaign around because other chicken companies could come in and make the same claim. They tried numerous approaches, but nothing worked. Scali described sitting in his office one day when Perdue came barging in. "I was just sitting there slackjawed and bemused by this Perdue character . . . he looked a little like a chicken himself, and he sounded a little like one, and he squawked a lot. . . . it just clicked." Obviously Perdue himself should be the spokesman in the commercials. Perdue wasn't excited about the idea. He admitted that he was shy and that another agency had proposed the same thing, which he thought was just pandering to his vanity. Scali talked him into it, and the commercials were instantly successful.

The slogan was: "It takes a tough man to make a tender chicken." One commercial showed Perdue in the chicken house in coveralls, a paper hat, and rubber boots talking about "clean livin'." He declared: "This is not to protect people from my chickens; it's to protect my chickens from people."

McCabe explained that Perdue has a personality that lent credibility to the product: "If Frank Perdue didn't look and sound like a chicken, he wouldn't be in the commercials." McCabe admitted that Perdue is not the usual CEO spokesman. "He always appears a little bit off the wall, a little bit irregular."[*]

Perdue Farms' advertising expenditures increased thirtyfold, and the annual revenues of the company rose from $58 million to more than half a billion dollars by 1983. This unlikely campaign has won several Clio awards and has been incredibly successful for both Perdue and the agency.

[*]"Annals of Business: CEO TV," *The New Yorker,* July 6, 1987, pp. 39–56.

ADVERTISING: STRATEGY AND CREATIVITY

All the advertising strategy decisions and all the message strategy decisions in the world cannot create a good ad. Strategy gives direction to an advertisement, but it does not give shape to it. The shaping, the designing, the crafting, the sculpting, of the message is an art. Strategy tells where you are headed, but it does not tell you how to get there.

After the strategy has been agreed upon, the next step in creating an advertisement is to come up with a creative concept that brings the message to life. Dull, but important, marketing phrases have to be transformed into attention-getting and memorable creative ideas.

What Makes an Idea Creative?

Creative ideas aren't limited to advertising. People such as Lee Iacocca, who rescued Chrysler from bankruptcy, and Steven Jobs, the inventor of Apple Computers, are highly creative. They are idea men, creative problem solvers, and highly original thinkers. Creative people are found in business, in science, in engineering, and yes, even in advertising.

Although definitions of creativity vary, all agree that the focus of creativity is the end result—the idea that comes out of creative thinking. Stern says that creativity results in a "novelty that is accepted as useful, tenable, or satisfying by a significant group of others. . . . The result represents a 'leap,' not merely a step away from that which existed before but a good distance away."[*]

The creative leap is what sets the advertisement apart. The springboard for the leap is a solid strategy statement. Advertising has to be creative, but it must also be strategic. The nature of this relationship is expressed in the philosophy of DDB Needham Worldwide, summarized as relevance, originality, and impact (R.O.I.).

original *One of a kind; unusual and unexpected.*

Originality   An advertising idea is considered creative when it is novel, fresh, unexpected, and unusual. **Original** means one of a kind. Any idea can seem creative to you if you have never thought of it before. But the essence of a creative idea is that no one else has thought of it either.

In classes on creative thinking, a teacher will typically ask people to come up with ideas about, for example, what you can build with ten bricks. Some ideas like a wall, will appear on many people's lists. Those are obvious and expected ideas. The original ideas are those that only one person thinks of.

An unexpected idea can be one with a twist, with an unexpected association, or catchy phrasing. A familiar phrase can become the raw material of a new idea if it is presented in some unusual or unexpected situation. An ad for Bailey's Irish Cream, for example, shows the product being poured into a wine glass over ice cubes. The twist is in the headline that reads: "Holiday on Ice."

A play on words is a good way to develop something unexpected. The American Cancer Society used the headline "Fry Now, Pay Later" for its safe tanning message. (See Ad 13.1.)

cliché *A trite expression, an overused idea.*

CLICHÉS   Unoriginal advertising is not novel or fresh; it is the common or obvious idea. Look-alike advertising copies somebody else's great idea. Unfortunately a great idea is only great the first time around. When it gets copied and overused, it becomes a **cliché**. Even though professionals continually disparage look-alike advertising, it remains a dominant advertising form. Although every-

[*]Morris I Stein, "The Investment Analyst: An Intermediary in the Creative Process," *Wall Street Transcript,* April 20, 1981, p. 61.

There is a proven connection between sun exposure and skin cancer, as well as to premature wrinkling. If you must be in the sun, use sunscreen and common sense.

AMERICAN CANCER SOCIETY

AD 13.1
This ad by the American Cancer Society illustrates creative use of a play on words. What other ads can you think of that use this device?
(Courtesy of DDB Needham Worldwide.)

relevance *That quality of an advertising message that makes it important to the audience.*

PRINCIPLE
If it doesn't conform to strategy, reject it.

one is searching for a great idea, not everyone is lucky or talented enough to find one.

Relevance   The hallmark of a creative idea is originality, but in advertising there is a second and equally important dimension, **relevance.** Advertising is a disciplined, goal-oriented field that tries to deliver the right message to the right person at the right time. The goal is persuasion that results in either opinion change or sales. Ideas not only have to be original, they also have to mean something important to the audience.

Advertising is a tough, problem-solving field where you don't have the luxury of waiting for a creative concept to appear. According to former advertising executive Gordon White, "It is creativity on demand, so to speak. Creating within strict parameters. Creativity with a deadline."*

EMPATHY   Advertising is directed at convincing people. Unlike a painting, a building, or a technological breakthrough, creativity in advertising requires

*Gordon E. White, "Creativity: The X Factor in Advertising Theory," in *Strategic Advertising Decisions: Selected Readings,* Ronald D. Michman and Donald W. Jugenheimer, eds. (Columbus, OH: Grid, Inc., 1976), p. 212.

empathy *Understanding the feelings, thoughts, and emotions of someone else.*

empathy, a keen awareness of the audience: how they think and feel, what they value, and what makes them take notice. A creative idea has to speak to the right audience with the right sales message. The purpose of advertising is first and foremost to sell the product, service, or idea. No matter how much the creative people or the client or the account executive may like an idea, if it doesn't communicate the right message or the right product personality to the right audience, then it doesn't work. Liking the idea simply isn't enough.

impact *The effect that a message has on the audience.*

Impact   To be creative, the idea must also have **impact.** Most advertisements just "wash over" the audience. A commercial with impact can break through the screen of indifference and focus the audience's attention upon the message and the product. An idea with impact helps people see themselves or the world in a new way. The classic ad campaign for V-8 vegetable juice pictured in Ad 13.2 demonstrates the impact of a creative idea when the various characters hit themselves on the forehead in the familiar gesture that says "Why didn't I think of that" while saying aloud: "I could have had a V-8." That ad expresses the impact and power of a relevant, new idea.

Effective Creativity   Many advertising professionals believe that creativity occurs only if the advertisement meets the objectives of the sponsor. "Marketing creativity is that thought behind a product or a line of products that sells the product," says Faith Popcorn, partner in a marketing consulting firm. "If you sell the product, you're as creative as you ever want to be."*

AD 13.2
A classic example of an ad with impact.
(Courtesy of DDB Needham Worldwide.)

*Roberta Reynes, "Creativity in Marketing," *Marketing Communications,* December 1980, p. 21.

However, there is a danger in focusing too heavily on the marketing objectives and ignoring the need for original, novel ideas. *Strategy hypnosis,* an extreme concentration on strategy, can stifle creative thinking. The environment can also block creative thinking. Bureaucracy, specialization, and time clocks hinder the spirit of exploration and playfulness necessary for creative thinking.

Perhaps the environmental factor most inhibiting to creative advertising is the *risk-aversive* nature of many large organizations. Typically a creative person will use a proven formula for an ad, knowing that the approach is safe and the ad probably won't fail, even though it may not be highly successful either. A new approach is always a gamble. The creative person who tries a new idea may be dismissed as lucky if the ad is successful or incompetent if it fails. Creative people often choose to play it safe when working with a multimillion-dollar investment.

The Creative Personality

Is creativity a personality trait we are born with, or can we be trained to be creative? Geneticists studying the issue contend that we are all born somewhat creative, able to combine complex and unrelated ideas and solve problems. However, creativity tests show that a person's score invariably drops about 90 percent between the ages of five and seven. By the time the average adult reaches age 40, only about 2 percent of the creativity of age 5 remains.*

Being Different   What causes this enormous creative loss? Actually, several factors are responsible. Most notably, creativity is smothered in the growing-up process. We are rewarded for complying and punished for being different. The human mind is taught from birth to accomplish certain tasks in specific ways. Parents and teachers are often more concerned with keeping children "well behaved" and "under control" than with developing their creative abilities. Thus, both our culture and our education stifle our capacity to be different.

Personal Characteristics   Although everyone has some problem-solving abilities, certain traits seem to be typical of creative problem solvers. The first is that they soak up experiences like sponges. They have a huge personal reservoir of material: things they have read, watched, or listened to, places they have been and worked, and people they have known.

Research has found that creative people tend to be independent, self-assertive, self-sufficient, persistent, and self-disciplined, with a high tolerance for ambiguity. They are risk takers and they have powerful egos. In others words, they are *internally driven.* They don't care much about group standards and opinions. They are less conventional than noncreative people and have less interest in interpersonal relationships.

They have an inborn skepticism and very curious minds. They are alert, watchful, and observant. They reach conclusions through intuition rather than through logic. They also have a mental playfulness that allows them to make novel associations. They find inspiration in daydreams and fantasies, and they have a good sense of humor.

In general, creative people tend to perform difficult tasks in an effortless manner and are unhappy and depressed when they are not being creative. In addition to having many positive characteristics, they also have been described as abrasive, hard to deal with, and withdrawn.

*Richard Bencin, "The Psychology of Creativity," *Marketing Communications,* December 1983, p. 43.

Leonardo da Vinci, Albert Einstein, and Pablo Picasso all excelled in different fields, but all three qualify as creative geniuses.
(Leonardo da Vinci and Albert Einstein courtesy of The Bettmann Archive and Pable Picasso courtesy of UPI/ Bettmann Newsphotos.)

What characteristics do creative thinkers *not* exhibit? They are not dogmatic (although they can be stubborn), and they have little patience with authoritarian people. They don't follow the crowd, and they like being alone. They aren't timid, and they don't care much what other people think.

Visualization Skills   Most copywriters have a good visual imagination as well as excellent writing skills. Art directors, of course, are good visualizers, but they can also be quite verbal. Stephen Baker, in his book *A Systematic Approach*

CHARACTERISTICS OF CREATIVE PEOPLE

Creative people in advertising tend to score high on the following personal characteristics, although not every person on the creative side scores high on every factor. How do you rate yourself?

	High	Medium	Low
• Intuitive	—	—	—
• Risk taker	—	—	—
• Enthusiastic	—	—	—
• Open to your feelings	—	—	—
• Motivated	—	—	—
• Nonconformist	—	—	—
• Hard worker	—	—	—
• Goal-directed	—	—	—
• Imaginative	—	—	—
• Self-confident	—	—	—
• Enjoy toying with ideas	—	—	—
• Ideas are a dime a dozen	—	—	—
• Persuasive	—	—	—

• Express feminine interests (for men)	—	—	—
• Express masculine interests (for women)	—	—	—
• Like the unknown	—	—	—
• Do not mind being alone	—	—	—
• Curious	—	—	—
• Interested in aesthetics	—	—	—
• Perceptive	—	—	—
• Self-demanding	—	—	—
• Observant	—	—	—
• Good-natured	—	—	—
• Independent	—	—	—
• Resourceful	—	—	—
• Original	—	—	—

Source: Adapted from a study by Roxanne Hovland, Gary Wilcox, and Tina Hoffman, "An Exploratory Study of Identifying Characteristics of Advertising Creatives: The Creative Quotient Test," 1988 Annual American Academy of Advertising Conference, Chicago, April 11, 1988.

to *Advertising Creativity,* describes "writers who doodle and designers who scribble" as the heart of the advertising concept team.*

Writers as well as designers must be able to visualize. Good writers paint pictures with words; they describe what something looks like, sounds like, smells like, and tastes like. They use words to transmit these sensory impressions. Most of the information we accumulate comes through sight, so the ability to manipulate visual images is very important for good writers. In addition to seeing products, people, and scenes in their "mind's eye," they also need to be able to form a mental picture of the finished ad while it is still in the talking, or idea, stage.

visualization *The ability to see images in the mind, to imagine how an ad or a concept will look when it is finished.*

Visualization is not a skill limited to print advertising. Copywriters, art directors, and producers work together to create radio and television commercials. In radio, copywriters have to be particularly good at painting with words and sounds to create an image in the listener's mind. In television, visualizing means you have to be able to think in terms of staging, movement, and story development. The ability to imagine how the ad or commercial will look is critical to people on the creative side of advertising.

The Creative Team Strategy statements are usually developed by account executives and advertising managers. Creative concepts are developed by the creative team—copywriters, art directors, creative directors, and producers. Sometimes the creative people are involved in the strategy decisions, and sometimes they are not. They use the strategy, however, as a foundation for the creation of an advertising message that brings the objectives, positions, and selling premises to life. Strategy is a foundation, not a framework.

Creativity involves finding different uses for common items or materials.
(Courtesy of Hirshhorn Museum/Art Resource.)

*Stephen Baker, *A Systematic Approach to Advertising Creativity* (New York: McGraw-Hill Book Co., 1979).

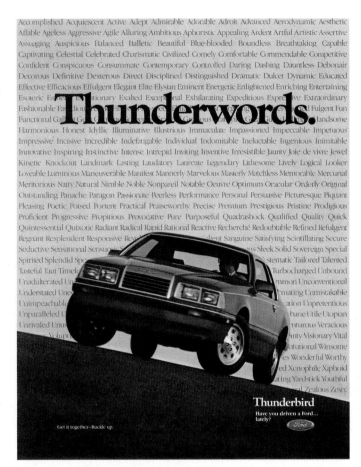

AD 13.3
A creative example of verbal association. The reader is supposed to associate all of the words in the ad with the Ford Thunderbird.
(Courtesy of Ford Motor Company.)

OMI pg. B23-327

Creative Thinking

You may wonder how creative ideas appear. There is a tendency to think that only certain people are creative. That is one of the myths of the advertising business, and people who work on the "creative side" in advertising deliberately maintain it. Actually creativity is a special form of problem solving, and everyone is born with some talents in that area. Research has consistently shown that all people are creative to some extent and can increase their abilities by learning to think creatively.

Furthermore, creativity is not limited in advertising to the "creative side." Advertising is a very creative business that demands imagination and problem-solving abilities in all areas. Media planners and researchers, for example, are just as creative as copywriters and art directors in searching for innovative solutions to the problems they face.

idea *A mental representation; a concept created by combining thoughts.*

Juxtaposition An **idea**, according to James Webb Young, a legendary advertising executive, is "a new combination" of thoughts. In his classic book *A Technique for Producing Ideas,* Young claimed that "the ability to make new combinations is heightened by an ability to see relationships."* An idea is a thought that is stimulated by placing two previously unrelated concepts together. The juxtaposition sets up new patterns and new relationships and creates a new way of looking at things. This phenomenon has been described as making the familiar strange and the strange familiar.

*James Webb Young, *A Technique for Producing Ideas,* 3rd ed. (Chicago: Crain Books, 1975).

free association *An exercise in which you describe everything that comes into your mind when you think of a word or an image.*

convergent thinking *Thinking that uses logic to arrive at the "right" answer.*

divergent thinking *Thinking that uses free association to uncover all possible alternatives.*

Association Creative thinking uses a psychological technique called **free association.** Young's definition of a new idea called for the juxtaposition of two seemingly unrelated thoughts. That is what happens in associative thinking. In free association you think of a word and then describe everything that comes into your mind when you imagine that word. Associative thinking can be visual or verbal—you can start with a picture or a word. Likewise you can associate by thinking of either pictures or words.

The advertisement for the Thunderbird automobile pictured in Ad 13.3 demonstrates visually how verbal association works.

Divergent Thinking Creative thinking is different from the way you think when you try to balance your checkbook or develop an outline for an essay in English class. Most of the thinking that students do in classrooms is rational and is based on a linear logic where one point follows from another, either inductively or deductively.

Creative thinking uses an entirely different process. J. P. Guilford, a well-known cognitive psychologist, distinguished between convergent thinking and divergent thinking.* **Convergent thinking** uses linear logic to arrive at the "right" conclusion. **Divergent thinking,** which is the heart of creative thinking, searches for all possible alternatives.

Convergent thinking neatly and systematically follows a logical route to an answer. Divergent thinking seeks alternative approaches rather than a correct or right answer. Convergent thinking, then, follows from the past and leads to predictable conclusions on the basis of what has gone before. Divergent thinking makes a series of breaks with the past and leads to surprising or unexpected alternatives.

Right and Left Brain In current neurophysiology the two types of thinking have been associated with different hemispheres of the brain. Left-brain thinking is logical and controls speech and writing; right-brain thinking is intuitive, nonverbal, and emotional. Most people use both sides of their brains, depending upon the task.

There are personality types, however. An artist is generally more oriented to right-brain thinking, whereas an accountant is more left-brained. A person who is left-brain dominant is presumed to be logical, orderly, and verbal. In contrast, a person who is right-brain dominant deals in expressive visual images, emotion, intuition, and complex interrelated ideas that must be understood as a whole rather than as pieces.†

The Process There is a tendency to think of a creative person as someone who sits around waiting for an idea to strike. In comic books that is the point where the light bulb comes on above the character's head. In reality, most people who are good at thinking up new ideas will tell you that it is hard work. They read, they study, they analyze, they test and retest, they sweat and curse and worry, and sometimes they give up. Major breakthroughs in science or medicine may take years, decades, even generations. That unusual, unexpected, novel idea doesn't come easily.

Despite differences in terms and emphasis, there is a great deal of agreement among the different descriptions of the creative process. It is agreed that the stages of the creative process do not occur in a systematic and orderly manner. The creative process is usually portrayed as following sequential steps. As long ago as 1926 an English sociologist named Graham Wallas first put names

*J. P. Guilford, "Traits of Personality," in *Creativity and Its Cultivation,* H. H. Anderson, ed. (New York: Harper & Brothers, 1959).

†Betty Edwards, *Drawing on the Right Side of the Brain* (Los Angeles: Tarcher, 1979).

to the steps in the creative process. He called them: *preparation, incubation, illumination,* and *verification.**

A more comprehensive process is suggested by Alex Osborn who, in addition to being a former head of the BBDO agency, also established the Creative Education Foundation:

1. Orientation: pointing up the problem
2. Preparation: gathering pertinent data
3. Analysis: breaking down the relevant material
4. Ideation: piling up alternative ideas
5. Incubation: letting up, inviting illumination
6. Synthesis: putting the pieces together
7. Evaluation: judging the resulting ideas†

Although the steps might vary and the names might differ, all creative strategies seem to share several key points. Researchers consistently have found that ideas come after the person has immersed himself or herself in the problem and worked at it to the point of giving up. *Preparation* is that essential period of hard work when you read, research, investigate, and learn everything you can about the problem.

After preparation comes a time of playing with the material, of turning the problem over and looking at it from every angle. This is also a period of teasing out ideas and bringing them to the surface. Most creative people develop a physical technique for generating ideas, such as doodling, taking a walk, jogging, riding up and down on the elevator, going to a movie, sharpening pencils, or eating strange foods. It is a highly personal technique used to get in the mood, to start the wheels turning. The objective of this stage is to generate as many alter-

*Graham Wallas, *The Art of Thought* (New York: Harcourt, Brace & World, Inc., 1926).
†Alex F. Osborn, *Applied Imagination,* 3rd ed. (New York: Scribners, 1963).

CONCEPTS AND CONTROVERSIES

THE CURSE OF THE CLIO

There is some debate in the advertising world concerning the various award programs for advertisements. Are award-winning advertisements really winners for the client as well as for the creative team? Some people argue that the creative team views advertising in a different light than the client does. Whereas one is concerned with originality and creativity, the other has only one criterion for judging an ad: Does it increase sales?

Whether or not this assumption is true, it is a fact that agencies have been fired shortly after winning awards for creative ads. Because the major advertising awards are called the Clio awards, the loss of clients by Clio winners has become known as the "Curse of the Clio." Harry McMahan, who has written extensively on television, analyzed the Clio winners one year and reported that:

* Four of the agencies that won Clios lost the accounts.
* Another Clio winner was out of business.
* Another Clio winner eliminated its television budget.

* Another Clio winner gave half the account to another agency.
* Another Clio winner refused to put the winning entry on the air.
* Of the 81 television classics picked by the Clio festival in previous years, 36 were by agencies that had either lost the account or gone out of business.

Clearly, winning an award for creativity does not guarantee success for an agency.

The "curse of the Clio" raises several difficult questions for people concerned with advertising. Does creativity matter? Who should judge creativity, clients or other creatives? Should creativity be measured by artistic standards or by the extent to which the advertisement achieves the client's goals? Which would you rather create, an ad that wins an award or an ad that increases sales for the client?

Source: David Ogilvy, *Ogilvy on Advertising* (New York: Vintage Books, 1985), p. 24.

natives as possible. The more ideas that are generated, the better the final concepts.*

The processes of analysis, juxtaposition, and association are mentally fatiguing for most people. You may hit a blank wall and find yourself giving up. This is the point that Young describes as "brainfag." It is a necessary part of the process.

Incubation is the most interesting part of the process. This is the point where you put your conscious mind to rest and let your subconscious take over the problem-solving effort. In other words, when you find yourself frustrated and exasperated because the ideas just won't come, try getting away from the problem. Go for a walk, go to a movie, do anything that lets you put the problem "out of your mind," because that is when the subconscious will take over.

Illumination is that unexpected moment when the idea comes. Typically the solution to the problem comes at the least expected time: not when you are sitting at the desk straining your brain, but later that evening just before you drop off to sleep or in the morning when you wake up. At an unexpected moment the pieces fit together, the pattern is obvious, and the solution jumps out at you.

One of the most important steps is the *verification* or evaluation stage, where you step back and look at the great idea objectively. Is it really all that creative? Is it understandable? Most of all, does it accomplish the strategy?

Most people working on the creative side of advertising will admit that many of their best creative ideas just didn't work. They may have been great ideas, but they didn't solve the problem or accomplish the right objective. Copywriters will also admit that sometimes the idea they initially thought was wonderful does not project any excitement a day or a week later.

Brainstorming   **Brainstorming** is a technique developed in the early 1950s by Alex Osborn.† Brainstorming uses associative thinking in a group context. Osborn would get a group of six to ten people together in his agency and ask them to come up with ideas. One person's ideas would stimulate someone else, and the combined power of the group associations stimulated far more ideas than any one person could think of alone.

The secret to brainstorming is to remain positive. Try to elicit the maximum number of ideas without any evaluation of their effectiveness. The rule is to defer judgment. Negative thinking during a brainstorming session can destroy the informal atmosphere necessary to achieve a novel idea.

Another type of divergent thinking uses such comparisons as analogies and metaphors. Young's definition of an idea also called for the ability to see new patterns or relationships. That is what happens when you think in analogies. You are saying that one pattern is like or similar to another totally unrelated pattern. William J. J. Gordon, a researcher in the area of creative thinking, discovered in his research that new ideas were often expressed as analogies. He has developed a program called *Synectics* that trains people to approach problem solving by applying analogies.‡

Developing the Skills   Understanding the creative process is the biggest step in learning to be more creative. Most people who think they aren't creative simply don't work hard enough. You must accumulate a great deal of information to produce good ideas. Be alert, be perceptive, observe everything that's

*Bruce G. Vanden Bergh, Leonard N. Reid, and Gerald A. Schorin, "How Many Creative Alternatives to Generate," *Journal of Advertising* 12 (1983): 4.

†W. J. J. Gordon, *The Metaphorical Way of Learning and Knowing* (Cambridge: Penguin Books, 1971).

‡*Ibid.*

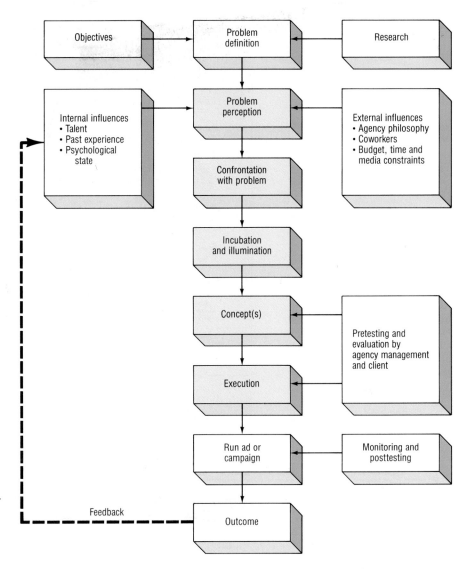

FIGURE 13.1
The creative process in advertising.

Source: Reprinted from *Marketing News,* published by the American Marketing Association. Bruce Vanden Bergh, "Take This 10-Lesson Course on Managing Creatives Creatively," *Marketing News,* March 18, 1983, p. 22.

happening around you. Read, wonder, and question. You can consciously develop a creative mind.

The mental digestion process takes time and effort. Develop your own getting-started techniques like doodling with words and pictures. Creative people often fill pads with what seems to be aimless doodling. They even sleep with notepads by their beds. In fact, the half-sketched ideas and phrases are the raw materials of ideas. This stage often leads to what seems to be a blind wall. Don't give up too easily; take a walk instead. Too many people give up too soon.

Another way to become more creative is to develop your associative thinking skills. You can practice free association by yourself. Just look around the room, pick out an object, relax, open your mind, and see what thoughts come to mind. The more often you do this, the more comfortable you will be with the process. You will find that the number and variety of associations increase. Strive for the funniest, silliest, craziest associations you can think of—that is how you develop the ability to come up with original associations.

Analogies are also useful exercises. Look around the room and pick out something. Ask yourself what that item is like—what it resembles, either physically or functionally. Functional analogies compare processes such as how something works or how something is used. A vacuum cleaner is like . . . an anteater, the tentacles of an octopus, a swimmer gasping for air. Keep playing

AD 13.4
An example of the "Big Idea." It makes an impact upon the viewer and yet appears obvious and simple.
(Courtesy of DDB Needham Worldwide.)

with the images—once again, the crazier the better. The creative mind is a muscle that can be strengthened through exercises like making associations and analogies, but it takes practice.

CREATIVE CONCEPT: THE BIG IDEA

creative concept *A "Big Idea" that is original and dramatizes the selling point.*

PRINCIPLE
Effective ads are built on strong creative concepts.

Behind every good advertisement is a **creative concept,** a "Big Idea" that makes the message distinctive, attention-getting, and memorable. Usually a Big Idea is simple and, after it has been developed, seems to be the "obvious" solution. You know a successful Big Idea because you will find yourself saying "I wish I had thought of that." For an example of a Big Idea see Ad 13.4.

This step is what advertising giant Otto Kleppner called "The Creative Leap."* To come up with the Big Idea, you have to move away from the safety of the strategy statements and leap into the creative unknown. The creative team's mission is to find an idea that has not been used before in order to communicate what might otherwise be a dull sales message.

Usually the concept is developed by a copywriter/art director team. These two people work together to generate as many ideas as they can, hoping that one of the ideas will be the Big Idea. Both people are good at thinking in words and pictures, so they work as a team rather than as specialists.

You might ask: Why not just run the strategy statement? It says everything we want said. The problem with strategy statements is that they are not distinctive, attention-getting, and memorable. They are dull outlines, platforms for in-house discussion and agreement, not messages that will persuade a consumer audience to buy or believe something.

The concept may come to mind as a visual, as a phrase, or as a thought that uses both visual and verbal expression. If it begins as a phrase, then the next step is to try to visualize what it looks like. If it begins as an image, then the next step is to come up with words that express what the visual is saying. The ideal con-

*Thomas Russell and Glenn Verrill, *Otto Kleppner's Advertising Procedure,* 9th ed. (Englewood Cliffs, New Jersey: Prentice Hall, 1986), p. 411.

cept is expressed simultaneously through both the visual and the verbal elements. Words and pictures reinforce one another. An example is the Dial ad pictured in Ad 13.5.

THE MESSAGE STRATEGY

After the creative concept has been decided upon, the next step in creating an advertisement is to decide on the message format. We are not talking about actually writing or designing the ad, but rather about deciding upon what the message will say and how it will say it. Should the message be hard-sell or soft-sell, informational or emotional? Should it build an image or attack a competitive position?

Even within a product category, there usually is no one right way. On liquor advertising, one creative director says that consumers should not be given a logical reason for buying liquor—"I think long copy, as far as taste, feel and smell goes, isn't necessary." He explains: "If I'm a consumer buying a $10 bottle of scotch, I don't need to know the whiskey is aged in charred barrels or that 'God's sun showered down on the grain.'"* Other creative directors for a liquor product may feel that a long narrative story about how the product is made is not appropriate but is interesting and attention-getting.

Some products in categories like insurance will find highly emotional copy to be effective, while their competitors are successful with humor or long, serious explanations of financial information. Although most copy is written short and tight, there are creative directors who stress information. Some feel that you can't give consumers enough information. Others believe in touching the emotions.

AD 13.5
This Dial ad demonstrates how words and pictures can work together to create impact.
(Courtesy of DDB Needham Worldwide.)

*Michael Schudson, *Advertising, The Uneasy Persuasion* (New York: Basic Books, 1984), p. 74.

Content Approaches

informational *Messages built on facts and logic.*

emotional *Messages built on psychological appeals such as fear and love.*

image *Messages built by associating or linking the product to symbols of life styles and desired values.*

Three general terms are used to describe the content of an advertising message: information, emotion, and image. The most common approach is **informational,** with the emphasis on facts, learning, and the logic of persuasion. **Emotional** messages use psychological appeals such as fear and love to touch our feelings. **Image** advertising tries to develop associations between the product and desired lifestyles, glamorous people, and symbols. The message is communicated through these linkages.

Sales Approaches

From the area of salesmanship comes another way to describe advertising messages: *hard-sell* or *soft-sell*. The difference between the two message strategies was the subject of a special issue of the *Topline* newsletter produced by the research company McCollum/Spielman & Company.

hard-sell advertising *Messages that emphasize a strong argument and call for action.*

The Hard Sell   **Hard-sell advertising** can be equated with informational advertising, particularly that end of the spectrum that uses strong arguments and pushy demands for action. The more common hard-sell approach, however, is direct, with an emphasis on tangible product features and benefits. In *Topline* these messages were described as "putting the product up front." Hard sell, says the report, "tries to convince the consumer to buy because it's very good, better, the best."*

Typical of the advertisements found by McCollum/Spielman is a commercial for Cheer that shows a mother and her teenage son arguing about the laundry. He concludes that Mom was right when he sees how All-Temperature Cheer removes the dirt from his shirts of different colors and different fabrics.

soft-sell advertising *Ads with indirect appeal that use mood, ambiguity, and suspense to create an intriguing message.*

The Soft Sell   McCollum/Spielman undertook to investigate the two message approaches because of the growing popularity of **soft-sell advertising.** Subtle, intriguing, and ambiguous commercials by Jordache, Calvin Klein, and Guess? have been getting a lot of attention lately as more and more advertisers sell moods and dreams rather than products. Obsession for Men, with its stark images and puzzling story lines, is an example of the strange images created by Calvin Klein for his products.

McCollum/Spielman found out that hard-sell messages have not become extinct, however. In a random 2-hour viewing of afternoon soap operas, they counted 36 hard-sell commercials out of a total of approximately 42 commercials run during the period. In a different study the company found that although hard-sell commercials might be less arresting than soft sell, nearly two-thirds of those studied enjoy acceptable levels of brand awareness. They also discovered that hard sell was clearly more persuasive than soft sell.

Stylistic Approaches

lecture *Instruction delivered verbally to present knowledge and facts.*

drama *A story built around characters in a situation.*

Most advertising messages use a combination of two basic literary techniques: lecture or drama. A **lecture** is serious structured instruction given verbally by a teacher. A **drama** is a story or play built around characters in some situation. Both techniques are used in broadcast advertising. Print advertising makes less use of drama and more use of an anonymous voice engaged in presenting a written lecture.

*"The Hard Sell: How Is It Doing?" *Topline,* August 1986.

Lectures Lectures are a form of direct address. Stylistically, the speaker addresses the audience from the television or written page. The audience receives the message "at a distance." A television-commercial lecture is like a platform speech. In a lecture the speaker presents evidence (broadly speaking) and employs such techniques as an argument to persuade the audience.

Some lectures work by borrowing expertise from authority figures or experts in certain technical areas, such as Bruce Jenner for Wheaties, Chuck Yaeger (a former test pilot) for Delco automobile parts, and "Marcus Welby, M.D." for decaffeinated Maxwell House coffee. Compared with unknown presenters, such "authorities" are more likely to attract audience respect and attention.

Because advertising lectures work by presenting facts, they face the same kinds of problems schoolteachers face. The audience often becomes distracted with other matters, discounts part or all of the evidence, makes fun of the source, or disputes every point. In many cases these responses dilute or even cancel the message the advertiser wants to convey.

Dramas A drama is a form of indirect address, like a movie or a play. In a drama the characters speak to each other, not to the audience. In fact, they usually behave as though the audience were not there. Members of the audience observe and sometimes even participate vicariously in the events unfolding in the story. They are "eavesdroppers."

Like fairy tales, movies, novels, parables, and myths, advertising dramas are essentially stories about how the world works. Viewers learn from these commercial dramas by inferring lessons from them and by applying those lessons to their everyday lives. The key word here is *infer*. Audiences learn from dramas by observation and inference, just as they learn from stories they hear and from other things that happen to them every day.

Use of the term *drama* is not intended to imply an intense emotional experience. Some drama ads are comic sketches, some are cartoons, and some are conversations about household products, medicines, or trivial everyday events. Some simply tell a story.

A commercial drama can be very powerful. The source of the power is the viewer's involvement. When a drama rings true, the viewer "joins" the drama, draws conclusions from it, and applies those conclusions to his or her own life. From the viewer's perspective, conclusions drawn from dramas are "mine," whereas conclusions urged in lectures are "ideas that other people are trying to impose on me."

To have this involving effect, a drama must appear realistic to the audience. If a drama is contrived or unrealistic, the viewer will reject both the drama and the message. When this occurs, the inferences the advertiser counted on being made will not be made.

One important thing to remember is that the drama should be intrinsic to the product. In other words, you aren't telling a cute or funny story just to be entertaining. There is a drama in every product, and the product must be central to the drama. The tendency in using drama is to forget or downplay the point of the ad. Even with dramatic forms, you still need a solid selling premise.

Combinations Many television commercials combine lecture and drama. One common format begins as a drama, which is then interrupted by a short lecture from the announcer, after which the drama concludes. One example of this form is a Charlie the Tuna ad. Charlie is a cartoon character who is placed in some situation where he aspires to "good taste." The commercial then turns to real-life product shots of tuna fish being used in meals while the announcer explains the quality of Starkist tuna. The commercial closes with Charlie realizing he is not good enough for Starkist, but vowing to keep trying.

Another common version of the combination is a commercial that is almost all drama until the end, when a tiny lecture, like the moral of a story, is added as a tag. In still another common version the message is mostly lecture, but the lecture is illustrated with minidramas that amplify the information.

Advantages and Disadvantages Dramas have a distinct advantage because they encourage the audience to draw their own conclusions from the action of the play. Such conclusions are more likely to be accepted than are the lecture-based conclusions that the advertiser attempts to impose upon the audience.

Despite the power of dramas, lectures are still the dominant commercial message format. One advantage of lectures is that they cost less to produce. Another advantage is that they are more compact and efficient. A lecture can deliver a dozen selling points in seconds, if need be. Because the current trend is toward shorter commercials, lectures may become more common because they are so efficient. It takes time to set up a dramatic scene and introduce characters. Another advantage is that a lecture gets right to the point. A lecture can be perfectly explicit; a drama relies on the viewer to make inferences.

AD 13.6
An example of a straightforward factual ad. Note the absence of humor, drama, and any other elements that might distract readers from the central message of the ad.
(Courtesy of BMW of North America, Inc.)

HOW PURISTS TELL A FUTURE CLASSIC FROM A CONTEMPORARY ANTIQUE.

Any automobile that attempts to court fashion will inevitably be betrayed by it.

In fact, it is the very effort to be "timely" that leads to the creation of instant artifacts — the dated gadgetry and gratuitous styling that turn today's status symbols into tomorrow's symbols of transience.

The BMW 633CSi is built on a different principle: To build a truly enduring automobile, you begin with the ideal of pure technology, then ever so gradually shape it into a car.

The 633CSi's technology has constantly anticipated needs rather than reacting to them. Its computer-controlled engine, amazingly agile suspension, and superior all-around performance—these have become standards for an industry that has long found its inspiration in BMW's.

Its bucket seats are not only made of fine leather but orthopedically fitted to the curvature of the spine. They will not be outmoded until human architecture changes.

It is constructed with almost unimaginable precision—to accuracies of up to 1/1,000th of a millimeter. And while beauty is in the eye of the beholder, no less informed a beholder than Motor Trend judged it "maybe the world's handsomest car."

It isn't surprising, then, that one critic called the 633CSi a car without which "you won't know how to judge anything else" (AutoWeek).

It isn't just built for purists. It is built by them.

We invite you to sample their work through a thorough test drive at the BMW dealer nearest you. **THE ULTIMATE DRIVING MACHINE.**

© 1984 BMW of North America, Inc. The BMW trademark and logo are registered. European Delivery can be arranged through your authorized U.S. BMW dealer.

Lincoln
MISLE IMPORTS
50th and "O" St.
(402) 483-2261

Formats and Formulas

In addition to these basic approaches, advertisers use a number of common formats, or formulas, for advertising messages. These include straightforward and factual messages, demonstrations, comparisons, image associations, playlets, problem-solution, slice of life, and spokesperson.

Straightforward Factual One of the most common formats is a straightforward factual message. These advertisements are usually factual and convey information without any gimmicks or embellishments. They are rational rather than emotional. Cigarette advertisements that make claims about low tar, for example, are usually presented in a straightforward manner. Business-to-business advertising also is generally factual in tone.

BMW, Volvo, and Saab use straightforward factual copy for their cars. In contrast, other car companies use pictures of their cars against pretty backgrounds such as mountains, deserts, or beaches. Ad 13.6 for BMW is an example of factual approach. The headline reads: "How purists tell a future classic from a contemporary antique." The focus of the body copy is on the advanced technologies used in its manufacture.

PRINCIPLE
Demonstrations have to be believable.

Demonstrations Two other types of message formats that are usually straightforward and rational in tone are demonstrations and comparisons. The demonstration focuses on how to use the product. The product's strengths take center stage. In demonstration, seeing is believing, so conviction is the objective. Demonstration can be a very persuasive technique.

Comparisons A comparison contrasts two or more products and usually finds the advertiser's brand to be superior. The comparison can be direct, in which a competitor is mentioned, or indirect, with just a reference to "other leading brands." Advertising experts debate the wisdom of mentioning another product, particularly if it is a category leader, so a direct comparison has to be handled carefully.

Playlets Playlets are short dramas that employ a number of specific formula messages to convey a message. They can use any number of appeals, from fear to family love to sex to humor. A mild threat appeal has been found to be a strong motivator, but research has found that strong fear appeals can turn the audience against the message.

Humor is often used in playlets in the hope that the goodwill and positive feelings generated by the message will carry over to the product. Humor is tricky, however, because not all people think the same joke is funny. Furthermore, humor can overwhelm the product. People might remember the punch line but forget the product name. For a humor ad to be effective, the selling premise needs to pivot around the point of the humor. Humor should *never* be used to poke fun at the product or its users.

PRINCIPLE
Humor should focus attention on the selling point.

Problem-Solution There are several dramatic formats that you will hear referred to in analyzing advertising messages. One is the problem-solution where the message begins with some problem and the product is presented as the solution to that problem. This is a common technique used with cleansers and additives that make things run smoother. Automotive products often use problem-solution. It is called the *product-as-hero* technique.

An ad for MONY Financial Services enumerates a series of financial disasters that might happen to a family. The solution to these problems, of course, is a financial plan based on MONY's insurance program. The headline dramatizes

AD 13.7
Wheaties uses professional athletes to emphasize the nutritional value of the cereal. Pictured here is Walter Payton, who played for the Chicago Bears.
(Courtesy of General Mills, Inc.)

the situation: "If only interest rates hadn't gone up. If only the stock market hadn't softened. If only the kids hadn't needed braces."

A variation on this technique is the *problem-avoidance* message where the problem is avoided because of product use. This is a form of threat appeal. It is often used to advertise insurance and personal-care products.

slice of life *A problem-solution message built around some common, everyday situation.*

Slice of Life   The much maligned **slice of life** is really just an elaborate version of a problem-solution message presented in the form of a playlet. It uses some commonplace situation with "typical people" talking about the problem. Procter & Gamble (P&G) is particularly well known for its reliance on the slice-of-life technique. The P&G version puts the audience in the position of overhearing a discussion where the problem is stated and resolved. There is something very compelling about listening in on a conversation and picking up some "tip." The solution, of course, is a P&G product.

PRINCIPLE
The spokesperson should not overpower the product.

Spokesperson   Using a person to speak on behalf of the product is another popular message technique. Spokespersons and endorsers are thought to build credibility. They are either celebrities we admire, experts we respect, or someone "just like us" whose advice we might seek out. One of the problems with a spokesperson strategy is that the person may be so glamorous or so attractive that the message gets lost. The spokesperson should be associated with the product, but the product should still be the center of attention; that may be difficult with glamorous endorsers.

Although anyone can be a spokesperson, endorsers usually fall into one of four categories:

1. A created character like the Pillsbury Doughboy or Madge the manicurist
2. A celebrity like Michael Jackson for Pepsi or Bill Cosby for Jell-O
3. An authority figure like a doctor for an over-the-counter drug product
4. A typical user who represents as closely as possible the targeted audience

Nonhuman celebrities are also used as spokespersons. The Max Headroom character has been used for Coke in some very tough competitive ads directed at Pepsi. This character has a peculiar appeal to teens with its computer-generated image and its stuttering, which seems to be interpreted as signifying a personality still in the process of developing and maturing.

CREATIVITY AND CONSUMER REACTIONS

Most advertising is directed toward consumers. The objective is to influence consumer behavior in a number of ways, ranging from product awareness to an actual purchase. Because people outside the industry often view advertising differently than the creative team does, ads that appeal to creatives do not always meet with public approval. For this reason advertisers increasingly seek consumer feedback during, as well as after, the creative process. Many advertisers feel that they can save themselves money and effort by discovering early on that a particular strategy will not work.

One recent case involved the Pillsbury company. Pillsbury was designing an advertising campaign for Figurine 100s, a measured-diet meal bar. The proposed commercials centered around the weight problems of many viewers. One commercial, for example, depicted "pies and cakes flying through the air and sticking to various parts of the body as in the expression, 'A moment on the lips, forever on the hips.'" Research conducted for Pillsbury, however, revealed that dieters found these ads tasteless and offensive. As one marketing research executive observed: "After all, what one dieter jokingly says to another is very different from when [Pillsbury] says something to them as a group." As a result of this feedback, Pillsbury changed the nature of its commercials, adopting a more informative tone.

Copy testing of proposed ads has revealed that a number of widely used strategies do not appeal to consumers. Consumers react negatively, for example, to commercials that exaggerate common problems ("waxy yellow floors") and to commercials in which the characters seem to be poorly treated by the announcer. Other major complaints included stereotyped characters and "stupid" dialogue. Some formats, such as side-by-side demonstrations and exchanging a proven brand for a different one (both commonly used for laundry detergents), lose their effectiveness over time.

Some advertisers, such as Procter & Gamble, have incorporated copy testing into the creative process. As one P&G executive observed: "When it comes to liking or disliking something, it's so monumentally straightforward. This is powerful communication directly from the heart of the respondents to the mind of the creative. I don't understand why everyone isn't doing it."

Exercise

You are in the process of creating an ad for a mouthwash. The ad involves what you consider to be comical (and harmless) scenes of people reacting to someone's bad breath. Market research informs you that many consumers consider such ads to be offensive. How would you react to this information? Would you change your entire approach? To what extent should creatives tailor their ads to conform to popular tastes? Should consumer feedback be a part of the creative process? How should this feedback be used?

Source: Advertising Age, November 24, 1986, pp. 522–23.

---

testimonial *An advertising format in which a spokesperson describes a positive personal experience with the product.*

A **testimonial** is a variation of the spokesperson message format. The difference is that people who give testimonials are talking about their own personal experiences with the product. Their comments are based on personal use, which has to be verifiable or the message will be challenged as deceptive.

All of these formats are commonly used in advertising. There are other ways to package the message—this list is not complete. Some advertising professionals would like to ban many of these techniques because they are so overused. But because they are so common, they do provide a way to analyze advertising messages.

Executions

execution *The form of the complete advertisement; how the ideas are expressed and what the ad looks like.*

In the advertising world, **execution** refers to the form of the complete advertisement. After the selling premise has been agreed upon and the "Big Idea" has been developed, it must be translated into an ad, which professionals call an execution. At that point all the group work and the group decision making stops and each person does whatever he or she does best—either writing or designing an ad.

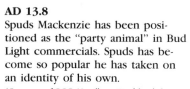

AD 13.8
Spuds Mackenzie has been positioned as the "party animal" in Bud Light commercials. Spuds has become so popular he has taken on an identity of his own.
(Courtesy of DDB Needham Worldwide.)

Artistic creativity is essential to successful advertising.
(Courtesy of Comstock.)

Leo Burnett, a master copywriter who founded a major agency in Chicago, summarized this stage of development: "After all the meetings are over, the phones have stopped ringing and the vocalizing has died down, somebody has to get out an ad, often after hours. Somebody has to stare at a blank piece of paper. Probably nothing was ever more bleak."* Out of that grim confrontation with the deadline and the empty piece of paper, and out of the imagination of one or two people working late, materializes a copy sheet, a layout, or a storyboard—the forms of an ad execution.

IMAGES AND ADVERTISING

Which is more important in an advertisement—the words or the picture? In print as well as in broadcast advertising a decision has to be made to emphasize either the images or the words. In times past, the words tended to dominate, with the visual seen as a supporting element, particularly in print. Contemporary advertising, however, has made more effective use of the visual as an important contributor to the content of the message.

The Power of the Visual

PRINCIPLE
What you show can speak more effectively than what you say.

An ad for Saab demonstrates the power of the visual by deliberately avoiding copy. The picture is taken from inside a car on a winding highway, looking over the driver's hands. The headline reads: "What we could tell you about the Saab 900 in the space below is no substitute for ten minutes in the space above." The "space below" where the body copy would normally be found was left blank in the layout.

Message Objectives Before deciding whether to emphasize words or pictures, a creative team has to consider the underlying strategy for the ad. For example, if the message is complicated, if the purchase is deliberate and well considered, or if it is a high-involvement product, then the more information the better, and that means words. If you are doing reminder advertising or trying to establish a brand image, then you may want less emphasis on words and more on the visual impression. Undifferentiated products with low inherent interest are often presented with an emphasis on the visual message.

Actually words and pictures are both important, and the best advertising uses the two to reinforce each other. But they do tend to do different things. Visuals are thought to be better at getting attention, although words can be strong if they are bold and don't have to compete with the visual. Pictures also communicate faster than words. You see a picture instantaneously, but verbal communication is deciphered word by word, sentence by sentence, line by line.

PRINCIPLE
Words and pictures work in combination to create a concept.

Visuals are thought to be easier to remember, although some verbal phrases can make a long-term impression, like "Where's the beef?" Many people remember messages as visual fragments. These are key images that they lock into their minds. You probably remember the word *home* in terms of the image of a specific house in which you have lived. Most people file memories using a visual index, although some people who are highly verbal may have difficulty remembering images. Most of us remember a print ad in terms of how it generally looked. We would have a difficult time describing all the details. Likewise a television commercial is remembered by some key visual image that is just a section or fragment of the entire commercial.

*Leo Burnett, "Keep Listening to That Wee, Small Voice," in *Readings in Advertising and Promotion Strategy,* Arnold A. Barban And C. H. Sandage, eds. (Homewood, Il: Irwin, 1968).

Visual Impact   Different people respond to words and pictures in different ways. When you think of a car, what do you think of, an image or a word? Some people are highly visual and automatically think and remember in images; other people are more verbal and would respond with a word like Ford or Ferrari.

The strength of the visual is demonstrated in an ad by the Burroughs company. It simply shows a brick wall. The impact comes after reading the headline which says, "Does talking to your computer company's service department conjure up a certain image?"

Research involving print advertising has found that more than twice as many magazine readers are captured by a picture in an ad as by the headline. Furthermore, the bigger the illustration, the higher the attention-getting power of the advertisement. Ads with pictures are noticed more than are ads with all type. Ads with pictures also tend to pull more readers into the body copy. In other words, the initial attention is more likely to turn to interest with a strong visual.

Similar research with television has found that the pictorial elements of a television commercial are better remembered. One study ranked the elements according to how well people remembered them. People tended to remember the picture first, then type on screen, then voices, and finally other sounds.

Purpose of the Visual

Obviously the most important role of the visual is to capture attention. Beyond that, look at a print ad and analyze how the visual communicates the essence of the message. Although the visual is illustrative, notice also how it expresses the central point, the pivotal idea.

Narration   In some advertisements, the picture itself tells much of the story. The legendary campaign for Hathaway shirts is an example. David Ogilvy created the elegant Hathaway man with his eye patch in 1951, suggesting a fascinating, but mysterious, lifestyle. The campaign continues to this day with contemporary men such as sportscaster Bob Costas and artificial-heart designer Robert Jarvik. It is a visual image—with relatively little reliance on words. The story development is left to the imagination of the reader.

Depiction   In other ads the idea is carried more by the words, and the visual illustrates, demonstrates, or emphasizes the point. In retail advertising, for example, a department store may feature housewares in an ad. The visual shows the line of dishes, what they look like, and what pieces are available. That is an illustrative function. The emphasis is on tangible product details.

Demonstration   With a new product, the visual may be used to demonstrate how it works or how to use it. Demonstrations are primarily visual, because it can be extremely difficult to show how something works with only verbal instructions. The picture, and particularly a series of pictures showing the steps, is a critical element in a demonstration. Ad 13.9 offers an example of a demonstration.

Symbolization   Intangibles such as quality, economy, value, speed, and flexibility are difficult to express in visuals. Abstractions like these are easier to communicate with words. Internal states like happiness, confidence, and satisfaction are also difficult to visualize. How do you show somebody looking "satisfied?"

Symbolism is the way we communicate intangibles visually. Symbols are images that represent something, usually by association. They substitute a *cue* for a concept. If you want to communicate stress, you can show a picture of a person snapping a pencil in half. Quality usually means something upscale like a fancy car, a mink coat, or a formal dinner. Associative thinking skills are important for people who communicate using abstractions and symbols.

Symbols are also important to the development of a product brand image. The Marlboro cowboy and the Charlie woman are classic examples of symbols that represent an attitude that the audience might want to identify with. These symbols do more than identify the product. The Pillsbury Doughboy is a lovable character that associates all kinds of warm, positive feelings with Pillsbury and baking. Mr. Goodwrench is the kind of friendly, helpful repairman you can trust—the image is fighting the common stereotype of an auto repairman as a

AD 13.9
This ad for Corning Lenses That Change is effective because it demonstrates, rather than just explains, how the glasses work.
(Courtesy of Corning Glass Works.)

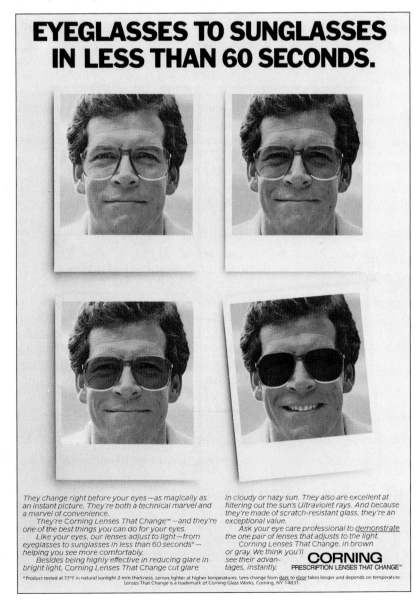

EYEGLASSES TO SUNGLASSES IN LESS THAN 60 SECONDS.

They change right before your eyes—as magically as an instant picture. They're both a technical marvel and a marvel of convenience.

They're Corning Lenses That Change™—and they're one of the best things you can do for your eyes.

Like your eyes, our lenses adjust to light—from eyeglasses to sunglasses in less than 60 seconds*—helping you see more comfortably.

Besides being highly effective in reducing glare in bright light, Corning Lenses That Change cut glare in cloudy or hazy sun. They also are excellent at filtering out the sun's Ultraviolet rays. And because they're made of scratch-resistant glass, they're an exceptional value.

Ask your eye care professional to demonstrate the one pair of lenses that adjusts to the light.

Corning Lenses That Change, in brown or gray. We think you'll see their advantages, instantly.

CORNING
PRESCRIPTION LENSES THAT CHANGE™

*Product tested at 77°F in natural sunlight 2-mm thickness. Lenses lighter at higher temperatures. Lens change from dark to clear takes longer and depends on temperature. Lenses That Change is a trademark of Corning Glass Works, Corning, NY 14831.

shyster. The Maytag repairman is not only friendly, he's lonely because Maytags are so dependable that he never gets to see customers. These symbols convey subtle yet complex meanings about the target, the target's lifestyle and values, and the product's benefits, in addition to serving as an identity cue for the brand.

Art Direction

As discussed in Chapter 4, the person who is primarily responsible for the graphic image of the advertisement is the **art director.** The art director "composes" the visuals in both print and video and "lays out" the ad elements in print. Artists may be used to do the specific illustrations or renderings, but the art director is the chief arranger of elements. He or she is responsible for the visual "look" of the message.

Photography versus Artwork   One of the primary decisions made by an art director is whether to use photography or artwork. Photography is the mainstay of the advertising business because it is "real" and adds credibility to the message. Seeing is believing, after all. Probably three-fourths of all advertising visuals are photographic. Of the photographs, around 80 percent are realistic. Illustrations in print and animation on television are used for fashion, fantasy, and exaggerated effects.

Styles of Photography   If the decision is to use photography, then there are different styles of images to choose from. A reportorial style uses dramatic black-and-white images to try to imitate photojournalism. Documentary style also uses black and white, but the style is more stark. Most products and product scenes, however, are shot in realistic full color, either in a studio, on a set, or on location.

Different photographers specialize in different types of shots. Some are great with fashion, others do buildings, some are good at landscapes, others know all the difficulties of shooting food, and still others specialize in shooting babies or animals. Each area demands specialized knowledge of how to handle lighting, staging, props, and models.

Styles of Artwork   If the layout calls for illustrations, the art director must decide which artist to use. Every artist has a personal style, although most good artists are able to shift styles somewhat to reflect the nature of the message. There is a big difference between a *loose* style, which is somewhat rough, primitive, or casual in appearance, and a *tight* style, which is detailed, perhaps even technical. Some artists are good at realistic effects, whereas others are better at abstract or highly stylized effects, as in fashion advertising. Some are good cartoonists.

Artists use a variety of techniques to create different effects, such as pen-and-ink sketches, oils, pastels, watercolor, wash drawings, scratchboards, and felt-tip pens. Computergraphics can be used to create almost any effect. Art created on a sophisticated computer is limited only by the artist's imagination and willingness to experiment.

WORDS AND ADVERTISING

Advertising writing is a special art form. It has an entirely different style than English essays or journalistic news stories. The structure is different; the language is different. In some ways advertising writing is more similar to poetry than to the usual styles of prose writing.

Copywriting

copywriter *The person who writes the text for an ad.*

Advertising writing is called *copy,* and the person who shapes and sculpts the words in an advertisement is called a **copywriter.** Copywriters are preoccupied with language. They listen to how people talk. They read everything they can get their hands on, from technical documents to comic books. They are tuned in to current expressions and fads. They understand technical communication as well as street language.

Versatility is the most common characteristic of copywriters. They can move from toilet paper to Mack trucks and shift their writing style to match the product and the language of their target. Copywriters don't have a style of their own because the style they use has to match the message. Some veteran copywriters specialize in certain types of writing, but beginners find themselves advertising all types of products. Except in a few rare cases, advertising copy is anonymous, so people who want a byline are generally not very happy as copywriters.

Stylistics

There is good writing and there is bad writing in advertising, just as there is in every other area of expression. Some of the characteristics that will be discussed here are features of good advertising writing, although all ads are not written that way.

Conversational   The best advertising copy sounds natural, like two friends talking to one another. It is not forced; it is not full of generalities and superlatives; it does not brag or boast. Conversational copy is written the way people talk. It uses incomplete sentences, fragments of thoughts, and contractions.

Because it is written as if it were a conversation, advertising copy can also be described in terms of *tone of voice.* In developing a statement of message strategy, copywriters are often asked to describe the tone of the ad. Hard-sell and soft-sell message approaches reflect a tone of voice. Look through some magazines and notice how the tone varies from ad to ad. Most ads, you will find, are written as if some anonymous announcer were speaking. But even in the anonymity there may still be an identifiable tone of voice. Some ads are angry, some are pushy, some are friendly, others are warm or excited.

PRINCIPLE ————————
Write to someone you know and match the tone of voice to the situation.

In order to get the right tone of voice, copywriters usually move away from the target audience description and concentrate on the typical user. If they know someone who fits that description, then they write to that person. If they don't, then they may go through a photo file, select a picture of the person they think fits the description, and develop a profile of that personality. They may even hang that picture above their desk while they write the copy.

Personal and Informal   One way that advertising differs from newswriting is in the use of pronouns. It is perfectly acceptable in copywriting to use "you" in direct address. As a matter of fact, a conscious attempt to use "you" will force copywriters to be more natural and less affected in their writing. It also forces them to think about the product in terms of the prospect and benefits.

"We" copy is advertising that is written from the company's point of view. It tends to be more formal, even pompous. It is also called **brag-and-boast copy.** Research has consistently found that this is the weakest of all forms of ad writing.

brag-and-boast copy *Advertising text that is written from the company's point of view to extol its virtues and accomplishments.*

"I" copy is used occasionally in testimonials or in dramas such as slice of life where a leading character speaks about a personal experience.

AD 13.10
Rather than using technical or for-
mal language, this ad relies on sim-
ple, conversational copy to make a
point. Would a different style of
copy have been effective here?
(Courtesy of The National Federation of Coffee
Growers of Colombia.)

PRINCIPLE _____
Keep it simple.

Simple   Advertising has to win its audience, and usually it is in competiton with some other form of programming or editorial matter. For that reason, the copy should be as easy to read as possible. Unless the rewards are exceptional, most people will shun advertising copy that taxes them. Simple ads avoid being gimmicky or too cute. They don't try too hard or reach too far to make a point. The Soloflex campaign is a good example of a simple concept simply expressed. The visual is of a well-built man taking off his shirt. There is no headline, but the short body copy is set in large type and serves as a long headline. The copy reads: "To unlock your body's potential, we proudly offer Soloflex. Twenty-four traditional iron pumping exercises, each correct in form and balance. All on a simple machine that fits in a corner of your home." The short slogan is a play on words: "Body by Soloflex."

Advertising copy uses short, familiar words and short sentences. If a technical term is used, it is defined immediately. Advertising copy avoids long, complex sentences and paragraphs. You will probably notice in print advertising that some of the paragraphs are only one sentence long.

Every attempt is made to produce copy that looks or sounds easy to understand. Long blocks of copy in print, which are too "gray" or intimidating for the average reader, are broken up into short paragraphs with many subheads. The equivalent of a long copy block in television advertising is a long speech by the announcer. Television monologues can be broken up by visual changes, such as shots of the product. Sound effects can also be used to break up the heaviness of the monologue.

Specific The more specific the message, the more attention-getting and memorable it is. The better ads won't say "costs less" but will spell out exactly how much less the product costs. There just isn't a lot of time to waste on generalities.

Concise Advertising copy is very tight. Every word counts because both space and time are expensive. There is no time or room for ineffective words. Coywriters will go over the copy a hundred times trying to make it as concise as possible. The tighter the copy is, the easier it is to understand and the greater its impact will be.

Positive Any message can be expressed as either positive or negative. You can say "Paint your house and the siding will last longer and weather better," or you can say "Paint your house because it looks terrible weathered with peeling paint."

PRINCIPLE _____
Keep it positive.

There are times when a threat or an appeal to the consumer's fears is appropriate. These are always negative messages, and they have to be handled carefully to avoid generating unnecessary consumer resistance. However, most advertising uses positive messages because the intention is to establish and reinforce positive feelings about the product. Positive associations are very important in developing brand images. You can't scare or threaten people into buying a product, and it is hard to make them want to buy something they have negative thoughts about.

adese *Formula writing that uses clichés, generalities, stock phrases, and superlatives.*

"Adese" Unfortunately advertising does have a style that is so well known that it is parodied by comedians. It is a form of formula writing, called **adese,** that violates all the preceding guidelines. Adese is full of clichés, superlatives, stock phrases, and vague generalities. Would you ever say things like this to a friend: "Now we offer the quality that you've been waiting for—at a price you can afford?" "Buy now and save." Can you hear yourself saying that aloud?

An ad by Buick for its Somerset line is full of adese. The headline starts with the stock opening: "Introducing Buick on the move." The body copy includes superlatives and generalities such as:

> "Nothing less than the expression of a new philosophy"

> "It strikes a new balance between luxury and performance; a balance which has been put to the test"

> "Manufactured with a degree of precision that is in itself a breakthrough"

> "Two coats of clear paint are added for an almost unbelievable luster."

Structure

Although different media make different demands upon the message, they all have a certain order in common: openings, middles, and closings. And the various pieces of an ad have the same functions, regardless of the medium.

Openings The most important part of any advertisement is the beginning. The initial impact is usually created by a combination of impressions from the visual and the words. In print the headline creates the initial impact; in television the opening comments create this impact. These initial words have to work with the visual to stop and grab the viewer or reader. Their primary function is to get attention. Copy research has proved that people make the decision either to read on or to look elsewhere after the first couple of seconds. Advertising messages have to stop the scanning and grab the audience's attention immediately.

Middle The purpose of the body of the message is to elaborate the selling points. The content is focused upon creating desire, intention, or preference. This is the persuasive heart of the message.

Certain elements in the body of the copy have other responsibilities, such as maintaining interest. This is particularly true in print, where photo captions and subheads are used as interest pegs. All the way through the message, whether print or broadcast, there has to be a strategy to keep the message interesting in order to retain the audience.

Closings The ending of the advertisement has several responsibilities. Its primary function is to point out the appropriate action as defined in the strategy. After reading or watching the advertisement, what should the audience do? Are they just supposed to feel good about the product; are they supposed to remember a name or a package design; should they associate the product with a certain lifestyle, situation, or type of person; should they make a note or tear out a coupon; or should they show up at the store the next morning for some spectacular sale? Whatever the objective, it should be clear from the closing what the consumer is to do. Every good salesperson knows that the most important part of sales is "closing the sale." Don't just leave the audience hanging.

The closing has another important function: memorability. This is the final chance the message has to make a lasting impression. It should conclude with something that will stick in the audience's mind. Slogans and taglines are used at the end because they are easy to remember. Product identification is also important. Show the product, the logotype, the signature, the trademark, or any other distinguishing product or brand features.

■ SUMMARY

- A creative concept must have relevance, originality, and impact.
- All people are born with creative skills, but most people lose these skills in the course of their lives.
- Creative people tend to be right-brain, rather than left-brain, dominant. These differences correspond roughly to divergent versus convergent thinking.
- The "Big Idea" is the creative concept around which the entire advertising campaign revolves.

- The two basic literary techniques used in advertisements are lectures and dramas. Some ads use a combination of the two.
- Common advertising formats include playlets, slice of life, spokesperson, straightforward factual, and comparisons and demonstrations.
- Effective copywriting is informal, personal, conversational, and concise. Forced, unnatural writing is referred to as *adese*.

■ QUESTIONS

1. What are some of the major traits of creative people?
2. Which characteristics of the advertising world do you think enhance creativity? Which discourage it?
3. What is the difference between convergent and divergent thinking? Give examples of each.

4. What are the advantages of using a lecture rather than a drama? What are the disadvantages?
5. What is a symbol? Why are symbols important to advertising?

■ FURTHER READINGS

BAKER, STEPHEN. *A Systematic Approach to Advertising Creativity.* New York: McGraw-Hill Book Co., 1979.

BARBAN, ARNOLD A., and C. H. SANDAGE, eds. *Readings in Advertising and Promotion Strategy.* Homewood, IL: Irwin, 1968.

DE BONO, EDWARD. *Lateral Thinking: Creativity Step by Step.* New York: Harper and Row, 1970.

GORDON, W. W. J. *The Metaphorical Way of Learning and Knowing.* Cambridge, MA: Penguin Books, 1971.

MORIARTY, SANDRA. *Creative Advertising.* Englewood Cliffs, NJ: Prentice Hall, 1985.

YOUNG, JAMES WEBB. *A Technique for Producing Ideas,* 3rd ed. Chicago: Crain Books, 1975.

14 Creating Print Advertising

Chapter Outline

Print Advertising
Writing for Print
Designing for Print
Print Production

Chapter Objectives

When you have completed this chapter you should be able to:

- Distinguish between the key features of newspaper and magazine advertising
- List the various elements of a print ad and their function
- Understand the process by which print ads are created
- Distinguish between letterpress, offset, gravure, and silk-screen printing

PRINT ADVERTISING

Paul Britten is an advertising expert who thinks big. His company, Britten Banners in Washington, D.C., specializes in oversized messages. For example, one of his clients, Perpetual American Bank, wanted a "birthday card" for the Statue of Liberty's 100th anniversary. But this was not to be your average birthday card. The bank wanted to hang it on the outside of their building in downtown Washington. How do you print something that's big enough to cover a building?

The football-field–sized birthday card created by Britten Banners measured 135 feet by 95 feet and cost $75,000 to produce. It was printed on a specially designed nylon-reinforced paper that made the "card" lightweight and durable. And the printing was done by silk screen, a process that can print on anything, regardless of size, shape, or surface.*

The Print Foundation

The foundation of modern advertising message strategy and design lies in the early print formats. The earliest mass-produced commercial messages either appeared in newspapers or as handbills. Thus many advertising guidelines originated with print, and print techniques, such as headline writing, are still seen as basic concepts. Many things have changed over the years. Television has had a tremendous impact on advertising. Visuals, which were limited in the early press to infrequent woodcuts, are now as important as words. But print advertising continues to be important and still serves as a foundation in the sense that its techniques are the easiest to understand and analyze. So we'll begin our discussion of media and their creative characteristics with newspapers and magazines.

The key elements of print advertising are divided between copy and art. The *copy* elements include headlines, underlines and overlines, subheads, body copy, captions, slogans, and taglines. **Art** refers to the visual elements, which include illustrations or photography, the type, logotypes (logos) and signatures, and the *layout* itself, which is the arrangement of all the elements.

art *The visual elements in an ad, including illustrations, photos, type, logos and signatures, and the layout.*

Newspaper Advertisements

Audience Interest   The local newspaper is unusual in that most people see newspaper advertising as a form of news. In fact, newspaper advertising is one of the few forms of advertising that is not considered intrusive. People consult the paper as much to see what is on sale as to find out what is happening in City Hall. For this reason, newspaper advertisements do not have to work as hard to catch the attention of an indifferent audience.

In addition, because the editorial environment of a newspaper is generally more serious than entertaining, the advertisements don't have to compete as entertainment, as television ads do. Therefore most newspaper advertising is straightforward and newslike. It announces what merchandise is available, what is on sale, how much it costs, and where you can get it.

PRINCIPLE
Advertising is news too.

Production Characteristics   Daily newspapers are printed at high speed on an inexpensive, rough-surfaced, spongy paper, called **newsprint,** that absorbs ink on contact. The demands of speed and low cost have traditionally made newspaper reproduction rather low-quality printing.

newsprint *An inexpensive but tough paper with a rough surface, used for printing newspapers.*

*"Turn Special Events into 'Banner' Events," *Image Maker*, Vol. 3, No. 2, p. 1.

Newsprint is not a good surface for reproducing fine details, especially photographs and delicate typefaces. Most papers can offer color to advertisers, but because of the limitations of the printing process, the color may or may not be **in register** (aligned exactly with the image).

We are accustomed to seeing news photographs that are somewhat "muddy," but most of us expect better quality from advertising. Although photographs are used in newspaper advertising, illustrations generally reproduce better. Illustrations in newspaper advertisements, like the Bullocks Wilshire ad pictured in Ad 14.1, are bold, simple, and specifically designed to reproduce well within the limitations of the printing process.

Most newspapers subscribe to an artwork service, called a *mat service,* that sends general and seasonal illustrations directly to the advertising department. This generic art satisfies the needs of most local advertisers. Larger newspapers may have their own graphic artists who are available to local advertisers. Some major advertisers may have their own art services through their trade associations, such as banks and savings and loan associations. Large department stores often have an in-house advertising staff that includes artists. Stores also hire **free-lance artists,** who provide original art for the store's ads.

AD 14.1

Despite the limitations of reproducing illustrations in newspapers, this ad manages to appear both artistic and informative.

(Courtesy of Bullocks Wilshire.)

This scene is changing, however. *USA Today* has pioneered much better quality reproduction for daily newspapers. Because the paper itself is of better quality, photographs and color reproduction are considerably better than those found in most newspapers. Significant use of color is an important part of the *USA Today* formula. Many newspapers are upgrading their technology to catch up with *USA Today,* so that quality color is more easily available to advertisers today.

Even fancy printing techniques are now possible. Some newspaper advertisements include decals and logos that have been printed with a special heat-transfer ink. These can be cut out of the paper and then ironed on T-shirts.

Magazine Advertisements

If the advertising ties in closely with the magazine's special interest, then it may be valued as much as the articles. For example, skiiers read the ads in the ski magazines to learn about new equipment, new technology, and new fashions. Readers of professional publications may cut out and file ads away as part of their professional reference library. For this reason magazine ads are often more informative and carry longer copy than newspaper ads do. Still, despite this built-in interest, ads must catch the attention of the reader who may be more absorbed in an article on the opposite page. To do that magazine advertising tends to be more creative than newspaper advertising, using beautiful photography and graphics with strong impact.

Production Characteristics   Magazines have traditionally led the way in graphic improvements. The paper is better; it is slick, coated, and heavier. Excellent photographic reproduction is the big difference between newspapers and magazines. Magazines do use illustrations, but they employ them to add another dimension, such as fantasy, to the visual message.

WRITING FOR PRINT

In Chapter 13 we talked about advertising copywriting in general. In this chapter we will examine the specific demands of print advertising. There are two categories of copy: display and body copy, or text. **Display copy** includes all those elements that the reader sees in his or her initial scanning. These elements, usually set in larger type sizes, are designed to get attention and stop the viewer's scanning. **Body copy**, the text of the message, includes the elements that are designed to be read and concentrated upon.

Headlines

Most experts on print advertising agree that the headline is the most important display element. The **headline** works with the visual to get attention and communicate the creative concept. This "Big Idea" is usually best communicated by a picture and words working together. For example, an ad for Bekins, a moving and storage company, showed a photograph of a personal check torn in half. It made sense when combined with the headline that completed the thought: "If a mover only does part of the job well, that's all he should be paid for."

The headline is the most important element of a print ad because most people who are scanning read nothing more. Researchers estimate that only 20 percent of those who read the headline go on to read the body copy.*

Functions   Because headlines are so important, there are some general guidelines for their development. A headline must *select* the right prospect, *stop*

*Philip Ward Burton, *Which Ad Pulled Best?* (Chicago: Crain, 1981).

Principle sidebars

PRINCIPLE
In magazine advertising, speak to their special interest.

PRINCIPLE
Color reproduction is better in magazines than in newspapers.

display copy *Type set in larger sizes that is used to attract the reader's attention.*

body copy *The text of the message.*

headline *The title of an ad; it is set in large type to get the reader's attention.*

PRINCIPLE
Tell as much of the story in the headline as possible.

the reader, *identify* the product and brand, *start the sale*, and *lure* the reader on into the body copy.

GAINING VIEWER ATTENTION Obviously stopping and grabbing is critical. As discussed in Chapter 8, this responsibility, shared with the visual, is a measure of the strength of the creative concept. An advertisement by General Motors that focused on its automotive testing used a picture of a car driving on rough cobblestones. The headline was unexpected. It read: "One way or another we will destroy this car."

One way to stop and grab readers is to involve them in completing the message. Involvement techniques can have tremendous impact. Questions can be puzzling, make you think, and invite you to participate in the development of the message. Furthermore, you feel compelled to read on to find out the answer.

A different kind of involvement technique is used by Kraft for its Macaroni & Cheese Dinner. The ad uses an incomplete headline, "Kraft Macaroni and ____," that the reader must complete after looking at the visual, which includes a chunk of cheddar cheese. This is a psychological principle called *closure* in which the reader completes the thought.

PRINCIPLE ____
Use your headline to flag the target.

SELECTING PROSPECTS Ideally a good headline will stop only those who are prospects; there is no sense attracting people who are not in the market for the product. A good headline selects out target audience members by speaking to their interests. An old advertising axiom is: "Use a rifle, not a shotgun."

An example of an ad that pinpoints its audience is one for Metropolitan Life that tries to sell insurance to women who are single parents. This is a very specific audience. Life insurance is not an easy product to sell to anyone, but this headline spoke to a person who may not have wanted to even think about life insurance: "Children growing up without their fathers should be able to live without their mothers too."

IDENTIFYING THE PRODUCT Product and brand identification is very important. At the very least, the headline should make the product category clear to the reader. The headline should answer the question: "What kind of product is this?" The more the brand is tied into the concept, the more likely you will be to leave some minimal identification with the 80 percent who look at the ad, read the headline, and then move on.

PRINCIPLE ____
Name the brand, if you can, in the head.

A series of ads for Goodyear Eagle radial tires was able to develop the association with high-performance vehicles and, at the same time, link the name of the brand to well-known sports cars. For example, one of the ads had two pictures of Formula One racing cars with a Ferrari Testarossa in between. The headline said: "The fact that all of these Ferraris are on Goodyear Eagle radials is no coincidence."

PRINCIPLE ____
Telegraph the selling premise in the headline.

INTRODUCING SELLING PREMISES Another function of a good headline is to introduce the selling premise. If the strategy calls for a benefit, a claim, a USP, a promise, or a reason why, that message should be telegraphed in the headline. If you have a strong sales point, lead with it.

Ford advertised its extended service plan with an advertisement that showed a miniature car in a bottle. A hand was in the process of screwing on the lid. This is another example of a creative concept that has a carefully integrated visual and headline. The headline emphasized saving money. It read:

"Put a $25 lid on major car repair costs."

INTRODUCING BODY COPY Finally, a good headline will lead the reader into the body copy. In order for that to happen, the reader has to stop scanning and start concentrating. This change is the reason only 20 percent of scanners become readers.

Action Headlines can be grouped into two general categories: direct and indirect action. *Direct headlines* are straightforward and informative, such as the

Ford headline about putting a "$25 lid on major car repair costs." They select the audience with a strong benefit, promise, or reason why. They identify the product category, and they link the brand with the benefit. Direct headlines are highly targeted, but they may fail to lead the reader into the message if they are not captivating enough.

Action techniques include news announcements, assertions, and commands. News headlines obviously are used with new-product introductions, but also with changes, reformulations, new styles, and new uses. A command headline politely tells the reader to do something. An assertion is used to state a claim or a promise.

Indirect headlines are not as selective and may not provide as much information, but they may be better at luring the reader into the message. They are provocative and intriguing, and they compel people to read on to find out the point of the message. They use curiosity and ambiguity to get attention and build interest.

An ad by 3M uses a provocative photo of a huge scruffy tennis shoe in a beautiful living room and an indirect headline to grab attention and stimulate interest. The headline reads: "How a dirty old sneaker made living rooms livable."

Techniques include questions, how-to statements, challenges, and puzzlements. A question headline can be effective if it addresses an important point. How to do something is a tremendously powerful message because it makes it possible for people to accomplish or achieve something on their own. Challenges and puzzling statements are used strictly for their provocative power. Safeway used a picture of an egg with a puzzling headline to introduce its testing procedures. The headline read: "You can't judge an egg by its cover."

All of these techniques require the reader to examine the body copy to get

AD 14.2
This Xerox ad uses a series of subheadings to attract and hold the reader's interest.
(Courtesy of Xerox Corporation. Photography by Lamb & Hall, Inc.)

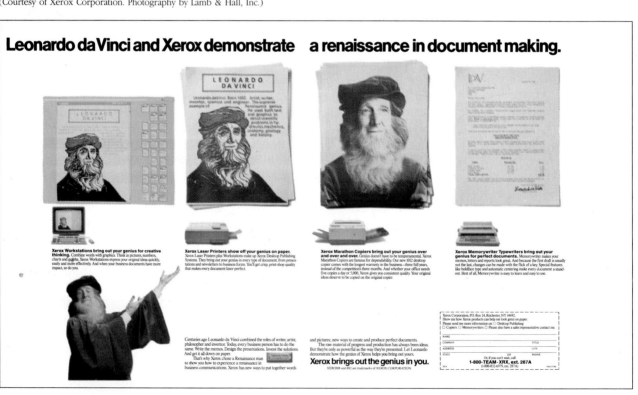

the answer or explanation. Sometimes these indirect headlines are referred to as "blind" because they give so little information. A blind headline is a gamble. If it is not informative or intriguing, the reader may move on without absorbing any product information.

Headline Writing   Writing a headline is tremendously challenging. Writers will cover notepads with hundreds of headlines and spend days worrying about the wording. Headlines are also carefully tested to make sure they can be understood at a glance and that they communicate exactly the right idea. *Split-run tests* (two versions of the same ad) in direct mail have shown that changing the wording of the headline, while keeping all other elements constant, can double, triple, or quadruple consumer response. That is why the experts, such as David Ogilvy, continue to state that the headline is the most important element in the advertisement.*

overline *A subhead that leads into the headline.*

underline *A subhead that leads from the headline into the body copy.*

Overlines and Underlines   An **overline** is a subhead that leads into the headline; an **underline** is a subhead that leads from the headline into the body copy. They are used to compensate for the limitations of direct and indirect headlines. The overline, for example, is a teaser. It may be used with a straightforward headline to spark some interest. An underline is a transition, a bridge, and it is used with indirect headlines. The underline provides the information that was missing in the "blind" headline.

These supplemental headings are useful with complex multipage layouts. For example, see the Leonardo da Vinci ad for Xerox pictured in Ad 14.2.

Other Display Copy

Subheads and Captions   Most people, if their interest is aroused by the visual and the headline, will scan the body of the advertisement to see if it looks interesting enough to read. Subheads and photo captions help to make that decision easier.

subheads *Sectional headlines used to break up masses of type.*

Subheads are sectional headlines. They are smaller in size than headlines but larger than body copy. They are sprinkled throughout the body copy to break up the gray type, to tease the reader's interest, and to identify the major points. They should be written just as carefully as the main headline. The Xerox "da Vinci" ad uses a series of four subheads to reinforce the "creative genius" concept as well as to focus attention on the four featured products.

captions *Short descriptions of the content of a photograph or an illustration.*

Captions, or cutlines, are used with the art because photos and illustrations can be interpreted in a number of ways. Captions not only help prevent misunderstanding but also are the next copy read after the headline. Because of the power of the visual, captions have very high readership. David Ogilvy insists that every photo should have a caption.†

tagline *A memorable phrase that sums up the concept or key point of the ad.*

Slogans and Taglines   Product and campaign slogans are also part of the copy package. Slogans were discussed in Chapter 8 as an important element in creating memorability. A **tagline** is a particularly memorable phrase from an individual advertisement that is repeated at the end of a single ad. It captures some key point of the ad. If it is repeated from ad to ad, then it becomes a slogan.

An example of a tagline that is used to wrap up the creative concept is found in the Xerox "da Vinci" ad. The tagline at the bottom of the ad reads: "Xerox brings out the genius in you."

*David Ogilvy, *Ogilvy on Advertising* (New York: Vintage Books, 1985).
†*Ibid.*

Copywriters employ a number of literary techniques to enhance the memorability of slogans and taglines. Some slogans use a startling or unexpected phrase; others use rhyme, rhythm, alliteration (repetition of sounds), or parallel construction (repetition of the structure of a sentence or phrase). This repetition of structure and sounds contributes to memorability. Notice the use of those techniques in the following slogans:

- BMW: "The Ultimate Driving Machine"
- Army: "Be all that you can be"
- *Wall Street Journal:* "The daily diary of the American dream"

Body Copy

The body copy is the text of the ad, the paragraphs of small type. The content develops the sales message and provides support, states the proof, and gives the explanation. This is the persuasive heart of the message. You excite consumer interest with the display elements, but you win them over with the argument presented in the body copy.

Candy bars, for example, might be seen by some writers as a difficult product about which to write an interesting message. However, the copy for Take Five* candy bar is fun, interesting, and easy to read all the way through. The headline asks:

"When to Take Five."

The body copy answers:

"—When you total up your dog's veterinarian bills and discover he's getting better medical care than you.

—When your credit card balance makes you the fourth biggest deficit spender after Argentina, Mexico and Brazil.

—When the number of candles on your birthday cake makes it necessary to blow them out with a fan.

—Whenever you bring work home on the weekend and actually do it.

—When you have a flat and the spare is in the garage.

—When you arrive in Toledo and your bags arrive in Taipei.

—Whenever the car repair bill is under $100.

—When your mother informs you she's taking up break-dancing.

—After taking 1st prize at a costume party and you didn't wear one.

—Anytime on Monday.

—When you discover that the CPA who found all those loopholes for you last year, is working for the IRS this year.

—After you finish reading all these reasons to take five and you're dying to try a Take Five bar.

—When you want light wafers, silky peanut creme, covered with Hershey's milk chocolate . . .

—When you want the richness of a candy bar without the heaviness of one, try a Take Five bar."

Types of Body Copy There are as many different kinds of writing styles as there are copywriters and product personalities. Some body copy is *straightforward* and written in the words of an unknown or unacknowledged source. A *narrative* style may be used to tell a story, and it may be either in the first person or the third person. A *dialogue* style lets the reader "listen in" on a conversation.

A liquor named Sambuca Romana uses historical stories in its advertising campaign. The following example started with a headline, followed by an underline:

*The TAKE FIVE candy bar material is reprinted by permission of the copyright owner, Hershey Foods Corporation, Hershey, Pennsylvania, U.S.A. TAKE FIVE and HERSHEY'S are registered trademarks of Hershey Foods Corporation.

PRINCIPLE

The headline catches their eye, but the copy wins their heart.

Lord Byron's Dilemma* (or, the lady or the Sambuca Romana)

The story tells of Lord Byron's adventures with Sambuca Romana in Venice:

> "The story is told that it was in a Venetian cafe, early for a rendezvous, that he first ordered the two drinks at one time. His coffee arrived and, just as he saw his contessa stepping from her gondola, the liqueur. As he started to his feet, somehow jostling the waiter, the Sambuca Romana spilled into the coffee. There was time for only one sip. He sipped, considered a moment, then sat down to finish the cup at his leisure.
>
> It was plain the lady would have to wait. The attraction of this sensuous new taste was greater than even hers.
>
> For the rest, we know Byron left Italy soon afterwards for Greece and his ultimate destiny. As for Sambuca Romana and coffee, the taste is history."

Dialogue is a little harder to write. It takes an ear for the language used by the target audience. An example of copy that reflects the witty urbanity of a contemporary couple has appeared in a series of ads for Paco Rabanne, a men's cologne. The dialogue runs without a headline:

> Hello?
>
> *What are you doing?*
>
> Taking a shower.
>
> *Right now?*
>
> No, right now I'm standing in a puddle of water.
>
> *You didn't say goodbye.*
>
> I didn't want to wake you.
>
> *Who could sleep when there's a hunk with no clothes on wandering around at five in the morning, knocking over the furniture?*
>
> I had to come back and dig out my sincere suit. Big meeting this morning. I get to say things like "bottom line" and "net net" with a straight face. What are you doing?
>
> *Lying here, thinking about you. You know, I can smell your Paco Rabanne. It's like you were still here.*
>
> I wish I were.
>
> *I couldn't go back to sleep, remembering everything. I wanted to hear your voice. It has the most interesting effect on me . . .*
>
> Maybe I should run over and read you a bedtime story or something.
>
> *Or something.*

Craftsmanship.   Body copy is very well crafted. Writers will spend hours, even days, on one paragraph. Copywriters will write a first draft, revise it, then tighten and shorten it. After many revisions it gets read by others, who critique it. It then goes back to the writer, who continues to fine-tune it. Body copy for most major ads is revised over and over.

Notice the craftsmanship in the following advertisement for a computer software product named Lotus 1-2-3. This copy is unusual in that it doesn't have a headline. Possibly the body copy is intended to be one long headline. At any rate, the emphasis is definitely on the text of the message. As you read it, notice the use of natural language, personal address, parallel structure, and alliteration:

> If you've ever scribbled on a yellow pad, a napkin, a tablecloth, a notebook or a memo pad,
>
> If you've ever used even the simplest tools of business to prepare a budget, predict a trend, plan a schedule or to analyze information of any kind.
>
> If you deal in straight lines, curved lines, credit lines or bottom lines,

*(Courtesy of Sambuca Romana, Morgan Furze, Ltd., Ft. Lee, N.J.)

If you've ever asked "what if," "why not," or "how come?"

If you've ever taken into account a variable, a sudden change of plans, a mid-course correction or the weather,

If you work in any kind of business, anywhere in the world, then you can use 1-2-3 software from Lotus.

That's what makes the world's most powerful analytical tool the world's most popular.

The copy ends with a tagline that functions as a headline: "More people use it because it does so much more."

Structure Two paragraphs get special attention in body copy: the *lead-in* and the *close*. The first paragraph of the body copy is another point where people test the message to see if they want to read it. Magazine article writers are particularly adept at writing lead paragraphs that pull the reader into the rest of the copy.

Closing paragraphs in body copy are difficult to write because they have to do so many things. Usually the last paragraph refers back to the creative concept and wraps up the "Big Idea" (see Chapter 13). Often the closing will use some kind of "twist," an unexpected tie-in with the concept. In addition, direct-action messages include some kind of *call to action* with instructions on how to respond. Even indirect-action advertisements, like brand-reminder ads in magazines, may use some kind of call to action, perhaps a reminder of where the product may be found.

*D*ESIGNING FOR PRINT

Layout and Design

Architects design buildings in their minds and then translate the details of the structure onto paper in a form known as a *blueprint*. The blueprint guides the construction of a building. It tells the builder what size everything is and what goes where.

The same thing happens in advertising. The art director takes the creative concept that has been developed with the copywriter and visualizes in his or her mind how the final ad will look. This visual inventiveness is characteristic of good designers.

layout *A drawing that shows where all the elements in the ad are to be positioned.*

Art directors manipulate the elements on paper to produce a **layout**, which is a plan that imposes order and at the same time creates an arrangement that is aesthetically pleasing. A layout is a map, the art director's equivalent of a blueprint. The art director positions and sizes the elements. These include the visual or visuals, the headline and other supplemental display copy, copy blocks, captions, signatures, logos, and other details such as boxes, rules, and coupons.

A layout has several roles. First, it is a communication tool that translates the visual concept for others so that the idea can be discussed and revised before any money is spent on production. After it has been approved, the layout serves as a guide for the production people who will eventually handle the typesetting, finished art, photography, and pasteup. In some cases the layout acts as a guide for the copywriter who writes copy to fit the space. It is also used for cost estimating.

Layout Styles The most common layout format is one with a single dominant visual that occupies about 60 to 70 percent of the area. Underneath it is a headline and a copy block. The logo or signature signs off the message at the bottom. A variation on that format has a dominant visual and several smaller visuals in a cluster. A panel or grid layout uses a number of visuals of certain sizes.

Less frequently you will see layouts that emphasize the type rather than art. Occasionally you will see an all-copy advertisement where the headline is treated as type art. A copy-dominant ad may have art, but it is either embedded in the copy or positioned at the bottom of the layout.

Developing Layouts   There are several steps in the normal development of a print layout. Most art directors—and sometimes copywriters at this stage—work with a form known as **thumbnails.** These are quick miniature versions of the ad, preliminary sketches (more like doodles) that are used for developing the concept and judging the positioning of the elements. In the early stages of development an art director may fill page after page with these thumbnails, trying to decide what the ad will look like and where the elements will be positioned.

The second step is a *rough layout.* Roughs are done to size but not with any great attention to how they look. Once again, a rough layout is for the art director's use in working out size and placement decisions. It is sometimes called a *visualization.* In newspaper ads the "rough" may be the only step before the layout goes to production.

Comps and Semicomps   In order to show the idea to someone or to test various concepts, the art director will usually move to the next step, which is a **semicomp** ("comp" is short for comprehensive). A semicomp is done to the exact size of the ad, and all the elements are exactly sized and positioned. It is done by hand, but because it is going to be presented to others, extra care is taken to make it look good.

In a semicomp the art is sketched in, usually with felt-tip markers. Color is added where appropriate. Shading for black and white is done with various gray markers to indicate tonal variations. The display type is lettered in to resemble the style of type in the final ad. The body copy is indicated by ruling in parallel lines that indicate the size of the body type and the space it will fill. Most advertising layouts are presented in either the rough layout or semicomp stage. The semicomp is used for most routine presentations.

On special occasions a full-blown **comprehensive** may be developed. This is an impressive presentation piece. Type may be set, particularly for the display copy. Body copy is often just nonsense type (also called *Greeking* type), either commercially available or cut out of another publication. It is supposed to be the right size and resemble the actual typeface specified for the ad. The art may be a rendering by an artist who specializes in realistic art for comps, or it may be cut out of another publication.

The idea is to make the comp look as much as possible like the finished piece. It is used for presentations to people who cannot visualize what a finished ad will look like from a semicomp. It is also used in important situations like new business presentations and agency reviews.

Design Principles

You begin a layout with a collection of miscellaneous elements, usually a headline (and perhaps an overline or underline), one or more pieces of art and maybe some accompanying captions, body copy complete with subheads, a brand or store signature, perhaps a trademark, a slogan or tagline. Local retail advertising will also include reminder information such as address, hours, telephone number, and credit cards accepted. Arranging all of these elements so that they make sense and attract attention is a challenge. These decisions are both functional and aesthetic. The functional side of a layout makes the message easy to perceive; the aesthetic side makes it attractive and pleasing to the eye.

thumbnails *Small preliminary sketches of various layout ideas.*

semicomp *A layout drawn to size that depicts the art and display type; body copy is simply ruled in.*

comprehensive *A layout that looks as much like the final printed ad as possible.*

Organization   The challenge to the designer is to impose some order on all this chaos. We know from research into perception that organized visual images are easier to recognize, perceive, and remember than visual images without any order.*

What do we mean by order? Basically we mean organization—imposing some pattern on the placement of the elements. Behind every layout is a pattern. If you take a piece of tracing paper and convert the major elements of any good ad to geometric shapes, a pattern will emerge. *Pattern* is a way of talking about the relationship of various elements to one another. A layout without any order lacks visual coordination of the elements.

Direction   The next thing you will notice when you study the tracing paper is that your eye follows some kind of path when it scans the elements. This path is determined by the ordering of the elements. The elements seem to follow one another according to some very carefully planned strategy.

In Western countries most readers scan from top to bottom and from left to right. That motion from upper left to lower right was tagged the **Gutenberg Diagonal** (see Figure 14.1) by graphics expert Edmund Arnold. Most layouts try to work with these natural eye movements, although directional cues can be manipulated in a layout to cause the eye to follow an unexpected path. The biggest problem occurs when the visual path is unclear.

DOMINANCE   Most good layouts have a starting point, called the dominant element. Within the design process, someone must determine the relative importance of the various elements in order to decide which one should be dominant. Normally the dominant element is a visual, but it can be a headline if the type is sufficiently big and bold to overpower the other elements. By definition there can be only one dominant element; everything else must be subordinate. This element is the **focal point** of the ad; it is the first thing you see.

VISUAL PATH   In most ads this starting point will be in the upper half of the layout, and frequently the upper left quarter. That is the natural point of entry for the eye. Likewise the natural ending point is the lower right corner, which is where you will often find a brand logo or store signature.

PRINCIPLE _____
The layout imposes structure on chaos.

Gutenberg Diagonal *A visual path that flows from the upper left corner to the lower right.*

focal point *The first element in a layout that the eye sees.*

FIGURE 14.1
The Gutenberg Diagonal.

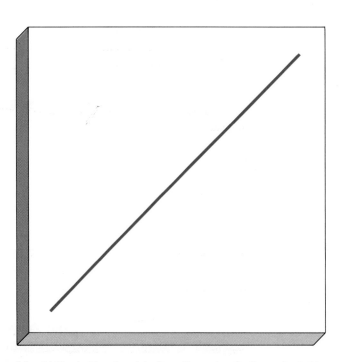

*Gerald Murch, *Visual and Auditory Perception* (Indianapolis: Bobbs-Merrill Co., 1973).

visual path *The direction in which the reader's eye moves while scanning a layout.*

PRINCIPLE _____
Use graphic signposts to make the visual path obvious.

PRINCIPLE _____
Think unity. Keep things together that go together.

margin *White space used to frame the ad content.*

bleed *An ad in which the printed area runs to the trim edge of the page.*

PRINCIPLE _____
If everything is bold, then nothing is bold.

The **visual path** that your eye follows in scanning the ad is a function of the pattern created by the arrangement. Built into the arrangement are signposts that tell you where to look next. Sometimes they are very obvious, like the direction of a model's gaze or a pointing hand. More often the pattern itself creates the order. Your eye will move from one element to another depending upon the descending visual importance of the element.

Unity You begin a layout with a collection of discrete elements. You end with a design in which all the elements have been fused into one coherent image: The pieces become a whole. For that to happen, the relationships have to be strong. The art and the headline work together to create a concept. The selling premise and creative concept work together to touch the right chord in the target. On a visual level the content of the message fuses with the form of the presentation. The ad's appearance should match its message. You wouldn't use delicate letters for an ad about Mack trucks, nor would you use fanciful art for an ad targeted to truck drivers.

CONSISTENCY Consistency is important to unity. Using one typeface rather than several is a good technique for creating unity, particularly for display copy. If there is a dominant artistic style, stick to it. Ultramodern type doesn't fit with an illustration that looks Victorian.

CONTIGUITY Neighboring elements that touch and align are another important aspect of unity. An old axiom in layout states: "Keep things together that go together." Captions need to adjoin the pictures to which they refer. Headlines lead into the text, so the headline should be over the body copy. Pictures providing a different view of the same thing should be grouped.

WHITE SPACE White space is not simply an area where nothing happens. It can be massed and used as a design element. It works in one of two ways: Either it frames an element in a sea of white, which gives it importance; or it separates elements that don't belong together. Because it sets things apart, white space is used as a prestige cue in layouts for upscale stores and products.

MARGINS Margins are an important part of unity. A **margin** is simply white space designed to frame the ad and separate it from everything surrounding it. When layout artists begin an ad, the first thing they do is draw the ad size (for a newspaper) or the page size (for a magazine), and then they draw a second set of faint guidelines that indicate the four internal margins of the ad.

Margins are critical in newspapers where ads frequently abut one another. In magazines, for a special charge, a full-page ad may **bleed** to the trim edge of the page, eliminating the margins altogether. Bleed pages are used for ads that are dominated by photographs. You wouldn't want the copy to run right to the trim edge because it might be trimmed off. Even bleed ads use an internal set of margins that determine the edge of the copy blocks.

Contrast Contrast indicates the importance of the various elements. Contrast makes one element stand out because it is different. People notice opposites, the unexpected. Contrast is also used to separate an ad from its surroundings. Because the newspaper environment is mostly black and white, an ad that uses color will stand out in contrast. In magazines, where most of the ads and editorial material use color, a black-and-white ad might stand out. Black-and-white ads, by definition, are high in contrast. They can create dramatic, high-contrast images. A small ad or illustration can dominate if it contrasts effectively with its surrounding.

Balance When an artist decides where to place an element, he or she is manipulating balance. A layout that is not in a state of visual equilibrium seems to be heavier on one side than the other. A layout that is out of balance is visually unpleasing and looks like a mistake.

There are two types of balance—formal and informal. *Formal balance* is symmetrical, left to right. Everything is centered. Formal balance is conservative and suggests stability. *Informal balance* is asymmetrical and creates a more visually exciting or dynamic layout. Informal balance is much harder to achieve because it requires manipulating and counterbalancing visual weights around an imaginary optical center. Counterbalancing uses the teeter-totter principle: larger figures are positioned closer to the fulcrum than smaller figures.

The concept of optical center is critical to informal balance. The **optical center** is the point on a page that our eyes see as the center. Because we tend to overemphasize the top half of the page, the optical center is slightly above the mathematical center (the point where the diagonals cross). This is an imaginary point. Sometimes the designer uses it to position the actual focal point of the ad, but more often it is just the point around which the elements are balanced.

optical center *A point slightly above the mathematical center of a page.*

Proportion Proportion is both an aesthetic and a mathematical principle that concentrates on the relative sizes of the elements. The basic idea is that equal proportions are visually uninteresting because they are monotonous. Two visuals of the same size fight with one another for attention, and neither provides a point of visual interest. Copy and art, for example, should be proportionately different. Usually the art dominates and covers two-thirds to three-fifths of the page area. The worst sin aesthetically is to use a layout that divides the page in half.

Simplicity The architect's axiom applies here: Less is more. The more elements you crowd into a layout, the more the impact is fragmented. Don't overload the layout. The fewer the elements, the stronger the impact. *Clutter* comes from having too many elements and too little unity. It is the opposite of simplicity.

It is possible, however, to create busy ads with numerous elements and still control the organization. Discount store advertising typically uses a form called an *omnibus* ad that is crammed with many items and big prices as a signal to the reader that the store has plenty of merchandise at good prices. This layout style can work if the elements are carefully organized, the pattern is obvious, and the visual path is logical.

Local retail advertising often tries to crowd as many elements as possible into the limited advertising space because the advertiser is trying to get maximum advertising out of a limited budget. Such ads can be a waste of the advertiser's money because the layout is not skillfully organized, the art looks like postage stamps, and the clutter makes the layout so unappealing that it is frequently ignored by most of its prospective readers. Those who lay out ads know that when you "feature" something in an ad, it has to stand out. People won't fight through clutter and disorganization. Make it hard for them to read and they won't bother to.

PRINCIPLE
Less is more, so when in doubt, delete.

Color

Color is used in advertising to *attract attention, provide realism, establish moods,* and *build brand identity.* Research has consistently shown that ads with color get more attention than ads without color. Full-color photos are more interesting than black-and-white photos. In newspapers, where color reproduction may not be very accurate, *spot color,* in which a second accent color is used to highlight important elements, has proved to be highly attention-getting.

Realism is important for certain message strategies; in those cases full-color photographs may be essential. Some things just don't look right in black and white: pizza, flower gardens, beef stroganoff, and rainbows, for example. You need color to do justice to the content.

Color has a psychological language that speaks to moods and symbolic meanings. Warm colors, such as red, yellow, and orange, are bright and happy. Pastels are soft and friendly. Earth tones are natural and no-nonsense. Cool colors, such as blue and green, are aloof, calm, serene, reflective, and intellectual.

Yellow and red have the most attention-getting power. Red is used to symbolize alarm and danger, as well as warmth. Yellow combined with black is not only attention-getting but also dramatic because of the contrast in values between the two colors. Black is used for high drama and can express power and elegance.

Metallic ink is popular with advertisers. Automotive advertising often uses a silver metallic ink. The gold industry has been running a campaign that uses 18-karat gold foil that is applied by heat.

Color association can be an important part of a brand image. Johnnie Walker Red has built a long-running campaign on all the warm associations we have with red, such as sunrises and sunsets, a fireplace, and a red setter. Kool cigarettes has used the color green so extensively that you can recognize the ad even when the product is obliterated. IBM uses the color blue so extensively that the company is sometimes referred to by people in the computer industry as "Old Blue."

PRINT PRODUCTION

The Art

The word *art* refers to the graphics, whether an illustration or a photograph. Although art directors lay out the ad, they rarely do finished art. If an illustration is needed, then an artist who works in the appropriate style is hired, usually free-lance. Fashion illustration is different from cartooning. If a photo is needed, then a photographer is hired. Both artists and photographers tend to have personal styles or specialties, and the right person has to be found for the visual. A recent article in *Adweek* reported that specialized free-lancers are being used more frequently as advertising agencies move into unusual media.*

composition *The process of arranging the elements in a photograph or an illustration.*

The layout guides the execution of the illustration or photograph. The photographer uses it to compose the image. **Composition** is a term used to describe how the elements in the picture are arranged and framed. Composition is different from a layout, which arranges all the elements in an ad, including the type as well as the visual. The composition problem may be complicated by overlapping elements. The photographer or artist has to allow room in the composition for these elements, which will be added later. The layout shows how much space is needed and where.

The Type

Most people don't even notice the letters in an ad, which is the way it should be. Good typesetting doesn't call attention to itself because its primary role is functional—to convey the words of the message. As George Lois, chairman and creative director at Lois Pitts Gershon Pon/GGK, stated: "It's important the typography doesn't get in the way of an idea."† But type also has an aesthetic role, and the type selection can, in a subtle way, contribute to the impact and mood of the message.

font *A complete set of letters in one size and face.*

Typeface Selection The basic set of typeface letters is called a **font** (see Figure 14.2). A type font contains the alphabet for one typeface in one size, plus

*Casey Davidson, "Agencies Learn the Art of Farming Work Out," *Adweek,* October 5, 1987, p. D14.
†Noreen O'Leary, "Legibility Lost," *Adweek,* October 5, 1987, p. D7.

FIGURE 14.2
This is an example of the widely
used Times Roman typeface.

14 pt

ABCDEFGHIJKLMNOPQRSTUV
abcdefghijklmnopqrstuvwxyz
1234567890

ABCDEFGHIJKLMNOPQRSTUVWXYZ ABCD
ABCDEFGHIJKLMNOPQRSTUVWXYZ ABCD

FIGURE 14.3
The top line is printed in serif letters; the bottom line in sans serif.

PRINCIPLE
Typefaces have distinctive personalities.

serif *A typeface with a finishing stroke on the main strokes of the letters.*

sans serif *A typeface that does not have the serif detail.*

italic *A type variation that uses letters that slant to the right.*

points *A unit used to measure the height of type; there are 72 points in an inch.*

picas *A unit of type measurement used to measure width and depth of columns; there are 12 points in a pica and 6 picas in an inch.*

the numerals and punctuation. The alphabet includes both capital letters, called *uppercase,* and small letters, called *lowercase.* You may want to specify *all caps,* which means every letter is a capital, or *U&lc* (upper and lower case), which means the first letter is capitalized and the others are lowercase.

Categories of Type. Most people don't realize that designers must choose among thousands of typefaces to find the right face for the message. Two of the major categories are serif and sans serif. The **serif** is the little flourish that finishes off the end of the stroke.

"Sans" means "without" in French, which is how you identify **sans serif** letters. They are missing the serif. Most of the sans serif typefaces are clean, blocky, and more contemporary in appearance.

Other categories include *cursive,* or *script,* typefaces, which look like handwriting, and *black letter* or Old English. These faces are copies of the kinds of letters in use when Gutenberg made his first type. They look like the lettering in early medieval manuscripts or Bibles. There are also hundreds of ornamental typefaces designed to look like everything from logs to lace.

Family Variations In addition to the thousands of typefaces in the various categories, there are variations within the typeface family itself. For example, any one typeface comes in a range of sizes. Figure 14.4 shows a typeface reproduced in different sizes.

The posture, weight, and width of a typeface also vary. Posture can vary from the normal upright letters to a version that leans to the right, called **italic.** The weight of the typeface can vary depending upon how heavy the strokes are. Most typefaces are available in *boldface* or *light,* in addition to the normal weight. Variation in width occurs when the typeface is spread out horizontally or squeezed together. These variations are called *extended* or *condensed.*

Printers' Measures To understand type sizes, you must understand the printers' measuring system. Type is measured in **points.** That's the smallest unit available. There are 72 points in an inch, so 72-point type is one inch high and 36-point type is half-an-inch high. The space between lines of type, called *leading* (pronounced "ledding"), is also measured in points. Normally one to two points of leading separate lines of body copy. Most designers consider type set in 14 points or larger to be display copy and type set 12 points or smaller to be body copy.

The width of columns, also called *line length,* is measured in **picas.** This is a bigger unit of measurement than the point. There are 6 picas in an inch and 12

6 POINT

ABCDEFGHIJKLMNOPQRSTUVWXYZABCDEFGHIJKLMNOPQRSTUVWXYZABC
abcdefghijklmnopqrstuvwxyzabcdefghijklmnopqrstuvwxyzabcdefghijklmnop　1234567890

8 POINT

ABCDEFGHIJKLMNOPQRSTUVWXYZ ABCDEFGHIJKLMNO
abcdefghijklmnopqrstuvwxyzabcdefghijklmnopqrstuvwx　1234567890

10 POINT

ABCDEFGHIJKLMNOPQRSTUVWXYZ ABCDEF
abcdefghijklmnopqrstuvwxyzabcdefghijkl　1234567890

12 POINT

ABCDEFGHIJKLMNOPQRSTUVWXYZ A
abcdefghijklmnopqrstuvwxyzabcd　1234567890

14 POINT

ABCDEFGHIJKLMNOPQRSTUVW
abcdefghijklmnopqrstuvwxyz 123456789

18 POINT

ABCDEFGHIJKLMNOPQRSTUVWXYZ　ABCDEFGHIJ

abcdefghijklmnopqrstuvwxyz abcdefghijklmnopqrstuvwxyz abc

1234567890

24 POINT

ABCDEFGHIJKLMNOPQRSTUVWXYZ　A

abcdefghijklmnopqrstuvwxyz abcdefghijklmno

1234567890

36 POINT

ABCDEFGHIJKLMNOPQRS

abcdefghijklmnopqrstuvwxyz a

1234567890

FIGURE 14.4
Examples of the different sizes available for the Times Roman typeface.

FIGURE 14.5
72 points = 1 inch
12 points = 1 pica
 6 picas = 1 inch
This ruler shows the relationship
between points, picas, and inches.

points in a pica. So 12-point type is exactly one pica high, or one-sixth of an inch. Column lengths are usually measured in inches. Figure 14.5 illustrates a pica ruler. The most common sizes for body copy are 9-, 10-, and 11 point.

Justification One characteristic of typeset copy as opposed to typewriter copy is the forced alignment of the column edges. With **justified** copy, like you are reading here, every line ends at exactly the same point. Because lines don't normally end so neatly, there has to be a system to force this alignment. It consists of taking the extra space at the end of the last word in the line and redistributing it back through the line at all the word breaks. Thus the spacing between words varies from line to line.

justified *A form of typeset copy in which the edges of the lines in a column of type are forced to align by adding space between words in the line.*

Justified copy is aligned on both the right and left column edges. Other options are available to advertisers. One variation is to let the right line endings fall where they will. This is called *ragged right.* You can also specify the opposite, *ragged left,* although that is a very unusual way to set type. If you want to specify that either edge be justified, then the phrase *flush left* or *flush right* is used. Another option is to set everything *centered,* which means neither the right nor the left edges align, but instead everything is centered around a vertical midpoint axis.

Legibility As previously mentioned, type selection is primarily functional. The objective of *legibility* is to convey the words as clearly as possible. Because reading is such a complex activity, the type should make the perceptual process as easy as possible. If the type is difficult to read, most people will turn the page. Research has discovered a number of type practices that can hinder the reading process.[*]

ALL CAPS One of the biggest problems that shows up consistently in legibility research is type set in all capitals. All caps slows down reading and causes many readers to give up. Although art directors like all caps because it gives a clean, rectangular look to the type, line after line of it will chase away all but the most dedicated readers.

REVERSE TYPE Another legibility problem is **reverse type,** a technique that creates letters that appear to be white against a dark background. If the letters are big, bold and few in number, then most people won't have any problem with reverse type. But if the letters are small and delicate, and if there is

reverse type *A style of typesetting in which letters appear to be white against a darker background.*

FIGURE 14.6

THIS LINE IS PRINTED IN ALL CAPS.

This line uses UPPERCASE and lowercase letters.

[*]Rolf Rehe, *Typography: How to Make It Most Legible* (Indianapolis: Design Research Publications, 1974).

a lot of type to be read, most people will give up. Ad 14.3 is printed in reverse type.

ORNAMENTALS   Unusual typefaces can also create legibility problems. Cursives and black-letter typefaces are particularly difficult to read. Ornamental faces are also difficult. Overly manipulated faces can also cause problems. Jeff Level, director of type research at Monotype Inc., has said: "A lot of people are thoroughly abusing typefaces today. They're stretching them, condensing them, and running them up against each other."*

SURPRINTING   **Surprinting** is a technique that prints the type over or across some other image. If the background is clear, surprinting might not cause a problem. However, background patterns of any sort can fight with the letter forms and actually obliterate them. Big and bold surprinting display type is generally acceptable. The problem comes when small, delicate type is surprinted over a discernible pattern.

The most useful rule for gauging legibility is: Don't play games with type.

surprinting *Printing type over some other image.*

PRINCIPLE
Play it safe. Don't fool around with the type.

Halftone Reproduction

There are two general types of images that have to be reproduced in print. A simple drawing is called **line art** because the image is just solid black lines on a white page. Photographs, however, are much more complicated because they have a range, or shades, of gray tones between the black and white. The phrase *continuous tone* is used to refer to images with this range of gray values.

Because printing is done with black ink, designers must be able to create the illusion of a range of grays. Continuous-tone art and photos must be converted to **halftones** in order to be printed. The *halftone process* begins when the original photograph is shot by another camera after a fine screen has been placed over the original. That screen looks just like the screen on your window, only finer. If the area on the original is dark, then the dot will fill the space; if the original is light, then the dot will be surrounded by empty white space. The image, in other words, is converted to a pattern of dots that gives the illusion of shades of gray, the shades being replicated by the various sizes of the dot pattern. If you look at a photograph in most newspapers, you can almost see the dot pattern with your naked eye. If you can't, look at the image through a magnifying glass. Figure 14.8 shows the dot pattern in a reproduced photo.

line art *Art in which all elements are solid with no intermediate shades or tones.*

halftones *Images with a continuous range of shades from light to dark.*

*O'Leary, "Legibility Lost," p. D7.

FIGURE 14.7
This figure contrasts the same image reproduced as line art (left) and a halftone (right).

FIGURE 14.8
An example of the dot pattern found in halftone reproduction.

FIGURE 14.9
These figures show the different screens for black and white and for color.

Screens The quality of the image depends upon how fine the screen is that is used to convert the original picture to a dot pattern. Because of the roughness of newsprint, newspapers use a relatively coarse screen, usually 65 lines per inch. (This is referred to as 65-line screen.) Magazines use finer screens, which may be 90, 110, 120, and on up to 200 lines per inch. The higher the number, the finer the screen and the better the quality of the reproduction.

Screens are also used to create various tint blocks, which can either be shades of gray in black-and-white printing or shades of color. A block can be printed solid or it can be *screened back* to create a shade. These shades are referred to as a range of percentages such as 100 percent (solid) down to 10 percent (very faint). Examples of screens are found in Figure 14.9.

Color Reproduction

Besides reproducing halftones, the other major problem for printers is the reproduction of full color. When you look at a slide, you see a full range of colors and shades. It would be impossible to set up a printing press with a separate ink roller for every possible hue and value. How, then, are these colors reproduced?

Process Colors The solution to this problem is to use a limited number of base colors and mix them to create the rest of the spectrum. Full-color images are reproduced using four distinctive shades of ink, called **process colors.** They are magenta (a shade of pinkish red), cyan (a shade of bright blue), yellow, and black.

Printing inks are transparent, so when one ink color overlaps another, a third color is created. Red and blue create purple, yellow and blue create green, yellow and red create orange. The black is used for type and, in *four-color printing,* adds depth to the shadows and dark tones in an image.

Color Separations The process used to reduce the original color image to four halftone negatives is called **color separation.** The negatives replicate the red, yellow, blue, and dark areas of the original. The separation is done photographically, beginning with original full-color images on slides. (Slides produce the most accurate and grain-free images.) Color filters are used to screen out everything but the desired hue. A separate color filter is used for each of the four process colors. Lasers are now used to scan the image and make the separations.

Printing Processes

Letterpress Four major printing processes are used in advertising. The oldest method, **letterpress,** is a form of relief printing, which means it prints from a raised surface. The old "hot metal" typesetting methods produced type with such raised images. A rubber stamp is a cheap form of relief printing. Letterpress is seldom used today except for sequential numbering and specialty printing effects.

Offset Lithography When **offset** printing emerged in the 1960s, many newspapers and magazines converted to this form of printing. Offset prints form a flat, chemically treated surface that attracts ink in the printing areas and repels it elsewhere.

A *camera-ready* original is shot photographically onto a thin aluminum *plate,* one plate for each color. The plate is chemically treated so that the image-carrying surfaces attract oil while the rest of the surface is covered with water. The plate is wrapped around a roller that revolves through a water bath and presses against an ink roller. The ink is greasy and doesn't stick to the water-

process colors *Four basic inks—magenta, cyan, yellow, and black—that are mixed to produce a full range of colors found in four-color printing.*

color separation *The process of splitting a color image into four images recorded on negatives; each negative represents one of the four process colors.*

letterpress *A type of printing that prints from an image onto a raised surface.*

offset *A type of printing that prints from a flat surface on the printing plate. The image is transferred to a rubber blanket that carries the impression to the paper.*

A JUGGLER'S LIFE.

She's 31 and a high school English teacher.

From 9 to 5 she lectures on the prose and cons of 20th century fiction.

Makes her home in Loveland, Colorado.

Married to Ron.

Mother to Bryan, 6 (only eats foods in primary colors).

Loves to escape on the back of an Appaloosa.

Has been known to quote:
"The highest form of bliss is living with a certain degree of folly." (Erasmus)

This Baby Boomer relies on the three R's—Reading, 'Riting and Redbook.

REDBOOK

REDBOOK. IT'S DIFFERENT BECAUSE SHE'S DIFFERENT.

FIGURE 14.10 (Cont.)
Red plate.

FIGURE 14.10
The following photos illustrate the process
of four-color separation. Yellow plate.

A JUGGLER'S LIFE.

She's 31 and a high school English
teacher.
From 9 to 5 she lectures on the prose
and cons of 20th century fiction.
Makes her home in Loveland, Colorado.
Married to Ron.
Mother to Bryan, 6 (only eats foods in
primary colors).
Loves to escape on the back of
an Appaloosa.
Has been known to quote:
"The highest form of bliss is
living with a certain degree
of folly." (Erasmus)
This Baby Boomer relies on the
three R's—Reading, 'Riting
and Redbook.

REDBOOK IT'S DIFFERENT
BECAUSE SHE'S DIFFERENT.

FIGURE 14.10 (Cont.)
Yellow and red plates.

She's 31 and a high school English
teacher.
From 9 to 5 she lectures on the prose
and cons of 20th century fiction.
Makes her home in Loveland, Colorado.
Married to Ron.
Mother to Bryan, 6 (only eats foods in
primary colors).
Loves to escape on the back of
an Appaloosa.
Has been known to quote:
"The highest form of bliss is
living with a certain degree
of folly." (Erasmus)
This Baby Boomer relies on the
three R's—Reading, 'Riting
and Redbook.

REDBOOK IT'S DIFFERENT
BECAUSE SHE'S DIFFERENT.

FIGURE 14.10 (Cont.)
Blue plate.

FIGURE 14.10 (Cont.)
Yellow, red, and blue plates.

FIGURE 14.10 (Cont.)
Yellow and blue plates.

FIGURE 14.10 (Cont.)
The finished ad with all four process colors.
(Courtesy of *Redbook*.)

FIGURE 14.10 (Cont.)
Black plate.

covered nonprinting parts of the image. The next step explains why this process is called "offset." The inked image is transferred to a rubber blanket on an adjoining roller and from that roller to paper.

Offset is now used for most printing jobs. It is clean and involves no heavy molten lead, as did older presses. Anything that can be photographed can be printed. The camera-ready original, variously called a *mechanical* or a *keyline,* is a pasteup of all the elements. In advertising agencies people who prepare the camera-ready materials are called *keyliners.*

Rotogravure   **Gravure** printing is the exact opposite of relief printing; the images are engraved into the surface of the plate. The printing is done from a

gravure *A type of printing that uses an image that is engraved, or recessed, into the surface of the printing plate.*

FIGURE 14.11
The major types of printing presses. *Top:* letterpress printing. *Center:* offset printing. *Bottom:* rotogravure.

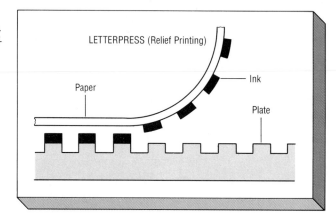

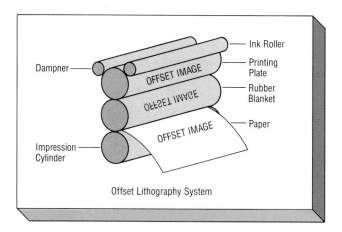

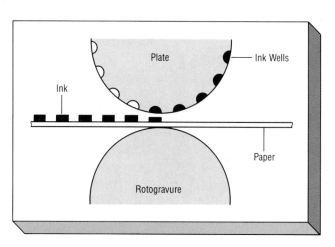

recessed image composed of tiny inkwells. Have you ever wiped your feet when you were wearing tennis shoes and then walked across a clean floor? You probably noticed that even though the surfaces of your shoes were clean, they still left a tread mark. That's because there was something in the treads that left an image on the floor. Gravure works well for photographic reproduction and for long runs because there is no wear on the printing surface. Quality magazines often use gravure printing, as do some Sunday newspaper photo sections and advertising inserts.

Flexography   A printing technique that is growing in popularity is flexography. *Flexography* is similar to offset in that it uses a rubber blanket to transfer the image to the page. It differs in that the ink is water-based and there is a different blanket setup on the press. Newspapers use flexography because the image is sharper and there is little ink ruboff.

Silk Screen   A relatively simple printing method based on a stencil process, **silk screen** is used to make small runs of posters and greeting cards. Beyond that, more complicated automatic equipment is now used by commercial printers for printing posters, T-shirts, decals, banners, point-of-sale materials, and advertising specialties such as pens and coffee mugs.

In silk screen a fine meshlike fabric, similar to silk, is tautly fastened across a frame. A design is drawn on a lacquer film that is then adhered to the screen. The printing areas are cut away with a knife or washed away chemically. A heavy opaque ink is then forced through the screen with a squeegee. It passes through the open areas but the film holds back the ink in the nonprinting areas.

Duplicating Ads   If an ad is going to run in a number of publications, there has to be some way to distribute a reproducible form of the ad to all of them. For letterpress, a *mat* made from a kind of papier-mâché is sent, along with a *proof* made from the original engraving. For gravure printing, film positives are sent to the publications. The duplicate material for offset printing is a "slick" proof of the original mechanical. These proofs are called *photoprints* or *photostats,* which are relatively cheap images. *Veloxes* or *C-Prints* are better-quality prints.

Binding and Finishing

A number of special printing effects are created at the end of the production process. These are mechanical techniques that embellish the image using such methods as embossing or foil stamping. The last step in production is the binding, where the pages of a publication are assembled.

Newspapers are folded, and the fold holds the sheets together. Magazines are folded, stapled or sewn, and trimmed. Sometimes a separate cover is glued on. During this binding process separate preprinted ads provided by the advertiser can be glued in. Such ads are called **tip-ins.** They are used when an advertiser wants particularly fine printing or wishes to include something that can't be accommodated in the normal printing process. Most perfume manufacturers, for example, are tipping in perfume samples that are either scratch-and-sniff or scented strips that release their fragrance when pulled apart.

Advertisers are searching for even more novel effects to add interest and impact to their magazine ads. Recent ads have included such novelty techniques as a sailboat that unfolds, called a *pop-up,* in the middle of a Merit cigarette ad that ran in *Time.* Honeywell used a similar pop-up to present an entire factory/office complex in *Business Week.* Maybelline has used a "peel 'n' brush" blusher sample in *Glamour.* Both Absolut vodka and Canadian Mist liquor have played holiday music in magazine ads via a tiny microchip. Probably the ultimate novelty was created for a Toyota ad to dramatize the slogan, "The new dimension in

silk screen *A form of printing where the nonimage areas, represented by a "block-out" film or lacquer, are adhered to a porous fabric, while ink is forced through the image areas that aren't blocked out.*

tip-ins *Preprinted ads that are provided by the advertiser to be glued into the binding of a magazine.*

FIGURE 14.12 A

This series of figures demonstrates some of the major steps involved in creating a print ad. The first step is a memo describing the ad and listing the body copy.

14.12 B

A rough layout. The rough contains little detail—note the nonsense type—and is used for size and placement decisions.

14.12 C

The mechanical. Used in offset printing, the mechanical is a photo-ready original with all of the elements properly placed. The various instructions are printed on transparent overlays.

14.12 D

The final proof.

(Courtesy of Maybelline USA.)

```
DDB NEEDHAM WORLDWIDE     303 E. Wacker Drive    Chicago, Illinois 60601-5282


CONTRASTS                               12/3/87 (CB)wc
PRINT
BLOOMING COLORS EYE SHADOW


FLAG:            COLOR PLAY

COPY:            Blooming Colors® Eye Shadows.  Bunches of
                 stand out, stay true colors.  SMART

                 Make your way through the crowd.  BEAUTIFUL










SMART.  BEAUTIFUL.  MAYBELLINE®.
c 1988 Maybelline Co.

/031
```

(A)

(B)

FIGURE 14.13
Screen printing.

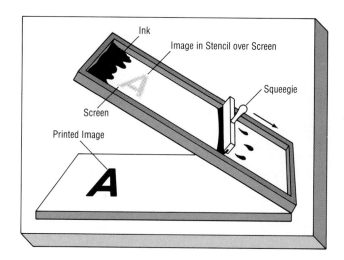

driving." Detachable cardboard binoculars gave a Viewmaster-like 3-D image of a Toyota Corolla on the road.*

New Technology

A new technology, based on computers and transmission by phone line using fiber optics or by satellite, has generated a revolution in print media. Computerized typesetting now makes it easy to transmit type electronically. Art can be *digitized* (broken into tiny grids, each one coded electronically for tone or color) and then transmitted. Fiber optics can send type, art, or even complete pages across a city for local editions of newspapers. Satellites make national page transmission possible for regional editions of magazines and newspapers such as *U.S.A. Today.*

Printing by personal computer, utilizing easy-to-use software, is taking over the low end of the typesetting function. In addition to typesetting, page layouts as well as advertising layouts can be done on a personal computer. This new approach to typesetting and layout is called *desktop publishing.* Graphics that can be drawn and modified on computers are now being used in many newspapers.

At the higher end of the typesetting function, many quality typesetting systems use some kind of computer-based *pagination* equipment that combines sophisticated computer typesetting with page layout capabilities.

Inkjet printing, which is a type of printing directed by computer, is becoming more common. It can speed up the entire printing process by eliminating many of the technical steps in printing, such as negatives and plate-making. It will soon be possible to go directly from the computer to a printed publication. This may make it feasible to customize the content of a publication, advertising as well as articles, to the interest of the reader, thus creating a new world of one-on-one publishing and, eventually, personalized target marketing.

*Bob Garfield, "Don't Gimme Gimmicks: Novelty Ads Flood Media," *Advertising Age,* November 9, 1987, p. 41.

■ SUMMARY

- Newspaper ads are more informative and less entertaining than other types of advertising.

- Magazines provide better reproduction of color and photographs than newspapers do.

- Headlines target the prospect, stop the reader, identify the product, start the sale, and lure the reader into the body copy.

- A layout arranges all the elements to provide a visual order that is aesthetically pleasing.

- Color is used in advertising to attract attention, provide realism, establish mood, and build brand identity.

- Typefaces convey meaning beyond the words; they help to create mood and impact.

- Color is reproduced as either spot color or process color, which involves a complicated process of color separation.

- The common printing processes are letterpress, offset, gravure, and silk screen.

■ QUESTIONS

1. What are the major features of a print ad? What is the purpose of each one?

2. What are the major steps involved in producing a print ad?

3. What are the process colors?

4. What is the difference between line art and halftones?

5. What is meant by "offset" printing? How did it get its name?

6. Collect a group of ads for department and discount stores. Compare their layouts. What does the layout "say" about the type of store and the merchandise it carries?

7. Think of ads you have seen in newspapers and magazines over the past 10 years. What trends, if any, do you notice? How do you account for these trends?

■ FURTHER READINGS

Burton, Philip Ward. *Which Ad Pulled Best?* Chicago: Crain, 1981.

Murch, Gerald. *Visual and Auditory Perception.* Indianapolis: Bobbs-Merrill Co., 1973.

O'Leary, Noreen. "Legibility Lost." *Adweek,* October 5, 1987.

Rehe, Rolf. *Typography: How to Make It Most Legible.* Indianapolis: Design Research Publications, 1974.

15

Creating Broadcast Advertising

Chapter Objectives

When you have completed this chapter you should be able to:

- Identify the critical elements in radio and television commercials
- Read and understand a radio script and a television script
- Compare and contrast radio ads and television commercials
- Understand the roles of the various people associated with television commercials, including the producer, director, and editor
- List the various stages in the production of a television commercial

ADVENTURES IN FILMING COMMERCIALS

Broadcast advertising is complex and challenging, and it can take you to exotic locations like the bottom of a murky, polluted canal in Venice, Italy. That is what a team of creatives from the Lowe Marschalk agency discovered when they were shooting a commercial for Grey Poupon Dijon Mustard. The eventful 2-day shoot could serve as a casebook on the difficulties of filming a spot in a foreign city—and on water.

At least the commercial started out on water. Halfway through the "Gondola" shoot, the French producer cried in distress, "Ze props, ze props! Zay fall into zah canal!" The props were not your ordinary theatrical props, but Limoges china, Baccarat crystal, and antique silver—a small fortune in symbols of elegant dining.

The director of production from the Nabisco Brands, the client, reportedly turned white and was ready to dive into the canal himself. Fortunately a young Venetian with a swim mask came to the producer's rescue and was able to retrieve every piece. Happily, this new commercial in the series of "One of Life's Finer Pleasures" turned out to be "an affordable one."*

This chapter discusses planning, writing, and producing commercials for radio and television. Television uses both audio and video, while radio uses audio alone to create pictures in the mind. Our discussion begins with radio advertising.

THE RADIO ENVIRONMENT

Imagine you are writing a musical play. This particular play will be performed before an audience whose eyes are closed. You have all the theatrical tools of casting, voices, sound effects, and music available to you, but no visuals. Imagine having to create all the visual elements—the scene, the cast, the costumes, the facial expressions—in the imagination of your audience. Could you do it?

This is how radio works. It is a theater of the mind in which the story is created in the imagination of the listener. The listeners are active participants in the construction of the message. How the characters look and where the scene is set come out of their personal experience. Radio is the most personal of all media.

PRINCIPLE
Radio creates images in the imagination of the listener.

Characteristics of the Radio Environment

Writing for radio is fun, but it is also very challenging because of the need to create an imaginary visual. Successful radio writers and producers have excellent visualization skills and a great theatrical sense.

Personal Radio is the most intimate of all media. It functions as a good friend in our culture, particularly for teenagers. Radio has one wonderful advantage over print media and that is the human voice, whether it is a newscaster's, a sportscaster's, a talk-show announcer's, or a singer's. The "boombox" on the shoulder or the earphones on a jogger reflect this intimate relationship.

*Debbie Seaman, "Grey Poupon's Unsinkable Series Charts Canals of Venice," *Adweek,* July 13, 1987, p. 28.

Most people who are listening to the radio are doing something else at the same time.
(Courtesy of J. F. Kainz/The Stock Option.)

Programming is oriented toward the tastes of particular groups of people. In that sense radio is a very specialized type of medium.

Inattention   There is a problem, however. Although radio is pervasive, it is seldom the listener's center of attention. Most people who are listening to the radio are doing something else at the same time, like jogging or driving. The listener's attention can focus on radio, particularly during programming that demands concentration like news and weather, but radio is generally a background medium.

Even though most people listen to radio with a divided mind, they remember the songs they hear. Sounds that are heavily repeated, like songs, can overcome inattentiveness. The primary challenge for radio advertisers is to break through the various distractions and get the audience to focus attention on the message. People tune in or tune out as something catches their attention or loses it. But understanding an advertising message requires more than just tuning in. Radio ads lack the equivalent of a newspaper ad headline that carries the heart of the message. Thus, for a message to have impact, the audience must be induced to listen with some measure of concentration. How many times have you stopped what you were doing to listen to a radio ad?

Intrusive   Radio advertising seeks to capture audience attention with one of two strategies. Some advertisements are primarily musical; they use a catchy tune and heavily repeated lyrics to embed the message in an inattentive mind.

The other strategy is to be intrusive. A message that is **intrusive** is one that forces itself on the audience, like the Oxy-5 commercials whose commanding voice has incredible recognition among teenagers around the country. Both television and radio use intrusive messages because of the inattention problem. However, most people dislike intrusive messages, and that causes a dilemma for people who create advertising and who know that intrusive techniques are essential.

Message Strategy

PRINCIPLE _____
Repeat product information as often as possible.

The radio message is ephemeral—it is here one moment and then it is gone. You cannot tune in to the middle of an ad and then go back to the headline, as you can with print. You can't "reread" a radio message. Repetition is used to overcome that problem. Key points are repeated, the product name is repeated, and any kind of numerical information that has to be included is also repeated.

Numbers are difficult to remember when they are given verbally. Phone numbers and addresses, for example, have to be repeated several times if they are to sink in. That is why advertisers avoid using phone numbers in radio commercials. People driving cars or walking down the street have a hard time finding a pencil to write down the number. Addresses are better conveyed as mental maps, such as "on Broadway across from K-Mart."

PRINCIPLE _____
Avoid giving numbers and complex information in radio commercials.

Complicated information is also difficult to convey on the radio. An inattentive audience is not likely to understand the logic of a sophisticated sales argument or a list of copy points. For that reason print advertisements, which are often complex, seldom translate easily to radio. Radio calls for different message tactics.

Radio is an ideal medium for reminder messages. Simple messages can promote product awareness and identification. Jingles are an effective means of repeating a name or slogan. Radio is also good for image advertising because of its ability to create pictures in the mind. Lifestyle associations can be reinforced through the theater of the mind.

WRITING RADIO COPY

Style

vernacular *Language that reflects the speech patterns of a particular group of people.*

Conversational   Radio copywriters write in a conversational style using **vernacular** language. Spoken language is different from written language. We talk in short sentences, often in sentence fragments and run-ons. We seldom use complex sentences in speech. We use contractions that would drive an English teacher crazy. Spoken language is not polished prose.

PRINCIPLE _____
For radio, write as you speak, not as you write.

Vernacular   Word choice should reflect the speech of the target audience. Slang can be hard to handle and sound phony, but copy that picks up the nuances of people's speech can sound natural when carefully written. Each group has its own way of speaking, its own phrasing. Teenagers don't talk like 8-year-olds or 80-year-olds. A good radio copywriter has an ear for the distinctive patterns of speech that identify social groups.

Tools

Radio uses three primary tools to develop messages: *voice, music,* and *sound effects.* These can be manipulated to create a variety of effects.

Voice   Voice is probably the most important element. Voices are heard in jingles, in spoken dialogue, and in straight announcements. Most commercials have an announcer, if not as the central voice, at least at the closing to wrap up the product identification. Dialogue uses character voices to convey an image of the speaker—a child, an old man, an executive, a Little League baseball player, an opera singer.

Music   Music is another important element. Don Wilde of SSC&B said at a symposium that "Music has been found to be more effective in persuasiveness than celebrity endorsements, product demos, or hidden camera techniques." He explained: "It falls just a little under humor or kids. If you write a humorous jingle on kids, you've got it made."*

In an earlier chapter we mentioned the use of jingles, catchy songs about a product that carry the theme and product identification. These finger-snapping, toe-tapping songs have tremendous power because they are so memorable. Jingles are good for product identification and reminder messages, but they do not effectively convey complex thoughts and copy points.

Jingles can be used by themselves as a musical commercial, or they can be added to any other type of commercial as a product identification. A straight announcer commercial, for example, might end with a jingle. Musical forms can be easily adapted to the station's programming. Most major campaigns that use radio produce a number of different versions of the jingle, each one arranged to match the type of music featured in the programming, whether it is country and western, rock, reggae, or easy listening.

Music can also be used behind the dialogue to create mood and establish the setting. The mood, whether it be that of a circus or that of a candle-lit dinner, can be conveyed through music. Music can be composed for the commercial, or it can be borrowed from an already recorded song. There are also a number of music libraries that sell stock music. This music is not copyrighted; however, there is no guarantee that other ads will not use the same music.

Sound Effects   **Sound effects** (SFX) are also used to convey a setting. The sounds of sea gulls and the crash of waves, the clicking of typewriter keys, and the cheers of fans at a stadium, all create images in our minds. Sound effects can be original, but more often they are found on records.

Scripting

Timing   Radio commercials are written for a limited time frame. The common lengths are 10, 20, 30, and 60 seconds. The 10-second and 20-second commercials are used for reminders and product or station identification. More elaborate messages are usually 30 or 60 seconds. The 60-second spot is quite common in radio, although it has almost disappeared in television, where the more common length is 30 seconds.

Forms   Radio **scripts** use a form and code that are commonly understood. The scripts are typed double-spaced with two columns. The narrow column on the left describes the source of the sound, and the wider column on the right gives the actual content of the message, either words or a description of the sound and music.

The typing style is important because typed cues tell the producer and announcer instantly what is happening. For example, anything that isn't spoken is typed in capital letters. This includes the source identification in the left column and all instructions and descriptions that appear in the right column. Underlining is used to call attention to music and sound effects in the right column so the announcer can see instantly that those instructions are not to be read over the microphone as if they were copy. If you write radio scripts often, you will probably use a preprinted form that sets up the columns and the identification information for the commercial at the top.

*Aliza Laufer, "Agency Panel Mulls the Impact of :15s on Jingle Biz at SAMPAC Symposium," *Back Stage,* February 7, 1986, p. 1.

PRINCIPLE _____
The simpler the jingle, the higher the memorability.

_____

sound effects (SFX) *Lifelike imitations of sounds.*

_____

scripts *Written versions of radio or television commercials.*

Project Help   11/17/87   DR/jks
"No Place Like Home"
:60 Radio
"INTRUSION ALARM"

ANNCR: There's someone walking around right next to me.

You probably don't hear him. That's the way he likes
it. Because he's an intruder. And an intruder in
your home steals much more than just your valuables...

He steals your privacy. Your security. Your sense
of home.

And no insurance check can begin to replace that.

SFX: ALARM

ANNCR: Now you definitely hear this.

This is the sound of the new Eversafe Intrusion Alarm.
It mounts easily on a door or a window. To keep
intruders out. And what you value in.

The Eversafe Intrusion Alarm is part of a full-line
of home safety and security products that you'll
find at the Eversafe Center. One place with all
the elements you need to create an entire security
system. To protect your home. From intruders, fire,
or even power blackouts.

So visit your Eversafe Center. You'll find it at
_____. And protect what's yours. With
Eversafe.

Cause there's no place like home.

AD 15.1
An example of a radio script.
(Courtesy of DDB Needham Worldwide.)

PRODUCING A RADIO COMMERCIAL

Taped Commercials

producer *The person in charge of all the arrangements for a commercial, including settings, casting, arranging for the music, and handling bids and budgets.*

mixing *Combining different tracks of music, voices, and sound effects to create the final ad.*

The radio **producer** is in charge of getting the commercial casted, recorded, mixed, and duplicated. All the sound elements are recorded separately or *laid down* in stages. Voices can be double- and triple-tracked to create richer sounds. There may be as many as 24 separate tracks for an ad. **Mixing** occurs when the tracks are combined, with appropriate adjustments made in volume and tone levels.

National radio commercials are produced by an advertising agency, and duplicate copies of the tape are distributed to local stations around the country. Commercials for local advertisers might be produced by local stations, with the station's staff providing the creative and production expertise. The recording is done in house using the station's studio.

Live Spots

An unusual experiment in "live" radio is happening in Chicago where the *Chicago Tribune* has hired two of the city's top radio personalities to ad-lib commercials while they banter on the air. The approach is the idea of Hal Riney & Partners. Media columnists are criticizing the ads for not sounding like ads. The "extemporaneous ad-lib announcement" involves reading an item—whether personal ad, column, or news story—from the *Tribune* and mentioning the paper's name. The ads are paid for and listed as 60-second commercials in the station's program log.*

THE TELEVISION ENVIRONMENT

Like most Americans, you probably have a love-hate relationship with television commercials. On the one hand, you may have a favorite commercial or campaign. The Bartles and Jaymes wine cooler commercials by the Hal Riney Agency have been amazingly successful using two elderly men to sell wine coolers to an audience composed primarily of young women because the characters are so captivating. On the other hand, you can probably identify a dozen commercials that you resent so much that you turn the channel or leave the room the minute they appear. You might hate the product or see the characters in the commercial as stupid and the message as insulting. Your reaction can be personal—different people like different things; strategic—you are not in the target for that particular product and the message isn't addressed to you; or factual—there are, after all, a number of dreadful commercials on television.

Characteristics of the Television Environment

Acceptance   People do like to watch commercials if the ads are well done. They watch excerpts from the annual Clio awards given for television advertising when they appear as an item on news broadcasts. Television shows on famous

An example of editing using an audiotape editing machine.

(© 1988 by Prentice-Hall, Inc. All rights reserved.)

*Julie Liesse Erickson, "Riney, *Tribune* Spark Interest in Radio Ad (Lib)," *Advertising Age,* November 9, 1987, p. 3.

JOHN BERNERS, COPYWRITER, YOUNG & RUBICAM, NEW YORK

Writing ads for radio and television might sound like an exciting, glamorous job. However it can also be hectic and exhausting. In the following excerpt a young copywriter describes a "typical" day that includes producing a radio advertisement.

Instead of mixing bits of many different days to form a day-long salad of typical moments, I will tell you a real day: Thursday, December 11, 1987.

On this day, I come in to work at 8:00 A.M. That's early for me. But since I meant to get here at 7:30, I still have that "uh-oh, I'm late" feeling, which is a vital component of a typical morning.

Now I just have time to make some last-minute revisions and type up radio scripts to be recorded at 9:00. (We young writers do lots of radio.)

With that done, I'm on my way to the recording session when I run into an account supervisor who tells me that the ending of a script I thought was done was killed last night by the chief client. Ugh.

So at 8:55 I have 5 minutes to come up with a new, snappy ending before the session starts. Of course, I fail. But I do come up with some eloquent reasons why I shouldn't be expected to create under these conditions.

It's 9. So I grab my papers and trot over to the studio with one script still trickling off into unresolved nothingness.

This morning's studio is next door. So I get there in 2 minutes, and we start recording the one complete script.

Now, in radio, unlike filming TV, there is no director on the set telling the actors how to act. *You* have to do it.

Working with the actors is fun. Some are famous. You recognize them from TV and movies. They're doing radio spots for extra money while in the Big Apple. During the session you can call everyone "babe" and wink at them and they think you're a bona fide Hollywood type just like them.

Directing actors is also challenging. If they're not reading it right, you have to act it out for them. And as you can imagine, you have to be careful of their egos. You can't tell an actor to read like Burgess Meredith if he thinks he's better than Burgess Meredith. It's up to you to do everything just right to get the best finished product, taking into account personalities, time constraints, and the limitations of your script.

In this morning's session, the first spot goes well. The actors click into their parts right away, and they're in and out in 25 minutes.

But as they exit, I once again face the problem of the unfinished script. The cast for this spot is already here waiting. Studio time is ticking at $500 an hour. And

---

ads and advertising bloopers consistently get high ratings. Lines from commercials can even take on a life of their own, such as "Do you know me?" from the American Express campaign and "Thanks, I needed that" from a Mennon Skin Bracer commercial. The Wendy's line "Where's the beef?" went from an immensely popular commercial to a catch phrase used by one political candidate, Walter Mondale, against another, Gary Hart, in the 1984 presidential primaries.

Intrusiveness   Most people give television more attention than radio. People watching a program they enjoy are frequently absorbed in it. The absorption is only slightly less than that experienced by people watching a movie in a darkened theater. Advertising is considered an unwelcome interruption because it disrupts concentration. This intrusiveness can be disconcerting and can cause the viewer to be even less receptive to the commercial message.

Another problem confronting television advertisers is the tendency of viewers to switch channels or leave the room during commercial breaks. Because of television viewers' strong patterns of avoidance, commercials have to be intriguing as well as intrusive.

Producing a major national commercial may take the work of hundreds of people and cost as much as half a million dollars. The "1984" commercial for Apple Computers that only ran once during the 1985 Super Bowl used a cast of

PRINCIPLE _____
Television commercials should be intrusive as well as intriguing.

all these people are standing around drumming their fingers and staring at me as I resume trying to think up a new, snappy ending.

My mind is blank. So I scribble out something I don't find funny at all just to get some words on paper. The client, who is understandably worried about time, paces by, looks over my shoulder, and says, "Good. Let's go with that." So we do. The session comes back to life and we finish up.

I'm actually relieved that someone else made the decision to go ahead and get it over with. The spot doesn't have a great ending now, but in that situation I probably wouldn't have thought of one no matter how long I sat there.

Sometime during all this, lunchtime went by. Lunch is purported to be a big part of the ad game. But that's only for big shots. Not kids like me. So in this itinerary, we omit lunch.

Around 2:30 I pick up my partner and we're off to a video editing house to finish up some commercials. The actual film was shot 2 weeks ago, and the spots are now in a phase called postproduction.

This is a tremendously important phase. With modern video equipment, the film you shot can be changed considerably as it's assembled into a commercial. You can create new objects, speed up, slow down,

zoom in, out, and sideways, change color, and so on. It's actually dangerous how many things you can do to a spot with this equipment. Lots of decisions have to be made on the spot, and the results are rewarding. My partner and I finish up the evening doing this, and call it a day.

(Courtesy of John Berners.)

200 and is estimated to have cost half a million dollars (see Ad 15.2).* Since that time even more expensive commercials have been produced. The expense only makes sense if the ads will reach large numbers of people.

THE NATURE OF COMMERCIALS

Message Strategy

Every advertising medium is different, and copywriters are adept at writing messages that take advantage of each medium's particular set of strengths. Television is unlike radio or print.

Action and Motion   Television is a visual medium, and the message is dominated by the impact of visual effects. But, you might observe, newspapers and magazines also use visuals. So what makes the difference in impact between television and print visuals? It is the moving image, the action, that makes television so much more mesmerizing than print. When you watch television you are watching a walking, talking, moving world that even gives the illusion of being three-dimensional. Good television advertising uses the impact of action and

PRINCIPLE
Television uses motion and action to create impact.

*David Carey, "Advertising in the '80s: A Roaring Comeback," *Financial World,* March 20, 1985, pp. 8–9.

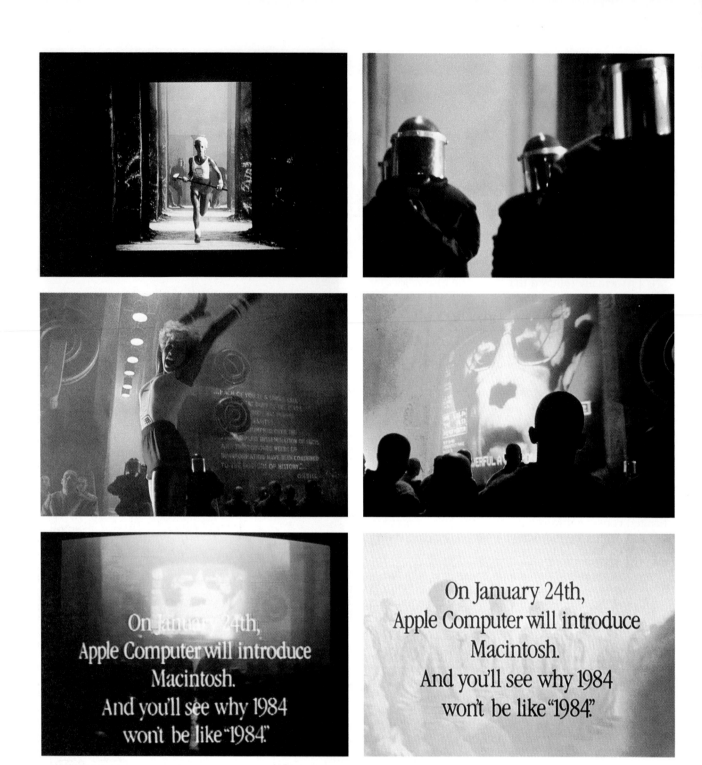

AD 15.2
The Apple "1984" ad was a major production that employed 200 people and cost half a million dollars.
(Photos courtesy of Apple Computer, Inc.)

motion to attract attention and sustain interest. The Bounce commercials that are built on the Pointer Sisters' song "Jump" are great examples of the power of the moving image (see Ad 15.3).

Storytelling   Stories can be riveting if they are well told, and television is our society's master storyteller. Most of the programming on television is storytelling. But stories do more than just entertain—they express values, teach behavior, and show us how to deal with our daily problems. Television shows like *The Cosby Show, Cagney and Lacey, St. Elsewhere, Hill Street Blues,* and *M*A*S*H* all include discussions of ethics or morals.

Effective television advertisements also use storytelling, both for entertainment value and to make a point. These little stories can be funny, warm, silly, or heart-rending, just as in real life. Slice of life is simply instruction in a soap opera format.

The computer industry is also taking advantage of television in big-budget battles to gain dominance in this growth market. IBM's use of the Charlie Chaplin character and M*A*S*H unit both play on television's storytelling power while capitalizing on the "everyman" values expressed in the original Chaplin character and the coping-under-pressure-with-humor camaraderie of the M*A*S*H team.

Emotion More than any other advertising medium, television has the ability to touch emotions, to make people feel things. This ability to touch the feelings

AD 15.3
This Bounce ad is a good example of the use of moving images—and a popular song—in a television commercial.

(Courtesy of D'Arcy Masius Benton & Bowles, Inc.)

BENTON & BOWLES
909 THIRD AVENUE
NEW YORK, N.Y.
(212) 758-6200

Client: PROCTER & GAMBLE CO.
Product: BOUNCE
Length: 45 SECONDS (PGBC 2505)
Title: "JUMP/FP"

1. (MUSIC UNDER) WOMAN: When towels feel this soft... CHORUS: Jump in...
2. WOMAN: Sheets feel this fresh. CHORUS: Jump.
3. WOMAN: And there's no cling to most anything.
4. CHORUS: Jump, jump, jump, jump.
5. WOMAN: You've got Bounce clothes.
6. (SINGS): Clothes you can't wait to jump into.
7. CHORUS: Jump. WOMAN SINGS: Feel the touch.
8. CHORUS: Jump in. WOMAN SINGS: You are the one,
9. you feel so good around me.
10. CHORUS: Jump, jump, jump, jump.
11. WOMAN: You could use this
12. or even this,
13. but Bounce is the softener more people use.
14. And they feel like this about their clothes.
15. So soft sweaters, sweet smelling linens,
16. no cling things.
17. CHORUS: Jump. WOMAN SINGS: Feel the touch.
18. CHORUS: Jump in. WOMAN: Bounce...
19. (SINGS): For clothes you can't wait to jump into.
20. CHORUS: Jump, jump, jump.

THE ENTERTAINMENT FACTOR

Television is a form of show business. The programs are intended to be entertaining. Some experts believe that in order to maintain viewers' attention through the commercial break, advertisements have to be just as entertaining as the media environment in which they appear.

William Bernbach, the creative genius behind the highly successful agency originally known as Doyle Dane Bernbach, has said: "What brand of vanity or indifference leads us to believe that we can, so to speak, sit alongside world-shaking events and even be noticed?" He concludes that "Only a message with a tremendous vitality carried in a dramatic graphic treatment will ever reach your consumer."*

Other experts insist that the purpose of advertising is to sell, not to entertain. They feel that a well-crafted sales message should be just as entertaining as the programming because the message is compelling. Sid Bernstein, in his column in *Advertising Age,* has written about the problems of creativity. He says that "if carried too far, 'creativity' can interfere with sales effect, or at least not help it very much."†

The problem may be more than the programming. The real challenge is the avoidance behavior of the audience. In order to keep viewers watching, the commercial has to make it worth their while to stay in their seats. There are some straight sales messages that are able to do this, but they are rare. More often, particularly with the *parity products* (products that are very similar and are mass-marketed on television), there is no strong sales message. The only thing that makes one product different from another is the advertising, so it *has* to be good. And on television, good often means entertaining.

But what does entertaining mean? The dictionary defines it as "diverting, amusing, or absorbing." To be diverting, advertising has to switch attention from the program to the product; to be amusing, it has to charm or please; to be absorbing, it has to catch the eye, fascinate the mind, and focus the attention.

What do you think about the entertainment factor in television advertising? Which commercials do you remember? Which commercials do you think work the best? Can you identify some commercials that are entertaining and others that are strong sales messages? Can a strong sales message be effective on television? Can it be as effective as an entertaining message? Do you think the entertainment factor gets in the way of the sales message?

*Albert C. Book and C. Dennis Schick, *Fundamentals of Copy and Layout* (Lincolnwood, IL: NTC Business Books, 1984).
†Sid Bernstein, "The Test for Ad Ideas," *Advertising Age,* November 16, 1987, p. 16.

PRINCIPLE _____
Television touches feelings.

of the viewer makes television commercials entertaining, diverting, amusing, and absorbing. Real-life situations with all their humor, anger, fear, pride, jealousy, and love come alive on the screen.

These emotions are pulled from natural situations that everyone can identify with. Hallmark has produced some real tear-jerker commercials about those times of our lives that we remember by the cards we get and save. Kodak and Polaroid have used a similar strategy for precious moments that are remembered in photographs.

The copy for a commercial for Dreyer's Grand Ice Cream (known as Edy's in some markets) illustrates the use of emotion. Peter Murphy, creative director at Hal Riney & Partners, who wrote the ad, explained: "We didn't want to show why Edy's is superior to other brands. We wanted to show how ice cream makes people feel." The writer interviewing Murphy observed that "the view of human nature brought out in that commercial comes from a place much deeper in his soul."* The copy is as follows:

> When we introduced Edy's Grand Ice Cream to towns and villages, some extraordinary things happened. A meter maid smiled and gave someone who needed a quarter a quarter. Baseball players asked the fans for their autographs. Hardly anyone forgot a birthday or an anniversary. All the flow-

*Art Kleiner, "The Culture of Marketing and the Marketing of Culture," *Whole Earth Review,* Spring 1987, pp. 74–80.

ers in all the flower shops were sold. The average age of someone with a balloon was 43. And generally speaking, it was the happiest people have been in a long time.

Demonstration Demonstration was discussed in Chapter 7 as an important message strategy. If you have a strong sales message that lends itself to demonstration, then television is the ideal medium for that message. Its realism makes the demonstration persuasive. Believability and credibility are high because we believe what we see with our own eyes.

Sight and Sound Television is an audio-visual medium—that is, it uses both sight and sound—and an effective television commercial fuses the audio and visual elements. One of the strengths of television is its ability to reinforce verbal messages with visuals or visual messages with verbal.

Hooper White, who has been making television commercials since the 1950s, says in his book *How to Produce an Effective TV Commercial* that "The idea behind a television commercial is unique in advertising." He explains that it is a combination of sight and sound: "The TV commercial consists of pictures that move to impart fact or evoke emotion and selling words that are not read but heard." He concludes: "The perfect combination of sight and sound can be an extremely potent selling tool."*

Advertising professionals have long known that memorability is much higher when commercials show the product and say the name at the same time. The long-running Bud Light campaign shows all the incredible number of things that come to mind when you think of the word "light" and at the same time dramatically fuses the name Budweiser with the word "light." Rather than focusing on a product benefit, it simply combines the brand name with the "light" category by dramatizing the word "light" with these unexpected visuals.

The point of audio-video fusion is that words and pictures must work together or else commercials will show one thing and say something else. Researchers have found that people have trouble listening and watching at the same time unless the audio and visual messages are identical.

The campaign for Van de Kamp's frozen fish, for example, uses a memorable audio-video device. The packages flip and flop like newly caught fish accompanied by a sound effect of flopping fish. There are a number of executions in this campaign, but they are all coordinated by this unusual audio-video logo.

Elements

Video The visual dominates the perception of the message in television, so copywriters use it as the primary carrier of the concept. The *video* elements include everything that is seen on the screen. Copywriters use visuals, the silent speech of film, to convey as much of the message as possible. Emotion is expressed most convincingly in facial expressions, gestures, and other body language. Good television writers try not to bury the impact of the visual under a lot of unnecessary words.

A tremendous number of visual elements must be coordinated in successful television ads. Because television is theatrical, many of the elements, such as characters, costumes, sets and locations, props, lighting, optical and computerized special effects, and on-screen graphics, are similar to those you would use in a play, television show, or movie. Because of the number of video, as well as audio, elements, a television commercial is the most complex of all advertising forms.

*Hooper White, *How to Produce an Effective TV Commercial* (Chicago: Crain Books, 1981).

POLAROID INSTANT CAMERAS & FILM
"CHRISTMAS"

CLIENT: POLAROID CORPORATION

COMM'L NO.: PDCF 4310
Page 1

(MUSIC UNDER)

ANNCR: (VO) Perhaps, even more than any other time of year,

this is the season

when millions of people discover

(SFX: CLICK OF CAMERA)

that Polaroid cameras do

what no other kind of camera can do.

AD 15.4
This Polaroid commercial is an example of an ad that touches the viewer's emotions. How does it do this? What other ads use this strategy?
(Courtesy of Polaroid.)

voice-over *A technique used in commercials in which an off-camera announcer talks about the on-camera scene.*

talent *People who appear in television commercials.*

Audio The audio dimensions of television ads are the same as in radio—music, voices, and sound effects—but they are used differently, depending on the relationship to the visual image. An announcer, for example, may speak directly to the viewer or engage in a dialogue with another person who may or may not be on-camera. A common manipulation of the camera-announcer relationship is the **voice-over,** in which there is some kind of action on the screen that is described by the announcer's voice, although the announcer is not visible. Sometimes a voice is heard *off-camera,* which means it is coming from either side, from behind, or from above.

Talent A television commercial has all the ingredients of a play. The most important element is people, who can be announcers (either on- or offstage), presenters, spokespersons, "spokesthings" (like talking butter dishes), and character types (old woman, baby, skin diver, policeman). People in commercials are called **talent.** In addition, some commercials have just parts of people, such as hands, feet, or the back of the head.

Depending upon what kind of people are being used, *costumes* and *makeup* can be very important. Historical stories, of course, need period costumes, but modern scenes may also require special clothing such as ski outfits,

LITTLE GIRL: What's this.

Thanks for the milk and cookies,

and thanks for the beautiful

Polaroid picture.

Love Santa.

ANNCR: (VO) Happy holidays from Polaroid.

AD 15.4 (Continued)

swim suits, or cowboy boots. The script should specify which costumes are essential to the story. Makeup may be important if you need to create a skin problem or to change a character from young to old.

PRINCIPLE _____
The most important prop is the product.

Props   In most commercials the most important *prop* is the product. The ad should reflect the essential properties of the product. Does it come in a package? Does it have a distinctive logo? How should it be depicted? Can you show it in use? What other props are necessary to make the story come together? Sometimes they are critical to the action, like a tennis racket in a tennis scene. Sometimes they are used just to set the scene, like the patio table and tray of drinks in the background behind the tennis players. The script should identify every important element in the scene.

set *A constructed setting where the action in a commercial takes place.*

Setting   The setting is where the action takes place. It can be in the studio, maybe something as simple as a table top or maybe a constructed **set** that represents a storefront. Commercials shot outside the studio are said to be filmed *on location.* In these cases the entire crew and cast are transported somewhere. The location could be an alley or a garage down the street, or it could be some exotic place like New Zealand.

AD 15.5
Lighting is one of the most important
elements in the production of a television commercial.
(Courtesy of Anheuser-Busch, Inc. and Genesis.)

Lighting   Lighting is another critical element that is usually manipulated by the director. Special lighting effects need to be specified in the script. For example, you might read "Low lighting as in a bar," or "Intense bright light as though reflected from snow," or "Light flickering on people's faces as if it were reflecting from a television screen."

Graphics   There are several types of visuals that are filmed from a flat card or generated electronically on the screen by a computer. Words and still photos are shot from a card. Words can also be computer-generated right on the screen. The **crawl** is computer-generated letters that appear to be moving across the bottom of the screen.

      Stock footage is a previously recorded image, either video, still slides, or moving film, that is used for scenes that aren't accessible to normal shooting. Examples are shots from a satellite or rocket and old World War II scenes.

Pacing   The speed of the action is another important factor in a television commercial. Pacing describes how fast or how slow the action progresses. Some messages are best developed at a languid pace; others work better done upbeat and fast. If the pacing is an important part of the message, then it needs to be explained in the script.

Filming and Taping

There are a number of ways to produce a message for a television commercial. It can be filmed live or it can be prerecorded using film or videotape. It can also be shot frame by frame using animation techniques.

crawl *Computer-generated letters that move across the bottom of the screen.*

Live In the early days of television most commercials were shot live. The history of advertising includes numerous stories about refrigerator doors that wouldn't open and dogs that refused to eat the dog food. These traumatic experiences explain why most advertisers prefer to prerecord a commercial rather than gamble on doing it live.

You will occasionally see live commercials using spokespersons such as Ed McMahon on the Johnny Carson show. These commercials project a warmth and an immediacy that prerecorded commercials lack. But the chance remains that something will go wrong. The most skilled announcer can still forget a line or mispronounce the name of the product.

Film Today about 90 percent of television commercials are shot on 16 mm or 35 mm film. Most of the film is shot as a negative and processed, after which the image is transferred to videotape. This transferring technique is called *film-to-tape transfer.*

Film consists of a series of frames on celluloid that, for advertising, is usually 35 mm wide. Actually each frame is a still shot. The film passes through a projector and the small changes from frame to frame create the illusion of motion. Film is shot at 24 frames per second. In film-to-tape transfer the film has to be converted to videotape that uses 30 frames per second.

Editing on film is done by cutting between two frames and either eliminating a segment or attaching a new segment of film. The term **cut,** which comes from this editing procedure, is used to describe an abrupt transition from one view of a scene to another.

Videotape Until the 1980s **videotape** was thought of as an inferior alternative to film. It was used primarily by the news side of the television industry because it records sound and images instantly, without a delay for film processing, and the videotape can be replayed immediately. Videotape's "cheap cousin" image has changed dramatically in the last decade. First of all, the quality of videotape has improved. The film-to-tape transfer has seen significant improvements. Also a number of innovations in editing have made the process more precise and faster; computer editing has improved accuracy and made special effects possible.

Animation **Animation,** which uses film rather than videotape, records drawn images one at a time, frame by frame. Cartoon figures, for example, are sketched and then resketched with a slight change to indicate a small progression in the movement of an arm or a leg or a facial expression. Animation is traditionally shot at 12 or 16 drawings per second. Low-budget animation uses fewer drawings, and consequently the motion looks jerky.

Because of all the hand work, animation is labor-intensive and expensive. It takes a long time to create an animated commercial because of the drawing time, but the introduction of computers is speeding up the process. Now illustrators need draw only the beginning and the end of the action sequence, and the computer can plot out the frames in between.

A variation on animation is called **stop action,** a technique used to film inanimate objects like the Pillsbury Doughboy, which is a puppet. The little character is moved a bit at a time and filmed frame by frame. The same technique is used with **claymation,** which involves creating characters from clay and then photographing them. The dancing raisins in the "Heard It Through the Grapevine" commercial by the National Raisin Board are the product of the claymation technique.

film *A strip of celluloid with a series of still images, called frames.*

cut *An abrupt transition from one shot to another.*

videotape *A type of recording medium that electronically records sound and images simultaneously.*

animation *A type of recording medium in which objects are sketched and then filmed one frame at a time.*

stop action *A technique in which inanimate objects are filmed one frame at a time, creating the illusion of movement.*

claymation *A technique that uses figures sculpted from clay and filmed one frame at a time.*

PLANNING AND PRODUCING COMMERCIALS

Planning Television Commercials

Lengths   The most common length for a commercial on broadcast television is 30 seconds. Because of the increasing costs of air time, 60-second commercials are becoming rare. Some network commercials now run in 20-second and 15-second formats. An advertiser may buy a 30-second spot and split it in half for two related products in the line. If the two messages are interdependent, the strategy is called *piggybacking*.

Scenes   A commercial is planned in scenes. These are segments of action that occur in a single location. Within each scene there may be a number of shots from different angles. A 30-second commercial is usually planned with three to four scenes; a fast-paced commercial may have six to eight scenes.

Key Frames   The writer and art director begin the planning together. The television equivalent of thumbnails is called a **key frame.** Because television is a visual medium, the message is developed from a key visual that contains the heart of the concept. The various concepts are devised, tested, and revised as key visuals. When a concept seems promising, the writer and art director move to a rough script and storyboard.

key frame *A single frame of a commercial that summarizes the heart of the message.*

Local Productions   Most local retail commercials are simple, relatively inexpensive, and are shot at the local station or production facility on videotape. The sales representative for the station may work with the advertiser to write the script, and the station's director handles the filming of the commercial. They may not have extravagant production techniques, but these commercials can be just as effective as any big-budget production.

Scripts and Storyboards

A print advertisement is created in two pieces: a copy sheet and a layout. Commercials are planned with two similar documents. A script is the written version with all the words, dialogue, lyrics, and description; the storyboard shows the number of scenes, the composition of the shots, and the progression of the action.

storyboard *A series of frames sketched to illustrate how the story line will develop.*

Storyboards   The **storyboard** is the visual plan, the layout, of the commercial. It uses selected frames to communicate how the story line will develop. It depicts the composition of the shots as well as the progression of action and the interaction of the audio with the video. A 30-second commercial will be planned with six to eight frames. These frames, of course, are stills. They don't show

AD 15.6
Examples of key frames from television commercials.

(Courtesy of The Pillsbury Company and The California Raisins™, © 1987 CalRab. Licensed by Applause Licensing.)

AD 15.7
Example of a television script.
(Courtesy of State Farm Insurance Companies.)

action; they can only suggest it by a pictorial progression. The art director must determine which visuals convey the most information. Underneath the frame will be a short version of the audio, just enough to locate the dialogue in relation to the video.

Television Scripts Like a radio script, a television script is a detailed document. It includes everything depicted on the storyboard plus all the descriptions necessary to assist the director or producer in finding the location or building the set, the talent agency in casting the talent, the composer/arranger in creating the music, and the producer in budgeting and scheduling the entire project.

The script is written in two columns with the audio on the right and the video on the left. The code—capitals, abbreviations, and underlining—is similar to that used for radio scripts. The key to the structure of a television script is the relationship between the audio and the video. The video is typed opposite the corresponding audio. Sometimes these are numbered to correspond to the frames on the storyboard.

TELEVISION TERMINOLOGY

Distance (camera to image): Long shot (LS), full shot (FS), medium shot (MS), wide shot (WS), close-up (CU), extreme close-up (ECU or XCU).

Camera Movement:

* Zoom in or out: The lens on the camera manipulates the change in distance. As you zoom in, the image seems to come closer and get larger; as you zoom back, it seems to move farther away and get smaller.
* Dolly in and out: The camera itself is wheeled forward or backward.
* Pan right or left: The camera is stationary but swings to follow the action.
* Truck right or left: The camera itself moves right or left with the action.

Transitions

* Cut: An abrupt, instantaneous change from one shot to another.
* Dissolve: A soft transition where one image fades to black while another image fades on.

* Lap dissolve: A slow dissolve with a short period in which the two images overlap.
* Superimposition: Two images held in the middle of a dissolve so they are both on-screen at the same time.
* Wipe: One image crawls across the screen and replaces another.

Action

* Freeze frame: Stops the scene in midaction.
* Stop action: Shots are taken one at a time over a long period. Used to record animation, claymation, or something that happens over a long period of time, like a flower blooming.
* Slow motion: Suspends the normal speed of things by increasing the number of frames used to record the movement.
* Speeded-up motion: Increases the normal speed by reducing the number of frames used to record the movement.
* Reverse motion: The film is run backward through the projector.

---

animatic *A preliminary version of a commercial with the storyboard frames recorded on videotape along with a rough sound track.*

photoboard *A type of rough commercial, similar to an animatic except that the frames are actual photos instead of sketches.*

Animatics and Photoboards As the concept is revised and finalized, the script becomes more detailed and the storyboard art more finished. A finished storyboard is equivalent to a comprehensive in print. To make the storyboard even more realistic, the frames may be shot on slides for presentation to the client. If the frames are recorded on videotape along with a rough sound track, the storyboard is called an **animatic.** Animatics frequently are used for client presentations and market research sessions. If frames are actual photographs of the action, which are more realistic, they are called **photoboards.** You have been looking at photoboards in many of the commercials depicted throughout this book.

The Team

A locally produced commercial uses the station's personnel for most of the production roles. Producing a major national advertisement, however, requires, in addition to a lot of time and a great deal of money, a number of people with specialized skills. The agency crew usually includes the copywriter, art director, and producer. The outside people include a production house, a director and shooting crew, a talent agency, a music arranger/director plus musicians, and a film or video editor. The client's advertising manager is also involved throughout the planning and production.

The copywriter, art director, and possibly a creative director and producer work together to develop the idea and translate it into a script and a storyboard. The art director develops the storyboard and establishes the "look" of the commercial, whether realistic, stylized, or fanciful. The copywriter writes the actual script, whether it involves dialogue, narrative, lyrics, announcement, or descriptive copy.

producer *The person who supervises and coordinates all of the elements that go into the creation of a television commercial.*

The **producer,** usually an agency staff member, is in charge of the production. He or she handles the bidding and all of the arrangements, finds the specialists, arranges for casting the talent, and makes sure the budget and the bids all come in together.

PENGUIN #1: Morning Fred. Morning Burt. Let's go boys!

That ice cream's not going to mine itself!

PENGUIN #2: Say, these Goldrush Bars are a real gold mine, eh, Burt?

PENGUIN #3: Right! Ice cream . . peanuts, caramel . . .
PENGUIN #2: . . . chocolatey coating . . .
PENGUIN #3: Yeah!

PENGUIN #2: Goldrush Bars sure look good, eh Burt? . . .

. . . Burt! Hey, Burt, don't eat all our profits!
PENGUIN #3: Sorry! I lost my head!

ANNCR: Goldrush Bars and new Goldrush Nuggets. Precious ice cream treats mined by penguins.

SFX: CLOSING WHISTLE
PENGUIN #3: Hey, Fred! Want to grab a cold one?
PENGUIN #2: Really funny!

ANNCR: Goldrush. In your grocer's freezer.

AD 15.8
An example of a photoboard. The script is incorporated below the different frames.
(Courtesy of DDB Needham Worldwide.)

---

director *The person in charge of the actual filming or taping of the commercial.*

The production house usually coordinates the entire shoot, working closely with the agency staff. The production house normally provides the director, but may instead use a free-lance director, particularly if that director's special "look" is desired for the commercial. The production house provides most of the technical expertise and equipment needed to produce the commercial. The **director** is in charge of the actual filming or taping; the look of the set and lighting; how long the scenes and pieces of action are; who does what and moves where; and how the lines are spoken and the characters played. The director manages the flow of action and determines how it is seen and recorded by the camera.

composer *The person who writes the music.*

arranger *The person who orchestrates the music, arranging it for the various instruments, voices, and scenes.*

editor *The person who assembles the best shots to create scenes and who synchronizes the audio track with the images.*

The music **composer** writes original music; the music **arranger** orchestrates the music for the various instruments and voices to make it fit a scene or copy line. The copywriter usually writes the lyrics or at least gives some idea of what the words should say. A composer who does a lot of commercials, like Barry Manilow, might write the lyrics along with the music. Musicians are hired as needed, from a complete orchestra to a marching band to a vocalist.

In a film production the **editor** becomes involved toward the end of the process and puts everything together. Film is shot from a number of different cameras, each representing a different angle. The audio is recorded on multiple tracks. The editor's job is to decide which are the best shots, how to assemble the scenes, and how the audio tracks work best with the assembled video.

Producing a Television Commercial

Commercials for local stores are relatively inexpensive to produce because they use the facilities and staff of the local station. The production process for a major national television commercial, however, is long and expensive. The 1987 annual study by the American Association of Advertising Agencies estimated production costs for the average commercial at $113,940. This was actually down 4 percent from 1985. However a similar study by the Association of National Advertisers found in 1985 that production costs for the average spot had increased 29 percent from the previous year to $125,000. That is a lot to pay for a single commercial.*

In addition to being expensive, the production of a major commercial is involved and complex. The script and storyboard are reviewed and approved by the client and become the basis for the production planning. The producer and staff first develop a set of *production notes*. These describe in detail every aspect of the production. They are important for finding talent and locations, building sets, and getting bids and estimates from the specialists.

Preproduction Before the commercial can be filmed or taped, a number of arrangements need to be handled. Once the bids have been approved, a preproduction meeting of the creative team and the producer, director, and other key players is held. The meeting attempts to outline every step of the production process and anticipate every problem that may come up. A detailed schedule is also finalized and agreed to by all parties.

The talent agency is in charge of casting, which is accomplished through a series of auditions. A location has to be found and arrangements made with owners, police, and other officials to use the site. If sets are needed, then they have to be built. Finding the props is a test of ingenuity, and the prop person may wind up visiting hardware stores, second-hand stores, or maybe even the local dump. Costumes may have to be made.

The Shoot Although the actual filming takes a rather short time, the setup and rehearsal can take incredible amounts of time. It may seem as though nothing is happening when actually everyone is busy setting up and checking specialized responsibilities.

The film crew includes a number of technicians, all of whom have to know what is happening and what they are supposed to do. Everyone reports to the director. If the sound is being recorded at the time of shooting, the recording is handled by a *mixer*, who operates the recording equipment, and a *mic* or *boom* person, who sets up the microphones. For both film and video recording, the camera operators are the key technicians.

*James P. Forkan, "Spot Production Costs Drop 4%," *Advertising Age*, October 26, 1987, p. 46.

Other technicians include the *gaffer,* who is the chief electrician, and the *grip,* who moves things such as the sets. The grip also lays track for the dolly on which the camera is mounted and pushes the camera on the dolly along the track at the required speed. The *script clerk* checks the dialogue and other script details and times the scenes. All of the technicians are supported by their own crew of assistants. A set is a very busy, crowded place.

The commercial is shot scene by scene, but not necessarily in the order set down in the script. Each scene is shot and reshot until all the elements come together. If the commercial is filmed in videotape, the director plays it back immediately to determine what needs correcting. Film, however, has to be processed before the director can review it. These processed scenes are called *dailies.*

Rushes are rough versions of the commercial assembled from cuts of the raw film footage. They are viewed immediately after the filming to make sure everything necessary has been filmed.

If the audio is to be recorded separately in a sound studio, it is often recorded after the film is shot to **synchronize** (sync) the dialogue to the footage. Directors frequently wait to see exactly how the action appears before they write and record the audio track. If the action occurs to music, then the music may be recorded prior to the shoot and the filming done to the music.

Postproduction For film, much of the work happens after the shoot. That is when the commercial begins to emerge from the hands and mind of the editor. In film a **rough cut** is a preliminary edited version of the story. The editor chooses the best shots and assembles them to create a scene. The scenes are then joined together. After the revision and reediting is completed, an **interlock** is made. The audio and film are separate, but they are timed, and can be listened to, simultaneously. The final version with the sound and film recorded together is called an **answer print.**

In order for the commercial to run at hundreds of stations around the country, duplicate copies have to be made. This process is called **dubbing,** and the copies are called **release prints.** Release prints are distributed on 16mm film or videotape. Because the industry now uses the film-to-tape transfer process, most production is done on videotape, thereby avoiding much of the film-laboratory work.

rushes *Rough versions of the commercial assembled from unedited footage.*

synchronize *Matching the audio to the video in a commercial.*

rough cut *A preliminary rough edited version of the commercial.*

interlock *A version of the commercial with the audio and video timed together, although the two are still recorded separately.*

answer print *The final finished version of the commercial with the audio and video recorded together.*

dubbing *The process of making duplicate copies of a videotape.*

release prints *Duplicate copies of a commercial that are ready for distribution.*

MESSAGE TRENDS

Cable and videocassettes are having a tremendous impact on television commercials. The nature of the advertising message has changed dramatically, and the percentage of the audience that watches the commercials has diminished. Clutter on the networks, the increasing costs of commercials, and smaller audiences have forced television commercials to become ever more competitive.

Shooting a television commercial is an expensive and complicated process.
(Courtesy of Hub Willson/The Stock Option.)

Length and Content

There are two observable trends in the length of television messages. As previously explained, network commercials are getting shorter, with 15-second spots becoming more and more common. In alternative media such as cable, videocassettes, and movie theaters, advertising messages are getting longer—often lasting 2 to 5 minutes. A new term, *infomercials,* has been introduced to refer to even longer commercials—some lasting 30 or 60 minutes—that provide extensive product information.

The informative commercials playing on cable and videotext and in theaters allow room for the development of longer messages. At the same time, the creative demands of the shorter commercials on network television call for simpler messages that are as concise and pointed as the messages on outdoor boards. Reminder ads with to-the-point brand imagery seems to work best in these short formats. The trends in message design, then, are to be more informative in the alternative media and more concise on traditional network television.

Zap-Proofing

The threat of zapping commercials makes the creative side of the message even more important. To survive in this new era when control over the message is in the hands of a viewer holding a remote-control device requires an "awesome creative effort" that will make "the commercials even better than the programs."[*] Len Sugarman, executive vice president and creative director at Foote, Cone & Belding, says that zap-proofing calls for "advertising that is more intriguing up front . . . more intriguing and beautiful."[†]

Arthur Meranus, executive vice president and creative director at Cunningham & Walsh, separates ads into those that use a traditional tell-it-upfront approach, sometimes referred to as the P&G approach, and those that use "some sort of likability in the beginning." The traditional commercials start by telling the viewer what the product is and what it promises. Meranus feels, however, that the trend is toward commercials that start with likability devices, such as the Bud Light sight gags.[‡] *Zap-proofing* commercials means designing them to be entertaining—dramatic, funny, puzzling, or emotional.

An example of zap-proof commercials on cable television is General Food's "shortcuts" series, which has kept fidgety audiences glued to the tube. A typical spot opens with a hostess promising to reveal a recipe for baked Brie cheese. The picture then dissolves to a 30-second commercial for some other GF product. Then comes the payoff as the commercial moves back to the cheese and shows how to insert the wheel of cheese into a precut hole in the french bread. The hostess explains that you bake it for 30 minutes. *Voila!* Instant success.[§]

Embeds

Another technique used to beat the zipping and zapping is to embed the commercial message in some kind of programming. For example, during the Texas Sesquicentennial, Media Drop In Productions produced a series of true tales about Texas featuring Willie Nelson. Included within the 45 vignettes were commercials for Wrangler jeans.

[*]Richard Christian, "Can Advertising Survive Split 30s, Zapping, Globalization, High Tech, Million Dollar Minutes, Narrowcasting, and Even More Accountability?" *Back Stage,* May 31, 1985, pp. 12, 24.
[†]"Can Ad Agency Creativity Combat Zapping, Zipping?" *Television/Radio Age,* November 11, 1985, pp. 63–65.
[‡]*Ibid.*
[§]"Advertisements That Aren't," *Marketing & Media Decisions,* July 1987, pp. 24–25.

Image Manipulation

Sophisticated computergraphic systems, such as those used to create the *Star Wars* special effects, have pioneered the making of fantastic original art on computers. At the same time, MTV has generated some of the most exciting video techniques to be seen anywhere on television. The messages are filled with action, unexpected visuals, and, most of all, imaginative special effects.

In the new computer-animated world television images are changing dramatically. Already the Quantel Paint Box system is being used by computergraphic specialists to create and manipulate video images. Eventually, as costs decrease, these systems will find their way into the art director's office and will expand the graphic capabilities of the agency and production houses—both for print and for video.

Computergraphic artists brag that they can do anything with an image using a computerized "paintbox"—they can make Robert Redford look 80 or Ronald Reagan look 30. They can look at any object from any angle or even from the inside out. Photographs of real objects can be seen on television as they change into art or animation and then return to life.

An example of computergraphics is a commercial by the computer production company Charlex for Pringles potato chips that shows six children munching on Pringles that appear to come out of their computers. The set is a collection of real elements, including desks, chairs, computers, students, and bookcases, but the scene is "perfectly colorized, cloned, and totally paintboxed, right down to shadows and lighting effects." The wide-angle pan reveals six children plucking Pringles from their computer screens. However, two of these youngsters were created via paintbox. Likewise only three computers actually existed in the original scene; the rest were cloned by paintbox.*

Television/Radio Age, November 11, 1985.

■ SUMMARY

Broadcast advertisements must be intrusive to overcome audience inattention.

The three tools used in radio commercials are voice, music, and sound effects.

Radio copy is simple, avoids complex information, and uses conversational language.

Television uses stories to entertain and make a point.

The production of a commercial begins with preproduction planning and continues through rehearsal, the shoot, and the postproduction editing.

■ QUESTIONS

1. What are the major characteristics of radio ads? How do these characteristics reflect the use of voice, music, and sound effects?

2. How does radio copy differ from television copy? From print copy?

3. Who are the key people involved in creating television commercials? How do they interact during the production process?

4. Think of an effective television commercial you have seen recently. Why was it effective? What types of creative efforts do you think went into producing this commercial? How long do you think it took to produce? How much do you think it cost?

5. How has the emergence of cable television and VCRs affected the nature of commercials? How might they affect advertising in the future?

■ FURTHER READINGS

BALDWIN, HUNTLEY. *Creating Effective TV Commercials.* Chicago: Crain Books, 1972.

HEIGHTON, ELIZABETH J., and DON R. CUNNINGHAM. *Advertising in the Broadcast Media.* Belmont, CA: Wadsworth Publishing Co., 1976.

ORLIK, PETER B. *Broadcast Copywriting.* Boston: Allyn and Bacon, 1982.

TERRELL, NEIL. *The Power Technique of Radio-TV Copywriting.* Blue Ridge Summit, PA: Tab Books, 1971.

WHITE, HOOPER. *How to Produce an Effective TV Commercial.* Chicago: Crain Books, 1981.

ZEIGLER, SHERILYN K., and HERBERT H. HOWARD. *Broadcast Advertising.* Columbus, OH: Grid, 1978.

INTERIORS
Clothing and Gifts
1988 Volume I, No. 1
Harry and David's
CHRISTMAS
THE RENOVATOR'S SUPPLY
Manufacturer & Importer of Fine Hardware, Plumbing & Lighting
SPRING '88 $3
FACE IT. YOU DON'T HAVE THE TIME TO SHOP THAT YOUR MOTHER DID.
TRY US. THIS CATALOG HAS OUR BEST PRICES.

16

Creating Direct-Response Advertising

Chapter Outline

As Personal as a Letter or a Telephone Call
Direct-Response Advertising
The Direct-Response Industry
Characteristics of Direct Response
The Players
The Media of Direct Response
Telemarketing

Chapter Objectives

When you have completed this chapter you should be able to:

- Define direct-response advertising
- Distinguish between direct-response advertising, direct marketing, and mail order
- Evaluate the various media that direct-response advertising can utilize
- Explain how modern technology has transformed the nature of direct response
- List the three types of firms that produce direct-response advertising

AS PERSONAL AS A LETTER OR A TELEPHONE CALL

Mary gets home from work on a Friday afternoon. She sinks into her favorite chair to read her mail. Actually she doesn't read the mail as much as sort through it. A bill, another bill—they both go into a stack unopened. A bank statement—that goes in another stack. It can wait until she has the energy to balance the checkbook. A detergent sample from Procter & Gamble—"Oh, good," she thinks. "I'll try it tomorrow when I do the wash." Another bill—that goes in the stack, too.

A form letter—she starts to toss it out but notices something on the envelope about a computer magazine for kids. She has been nagging her son Mike about all the time he spends playing games on his computer and hopes she can find some ideas in the ad. She opens the envelope and reads the letter. It is addressed to parents and refers specifically to that problem. Apparently the magazine will introduce more challenging activities for the kids. She also notices from the reply card that she can get the first issue for free and does not have to pay if she doesn't like it. She decides it is worth a try.

The telephone rings and she answers to hear someone ask her if she needs to have her carpets cleaned. Her first response is to hang up; she really hates to be interrupted by people selling her things over the phone. Then she thinks about the dog smell in the carpet in the upstairs bedroom. She's tried a dozen products and can't get that smell out, so she asks the salesperson about it and makes an appointment to have one of their cleaning reps come by to give her an estimate.

Returning to her mail, Mary finds another bill, which goes into the stack. The last piece of mail is one of those gift catalogs. She really likes to get catalogs, so she takes a minute to scan through it.

She remembers her mother's birthday is next month and notices that the company is having a sale on her mother's Franciscan dishes. Maybe she ought to order some of the serving pieces. As she turns to the back cover, she notices a toll-free number. She decides to make the call right now while she is thinking about it, so she digs her credit card out of her purse and calls in the order.

This vignette illustrates how direct-response advertising works. For busy people, shopping at home is a convenience. They can browse and read on their

FIGURE 16.1
The direct-response flow chart.

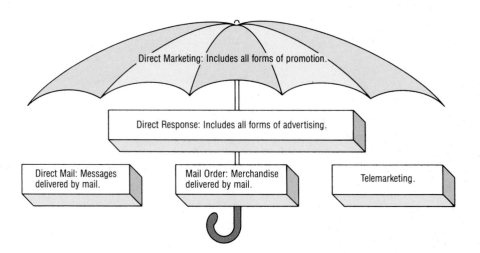

own time at their own pace. There are no parking hassles, no lines, no unfriendly clerks. Direct marketing that establishes a one-on-one relationship with the consumer is remaking the face of retailing in America.

DIRECT-RESPONSE ADVERTISING

direct-response advertising *Advertising that solicits a response from the prospect without the intervention of a third party.*

direct marketing *A selling method that establishes a one-on-one relationship with customers; it can include direct-response advertising and other promotional techniques.*

PRINCIPLE
Direct marketing always involves a one-on-one relationship with prospects.

direct mail *A form of advertising that uses the mail to carry the message.*

mail order *A form of marketing that uses the mail to deliver the product.*

Direct response is an area with a lot of terms that have similar meanings. The Direct Marketing Association defines **direct-response advertising** as "any paid advertising where the intention is to solicit a direct response by including a response device."* Direct response can use any medium—mail, telephone, television, radio, newspapers, or magazines.

Direct Marketing

Direct marketing is even broader in scope than direct response. **Direct marketing** is a selling method that utilizes direct-response advertising and other promotional techniques to make a contact and solicit a response. A direct marketing program can also include sales promotion and product publicity. Direct marketing always involves a one-on-one relationship with prospects and customers built around the maintenance of a data base of customer names.

Direct Mail

One of the earliest forms of direct-response advertising is **direct mail.** In fact, this term is still used by some people to refer to the entire advertising category. Direct mail, however, is limited to *messages that are delivered by mail.* Consumers can respond by mail or telephone. **Mail order,** a variation on direct mail, usually refers to *merchandise that is delivered by mail* directly from seller to consumer without a middleman. The order can be placed by mail, by telephone, or by computer terminal.

THE DIRECT-RESPONSE INDUSTRY

Direct-response advertising is one of the fastest-growing segments of the advertising industry, and direct marketing is one of the fastest-growing segments of retailing. Direct response has been an important advertising area for over a century. The first major venture by an important national company into mail order was the publication of the Montgomery Ward catalog in 1872.†

The Direct Mail/Advertising Association was founded in 1917. Currently known as the Direct Marketing Association (DMA), it has long been active in industry research and professional training programs. One of DMA's most successful programs is a seminar for college students sponsored by one of its divisions, the Direct Marketing Educational Foundation.

Characteristics of the Industry

Growth Direct response is a rapidly growing field. Sales are increasing at an annual rate of 9.5 percent, as compared to the 6.4 percent growth of sales in retail stores. In 1986 direct response generated $133 billion in sales.‡ In a special section of *Target Marketing* called "Outlook '87," Postmaster General Preston Tisch claimed that about 14 percent of all retail purchases are a result of

*Kenneth C. Otis II, "Introduction to Direct Marketing," DMMA Manual Release 100.1, April 1979, p. 1.
†*Ibid.*
‡*Direct Marketing,* February 1988, p. 33.

AD 16.1

This direct-response ad includes both a toll-free number and a reply form, making it very easy for interested consumers to join the program.

(Courtesy of Rapp & Collins, New York.)

direct-mail transactions. He predicted that this total would reach 20 percent by 1990.* Of course, direct mail is only one part of direct marketing.

Direct marketing is now one of the selling methods applied in virtually every consumer and business-to-business category. For example, direct marketing is used by IBM, Digital Equipment, Xerox, and other manufacturers selling office products. It is used by almost every bank and insurance company. It is used by the airlines and hotels and cruise lines, as well as by resorts and government tourist agencies. It is used by packaged-goods marketers such as General Foods, Colgate, and Bristol Myers; by household product marketers such as Black and Decker; and by automotive companies such as Ford, Buick, and Cadillac. Direct marketing is also employed for membership drives, fund raising, and solicitation of donations by nonprofit organizations such as the Sierra Club, Audubon Society, and political associations.

Direct-response advertising represented 17 percent of the media expenditures by advertisers in 1986 for consumer advertising. This category has been increasing at an annual rate of over 10 percent, which makes it the third-fastest growth area for media expenditures.† Direct response is also becoming increasingly important in business-to-business advertising.

*"Outlook '87," *Target Marketing,* January 1987, pp. 25–28.

† Mary Lou Roberts and Paul B. Berger, *Direct Marketing Management: Text and Cases* (Englewood Cliffs, NJ: Prentice Hall, 1989).

Reasons for Growth   Direct-response advertising is growing for both social and technological reasons, including the increase in the number of women in the work force and in the number of single-parent homes. Both men and women are doing the household shopping, usually after work and on weekends. They are busy people, and they would rather be doing anything other than driving through a parking lot looking for that elusive place to park.

Technology   Numerous technological advances have made direct-response advertising more efficient for marketers and more acceptable to shoppers. The introduction of the zip code by the U.S. Postal Service, for example, made it possible to target direct mail geographically and even demographically within a region. Likewise the introduction of the **toll-free number** (800 number) by AT&T made it much easier for consumers to respond.

Computers   The technology that has made the biggest impact on direct marketing is the computer. Advertisers and service firms use the computer to manage lists of names, handle addressing, and feed personalized addresses into the printing process. Consumers are just beginning to use their personal computers at home to reach marketers with computerized shopping services.

Credit Cards   Another major factor has been the introduction of credit cards. With an automatic billing system available, a customer can call in an order and give a number for billing. The order is filled immediately; the company does not have to wait for a check to be mailed and clear the bank.

toll-free (800) number *A call that is free to the caller and paid for by the number being called.*

PRINCIPLE ————
The growth in direct-response advertising has come about because of computers, zip codes, 800 numbers, and credit cards.

CHARACTERISTICS OF DIRECT RESPONSE

Direct response is different from other types of advertising because it uses some form of two-way communication and a reply device. Action objectives make it possible to measure the response and determine what works and what doesn't. The targeted audience tends to be smaller than for other forms of media advertising. One reason for this is that direct-response advertising is tightly targeted to people who are already identified as serious prospects. It is a more expensive, but also a more efficient, form of advertising. Lists of addresses and telephone numbers are essential parts of the data base for this form of advertising.

FIGURE 16.2
The armchair shopper.

Tightly Targeted

The most important characteristic of direct-response advertising is that it can be tightly targeted. With some media, such as mail or telephone, it can even be targeted directly to an individual rather than to a mass population. This advantage allows the marketer to personalize the message far more than in other advertising forms.

With computers and extensive data bases on prospects, direct mail, for example, can be targeted to very specific types of people—not just to consumers but also to potential customers—who actually are in the market for the product. Furthermore, the letter can be personally addressed and the message can be tailored to that person's interests. In their book on direct marketing Mary Lou Roberts and Paul Berger call this "precision targeting."*

Interactive

A number of characteristics distinguish direct-response advertising from other types of promotion. One of the main differences is that it is **interactive,** a transaction between the advertiser and the customer. It is the most personal of all types of advertising. There is a direct communication link between advertiser and target. In direct mail it is a letter; in telemarketing it is a phone call. In conventional media it is an ad with a response device.

Reply Device Direct response uses some form of two-way communication, either an interactive medium like the telephone or a self-contained response mechanism like a reply card. Direct response always includes at least one reply technique, either a telephone number (usually toll-free for national advertising), an order card or inquiry form, or a return envelope.

Measurable Action Objectives

Direct advertising usually includes stated action objectives, generally a purchase or requests for additional information. Not only is the response direct, it is usually immediate. Other forms of advertising are limited to indirect communication objectives like awareness or attitude change.

One benefit of having specific action objectives is that direct-response advertising is measurable. In fact, it is one of the most frequently tested areas in all of advertising. Advertisers often use split-run techniques and variations on the message to test the strength of the offer and the creative strategy.

Data Bases

Targeting, in the new age of direct response, means being able to access and manipulate huge files of information, called a **data base,** that includes names, addresses, telephone numbers, and demographic and psychographic information. CCX, for example, is a data-base program that stores more than 1 billion names and allows list users to mix and match information.

List brokers have thousands of lists tied to demographic, psychographic, and geographic breakdowns. They have classified their data on America's households down to the carrier routes. For instance, one company has identified 160 zip codes it calls "Black Enterprise" clusters, inhabited by "upscale, white-collar, Black families" in major urban fringe areas. If you want to target older women in New England who play tennis, most major firms would be able to put together a

*_Ibid._

merging *The process of combining two or more lists of prospects.*

purging *The process of deleting repeated names when two or more lists are combined.*

PRINCIPLE
Computerized lists can be merged and purged to create custom-designed lists of highly targeted prospects.

list for you by combining lists, called **merging,** and deleting the repeated names, called **purging.**

The secret is the power of the computer to manage the incredible wealth of descriptive data that is now being accumulated along with the lists. Most list brokers have standard lists for sale, but in addition they can sort, merge, and purge lists to custom-design one to fit a particular prospect profile.

Stan Rapp and Tom Collins see the computerized data base as revolutionizing marketing. In their book *MaxiMarketing* they explain: "The trend is as clear as the name on your checkbook. From mass marketing to segmented marketing to niche marketing to tomorrow's world of one-to-one marketing—the transformation will be complete by the end of the eighties."*

THE PLAYERS

Advertisers

There are more than 12,000 firms engaged in direct-response marketing whose primary business is selling products and services by mail or telephone.† This number does not include the many retail stores that use direct marketing as a supplemental marketing program. Traditionally the product categories that have made the greatest use of direct marketing have been book and record clubs, publishers, insurance, collectables, packaged foods, and gardening firms. A recent study sponsored by the DMA identified the most common users of direct-response advertising.‡

Direct-response consumer categories include:

1. Apparel (including jewelry)
2. Home furnishings
3. Periodicals
4. Appliances
5. Books
6. Records
7. Gardening

Direct-response business categories include:

1. Computer technology
2. Books
3. Office supplies
4. Computer office supplies

Some of the largest direct-marketing firms are well known because they are major retail firms and use national advertising, but others are not as familiar because they only engage in direct marketing. Among the largest U.S. direct marketers are Sears, J. C. Penney, Time, and the American Automobile Association.§

Agencies

Three types of firms are involved in direct-response advertising: advertising agencies, independent agencies, and service firms.

---

*Stan Rapp and Tom Collins, *MaxiMarketing* (New York: McGraw-Hill Book Co., 1987), p. viii.
†Roberts and Berger, *Direct Marketing Management.*
‡Neil Doppelt, "Measuring Direct Marketing: DMA's Industry Statistics Survey," *DMA Focus,* January/February 1987, p. 7.
§Arnold Fishman, "The 1986 Mail Order Guide," *Direct Marketing,* July 1987, p. 40.

TABLE 16.1
The Largest U.S.
Direct-Response
Agencies

Agency	1986 U.S. Gross Billings (in millions)
Agencies Reporting Fees and Commissions Only:	
1. Wunderman, Ricotta & Kline	$224.5
2. Ogilvy & Mather Direct	207.4
3. MARCOA DR Group Inc.	110.0
4. Grey Direct International	94.0
5. Kobs & Brady Advertising Inc.	81.0
6. Chapman Stone & Adler Inc.	80.4
7. Rapp & Collins Direct Response Group	80.1
8. FCB Direct	78.4
9. Barry Blau & Partners	63.1
Agencies Reporting Fees, Commissions, and Internal Production Revenues:	
1. The Direct Marketing Group Inc.	$138.7
2. Krupp/Taylor	64.8
3. The Direct Marketing Agency Inc.	60.4
4. Epislon	47.8
5. Customer Development Corp.	40.5
6. Direct Mail Corporation of America	40.0
7. Computer Marketing Services Inc.	37.5
8. Grizzard Advertising Inc.	13.7
9. Manus Services Corp.	12.4
10. Marketing Communications Inc.	11.7

Source: Reprinted from "Top Direct Agencies Hold Rank," *Marketing News,* April 24, 1987, p. 18, published by the American Marketing Association.

Advertising Agencies First are the *advertising agencies, whose primary business is general media advertising.* These agencies might have a department that specializes in direct response or they might own a separate direct-response company. Many major advertising agencies that want to provide integrated, full-service promotional programs for their clients are buying direct-response companies because this is such an important part of the corporate promotional program.

Independent Agencies The second category is the *independent, full-service, direct-response agency.* These companies specialize in direct response, and many of them are quite large.

Service Firms The third category is the *service firms that specialize in supplying such services as printing, mailing, and list brokering.*

The largest direct-response agencies include some firms that specialize only in direct response and others that are affiliated with major agencies. The largest firms for 1986 are listed in Table 16.1.

Consumers

Most people have a love-hate relationship with direct-response advertising. They complain about the "junk" mail that clutters their mailbox. They hate to get telephone calls at dinnertime asking for donations no matter how good the cause is. They talk back to the salesperson on television who is demonstrating a new screwdriver. However, they respond. They buy from direct-mail letters and catalogs, they listen to the personal sales pitch over the telephone, and they call in orders. Sid Bernstein reported in his column in *Advertising Age* on a service that lets people who object to direct mail have their names taken off the lists. Bernstein found that twice as many called to have their names added as did to have their names removed.[*]

[*]Sidney Bernstein, "Mail Order Is Burgeoning Giant," *Advertising Age,* March 26, 1979.

New Shoppers Although people might dislike the intrusiveness of direct-response advertising, they appreciate the convenience. Postmaster General Tisch observed that it is "a method of purchasing goods in a society that is finding itself with more disposable income but with less time to spend it."*

Stan Rapp described this new consumer in his speech to the DMA annual conference as "a new generation of consumers armed with push-button phones and a pocket full of credit cards getting instant gratification by shopping and doing financial transactions from the den or living room." He pointed to the tremendous success of Domino's Pizza, with its home delivery service, as the fastest-growing sector of the $12-billion pizza market.†

The push-button shopper is a new breed. It takes some daring to order a product you can't see, touch, feel, or try out. It is not like shopping at a retail store. This new breed of consumer is self-confident and willing to take a chance but doesn't like to be disappointed.

Expectations Barbara Berger Opotowsky, president of the Better Business Bureau of Metropolitan New York, describes direct response as "an act of faith." She explains: "If the company does not meet the expectations created by the promotion, the customer may lose faith not only in that firm, but in all direct-marketing offers. You know what happens when you've been burned. You tend to say, 'I've learned my lesson, I'll never try that again.'" She comments that "There is no industry in which strong customer relations are more important than the direct-marketing industry."‡

The biggest problem identified by Opotowsky is unrealistic expectations. Sometimes the shopper just doesn't read the ad carefully enough. Sometimes the ad doesn't tell enough of the story to give a good picture of the product. Sometimes the puffery and hype get out of control, and the description bears little resemblance to the actual product.

One recent case involved a miniature electronic piano. It was really a toy, about the size of a cassette. Two of the firms described it as being like an instrument: "Easiest-to-play model, fully electronic, soft-touch keyboard." Their customers complained that they had been deceived. Two other firms sold the identical product for a similar price but included a picture and the size specifications. They received no complaints.

CUSTOMER RELATIONS Spiegel, a catalog marketer that is now adding new customers at a rate of 1 million per year, is very conscious of the need for a good customer-service program. Henry A. Johnson, vice chairman of Spiegel, describes the company's three levels of service. The first is accuracy: every product is described and depicted realistically. The second is immediate correction of any error. The third level is a strong customer-relations program with trained people to answer questions, take orders, and handle complaints.§

THE MEDIA OF DIRECT RESPONSE

Direct response is a multimedia field. All conventional advertising mass media can be used, as well as others that you might not think of as media, such as the telephone and postal service. Sometimes the media are used in combination. A mail offer, for example, may be followed up with a telephone call. Advertisers are allocating increasing sums of money to direct-response media. In 1987 expenditures on telephone and direct mail alone totaled almost $65 billion.‖

*"Outlook '87," pp. 25–28.

†"Looking into the Future of Direct Marketing," *Direct Marketing,* May 1987, pp. 144–45, 153.

‡Barbara Berger Opotowsky, "Consumer Confidence: The Future of Direct Marketing," *Directions,* March/April 1987, pp. 6, 12.

§"Outlook '87," pp. 25–28.

‖*Direct Marketing,* February 1988, p. 33.

WHEN IS EXPENSIVE CHEAP?

Although direct-response advertising, particularly direct mail and telemarketing, can be very efficient, it also can be very expensive. Costs per thousand can reach $200, $300, or even $400.

Package-goods manufacturers, for example, debate the use of direct response because the cost per thousand is so high. RJR Nabisco chairman—CEO J. Tylee Wilson insisted that the "jury is still out on direct mail." He explained: "Computers let us target to the finest demographic detail, which is terrific. But it's also terrifically expensive."*

Most direct-response experts feel the strategy is cost-effective because the audience is so carefully targeted. The advantage is in not having wasted reach. Nancy Shalek, president of Wexler & Shalek, said, in response to Wilson's comment: "If the product is aimed at the mass market, then it becomes ridiculously expensive and meaningless. But if you narrow your focus and segment the audience, then it's cost effective."

Many experts feel that direct response compares favorably with mass media advertising when you consider the question of wasted reach. *MaxiMarketing* authors Stan Rapp and Tom Collins cited a study that compared the cost of a television spot with direct response. The hypothetical television spot cost $138,000 and reached an audience of 11.5 million, giving a cost per thousand of $12. However, these numbers assumed that everyone who saw the commercial (1) used the product category and (2) remembered the ad. In fact, if only 25 percent of the households watching used the product and only 20 percent of these people remembered the ad the next day, then the true cost of delivering that one 30-second commercial was really $230 per thousand, about the same as for a direct mailing to a list of users.†

*"Street Talk," *Advertising Age,* November 24, 1986, p. 58.
†Stan Rapp and Tom Collins, *MaxiMarketing* (New York: McGraw-Hill Book Co., 1987), pp. 44–45.

It may come as a surprise that telemarketing is so large. It is clearly the growth area in direct response. The expenditure, however, includes both incoming and outgoing calls. In other words, any telephone call related to direct marketing comes under this category, including offers, orders, inquiries, and service calls. The calls placing orders may be in response to ads in any of the media. Direct mail, which is one of the most visible areas, is much smaller in terms of expenditure. Television is high on the list because of the costs of production and airtime.

Direct Mail

Direct mail provides the foundation for the direct-response industry. A direct-mail piece is a complex, self-standing advertising message for a single product or service. It may be as simple as a single-page letter or as complex as a package consisting of a multipage letter, a brochure, supplemental flyers, and an order card with a return envelope.

Direct mail has increased dramatically in recent years. Total business mail handled by the Postal Service has grown from 30 billion pieces in 1980 to more than 54 billion in 1986. It now accounts for more than 37 percent of the total mail volume, an increase of 30.5 percent since 1982.*

Most direct mail is sent using the third-class bulk mail permit, which requires a minimum of 200 identical pieces. Third class is cheaper than first class, but it takes much longer to be delivered. Estimates of nondelivery of third-class mail run as high as 6 to 8 percent.

Assistant Postmaster General John R. Wargo estimates that the volume of third-class mail may surpass first class sometime during the 1990s. He also notes that a typical household receives an average of 17 pieces of third-class mail each

*"Outlook '87," pp. 25–28.

week. Even this number does not tell the whole story because not all direct-mail ads are sent third class. In fact, as much as 10 percent of all first-class mail is also direct response.*

Characteristics   Direct mail demonstrates, more than any other medium, how a message can sell a product without the help of a salesperson. Because direct mail is a self-contained sales message, it has to deliver all the information and all the incentives necessary to make a sale. If it didn't work, it wouldn't be used. The response rates of direct mail are generally higher than those of any other medium used in direct marketing.†

Tight targeting is one of direct mail's strengths. Although media advertising is limited to the circulation of the publication or the audience of the station, direct mail can select its own group of prospects. This selectivity is matched by direct mail's flexibility. Messages can be sent to any postal address at any time of the year in any size or shape acceptable for mailing. Anything, including product samples, computer discs, and videocassettes, can be included.

Message Format   Direct mail can be anything and look like anything, but most pieces follow a fairly conventional format. The packaging usually includes an outer envelope, a letter, a brochure, supplemental flyers or folders, and a reply card with a return envelope. Ad 16.2 illustrates the contents of an envelope.

AD 16.2
All of the items in this photo were included in a direct-mail envelope from American Demographics.
(Courtesy of American Demographics.)

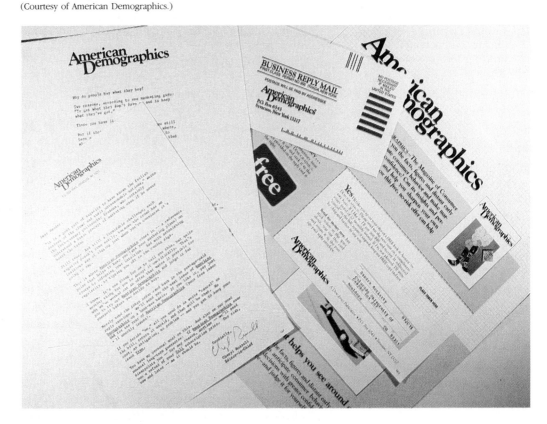

*"Print Executives Say Direct Mail Growth Is Strong Draw, Although It's Still Healthy," *DM News,* July 1, 1987, p. 8; and Herbert Katzenstein and William S. Sachs, *Direct Marketing* (Columbus: Merrill Publishing Co., 1986), pp. 254–55.

†Katzenstein and Sachs, *Direct Marketing.*

THE OUTER ENVELOPE   One of the most important elements in direct mail is the outer envelope. The critical decision is whether to read the mailing or throw it out, and that decision is made on the basis of the outer envelope. Actually the industry estimates that three-fourths of the pieces do get read. Ad 16.3 gives examples of outer envelopes.

Advertisers use a number of techniques to get people to open the envelope. One is to state the offer on the outside: "Save $50 on a set of china." If an incentive is part of the offer, then that might be used: "Order now and get a free telephone." A *teaser* statement or question might be used to spark curiosity: "What is missing from every room in your house?" A "peek-through window" may be used to show part of the product, or a "show-through envelope" can call attention to the message design of the brochure and the quality and colorfulness of the graphics.

THE LETTER   The letter is next in importance because it is seen after the envelope (see Ad 16.4). It highlights and dramatizes the selling premise and explains the details of the offer. Most letters are two to four pages long, although many are longer. Research has found that people with any interest in the product will read everything in the letter. The letter has to carry the full weight of the marketing, advertising, and sales effort.

Bill Jayme, one of the best copywriters in direct-response advertising, commented that people "often ask why we in direct marketing are so verbose. Letters that can run to eight pages. Brochures the size of a bedsheet." He ex-

AD 16.3
Examples of direct-mail envelopes. What characteristics of these envelopes would encourage recipients to examine the contents?

(Courtesy of Motorola Communications & Electronics, Inc.)

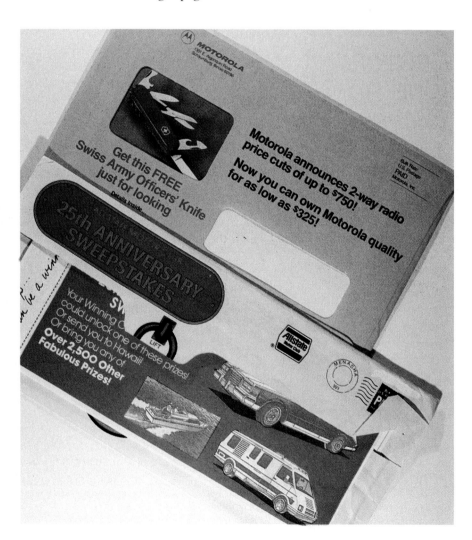

WITH THIS CARD YOU AND YOUR SPOUSE ARE INSTANTLY ELIGIBLE FOR IMPORTANT ALLSTATE MOTOR CLUB PRIVILEGES, LIKE 24 HOUR EMERGENCY ROAD SERVICE.

...AND IT CONTAINS YOUR CHANCE TO WIN ANY OF OVER 2,500 FABULOUS PRIZES IN THE ALLSTATE MOTOR CLUB 25TH ANNIVERSARY SWEEPSTAKES!

NOTE: MEMBERSHIP IS NOT REQUIRED TO BE ELIGIBLE TO WIN A PRIZE.

DEAR RON PERRELLA,

HAVE YOU EVER SAT BEHIND THE WHEEL OF A LUXURIOUS BRAND NEW CADILLAC SEVILLE? HAVE YOU EVER DREAMED OF OWNING ONE? PARKING IT IN YOUR GARAGE? BEING THE ENVY OF YOUR NEIGHBORHOOD?

RON PERRELLA IF YOU'RE OUR GRAND PRIZE WINNER YOU CAN HAVE THAT CADILLAC FOR YOUR VERY OWN! PLUS $25,000 TO USE ANY WAY YOU WANT!

OR, IF YOU'RE OUR FIRST PRIZE WINNER...YOU CAN HAVE YOUR CHOICE OF A NEW CHRIS CRAFT CABIN CRUISER OR A WINNEBAGO LESHARO RV!

AND THERE ARE OVER 2,500 OTHER FABULOUS PRIZES YOU CAN WIN!

AD 16.4
An example of a direct-marketing letter designed to attract the customer's attention.
(Courtesy of Allstate Motor Club, Inc.)

plains why: "Because a single mailing package must in one fell swoop do the work, in more conventional selling, of many hundreds of people."*

The style of the letter is personal. It usually begins with a personal salutation that includes the target's name. The tone is a little different from that of traditional media advertising. It points out things about the offer as a friend might. The first paragraph works like a headline to convince the reader to stay with the message all the way through. It may dramatize the selling premise, spark curiosity, or make some incredible statement as a way to build interest.

The body of the letter provides support, explanation, proof, documentation, and details. This is serious hard-sell copy. One critical part of the letter is the postscript (P.S.). Because the postscript is highly attention-getting, most writers use it to wrap up or restate the offer.

THE BROCHURE Accompanying the letter is a brochure that features the product in glowing color. The letter uses words; the brochure uses graphics to create impact. The product is displayed in as many attractive settings as possible. Demonstrations and how-to-use visuals are included, if appropriate. These can be one-page flyers, multipanel folders, multipage brochures, or spectacular **broadsheets** that fold out like maps to cover the top of a table. Smaller, supplemental pieces may also be used as postscripts or for additional details or incentive offers.

broadsheets *Large brochures that unfold like a map.*

THE ORDER CARD Usually an order card with its own envelope is included. The order form may also contain a toll-free number to give the customer

*John Francis Tighe, "Complete Creative Checklist for Copywriters," *Advertising Age,* February 9, 1987, pp. 24, 69.

FIGURE 16.3
The many roles of direct response.

a choice in how to respond. Order cards sometimes have involvement devices such as tokens, stickers, stamps, and scratch-off boxes.

Message Functions The functions of a direct-mail message are similar to the steps in the sales process. The mailing plays many roles. First it has to get the attention of the targeted prospect. Then it has to create a need for the product, show what it looks like, and demonstrate how it is used. Furthermore it has to be able to answer questions like a good salesperson and reassure the buyer. It might have to provide critical information about product use. It must inspire confidence, minimize risk, and establish that the company is reputable. Finally it has to make the sale, which involves explaining how to buy, how to order, where to call, and how to pay or charge the purchase. There may even be an incentive to encourage a fast response. Figure 16.3 illustrates the different roles of direct-response advertising.

The List   A direct-mail ad can only be effective if the mailing list targets the appropriate customers. If the prospects are not in the market for the product, then even the best direct-mail package will be thrown away.

The biggest problem with computer-generated lists is accuracy. Updating mailing addresses is a constant activity in a mobile society. Other errors include addressing a man as a woman (and vice versa) and misspelling names.

The Catalog Marketplace

A catalog is a multipage direct-mail publication that lists a variety of merchandise. The big books are the ones produced by such retail giants as Sears Roebuck, Montgomery Ward, and J. C. Penney. The Spiegel company is a major catalog merchandiser that doesn't have retail outlets (see Ad 16.5). Saks Fifth Avenue, Nieman-Marcus, and Bloomingdale's are major retailers that support their in-store sales with expensive catalogs.

AD 16.5
Spiegel produces one of the best-known catalogs. All orders are placed through the catalog; there are no retail outlets.

(Courtesy of Spiegel, Inc.)

LANDS' END: A DIRECT-MARKETING SUCCESS STORY

Over the past 25 years Lands' End has become one of the most successful direct merchants in the United States. Customers can use Lands' End catalogs to order clothing, shoes, and soft luggage without leaving their homes. The company's success stems in part from its policy of supplying quality merchandise at reasonable prices, backed by excellent customer service. However, customers might never have heard of Lands' End had it not been for an aggressive—and effective—advertising campaign.

Lands' End was founded in 1963 by former copywriter Gary Comer. By 1980 the company was offering its line of quality "cut and sewn" clothing and luggage to about 400,000 customers, and sales were growing at better than 50 percent annually.

Despite this success, Comer remained convinced that his company had not realized its full potential. He consulted consumer-media specialist Richard C. Anderson, who recommended an ambitious, 5-year consumer-advertising plan that would focus on building a national reputation for quality, value, and service. The strategy ultimately called for placing Lands' End ads in the medium best suited to attract the targeted audience of upscale professional people—consumer magazines such as *New York, Smithsonian,* and *Travel and Leisure.* The ads were to be full page, black and white, with simple artwork (no photography) and detailed descrip-tive copy. Ads included an address and toll-free number that consumers could use to order a free catalog. However, this was not the primary purpose of the advertising.

This long-range image-building approach was a major departure from conventional mail-order advertising, which measured success by such short-term results as cost per inquiry and revenue per ad.

The campaign proved so successful that it was extended beyond the "5-year mark" right through to the present. As indicated by the enclosed ads, the style of the campaign is essentially unchanged. How effective was the campaign? In fiscal 1988 (ending January 31, 1988) company sales totaled over $336.3 million, which is about 20 times what they were before the campaign was initiated in 1980. The accompanying table lists the company's sales growth since 1985.

Lands' End provides an example of how a well-managed company that produces quality goods can use a creative advertising approach to create a success story.

Fiscal Year	Net Sales (in millions)	% Increase
1988	$336.3	26.9
1987	265.1	16.7
1986	227.2	31.9
1985	172.2	39.5

The ad on the left was the first ever run by Lands' End; the one on the right is a recent one. Note the consistency of style.

(Courtesy of Lands' End, Inc. Copyright 1988 Lands' End, Inc.)

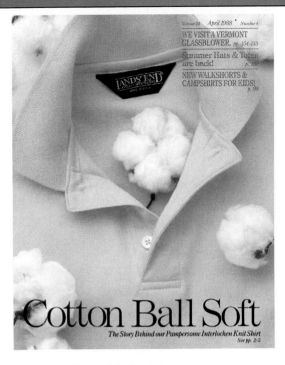

Examples of Lands' End catalogs.
(Courtesy of Lands' End, Inc. Copyright 1988 Lands' End, Inc.)

Sample pages from a Lands' End catalog, including a return envelope.
(Courtesy of Lands' End, Inc. Copyright 1988 Lands' End, Inc.)

AD 16.6

This catalog from the Metropolitan Museum of Art in New York City advertises
many upscale products.

(Courtesy of the Metropolitan Museum of Art.)

Specialty Catalogs   The growth in this field, however, is in the area of specialty catalogs. There are catalogs for every hobby as well as for more general interests such as men's and women's fashions, sporting goods, housewares, gardening, office supplies, and electronics. There are catalogs specifically for purses, rings, cheese and hams, stained-glass supplies, garden benches, and computer accessories—to name just a few. For example, Balducci's fruit and vegetable store in Greenwich Village, New York City, produces a catalog promising overnight delivery of precooked gourmet meals.

Some of these retailers have their own stores, such as L. L. Bean, Williams-Sonoma, Royal Silk, and Banana Republic. Others, such as Hanover House and FBS, only offer their merchandise through catalogs or other retailers. Levi's, for example, has always depended on other retailers to distribute its products, but it is now planning a catalog that, for the first time, will make the entire Levi's line available to its customers. Some of the merchandise is relatively inexpensive, like the Hanover line, which is usually $10 or less. Others are much more upscale. Nieman-Marcus, Sakowitz, Steuben, and Tiffany all offer items priced in the thousands of dollars. The catalog in Ad 16.6 is an example of upscale advertising.

J. Tylee Wilson claimed that in 1986 "consumers were buried under 10 billion catalogs—up from 4.7 billion 5 years ago."* Catalogs are the chief benefi-

*Quoted by Rose Harper in "Outlook '87."

ciaries of the social changes that are making armchair shopping so popular. Many of the consumers who receive these books would probably argue with Wilson's choice of the word "buried." Catalogs are so popular that direct-response consumers receive mailings offering them lists of catalogs available for a charge. People pay for catalogs the way they pay for magazines. An increasing number of catalogs can now be purchased at newsstands.

Designing the Catalog Message   The most important part of the catalog message is the graphics. Products are displayed in attractive settings showing as many details and features as possible. People scan through a catalog and look at pictures. Only after they have been stopped by the visual do they look down to the copy block. Copy is at a minimum and provides such details as composition, fabric, color, sizes, and pricing.

Some catalogs are low-budget, particularly those in special-interest areas such as hobbies and professional supplies. A catalog for woodworkers or plumbers might be printed on cheap paper in black and white. Most general-interest catalogs, however, are moving to quality reproduction with slick paper and full-color printing. The fashion catalogs are often shot at exotic locations, and the reproduction values are excellent.

Some catalogs are designed to create an image, such as the Banana Republic and Caswell-Massey catalogs, which come in unusual sizes and use distinctive illustrative styles (see Ad 16.7). Caswell-Massey is an apothecary that dates back to colonial days and carries an unusual assortment of soaps, brushes, after-shave lotions, and colognes. Banana Republic specializes in the "jungle look" in fashion, and each catalog features a story about some expedition to an exotic location.

A woman ordering merchandise directly from a catalog.
(Courtesy of Teri Stratford.)

AD 16.7
Caswell-Massey and Banana Republic use distinctive catalogs to advertise their merchandise.

(Courtesy of Caswell-Massey Co. Ltd. and Banana Republic.)

AD 16.7 (Continued)

Electronic Catalogs   Catalogs are becoming available in videocassette and computer disk formats. Buick has developed an "electronic catalog" on computer disk. The message is interactive and features animated illustrations. It presents graphic descriptions and detailed text on the Buick line, including complete specifications, and lets you custom-design your dream car.* At present the electronic catalog is being marketed to readers of computer magazines.

Video catalogs are being considered by a number of advertisers. Video offers a dynamic live presentation of the product, its benefits, and its uses. With one-half of American homes owning VCRs, this medium is becoming increasingly important. Cadillac developed a video brochure for Allante, its new luxury car. Air France and Soloflex are also investigating videos for in-home promotions.

*"Software Beats Hard Sell at Buick," *Advertising Age,* November 24, 1986, p. 59.

AD 16.8
An example of a video catalog produced by Royal Silk.
(Courtesy of Royal Silk.)

Print Media

Ads in the mass media are less directly targeted than direct mail, catalogs, or telemarketing. However, they can still provide the opportunity for a direct response. Ads in newspapers and magazines can carry a coupon, an order form, an address, or a telephone number for customers to respond to. The response may be either to purchase something or to ask for more information. In many cases the desired response is an inquiry that becomes a sales lead for field representatives.

In *MaxiMarketing,* Rapp and Collins discuss the power of *double-duty advertising* that combines brand-reinforcement messages with a direct-response campaign to promote a premium, a sample, or a coupon. Giorgio perfume, Cuisinart, and Ford all use multifunctional advertising in magazines that works two or more ways, including direct response.*

Inserts Newspapers also carry preprinted inserts that call for some kind of direct response. Not all inserts are direct response, but some are designed to stimulate an immediate sale and, for this purpose, carry a reply device. The preprinted inserts allow more room for the sales message and better-quality reproduction.

Reply Cards In magazines the response cards may be either *bind-ins* or *blow-ins.* These are free-standing cards that are separate from the ad. Bind-in cards are stapled or glued right into the binding of the magazine adjoining the ad. Ad 16.9 for *Encyclopaedia Britannica* uses bind-in cards. They have to be torn out to be used. Blow-in cards are blown into the magazine after it is printed by special machinery that "puffs" open the pages. These cards are loose and may fall out in distribution, so they are less reliable.

Broadcast Media

Television Television is a major medium for direct marketers who are advertising a broadly targeted product and who have the budget to afford the ever-increasing costs of television advertising. Direct-response advertising on television used to be the province of the late-night hard sell with pitches for vegematics and screwdrivers guaranteed to last a lifetime. As more national marketers such as Time Inc. move into the medium, the direct-response commercial is becoming more general in appeal.

CABLE TELEVISION   Cable television lends itself to direct-response commercials because the medium is more tightly targeted to particular interests. For example, ads on MTV for products targeted to the teenage audience can generate a tremendous response. Sales are soaring on the Home Shopping Network (HSN), a cable network that displays merchandise in living color. From 1986 to 1987 HSN sales rose 296 percent to become one of the top ten direct-order marketers.†

J. C. Penney is the first major retailer to go on air via a cable hookup. Its new interactive home-shopping service will be called Teleaction. Penney says it will invest $40 million in the new "video catalog" service. Customers will be able to order the merchandise on screen by using their push-button phones.‡

---

*Rapp and Collins, *MaxiMarketing,* p. 171.
†"Home Shopping Network Expands Its Game Plan," *Advertising Age,* June 22, 1987, p. 44.
‡"Penney Says Teleaction to Start by September," *Advertising Age,* June 8, 1987, p. 82.

AD 16.9
This ad for the *Encyclopaedia Britannica* uses bind-in cards.
(Courtesy of Encyclopaedia Britannica.)

Radio   Radio has not been a dynamic medium for direct-response advertising. Most experts see the radio audience as too preoccupied with other things to record an address or a telephone number. Home listeners, however, are able to make a note and place a call, and local marketers have had some success selling merchandise this way.

Radio's big advantage is its targeted audience. Teenagers, for example, are easy to reach through radio. There has even been some success selling products such as cellular phones and paging systems specifically to a mobile audience.

*T*ELEMARKETING

telemarketing *A type of marketing that uses the telephone to make a personal sales contact.*

The telephone system is a massive network linking almost every home and business in the country. More direct-marketing dollars are spent on telephone ads using **telemarketing** than on any other medium. The telephone combines personal contact with mass marketing.

Costs

Personal sales calls are very expensive but very persuasive. Telemarketing is almost as persuasive, but a lot less expensive. A personal sales call may cost anywhere from $50 to $100 when you consider time, materials, and transportation. A telephone solicitation may range from $2 to $5 per call. That is still expensive, though, if you compare the cost of a telephone campaign to the cost per thousand of an advertisement placed in any one of the mass media. Telemarketing is four to five times as expensive as direct mail.*

If this medium is so expensive, why would anyone use it? The answer is that the returns are much higher than those generated by mass advertising. Telemarketing has to be efficient to be justifiable. The revenue has to justify the bottom-line costs.

Characteristics

Telemarketing is personal; that is its primary advantage. The human voice is the most persuasive of all communication tools. Although many people regard a telephone solicitation as an interruption, there are still large numbers who like to talk on the telephone. Some people are flattered by receiving a telephone call, even if it is just a sales pitch.

Two-Way   Telephone conversations are also two-way. There is a conversation in which the prospect can ask questions and give responses. This conversation can be tailored to individual interests. Furthermore, if the person isn't a prospect, the caller can find out immediately and end the call.

There is another important aspect of this two-way communication system. Just as the marketer can call the prospect, the customer can call the company. When you think of telemarketing you probably just think of the telephone solicitation, but that is only half the picture. The telephone is also used by the consumer to place orders and to call with questions and complaints. The telephone is a very important tool in *customer service* as well as in getting and taking orders.

wide area telephone service (WATS) *A system of mass telephone calling at discount rates.*

Technology   Two technological changes have spurred the use of telemarketing. The first is the **wide area telephone service** (WATS line), a system pro-

*Katzenstein and Sachs, *Direct Marketing*.

vided by the telephone company that is similar to bulk mail. The price is discounted with use; the more calls made from a single location, the cheaper the cost of each individual call.

The WATS line has made it possible for telemarketers to set up "phone factories" with multiple lines, banks of telephones, and hundreds of trained callers. This mass production of telephone calls has made telemarketing economically feasible.

The other innovation is the incoming WATS line, which we have referred to previously as the 800 number or toll-free number. The number isn't free, of course; the charges go to the company being called rather than to the caller.

Telemarketing Firms   Most companies that use telemarketing hire a specialized company to handle the solicitations and order taking. They do this because most of the activity occurs in bunches. If a company advertises a product on television, for example, the switchboard will be flooded with calls for the next 10 minutes. Companies that do occasional direct-response advertising don't have the facilities to handle a mass response. A service bureau that handles a number of accounts is more capable of handling the bursts of activity that follow promotional activities.

The Message

The most important thing to remember about telemarketing solicitations is that the message has to be simple enough to be delivered over the telephone. If the product requires a demonstration or a complicated explanation, then the message might be better delivered by direct mail.

The message also needs to be compelling. People resent intrusive telephone calls, so there must be a strong initial benefit or reason-why statement to convince prospects to continue listening. The message also needs to be short; most people won't stay on the telephone longer than 4 to 5 minutes for a sales call. That, of course, is still a lot longer than a 30-second commercial.

■ SUMMARY

- Direct marketing always involves a one-on-one relationship with the prospect. It is personal and interactive.
- The growth in direct-response advertising has been stimulated by technologies such as computers, zip codes, toll-free numbers, and credit cards.
- Direct-response advertising can use any advertising medium, but it has to provide some type of response or reply device.
- Direct-response advertising has benefited from the development and maintenance of a data base of customer names, addresses, telephone numbers, and demographic and psychographic characteristics.

- The new push-button consumer is busy and appreciates the convenience of shopping at home or at the office.
- A direct-mail advertising piece is a complex package using an outer envelope to get attention, a cover letter, a brochure, an order card, and a return envelope.
- Catalogs are so popular that consumers will pay to get their names on the mailing lists.
- Telemarketing is the biggest direct-response area; it combines the personal contact of a sales call with mass marketing.

■ QUESTIONS

1. What are the major advantages of direct-response compared to other forms of advertising? The major disadvantages?
2. What types of firms produce direct-response advertising?

3. What is telemarketing? How has it affected the advertising industry?
4. What types of media work best for direct response? Why?

■ FURTHER READINGS

KATZENSTEIN, HERBERT, and WILLIAM S. SACHS. *Direct Marketing.* Columbus, OH: Merrill Publishing Co., 1986.

"Looking into the Future of Direct Marketing." *Direct Marketing,* May 1987, pp. 144–45, 153.

RAPP, STAN, and TOM COLLINS. *MaxiMarketing.* New York: McGraw-Hill Book Co., 1987.

ROBERTS, MARY LOU, and PAUL D. BERGER. *Direct Marketing Management: Text and Cases.* Englewood Cliffs, NJ: Prentice Hall, 1989.

UNI-TEL

YELLOW PAGES

LEHIGH VALLEY
MAR. '87 - FEB. '88

 RESIDENTIAL WHITE PAGES

 MONEY SAVING COUPONS

 ALPHABETICAL BUSINESS SECTION

 CLASSIFIED YELLOW PAGES

 YELLOW PAGES INDEX

17

Creating Yellow Pages and Out-of-home Advertising

Chapter Objectives

When you have completed this chapter you should be able to:

- Understand how consumers use the Yellow Pages to search for information about stores, products, and services
- Describe the characteristics of a well-written and well-designed Yellow Pages ad
- Explain the importance of graphics in poster design
- Understand the effect of a moving audience on the design of a billboard
- Explain the difference between interior and exterior transit advertisements
- Identify innovative media to use to deliver sales, reminder, and action messages

_H_OW TO WALK FOR HELP

OMIT 434½ - 439

Our friend John from Chapter 8 has decided to build that new deck on the side of his house. He knows the underground electrical line coming into the house cuts across the yard in the same area where he wants to put his new deck, and until he locates those lines he doesn't know quite exactly where to build the deck. Who can help him find those lines? He decides to try the Yellow Pages. On the way back into the house he trips and twists his ankle. He limps into the house, gets the telephone book, sinks into his favorite chair, and starts to look for some help.

But where to look? Stumped, he decides to begin with the index at the back of the book. First he looks for "power lines." He finds Power Companies, Power Line Contractors—which might be a possibility—Power Plant Equipment, Power Plants, Power Press, and Power Tools. Nothing here sounds quite right, so he turns to "utilities." Aha! Here he finds Utilities Underground Cable, Pipe & Wire Locating Service. Looking in the book under that heading, he finds five services listed.

While he's thumbing through the Yellow Pages, his aching ankle reminds him that he might need to rent crutches. What kind of store rents crutches? And is there any such store nearby? Sure enough, he finds a listing for "crutches" in the telephone book, but he's not sure they are for rental, so he keeps looking. Under Hospital Equipment and Supplies he finds a "rental" category. That sounds like what he wants. Turning to that category in the book, he finds several pages of stores that rent all kinds of hospital and invalid equipment. He even finds one in his neighborhood; he knows exactly where it is located because the accompanying display ad includes a map.

That is how the Yellow Pages "lets your fingers do the walking," to quote one of the most famous advertising slogans of all time. The slogan works so well because it so clearly dramatizes the benefits of using the Yellow Pages.

_Y_ELLOW PAGES ADVERTISING

The Audience

The behavior of consumers using the Yellow Pages is considerably different from that of consumers using other forms of mass-media advertising. For this reason directory advertisements are designed differently from other ads. The Yellow Pages is consulted by consumers who are interested in buying something. They know what they want, they just don't know where to find it.

Almost 90 percent of those who consult the Yellow Pages follow up with some kind of action.* Because a Yellow Pages ad is the last step in the search for a product or service by a committed consumer, the ads do not have to be intrusive.

PRINCIPLE
Yellow Pages advertising is not intrusive because the audience is looking for the information in the ad.

Functions of the Ad

Directional   Consumer advertising generally attempts to create desire for a product. Yellow Pages advertising, in contrast, need not create desire or awareness because consumers consulting the directory already know what they want. Instead Yellow Pages advertising is considered **directional** in that it points the

directional _Advertising that channels the buyer to the store where the product or service is available._

---

* "How to Write an Ad for the Yellow Pages." Ad by Southwestern Bell Telephone that ran in local community newspapers.

consumer to the store where the product or service is available. It channels the buyers. Many ads, for example, provide an 800 number to help you locate a local dealer.

Although the advertisement doesn't have to attract the attention of an indifferent audience, it does have to stand out in a competitive environment. Once they locate the category, most consumers tend to "browse" through the listings. The decision about which store to call or visit will be based on certain criteria. The most important decision factor is *convenience,* especially location and hours. Most people prefer to shop at the nearest store. Large directories in major metropolitan areas often group businesses by geographical area. Other factors that affect the consumer's decision include the scope of the services or product lines available and the reputation or image of the store.

Creating the Yellow Pages Ad

Index and Headings   The most important feature of Yellow Pages advertising is the category system. Because consumers must be able to find the product, store, or service in the directory, category headings are extremely important.

AD 17.1
Since the breakup of AT&T the number of Yellow Pages directories has increased, which has led to greater competition.
(Courtesy of Bell Atlantic.)

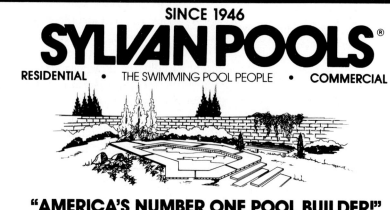

AD 17.2
This ad for Sylvan Pools contains a great deal of valuable information, including several telephone numbers and locations.
(Courtesy of Bernard Hodes Telephone Marketing Services, Inc.)

If there is any doubt about where people would look, then the best practice for an advertiser is to use multiple ads that cover all possible headings. For example, a store selling radios may be listed under appliances or even under television. The critical thing for an advertiser is to know how people search for the store or service and to make sure information is found under every possible heading that they might use.

Critical Information   Certain pieces of information are critical to a Yellow Pages ad. In addition to location and hours of operation, the telephone number must be included. The Yellow Pages, after all, is a directory of phone numbers, and many consumers will call to see if the product is available before making a trip. Note the multiple telephone numbers listed in Ad 17.2.

Writing   Yellow Pages specialists advise using a real headline that focuses upon the service or store personality rather than a label headline that just states the name of the store. The ad should describe the store or the services it provides unless the store's name is a descriptive phrase like "Overnight Auto Service" or "The Computer Exchange." In Ad 17.3, because "Crown" gives no clue as to the product, the advertiser uses a descriptive headline and a photo.

Complicated explanations and demonstrations don't work very well in the Yellow Pages. Any information that is timely or changeable can become a problem because the directory is only published once a year.

The Design   Among the key design elements of Yellow Pages ads are size, image, and graphics.

SIZE   When people browse through the ads in a category, their choice of a company or product is often influenced by the size of the ad. One study reported that the larger the ad, the more favorable the consumer perception.*

*Dennis Hinde and Gary Scofield, "Is Bigger Better in Yellow Pages Ads?" *Journalism Quarterly,* Spring 1984, pp. 185–87.

IMAGE   People make decisions based on the reputation and image of the store. This unique personality should be reflected in the design of the ad. Is it a high-quality, upscale, expensive store? Is it nostalgic or classy or exclusive? When you look through the Yellow Pages for restaurants, women's clothing stores, or hair stylists, can you tell something about the personality of the store from the ad? This personality is communicated through the headline, the illustration, the layout, and the use of type.

GRAPHICS   In addition to communicating a store image, the design performs several other functions. In a competitive market design helps an ad stand out. An illustration, for example, can make an ad more visible. The attention-

AD 17.3
This ad uses a strong benefit head-line that also ties in the name of the product.
(Courtesy of Bernard Hodes Telephone Marketing Services, Inc.)

AD 17.4
This ad for a beauty shop tries to convey a store image as well as consumer information.
(Courtesy of At Rainbow's End.)

HANDLE WITH CROWN

Call today and take advantage of Crown's durable, heavy duty equipment including: Forklift Trucks–Narrow Aisle Trucks–Stockpickers–Stackers–Pallet Trucks–Racks–Shelving–Personnel Carriers–In-Plant Office–Dock Equipment

CROWN lift trucks

Direct Factory Branch

P.O BOX 000, Anytown, USA

000-0000

Sales-Service-Rentals-New & Used
Immediate delivery on many models

AT RAINBOW'S END
"Where Your Beauty Begins"

- CHINA SILK NAILS
- BACKSCRATCHER FIBERGLASS NAILS
- OR WRAP YOUR NATURAL NAILS
- AIR BRUSHING
- NAIL DESIGN
- MANICURE
- PEDICURE
- PARAFFIN THERAPY MANICURES
- SEBASTIAN SKIN CARE COSMETICS

- ALOE VERA SKIN CARE COSMETICS
- BODY WRAPS
- FULL BODY MASSAGE
- CELLULITE MASSAGE
- GIFT CERTIFICATES
- MAKE UP & SKIN CARE LESSONS
- EAR PIERCING
- JEWELRY AND PERFUMES
- WE SHIP PACKAGES

TWO LOCATIONS

Arvada Plaza
9334 W. 58th Avenue
422-3232

Chambers Plaza
15179 E. Colfax #C
343-9898

AD 17.5
This ad for CareUnit demonstrates that most effective Yellow Pages layouts are
bold and visually well organized.
(Courtesy of Comprehensive Care Corporation.)

getting elements should also be big and bold. Spot color, which is becoming
available at an additional cost, contributes tremendously to the impact of the ad.
Ad 17.5 is designed to stand out against the competition.

Simplicity is very important. Specialists advise advertisers to keep the number of elements to a minimum. If you must use a lot of pieces, then organize the
layout carefully so that the visual path is clear and things that belong together are
grouped together. A fanciful display type may be used for the headline to communicate an image, but try to avoid using a variety of faces in a variety of sizes.
Use *bullets* (a series of dots) rather than an extended piece of body copy to list
important points.

Photographs don't reproduce well in phone books, given the quality of the
paper and printing. Line drawings work better, although a high-contrast photo
may be acceptable. Avoid any graphic that has a lot of detail. Full-color art and
photos don't reproduce well. Maps are very important but they need to be
simplified to show only major streets in the immediate neighborhood.

POSTERS

Development of the Poster

A poster is a large placard or sign that is posted in a public place to announce or
publicize something. Almost every culture throughout history has left behind
some form of public message (see Chapter 1). For this reason posters have been
called the oldest form of advertising. Even after a culture has disappeared, its
messages have remained.

A *Visual Message*   Early posters and signs were primarily pictorial or symbolic because most of the population couldn't read. A sculptured wooden shoe over the door indicated the shoemaker; a sign of a lady with a crown indicated the Queens Crown pub. Graphics remain central to the design of posters as well as outdoor advertising.

Aesthetics   Posters and other advertising signs have achieved "art" status and are collected and valued for their aesthetics. Posters became masterpieces following the invention of lithography. During the nineteenth century such artists as Manet, Toulouse-Lautrec, and Beardsley produced posters advertising events such as plays and bicycle races.

Poster competitions for artists are popular even today. Posters, both historic and contemporary, are found on display in galleries and museums. The Swiss and English governments have sponsored programs to encourage posters as art. Posters are probably the only advertising medium that has received such encouragement.*

Message Design

Graphics   As mentioned earlier, posters are characterized by a strong graphic impact. Even if a poster is predominantly type, the type will be designed artistically for maximum impact. The key to most posters, however, is a dominant visual with minimal copy.

PRINCIPLE _____
Strong graphics are central to the design of posters.

Location   Posters are found on buildings, walls, lampposts, bulletin boards, hallways, subway platforms, and bus shelters—anywhere people collect or pass by in great numbers. *Station posters* are a form of transit advertising that uses posters in bus shelters and subway platforms. In Europe and on university campuses special structures called **kiosks** are designed for public posting of notices and advertisements. Some of these locations are places where people walk by; others are places where people wait. The location has a lot to do with the design of the message.

kiosks *Multisided bulletin board structures designed for public posting of messages.*

If people are moving, then the design needs to be simple and easy to read instantly. If people are waiting, then the advertiser has a captive audience, and the poster can present a more complicated message.

OUTDOOR ADVERTISING

billboards *Large structures erected on highways and roads for the display of huge advertising posters.*

Billboards are oversized versions of posters. They are designed to be seen by people traveling by in cars. This is a most unusual situation in that the audience is moving and the advertising is stationary. The word *billboard* goes back to the nineteenth century. At that time advertising posters were called "bills." Enterprising entrepreneurs began leasing space on wooden boards in high-traffic areas where these bills could be posted—hence "billboards."

RSAD – END

The Outdoor Industry

Outdoor advertising is a big industry. It is seen all day, every day. It can't be turned off or tuned out. Because of its continuous presence, it is a constant reminder.

Format   The format of outdoor advertising has a tremendous impact on its message design. The format is extremely big and extremely horizontal, and visu-

*Sally Henderson and Robert Landau, *Billboard Art* (San Francisco: Chronicle Books, 1981); and *The Big Outdoor* (New York: The Institute of Outdoor Advertising).

als and layouts are forced to accommodate these dimensions. Television screens are slightly horizontal, and magazine and newspaper pages are vertical. A design for a magazine or newspaper page doesn't transfer very well to a billboard because of the elongated horizontal dimension.

All three of the standardized poster panel sizes (see Chapter 11) maintain a basic 2 ¼:1 proportion. The *painted bulletin* used for local advertising is even more horizontal than poster panels; the proportion is 3 ½:1.

EXTENSIONS   Extensions can be added to painted billboards to expand the scale and break away from the limits of the long rectangle. The extensions are limited to 5 feet 6 inches at the top and 2 feet at the sides and bottom. These embellishments are sometimes called **cutouts** because they present an irregular shape that reflects something such as a mountain range or a skyscraper.

The Nike campaign created by the Chiat-Day agency uses outdoor displays that are distinctive and memorable because they are so dynamic. The action is focused on a sports figure with an extension of an arm, a leg, or a head outside the limits of the board (see Ad 17.6).

Under these circumstances it should be clear that the primary objectives of the message are awareness, announcement, and reminder. Detailed explanations are not possible; there is no time for elaboration of copy points.

Message Design

The Message   Outdoor messages differ from other advertising messages. Some of the key elements are discussed below.

CONCEPT   Effective outdoor advertising is built on a strong *creative concept* that can be instantly understood. The idea needs to be creative because the message has to get attention and be memorable. Most of all, it has to make the point quickly. For example, a billboard for a doughnut store announcing that it now sells cookies featured a huge, one-word headline filling the entire board that read: "Goody." The two O's in the middle were both round cookies. The underline read: "Winchell's has gone cookies." The concept was expressed in both words and visuals.

COPYWRITING   The copy on a billboard is minimal. Usually there is one line that serves both as a headline and as some kind of product identification. The most important characteristic is *brevity.* The words are short, the phrases are short, and there are no wasted words. Some books suggest that no more than six to seven words be used. The headline is usually a phrase, not a sentence. There is nothing equivalent to the body copy found in a print ad.

AD 17.6
An example of the action-oriented billboards produced for Nike by Chiat-Day.
(Courtesy of Nike.)

AD 17.7
The words and visuals in the Spuds billboard work together to form a
single creative concept, "The Party Animal."
(Courtesy of Anheuser-Busch, Inc.)

The best copy for outdoor is a short, catchy phrase. It needs to catch
attention, but it also needs to be captivating in order to be memorable. Often the
phrase will be a play on words or a twist on a common phrase, such as the
McDonalds' billboards.

For example, a billboard for Orkin pest control showed a package
wrapped up with the word "Orkin" on the tag. The headline read: "A little
something for your ant." A billboard for Best Food mayonnaise showed a
butcher block with tomatoes, lettuce, cheese, and rye bread sitting next to the
mayonnaise bottle. The headline read: "Best on the block."

The Design Because billboards must make a quick and lasting impression,
design is critical to their effectiveness.

LAYOUT The integration of art and headline is critical for the development of a strong concept. The layout is compact with a very simple visual path,
usually beginning with a strong graphic, followed by a catchy headline, and
ending with some kind of product identification. The relationships should be so
clear and so integrated that the elements are perceived as one whole concept
(see Ad 17.7).

GRAPHICS The most important feature of billboard design is high visibility. *Visibility* means that a billboard is conspicuous; it is noticeable; it bursts into
view. The illustration should be an eye-stopper.

What makes something visible? Size is one factor. A billboard is the world's
biggest advertising medium. It offers a grand scale, much larger than life, and
therefore can create tremendous impact. You can depict a 25-foot-long pencil or
a pointing finger that is 48 feet long. The product or the brand label can be
hundreds of times larger than life. Most elements on a billboard are big and
bold—the type as well as the illustrations.

Bold, bright color is another characteristic of impact. The outdoor industry
has done significant research on color and color combinations. It has found that
the greatest impact is created by maximum contrast between two colors. The
strongest contrast, for example, comes from dark colors against white or yellow.

Yellow adds tremendous impact as well as contrast. Bright colors also add impact. The visibility problem is compounded by the fact that outdoor boards are seen at all times of the day and night under all kinds of lighting conditions. The most visible billboards use bright, contrasting colors.

Another aspect of visibility is the clarity of the relationship between foreground and background. In outdoor advertising the best practice is to make this distinction as obvious as possible. A picture of a soft drink against a jungle background will be very hard to perceive when viewed from a moving vehicle at a distance. The background should never compete with the subject.

TYPOGRAPHY   Type demands unusually sensitive handling. It has to be easy to read at a distance by an audience in motion. The outdoor industry has researched type legibility on billboards. Among its conclusions is to avoid all-capital letters because that is the hardest typographical form to read. Ornamental letters, depending upon how fanciful they are, can also be hard to read, as can script and cursive letters. Anything that is unusual can create legibility problems. Experts in outdoor advertising advise using simple, clean, and uncluttered type.*

DISTANCE   Planning for reading at a distance is an important aspect of billboard design. The Institute for Outdoor Advertising has developed a poster distance scale viewer that designers use in planning the layout. Designers realize that a layout on a desk has a very different impact than a billboard by the side of a highway. The viewer lets them evaluate the design as it would be seen at a distance from a moving car.

PRODUCT IDENTIFICATION   Product identification is another important aspect of the design of outdoor advertising. Most billboards focus attention on the product. The distinctive label on a cold, dripping Perrier bottle filled the entire space on one billboard. Underneath was the headline: "It's only natural." The red Smirnoff label with its distinctive typeface appeared on another board next to an olive and a lemon peel. The headline was a play on words: "Olive 'R Twist."

Production of Outdoor

Types of Billboards   The two most common types of billboards are poster panels and painted bulletins.

POSTER PANELS   The design for an outdoor board is supplied by the advertiser or agency. For poster panels, the art is printed on a set of large sheets of paper. Thousands of copies can be printed and distributed around the country. The sheets are then pasted like wallpaper on existing boards by the local outdoor advertising companies who own the boards.

PAINTED BULLETINS   Painted billboards are prepared by artists working for the local outdoor advertising company. They are hand-painted either on location or in the shop on removable panels that can be hoisted up and attached to the billboard frame.

Painting a large-scale image takes an unusual eye because the details are so much larger than life. Up close the work looks like an impressionistic painting because the colors, contrasts, and shading patterns are so exaggerated. From a distance the details blend together to create a recognizable image.

Special Effects   As a result of modern technology, outdoor ads can now utilize a number of special effects.

LIGHTING   Lighting is a very important aspect of outdoor advertising. Illuminated billboards against a nighttime sky can create a compelling visual. In urban areas illuminated boards may be combined with special lighting effects that blink and change colors. Neon may even be added. These displays are called

*A Creative Guide to Outdoor Advertising, (New York: Institute of Outdoor Advertising).

Times Square in New York offers many examples of the elaborate outdoor ads known as spectaculars.

(Courtesy of Comstock.)

spectaculars *Billboards with unusual lighting effects.*

holography *A technique that produces a projected three-dimensional image.*

kinetic boards *Outdoor advertising that uses moving elements.*

spectaculars. Las Vegas and Times Square in New York display many examples of lighted spectaculars.

A new *backlighting* technique used for nighttime showings appears to make the background of the board disappear so that the image pops out against the black sky. Another experiment involves the use of an internally illuminated transparent polyvinyl that gives the appearance of a luminous image projected onto a screen. Some advertisers are experimenting with **holography,** which can project a three-dimensional image from a board or onto a board.

SHAPE Designers have been searching for decades for techniques to break away from the rectangular frame of most boards. Extensions help, but advertisers are also experimenting with designs that create the illusion of 3-D effects by playing with horizons, vanishing lines, and dimensional boxes.

Inflatables are even closer to 3-D. Giant inflatable liquor bottles and cigarette packs made of a heavyweight stitched nylon inflated by a small electric fan have been added to outdoor boards. An especially impressive billboard for Marineland shows a 3-D creation of Orca, Marineland's killer whale, bursting through the board.

MOTION Revolving panels, called **kinetic boards,** are used for messages that change. These two-, three-, or four-sided panels can contain different messages for different products or they can be used to develop a message that evolves. Two- or three-sided stationary panels can be used to create a message that changes as the viewer passes by—different angles giving different versions of the message.

Motors can be added to boards to make pieces and parts move. Disklike wheels and glittery things that flicker in the wind have all been used to create the appearance of motion and color change. Special effects include techniques to make images squeeze, wave, or pour.

TRANSIT ADVERTISING

The Industry

Transit advertising is primarily an urban advertising form that uses vehicles to carry the message to people. The message is on wheels, and it circulates through the community. Occasionally you might see trucks on the highway that carry messages. Many semitrailer trucks carry graphics to identify the company that owns them. Some of these graphics are beautiful, such as the designs on the sides of the Mayflower Moving trucks and the Steelcase trucks. In addition to this corporate identification, the sides of trucks may also be rented out for more general national advertising messages. Trucks are becoming moving billboards on our nation's highways.

interior transit advertising *Advertising on posters that are mounted inside vehicles such as buses, subway cars, and taxis.*

exterior transit advertising *Advertising posters that are mounted on the sides, rear, and top of vehicles.*

The Audience

There are two types of transit advertising—interior and exterior. **Interior transit advertising** is seen by people riding inside buses, subway cars, and some taxis. **Exterior transit advertising** is mounted on the sides, rear, and top of these vehicles, and it is seen by pedestrians and people in nearby cars.

An example of exterior advertising panels.
(Courtesy of Andy D'Angelo/The Stock Option.)

Targeting Transit messages can be targeted to specific audiences if the vehicles follow a regular route. Buses that are assigned to a university route will have a higher proportion of college students, whereas buses that go to and from a shopping mall will probably have a higher proportion of shoppers.

Message Design

car cards *Small advertisements that are mounted in racks inside a vehicle.*

Interior Transit Interior advertising in buses and subways uses a format called **car cards.** These cards are mounted in racks above the windows and in panels at the front and back of the vehicle. The car cards are horizontal, usually 11 inches high by either 28, 42, or 56 inches wide.

Interior advertising is radically different from exterior transit advertising. People sitting in a bus or subway car are a captive audience. Their ride averages 20 to 30 minutes. Some read books or newspapers, but most watch other riders, look out the window, and read and reread the ads. In addition, most people who commute on mass transit ride both ways, so the messages get studied twice.

PRINCIPLE
Interior transit advertising uses longer and more complex messages because it can be studied.

As a result, car cards can have longer and more complex messages than outdoor or exterior panels. The only problem with length is visibility. The messages are read from a distance and frequently at an angle. The type must be big enough to be legible given this seating problem.

Car cards offer other opportunities for extending the message. Many cards come with *tear-offs* and *take-ones.* Tear-offs are pads of coupons or other information that are glued to the car card. Take-ones are pockets filled with flyers or leaflets. Both can be used for coupons, recipes, or just to provide information in more depth.

PRINCIPLE
Exterior transit advertising is designed like small billboards with simple, bold, and catchy messages.

Exterior Transit Exterior advertising panels are very similar to outdoor boards and are designed using the same guidelines. The only difference is that the vehicle carrying the message, as well as the reader, may be in motion. This makes the perception of the message even more difficult. Exterior panels are designed like small billboards: simple, bold, catchy, and legible.

*M*OVIE ADVERTISING

trailers *Advertisements that precede the feature film in a movie theater.*

Most movie theaters will accept filmed commercials to run before the feature. Called **trailers,** these advertisements are similar to television commercials but are usually longer and better produced. Theater messages are usually 45 seconds or 1 minute in length. This gives more time for message development than the typical 30-second television spot. There is even talk of 2-minute minifilms for theater showings.

The Audience

There may be some limited targeting of these messages in terms of location and the type of audience attracted by various kinds of movies. The important audience factor, however, is the attention and concentration generated by the theater environment. The projection of larger-than-life images in a darkened theater is totally unlike the experience of watching television. The impact of the large screen makes for a compelling image that commands total attention. It is very difficult for the audience to turn off or tune out whatever is happening on that screen.

PRINCIPLE
Theater advertising is the most compelling form of advertising because of the impact of larger-than-life images in the dark on the big screen.

That is also one of theater advertising's biggest problems. Some people resent the compelling nature of the message. Because they have paid money for entertainment, they dislike being forced to watch a commercial. This issue is discussed in more detail in the "Concepts and Controversies" box.

THEATER ADVERTISING: DO YOU GET WHAT YOU PAY FOR?

In January 1988 two Boulder, Colorado, dedicated movie-goers were picketing outside a movie theater complex rather than standing in line for tickets. The two women, Marsha Faulconer and Julie Golden, spent the chilly evening urging other movie-goers to voice their displeasure at the advertisements shown before the feature movies.

The two explained that they saw one too many ads inside a movie theater the week before and decided to take their pet peeve public. Golden explained, "I have heard people boo and hiss in the theater and I decided to be more vocal."

The manager explained that the theater limits its commercials to no more than three per film. The theater runs ads for everything from cars to credit cards to the Marine Corps. The manager said he has only re-

ceived ten written complaints about the ads in the past 5 years. He also pointed out that the decision to run ads is not up to the individual theater, but is made by the motion picture companies and distributors.

The two protesters do not intend to start a national campaign, but their complaints have touched a nerve. The assistant manager of the theater even admitted that some of the ads, such as one running for American Express, irritated her as well; however, she thought others are well done enough to be entertaining.

What is your position on theater advertising? Is it a useful way to reach an audience? What can be done to make these messages more acceptable?

Barry Bortnick, "Just Saying No to Movie Ads," *Daily Camera*, January 30, 1988, p. 1B.

Message Design

The critical feature of theater advertising is that it must function as entertainment. People in theaters have a low tolerance for hard-sell messages. Dramas and MTV techniques, with their music and intense imagery, have been particularly effective with theater advertising.

INNOVATIVE MEDIA

Sales Messages

New and novel media are constantly being utilized as vehicles for advertising messages. Pay telephones are beginning to carry advertising space. This can be a highly targeted medium. If you want mall shoppers, then you can reach them at telephone booths in malls; if you want travelers, use the airport telephones; if you want college students, advertise on campus pay telephones.

indicia *The postage label printed by a postage meter.*

Companies that have their own postage meters use the **indicia** for printed messages on the envelopes of the correspondence. Some people have even suggested that the government sell space on postage stamps for advertising messages.

Even garbage and trash cans on the city streets are being used for short messages. These advertisements can carry short copy lines and product symbols. Bus-stop benches are also available for short copy such as slogans, although visuals don't work well on benches.

Reminder Messages

Blimps have been around for decades and, of course, the Goodyear Blimp is a classic example of brand-reminder advertising. Planes pulling banners have been used over major outdoor events such as fairs and football games. More recently, hot air balloons have carried commercial messages.

The Goodyear Blimp is a creative form of brand-reminder advertising.
(Courtesy of Goodyear.)

Athletic competition makes heroes, and heroes are good message endorsers. Consequently almost every sports event is a display for special-interest advertising. All the tennis, skiing, swimming, and golf equipment manufacturers prominently display their brands on the course or on the athletes' clothing.

Other sponsors, such as beer companies, simply like to affiliate with an attention-getting event such as the Indy 500 or the Super Bowl. The Indy cars are covered with decals for the sponsors who underwrite the cost of getting the car into the race and on the track.

Action Messages

Grocery carts now have placard space that can be rented. These are reminder messages, but they function like point-of-purchase advertising (see Chapter 18). They confront the shopper at the moment when he or she is ready to make a purchase.

Coupons are being printed on the back of tickets to major events like college football games. Coupons are also showing up on the back of grocery store receipts.

THE MALE GOLFER

In our society professional sports and advertising have become inseparable. Every major sporting event from the Super Bowl to the Indy 500 has its commercial sponsors. In turn, sports figures are often used as spokespersons because so many people identify with them. By examining a lifestyle study of male golfers, we can decide whether the endorsement of a sports celebrity and other promotional techniques are likely to help sell a product.

Profile

The study focuses on men who played golf 12 times or more within the previous year. Male golfers are a distinct group who represent only 7 percent of the total male population. According to the study, male golfers are more likely than men in general to be over the age of 45 and to be retired, and they are less likely to have children living at home. They more frequently have attended college and have household incomes higher than $30,000. Golfers are also self-confident and consider themselves leaders.

Because golfers earn a high income, they tend to be less price-conscious than men in general. Most golfers are more concerned with the quality of a product than the price. They are less likely than men in general to pay cash for all their purchases, to check prices, and to shop for specials.

Golfers are also more active than men in general. They take part in social activities, including dinner parties, sporting events, and cultural activities, such as visiting museums and libraries. They are also more physically active, taking part in exercise and sports activities.

Golfers tend to have liberal views on television and advertising. They are less concerned about the amount of sex and violence on television, and they are less likely to oppose television advertising of alcoholic beverages or ads directed toward children.

Golfer Bernhard Langer endorsing certain brands of sporting goods.
(Courtesy of Dave Cannon/Allsport.)

Exercise

What types of special advertising techniques would appeal to male golfers? Do you think they would use sporting goods that are endorsed by a professional golfer? Does it make sense to spend money promoting these products to male golfers, given the fact that so few men fit into this category?

Source: Needham Harper Worldwide, "Life Style Profile: The Male Golfer," prepared by Diana Kinzie, October 1985.

■ SUMMARY

- The Yellow Pages is the most universal advertising medium.
- Yellow Pages ads focus on the service offered or the store personality.
- Posters are the oldest form of advertising.
- Posters are graphic, and the focus of the message is the visual.
- Outdoor advertising delivers messages to moving audiences using "quick-impact" techniques such as strong graphics and short, catchy phrases.

- A billboard is the largest advertising medium.
- National billboards are distributed as preprinted posters; local billboards are original, hand-painted art.
- Interior transit messages can be studied; exterior messages must be seen in a glance.
- Theater advertising is the most compelling form of advertising because of the impact of larger-than-life images on the big screen.

QUESTIONS

1. Why is Yellow Pages advertising described as "directional?"

2. Outdoor advertising is described as "quick impact." What does that mean? How do you design effective messages for this medium?

3. Explain what design techniques are used to increase the visibility of outdoor advertising messages.

4. What are the differences in message design and content between interior and exterior transit advertising?

FURTHER READINGS

The Big Outdoor. New York: The Institute of Outdoor Advertising.

A Creative Guide to Outdoor Advertising. New York: The Institute of Outdoor Advertising.

FLETCHER, ALAN D. *Yellow Pages Advertising.* Chesterfield, MO: American Association of Yellow Pages Publishers, 1986.

HENDERSON, SALLY, and ROBERT LANDAU. *Billboard Art.* San Francisco: Chronicle Books, 1981.

"Multiple Directories: A Publisher's Point of View." *Update,* Summer 1986, pp. 2–3.

"Yellow Pages Co-op Advertising: The $2 Billion Advertisers Bonanza." *Update,* Summer 1986, pp. 4–5.

CHEE·TOS®

Cheese puffs—baked or fried puffed cheese snacks—are a small part of the larger category of salty snack products. Nearly all American households buy salty snacks; nearly 50 percent buy cheese puffs.

CHEE·TOS®, introduced in 1963, is the best-selling brand of cheese puffs. Planters is a distant second with about a quarter of the sales volume of CHEE·TOS®. Borden, Anheuser Busch, and a variety of private-label and regionally popular brands make up the rest of the market. When CHEE·TOS® puffs sell well, so do other cheese puffs; when CHEE·TOS® sales decline, so do those of the other brands. Between 1968 and 1977, sales of CHEE·TOS® puffs grew significantly, increasing in some years by as much as 15 percent. During these years, the advertising campaign featured a mouse and the slogan "CHEESE THAT GOES CRUNCH®." Importantly, the advertising focus was on fun.

In 1978, after a period of sustained growth, sales began to level off. During this time, CHEE·TOS® brand had shifted its advertising focus from fun to the product's ingredients ("real cheese"). In addition, a variety of CHEE·TOS® branded flavors were on the market at that time, cluttering the product line. This confused the customer and Frito-Lay's sales force, resulting in overall softness in CHEE·TOS® brand sales.

In 1985 the company thinned its product line to two flavors—regular and CHEDDAR VALLEY® Sharp—and decreased the price difference between CHEE·TOS® puffs and its major competitors. It also reintroduced the idea of fun along with the "CHEESE THAT GOES CRUNCH®" slogan in its advertising. Sales rebounded in 1985, showing an increase of 7 percent.

In 1986 DDB Needham, the advertising agency for CHEE·TOS® brand, created and introduced a new cartoon character—CHESTER CHEETAH®. CHESTER CHEETAH® was intended to personify the fun that had been successful in earlier campaigns. He also was intended to appeal to "the kid in all of us."

CHESTER CHEETAH® reflects characteristics of CHEE·TOS® puffs themselves: CHEE·TOS® puffs are orange and "go fast"; CHESTER CHEETAH® is orange and "goes fast." CHEE·TOS® puffs are cheesy and lovable; CHESTER CHEETAH® is cheesy and lovable too. CHESTER CHEETAH'S® primary personality trait is his "cool." He is a laid-back, easygoing dude. He has a positive outlook on life (like buyers of cheese puffs). The only time CHESTER CHEETAH® isn't cool is when he thinks about CHEE·TOS® puffs; then he loses all self-control. Every attempt to get his paws on them results in failure and in some hilarious mishap for CHESTER CHEETAH®.

In CHEE·TOS® brand advertising, CHESTER CHEETAH® always behaves exactly the same way, and advertising situations remain faithful to his persona:

- *Cool:* The essence of CHESTER CHEETAH® is always being cool but losing his cool over CHEE·TOS® puffs.
- *The plot:* CHESTER CHEETAH® is always chasing CHEE·TOS® puffs. The plot of every CHESTER CHEETAH® commercial is some variation of that chase.
- *Language:* CHESTER CHEETAH'S® language is the colloquial dialect of "hip" young Americans. He expresses himself in rhyme with colorful and memorable words.
- *Behavior:* CHESTER CHEETAH® behaves in two ways: He either does something cool, or he recklessly chases CHEE·TOS® puffs. In commercials we see CHESTER CHEETAH® simply relaxing or engaging in activities popular with contemporary American youth, like playing sports, listening to music, or just taking it easy in a fun setting.
- *Wardrobe:* CHESTER CHEETAH® wears high-top sneakers and sunglasses. Any additional clothing is limited to accessories that fit specific situations. If he were skiing, for instance, he might wear mittens and a scarf. Unlike the Pink Panther, however, he never disguises himself.
- *"The Crunch":* CHESTER CHEETAH® gets "crunched" when he is just about to get his paws on CHEE·TOS® puffs. As a result of his concentration on the product, he inevitably overlooks some flaw in his plan that causes him to miss the target. The line "IT'S NOT EASY BEING CHEESY®" signals CHESTER CHEETAH'S® return to coolness and is his recognition that he lost his cool because of his urge for CHEE·TOS® puffs.

In CHESTER CHEETAH'S® first year as a "spokescat," his commercials were shown on American television as well as in Puerto Rico, Australia, and Canada. CHEE·TOS® brand sales rose, despite a modest advertising budget. A recent Frito-Lay image study found that approximately 40 percent of mothers and 75 percent of children were familiar with CHESTER CHEETAH®. In CHESTER CHEETAH'S® second year, Frito-Lay employed CHESTER CHEETAH® in several new commercials, published a CHESTER CHEETAH® calendar and poster, and marketed a stuffed CHESTER CHEETAH® doll, CHESTER CHEETAH® drinking glasses, and licensed a line of CHESTER CHEETAH® clothing. With CHESTER CHEETAH® as the hero of CHEE·TOS® advertising, the brand continues to lead the category, with no sign that his appeal to cheese puff users is even beginning to fade.

Questions for Discussion

1. Can you think of characters other than CHESTER CHEETAH® that were created to capture the personality of a product? Give examples. Do you think this strategy is effective? Why or why not?

2. In what ways is CHESTER CHEETAH® a good "spokescat" for cheese puffs? What might his appeal be for the typical heavy cheese puffs buyer?

3. How long do you think the CHESTER CHEETAH® image will attract consumers? What options are available to Frito-Lay should the campaign lose its effectiveness?

(Courtesy of Frito-Lay, Inc.)

18

Sales Promotion

Chapter Outline

Sales Promotion: Trick or Treat?
Defining Sales Promotion
The Size of Sales Promotion
The Role of Sales Promotion in Marketing
The Role of Sales Promotion in Advertising
Types of Sales Promotion
Suggestions for Success

Chapter Objectives

When you have completed this chapter you should be able to:

- Distinguish between sales promotion and advertising
- Explain how promotion and advertising work together within the marketing mix
- List several types of promotions, both for consumers and for resellers
- Understand why advertisers are spending increasing sums of money on sales promotion
- Explain the advantages and disadvantages of sales promotion as compared to advertising

SALES PROMOTIONS: TRICK OR TREAT?

Every Halloween since 1979, millions of kids run home from school clutching not only their costumes and paper jack-o'-lanterns, but also a brightly decorated plastic bag stuffed with coupons and product samples.

The kids probably thought their teachers were sending home a treat for their parents, but the real trick was getting the schools involved in a large-scale commercial venture. Sampling Corporation of America, a large promotion company, started the program and now distributes the sample bags free to 10 million 6-to-12-year-olds, covering half the country's households with children in that age group. "We can do something that major brands can't do for themselves. We can get products and coupons home to parents through the schools," says Stephen Kaplan, Sampling's executive vice president. "That's what we specialize in. We distribute samples and coupons in an environment that will maximize their usage and reinforce the brand name and existence."

Packed inside the bags are reflective safety stickers to wear while trick-or-treating, a safety poster, and a booklet for parents containing ideas for simple costumes, makeup, party games, safety tips, and, of course, coupons. Usually several product samples are included, most typically candy, snacks, an aseptically packaged juice box, and, sometimes, toothpaste. The promotion has the support of the National Safety Council, and the schools hand out the bags in conjunction with either a police officer or a teacher giving a safety speech that adds further credibility to the program.

Is the program successful? According to Burke Market Research, both brand and total advertising awareness for one brand included in the program increased by 40 percentage points. Usage of the brand increased by 35 percentage points, and actual purchases of the brand increased by 20 percentage points. Consumers also responded well to the coupons, with 17 percent using them and 65 percent indicating plans to do so.

This proven success has prompted 80 percent of the sponsors to continue, with about eight national brands participating every year. The rate for a page insert in the parent pamphlets is $147,500; this includes the company's brand logo on the bag and all other materials plus sales support materials.

It appears that Sampling Corp. has solved the mystery of promoting to young kids and their families through the schools. It is now developing a similar campaign for summer safety with bags of samples, coupons, stickers, and posters that reinforce awareness of water, bicycle, fire, and general safety rules.*

The promotional strategy employed by Sampling Corporation suggests an important change in the way marketers are communicating with audiences today. No longer is advertising the best alternative for all companies. Sales promotion now appears to be equally good at capturing the minds, hearts, and wallets of consumers and resellers.

The emergence of sales promotion has created a great deal of turmoil and confusion. Take one of the users of Sampling Corporation—Kraft, Inc. Things were once simple for an advertiser like Kraft. In order to sell macaroni-and-cheese dinners, salad dressings, and handy snacks, the company merely had to run commercials on the "Big Three" network affiliates, on one or two locals, and in three or four women's magazines, and they were able to reach the great

*Joanne Y. Cleaver, "Promo Dresses Up for Halloween," *Advertising Age,* November 16, 1987, pp. S-12, S-13, S-14.

majority of their market. Not anymore. Cable television, videocassette recorders, and independent stations have splintered the mass television audience. Meanwhile, more magazines are catering to specific target audiences. The cost of media is growing, and the rising number of women in the labor force makes it more difficult to reach the crucial female audience through mass media.

So what has Kraft done? Instead of pumping more money each year into traditional advertising media, they are increasing their expenditures on sales-promotion techniques, such as cents-off coupons, rebates, giveaways, and sweepstakes that better reach market segments.

Advertising agencies, already faced with higher client expectations and cost problems (see Chapter 4), have been hit by 30-to-40-percent reductions in media budgets by their major clients. Agencies initially reacted to this trend by arguing that advertising was a far more effective communication device than sales promotion. Some still believe this. Others have come to realize that sales promotion is here to stay, and they are learning how to incorporate it into the advertising campaign. Yet there is still a great deal of confusion about the definition of sales promotion, its role in marketing, and how it should interact with advertising.

DEFINING SALES PROMOTION

sales promotion *Those marketing activities that add value to the product for a limited period of time to stimulate consumer purchasing and dealer effectiveness.*

The evolution of **sales promotion** has also changed the way experts define the practice. At one point, the official definition of sales promotion proposed by the American Marketing Association was: "Marketing activities, other than personal selling, advertising, and publicity, that stimulate consumer purchasing and dealer effectiveness, such as displays, shows, exhibitions, demonstrations, and various nonrecurrent selling efforts not in the ordinary routine."* This somewhat bland definition has been replaced in this book by one that more accurately portrays modern sales promotion: Those marketing activities that *add to the basic value* of the product for a *limited time period* and thus *directly stimulate* consumer purchases and increase sales-force and reseller effectiveness.

PRINCIPLE
Sales promotion offers an extra incentive for consumers to take action.

This definition implies, first, that sales promotion offers an "extra incentive" for consumers to take action. Although this extra incentive is usually in the form of a price reduction, it may also be additional amounts of the product, cash, prizes, premiums, and so on. Second, sales promotions usually include specified limits that may take the form of an expiration date or a limited quantity of the merchandise. Finally, sales promotion has three somewhat different goals, which relate to its three target audiences: (1) to increase immediate *customer* sales, (2) to increase support among the marketer's *sales force,* and (3) to gain the support of *middlemen* (resellers) in marketing the product.

THE SIZE OF SALES PROMOTION

Determining the actual size of sales promotion is difficult and varies according to which agency collects the data. For example, the most recent estimates provided by Robert Coen, senior vice president at McCann-Erickson/New York, put 1986 expenditures on sales promotion at $106.7 billion (see Table 18.1). That figure represented a 13 percent increase over the previous year, compared to 7 percent for advertising.† Today more money is spent on sales promotion than on advertising.

*American Marketing Association, *Marketing Definitions: A Glossary of Marketing Terms* (Chicago: 1960), p. 20.
†*Marketing and Media Decisions,* July 1987, pp. 153–54.

TABLE 18.1
Sales Promotion
Figures for 1986

Sales Promotion			% Increase over 1985
Direct mail	$17,145	16%	+11%
P-O-P/display	13,302	12%	+20
Premiums and incentives*	14,044	13%	+10
Meetings and conventions	34,119	32%	+10
Trade shows & exhibits	6,208	6%	+ 7
Prom. advertising	8,052	8%	+ 6
Print/A-V/misc.	9,333	9%	+18
Coupon redemption	4,497	4%	+14
Total	**$106,700**	**100%**	**+13**

*Includes $904 million in sweepstakes and contests.
Source: Marketing and Media Decisions, July 1987, pp. 153–54.

Reasons for the Growth of Sales Promotion

So why are companies spending more and more money on sales promotion? Several reasons exist.

PRINCIPLE ————————
*Unlike most advertising, sales pro-
motion stimulates immediate sales.*

Short-Term Solutions   "It's a matter of short-term vs. long-term thinking," says Robert Prentice, a marketing consultant and expert on promotion strategy.* He and others say that product managers are under pressure to generate quarterly sales increases. Because advertising often produces long-term benefits, advertisers are investing more money in sales promotion, which generates immediate results.

Need for Accountability   Another reason for the growth is the accountability of sales-promotion techniques. It is relatively easy to determine whether a given sales promotion strategy accomplished its stated objectives. Moreover, this assessment can be done rather quickly. Providing accountability is critical at a time when marketers want to know exactly what they are getting for their promotional dollars.

Economic Factors   Advertisers also cite economic reasons for the shift. While advertising budgets have remained fairly constant, television advertising prices have climbed. In addition, since 1977, newspapers and magazines have more than doubled their fees.† Therefore, advertisers feel pressured to invest their money in areas like sales promotion that produce immediate, tangible results.

Consumer Behavior   Other reasons for the move toward sales promotion reflect changes in the marketplace. For instance, shoppers today are better educated, more selective, and less loyal to brand names. In addition, many new markets are developing because of demographic shifts. The affluent "gray" market, the "new man," the "Yuppie," and the working woman are all markets that appear responsive to the benefits of sales promotion. From the consumer's perspective, sales promotion reduces the *risk* associated with purchase. This attitude was reinforced during the recession of the 1970s when people were desperately looking for opportunities to save. That economic downturn introduced many consumers to the benefits of sales promotion, and they apparently enjoyed the experience.

*Paul L. Edwards, "Sales Promotion Comes into Its Own," *Advertising Age,* July 28, 1986, p. 65.
†Kevin T. Higgins, "Sales Promotion Spending Closing in on Advertising," *Marketing News,* July 4, 1986, p. 8.

The Product Life Cycle   Although we are constantly bombarded with the terms "new" and "improved," very few entirely new product categories have emerged since World War II. Today's marketplace is characterized by mature product categories and considerable consumer experience and knowledge. In most industries the battle is for market share rather than general product growth. Although advertising remains the best tool for launching new products, sales promotion is often the most effective strategy for increasing share and volume. For example, experts estimate that over 80 percent of coffee sales are due to some sort of sales promotion.*

The Pricing Cycle   Retail pricing has also been a factor in creating opportunities for the increased use of sales promotion, particularly in the highly volatile supermarket environment. Prices soared in the inflationary cycle of the 1970s as the result of increased costs of labor, raw materials, and manufacturing. This situation led to the growth of low-priced private-label brands and the emergence of generic products. Having adjusted to these lower-priced goods, consumers have come to expect constant short-term price reductions such as coupons, sales, and price promotions.

The Power of the Retailer   The final reason for the growth of sales promotion is the increasing power of the modern retailer. Very simply, of the $106 billion spent on sales promotion, over half is used to maintain in-store distribu-

(Courtesy of United Feature Syndicate.)

*Stan Rapp and Thomas L. Collins, *MaxiMarketing* (New York: McGraw-Hill Book Co., 1987), p. 142.

tion, to obtain desirable shelf location, and to promote special in-store merchandising support.*

It is estimated that quite soon just a few retailers will dominate retail distribution. The increased concentration of buying power among fewer and fewer retail accounts has enabled retailers to demand the financial support of manufacturers through sales-promotion techniques.

THE ROLE OF SALES PROMOTION IN MARKETING

As explained in Chapter 3, sales promotion is just one element of the promotional mix available to the marketer. Because of its unique characteristics, however, sales promotion can accomplish certain communication goals that the other elements cannot. For example, research suggests that sales promotion excels at the following:

1. Obtaining trial of a new product
2. Establishing a purchasing pattern by persuading triers to rebuy
3. Increasing consumption of a product
4. Neutralizing competitive promotions
5. Affecting the sales of companion products

Conversely, sales promotion cannot:

1. Build brand loyalty
2. Reverse a declining sales trend
3. Convert rejection of an inferior product into acceptance†

Sales promotion should be incorporated into the company's strategic marketing planning, along with advertising, personal selling, and public relations. This means establishing sales-promotion goals and selecting appropriate strategies. A separate budget should be set up for sales promotion. Finally, management should evaluate the sales promotion performance.

Although all these elements are important, setting promotional objectives is particularly important. Our definition of sales promotion implied three broad objectives:

1. To stimulate demand by industrial users or household consumers
2. To improve the marketing performance of middlemen
3. To supplement and coordinate advertising, personal selling, and public relations activities

The more specific objectives of sales promotion are quite similar to those of advertising. For example, in order to *get customers to try a new product*—Pert Shampoo—Procter & Gamble sent out over 60 million free samples through the mail. To *encourage present customers to use the product in greater quantities* United Airlines, American Airlines, and other large airlines introduced frequent-flyer programs. To *increase the amount of impulse buying by consumers* Miller Brewing set up an end-of-the-aisle display manned by ex–football star L. C. Greenwood. Finally, in order to get *greater cooperation from retailers,* Homer Formby brought store managers to central locations for 3 days of training, wining, and dining.

Thus sales promotion has become an important element in the strategy of many marketers. Like advertising, it is not right for everyone, and it will be effective only if it is carefully managed.

*Keith M. Jones, "Held Hostage by the Trade?" *Advertising Age,* April 27, 1987, p. 18.
†Don E. Schultz, Dennis Martin, and William P. Brown, *Strategic Advertising Campaigns,* 2nd ed. (Lincolnwood, IL: Crain Books, 1984), pp. 388–90.

THE ROLE OF SALES PROMOTION IN ADVERTISING

Differences and Similarities

What are the differences and similarities between advertising and sales promotion? Among the major differences are the following:

Advertising . . .	Sales promotion . . .
• Is interested in creating an image; this takes time.	• Is interested in creating immediate action, preferably a sale.
• Relies heavily on emotional appeals.	• Relies heavily on rational appeals.
• Tends to add intangible value to the good or service.	• Tends to add tangible value to the good or service.
• Makes a moderate contribution to profitability.	• Makes a high contribution to profitability.

However, the two have much in common. According to Leonard Lodish, international expert on sales promotion, advertising and sales promotion share the same roles: to increase the number of customers, and to increase the use of the product by current customers. Both tasks attempt to change audience perceptions about the product or institution, and both attempt to make people do something.* Of course, the specific techniques used to accomplish these tasks differ.

Introducing a New Product

One area in which advertising and promotion work well together is the introduction of new products and services. Suppose we are introducing a new corn chip named Corn Crunchies. Our first problem is to create awareness of this product. This is the real strength of advertising. However, sometimes advertising should be combined with an appropriate sales-promotion device calling attention to the advertising and the brand name. Possibilities are colorful point-of-purchase displays, a reduced introductory price, and a special tie-in with a well-known chip dip company.

Creating awareness will only take the product so far. Corn Crunchies must also be perceived as offering some clear benefit compared to competitors to convince consumers to purchase it. Advertising promotes this perception through informational and transformational executions. Sales promotion enhances the message by offering coupons as part of the ad (known as an *overlay* ad), mailing free samples of Corn Crunchies to households, and conducting a contest in conjunction with the product introduction during the July 4th holiday. If we have successfully implemented this *pull strategy*, consumers will be convinced of the value of Corn Crunchies and go to their supermarkets and demand that the product be stocked. They will *pull* it through the channel of distribution.

Unfortunately creating awareness and desire means nothing unless the product is available where the consumer thinks it should be. Somehow resellers (the trade) must be convinced that the product will move off the shelves before they will stock it. Therefore, a *push promotional strategy* is used. This means that we convince members of the distribution network to carry and market Corn Crunchies. We literally *push* the product through the channel. This is accomplished through two devices, *trade advertising* and *trade sales promotion.* Trade advertising directed at wholesalers and retailers can be effective in providing resellers with important information. In addition, trade sales-promotion tech-

*Leonard M. Lodish, *The Advertising and Promotion Challenge* (New York: Oxford University Press, 1986).

niques, especially price discounts, point-of-purchase displays, and advertising allowances, help to gain shelf space.

After the initial purchase we want the customer to repeat purchase, and we want retailers to allocate more shelf space to Corn Crunchies. This means that advertising copy changes to remind customers about the positive experience they had with the product, and sales promotion reinforces their loyalty with coupons, rebates, and other rewards. Retailers will be rewarded as well.

Sales promotion is not a replacement for advertising. If advertising makes people aware of the product and establishes some sort of customer interest, sales promotion brings the customer closer to the point of purchase—the final stimulus to act. The two strategies should work together to create a greater effect than either could alone.

TYPES OF SALES PROMOTION

Sales promotion strategies are divided into three primary types: end-user or consumer, reseller or trade, and sales-force. Because only the first two have implications for advertising, we will not discuss sales-force strategies here.

Consumer Sales Promotion

Consumer sales promotions are directed at the ultimate user of the good or service. They are intended to "presell" consumers so that when they go into a store they will be looking for a particular brand. Most often, consumer sales promotions are the responsibility of the product manager, along with the advertising campaign planner, the advertising department, or a sales promotion agency or advertising agency.

The primary strengths of consumer sales promotions are their variety and flexibility. There are a large number of techniques that can be combined to meet almost any objective of the sales-promotion planner. This flexibility means that sales promotion can be employed by all kinds of businesses. Figure 18.1 indicates how promotional dollars are allocated among the various sales promotion activities. Figure 18.2 displays the level of consumer participation in the various promotions.

FIGURE 18.1
This figure illustrates how sales promotion monies are divided among the various forms.
Source: Russ Bowman and Industry Associates, *Marketing & Media Decisions,* July 1987, p. 154.

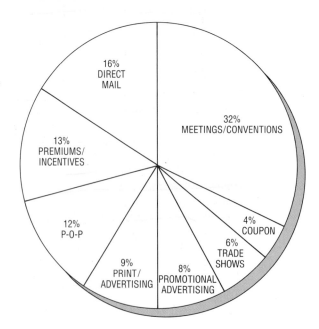

FIGURE 18.2

Source: UMS Consumer Survey and *Marketing & Media Decisions,* September 1987, p. 124.

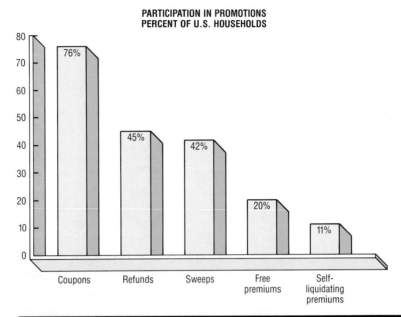

PARTICIPATION IN PROMOTIONS
PERCENT OF U.S. HOUSEHOLDS

AD 18.1
A unique coupon that is redeemable on any of these SmithKline consumer products.
(Courtesy of SmithKline Consumer Products.)

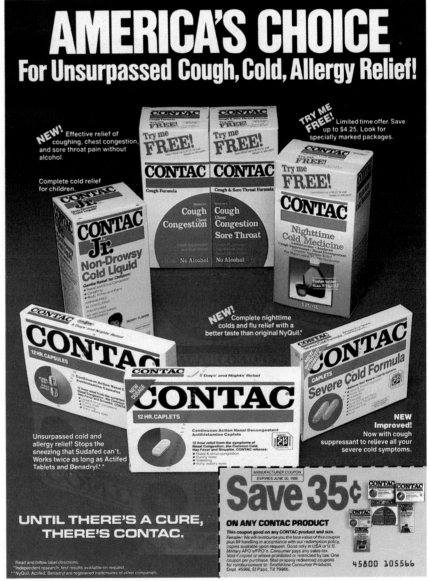

AD 18.2
Budget combines a coupon with a premium.
(Courtesy of CPM Incorporated.)

Price Deals   A temporary reduction in the price of a product is called a **price deal.** Price deals are commonly used to encourage trial of a new product, to persuade existing users to buy more or at a different time, or to convince new users to try an established product. They are effective only if price is an important factor in brand choice or if consumers are not brand loyal.

There are two principal types of consumer price deals: cents-off deals and price-pack deals. *Cents-off deals* are a reduction in the normal price charged for a good or service (for example, "was $1,000, now $500," "50 percent off"). Cents-off deals can be announced at the point of sale or through mass or direct advertising. Point-of-sale announcements include the package itself and signs near the product or elsewhere in the store. Advertising includes sales flyers, newspaper ads, and broadcast ads. Both types of cents-off deals can be initiated by either the manufacturer, the wholesaler, or the retailer.

Price-pack deals provide the consumer with something extra through the package itself. There are two types of pack deals, bonus packs and banded packs.

coupons *Legal certificates offered by manufacturers and retailers that grant specified savings on selected products when presented for redemption at the point of purchase.*

Bonus packs contain additional amounts of product free when a standard size of the product is purchased at the regular price; for example, Purina Dog Food with 25 percent more in the bag. Often this technique is used to introduce a new large-size package of the product. When one or more units of a product are sold at a reduced price compared to the regular single-unit price, a *banded pack* is being offered. Sometimes the products are physically banded together. In most cases the products are simply offered as two-for, three-for, five-for, and so on.

Coupons **Coupons** are legal certificates offered by manufacturers and retailers that grant specified savings on selected products when presented for redemption at the point of purchase. *Manufacturer-sponsored coupons* can be redeemed at any outlet distributing the product. *Retailer-sponsored coupons* can only be redeemed at the specified retail outlet. The primary advantage of the coupon is that it allows the advertiser to lower prices without relying on cooperation from the retailer.

Manufacturer-sponsored coupons can be distributed directly (direct mail, door-to-door); through media (newspaper/magazine ads, free-standing inserts); in or on the package itself; or through the retailer (co-op advertising). Manufacturers also pay retailers a fee for handling their coupons. Producers of packaged goods issued 180 billion coupons in 1985, with a face value of about $50 billion. According to A. C. Nielsen, consumers redeemed 6.5 billion of these, saving more than $2 billion on their shopping bills.*

contests *Sales-promotion activities that require participants to compete for a prize on the basis of some skill or ability.*

sweepstakes *Sales-promotion activities that require participants to submit their names to be included in a drawing or other type of chance selection.*

Contests and Sweepstakes The popularity of contests and sweepstakes grew dramatically during the 1980s. These strategies create excitement by promising "something for nothing" and offering impressive prizes. **Contests** require participants to compete for a prize or prizes on the basis of some sort of skill or ability. **Sweepstakes** require only that participants submit their names to be included in a drawing or another chance selection.

A good contest or sweepstakes generates a high degree of consumer involvement, which can revive lagging sales, help obtain on-floor displays, furnish merchandising excitement for dealers and salespeople, give vitality and a theme to advertising, and create interest in a low-interest product. Contests are viewed favorably by advertising designers because the copy tends to write itself as long as it is supported by background enthusiasm and excitement. Ad 18.3 illustrates a sweepstakes run by two famous companies.

refund *An offer by the marketer to return a certain amount of money to the consumer who purchases the product.*

Refunds Simply stated, a **refund** is an offer by the marketer to return a certain amount of money to the consumer who purchases the product (see Ad 18.4). Most refunds encourage product purchase by creating a deadline. The details of the refund offer are generally distributed through print media or direct mail. General information may be delivered through broadcast media. Refunds are attractive because they stimulate sales without the high costs and waste associated with coupons. The key to success is to make the refund as uncomplicated and unrestrictive as possible. The refund may take the form of a cash *rebate* plus a low-value coupon for the same product or other company products, a high-value coupon alone, or a coupon good toward the brand purchased plus several other brands in the manufacturer's line.

Refunds have proved to be a very effective promotional device. According to Shopper's Pay Day, a research firm, money refund offers generate five times as much business as product coupons for comparable values.†

---

*Felix Kessler, "The Costly Coupon Craze," *Fortune,* June 9, 1986, pp. 83–84.
†Ronnie Telzer, "Rebates Challenge Coupons' Redeeming Values," *Advertising Age,* March 23, 1987, pp. S-18, S-20.

AD 18.3

This ad illustrates a sweepstakes initiated by Miles Labs, makers of Alka-Seltzer, and H&R Block.

(Courtesy of H&R Block and Miles Incorporated.)

Consumer Products Division

MILES LABORATORIES, INC.

P.O. Box 340
Elkhart, IN 46515
Phone (219) 264-8988
TWX 810/294-2259

CLIENT: MILES LABORATORIES
PRODUCT: ALKA-SELTZER
TITLE: "TIME LAPSE"

COMM'L NO.: MIAS 7304
LENGTH: 30 SECONDS

(MUSIC)
ANNCR: So you're doing your own taxes again.

WOMAN: 'Night, Harry.
MAN: Um hum.

ANNCR: But with the new tax laws for '87, you might have bitten off more than you can chew.

WOMAN: Morning, Harry.

ANNCR: So when taxing head and stomach aches write you off,

send Alka-Seltzer to the rescue.

MAN: Hello, H&R Block?

ANNCR: And get help fast.

TAX PREPARER: All done.

MAN: I feel better already.

ANNCR: Alka-Seltzer and H&R Block. Where more Americans find fast relief.

HENRY BLOCK: Win a lifetime of tax time relief. Enter the Alka-Seltzer H&R Block Sweepstakes.

---

premium *A tangible reward received for performing a particular act, such as purchasing a product or visiting the point of purchase.*

Premium Offers   A **premium** is a tangible reward received for performing a particular act, usually purchasing a product or visiting the point of purchase. The toy in Cracker Jacks, glassware in a box of detergent, or a transistor radio given for taking a real estate tour are examples of premiums. Premiums are usually free. If not, the charge tends to be quite low. Over $6 billion was spent on premiums in 1986.*

DIRECT VERSUS MAIL   There are two general types of premiums: direct and mail. *Direct premiums* award the incentive immediately, at the time of purchase. Approximately $1.8 billion was spent on this area in 1985.† There are four variations of direct premiums:

Incentive Marketing, December 1986.
†"Prizes Become More Sophisticated," *Advertising Age,* May 2, 1985, p. 46.

1. Store premiums: given to customers at the retail site
2. In-packs: inserted in the package at the factory
3. On-packs: placed on the outside of the package at the factory
4. Container premiums: the package is the premium

   Mail premiums (a $1.8-billion industry) require the customer to take some action before receiving the premium. The original mail premium is called a *self-liquidator*. Self-liquidators usually require that some proof of purchase and payment be mailed in before receiving the premium. The amount of payment is sufficient to cover the cost of the item, handling, mailing, packaging, and taxes, if any. The food industry is the largest user of self-liquidating premiums (see Ad 18.5). The *coupon plan* or *continuity-coupon plan* is the second type of mail premium. It requires the customer to save coupons or special labels attached to the product that can be redeemed for merchandise. This plan has been used by cigarette and diaper manufacturers. The final type of mail premium is the *free-in-the-mail* premium. In this case the customer mails in a purchase request and

AD 18.4
Refunds are very popular in the automobile industry.
(Courtesy of Subaru of America.)

UP TO
$1500
CASH BACK.
OR 3.9%APR
ON A
SUBARU.

We've just made a great deal on a Subaru better than ever. When you buy a 1987 Subaru you can choose up to $1500 cash back* or 3.9% A.P.R. financing.**
So if getting that much cash back wasn't enough to get you into a Subaru showroom, 3.9% financing should be. Just be sure and visit your Subaru dealer before Aug. 3. After that, all you'll have are the usual reasons to buy a Subaru. Like durability, reliability, performance and quality.

SUBARU.
OFFER ENDS AUGUST 3RD

*Dealer participation may affect final price. At participating dealers, you must choose from select models from dealer inventory by August 3, 1987.
**3.9% Annual Percentage Rate financing for 24 months, to qualified buyers through Marine Midland Automotive Financial Corp. on select Subaru models at participating dealers.

proof of purchase to the advertiser. For example, the "Opportunity Calling" program sponsored by AT&T offers premiums at a greatly reduced price depending on the amount of long-distance billing.

One advantage of premiums is their ability to enhance an advertising campaign or a brand image. The best examples of this strategy are those brands or companies that are symbolized by characters such as the Campbell Soup Kids, Charlie the Tuna, Tony the Tiger, Cap'n Crunch, Ronald McDonald, and the Pillsbury Doughboy.

Specialty Advertising   Advertising specialties are similar to premiums, except that the consumer does not have to purchase anything in order to receive the item. These items normally have a promotional message printed on them somewhere. Although specialties are often given away as year-end gifts (the calendar hanging in the kitchen), they can be used throughout the year in particular sales situations. For example, some specialties, including pens, pencils, and organizers, are ideal for desktops. Other items work well because they are attention-grabbing novelties. Balloons, fans, litter bags, and tote bags are in this cate-

AD 18.5
This ad, featuring the rock group Genesis, is an excellent example of a self-liquidating premium.
(Courtesy of D. D. B. Needham and Genesis.)

AD 18.6
Purina provides a sample in conjunction with an advertisement.
(Courtesy of Ralston Purina Company.)

gory. The ideal specialty item is something that is kept out in the open where a great number of people can see it, such as a calendar or penholder with the company's name on it.

trading stamps *A sales-promotion program that involves giving consumers stamps that can later be traded in for merchandise.*

Trading Stamps   The 1950s and 1960s were the heyday of **trading stamps,** a program in which the customer usually gets one stamp for every dime spent in participating stores. The trading stamp industry may never again experience the tremendous success of those decades, when over 250 firms distributed stamps, but such programs are far from dead. A 1982 survey conducted by Sperry & Hutchinson Company, Inc. (S&H), discovered that 20 million households saved trading stamps from food stores, drugstores, and other retail establishments. Of the respondents who saved stamps, 14 percent were new savers (last 2 years), and 78 percent of these people were between 18 and 34 years old.*

sampling *An offer that allows the customer to use or experience the product or service free of charge or for a very small fee.*

Consumer Sampling   **Sampling** allows the consumer to experience the product or service free of charge or for a small fee. It is a very effective strategy

*"Are Trading Stamps Making a Comeback?" *Marketing News,* August 17, 1986, p. 6.

for introducing a new or modified product or for dislodging an entrenched market leader. To be successful, the product sampled must virtually sell itself on the basis of a certain uniqueness and ability to create a strong positive impact with minimal trial experience.

Samples can be distributed to consumers in several ways. The most common method is through the mail. An alternative is to hire companies specializing in door-to-door distribution. Advertisers can design ads with coupons for free samples, place samples in special packages, or distribute samples at special in-store displays. To illustrate a very successful sampling program, each year *Rolling Stone* magazine sponsors a Spring Break Showcase in Daytona Beach, Florida. All national advertisers are offered booths through which they may distribute free samples. In 1986 products given away included DC Comics, Diet Coke, Ralph Lauren's Chaps cologne, Wilkinson Sword razor blades, and VLI Today's Sponge.*

In general, retailers and manufacturers maintain that sampling can boost sales volume as much as five to ten times during a product demonstration and 10 to 15 percent thereafter. Sampling is generally most effective when reinforced on the spot with product coupons. Most consumers like sampling because they have not lost any money if they do not like the product.† Although all of these consumer sales promotion techniques can be effective alone, they can also be combined to create a tremendous impact. The Nestlé Foods Corporation did just this with the material shown in Ad 18.7.

PRINCIPLE

Sampling, which allows the consumer to try the product or service free, is effective for new product introductions.

AD 18.7

Nestlé Foods positioned three of its products—Raisinets®, Goobers®, and Crunch™—as the "Home Video Candy" in a promotion where consumers could redeem a mail-in certificate with any VCR movie rental receipt along with proof of purchase and receive a $2 cash rebate. The certificate was available in free-standing inserts and at point-of-purchase displays, and the three candy products were packaged in a take-home pack. The promotion was developed by Saxton Communications Group, New York.

(Courtesy of Nestlé Foods Corporation.)

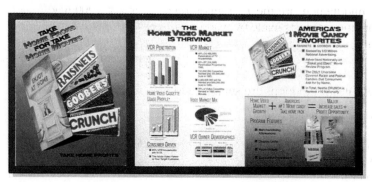

*Mark Bittman, "'Free' Samples a Costly but Effective Opportunity," *Advertising Age,* February 2, 1987, p. S-16.

†*The Wall Street Journal,* August 28, 1986, p. 19.

AD 18.8
Companies such as A. G. Industries advertise to potential users of P-O-P.
(Courtesy of A.G. Industries, Inc.)

Reseller (Trade) Sales Promotion

Resellers, or middlemen, are the 1.7 million retailers and 300,000 wholesalers who distribute the products made by manufacturers to other resellers and ultimate users. The manufacturer usually is certain the product is acceptable only if resellers are willing to carry and *push* it. Sales promotion is used to bring resellers to that point of conviction.

Reseller sales promotions are supposed to accomplish four overall goals:

1. Stimulate in-store merchandising or other trade support (for example, feature pricing, superior store location, and/or shelf space)
2. Manipulate levels of inventory held by wholesalers and retailers
3. Expand product distribution to new areas of the country or new classes of trade
4. Create a high level of excitement about the product among those responsible for selling it

The ultimate gauge of a successful reseller promotion is whether sales increase among ultimate users.

A great many promotional devices that are designed to motivate middlemen to engage in certain sales activities are available to the manufacturer. The major ones are discussed in the following paragraphs.

point-of-purchase display *A display designed by the manufacturer and distributed to retailers in order to promote a particular brand or line of products.*

Point-of-Purchase Displays   A **point-of-purchase display** (P-O-P) is designed by the manufacturer and distributed to retailers in order to promote a particular brand or group of products. Although the forms vary by industry, P-O-P can include special racks, display cartons, banners, signs, price cards, and mechanical product dispensers. Point-of-purchase is the only advertising that occurs when all the elements of the sale—the consumer, the money, and the product—come together at the same time. As we move toward a self-service retail environment in which fewer and fewer customers expect help from sales clerks, the role of point-of-purchase will continue to increase. According to the Point of Purchase Advertising Institute (POPAI), only 19 percent of consumers have a specific purchase in mind when they walk into a store. It is the other 81 percent that P-O-P is directed toward.*

PRINCIPLE
Point-of-purchase brings all the elements of the sale together: the consumer, the product, and the money.

Point-of-purchase is a big-business effort ($8.2 billion in 1985) that must be well thought out if it is to be successful. Advertisers must consider not only whether P-O-P is appealing to the end user but also whether it will be used by the reseller. Retailers will use a P-O-P only if they are convinced that it will generate greater sales.

A P-O-P should be coordinated with the theme used in advertisements. This not only acts as a type of repetition, it also creates a last-minute association between the campaign and the place of decision.

Contests and Sweepstakes   As in the case of consumer sales promotion, contests and sweepstakes can be developed to motivate middlemen. Contests are far more common, primarily because contest prizes are usually associated with the sale of the sponsor's product. A sales quota is set, for example, and the company or individual who exceeds the quota by the largest percentage wins the contest.

The need to create the desired amount of excitement and motivation has forced designers to develop spectacular contests with very impressive prizes. In 1985, for example, $1.45 billion was spent on merchandise and $771 million was spent on travel.† Frequent contests quickly lose their excitement. Contests are effective only if they take place periodically. If conducted properly, contests can provide short-term benefits and can improve the relationship between the manufacturer and the reseller.

Trade Shows   Many industries present and sell their merchandise at trade shows that allow demonstrating the product, providing information, answering questions, comparing competing brands, and writing orders. In turn, trade shows permit manufacturers to gather a great deal of information about their competition. In an environment where all the companies are attempting to give a clear picture of their products to potential customers, competitors can easily compare quality, features, prices, and technology.

Because of the tremendous importance of trade shows, companies spend a great deal of money each year (approximately $7 billion) planning and staging them.‡ For some companies, this expense represents most of their promotional expenditure.

---

*J. Max Robbins, "Making Point-of-Purchase More Pointed," *Adweek,* November 10, 1986, p. 8.
†Monci Jo Williams, "The No-Win Game of Price Promotion," *Fortune,* July 11, 1985, p. 92.
‡Melanie Rich, "Regional Shows Give Small Marketers an Even Break," *Marketing News,* May 10, 1985, p. 15.

push money (*spiffs*) *A monetary bonus paid to a salesperson based on units sold over a period of time.*

dealer loader *A premium given to a retailer by a manufacturer for buying a certain quantity of product.*

trade deals *An arrangement in which the retailer agrees to give the manufacturer's product a special promotional effort in return for product discounts, goods, or cash.*

Push Money **Push money,** or *spiffs,* is a monetary bonus paid to a salesperson based on units sold over a period of time. For example, a manufacturer of air conditioners might offer a $50 bonus for model EJ1, $75 for model EJ19, and $100 for model EX3 between April 1 and October 1. At the end of that period each salesperson sends in evidence of total sales to the manufacturer and receives a check for the appropriate amount.

Dealer Loaders A **dealer loader** is a premium (comparable to a consumer premium) that is given to a retailer by a manufacturer for buying a certain amount of product. The two most common types of dealer loaders are called *buying loaders* and *display loaders.* Buying loaders award gifts for buying a certain order size. Display loaders award the display to the retailer after it has been taken apart. Both techniques can be effective in getting sufficient amounts of a new product into retail outlets or in getting a point-of-purchase display into the store. The underlying motivation for both arrangements is to sell large amounts of the product in a short period of time.

Trade Deals **Trade deals** are the most important reseller sales-promotion technique. A retailer is "on deal" when she or he agrees to give the manufacturer's product a special promotional effort that it would not normally receive. These promotional efforts can take the form of special displays, extra purchases, superior store locations, or just greater promotion in general. In return, retailers sometimes receive special allowances, discounts, goods, or cash.

No one knows exactly how much money is spent on trade deals; experts estimate approximately $8 billion to $12 billion annually.* In some industries, such as grocery products, electronics, computers, and automobiles, trade deals are expected. A manufacturer would find it impossible to compete in these industries without offering trade discounts. In fact, the requirement to "deal" has become so prevalent that many advertisers fear that it is now more important in determining which products receive the greatest promotion than the value of the product or the expertise of the manufacturer. In the grocery field, for example, approximately 60 percent of all manufacturers' sales are accompanied by a trade deal averaging about 12 percent of the asking price.†

TYPES OF TRADE DEALS There are two general types of trade deals. The first is referred to as *buying allowances* and includes situations in which a manufacturer pays a middleman a set amount of money for purchasing a certain amount of the product during a specified time period. All the retailer has to do is meet the purchase requirements. The payment may be given in the form of a check from the manufacturer or a reduction in the face value of an invoice.

The second category of trade deals includes advertising and display allowances. An *advertising allowance* is a common technique employed primarily in the consumer-products area in which the manufacturer pays the wholesaler or retailer a certain amount of money for advertising the manufacturer's product. This allowance can be a flat dollar amount, or it can be a percentage of gross purchases during a specified time period. *Cooperative advertising* involves a contractual arrangement between the manufacturer and the middlemen whereby the manufacturer agrees to pay a part or all of the advertising expenses incurred by the middlemen. A *display allowance* involves a direct payment of cash or goods to the retailer if the retailer agrees to set up the display as specified. The manufacturer requires the retailer to sign a certificate of agreement before receiving payment.

*Higgins, "Sales Promotion," p. 8.
†Jones, "Held Hostage," p. 18.

Introducing new Fudge Jumbles in three flavors

BROWN SUGAR OATMEAL

COCONUT OATMEAL

PEANUT BUTTER OATMEAL

It's refreshingly different

That means increased sales in your dessert baking mix section

- unique three layer bar satisfies consumer need for dessert variety
- contains real oatmeal, coconut, peanuts and brown sugar fulfilling consumer demand for "wholesome" desserts
- appeals to families and adults as a hand-held snack bar or as an after-dinner dessert
- 83% of consumers who tasted Fudge Jumbles said they would buy*
- available exclusively from Pillsbury

* Home Use Test, July 1982

AD 18.9
An example of the type of advertising, directed at resellers, that accompanies trade deals.
(Courtesy of The Pillsbury Company.)

*S*UGGESTIONS FOR SUCCESS

It should be obvious by now that sales promotion is a very diverse area. Trying to become an expert on all aspects of sales promotion may be unrealistic, and special skills in certain areas may be best learned on the job. Carmela Maresca, vice president–management supervisor for Ogilvy & Mather Promotions, and Leslie R. Wolff, vice president of the Creative Director, offer 12 tips on how to create a successful sales promotion:

1. Don't discount the basic product. Add value.
2. Brand your promotions. They should be exclusive to you.
3. Focus on the future. Look for ways to develop repeat business.
4. Theme your promotions. Have them reinforce the advertising.
5. Make your promotions targeted and quantifiable.
6. Look for ways to reward your best, most frequent customers.
7. Look for cross-promotional opportunities where you can come out on top.
8. Look for ways to make your customers feel good about you.
9. Strive to present the promotion in a first-class way.
10. Make the promotion exciting and rewarding for your staff and the consumers to participate in.

11. Make the promotions fun and easy to execute.

12. Test your promotions.*

It is apparent that sales promotion will continue to grow as a promotional alternative. Whether it will diminish the importance of advertising is still debatable, but certainly the varieties and styles of sales promotion are changing the world of advertising.

■ SUMMARY

Sales promotion is designed to promote short-term profits, whereas advertising promotes long-term goals.

Sales promotion works in tandem with advertising during different stages of the product-adoption process.

Sales promotion can be directed at either final consumers or resellers.

Among the most popular consumer promotions are coupons, refunds, contests and sweepstakes, premiums, and consumer sampling.

Reseller sales promotions include point-of-purchase displays, trade shows, push money, and dealer loaders.

■ QUESTIONS

1. What is sales promotion? What are the broad goals of sales promotion in terms of its three target audiences?

2. Why has sales promotion grown so rapidly in recent years?

3. How do sales promotion and advertising differ? What objectives is each one best suited to achieve?

4. What are the four goals that reseller sales promotions attempt to achieve?

5. You have just been named product manager for Bright White, a new laundry detergent that will be introduced to the market within the next 6 months. What type of sales promotion strategy would work best for this product? What types of advertising would enhance this strategy? What would your target audience be?

■ FURTHER READINGS

Jones, Keith M. "Held Hostage by the Trade?" *Advertising Age,* April 27, 1987, p. 18.

Lodish, Leonard M. *The Advertising and Promotion Challenge.* New York: Oxford University Press, 1986.

"Panelists Give 12 Tips on How to Improve Promotions." *Marketing News,* May 8, 1987, p. 7.

Schultz, Don E., Dennis Martin, and William P. Brown, *Strategic Advertising Campaigns,* 2nd ed. Lincolnwood, IL: Crain Books, 1984.

*"Panelists Give 12 Tips on How to Improve Promotions," *Marketing News,* May 8, 1987, p. 7.

19 *Public Relations*

DON'T READ

Chapter Outline

Describing Public Relations
Who Actually Performs Public Relations Activities?
Comparing Public Relations and Advertising
Using Advertising and Public Relations Together
Public Relations and Integrated Marketing Communications
Arenas in Which Public Relations Operates
Evaluating Public Relations

Chapter Objectives

When you have completed this chapter you should be able to:

- Understand what public relations is, how it differs from advertising, and what its advantages are
- Explain how public relations, advertising, and other marketing communications can work together to achieve greater benefit for an organization
- Identify the areas in which public relations operates and some of the activities performed in those areas
- Understand the value and importance of measuring the results of public relations efforts

DESCRIBING PUBLIC RELATIONS

In Chapter 3 we discussed the concept of *integrated marketing communications* (IMC), in which the various elements of the marketing mix work together to increase the effectiveness of the marketing effort. One element of this mix is public relations. Public relations is not advertising, but it increasingly works in tandem with advertising to produce an integrated message. This chapter will describe what public relations is and what it does, and will then explain how public relations and advertising can complement each other.

Public relations is not easy to define. It is often defined by what it is not. Public relations is *not* advertising. It isn't just press agentry, such as promoting circuses, movies, and galas. Neither is it lobbying or influence peddling.

Although numerous definitions of **public relations** exist, there is no universally accepted definition of the discipline. The National Assembly of the Public Relations Society of America has endorsed a description of public relations that states, in part:

> Public relations serves a wide variety of institutions in society such as business, trade unions, government agencies, voluntary associations, foundations, hospitals and educational and religious institutions. To achieve their goals, these institutions must develop effective relationships with many different audiences or publics such as employees, members, customers, local communities, shareholders, and other institutions, and with society at large.
>
> The managements of institutions need to understand the attitudes and values of their public in order to achieve institutional goals.
>
> As a management function, public relations encompasses the following:
>
> - Anticipating, analyzing, and interpreting public opinion, attitudes and issues that impact, for good or ill, on the operations and plans of the organization.
> - Counseling management at all levels in the organization with regard to policy decisions, courses of action, and communication, taking into account their public ramifications and the organization's social or citizenship responsibilities.

public relations *A management function enabling organizations to achieve effective relationships with their various audiences through an understanding of audience opinions, attitudes, and values.*

TABLE 19.1
Listed Below Are the 15 Largest U.S. Public Relations Firms with Their Annual Income and the Number of People They Employ

Agency	Fee Income	Employees
1. Hill and Knowlton	$100,202,000	1,800
2. Burson-Marsteller		1,875
3. Ogilvy & Mather PR Group	31,000,000	640
4. Manning, Selvage & Lee	21,674,000	334
5. Daniel J. Edelman	20,871,013	336
6. Doremus Porter Novelli	20,846,942	289
7. Fleishman-Hillard	18,363,221	223
8. Ketchum Public Relations	17,775,000	234
9. Golin/Harris Communications	17,375,000	296
10. Ruder Finn & Rotman		260
11. Regis McKenna	12,660,000	149
12. Rogers & Cowan	10,469,643	137
13. Howard J. Rubenstein Assocs.		120
14. Creamer Dickson Basford	8,000,000	120
15. The Rowland Co.		90+

Source: J. R. O'Dwyer Company, Inc., New York.

• Researching, conducting, and evaluating, on a continuing basis, programs of action and communications to achieve informed public understanding necessary to the success of an organization's aims.*

PRINCIPLE ⎯⎯⎯⎯⎯⎯⎯⎯⎯
Public relations attempts to create positive opinions.

This definition treats public relations as a management function that is practiced by companies, governments, trade and professional associations, and other nonprofit organizations such as hospitals, universities, and religious groups. Its audiences may be external (customers, the general public) and also internal (employees, stockholders). Its purposes are to create positive opinions about the organization, promote products and services, raise operating funds and capital, and generate support.

Traditionally, public relations has been thought of as a communications tool. But as the above description indicates, public relations functions best when it is integrated into management research, planning, and decision making.

WHO ACTUALLY PERFORMS PUBLIC RELATIONS ACTIVITIES?

In most companies and other organizations the public relations function is clearly defined and staffed. In larger organizations this function may be the responsibility of a department that can range in size from a few managers to 50 or more people.

In addition, public relations agencies abound in the United States. Thousands of these agencies, large and small, serve clients in virtually every city in the country. Most public relations agencies contain only a handful of practitioners. Many specialize in just one subject area or one community. The larger agencies have hundreds of employees in offices in major U.S. and foreign media centers.

Public relations agencies charge fees for their services, which are usually determined by the level and cost of personnel assigned to an account. The annual fee from a large client may be $750,000 and in some cases may exceed a million dollars. Because these sums are considerably smaller than the sums received by advertising agencies, the major U.S. public relations firms are smaller than the big advertising agencies.

COMPARING PUBLIC RELATIONS AND ADVERTISING

Similarities

Like advertising, public relations programs are often implemented through mass media channels. Advertising and public relations also have common planning steps, including audience and market research, setting objectives, segmenting and selecting target audiences, and establishing communications strategies.

Differences

PRINCIPLE ⎯⎯⎯⎯⎯⎯⎯⎯⎯
Rather than purchasing time and space, public relations experts persuade the media to use the information in articles and programs.

To communicate messages, advertisers purchase time and space in media, including television, radio, newspapers, magazines, transit media (for example, buses and subways), and billboards. Public relations practitioners have a different approach to the media. Rather than purchasing time or space to communicate their messages, they seek to *persuade* media "gatekeepers" to carry their information.

These "gatekeepers" include writers, producers, editors, talk-show coordinators, and newscasters. The public relations message placed with gatekeepers

*Public Relations Society of America, "Official Statement on Public Relations," *Public Relations Journal, 1986–1987,* Public Relations Society of America Register Issue, June 1986, p. 6.

**TABLE 19.2
Agencies and Clients**

Listed below are the five largest public relations agencies, their parent organizations, and some of their better-known clients.	
Agency	**Clients**
Hill and Knowlton
Subsidiary of JWT Group, Inc.	Aetna
Celestial Seasonings
Eastern Airlines
B. F. Goodrich Co.
U.S. Satellite Broadcasting Co.
Burson-Marsteller
Subsidiary of Young &
Rubicam, Inc.	Beatrice Foods Co., Inc.
Bethlehem Steel
Coca-Cola Co.
Quaker State Oil
U.S. Postal Service
The Ogilvy & Mather
Public Relations Group
Division of Ogilvy &
Mather Worldwide	Dow Jones
Frito-Lay, Inc.
General Foods Corp.
Memorex Computer Supplies
Shell Oil Co.
Doremus Porter Novelli	Audi of America
Export-Import Bank of the U.S.
General Mills, Inc.
GTE
National Institutes of Health
Manning, Selvage, & Lee, Inc.
Subsidiary of D'Arcy Masius
Benton & Bowles	American Motors
Disneyland Hotel
National Coffee Assn.
The Sporting News
Upjohn Co.

Source: J. R. O'Dwyer Company, Inc., New York.

finds its way into news and feature stories, editorials, op-ed pieces (on the page opposite the editorial page in newspapers), entertainment reviews, syndicated columns, news and talk shows, and other television and radio programs.

For example, the American Association of Retired Persons (AARP), the nation's largest organization of people aged 50 and older, has undertaken a national program to reduce health-care costs without sacrificing the quality of care. Part of this program involves educating older consumers about these issues. To reach this large audience, the AARP can *advertise*—that is, create print advertisements and purchase space in newspapers to carry the ads. The organization can also persuade television talk shows to invite AARP spokespersons to appear and encourage radio call-in programs to air the association's view of the issues. The latter two uses of the media are *public relations* tactics.

In addition to these media approaches, public relations utilizes numerous nonmedia channels to communicate its messages. Examples are speeches to business, professional, and other target audiences; programs channeled through civic, social, and religious organizations; information in corporate and other newsletters; videotapes for employees and organization members; classroom education (for instance, a curriculum module on good grooming offered by a cosmetics company to junior high schools); retail messages; trade-show programs; and participation in conferences and conventions.

Advantages of Advertising

Advertising has certain characteristics that distinguish it from public relations. Because advertisers pay the media for time and space, they can present their messages exactly as they wish (limited only by FTC and industry standards). But public relations practitioners do not have this control over message content.

Among the services provided by public relations agencies is training spokespersons for various causes and institutions.

(Courtesy of Doremus Porter Novelli.)

They may plant the seed of an idea, but the final message will be shaped by the magazine writer, the television news editor, or the columnist. Also, advertisers can buy *frequency* (the number of times an ad or a commercial will appear) and *reach* (the percent of the target audience exposed to the message). In public relations the media control these conditions.

Advantages of Public Relations

Although public relations has little control over the exact content of the message or the timing and frequency of message delivery, there are other aspects of communication in which public relations has advantages that advertising does not. The major advantages of public relations over advertising are *credibility* and *message length*.

PRINCIPLE _____

Public relations people have less control over placement and content of their messages than do advertisers, but their messages are more believable.

Credibility   The advantage in credibility stems from the fact that when viewers, listeners, and readers are exposed to an ad they know it is an ad. They understand that the message was created and paid for by the sponsoring organization. But a message from an organization that is accepted by a medium and worked into its editorial, news, feature, or program content has the credibility of media "endorsement." In other words, information delivered through the non-advertising portion of the media is usually more disarming and believable.

Message Length   A second advantage of public relations is message length. Usually a news or feature treatment of an issue is longer than a television commercial, which normally runs for a minute or less.

USING ADVERTISING AND PUBLIC RELATIONS TOGETHER

As discussed at the beginning of the chapter, public relations and advertising work best when they work together. For example, an engaging advertising idea such as Mike the Chimp as a personality for General Mills Fruit Loops can be extended and reinforced through the public relations tactic of placing Mike on a multicity media tour to serve as a "spokesprimate" for the brand.

Another combination of advertising and public relations involves using one discipline to fill in media gaps or seasonal periods when the other is not engaged. Take, for example, Freixenet sparkling wines from Spain. Most of the company's sales, and hence much of its advertising, take place during the December-January holiday season. To ignore the summer months, however, would be to miss out on other sales opportunities. So the company's public relations agency places articles and features during this period to maintain awareness and promote summer uses (such as picnic drinks) of Freixenet products.

In cases where advertising is not permitted or is considered inappropriate, public relations becomes the primary means of reaching and persuading target audiences. For example, it is illegal to advertise prescription drugs directly to consumers. These products may only be advertised to health-care providers. In order to create a "pull" strategy (see Chapter 1) public relations is employed. The new indications (or symptoms) for which a prescription drug can be used might serve as a news item. Increased incidence (occurrence) of a disease that can be treated by a particular drug might also make the news. A physician spokesperson may be placed on a talk show to discuss proper uses of a class of medications. In each case the pharmaceutical company's public relations staff and agency strive to get their product mentioned in the news and feature stories and on television.

Although advertising is becoming more common among physicians, dentists, lawyers, architects, and other professionals, public relations remains the primary means of communicating these services. Tactics can include brochures and pamphlets, speeches given before community groups, professional papers delivered at conferences and symposia (and then publicized in both professional and lay media), and feature stories in local newspapers.

*P*UBLIC RELATIONS AND INTEGRATED MARKETING COMMUNICATIONS

It seems obvious that public relations and advertising should work together with trade and consumer promotion, direct-response marketing, and personal selling to achieve an organization goal. However, such coordination is more the exception than the norm.

As "spokesprimate" for Fruit Loops, Mike the Chimp undertakes public relations tours for General Mills.
(Courtesy of Doremus Porter Novelli.)

Freixenet uses public relations to maintain consumer awareness of its products during the summer.
(Courtesy of Doremus Porter Novelli.)

The Problem of Specialization

Traditionally, public relations, advertising, and the other marketing communications fields have operated relatively independently. There are several reasons for this. Each field's services are usually provided by a different "supplier" to a company or other organization. Thus advertising is planned, created, produced, and placed in the media by an advertising agency; public relations efforts are conceived and implemented by a public relations agency; and so forth. Only among smaller, less-specialized agencies are the different disciplines all under one roof.

In companies, nonprofit groups, and other organizations, advertising and public relations have also been compartmentalized. As a result, neither side has understood the other very well. Advertising has usually been well integrated into the organization's marketing management structure, whereas public relations has often been relegated to a separate department that is brought in on occasion to help publicize a product.

The Move Toward Integration

Today this separation is breaking down, and the move toward integrated marketing communications is gaining momentum. The advantages of integration are considerable. Most important is the increased effectiveness that results from adopting common strategies and delivering consistent, uniform messages from all sources to the audience. Evidence increasingly demonstrates that integrating marketing communications can increase sales and achieve other objectives.

Another reason for the integration of advertising, public relations, and other marketing techniques is the rapid increase in mergers among agencies. Although a few advertising agencies have long had public relations departments or owned public relations agencies, a recent trend has emerged: "super-agencies" containing companies that perform advertising, public relations, direct-response, promotion, and other specialty services. These super-agencies have adopted integrated marketing communications to help their clients sell more goods and services and to increase their own revenues and profits by attracting more of their clients' marketing dollar.

A recent survey of managers in "client" organizations indicated that although most of them welcome the integration of advertising and public relations, this process is just starting to occur in most organizations.* Survey respondents considered public relations to be an effective marketing communications tool, designed primarily to make consumers more aware of the product and to improve the product's image rather than to generate an immediate increase in sales. They also thought of public relations as a tool to reinforce, rather than to expand, advertising message coverage. In addition, managers predicted that public relations will increase in importance within the marketing communications mix because of rising media costs for ads and the increasing clutter of advertising, which tends to lower attention and message recall. Managers compared these negative trends in advertising to the lower costs and higher value of public relations.

PRINCIPLE
Public relations can be an important marketing tool in an integrated marketing communication program.

Problems of Integration

Planning   Integrating advertising and public relations is not easy. The first need is for common planning. The various disciplines must cooperate to produce an integrated marketing communications plan. Included in this planning phase is integrated research. Marketing research expenditures can be better utilized if they benefit all parts of the communications mix. At present it is more common for the client or the advertising agency to conduct research and for the public relations practitioners to become involved later, learning what they can from the completed studies.

Staffing   Another requirement for making advertising, public relations, and related disciplines work together is integrated staffing. Practitioners from each area must be placed in a common operating structure with oversight and coordination. Without this operating relationship, coordinated planning, creative development, implementation, and evaluation are unlikely.

A RENAS IN WHICH PUBLIC RELATIONS OPERATES

marketing public relations *An area of public relations activity involving the marketing of products and services.*

Probably the most common arena for public relations activities is in the marketing of products and services. In fact, this area is often known as **marketing public relations.** This is an unfortunate designation because it suggests that other arenas of public relations do not involve marketing approaches. In fact, any of the areas discussed in this section can benefit from a public relations approach that is based on marketing analysis, planning, implementation, and control.

Products and Services

Public relations can play a significant role in promoting products and services such as breakfast drinks, toys, medications, professional services, and public transportation. It can contribute to the audience's positive perceptions of the product or service. Public relations can also contribute, through media and nonmedia channels, to the behavior changes that are the usual objectives of marketing efforts: trial, purchase, and repeat purchase.

To cite one example, Tang, the orange breakfast drink, is a well-known trademark of General Foods. To boost declining sales, General Foods intro-

*Thomas R. Duncan, "Marketing Public Relations: A Survey of the Need for Integration," unpublished paper, Ball State University.

duced new Sugar-Free Tang as the first and only sugar-free, low-calorie orange breakfast drink. The program emphasized public relations to increase trade interest, heighten consumer awareness, and improve sales. Tang's primary market was mothers of younger children. This led to the creation of the 1986 Tang March Across America for Mothers Against Drunk Driving (MADD), the first coast-to-coast walk for this cause.

The Tang public relations agency, Doremus Porter Novelli, trained MADD representatives as spokespersons and booked them on media interviews throughout the march. More than 60 government officials and celebrities participated, including the mayors of New York, Los Angeles, and Chicago. News releases, media alerts, and television and radio public service announcements were sent to local media in each city along the march. Promotions were set up with radio stations. Product samples and promotion items were made available at each march site. The program included a free-standing newspaper insert (FSI) containing a cents-off coupon for Tang and the promise of a 10-cent donation to MADD for each coupon redeemed.

Tang received positive media treatment for its social involvement. Publicity included several thousand newspaper and magazine articles and local and network television news coverage, including four segments on *Today* and *Good Morning America*. The program ultimately produced a 12-percent sales increase for Tang as well as the largest corporate contribution ever received by MADD.

Corporate Communications

One area in which public relations and advertising work well together is corporate communications. This field is more important than ever in today's world where mergers, acquisitions, and broad-scale corporate restructuring are blurring previous corporate images.

The public relations part of a corporate communications effort demands the same careful planning as all other communications activities. Public relations

The Tang March Across America was a major public relations success that raised a great deal of money for MADD.
(Courtesy of Doremus Porter Novelli.)

tactics include arranging print and broadcast interviews with company officials, preparing feature stories for placement with publications, organizing press conferences, setting up speaking engagements before target audiences such as business and economic organizations, writing annual and quarterly reports, and producing employee videotapes. These programs can contribute to increased public, stockholder, government, and industry understanding of the company and stimulate corporate growth.

A Case Study: Dun & Bradstreet   A classic example of what a well-planned public relations program can do for an organization involved the firm of Dun & Bradstreet (D&B). Research indicated that D&B's world leadership in providing credit information to businesses dominated the business market's perception of the company. As a result, many businesses were unaware of D&B's other informational capabilities.

To promote D&B's publishing, marketing, and business-information services, D&B and its agency aimed a public relations program at present and potential customers, government economists, the financial community, and the media. They created a flow of business information to promote the company's other "brand names," including Moody's Investor Service and A. C. Nielsen Research. News releases, regional economic forecasts, and a spokesperson program (using a media-trained chief economist) secured extensive media coverage in the United States, Canada, Great Britain, and West Germany. Major stories appeared in *Fortune, The New York Times,* and the *Wall Street Journal* emphasizing D&B's leadership role in the business-information industry. The media coverage reached an estimated 890 million readers during the program's first year, and calls to D&B's economic analysis department for business information increased by 280 percent.

Public Affairs and Government Relations

Government policy initiatives, organized consumer action, international events, community politics, and investor activism—these and other developments that occur daily in the public sector have a direct impact on corporations, trade and professional associations, and other organizations. Organizations must analyze and address public-affairs opportunities and problems just as they would any other marketing or business development that affects them.

Public relations involvement in this area includes conducting surveys and other research, building coalitions, encouraging grass-roots activities, and using the media to promote their message.

A Case Study: The Elderly   One example of such a public relations campaign involves a segment of the population that is growing in numbers and political strength—the elderly. Skyrocketing costs threaten the financial stability of the Medicare program and older people's access to quality health care. The AARP is working to address this problem.

A national communications program, including an extensive public relations role, is under way, based on the theme "Cut the Cost, Keep the Care." The campaign focuses on consumer action, political action, and promotion of healthy behaviors. The program is targeted to AARP's 24 million members and uses AARP volunteers to contact and influence policy makers and health-care providers. Doremus Porter Novelli, AARP's public relations agency, conducts training sessions to teach volunteers how to use the media effectively and serve as campaign spokespersons. These volunteers then appear on radio and television programs. Other activities include staging special events to attract attention

DUN & BRADSTREET REDEPLOYS THE RICHES

In a flurry of acquisition and divestiture, Dun & Bradstreet has sold five companies and bought 33. It still has cash for more. To whatever it buys, the company brings the technological muscle that makes it a leader in the business of business information. ■ *by Stuart Gannes*

Joyce "the Voice" Gordon records messages in a New York studio for DunsVoice, an automated service customers phone for credit information.

WITH HIS deep-throated Nixonian baritone, Charles W. Moritz, chairman and chief executive of Dun & Bradstreet, likes to note the importance of tradition at the 144-year-old company. Yet he is changing the face of the business information giant. In a mere 18 months, Dun & Bradstreet has sold its TV broadcasting and book-publishing properties, while investing $1.8 billion in a breathtaking 33 acquisitions and dozens of internal development projects. The company is debt-free and has $650 million in cash and marketable securities in the till. Deciding how to invest that money is the biggest challenge Dun & Bradstreet faces.

Moritz won't say where or when his next move will come, but his strategy is clear. He has devised a two-pronged expansion plan to make Dun & Bradstreet the world's leading provider of what he calls "products and services that help business people do their job." First, he is sinking the proceeds from divestitures into high-growth acquisitions in the U.S. and Europe. Second, he is spending millions to squeeze more profits out of a private treasure trove of facts and figures—databases, in computer lingo. Dun & Bradstreet Credit Services, for example, tracks the credit history of seven million businesses. Donnelley Marketing, the company's direct mail operation, keeps current addresses and other data on 75 million U.S. households. Through computer technology Dun & Bradstreet is transforming these proprietary databases into a stream of new information products tailored to the varying needs of millions of disparate customers.

Moritz is moving at a time of intense interest in the "information industry." The exact nature of this industry is frustratingly fuzzy. Until recently it was the domain of traditional media companies, magazine, newspaper, and book publishers, and TV and radio broadcasters. Now the definition is expanding to include the business of selling computer generated data and data services that massage the information. Scores of companies have claimed turf in the information industry. They range from data network operators to telephone service providers to banks. GE Information Services, a division of General Electric, says it is an information industry leader because it operates the world's largest private telecommunications network. AT&T and its seven offspring all see themselves as information industry powerhouses. Claiming to be a player, Citicorp says, "Information about money has become almost as important as money itself." Publishers and broadcasters also insist they can grab pieces of the market for computerized data.

Yet security analysts regard Dun & Bradstreet and other compilers of business statistics like Dow Jones (owner of the *Wall Street Journal*) and McGraw Hill (owner of Standard & Poor's) as the purest, most attractive information industry plays. Beginning a decade ago, these companies computerized their records, partly to control internal costs. They have since realized that widespread use of remote terminals and personal computers equipped to receive data from mainframes has created a vast new market for electronically generated information.

Dun & Bradstreet's profits have been superb. They're down for the last four quarters, but that's mainly because nonrecurring gains on the sale of properties had pumped up profits the year before. Dun & Bradstreet's three main operating divisions—business information services, publishing, and marketing services—all chalked up record operating revenue and income last year. And the company ranked 23rd in return on shareholders' equity on FORTUNE's directory of the 500 largest U.S. service corporations; over the past ten years, return on equity has averaged more than 25%.

Wall Street investment firms widely recommend the stock, even though it recently hit a record high and is selling at more than 20 times earnings. "If somebody wanted to take over Dun & Bradstreet he might have to pay 40 times earnings, and it might still be a good deal," says Victoria A. Butcher, who follows the company for the New York brokerage firm of F. Eberstadt & Co.

Chairman Moritz, 48, and President Robert E. Weissman, 44, took over in January. "They are very different individuals, and each is making a major contribution," says Harvard economics professor John R. Meyer, a Dun & Bradstreet director since 1961. Moritz, who has a marketing background, began his career as an account executive at Reuben H. Donnelley, acquired by Dun & Bradstreet in 1961 and now the largest publisher of Yellow Pages other than the telephone companies. "I've always been conscious of the needs of the customer," he says. "When people come to me with a new business proposal, I tell them, 'Put it in

terms a customer can relate to.' " Weissman, who is chief operating officer, is an admitted "techie." He hacks away at the personal computer in his office, compiling private databases on everything from jokes and Christmas card addresses to a shopping list of compact audio disks.

In 1983 Moritz, Weissman, and ten senior managers drafted a 28-page corporate strategy statement that laid out Dun & Bradstreet's new policy on acquisitions and internal development. Moritz carries a copy in his briefcase at all times. Although he won't let outsiders see the document, Moritz says, "The word 'customer' is the most frequent word in there." The statement was approved by his predecessor, Harrington Drake, in late 1983. The effects soon rippled through the Dun & Bradstreet empire. In January 1984 the company sold Funk & Wagnalls, a publisher whose reference books retail in supermarkets. Dun & Bradstreet says Funk & Wagnalls failed to meet objectives for profitability and growth. Four days later the company completed the sale of Corinthian Broadcasting Corp., which owns six TV stations, to Dallas-based A.H. Belo for $606 million. The problem there wasn't lack of profits or

growth. With 1983 earnings of $47.2 million on revenues of $100.6 million, says Moritz, "Corinthian was a hell of a good business, but we saw it was going to require a whole set of management skills that we weren't really that good at."

Dun & Bradstreet has done plenty to offset the divestitures. It made 23 acquisitions in 1984, and ten this year. The best known are Datastream, a British investment analysis firm, and the U.S. division of Britain's Thomas Cook travel agency. Others include market research and insurance services companies, specialty software developers, six more publishers of Yellow Pages, and technical magazines. Many are cash-hungry businesses growing 30% to 50% annually.

INTERNAL DEVELOPMENT projects got an infusion of $140 million. The databases range from Credit Services and Donnelley Marketing to Moody's Investors Service, which publishes corporate financial profiles, and Official Airline Guides, which sells up-to-date airline schedules to travel agents and companies. Research expenditures, mostly on computer software to manipulate these data, increased more than

30% last year. "We've been able to take an existing database, reformat it, spin it around, and develop a whole slew of new products for our customers," explains Moritz. Ten years ago, Dun & Bradstreet credit reports were as uniform as Model T Fords. Today they challenge Heinz for variety.

Dun & Bradstreet can tailor products to specific customers. The company can electronically comb the credit information database and generate reports on individual companies or industry groups. Topics range from a firm's bill payment history to the number of contracts it has with federal agencies. "Gillette's razors help it sell more blades," says James E. Rutter, an executive vice president who runs Dun & Bradstreet Credit Services.

Take, for instance, Donnelley Marketing. Its database of consumers—gleaned from census tracts, telephone listings, auto registrations, and other public sources—grew out of its direct mail business, which distributes grocery coupons to households. Moritz explains how he thought about expanding the business: "As long as we viewed this as a mailing list, we were putting blinders on. We asked what would happen if we said, 'This is

Reprinted through the courtesy of the Editors of FORTUNE
© 1985 TIME INC.

Dun & Bradstreet's public relations campaign resulted in widespread publicity for the company's varied informational services, as illustrated in this edition of *Fortune* magazine.
(Courtesy of Doremus Porter Novelli.)

This picture illustrates one way in which public relations practitioners can affect the policy-making process. A public relations firm helped to arrange a briefing breakfast between AARP members and a group of congressmen.
(Courtesy of Doremus Porter Novelli.)

on Capitol Hill and around the country and putting out guidebooks and consumer-education materials.

The AARP campaign has helped to reduce increases in the cost of health-care products and services. Legislation addressing quality-care programs was passed by the Congress with AARP support. Moreover, the Association has come to be seen by its members, policymakers, and the media as a leader in shaping health-policy issues.

Financial Relations

To attract the financial community and the investing public, adequate corporate performance is necessary but not always sufficient. Therefore corporations often design communications programs to promote their financial strengths to securities analysts, brokers, institutional investors, and other concerned parties. The objective of these programs is to gain increased investor and media recognition, which in turn contributes to capital formation and business expansion.

These communications programs can include such activities as:

- Presenting up-to-date profiles of a company to investment bankers, brokers, analysts, and others
- Setting up presentations and meetings between corporate officers and their financial audiences
- Getting articles on the company and its management into the business and financial media
- Developing and implementing stockholder communications.

Crisis Management

Product recalls, hostile takeovers, bankruptcies, factory accidents, contaminated products, and many other crisis situations call for effective public relations support. The public relations effort must be integrated within crisis management. It may include establishing early warning systems, writing contingency plans, providing financial analysis and counseling, overseeing media relations, and preparing spokespersons and crisis teams.

Lysol: Crisis Management in Action   For example, for 10 years beginning in 1978, Sterling Drug, Inc., and its Lehn & Fink Division struggled to protect their "Lysol" brand name of household disinfectants from claims that Lysol products contained dangerous chemicals. The problem began when a railroad tank car containing chemicals spilled into the backyards of dozens of homes near Belleville, Illinois. In the ensuing class-action suit against Monsanto, the maker of the chemicals, a lawyer for the plaintiffs dramatized the danger of the chemicals by saying in court that they contained dioxin, "which is used in Lysol."

Lehn & Fink did not use dioxin in the manufacture of Lysol. To prove this, the company commissioned an independent laboratory to test its products and to verify that they did not contain dioxin. While these tests were being conducted, the company turned to its public relations agency to develop a program for dealing with the media. The concern was that statements about dioxin in Lysol would severely injure product sales.

The public relations plan identified a number of situations that might arise and set forth strategies for dealing with each one. Many statements and question-and-answer documents were prepared to address any possible results from the testing. As the case dragged on, the agency developed follow-up plans for possible new charges against Lysol.

The case finally went to summation in the fall of 1987. The Lehn & Fink public relations agency covered the closing arguments at the trial and provided each reporter at the proceedings with a statement correcting the misinformation about Lysol products.

The agency then tracked media stories about the trial to ascertain whether dioxin was still being connected with Lysol. In those few cases where necessary, additional media contacts were initiated to correct the misinformation. As a result, although the trial was covered by national media, every mention of Lysol included a statement that its manufacturer had conducted independent tests showing there was no dioxin in any Lysol products.

Nonprofit Organizations

Long before they embraced marketing, most nonprofit organizations had well-functioning public relations departments. Now marketing is becoming a key management function in government agencies, colleges and universities, hospitals, voluntary health and social organizations, and religious groups. These institutions use marketing to increase membership, influence social behavior, improve fund-raising, attract clients and patients, and achieve other organizational objectives.

Now these nonprofit organizations are wrestling with the question of whether marketing and public relations should work together. Although most marketers recognize that public relations is part of the marketing mix, public relations practitioners in nonprofit organizations tend to view their discipline as separate from, or at best only marginally related to, the marketing function. Community hospital public relations departments are an example. They have typically seen themselves as responsible for the overall image of their institutions and distinct from the newer departments of marketing.

Another example is the United Way of America. This organization has been working for a decade to incorporate marketing into its management process. It has established a national marketing committee and held a conference (hosted by IBM) of marketing, advertising, and public relations executives to discuss

This press briefing for the Third International Conference on AIDS illustrates the role that public relations can play in health education. (Courtesy of Doremus Porter Novelli.)

how to integrate these disciplines for the purpose of furthering the United Way movement.

Case Study: The California State Lottery   As an example of public relations within a nonprofit organization, consider the case of the California State Lottery (CSL).

California set out in 1985 to establish the biggest lottery in the world, with 34 percent of the proceeds going to the state's public schools. The first game consisted of instant scratch-off tickets. One year later "Lotto 6/49" was introduced. An integrated marketing communications program was necessary to build and sustain public interest and participation. Advertising was used to create awareness. Promotions were offered to recruit retailers and attract consumers to the lottery. Public relations was employed to help build anticipation for the kickoff, educate people about how to play (and win), and promote the lottery's benefits to the public schools.

Initial public relations activities included a press conference in the governor's office, major publicity tied to the delivery of hundreds of millions of tickets, a ten-city media tour, parades, concerts, and a gala opening event at the Hollywood Bowl. Lotto 6/49 was later introduced with another major campaign, including "how-to-play" demonstrations in malls throughout the state.

Sustaining interest is an important objective of the ongoing public relations effort. A 30-minute television program is aired weekly (and promoted heavily) on a statewide network in which players spin a wheel for dollar prizes. Media events and tours are held with "instant millionaires" from both lottery games. Awareness programs and various ticket promotions are conducted regularly.

Over 21 million tickets were sold the first day of the California State Lottery, and the one billionth instant ticket was sold only 4 months later—the most successful launch in history. In its first year the CSL sold $2 billion in tickets. Marketing communications—including public relations—have helped the CSL to maintain these sales levels.

EVALUATING PUBLIC RELATIONS

Measuring the effectiveness of public relations has been a problem, which is a major reason that public relations has not been accepted as an efficient and effective approach to behavior change. Consider the evaluations that were offered in support of effective public relations programs during a recent industry awards competition:

- "Everyone agreed it was a popular event."
- "A college journalism student requested a copy of our program plan."
- "Achieved unaided awareness among New York City cab drivers."
- "Our client has approved a new timetable for the coming year."
- For a sports program: "Nobody died, nobody got hurt."

Obviously we need better standards for gauging the effectiveness of public relations efforts.

Evaluating public relations differs in several ways from evaluating advertising. One major difference relates to the lack of control public relations practitioners exercise over whether their message appears in the media and what it will look like if it does appear. Advertisers at least know the exact nature of their messages and the schedule of exposure to target audiences. Public relations practitioners must devote significant effort just to identifying and tracking the output of a campaign.

Public relations measurement may be divided into two categories: *process evaluation* (what goes out) and *outcome evaluation* (effect on the audience).

Process Evaluation

process evaluation *Measuring the effectiveness of media and non-media efforts to get the desired message out to the target audience.*

Process evaluation examines the success of the public relations program in getting the message out to the target audiences. It focuses on media and non-media approaches with such questions as:

- How many placements did we get? For example, how many articles were published? How many times did our spokespersons appear on talk shows? How much airplay did our public service announcements receive?

A scene from a weekly television program in which contestants spin a wheel to win prizes in the California State Lottery. This program is part of a public relations campaign that has helped to make the lottery a huge success.

(Courtesy of Doremus Porter Novelli.)

These public relations practitioners are reviewing the placement of their message on television.
(Courtesy of Doremus Porter Novelli.)

- What was the quality of our placements? For example, what key points were communicated? What was the length and the position of the articles? Were our photos shown? Were our charts used?
- How many speeches were made by company executives? How many high-level business executives did they reach?
- How many representatives of our target audience attended our seminars? Did they follow up with requests for additional information?

These process-oriented questions are important because tracking output enables a public relations practitioner to understand how well the program is working and what adjustments might be necessary. Output does not, of course, necessarily lead to results. But it is obvious that if the messages are *not* reaching the audiences as planned, positive results are unlikely.

Outcome Evaluation

outcome evaluation *Measuring the effectiveness of public relations efforts in changing audience awareness, knowledge, attitudes, or behavior.*

Outcome evaluation of public relations efforts focuses on the effects of the program on target audiences. Research techniques for measuring the effects of public relations are similar to those used to measure the effects of advertising, such as pre- and posttracking systems and test and control markets. The questions such research addresses include:

- Are the target audiences aware of our issue/product/service?
- What do the audiences remember about the campaign? Do they understand the key (strategic) issues or message points?

- Has there been a change in audience knowledge, attitudes, or reported behavior (as measured in the pre- and posttracking)?
- Can we associate actual behavior change (for example, product trial, repeat purchase, voting, joining) with the public relations effort?

Problems of Outcome Evaluation   Several difficulties are encountered in evaluating the outcome of public relations efforts. As with advertising, it is hard to assess the public relations contribution within a larger marketing communications mix. In fact, because public relations programs have smaller budgets and, presumably, more modest effects, results are even more difficult to isolate and measure than they are for advertising. In addition, unless the program is directly aimed at changing a specific audience behavior, such as product purchase, "success" is ambiguous and hard to ascertain. This is also true of "image" campaigns, such as corporate communications or community relations. How do you determine whether a public relations campaign has changed popular attitudes toward a product or organization? And even if a positive change in awareness and attitudes is achieved, it is difficult to know whether these changes will lead to desired behaviors, such as receptivity to salespeople, donations, or a purchase.

■ SUMMARY

Public relations is a management function that is practiced by companies, governments, trade and professional associations, and nonprofit institutions.

Advertising and public relations are separate activities, but the two work best when they are integrated.

Both advertising and public relations use a number of different media. Public relations practitioners often have less control over their messages than do advertisers.

Public relations activities can be performed by a department within a large organization or by a public relations agency.

Public relations is similar to advertising in that it must be evaluated, although its direct effects upon the audience are difficult to establish.

■ QUESTIONS

1. Why is public relations a management function?
2. What factors have served to encourage the integration of public relations with advertising? What factors have discouraged this process?
3. What are the major areas in which public relations is used? Give examples.
4. Why has a lack of effective evaluation impeded acceptance of public relations as a legitimate approach to behavior change?
5. What are the major research techniques used in formative evaluation, process evaluation, and outcome evaluation?

■ FURTHER READINGS

CANTOR, BILL. *Inside Public Relations: Experts in Action.* New York: Longman, 1984.

CUTLIP, SCOTT M., and ALLEN H. CENTER. *Effective Public Relations.* Englewood Cliffs, NJ: Prentice Hall, 1982.

NAGER, NORMAN R., and RICHARD H. TRUITT. *Strategic Public Relations Counseling.* New York: Longman, 1987.

20

Advertising Campaigns

DONT' READ

Chapter Objectives

When you have completed this chapter you should be able to:

- Understand the role of the situation analysis in identifying key problems to be solved by the advertising
- Understand how the basic strategy decisions are developed for an advertising campaign
- Analyze how the message strategy solves the key problem
- Explain how the media plan relates to advertising objectives and message needs
- List and explain the items found in a campaign budget
- Explain how the effectiveness of an advertising campaign is evaluated

WAR STORIES, TECHNOBABBLE, AND POWER TALK

Late on a December afternoon in a conference room in the Hill, Holliday, Connors, Cosmopulos agency the loudest sound in the crowded room was the sound of ideas dying. The Boston agency was presenting to Kenneth A. Olisa, the new marketing chief of Wang Laboratories, the agency's most important client. It was one of those painful experiences that agency people don't forget.*

Wang was in deep trouble, losing both market share and key executives as its quarterly losses filled the news columns in the business pages. Its new operations chief, Ian Diery, and marketing chief Olisa had persuaded the company to spend millions of dollars on a new advertising campaign—a difficult decision at a time when Wang was going through the painful process of laying off thousands of workers.

Now it was Hill, Holliday's turn to be in deep trouble. Here was Olisa with a multimillion-dollar budget waiting for a big-splash campaign. One after another, HHCC's best and brightest sketched out ideas, and one after another they fizzled. As evening turned into night the mood in the room grew darker and darker.

To ease the tension, Olisa, an intense salesman, started to explain the company's problems to the agency staff, problems as seen by the front-line salesmen in the brutally competitive computer industry. Slipping into computer speech, he started talking about his experiences setting up complex computer networks for management information systems (MIS) officers. He talked about connectivity and integration and IBM, DEC, SNA networks, nodes, mainframes, and Wang VSs. He told them about one MIS executive who walked behind the computer to check the wires connecting all the various types of equipment to make sure Olisa wasn't pulling something. He told one war story after another.

No one knows who caught the idea first, but by the time the room cleared after 10:00 P.M., Wang and Hill, Holliday had a campaign. Ten weeks later HHCC was ready to go on air and in print with a campaign for Wang built around these war stories and told in the language of an intensely competitive computer salesperson. The campaign was daring, broke a lot of rules, and has become an advertising classic. The story of this ground-breaking advertising will be the focus of our discussion of advertising campaigns in this chapter.

ADVERTISING CAMPAIGNS

advertising campaign *A comprehensive advertising plan for a series of different but related ads that appear in different media across a specified time period.*

In Chapter 7 we talked about the use of military metaphors for advertising planning. The word *campaign* is another military term adopted by the advertising industry. An **advertising campaign** is a comprehensive advertising plan for a series of different but related ads that appear in different media across a specified time period. The campaign is designed strategically to meet a set of objectives and solve some critical problem. A campaign is a short-term plan that usually runs for a year or less.

Theme and Variations

The Wang "Salesperson" campaign, for example, had four different executions that ran on television and radio and in magazines. Holding the various ads

*William Glaberson, "The Human Drama Behind a Hot Ad," *The New York Times,* May 17, 1987, pp. 1, 8.

" A big international banker out of London...we shared a cab from Kennedy. He's on a stop-over to Hong Kong fresh from deregulation and the Big Bang. Well, according to him anybody with a pair of wing tips and a power tie is in the banking business in London now. Nobody outside the business knows the business...least of all the computer companies. I say to him let me set you up with some of our banking people in Hong Kong while you're there. I figure we can **fix him up with a Wang PBX...a Wang VS computer...consultant help...SWIFT...market feeds...networks...soup to nuts—U.S...U.K...Hong Kong—anywhere he wants.** So I arrange a meeting. Got a call this morning. He's going with us on a $10 million banking system. How's _that_ for a nice little cab ride?"

WANG MAKES IT WORK.

"Let me tell you a story about connectivity and networking that I think you'll get a kick out of. We invite this guy to our Executive Briefing Center...the EBC...for a demo. He basically challenged us to talk to him about anything other than word processing. And we're showing him data processing...voice...graphics...way beyond anything he's even read about. Heavy, heavy processing and _real_ programming. He's impressed. The last thing we talk about is integration. And we've more or less duplicated his computing environment in the Briefing Center. **So we take a DEC workstation and via a Wang PBX we get it talking to his own IBM mainframe through our Wang VS.**  Oh...and I forgot to mention that the DEC workstation is also passing data back and forth to an IBM PC on the other side of the room via Wang Office.** The guy applauds. Then guess what? Guess. He checks the wires. Right. He checks the wires from his PC to make sure we're not...you know. I'll never forget it."

WANG MAKES IT WORK.

AD 20.1
Examples of the print ads used in the Wang campaign. Note the use of technical terms in the copy.

(Courtesy of Wang Laboratories, Inc.)

together was a single concept that provided continuity across the various messages and different media. The Wang campaign was built around the idea of computer salespeople and their pride in coming up with solutions for the information problems of their clients.

THE STRUCTURE OF A CAMPAIGN PLAN

A campaign plan summarizes the marketplace situation and the strategies and tactics for the primary areas of creative and media, as well as the supporting areas of sales promotion, direct marketing, and public relations. The campaign plan is presented to the client in a formal business presentation. It is also summarized in a written document called a *plansbook*.

Situation Analysis

situation analysis *A section of an advertising campaign plan that summarizes the relevant research findings about the company, the product, the competition, the marketplace, and the consumer.*

The first section of most campaign plans is a **situation analysis** that summarizes all the relevant information the agency has compiled on the product, the company, the competitive environment, the industry, and the consumers. This information is obtained using primary and secondary research techniques.

The situation facing Wang included declining sales and market share, changes in upper management, and staff layoffs.* Under these circumstances, using a novel, unusual advertising strategy was a gutsy thing to do.

On the plus side, Wang did have a foothold in most of the Fortune 500 and 1000 companies through its word-processing installations and its premier computer line, the VS series. Unfortunately, the company was seen primarily as specializing in word processing and had never been able to develop a strong position in data processing or management information systems.

Recently, however, Wang had been first in the development of a new, integrated front-office system that could scan documents, store them, and work on them through a conventional computer keyboard.† In addition, Wang had developed systems that linked different systems, a feature called "connectivity." Wang believed that most offices already had information-processing technology in place, so it designed its networking systems to connect and enhance these systems rather than to replace them.

Advertising Strategy

After the situation analysis, most advertising campaign plans focus on the key strategy decisions that will guide the campaign. These were discussed in detail in Chapter 7, and they include such activities as identifying the key problems and opportunities, specifying the objectives for the advertising, targeting the appropriate audience, identifying the competitive advantage, and locating the best position. These are the foundation decisions that will guide the overall plan.

Key Issues According to Terri Keeler, Hill, Holliday account executive for Wang, three issues had been identified that needed to be addressed by the advertising campaign.‡ The first and most serious was the perception that Wang was just a word-processing company. In reality, word processing only accounted for 10 percent of Wang's business. Therefore there was an opportunity to focus on information systems and networking, which was Wang's most important area. The second issue identified by Keeler, reliability, related closely to the first. Wang needed to upgrade its credibility in areas beyond word processing. The

*Tom Weisend, "Client Profile: Wang Goes Back on the Offensive," *Adweek,* March 16, 1987, p. 8.
†"Wang's New Image Reflected in Profits," *Information Week,* October 4, 1987, pp. 40–45.
‡Weisend, "Client Profile," p. 8.

INSIDE THE ADVERTISING WORLD

PHYLLIS LEVY, CATEGORY GENERAL MANAGER OF THE ITALIAN FOODS BUSINESS UNIT, CAMPBELL SOUP COMPANY

As general manager at the Campbell Soup Company, Phyllis Levy becomes involved in advertising campaigns for many well-known Campbell food products. Her description of a workday includes references to a very wide range of problems, issues, and administrative tasks.

Time/Place	Attendees	Issues
8:40–9:00 Office	—	Day preparation, phone calls, open door for staff
9:00–9:30 Office	—Manager of Purchasing	Cost, procurement, and supply review for all lines' base ingredients
9:30–10:00 R & D Kitchens	—Prego Product R & D Group —Prego Brand Group	Product inspection for competitive taste testing
10:00–11:00 Marketing Conference Room	—Franco Brand Group —DDB Needham (Advertising Agency) Account Group	Franco copy strategy review and creative development next steps
11:00–11:30 Office	—Prego Brand Group	Review and confirmation of sales projections and objectives
11:30–12:00 Office	—VP/Business Planning and Controller	Prego base business building ideas
12:00–1:30 Rose Room at CSC	—Category General Managers —Herb Baum, President, CSC U.S.	Quarterly "open door" lunch with Campbell's President
1:30–2:00 Office	—Unit's Controller and Asst. Controller —Beans Brand Manager —Director of Logistics	Ways to improve Plant scheduling and cost for Beans
2:00–3:00 Office	—	Time at desk to read, think, plan; return phone calls
3:00–3:30 Office	—New Product Manager of Camden Plant	Introductory meeting; review of Unit's needs in Plant vs. Plant Manager's production requirements
3:30–4:30	—VP/Business Planning and Controller	11:30 meeting continued . . . Prego base business building ideas
4:30–5:00	—Director of Market Research and Development	Discussion to resolve a personnel transfer

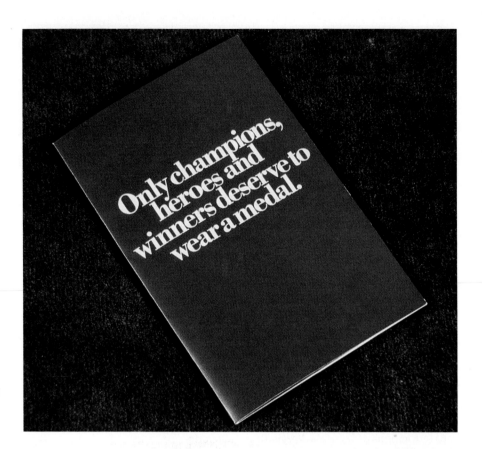

These photos depict the contents of an Employee Package, which is used to present a campaign to the client's employees.

third issue involved using advertising to improve sales and develop leads for the sales staff.

Objectives The advertising objectives developed for the Wang campaign to resolve these three issues included:

- Correcting the existing perceptions about Wang
- Strengthening Wang's credibility by creating an opportunity for dialogue with prospects
- Improving sales by using a call-to-action that puts the prospect in direct contact with the sales force

Target Audience

The Wang campaign targeted a narrow audience—top management, presidents, CEOs, vice presidents, and department managers in companies with over $100 million in revenue. In particular it focused on senior information systems directors (MIS) who evaluate computer systems or senior management executives who influence what information systems the office buys.

Clearly Wang wasn't trying to talk to "the rest of us" as did the Apple campaign. Wang focused on people who are busy, independent, successful, and powerful. They spend little time with mass media, are largely immune to advertising, and have little patience with the generalized messages, songs, and pleasant patter heard on many commercials. Wang knew that to reach these people advertising had to break through the clutter and their disinterest. The message strategy was to talk to them in their own language and demonstrate that Wang understood their information-processing problems.

Competitive Advantage Wang's advantage lies in its understanding of its customers' business needs. This was summarized in five communication messages described in the Wang campaign plan as follows:

1. *Systems for today and tomorrow* The Wang VS computer is the premier application processor in the industry. It can manage all four forms of information: voice and image, as well as words and data.
2. *Multivendor environment* Wang is committed to developing products and systems that can integrate both Wang and non-Wang systems.
3. *Realization of past investments* Most customers have information processing technology in place. Wang's networking systems are designed to enhance the investment already made—not replace it.

FIGURE 20.1
Target audience.
Courtesy of Wang Laboratories, Inc.

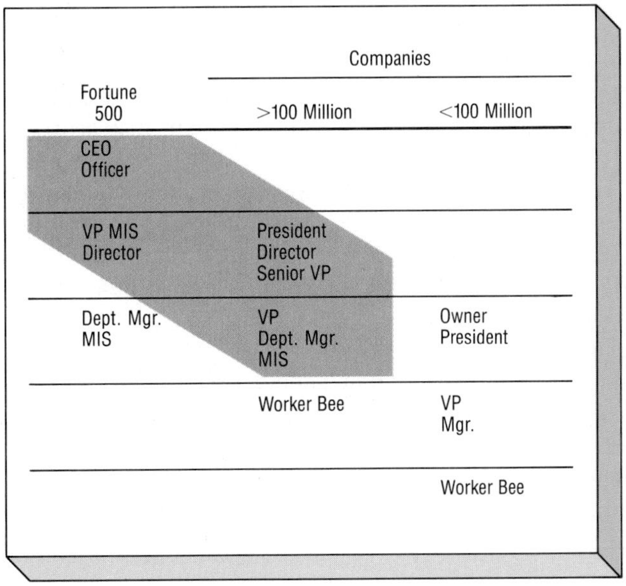

USERS OF MICROWAVE OVEN PRODUCTS

Advertising campaigns are designed to make consumers aware of products by repeating and varying themes in different media. A campaign requires more creative and financial resources than a single ad. Before preparing a series of ads and selecting different media, the advertiser must collect data on potential customers. It must consider how these people react to advertising, what their consumer habits are, and which media they prefer.

An example of this process is a lifestyle study conducted in the 1980s of female consumers who use convenience foods. Part of this study focused on users of microwave oven products.

Profile

According to the study, users of microwave oven products, hereafter referred to as "users," are somewhat older than women in general and are more likely to have children between the ages of 6 and 12. They more frequently have household incomes over $30,000, although they work at similar jobs and have educational levels similar to those of women in general.

Microwave products appeal to women with a busy lifestyle. Compared to women in general, users more frequently agree that "Everyone in our family is always on the run" and disagree with the statement, "I have a lot of spare time." Users take part in many cultural and social activities, including attending lectures and classical concerts, visiting museums, and going to movies and restaurants. They enjoy sports and are more likely to take an exercise class. They plan more family activities, such as trips to amusement parks, cookouts, and camping trips. They also eat out more often than nonusers.

As consumers, users tend to describe themselves as impulse buyers. They try new products more often, shop more frequently at convenience stores, and prefer name brands to store or generic brands. They are less likely to make a complete list before going shopping, to check prices on small items, to shop for specials, and to use coupons.

Perhaps because of their busy lifestyles, users place somewhat less emphasis on home cooking than do women in general. They are more likely to agree that "Meal preparation should take as little time as possible." A higher percentage disagree that "Baking shows that a women cares about her family" and "I like to cook." Users prefer single-serving packages because they often prepare different entrees for different family members. They also use other convenience foods, such as prepared stuffing and instant mashed potatoes. They use their microwave ovens for preparing foods not specifi-

cally designed for microwave cooking and for defrosting and reheating foods. Even though they are more likely to diet, they keep many sweet and salty snacks in the house. They are less concerned with restricting their intake of caffeine, salt, and cholesterol than women in general.

In terms of their media habits, users frequently read newspapers and watch television news programs. They also read more home and family magazines and watch prime-time dramas, detective shows, and cable television. They have a more favorable attitude toward advertising than do women in general. Almost 80 percent claim that advertising "helps me make better buying decisions."

Exercise

You are planning to introduce a new line of frozen dinners that are designed for use in microwave ovens. What themes could you emphasize in your ads? Which media would you choose? Develop a campaign. How would you vary each advertisement and still get your message across? How can a group of ads using different media be more effective than a single ad repeated over and over?

Source: Needham Harper Worldwide, *New Business Development Life Style Profile,* prepared by Kathy Kovacic, July 1986.

4. *Sensitivity to the user* Wang has a reputation for transforming complex technology into easy-to-use functionality. Also, Wang has a track record of integrating newer technology into older systems, eliminating the trauma normally experienced by users undergoing an upgrade.

5. *Long-term relationship* Wang has been an industry leader for 35 years, number one in word processing, and now with the unique VS system, Wang can become a leader in integrating entire operations. Customers can count on Wang to continue this leadership role throughout the 1990s—and beyond.

Positioning Strategy A product's position refers to how it is seen in the marketplace by the target audience. For Wang, changing customer perception is a critical part of the campaign strategy. Customer perception maps presently rate Wang high on quality but lower on reliability. The campaign was designed to move Wang's position higher on the reliability dimension to make the company more competitive with IBM and Digital (DEC).

In terms of the company's overall position in the marketplace, Wang's biggest strength is seen as *connectivity,* and the company's position statement focuses on this factor: *Wang offers connectivity, the ability to integrate Wang products and other vendor products into the overall corporate information network.*

Creative Plan

Finding the right creative approach is the most important part of the advertising plan. The creative approach is expressed through the message strategy; the theme, creative concept, or "Big Idea"; and the development of the theme in various executions.

Message Strategy The message strategy developed by HHCC for the Wang campaign was to speak to customers *in their own language* about their office information needs and problems. To demonstrate that Wang understands these needs the message was to challenge the consumer *to challenge Wang* to come up with a solution. To overcome the credibility problem the advertising needed to provide an effective *call-to-action* that would generate a one-on-one dialogue.

Creative Concept The concept, or theme, grew out of Kenneth Olisa's war stories. The creative team of HHCC creative director Don Easdon and copywriter Bill Heater pulled the concept together and wrote the ads. The idea was for the audience to listen in on a conversation where one salesperson is telling another about some successful strategy used to sell Wang computers. The stories were real; the salespeople were actors. The slogan "Wang makes it work" was used for continuity throughout the campaign.

The War Stories The story begins with the salesperson setting the stage: "I was doing a seminar on network management in Atlanta," or "Let me tell you a story about connectivity and networking that I think you'll get a kick out of." Then it describes in a clipped conversational style the challenge set up by the customer and how Wang understands the client's problem:

> "Management's screaming for operations help. His PC users are banging on the table for more power. He's mad at his vendors. He's even mad at me. His wife's mad because he's never home. I mean, he's getting it from all sides and the sad part is it's starting to look like it's his fault, which it isn't."

Then the salesperson comes up with the solution:

> "All I wanted to recommend is that he put in a Wang VS to tie his systems together. Don't trash his old systems. Make his PC users happy. . . . Get management off his neck . . . keep his meat and potatoes applications that he's spent so much time developing . . . and tie it all together with our VS."

"This company's MIS Director bought several systems . . . multiple vendor deal . . . a few years ago. All over-the-hill now. But now of course, management's screaming for operations help. His PC users are banging on the table for more power. He's mad at his vendors. He's even mad at me. His wife's mad because he's never home. I mean, he's getting it from all sides and the sad part is it's starting to look like it's his fault, which it isn't. So, I went to see him.

All I wanted to recommend is that he put in a Wang VS to tie his systems together. Don't trash his old systems. Make his PC users happy . . . get them into the swing of things. Get management off his neck . . . give them the systems they want . . . keep his meat and potatoes applications that he's spent so much time developing . . . and tie it all together with our VS. Perfect solution. Perfect, and when he saw that . . . tears came to his eyes. Well . . . not really. It wasn't quite like that."

AD 20.2

An example of a successful Wang television commercial.

(Courtesy of Wang Laboratories, Inc.)

Computerspeak   The approach was different from other computer ads because it used technical computer jargon (called "technobabble" in the press) mixed in with the so-called "power talk." The following examples from the Wang ad copy demonstrate this combination:

Computerspeak:

"So we take a DEC workstation and via a Wang PBX we get it talking to his own IBM mainframe through our Wang VS."

"The topic was making SNA work without IBM and the hall was filled with MIS guys who don't believe it can happen. . . .

"Five IBM look-alike mainframes . . . a Wang VS . . . a VS computer at each node . . . hundreds of them . . . and thousands of our workstations"

Power Talk:

"Anybody with a pair of wing tips and a power tie is in the banking business in London now."

"No IBM iron anywhere."

Most computer companies have shied away from using technical jargon in their advertising, particularly on television because of its mass audience. The agency knew it was a gamble. Terri Keeler insists however, that "It is a mistake to underestimate how many people are conversant with computer terms."* Today most business executives and CEOs know how to work with computers. Furthermore, the agency felt that the commercials could work with executives who didn't understand the jargon *because* it was so attention-getting. The uninitiated could grasp the idea even if they didn't understand the terms. For the 20,000 or so big company computer buyers, people who understand this computerese shorthand, "the high-tech jargon jumps out like a native language heard far from home."†

Jane Carpenter, Wang's advertising manager, said that computer-specific terms were necessary to make the ads stand out. "We wanted the ads to be

*Skip Wollenberg, "Wang's New Pitch—Jargon," *The Boston Globe,* April 21, 1987, p. 30.
†Glaberson, "Human Drama," pp. 1, 8.

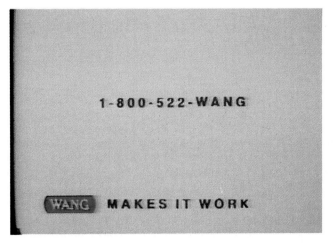

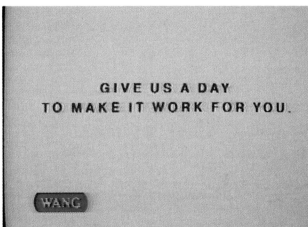

Wang makes it work.

Give us a day to make it work for you.

intrusive," she explained. Paul Henning, a Wang public relations executive, concurred that business executives would pay more attention to ads that "speak their language.*

Sales Leads   Another important goal of the creative approach was to *drive sales.* The concept of the customer challenge carried over to the call-to-action that specified contacting a Wang sales representative. Every ad ended with the line, "Give us a day to make it work for you," followed by an 800 number. The print ads invited the reader to visit the Wang Executive Briefing Center (EBC) for a customized 6-hour demonstration. The EBCs were set up with a variety of equipment systems that could be rearranged to duplicate as closely as possible the executive's existing office.

The Risk   This risky approach had some experts in the advertising industry shaking their heads. But the campaign caught the attention of the mass media as well as busy business executives. It was featured on Ted Koppel's *Nightline* and *The Today Show. Newsweek, The Boston Globe,* and *The New York Times* have run feature articles on the "war story" campaign. *The New York Times* explains that "there was something fascinating about the strange computer-speak dialect."†

Direct-Response Plan

Direct response (see Chapter 16) is used as part of an advertising campaign to stimulate action. To be effective it needs to tie in with the creative concept and support the overall message strategies. While the Wang advertising was intended to capture audience attention and build a new image of credibility for Wang in office information management, a supporting direct-response effort was designed to pull the target consumer into the EBC for a customized demonstration.

The high-impact mailers were designed as boxes. On the outside of the lid was a message similar to the copy in the ads. As the box opened up it became a three-dimensional brochure with the conversational copy continuing on the inside flaps. A small brochure was mounted on the last flap of the first mailer with more specific information about the Wang family of services. Inside each box in a special compartment was an involvement device that dramatized the invitation to visit the EBC.

Mailer #1 used a puzzle theme. The copy began:

*Wollenberg, "Wang's New Pitch," p. 30.
†Glaberson, "Human Drama," pp. 1, 8.

He had IBM equipment, DEC, HP, PCs, minis, the works . . . but nothing worked together. When I told him we could make it work, he said I know, I've seen the ads, but how can a word-processing company make it happen? I told him it was like a puzzle . . . but that he was missing a piece—and that we have it.

The inside panels continued developing the jigsaw-puzzle metaphor, and a small box inside contained an actual puzzle with the pieces representing different types of equipment from different companies all tied together with a Wang system. The brochure concluded with "Wang makes the pieces fit" and invited the executive to a demonstration at the EBC. The mailer also contained a postage-paid reply card arranging the demonstration.

The second and third mailers were all similar in design—boxes that unfolded as brochures. The second one included a roll of film and invited the executive to "take a picture at the demonstration and let your technical buddies look it over back at the office." The third mailer included a stopwatch to communicate to these executives that Wang understands their time constraints and busy lifestyles but feels that time spent at the Wang EBC demonstration is time well spent toward solving their business problems.

The mailers were sent to approximately 20,000 top-level business executives and MIS directors in Fortune 1000 companies over a 3-month period.

Sales Promotion Plan

Sales promotion (Chapter 18) is used in an advertising campaign to inform the sales force and others in the distribution channel about the campaign. It can also include incentives to encourage support activities by people in the trade as well as merchandising materials for in-store promotions.

The Wang sales promotion plan contained two pieces. The first was a *campaign awareness piece,* a media kit that was distributed to the sales force in regional and district meetings. The kit included a cover letter from a senior vice president, television storyboards, print ads, and the media schedule. The second was an *informational brochure* giving an overview of the Wang family of systems. It was designed to be used both as a sales call leave-behind and as a response for requests for more information.

Media Plan

The media plan in an advertising campaign identifies the media vehicles to be used, the scheduling, and the costs. An important aspect of media planning is estimating the number of impressions needed to accomplish the overall advertising objectives. This evaluation is stated in terms of *reach and frequency objectives.* The challenge to the media planner is to reach these objectives with the most efficient media buy.

Media Strategy   Among the key elements that were included within the media strategy were geographic emphasis, scheduling, and media objectives.

Geographic Emphasis   Wang's overall strategy was to engineer a national roll-out beginning with seven key cities: Atlanta, Boston, Chicago, New York, Los Angeles, San Francisco, and Washington, D.C. These cities were targeted because they headquartered many Fortune 1000 companies and other firms that use information systems. The first EBCs were to be located in these cities. The media plan also focused on these seven cities and bought local television and radio as well as regional editions of national publications. As more EBCs are set up, the campaign will move from this regionalized schedule to one that permits national media use.

TABLE 20.1
ADI Chart

ADI	% U.S. Adults	% U.S. P/M's	% Large & Medium Systems Installed Base	P/M CDI	Concentration Fortune 1000 Headquarters
1 New York	7.8	9.6	8.1	84	25.6
2 Los Angeles	5.3	6.0	6.0	100	6.2
3 Chicago	3.5	4.0	6.1	153	8.2
4 Philadelphia	3.0	3.2	3.4	106	3.0
5 San Francisco	2.3	3.1	4.2	135	4.4
6 Boston	2.3	3.0	3.2	107	1.8
7 Detroit	1.9	2.0	2.3	115	1.8
8 Dallas-Ft. Worth	1.7	1.8	2.7	150	2.8
9 Washington DC	1.8	2.8	3.7	132	1.2
10 Houston	1.7	1.8	2.5	139	3.0
11 Cleveland	1.6	2.0	1.8	90	2.4
12 Pittsburgh	1.4	1.3	1.4	108	3.2
13 Seattle	1.3	1.4	1.3	93	1.4
14 Miami	1.4	1.3	1.0	77	1.2
15 Atlanta	1.3	1.4	1.4	100	1.6
16 Minneapolis-St. Paul	1.4	1.6	1.8	113	3.4
17 Tampa	1.2	0.8	0.6	75	0.4
18 St. Louis	1.2	1.2	1.6	133	1.8
19 Denver	1.1	1.4	1.8	129	0.4
20 Sacramento	1.0	0.9	0.4	44	0.0
21 Hartford	1.0	1.2	1.4	117	1.6

Courtesy of Wang Laboratories, Inc.

Scheduling   The initial campaign was concentrated in a 4-month period from March to June 1987, just prior to the end of the fiscal year when many corporations make major purchases. The intent was to deliver maximum impressions to the target audience during a limited period of time in order to create impact and change consumers' perceptions of Wang as quickly as possible.

Media Objectives   HHCC used a reach campaign targeted to a narrow audience. The media plan estimated that in the seven markets the media schedule would reach approximately 1.2 million potential Wang customers. Because of the compressed time frame, it was also possible to build a high level of frequency. The overall reach was estimated at 60 percent, with an average frequency of five impressions per week. Table 20.2 illustrates how these estimates were developed by matching the campaign's communication goals to the media objectives.

Media Selection   The dialogue-intensive creative message required media that delivered strong audio messages. The campaign was designed for television,

TABLE 20.2
Setting Media Objectives

Communication Goal	Reach	Frequency
Awareness: build awareness of new campaign	High	Mid
Image: overcome negative perception	High	High
Purchase cycle: generally long, but need to motivate audience before end of fiscal year	Low	High
Creative: easy format to understand	—	Mid
Wang Objectives	60%	5+

Code:

	Reach	Frequency
High	67%+	6+
Mid	33–67%	3–6
Low	0–33%	0–2

| | Average market target delivery reach and frequency over schedule | | | | | |
| | 4 Weeks | | | Total Schedule | | |
	Reach	Freq.	GRPs	Reach	Freq.	GRPs
TV	84%	4.8	400	91%	8.8	800
Radio	60%	7.3	440	65%	13.5	880
Print	67%	6.1	412	70%	11.8	824
Total	95%	13.2	1,252	95%	26.3	2,504
Total schedule						
3+	80%			88%		
6+	61%			77%		
Goal at 6+	60%					
Index to goal	(102)					

Courtesy of Wang Laboratories, Inc.

but it also translated well to radio. Print ads reinforced the campaign message in business magazines.

This strategy could be considered a risky approach to media selection. Television is an unusual medium to use for a narrow target audience, particularly when the message contains so much technical language. Furthermore, Wang hadn't done much televsion advertising in previous years. "Some people might have said that in view of the tough times Wang has had, TV is too expensive," said Diery. "But TV is the most powerful medium mankind has ever known, so I countered that we couldn't afford *not* to be on it."*

Selection Criteria   Wang used four criteria in selecting media vehicles for the campaign:

1. Regional capabilities: No media were recommended that could not be purchased on a local or regional basis in line with the roll-out strategy.
2. Target-audience coverage: Wang needed to reach as many potential customers as possible to alter the existing perception.
3. Editorial environment: The media environment had to be consistent with the need to project an authoritative and credible image.
4. Frequency generation: Consumers needed to be exposed to a variety of creative executions to ensure they would be moved to respond.

Broadcast Ads   Television and radio commercials used a flighting schedule that ran for 4 weeks in March and the last 2 weeks of both April and May. Approximately 12 television spots and 55 radio commercials per week aired during thse periods.

The television programs were selected to reach the target, given these people's busy lifestyles and general disinterest in most television programming. The vehicles included sporting events such as college and professional basketball games; primetime shows such as *60 Minutes, 20/20, Hill Street Blues,* and *L.A. Law*; weekday and Sunday morning programs such as *The Today Show, Good Morning America,* and *Sunday Morning with Charles Kuralt*; and the late news. Forty percent of the commercials were 60-second spots; the remainder were 30-second spots. The ads achieved approximately 100 GRPs per week.

The radio spots were scheduled for morning and afternoon drive time and during weekends on leading adult-contemporary, news, and information stations. The schedule achieved approximately 110 target GRPs per week.

Print Ads   The print ads ran throughout the campaign in local newspapers and for 8 weeks in regional editions of *The Wall Street Journal.* Regional editions of *Business Week, Fortune, Newsweek,* and *Time* were also used every

*Weisend, "Client Profile," p. 8.

FIGURE 20.2 — Wang Laboratories, Inc. average market schedule

	February				March					April				May				June					TOTAL SCHEDULE DELIVERY
	26	2	9	16	23	2	9	16	23	30	6	13	20	27	4	11	18	25	1	8	15	22	
SPOT TELEVISION Late news, early news, sports, prime and Sunday news Approx. 12 spots/wk.					100 pts/wk 4 Wks. ← →					100 2 ← →				100 2 ← →									800 GRPs 91%/8.8x
SPOT RADIO AM & PM drive Weekend news Approx. 55 spots/wk.					100 pts/wk 4 Wks. ← →					110 2 ← →				110 2 ← →									880 GRPs 65%/13.5x
NEWSPAPER (12x) Major dailies Business section or Sunday edition (S)					X X (S)	X	X	X	X	X X (S)	X	X		X	X								824 CRPs (all print) 70%/11.1x
Wall Street Journal (7x)					X	X	X	X		X	X			X									
Time						X		X			X		X										
Business Week						X			X	X				X									
Fortune					← → ← →				← →				← →									
Newsweek						X		X		X			X										
Network Radio																							
CBS & ABC—I Approx. 22 spots/wk.					23 pts./wk. ← →																		114 GRPs 20%/5.7x
																	TOTAL SCHEDULE:						2,618 GRPs 95%/27.6x

FIGURE 20.2
Wang Laboratories, Inc. average market schedule.
Courtesy of Wang Laboratories, Inc.

FIGURE 20.3 — Wang media schedule

FIGURE 20.3
Wang media schedule.
Courtesy of Wang Laboratories, Inc.

other week during an 8-week period at the end of the campaign. The intent was to use authoritative and prestigious media vehicles that provide a credible editorial environment for the message.

Research and Evaluation

Research is used in three ways in advertising campaigns. Concept-testing research is used to evaluate the strength of the message strategy. Copy-testing research is used to evaluate the impact, effectiveness, and understandability of the various executions.

The third use of research is for evaluation during and after the campaign. A **tracking study** is a type of postevaluation that compares message objectives, such as awareness levels, before the campaign begins and after it is over. Intermediate tests can be conducted if there is time and opportunity to modify the campaign according to the results. (Research is discussed in more detail in Chapters 6 and 21.)

The Wang campaign plan included a comprehensive two-part research program: (1) a qualitative creative communications pretest; and (2) a quantitative pre- and posttracking of the campaign in each EBC market. The creative pretest consisted of in-depth interviews with 45 representatives of the primary target audience, including departmental senior managers in Fortune 1000 companies and senior MIS managers. All respondents were directly involved in analyzing and mailing decisions concerning data-processing equipment. The interviews also included a mix of Wang and non-Wang users in the New York, Atlanta, and San Francisco markets.

The tracking study involved two waves of tests. The first was conducted prior to the introduction of the campaign, and the second was conducted immediately after the completion of the campaign. Each wave consisted of 150 telephone interviews of Wang's key targeted executives in each EBC market.

Campaign Budget

The largest item in an advertising campaign budget is usually media time and space. Production of print and broadcast ads can be included, or it can be listed separately. Direct-response and sales promotion costs directly associated with the campaign are also included in the total budget, as are the costs of research and testing.

The total budget for the Wang "Salesperson" campaign was around $10 million. Approximately 85 percent of that amount was budgeted for media time and space. Table 20.4 breaks down the campaign budget.

AD 20.3
Wang television commercials used actors relating real-life "war stories." The strategy was highly successful.
(Courtesy of Wang Laboratories, Inc.)

*T*HE WANG SUCCESS STORY

In addition to being one of the most widely discussed campaigns in the business community, the Wang "Salesperson" campaign also contributed to increased sales and share of market. The first two quarters of the fiscal year ending in June 1987 showed losses totaling $70 million. The third quarter showed a slight profit, and the fourth quarter a substantial one, reflecting the impact of the campaign.*

In terms of direct measures, calls to the 800 number jumped dramatically after the campaign was under way. The reply cards in the direct-response mailings generated a substantial increase in sales leads.

The tracking study results were even more impressive. The unaided brand

*"Wang's New Image," pp. 40–45.

TABLE 20.4
Total Campaign Budget

Media	85%
Production	6%
Direct marketing	5%
Research	2%
Sales materials	1%

awareness of the MIS directors rose from 12 to 20 percent, an increase of 67 percent. Awareness of Wang as a microcomputer company increased from 71 percent to 86 percent. Advertising-campaign awareness more than doubled, testifying to the attention-getting impact of the campaign. The purchase consideration of potential Wang customers experienced impressive gains: unaided consideration jumped by 75 percent, and aided consideration more than doubled. Wang's overall image showed strong improvement, with an increase in positive evaluations of 61 percent. The concept of multivendor connectivity was strongly communicated by the campaign, and Wang's ratings on its perceived ability to deliver on this selection criteria more than doubled. Interest and purchase intention in Wang as a provider of this technology rose considerably.

The campaign discussed here ran in the spring of 1987 and was followed by a hiatus in summer. In the late fall of 1987 a second version of the campaign began to run, with three new creative executions mixed in with the original four. This version of the campaign ran through the spring of 1988.

The campaign has won several awards and has generated a number of spoofs that the Wang executives find flattering. Wang officials believe that they and Hill, Holliday have come up with a ground-breaking concept that has created a new genre of advertising.

SUMMARY

The situation analysis includes primary and secondary research findings about the company, product, competition, marketplace, and consumers.

The strategy section of a campaign plan identifies the key problem, the advertising objectives, the target audience, the competitive advantage, and the position.

The creative plan includes a theme, or creative concept, and variations, or executions, for different media, situations, and times of the year.

The media plan includes media objectives, media selection, geographic strategy, timing schedules, and a budget.

The overall advertising campaign budget includes the media time and space costs, production costs, sales promotion and public relations costs, direct-response costs, and research costs.

Research for an advertising campaign includes concept and execution testing, as well as postevaluation that evaluates the campaign against its objectives.

QUESTIONS

1. What is a creative concept, and what is its role in an advertising campaign?

2. How does the targeting decision affect the development of both the creative and the media plans?

3. What two pieces of information do you expect to find in the media objectives section of the media plan?

4. Develop a research proposal in outline form for a program that you would recommend to evaluate the effectiveness of the most current campaign for Pepsi, Coca-Cola, Burger King, or McDonald's (your choice).

FURTHER READINGS

AAKER, DAVID A., and JOHN G. MYERS. *Advertising Management,* 3rd ed. Englewood Cliffs, NJ: Prentice-Hall, Inc., 1987.

ANDREWS, KIRBY. "Communications Imperatives for New Products," *Journal of Advertising Research,* Vol. 26, No. 5, 1986, pp. 29–32.

HOGAN, BOB. "Print's Place in the Media Mix," *Inside Print,* March 1987, pp. 39–42.

SCHULTZ, DON E., DENNIS MARTIN, and WILLIAM P. BROWN. *Strategic Advertising Campaigns,* 2nd ed. Chicago: Crain Books, 1984.

21 *Evaluative Research*

Chapter Objectives

When you have completed this chapter you should be able to:

- Explain why advertisers devote time and money to research
- Distinguish between evaluative and diagnostic research
- Identify the three major evaluative research methods and what each one claims to test
- Evaluate the strengths of various forms of testing
- Understand the concerns surrounding the issues of validity and reliability

*E*VALUATIVE RESEARCH: AN OVERVIEW

This chapter describes a problem that is so difficult and so important that anyone who can solve it will become a millionaire very quickly. The problem is: develop a way to measure the sales effects of advertisements. The method must be affordable, reliable, and valid.

The chapter will describe the most important elements of that knotty problem and will show how advertising researchers have tried to solve it. Read carefully. The instant million is waiting.

Chapter 6 discussed the ways in which advertisers use research to supply feedback to people who create advertisements. This is referred to as *diagnostic research*. The other major use of research in advertising comes after the ad has been produced. Several key questions concerning the ad's effectiveness must be answered: Who has seen the ad? How did they feel about it? Did it affect their feelings about the product? Would they buy the product? Is the campaign worth pursuing, or should the advertiser adopt a new strategy? Research designed to answer these questions is referred to as **evaluative research.**

Once an advertisement has been produced, the advertiser must decide whether to run it frequently or rarely, nationally or in some limited test areas only. Those are extremely important decisions because they always represent major investments of marketing resources.

Even after the advertiser has decided where and how long to run the campaign, second thoughts can arise. Sales may fall, or they may not increase as rapidly as expected. Is the advertising at fault? Would sales be better if the advertising were "working harder?"

Because media investments are so large, and because it is so difficult to determine how well the advertising is working, advertisers are interested in testing the effectiveness of finished ads. Finished advertisements cannot easily be altered, but if they are found to be defective, they can be replaced.

A great many research suppliers offer advertising testing services, and some of the largest advertisers maintain their own advertising-testing systems. The most widely used tests of finished advertisements employ some variation of

evaluative research *Research intended to measure the effectiveness of finished or nearly finished advertisements.*

Agency people meeting with a client to discuss the effectiveness of a campaign.
(© 1988 by Prentice Hall.)

Advertisers must rely on more than intuition and faith when trying to assess the effectiveness of their efforts.

(© 1977 by Sidney Harris-American Scientist Magazine.)

"I THINK YOU SHOULD BE MORE EXPLICIT HERE IN STEP TWO."

one of three distinctive methods. One method tests *memorability* by measuring recall or recognition. The second tests *attitude change,* or change in intention to purchase the advertised brand. The third tests changes in actual *buying behavior.* For reasons to be described later, the first two of those approaches are much more widely used than the third.

*R*ECALL TESTS

recall test *A test that evaluates the memorability of an advertisement by contacting members of the advertisement's audience and asking them what they remember about it.*

The idea behind a **recall test** is simple: If an advertisement is to affect behavior, it must leave a mental "residue" with the person who has been exposed to it. One way to measure an advertisement's effectiveness, therefore, is to contact consumers and find out what they remember about it.

The traditional recall procedure generally works as follows: A finished commercial is run on network television within a regular prime-time program. The next evening interviewers in three or four cities make random telephone calls until they contact about 200 people who were watching the program at the exact time the commercial was carried. The interviewer then asks the respondent a series of questions:

- Do you remember seeing a commercial for laundry detergent?
- (If no) Do you remember seeing a commercial for Brand X laundry detergent? (Memory prompt)
- (If yes to either of the above) What did the commercial say about the product? What did the commercial show? What did the commercial look like? What ideas were brought out?

The answers to the third set of questions are written down verbatim.

The nature of those questions is important. Respondents are not asked, "Please tell me about all the commercials you remember seeing on TV last night," or "Please tell me about any detergent commercials you remember." The traditional recall test requires that the respondent link a specific brand name, or at least a specific product category, to a specific commercial. If the questions were more general, the answers would be quite different.

PRINCIPLE

In spite of much research, the relationship between day-after recall scores and sales effectiveness is still unknown.

Analyzing Test Results

The results of the recall test are analyzed by examining the verbatim responses to determine how many viewers remembered something specific about the ad. If an answer indicates that the viewer was merely guessing or remembering other advertising, that viewer is not counted as having recalled the commercial.

Even though some recall test "verbatims" are surprisingly detailed, many are so sketchy that it is hard to be sure the respondent was remembering a specific commercial. Here are some typical "verbatims." Which indicate recall of the specific commercial being tested?

- Nothing except they showed a can and people eating and enjoying it. I remember nothing else.
- It was two little kids that were bored with lunch and one little kid who was happy with lunch because his mother had Spaghettios. Then this little cartoon king pops out of the can and says dinner would be better with Spaghettios. Then they just show the can of Franco-American Spaghettios. It just demonstrated the product. It was cute, the kids. It's different than having ordinary spaghetti because it's circles. It's easy to make. It's nice to have around when you have kids.
- There were children on the spaghetti song. I was busy at the time and was knitting. Some children eating spaghetti with a spoon, then I got up and went in the bedroom for some more yarn. I like the Franco-American products. Just the song I remember, but I can't remember the words. Same thing, it's convenient, appeals to children, it's a canned food.
- They had little meatballs in them. (In the Spaghettios, isn't that what we've been talking about?) They had little kids. You're lucky I even saw what I did.*

The proportion of viewers who are counted as having proved recall usually ranges from zero to 60 or 70 percent. Across a range of product categories, the average recall score for 30-second commercials is about 20 percent. In other words, about one in five of those who view a commercial can recall something about it the following day.

Variations on Recall Tests

The traditional recall test procedure has seen many variations. In one version respondents are prerecruited to watch a specific program. That variation reduces research costs because very few contacts are wasted. Otherwise thousands of telephone calls are required to locate 200 viewers of the previous night's program.

In another variation respondents are exposed to commercials in a theater setting and telephoned at home 24 or 72 hours later. Other times respondents are prerecruited to watch a program telecast from a local cable television station. The latter two variations are popular because, unlike recall tests that employ network television, they can be used to test rough executions.

Assessing Recall Tests

Recall tests have several advantages over other methods of testing television commercials. One is that they have been around for a long time, almost since the beginning of commercial television. Advertisers are accustomed to using them. Among some advertisers they have become part of the corporate culture, an ingrained tradition.

Because recall tests have been so popular, research companies that conduct them have accumulated "norms"—records of results that serve the same purpose as batting averages. Norms allow the advertiser to tell whether a partic-

PRINCIPLE

For well-known brands, the change produced by one exposure to one advertisement may be too small to measure accurately.

*Courtesy of Campbell Soup Company.

ular commercial is above or below average either for the brand or for its product category. Without norms the advertiser could not determine whether a score of 23, for example, is good, bad, or average. Like students, commercials are graded with reference to the others being tested.

reliability *A characteristic that describes a test that yields essentially the same results when the same advertisement is tested time after time.*

Reliability A third advantage of recall tests is **reliability.** In this context the term *reliable* means that the commercial gets essentially the same score every time it is tested. Reliability is important because recall test scores, like all test scores, incorporate a certain amount of random *measurement error*. Measurement errors are due to differences among interviewers, differences among the programs that carry the commercials, and a host of other factors that influence the test results and vary from time to time. When the amount of measurement error is high, as it is in some other methods of testing television commercials, scores vary from test to test—a high score this time, a low score next time, a medium score the time after. When results are that inconsistent, the test is obviously of little value.

Recall tests are more reliable than most. That fact alone helps to explain why they remain popular with advertisers.

Validity Reliability is only one measure of the value of test results. An advertiser who uses a recall score to evaluate an advertisement is acting on the assumption that a recall score reflects the ad's ability to sell the product.

Considering that recall tests are among the oldest and most widely used of all advertising testing methods, you might assume that advertisers know the relationship between recall and sales effectiveness. Not so. Despite many years of experience and debate, the relationship between recall and sales effectiveness is still unknown. Many researchers, and most of advertising's creative leaders, believe that the relationship between recall and selling power is close to zero.

The technical term for the subject we are discussing is **validity.** When an advertiser uses a recall test to decide an advertisement's fate, the advertiser is assuming that recall is a valid measure of the advertisement's selling power.

If the validity of recall is unknown, why do so many advertisers use a recall test to evaluate their advertising? One reason is that the recall test is a relatively reliable measure of *something,* and many advertisers believe that that something must be a quality related to advertising effectiveness. It just seems to make logical sense that a well-remembered advertisement will, on the average, be more effective than an advertisement that left little detectable impression in the viewer's mind.

PRINCIPLE
Many physiological tests are so sensitive to outside influences that their test-retest reliability is unacceptably low.

validity *The ability of a test to measure what it is intended to measure.*

Recall Tests and Decision Making

The most fundamental reason that advertisers continue to use recall tests is that recall tests help them make decisions. The decision to run or not to run an advertisement is difficult because it affects the careers of all those involved in creating and approving the advertising. Furthermore, the decision to run or not to run an advertisement involves limited—and sometimes very large—resources. It therefore affects the welfare of everyone associated with the brand.

Consider, for example, a typical commercial for a well-known brand. A dozen members of the agency's creative department may have had a hand in it, even though only one creative team will have been responsible for its final form. Members of the research department may have contributed to the content of the commercial, especially if it is a significant departure from previous commercials in the campaign. Members of the account service department, and possibly even

INSIDE THE ADVERTISING WORLD

SOME THINGS I THINK I KNOW ABOUT STUDYING TELEVISION COMMERCIALS
JOHN S. COULSON, PARTNER COMMUNICATIONS WORKSHOP, INC.

A former vice president in charge of research at the Leo Burnett agency, John Coulson is now a partner in a creative and marketing research company that specializes in developing and evaluating new products and corporating communications. In both capacities he has evaluated numerous television commercials. The following observations are based on his research experience.

1. **No single set of measurements will serve to evaluate all commercials.** A commercial is a very complex subject with many different goals. It is part of a total advertising program that is part of a total marketing program. Studying it out of context can produce highly irrelevant information.

2. **A key element in the success of a commercial is the type of person the advertiser wishes to influence.** Some people are more receptive to a particular brand's advertising than are others. For example, product and brand users are more receptive to the message than are nonusers. Trier-rejectors show even less interest and acceptance. Generally women are more accepting than

men, older adults than younger adults, and children than adults.

3. **The most basic rule for a successful commercial is that the viewers know what product or brand is being advertised.** Occasionally a competitive brand is misidentified as the advertiser. The product or brand should be an organic part of the commercial rather than an element that seems to have been added on to it.

4. **The commercial's ability to create product recall is largely independent of the commercial's effect on the viewer's attitudes toward the product.** Recall is a measure of the commercial's efficiency and is related to the advertising weight, not to its effectiveness.

members of top agency management, will have discussed and recommended the commercial to the client. On the client side, the brand manager, members of his or her staff, and possibly members of other departments will have been involved in the process.

If the commercial is ultimately deemed a success, those most involved in creating and approving it will receive much credit. If for any reason the commercial is deemed a failure, sharp, critical questions will be asked: "Who approved that ad in the first place?" "Shouldn't we be spending our marketing dollars in some better way?"

Aware of the consequences and beset on all sides by uncertainty, decision makers need something to help justify their decisions. In so tense a setting a recall test, or any other test that has become part of the corporate culture, can play a decisive role, even when no one is really sure that it is a valid measure of the value of the advertisement.

RECOGNITION TESTS

recognition test *A test that evaluates the memorability of an advertisement by contacting members of the audience, showing them the ad, and asking if they remember it.*

One way to measure an advertisement's effectiveness is to ask people to recall it. Another way is to ask people if they remember having seen it. The latter kind of test is generally called a **recognition test.** Like recall tests, recognition tests were first used to evaluate print advertising. One of the earliest, and still one of the most popular, recognition tests is named after its inventor, Daniel Starch.

5. One effective commercial format is to provide news that is relevant and important to viewers. Information about a product can be news to the public for a long time, particularly if it can be given a fresh twist. Advertisers frequently feel that news is stale long before the public does.

6. When an idea projected by the commercial as news is seen by the public as trivial or irrelevant, the commercial will almost always be a failure.

7. When a commercial is delivering news of real interest to its viewers, liking the commercial or empathizing with its situation is generally not critical to its effectiveness. Instead clarity and simplicity are important.

8. A basic mistake of advertising is trying to cover too many ideas. It is more than twice as difficult to deliver two ideas as one idea, and delivering three or four ideas almost always produces a jumble that is quickly forgotten.

9. The believability of a product idea in a commercial is not always important to the commercial's success. If the product is relatively low priced, consumers might purchase it to test certain claims that they find difficult to believe.

10. An attractive spokesperson who is appropriate for the product or brand attracts attention and makes the message more believable and compelling.

11. Viewers are wary about the use of known spokespeople in advertising. If the spokespeople are not appropriate for the commercial, viewers consider them to be phony and reject their message.

12. In addition to informative commercials, another widely used approach to television advertising is a mood or emotional commercial designed to create greater awareness of, and favorable reaction to, the product or brand. Many commercials successfully combine the two approaches.

13. Appropriate music can enhance the mood of a commercial. Music can make a commercial more memorable and improve consumer attitudes toward the product.

14. For mood commercials, likability and empathy are far more important than clarity and simplicity.

15. Although the finished production can make a real difference in how viewers react to a television commercial, studying animatics generally can indicate how effective the commercials will be. There are some notable exceptions: (1) When the animatic is not clear because it is an animatic and not finished; (2) When appetite appeal from the appearance of food is a key element in the commercial's effect; (3) When commercials demonstrate softness and appearance in a hair commercial; (4) When a celebrity is used in the finished commercial who cannot be identified from the animatics; and (5) When actors perform tongue-in-cheek, which allows acceptable exaggeration in a finished commercial. In most other cases almost all measures of a finished commercial match those of the animatic from which it is produced.

(Courtesy of John S. Coulson, Communications Workshop, Inc.)

The Starch Test

The Starch test (see Figure 21.1) is used to evaluate print advertisements that have already been run in a specific issue of a publication. In the Starch procedure, interviewers locate people who, prior to the interviewer's visit, have glanced through or read the specific magazine issue being studied. After verifying that the respondent at least looked through the study issue, the interviewer proceeds page by page, through a copy of the issue distributed in the geographic area where the interviewing is being conducted, asking whether the respondent remembers having seen or read each ad being tested.

In the issue copy used in the interview, each studied ad is assigned an item number and is broken down into component parts (such as illustration, headline, logo, or main body of print) that are identified by codes. If the respondent says he or she remembers having seen an ad in that particular issue, the interviewer then asks a prescribed series of questions for each component part of the ad to determine exactly how much of the ad has been seen and read. The Starch procedure produces three scores:

1. *Noted:* The percentage of respondents who say they noticed the ad when they looked through the magazine issue on some previous occasion.
2. *Associated:* The percentage of respondents who said they noticed a part of the ad that contains the advertiser's name or logo.
3. *Read Most:* The percentage of respondents who reported reading 50 percent or more of the written material in the ad.

FIGURE 21.1
An example of a Starch test of a
well-known ad.
(Courtesy of Starch INRA Hooper and IBM.)

The Starch test competes with a recall-based approach to measuring magazine advertisements. When a recall test is used to evaluate print ads, respondents
who have looked through the magazine at home go through a deck of cards
containing brand names. When the respondent says, "Yes, I remember having
seen an advertisement for that brand," the interviewer asks the respondent to
describe everything he or she can remember about the ad. Responses are taken
down verbatim and studied later to determine whether the respondent was
remembering the specific advertisement being tested.

Assessing the Starch Test   Compared with a recall test, the Starch procedure
has some valuable advantages. First, because the questions asked of Starch respondents are relatively easy, the Starch interview proceeds more rapidly. An
easier interview allows more advertisements to be tested, which in turn lowers

the cost per advertisement. Lower cost implies a better investment of the advertiser's research resources.

RELIABILITY   The Starch procedure is very reliable. Repeated evaluations have shown that Starch scores are remarkably consistent. In fact Starch tests are substantially more reliable than recall tests in the print medium.

VALIDITY   What about validity? In one study of the Starch procedure researchers used a magazine that had not yet been distributed. They asked the usual Starch questions even though the respondents could not possibly have seen the specific advertisements being tested. The researchers found, as they had suspected, that respondents claimed to recognize many of the advertisements that had not yet been published. But they also found, much to their surprise, that when Starch scores from the prepublication study were compared with Starch scores obtained later in the normal manner, ads that scored high in the prepublication study also scored high in the real study, and ads that scored low in the prepublication study also scored low in the real study! That unexpected outcome led to the conclusion that whatever the Starch procedure measures, it certainly does *not* measure memory only. And it led some researchers to conclude that the Starch procedure therefore is not valid.*

However, the Starch test obviously measures something very consistently. What could that be? Subsequent investigations have suggested that when a Starch respondent says, "Yes, I looked at that ad when I went through the magazine," the respondent is really saying, "Ads like that usually attract my attention." And when the Starch respondent says, "I didn't see that ad," he or she is actually saying, "I usually ignore that kind of advertising." If that interpretation is correct (and many researchers believe that it is), a Starch score actually represents a kind of consumer vote on whether the advertisement is worth more than a passing glance.

Therefore, although the Starch test is not a valid measure of memory, it is a reliable measure of something. That something is probably attractiveness, a quality most advertisers want in their advertising. Given that conclusion, and given the low cost of the Starch procedure, the Starch test continues to play a major role in evaluation of print advertisements.

ATTITUDE-CHANGE TESTS

attitude-change test *A test that evaluates the effectiveness of an advertisement by measuring whether the ad affects consumers' intentions to buy a brand.*

The basic format for an **attitude-change test** is this: Consumers are first asked how likely they are to buy a specific brand. They are then exposed to an advertisement for that brand. After exposure they are again asked about what they intend to purchase. Results are analyzed to determine whether intention to buy has increased as a result of exposure to the advertisement.

Types of Attitude-Change Tests

Research companies that conduct attitude-change tests often invite consumers to a theater to see a "preview of a new television show." Before the audience sees the program, they fill out a questionnaire that asks about their preferences for various brands. They watch a television program, complete with commercials. They then answer questions about their reactions to the entertainment, and they respond to the brand-preference questions again.

At the beginning of the session most members of the audience believe that their major task will be to evaluate the entertainment. However, before the session is over, most respondents have figured out that the commercials are the

*Valentine Appel and M. I. Blum, "Ad Recognition and Response Set," *Journal of Advertising Research,* June 1961, pp. 13–21.

LIFESTYLE

AGENCY PEOPLE: WHO ARE THEY?

Advertisers spend a great deal of money on research to learn about consumer attitudes and preferences. They incorporate this information into both individual ads and entire campaigns. Rather than spend this money, advertisers might be tempted to rely on their own feelings and "gut" reactions to advertisements. This raises the question: Can advertisers assume that people in advertising agencies share the same opinions and beliefs as consumers in general? The answer, apparently, is that they cannot. A study conducted in the 1970s by the advertising agency Needham, Harper and Steers (now DDB Needham) of its own creative, research, media, and account services personnel discovered major differences between their views and those of a general cross section of consumers.

Profile

The study found agency people to be more optimistic, self-confident, cosmopolitan, and liberal on social and political issues than consumers in general. They were more likely to agree that their greatest accomplishments lay ahead of them and less likely to concur with the statement, "I dread the future." Consider the following data.

- Agency people were twice as likely to agree with the statement, "I like to visit places that are totally different from my home."
- Eighty-six percent of agency people, but only 32 percent of consumers in general, preferred to live in a large city rather than a small town.
- Over 90 percent of agency people, as opposed to only 30 percent of consumers in general, disputed the contention that women did not belong in the working world.
- Agency people were far more likely to disagree with the statements that "Communism is the greatest peril in the world today" and "There should be a gun in every home."

Exercise

You work for a major advertising agency, where you helped produce a series of ads for an insurance company. Your colleagues considered the ads both creative and forceful, and they predicted a successful campaign. How would you treat this type of feedback? Would you be satisfied with their conclusions, or would you want additional feedback? What types of tests or research would you utilize? In the long run, which would you consider more important, your colleagues' reactions or consumers' responses?

Source: "Uses of Values and Life Styles in Marketing," paper presented by William D. Wells to the American Marketing Association Conference, Palm Beach, Florida, May 29, 1980.

research company's principal interest. Although some respondents react negatively when they realize their cooperation has been secured through false pretenses, most go along with the instructions and willingly give their opinions.

In some variations on the basic attitude-change format, respondents are telephoned at home and asked to watch a program at a certain time. During the course of the recruitment interview they are asked about their brand preferences. After the program has been telecast, they are recontacted and asked the brand preference questions a second time. In still another variation of the attitude-change test, respondents are exposed to commercials only, without program material. In all such variations the same basic procedure is followed: pretest—exposure—posttest, with a comparison of purchasing intentions before and after exposure to the advertisement.

A Case Study A good example of the ways in which testing can contribute to a successful campaign involves General Mills. In the early 1980s the company launched a vigorous campaign to promote its Betty Crocker line of products. The goal was to consolidate a limited budget, which had been divided among several brands, behind the entire dessert line. This process involved updating the prim, conservative, housewife image associated with Betty Crocker. At the same time the company had to avoid drastically changing a personality that had become a standard in product advertising. As one company official explained: "While we didn't want to turn Betty into a swinger, we did want to present a more current image with more fun and a livelier tone." Not surprisingly, General Mills decided to test the new ads carefully.

Betty Crocker's ad agency, DDB Needham Worldwide, suggested a series of commercials revolving around the line, "You sweettalker, Betty Crocker." Central to these ads were close-ups of delicious Betty Crocker products such as muffins and brownies (see Ad 21.1).

After three rough commercials had been produced, General Mills tested them with six groups of women. The results confirmed the idea that consumers were willing to accept a Betty Crocker ad that they considered lighter, teasing, and even slightly sexy as long as it was done tastefully. Encouraged by these results, the agency produced a number of commercials that included such lines as, "Lead me on," "Butter me up," and "Tease me."

The next step was to show these commercials to a number of women who were subsequently interviewed one-on-one. These interviews indicated that the "new image" was viewed in a positive light as long as the ads did not exceed certain boundaries. For example, many women found certain aspects of the "Lead me on" commercial offensive. As a result the company edited the commercial by removing such phrases as "Honey," "Angel," and "Don't do that to me."

The final stage of research involved attitude-change tests. Included in these tests were the original and revised "Lead me on" ads, the "Butter me up" and "Tease me" ads, and some ads that the company was already using. The results

AD 21.1
A scene from the Betty Crocker "sweet talker" commercial. General Mills modified this ad after receiving consumer feedback.
(Courtesy of General Mills, Inc.)

indicated that the new ads were more effective than those already on the air. Moreover, viewers preferred the revised "Lead me on" ad to the original.

This series of tests helped to convince General Mills that it could update the Betty Crocker image without hurting sales. The company proceeded with the campaign, and its share of the dessert-mix category increased. The campaign achieved high awareness scores and updated the Betty Crocker image.

The Validity Issue: Audience Composition

The validity of the attitude-change test depends in part upon whether participants in the experiment constitute a good sample of the prospects the advertiser is trying to reach. A dog-food advertiser, for example, would not be interested in responses from people who do not own dogs. That requirement creates a problem because, unless the audience has been specially recruited to contain only dog owners, many of the responses from a typical theater audience will come from people who are not purchasers of dog food.

Audience composition becomes especially important when the target audience is relatively small. Denture wearers, heavy users of pain relievers, and potential buyers of expensive European cars will be tiny minorities of the audience in any normal theater test. Yet their reactions are the only reactions the advertiser really wants.

The audience-composition problem can become still more complex. A dog-food advertiser may be interested not in dog owners but rather in the member of the household who decides which brand of dog food to purchase. In an average theater audience less than half the people would own dogs. If the analysis is limited to those who select the brand, the number may become unacceptably small.

Because perfectly appropriate samples are so difficult to get, advertisers are tempted to ignore audience composition and take findings from the entire group. To anyone concerned with validity, that decision is understandable but wrong.

Other Limits on Validity

Further threats to validity are created by the exposure situation. The theater setting is a highly artificial environment. To what degree do reactions in the theater setting correspond to reactions that would occur at home?

When the advertisement being tested is for a well-known brand, the amount of change created by one exposure to one commercial is almost always very small. Small changes tend to be unreliable. When all changes are small, the advertiser cannot tell whether the difference between two commercials is small but real or whether the difference is due to some random combination of factors that accidentally affected the results of the test. The small size and consequent unreliability of attitude-change test scores for well-known brands is an important limitation. The better known the brand is, the more unreliable the attitude-change score will be. However, the better known brands are the heaviest users of advertising and of advertising testing. Thus the attitude-change test is, in this respect, least valuable where it is most needed.

Despite its well-known limitations, the attitude-change test is widely used. Advertisers continue to use it for the same basic reason they continue to use recall tests: The tests provide them with *some* concrete basis for making very difficult decisions. Although this reliance on an admittedly imperfect method is understandable, it produces many highly questionable decisions.

PHYSIOLOGICAL TESTS

OMIT 523-526

physiological tests *Tests that measure emotional reactions to advertisements by monitoring reactions such as pupil dilation and heart rate.*

All of the methods discussed thus far require consumers to make verbal responses: Do you remember seeing a commercial for a detergent? As you were looking at the commercial, what thoughts or ideas went through your mind? Which brand do you intend to buy? The value of those questions depends in large part upon respondents' ability to observe their own reactions and to report those responses accurately and thoroughly.

Aware of the shortcomings of verbal response, investigators have tried to use **physiological tests** to evaluate emotional reactions to ads. They reasoned that physiological measurements might pick up responses that the person was unable or unwilling to report.

Advertisers use a number of physiological measurements. Among the most common are:

- *Heart rate:* the heart speeds up in an emotional response.
- *Pupil dilation:* the pupil of the eye dilates when a person sees something especially interesting.
- *Galvanic skin response:* emotional reactions produce measurable changes in the electrical conductivity of the skin.
- *Electroencephalographic (EEG) response:* electrical activity in the brain changes as the brain processes information.

Assessing Physiological Tests

Without going into detail about any of the physiological tests, it can be said that, despite some apparent advantages, physiological measurements have not yet fulfilled their promise. Validity has been a problem because physiological reactions are often caused by factors that have little or nothing to do with the content of the ad, such as minor changes in the testing environment, changes in brightness or color of the advertisement, or random thoughts. Such instability leads to questions about what exactly is being measured. It also produces reliability problems—inconsistent findings when the same ad is tested more than once.

TABLE 21.1   This Table Lists the Responses of Advertisers and Agencies to Questions Concerning the Use of Different Tests. What Trends Do You See? Could You Have Anticipated These Responses? Why or Why Not?

Total Respondents	Total		Agencies		Advertisers	
	No. 112	% 100.0%	No. 39	% 100.0%	No. 73	% 100.0%
Undertake preliminary, background, or strategic research in preparation for advertising campaigns	104	92.9	39	100.0	65	89.0
Evaluate copy ideas, storyboards, and other formats prior to rough commercial	85	75.9	34	87.2	51	69.9
Evaluate rough commercial execution of other formats prior to finished commercial	102	91.1	38	97.4	64	87.7
Evaluate finished commercials	105	93.8	35	89.7	70	95.9
Evaluation of television campaigns	98	87.5	37	94.9	61	83.6
Test competitive commercials	73	65.2	27	69.2	46	63.0
Test commercials for wearout	29	25.9	9	23.1	20	27.4

Source: Benjamin Lipstein and James P. Neelankavil, "Television Advertising Copy Research: A Critical Review of the State of the Art," *Journal of Advertising Research,* April/May 1984, p. 21.

INNER RESPONSE: AN UPDATE IN PHYSIOLOGICAL TESTING

Inner Response, Inc., studies consumers' emotional reactions to advertisements by measuring electrical conductivity of the skin. In recent years the company has taken a standard physiological test, the galvanic skin response (GSR), and, with the aid of microcomputers, improved and streamlined the process by which the measure is recorded.

Since the late 1920s researchers have used physiological measurements to record the reactions of consumers to advertising. Many advertisers, however, remained skeptical of these tests. Because the measures were taken and analyzed through tedious manual labor, samples were often small. The required equipment was often large and cumbersome, preventing investigators from collecting measurements in several locations for each study.

These problems were alleviated by the introduction in the 1980's of modestly priced, portable computers and physiological measurement apparatus that allowed investigators to take GSR measurement to the field. Investigators now can cope with large volumes of data generated by large samples. As a result, physiological tests now rival high-quality paper-and-pencil measures in reliability.

In addition physiological measures have one major advantage over paper-and-pencil measures—their continuous nature. Questionnaires can be administered before and after presentation of a television commercial, but not during. GSR, on the other hand, can indicate which parts of a message attract interest or attention. Thus researchers can contrast the responses of subjects who indicate after the commercial that they are more interested in purchasing the product and those who are not. Studying the subjects' physiological profiles indicates which elements of the commercial were instrumental in influencing consumers' attitudes.

The GSR, or, as most physiologists prefer, the electrodermal response, is produced by signals sent from the central nervous system through the autonomic nervous system. It is one of several changes that occur in the body when a person "pays particular attention" to something. Collectively these changes are referred to as the *orienting response,* or OR. OR measures indicate that the brain has ordered all of the sensory organs (ears, eyes, touch) to become more sensitive, thus enabling the viewer to absorb more information. When the stimulus for OR is a television commercial, the result is a physiological map of the highlights of the commercial from a viewer's perspective.

Inner Response measures the orienting response through the skin of the palm. Small sensors only a little larger than pencil erasers are held to the palm with tape or an elastic band as the viewer watches a commercial. The sensors are attached to special equipment that records the electrodermal response at a rate of ten times per second. The computer then analyzes the string of numbers, identifying the peaks and valleys that mark the presence of an OR. As many as eight viewers can be measured simultaneously as they watch a commercial. The computer screen displays a continuous record of their responses.

Consider this illustration of the value of electrodermal recording in analyzing the effectiveness of one television commercial:

> The commercial was developed for a photo-processing firm. It began with a typical family scene in which a young mother and father were trying to persuade a baby daughter to smile for the camera. The scene then shifted to an attractive sales representative who explained the reasons to use the processor's service. Near the end of the commercial the finished photograph of the baby daughter appeared in close-up for a few moments.

Those sample viewers who indicated that they were more likely to use the service after viewing the commercial produced larger ORs at the beginning and end of the commercial (see graph) in those scenes where

(Courtesy: Myrna Powell.)

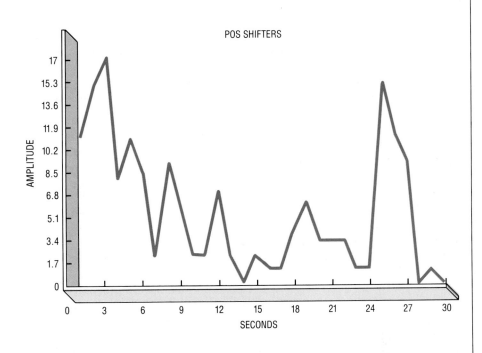

POS SHIFTERS

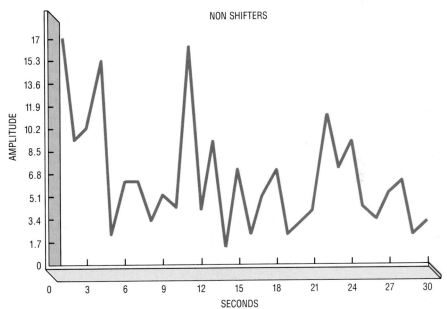

NON SHIFTERS

Photo finisher

the little girl appeared. They produced fewer and smaller ORs during the arguments presented by the sales representative. In general they responded to the emotional appeal of the child being photographed by loving parents, but they were less interested in the reasons offered by the sales representative. Those who were not persuaded by the commercial demonstrated almost the opposite pattern.

Armed with this research data, the advertiser and its agency were in a good position to reevaluate their strategic sales arguments and the format of the execution to make the commercial even more effective in attracting more customers for their photo-processing service.

The Test Environment   Most of the physiological tests require that respondents report to a laboratory, a setting that is hardly conducive to natural responses. Also, many of the tests require that respondents be attached to unfamiliar laboratory instruments, sometimes for extended periods of time. These requirements reduce the representativeness of samples because many potential respondents cannot be persuaded to submit to such unusual and possibly threatening procedures. They also reduce the representativeness of the environment in which the advertisement is shown.

Further, no one has been entirely sure how to interpret any of the physiological tests. A change in emotional response may mean that the consumer likes the advertisement or that the consumer likes the product. But then again, it may mean that the consumer is irritated or upset by something in the advertisement or by something in the testing situation itself. Researchers have had a hard time deciding what bearing any of that might have on the advertisement's intended effect.

FRAME-BY-FRAME TESTS

Recall tests, recognition tests, and attitude-change tests all collect consumers' responses to the advertisement as a whole. They all produce one number, or one collection of numbers, that summarizes the advertisement's overall effect.

However, a great deal goes on while a television commercial unfolds. Even though the commercial may be very brief, it always contains a sequence of separate parts. As those parts progress, viewers' responses to the commercial change as well.

Types of Frame-by-Frame Tests

frame-by-frame tests *Tests that evaluate consumers' reactions to the individual scenes that unfold in the course of a television commercial.*

Researchers have attempted to track those changes in several different ways. In one form of **frame-by-frame test** viewers turn a dial or press numbers on an electronic keypad to indicate moment-to-moment reactions to what they are seeing on the screen. That procedure produces a "trace"—a continuous record of ups and downs. When the trace is correlated with the commercial frame by frame, it provides a record of which parts of the commercial increased attention (or liking or whatever is being measured) and which parts reduced it.

In another form of frame-by-frame test viewers wear electrodes that measure the electrical conductivity of the skin. As various parts of the commercial provoke emotional response, electrical conductivity changes, producing an "emotional-reaction" trace line.

Assessing Frame-by-Frame Tests

Scene-by-scene responses can be useful because they provide some guidance as to how the commercial might be improved. If a commercial gets a low recall score or a low attitude-change score, no one can be really sure what change or changes will bring that score up. But because the trace line goes up in response to some scenes and down in response to others, it provides direct clues as to which parts of the commercial need further work.

As usual, reliability and validity are difficult to establish. Traces can be unstable from person to person and from group to group. This means that atypical respondents or groups can provide guidance that seems useful but is wrong. Further, the relationship between the trace's form or level and the advertisement's ultimate effect is uncertain. Even in those investigations in which the trace can be shown to be reliable, the question remains: Exactly what is the trace a reliable measurement of?

Nevertheless frame-by-frame analysis brings something to advertising research that other methods do not. It provides an opportunity to look inside a commercial, and it offers clues as to what scenes produce what kind of response. Because that is such a valuable advantage, more and more advertisers are experimenting with the frame-by-frame approach to evaluation.

*I*N-MARKET TESTS

in-market tests *Tests that measure the effectiveness of advertisements by measuring actual sales results in the marketplace.*

In-market tests evaluate advertisements by measuring their influence on sales. In view of all the problems discussed thus far, a sales-impact measurement might appear to be the only measurement that an advertiser should accept. However, such measurements are both difficult and costly to conduct.

One problem is that sales of any brand are produced by a tightly interwoven net of factors including economic conditions, competitive strategies, and all of the marketing activities in which the advertiser is engaged. Within that complicated set of interrelationships the effect of any single advertisement is extremely difficult to detect. Even with the benefit of a carefully designed large-scale (and therefore costly and time-consuming) experiment, the effect of a single advertisement may be entirely lost.

Another reason sales are not a popular criterion is that by the time sales figures become available, most of the important investments have been made. The advertisement has been produced; media costs have all been incurred. When the purpose is to evaluate an advertisement, sales results become available very late in the game.

Simulated Test Markets

simulated test market *Research procedure in which respondents are exposed to advertisements and then permitted to shop for the advertised products in an artificial environment where records are kept of their purchases.*

Some of those problems can be avoided by using **simulated test markets** (STM). In a simulated test market the research company conducting the test exposes respondents to advertising and then places them in a shopping environment where records can be made of their purchases. Later the researchers re-contact respondents who have chosen the advertiser's brand to ask if they would purchase the same brand again. The two numbers produced by that pair of interviews are *trial*—the proportion of respondents who chose to try the brand after seeing an advertisement for it—and *repeat*—the proportion of respondents who, having tried the product, chose to purchase the same brand again.

In spite of the obvious artificiality of simulated test markets, research companies that conduct them have developed formulas that, using trial-and-repeat numbers, have proved to be remarkably accurate predictors of later in-market success. One of the reasons for this accuracy is that the trial-and-repeat numbers collected in simulated test markets are much closer to what happens in the real marketplace than are the recall and attitude-change tests discussed earlier in this chapter.

Single-Source Data

In the other major substitute for a full in-market test, the research company conducting the test arranges to control the television signal received by the households in a community. The company divides the households into equivalent matched groups. The company then sends advertisements to one group of households, but not to the other, and collects exact records of what every household purchases. Because exposure records and purchasing records come from the same household, the data collected in this way are known as *single-source data.*

In principle, single-source data produce exceptionally dependable results. The advertisements are real advertisements, received under natural conditions in the home. The resulting purchases are real purchases, made by real consumers for their own use. The method is, however, very expensive, and it usually requires months to produce usable results. It is therefore not usually considered an acceptable method for routine testing of individual ads.

Once again the advertiser must make trade-offs. The procedures that come closest to duplicating the most important features of the natural environment are too expensive or time-consuming to be used on a regular basis. The procedures that are fast and affordable have so many obvious defects that their reliability and validity are very much in doubt. Faced with such trade-offs, advertisers either rely on their unaided judgment, which may be less reliable and less valid than any of the research techniques, or they temper their judgment with research findings that, although far from perfect, are much better than no help at all.

In this dilemma the advertiser joins the government official, the military leader, the business executive, the economist, the physician, and the educator. When decisions are complex and important, research cannot tell the decision maker what to do. However, research can provide guidance, and when that guidance is used skillfully, it contributes to decisions that generally turn out to be better than decisions made without any input from the audience that will ultimately determine the success or failure of the ad.

■ SUMMARY

Diagnostic research is conducted while an ad is being created; evaluative research is conducted on a completed or almost completed ad.

Different research methods test ads for memorability, attitude change, and buying behavior. Of the three tests, those for buying behavior are the most difficult and expensive to conduct.

The major research tests are recall tests, recognition tests, attitude-change tests, physiological tests, frame-by-frame tests, and in-market tests.

Reliability and validity are major problems in all forms of testing.

Despite all of the testing that is conducted, advertisers are still uncertain as to the exact relationship between advertising and consumer behavior.

Although all forms of testing have shortcomings, decisions made with the help of test results are generally superior to decisions made without this information.

■ QUESTIONS

1. In many colleges and universities students are asked to rate the professor at the conclusion of the course. What factors affect the reliability of such ratings? What factors affect their validity?

2. In the recall test of advertisements, and in the typical academic "blue book" exam, respondents are asked to pull information out of memory to answer questions. For both testing situations, what factors affect reliability? What factors affect validity?

3. Both the Starch procedure and the typical academic multiple-choice test are recognition measures. For both procedures, what factors affect reliability? What factors affect validity?

4. As noted at the beginning of this chapter, an affordable, reliable, and valid test of an advertisement's sales effectiveness would make its inventor a millionaire. Which of the methods discussed in this chapter come closest to being affordable, reliable, and valid all at the same time? How could those methods be improved?

5. Some people reject the value of evaluative testing and argue that advertisers should rely on "gut" feelings. How would you respond to this argument?

FURTHER READINGS

HONOMICHL, JACK. "TV Copytesting Flap: What to Do About It." *Advertising Age,* January 19, 1981, p. 59.

KILEY, DAVID. "Trouble in the Glass Bubble: Suit Exposes Flaws in Simulation Testing." *Adweek's Marketing Week,* August 24, 1987, p. 4.

LIPSTEIN, BENJAMIN, and JAMES P. NEELANKAVIL. "Television Advertising Copy Research: A Critical Review of the State of the Art." *Journal of Advertising Research,* April/May 1984, p. 21.

RAPP, STAN, and TOM COLLINS. "Research Fails to Tell if Ads Sell." *Advertising Age,* November 17, 1986, p. 50.

SINGH, SUERNDRA N., MICHAEL L. ROTHSCHILD, and GILBERT A. CHURCHILL, JR. "Recognition versus Recall as Measures of Television Forgetting." *Journal of Marketing Research,* February 1988, pp. 72–80.

Blood Center of Southeastern Wisconsin

The Blood Center of Southeastern Wisconsin (formerly called the Milwaukee Blood Center) is a major regional blood center that serves the six counties of southeastern Wisconsin. This area is the most densely populated part of the state, containing nearly 2 million people, almost one-third of the state's population. The Blood Center is a self-supporting, nonprofit organization that provides blood and blood components to the 31 hospitals in that region. All of the blood is donated by volunteer donors. The Center charges the hospitals only for the costs of recruiting donors; drawing, testing, and separating the blood; and delivering the blood to hospitals.

Because all donations are voluntary, the Blood Center can collect adequate supplies only with the assistance of an effective recruiting campaign. Historically this campaign reflected the economic life of the region. Economically, southeastern Wisconsin has been dominated by heavy-machinery manufacturing firms and other "smokestack" industries. The Blood Center conducted much of its recruiting through these major employers. It relied heavily on mobile blood drives in which it moved the equipment to the large industrial plants and collected blood from donors during working hours.

During the 1970s these industries became less competitive in the world market, which led to a major economic shift in the region. Many firms moved their plants to the South and West or, in some cases, overseas. Some workers relocated to keep their jobs; others became unemployed. Since the 1970s more than 70,000 industrial jobs were eliminated or relocated to plants outside the southeastern Wisconsin region.

Exhibit A
The Blood Center serves the six county region which includes: Kenosha County, Milwaukee County, Ozaukee County, Racine County, Washington County, and Waukesha County.

TABLE 1

Regular blood donors are:	Regular blood donors are not:	What donors like:	What donors dislike:
More likely to be male	Full-time homemakers	Adventure	TV news programs
25 to 54 years old	Quiet	Cultural events	Traditional family roles
College-educated	Insecure	Movies	Staying at home
Parents	Afraid to take chances	Sports	
Financially well-off	Troubled by change	Shopping	
Charitable	Tense	Reading the newspaper	
Community-minded	Concerned about nutrition	M*A*S*H	
Sociable	Interested in health foods	TV movies and specials	
Self-confident	Intensely bothered by sex or	Middle-of-the-road music	
Risk takers	violence on television	Popular music	
Busy	Unwilling to help around the	Alcoholic beverages	
Politically and socially	house (males)	Volunteer work	
liberal		Reading	
Dieters; concerned about			
weight			
Do-it-yourselfers			
Impulsive shoppers (females)			
Adaptable to social changes			

This development had a major impact on the policies of the Blood Center. No longer could the center rely on mobile drives at industrial plants to supply the amounts of blood needed by local hospitals. By the late 1970s the Center was forced to ship in thousands of units of blood each year to compensate for the decline in donations.

The declining effectiveness of the mobile drives convinced the Blood Center to abandon this practice in favor of multiple fixed-site locations, that is, *permanent* donor centers. This change, in turn, forced the Center to adopt an entirely new recruitment strategy. In the past the Center had recruited large organizations to supply donors. The transition to permanent sites required the Center to recruit *individual donors*, which it had not done previously. To implement this strategy, the Center needed some means of identifying the target audience. Like many nonprofit firms, it turned to marketing to accomplish this goal. In 1983 a consortium of 15 blood centers, including the Wisconsin Center, agreed to participate in a major lifestyle study conducted by Needham, Harper & Steers (now DDB Needham Worldwide). The consortium added one question to the study: "How often in the past 5 years have you donated blood?" As a result of that study, the Center initiated major changes in its recruitment policies.

What did the study reveal? Among other things the results outlined several major differences in the values and lifestyles of donors and nondonors. The frequent blood donor was between the ages of 25 and 54, college-educated, had a relatively high income, and lived in a household with children

and a working spouse. Female donors generally held jobs. Regular donors led active lives and participated in a number of activities, including attending lectures, going to movies, and playing sports. They did not watch a great deal of television, but when they did, they tuned in to dramas and comedies about social issues such as *M*A*S*H* and *Lou Grant*. For news, donors preferred to read newspapers and listen to the radio, rather than to watch television. They also enjoyed reading and working on do-it-yourself projects. Donors were more likely to perform volunteer work and donate time and money to charities than were nondonors. They were self-confident and saw themselves as leaders. Thus the profile of the "typical" donor was that of a young, well-off, well-educated, self-confident, community-minded person. This was the audience to which the Center had to appeal.

These survey results convinced the Center to reassess its traditional policies. Among the major changes it implemented were the following:

1. **Retaining Donors** The lifestyle study convinced the Center to place greater emphasis on retaining the services of previous donors. Many people who had not donated blood in a while did not consider themselves donors but, rather, "between donations." Although they were eligible and willing to donate again, because the Center had failed to contact them they assumed their services were not needed. The Center addressed this situation by instituting a major donor-retention pro-

Exhibit B
The Blood Center of Southeastern Wisconsin headquarters building.

The Blood Center
in Racine

August, 1983

SOMEBODY HAS TO THINK ABOUT KIDS LIKE
KYLE..............

Kyle, who lives in this area, is like
any other four-year-old boy, except
that almost every day he must have a
transfusion of a blood component called
Factor 8 -- the clotting element that
most of us have in our blood. Kyle was
born without that element. He has a
blood disorder called hemophilia.

Factor 8 is available to Kyle because
people like you make volunteer blood
donations in our community. Kyle is
just one of the people you could help
by donating blood in Racine.

Exhibit C

gram. In addition, the training program for the nurses who drew the blood, which formerly had stressed clinical knowledge, was expanded to include social skills. The Center felt that a comfortable environment would encourage donors to return. Finally, because the lifestyle study indicated that donors were heavy users of greeting cards, the Center began to send thank-you cards to donors to make them feel that they had performed a valuable public service.

2. **Family Strategies** When the Center learned that donors were more likely to have children living in the home, they began to develop promotional materials that featured children who had survived an emergency only because blood had been available (Exhibit C). The Center also involved the local high schools in blood drives at which students, parents, and faculty are regular donors. These drives currently supply about 10 percent of all blood collected in the region.

3. **Education**   Prior to this study, most of the literature produced for recruitment purposes was relatively simple and "cutesy"; it was designed for a general audience. After discovering that donors tended to be well educated, the Center increased the amount of information in its literature and conducted focus groups to determine the type of information that would appeal to people who fit the donor profile. The result was literature that addressed the needs and questions of the target group. Also successful was a brochure that explained what happens to the blood after it is donated (Exhibit D). Finally the Center began to target institu-

tions, such as law firms, colleges, and accounting firms, that employ better-educated people.

4. **Work and Income Patterns** The study portrayed typical donors as belonging to two-income, economically secure households. This information helped the Center to target its audience. For example, direct-mail campaigns became more efficient when they concentrated on the zip codes of the more affluent neighborhoods. Staff members visited small companies to request them to allow their employees to visit a local center on company time. In addition, the Center took steps to streamline the donation process to accommodate busy working couples. It also changed the hours of the donor centers so that people could stop by after work or during the evening.

5. **Media**   Having learned that donors were relatively heavy users of radio and relatively light users of television, the Center approached the major local radio stations and persuaded them to carry messages aimed at the target audience (Exhibit E). Television was not neglected, however. Because the study revealed that donors enjoyed watching M*A*S*H, the Center asked Alan Alda, one of the principal characters on the show, to film donation appeals. Alda agreed, and the appeal produced unusually favorable results.

6. **Leadership**   Donors tended to see themselves as leaders; the Center used this information by asking donors to "lead" others—friends and family—into the process of donating blood.

These strategies achieved the desired results. By the mid-1980s the Blood Center, instead of shipping in blood, was supplying 6,000 units to other centers. Nearly two-thirds of all blood was collected at the fixed sites, which was the highest percentage of any center in the country. The attempts to retain donors dramatically decreased the number of people whose names were removed from the donor lists. The appeals to leadership were also successful. For example, in one promotion in which 1,200 people were asked to donate, the Center actually received over 2,200 donations because of other people the donors brought with them. The Center was so satisfied with these results that it planned to have the lifestyle study updated every 3 years.

Questions for Discussion

1. How would you classify the various strategies that the Blood Center employed in its campaign? How would you account for their success? Do you see this case as an appropriate use of research techniques? Why or why not?

2. Examine the data shown in Table 1. On the basis of this information, can you think of other strategies the Center might have employed?

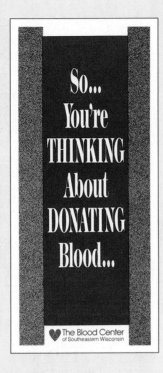

Exhibit D

3. Can you think of other examples of the use of marketing and advertising strategies by nonprofit organizations? Why do many experts feel that this trend will become more common in the future?

Ronald Franzmeier, *Use of Lifestyle Profiles at the Blood Center of Southeastern Wisconsin,* January 26, 1988, and *Lifestyle Profile of Frequent Blood Donors,* prepared by Jennifer Morrow and Anne Schiefelbein, Needham, Harper & Steers, Inc., August 5, 1982.

The Blood Center
of Southeastern Wisconsin

```
         The Blood Center of Southeastern Wisconsin
                 Public Service Announcement

"Feel Good":  30 second radio

ANNCR:    Some people have never given blood because they don't
          know how it feels.

VOICE 1: When you know you're helping people, it feels good.

VOICE 2: You don't get a chance to sit with your feet up that
         often.

ANNCR:    The Blood Center needs your blood.  All you'll get for
          it is a snack -- and a very good feeling.  So join
          donors like Howard Grenette.

GRENETTE: After I gave blood, I emotionally felt a high,
          because I knew that giving blood is like giving a pint
          of life to somebody.

ANNCR:    Go out of your way and give a little to The Blood
          Center nearest you.  It will make you feel good all
          over.
```

1701 West Wisconsin Avenue
Milwaukee, Wisconsin 53233
(414) 933-5000

Exhibit E

22 Corporate, Business-to-Business, and Retail Advertising

Chapter Outline

Corporate Advertising
Business-to-Business Advertising
Business-to-Business Advertising Media
The Integrated Business Advertising Plan
Retail Advertising
Cooperative Advertising
Retail Advertising: Creativity, Media, and Research

Chapter Objectives

When you have completed this chapter you should be able to:

- Distinguish between corporate and business-to-business advertising
- Explain business-to-business advertising objectives
- List the different markets in the business arena and the various media used in business advertising
- Understand how local retail advertising differs from national brand advertising
- Understand how cooperative advertising works

CORPORATE ADVERTISING

So far much of our discussion has centered on how advertising strategy is developed to influence the demand for products and services in the *consumer* market. Not all advertising, however, is directed at consumers. In this chapter we will discuss two other important areas of advertising, corporate and business-to-business advertising. *Corporate advertising* is a special type of advertising that is used by business organizations to create and nurture positive attitudes toward their company. Companies employ *business-to-business advertising* to influence the demand for products and services used in the business market. These ads usually appear in specialized publications that most of us never see.

When an organization wants to influence consumer attitudes, public opinion, or other important publics such as suppliers, stockholders, government, and employees, it uses **corporate advertising.** Corporate advertising promotes the company rather than its products or services because it is designed to convey a favorable impression of a firm's policies, products, and overall corporate health. Many organizations, however, question the effectiveness of corporate advertising. Perhaps this is because management fails to set out specific, measurable objectives when embarking on a corporate advertising campaign. A series of studies sponsored by *Time* magazine concluded that companies that used corporate advertising fared better in terms of *awareness, familiarity, and overall impressions* than did firms that used no corporate advertising. Not only did corporate advertisers rank higher in the areas of competent management, quality products, and higher dividends, but they also spent far less for total advertising—$38 million, compared to $251 million for those that did no corporate advertising.*

> **corporate advertising** *Advertising used by businesses to influence consumer attitudes and public opinion.*

Types of Corporate Advertising

When a corporation wants to influence publics in the marketplace, it uses different types of corporate advertising strategies. Depending on the needs of a particular situation, the audience or public to be addressed, and the message to be communicated, an organization can use *corporate identity advertising, institutional advertising,* or *public relations advertising.*

> **corporate identity advertising** *Advertising used to enhance or maintain a company's reputation.*

Corporate Identity Advertising **Corporate identity advertising** is used by firms that want to enhance or maintain their reputation among specific audiences, such as the general investment community, or establish a level of awareness of the company's name and the nature of its business. For example, to increase awareness of what 3M stood for among younger (ages 25–34) middle managers who purchased its products, 3M used the positioning strategy, "One thing does lead to another," shown in Ad 22.1.†

Most large corporations spend a great deal of energy creating and protecting their corporate identities, which are expressed through the company name, logo, trademark, and corporate signature. When an organization decides to change any one of these it must communicate that change to the public. Such changes are communicated through corporate identity advertising. Prominent

---

*"Firms That Use Corporate Ad Rate Better," *Industrial Marketing,* May 1978, p. 7.
†Karl E. Kaufmann and Bruce Sutherland, "3M Corporate Advertising," *Seventh Annual ARF Business Advertising Research Conference* (Advertising Research Foundation: The New York Hilton, October 17, 1985).

Profound truth: One thing does lead to another.

Here's how it works at 3M...

© 3M 1985

AD 22.1
This 3M ad was designed to increase brand awareness among younger consumers.
(Courtesy of 3M.)

examples include Nissan (formerly Datsun), IBM (easier to remember than International Business Machines), and Exxon (formed from such companies as Esso, Humble Oil, and Standard Oil of New Jersey).

institutional advertising *Advertising used to communicate with suppliers, dealers, or customers.*

Institutional Advertising **Institutional advertising** objectives usually center on positioning the company in the market; correcting communication problems with suppliers, dealers, or customers; reporting the company's achievements; or improving employee morale.

public relations advertising *Advertising used to bring about a change in audience attitudes or to express concern for environmental or social issues.*

Public Relations Advertising Firms use **public relations advertising** to express their concern for environmental or social issues, to bring about a change in audience attitudes toward the company or its products, or to enhance the firm's image with government, employees, suppliers, or stockholders. For example, during the breakup of AT&T in the early 1980s, Pacific Telesis Group faced a problem with the financial community, who viewed the firm as a high-risk investment. Among its other problems, Pacific Telesis had the lowest earn-

AD 22.2
An example of a public relations ad.
(Courtesy of Pacific Telesis Group.)

ing record of the seven Regional Bell Holding Companies that began operating independently on January 1, 1984. However, in preparation for the AT&T divestiture, Pacific Telesis embarked on a strategic plan to turn the firm around. All that remained to be accomplished was to communicate these changes to the financial community. Pacific Telesis accomplished this through the use of public relations advertising. In their first print ad (see Ad 22.2), they set out the whole story—from the company's financial health, to its marketing strategy, to the strength of its top management team.*

Most organizations seem to realize the need to use corporate advertising to communicate their views and to correct problems with the public. The problems encountered in the use of corporate advertising are knowing when to use it and what to say.

Corporate advertising should be as well thought out and planned as any other type of advertising. That is, problems and opportunities should be identified and corporate objectives established before the campaign is developed. To ensure that objectives have been obtained, the effectiveness of the advertising strategy should be evaluated. The direction for the Pacific Telesis advertising campaign, for instance, came from a survey that showed that AT&T share owners and financial analysts perceived the firm as financially strapped and technologi-

*William R. Brittingham, "How a Brand New $16-Billion Company Assesses Its Communication Needs," *Sixth Annual ARF Business Advertising Research Conference* (Advertising Research Foundation: Grand Hyatt Hotel, New York City, October 4, 1984).

cally outdated. Did the campaign work? According to Pacific Telesis, the objective was achieved. Stock analysts' reports now recommend Pacific Telesis for current purchases and view it as a top choice among the Bell regionals.

BUSINESS-TO-BUSINESS ADVERTISING

What Is Business-to-Business Advertising?

Business-to-business advertising is directed at people in business who buy or specify products for business use. As Figure 22.1 shows, these people work in a diversity of business areas such as commercial enterprises (retailing and manufacturing), government agencies (federal, state, and local), and nonprofit institutions (universities and hospitals), and purchase a wide variety of products. Although personal selling is generally the most common method of communicating with business buyers, business advertising is used to create product awareness, enhance the firm's reputation, and support salespeople and other channel members. A purchaser in the business market, just as a consumer, "gathers information about alternatives, processes this information, learns about available products, determines which alternatives match the perceived needs most closely, and carries through by making a purchase."*

FIGURE 22.1
The diversity of business markets and products purchased.

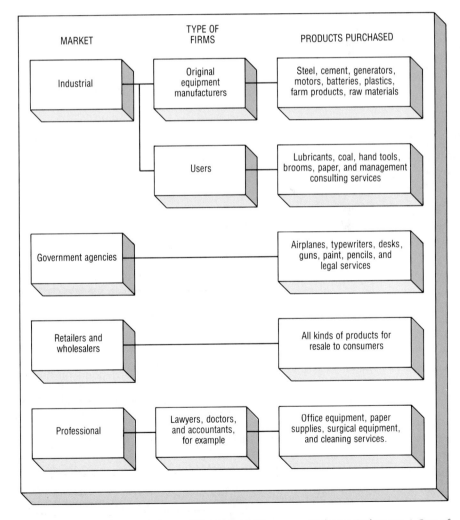

*Edward F. Fern and James R. Brown, "The Industrial/Consumer Marketing Dichotomy: A Case of Insufficient Justification," *Journal of Marketing 48* (Spring 1984): 68–77.

AD 22.3

A business ad for the Allen-Bradley Company of Milwaukee.
(Courtesy of Allen-Bradley, a Rockwell International Company.)

In the business arena, however, many people can be involved in the purchasing decision: people from different functional areas, such as marketing, manufacturing, or purchasing, who have varying information needs. For example, when a purchasing decision might result in a product change, such as altering the product's materials or packaging, marketing interest centers on product salability; manufacturing on production costs. Thus business advertising is also used to (1) reach the various influencers involved and (2) communicate the different information needs.

Types of Business-to-Business Advertising

Information needs also depend on the type of business market the business advertiser is trying to reach. The business arena comprises five very distinct markets, each of which tends to purchase products and services quite differently from the others. These markets are most frequently referred to as the *industrial, government, trade, professional,* and *agricultural* markets.

industrial advertising *Advertising directed at businesses that buy products to incorporate into other products or to facilitate the operation of their businesses.*

Industrial Advertising Original equipment manufacturers (OEMs), such as IBM and General Motors, purchase industrial goods and/or services that either become a part of the final product produced or facilitate the operation of their businesses. Information needs, then, depend on what the product is being purchased for. **Industrial advertising** is directed at businesses that buy products to incorporate into other products or to facilitate the operation of their businesses. For example, when General Motors purchases tires from Goodyear, information needs focus on whether the purchase will contribute to a successful finished product. On the other hand, when Goodyear purchases products, such as packaging material to ship the tires it manufactures to General Motors, information needs focus on prompt, predictable delivery.

Government Advertising   The largest purchasers of industrial goods in the United States are the federal, state, and local governments. These government units purchase virtually every kind of good—from $437 hammers to multi-million-dollar Polaris missiles. Interestingly, however, you seldom see advertisements targeted directly to government agencies. Perhaps this is because government agencies normally notify potential suppliers through advertising that they are in the process of taking bids. Supplier reputation, however, plays an important role in the selection decision. And because government buyers are responsible to, and influenced by, numerous interest groups that specify, legislate, evaluate, and use the goods and services that governments purchase, corporate image advertising is one way of influencing the government market.*

trade advertising *Advertising used to influence resellers, wholesalers, and retailers.*

Trade Advertising   **Trade advertising** is used to persuade resellers, wholesalers, and retailers in the consumer market to stock the products of the manu-

AD 22.4
AT&T, which does a great deal of consumer advertising, also advertises to other businesses.
(Courtesy of NW Ayer/New York.)

*"Selling to the Government Market: Local, State, and Federal," *Government Products News* (Cleveland, OH: Government Product News, 1977).

facturer. Because resellers purchase products for resale to ultimate consumers, they will want information on the profit margins they can expect to receive, the product's major selling points, and what the producer is doing in the way of consumer advertising and other promotional support activities.

professional advertising *Advertising directed at people such as lawyers, doctors, and accountants.*

Professional Advertising **Professional advertising** is directed toward a diverse group of people such as lawyers, accountants, management consultants, doctors, funeral directors, and marketing research specialists. Information

We Cover the U.S. and 37

Major Markets

Atlanta	Houston	Philadelphia
Baltimore/	Indianapolis	Phoenix
Washington	Jacksonville	Pittsburgh
Birmingham	Kansas City	Portland
Boston	Los Angeles	Raleigh/Durham
Buffalo/Rochester	Memphis/Little Rock	Salt Lake City/Boise
Chicago	Miami	San Diego
Cincinnati	Milwaukee	San Francisco
Cleveland	Minneapolis	Seattle
Columbus	Nashville	St. Louis
Dallas	New Orleans/Mobile	Tampa
Denver	New York	
Detroit	Orlando	
Hartford/New Haven		

Nielsen
SCANTRACK®
Services

THE NIELSEN RESEARCHER Summer 1987 Volume 1, Number 3

PUBLISHED BY
Nielsen Marketing Research
Marketing Communications Department

DESIGN
Higgins, Hegner, Genovese—Chicago

EDITOR
Bill McNair

TO OUR CUSTOMERS
The Nielsen Researcher is published three times per year for Nielsen Marketing Research customers and employees.

EDITORIAL COMMITTEE
Bob Bregenzer, V.P.—Director of Communications
Tom Busyn, V.P.—Manager Test Marketing Services
Ed Case, V.P.—Director Trade Services
Frank Herold, Exec. V.P.—Director of Sales and Marketing
Butch Janes, V.P.—Marketing Manager
Bert Kretch, Exec. V.P.—Managing Director Nielsen Marketing Research US
Steve Weinberg, V.P.—National Sales Director

READER COMMENTS, SUGGESTIONS AND CONTRIBUTIONS ARE WELCOME. SEND THEM TO:
The Nielsen Researcher
Nielsen Marketing Research
Nielsen Plaza
Northbrook, IL 60062-6288

ISSN NO., 0885-6206

Copyright 1987 A.C. NIELSEN COMPANY PRINTED IN USA

Nielsen Marketing Research
a company of
The Dun & Bradstreet Corporation

ATLANTA 400 Northridge Road; Suite 1200; Atlanta, GA 30350-1877 (404) 393-1010 ■ BOSTON Wellesley Office Park; 40 William Street; Wellesley, MA 02181-3989 (617) 237-6100 ■ CHERRY HILL Commerce Center; Suite 260; 1820 Chapel Avenue West; Cherry Hill, NJ 08002-4610 (609) 662-1235 DALLAS 333 West Campbell Road; Suite 350; Richardson, TX 75080-3515 (214) 669-1900 ■ DEERFIELD 707 Lake Cook Road; Deerfield, IL 60015-4999 (312) 480-6800 ■ FT. MITCHELL 211 Grandview Drive; Ft. Mitchell, KY 41017-2798 (606) 331-7800 ■ HACKENSACK Continental Plaza; 433 Hackensack Avenue; Hackensack, NJ 07601-6316 (201) 343-3600 ■ MENLO PARK 70 Willow Road; Menlo Park, CA 94025-3652 (415) 321-7700 NEW YORK 1345 Avenue of the Americas; New York, NY 10105-0302 (212) 262-5160 ■ NORTHBROOK Nielsen Plaza; Northbrook, IL 60062-6288 (312) 498-6300 ■ WESTPORT Carriage Hill North; 1221 Post Road East; Westport, CT 06880-5430 (203) 226-6851

PUBC 482/7-87/24,000/AR/MRS

AD 22.5
Nielsen's advertisement informs its audience, marketing researchers, of the diversity of markets tracked through SCANTRACK. SCANTRACK tracks product shelf movement.
(Courtesy of the Nielsen Researcher.)

needs depend on both the advertiser's product and the desired audience. Physicians, for example, want information on the healing nature of the drugs that they prescribe, whereas marketing research specialists want to know what markets a firm such as Nielsen Marketing Research (see Ad 22.5) covers in its product-movement analysis.

agricultural advertising *Advertising directed at large and small farmers.*

Agricultural Advertising **Agricultural advertising** promotes a variety of products and services, such as animal-health products, farm machinery and equipment, crop dusting, and fertilizer. Large and small farmers want to know how industrial products can assist them in the growing, raising, or production of agricultural commodities.

Business Versus Consumer Advertising

Market Concentration As we have indicated, the market for a typical business good is often relatively small when compared to the market for a typical consumer good. In some cases, particularly where an original equipment manufacturer (OEM) is concerned, it might even be geographically concentrated. (For example, our major manufacturing plants are primarily located in the Northeast and Southeast and on the Pacific Coast.) Media choice for business advertising, then, is often limited to industrial or business publications.

Multiple Influencers As previously mentioned, in contrast to the consumer market, decision making in the business arena tends to be shared by a group of individuals. In fact, it isn't uncommon for as many as 15 to 20 people to be involved in a particular purchasing decision. Advertising message strategy, then, centers on delivering different concepts to multiple influencers. To reach these diverse groups, business advertisers normally develop different communication strategies that are placed in those media that best reach the desired audiences.

Purchasing Objectives As you can see in the Winzeler advertisement (Ad 22.6 on the next page), purchasing objectives in the business market for the most part center on rational, pragmatic considerations such as price, service, quality, and assurance of supply.

Price Buyers in the business arena are more concerned than ordinary consumers with the cost of owning and using a product. In evaluating price, then, they consider a variety of factors that generate or minimize costs, such as: What amount of scrap or waste will result from the use of the material? What will the cost of processing the material be? How much power will the machine consume?

Services Business buyers require multiple services such as technical assistance, availability of spare parts, repair capability, and training information. Thus the technical contributions of suppliers are highly valued wherever equipment, materials, or parts are in use.

Quality Organizational customers search for quality levels that are consistent with specifications. Thus they are reluctant to pay for extra quality or to compromise specifications for a reduced price. The crucial factor is uniformity or consistency in product quality that will guarantee uniformity in end products, reduce the need for costly inspections and testing of incoming shipments, and ensure a smooth blending with the production process.

Assurance of Supply Interruptions in the flow of parts and materials can cause a shutdown of the production process, resulting in costly delays and lost

Five good reasons to buy Winzeler custom molded gears

1. **CONSISTENT QUALITY** Our advanced molding facility meets your most exacting requirements. Strict tolerances are maintained throughout production.

2. **ON-TIME DELIVERY** Promises don't keep production lines running. Parts do. Winzeler has been supplying the parts you need, on time, for over 45 years.

3. **CRAFTSMANSHIP** Highly skilled tool makers, working closely with our planning and gear engineering people, develop the finest tooling available. And quality tooling insures quality gears.

4. **QUALITY CONTROL** We have the latest gear checking equipment, to insure your parts meet exact specifications.

5. **EXPERIENCE** Our many years of gear making has given us the experience you need to solve your molded gear problems. Call us and get the finest molded gears at a cost-effective price.

   For more reasons why you should choose Winzeler, send for your free facilities and capabilities brochure.

Call Toll Free 1-800/621-2397
In Illinois, Call 312/867-7971

7355 W. Wilson Ave. • Chicago, IL 60656

Precision Made Molded and Stamped Gears

sales. To guard against interruptions in supply, business firms rely on a supplier's established reputation for delivery.

Business-to-Business Advertising Objectives

The average cost of an industrial sales call is approximately $178.96.* Business-to-business advertising enables a business marketer to reach a large portion of the market at a lower cost. For example, according to a recent study, the *adjusted* cost per thousand for ads by Minolta, IBM, and Toshiba in the same issue of *Time* magazine ran from $49.71 to $51.78.†

Although business advertising is an economical means of reaching large numbers of buyers, it is primarily used to assist and support the selling function. Thus business advertising objectives center on creating company awareness, increasing overall selling efficiency, and creating and maintaining demand at the distributor level.

Creating Company Awareness Effectively planned business advertising assists the industrial salesperson by increasing customer awareness of, and interest in, the supplier's product. When buyers are aware of a company's reputation, products, and record in the industry, salespeople are more effective.

Increasing Overall Selling Efficiency Salespeople are frequently unaware of people within a firm who are in a position to exert influence on a purchasing decision. These influencers, however, do read trade magazines and general business publications, and they can be reached through advertising. By responding to these ads, unknown influencers often identify themselves, making it possible for salespeople to contact them. And for some producers, particularly producers of industrial supplies, advertising may be the only way of reaching broad groups of buyers efficiently.

Supporting Channel Members Business advertising frequently provides an economical and efficient supplement to personal selling by providing information to distributors and resellers as well as end markets. It can reassure middlemen that the end markets are aware of the company's products. At the same time it can answer the most common resellers' questions, such as what profit they can expect on a product and what the producer is doing in the way of consumer advertising and other promotional support. Rarely can a sales force be deployed to reach all potential distributors and resellers often enough to satisfy all of these information needs.

Does Business Advertising Sell?

Although few business marketers today rely exclusively on their sales forces to reach potential buyers, the effectiveness of business advertising has been questioned by many people. Recently, however, the Advertising Research Foundation (ARF) and the Association of Business Publishers (ABP) undertook to study the link between business advertising and industrial product sales and profits. The researchers monitored product sales and the level and frequency of their advertising schedules for a period of 1 year. To ensure that the study's findings could be applied to a wide range of industries and products, three very different products were monitored: a portable safety device that sold for less than $10; a commercial transportation component package that sold for around $10,000;

*"From a Reporter to a Source: A New Survey of Selling Costs," *Sales & Marketing Management,* February 16, 1987, p. 12.

†Joan Treistman, "Where the Reader Eye Roams," *Business Marketing,* April 1984, pp. 110–18.

and highly specialized laboratory equipment priced between $5,000 and $10,000. Despite the diversity in price, product life, purchase complexity, and distribution channels, the study found that:

- Business-to-business advertising creates more sales than would occur without advertising.
- Increased advertising frequency results in increased product sales.
- It pays to advertise to both dealers and end users when a product is sold through dealers.
- Increased advertising frequency can increase sales leads and generate higher profits.
- It takes 4 to 6 months to see the results of an advertising program.
- The use of color in advertising can make a dramatic difference.
- The effectiveness of an advertising campaign can keep working long after the campaign has ended.
- Advertising can favorably affect purchasers' awareness of, and attitudes toward, industrial products.*

*B*USINESS-TO-BUSINESS ADVERTISING MEDIA

Although some business advertisers use traditional consumer media, most rely on general business or trade publications, industrial directories, direct marketing, or some combination thereof.

General Business and Trade Publications

horizontal publications *Publications directed to people who hold similar jobs in different companies across different industries.*

vertical publications *Publications directed to people who hold different positions in the same industries.*

General business and trade publications are classified as either horizontal or vertical. **Horizontal publications** are directed to people who hold similar jobs in different companies across different industries. **Vertical publications** are targeted toward people who hold different positions in the same industries. Advertisers select publications on the basis of whom they want to reach and what their goals are.

General business publications such as *Fortune, Business Week,* and *The Wall Street Journal* tend to be read by business professionals across all industries because of their general business news and editorials. Specialized business publications such as *Advertising Age, Purchasing,* and *Chemical Week* are targeted to people across industries who are responsible for a specific task or function, such as advertising, or who are interested in a particular technology, such as chemicals. Other specialized business publications, such as *Iron Age* and *Steel,* however, are targeted to people in a specific industry and are therefore classified as vertical publications.

Directory Advertising

Every state has an industrial directory, and there are also a number of private ones. One of the most popular industrial directories is the New York–based *Thomas Register.* The *Register* consists of 19 volumes that contain 60,000 pages of 50,000 product headings and listings from 123,000 industrial companies selling everything from heavy machine tools to copper tubing to orchestra pits.

Direct Marketing

In addition to trade magazines and general business publications, business advertisers use various other vehicles such as direct mail, catalogs, and data sheets

*Michael J. Naples and Rolf M. Wulfsberg, "The Bottom Line: Does Industrial Advertising Sell?" *Journal of Advertising Research,* August/September 1987, pp. RC3–RC16.

data sheets *Advertising that provides detailed technical information.*

to reach their markets. Business advertisers often use direct mail to prepare the groundwork for subsequent sales calls. Catalogs and **data sheets** support the selling function by providing technical data about the product as well as supplementary information concerning price and availability.

Consumer Media

Consumer media, in spite of wasted circulation, can be very effective owing to the lack of competition from other business advertisers. Because the message exposure occurs away from the office, it also encounters less competition from the receiver's other business needs. Consumer media are also an excellent means of reaching a market where market coverage is limited geographically. One industrial supplier of food equipment, for example, has been quite successful in his use of television for generating sales inquiries. When he discovered that his average sales call cost $200, he began to advertise heavily on television and backed it with direct mail and classified ads in local newspapers and a 24-hour, toll-free answering service.*

The Use of Publicity in the Business Market

Publicity, because of its high credibility and low cost, is a very effective promotional tool. When favorable editorial material about a company or its products is placed in the media, it generates sales leads and brings about better relationships with customers. Evidence indicates that industrial customers regard technical editorial material in trade journals as an important source of information in the buying process.† Thus technical articles, frequently referred to as "signed articles," in trade publications are excellent vehicles for reaching industrial customers.

*T*HE INTEGRATED BUSINESS ADVERTISING PLAN

People in business advertising departments typically participate more heavily in the actual creation and placement of advertising strategy than their counterparts in consumer organizations. This is because most business advertising and sales promotion are noncommissionable to advertising agencies—direct mail, catalogs, and trade show exhibits, for example. Additionally, business advertising tends to be technical, and this generally requires that experts within the firm prepare copy and artwork.

A well-written action plan, as developed in the box on the next page entitled "Anatomy of a Business Advertising Plan," should cover specifically what is to be communicated, when it is to be communicated, and through what media it is to be implemented. It should also incorporate all promotional plans included in the overall advertising strategy.

*R*ETAIL ADVERTISING

Most discussions of advertising focus on commercials that run on the Super Bowl, full-page ads in *Time* magazine, or copy strategies used by companies like Procter & Gamble. Often overlooked is local retail advertising, which accounts for nearly half of all the money spent on advertising.

The amount spent on advertising varies by retail category. A study by *Chain Store Age Executive* reported that discount stores spend about 2.9 percent

---

*Joseph Bohn, "Food Equipment Maker Tries Local Television," *Business Marketing,* June 1983, p. 12.
†Gordon M. Zinkham and Lauren A. Vachris, "The Impact of Selling Aids on New Prospects," *Industrial Marketing Management 13* (1984): 187–93.

ANATOMY OF A BUSINESS ADVERTISING PLAN

Marketing objective	Increase Acme's market share in the industry from 12% to 18% over the next 12 months, beginning January 19xx.
Advertising objectives	Increase awareness in existing market of Acme Widgets from 35% to 55% over the next 12 months. Create awareness in new market of Acme Widgets from 0% to 20% over the next 12 months.
Target market and audience	Widget processing industry, plant engineers, product designers, and purchasing agents.
Communication strategies	
Advertising	Prepare advertising copy to emphasize the production and purchasing benefits of one source of Widget product applications. Develop headline and illustrations to draw attention to the problems of multiple sourcing. Run 6 two-page, four-color spreads every other month in *Widgeting World.* Run one-half-page black-and-white ad each month in *Widgeting Product News* offering free technical manual "Widgeting Cross Sectional Dimensionality." Insert "800" toll-free number. Run 4 four-color spread in June, July, September, and October issues of *ABC Monthly Roundup* and *ABC Process Times* announcing widgeting "breakthrough" cost superiority, without maintenance or quality deficiency, compared to ABC process. Emphasize Acme Widget new wider size range, technical top line, and free offer of Widgeting Versatility technical manual.
Direct Mail	Rewrite "The Acme Widget Advantage" product brochure, emphasizing new wider range of sizes. Complete rewrite, editing, approval, and production by March 20, 19xx.

Mail brochure and letter to customer list in April 19xx, and to sales department's "hit list" the same month.

Distribute brochure in bulk to district sales offices and distributor list in February.

Telemarketing	Hire telemarketing consultant in January to set up incoming telephone program. Complete upgrade by March.
Sales promotion	Schedule trade show for new market prospects for July 19xx at Cleveland Widget Expo. Promote trade show through invitations mailed with technical manual to new market sales leads. Complete invitation and trade show schedule outline by March 31. Complete trade show planning by June 15. Offer free "Widgeting Versatility" manual in nine fractional ads, April through December, in *Production Unlimited* and *Factory Engineering Extra,* inserting "800" toll free phone number. Run same ad in *Perfect Plant* postcard mailing in September.
Publicity	Write and distribute press release and product brochure to *Widget Industries'* editorial department in January, emphasizing user and purchasing benefits of new larger-size range of Acme Widget Line. Distribute technical manual and press releases with a short synopsis to *Factory Engineering* editorial department in June. Research and write application case history, emphasizing the role of the wide range of widget sizes available from single-source Acme, for presentation to editor of *Widgeting World* in April for possible late spring or early summer publication.

Source: Adapted from Robert A. Kriegel, "Anatomy of a Marketing Communications Plan," *Business Marketing Magazine,* July 1983, pp. 72–78.

of sales, apparel retailers 2.6 percent, drugstores 2.0 percent, and supermarkets only about 1.3 percent.*

Just as advertising is part of the marketing mix for nationally promoted products and services, it also plays an important role in the marketing or merchandising mix for retailers. Therefore to understand **retail advertising,** it is first necessary to understand how retailing differs from national marketing.

Local Versus National Marketing

Philip Kotler of Northwestern University defines **retailing** as "all the activities involved in selling goods or services directly to final consumers for their personal, non-business use."† The primary differences between retail and national marketing center around *geography* and *consumer contact*. Retailing focuses on a much smaller geographic area. Most retail activity takes place within only a section of a single area of dominant interest (ADI). Retailing also involves direct contact with consumers. Whereas national product and service companies are primarily interested in creating consumer awareness of their brands, retailers are primarily concerned with attracting customers.

Trends in Retailing

Location Several developments in retailing over the past 30 years have changed the nature of retail advertising. One of the most significant has been the relocation of retail activity from city centers to suburbs. With the growth of suburbs has come the development of *shopping centers,* or malls. These merchants benefit from group promotions for the entire shopping center as well as from their own individual advertising.

Consolidation Ownership consolidation, especially among department stores, has brought mass merchandising to many stores that formerly operated on a smaller scale. Along the same lines has been the continued expansion of **franchising.** Today even the "mom and pop" ethnic restaurants are facing national competition from chains such as Chi Chi's (Mexican) and The Olive Garden (Italian). Most of these operations provide well-developed retail advertising programs for their franchisees.

Direct Marketing Competition In addition to competing against an increasing number of stores, the local retailer must compete against an increasing number of out-of-town companies that market directly to consumers with catalogs and 800 numbers.

Price Advertising In recent years retail advertising has focused on price, more specifically on sale or discounted prices. Many retailers now use any reason they can find to have a sale (Presidents' Day, Tax Time, Overstocked). There are also EOM (end-of-month) sales and even hourly sales (Ayre's 14-Hour Sales, K-Mart's Midnight Madness Sale). This trend has led to retailers' complaints about the disappearance of consumer loyalty as people move from store to store searching for the best price.

As strange as it may seem, the items that retailers advertise at reduced prices are often not the ones they really want to sell. In order to offer a reduced price retailers generally have to sacrifice part of their profit on each of these products. Sometimes stores even offer items for less than they paid for them merely to attract consumers to the store. These items are called **loss leaders.**

Chain Store Age Executive, December 1986, p. 13.

† Philip Kotler, *Principles of Marketing,* 2nd. ed. (Englewood Cliffs, NJ: Prentice Hall, 1980), glossary.

retail advertising *A type of advertising used by local merchants who sell directly to consumers.*

retailing *The selling of small quantities of goods directly to consumers.*

PRINCIPLE _____
Retail advertising's primary concern is attracting customers to the store.

franchising *Permission granted by a manufacturer, distributor, or supplier to a local merchant to sell the company's product.*

loss leaders *Products advertised at or below cost in order to build store traffic.*

TABLE 22.1
Top 15 Specialty Chains

Rank	Chain	Type	Sales (in millions)
1	The Limited	Apparel	$3,143
2	Mervyn's	Apparel	2,862
3	Radio Shack	Consumer electronics	2,700
4	Toys 'R Us	Toys	2,445
5	Marshall's	Apparel	1,410
6	Petrie Stores	Apparel	1,198
7	Circuit City	Consumer electronics	1,011
8	T. J. Maxx	Apparel	1,010
9	Zale	Jewelry	939
10	Volume Shoe	Shoe	934
11	Gap Inc.	Apparel	848
12	Levitz	Furniture	831
13	Kinney Shoe	Shoe	700
14	Highland Superstores	Consumer electronics	656
15	Waldenbooks	Books	650

Source: Reprinted from *Stores Magazine*, © 1987 National Retail Merchants Association.

TABLE 22.2
Top 15 Department Stores

Rank	Store	Units	Volume (in millions)
1	Dillard's (Little Rock)	115	$1,851
2	Nordstrom (Seattle)	53	1,629
3	Macy's (New York)	22	1,575
4	Dayton Hudson (Minneapolis)	37	1,566
5	Macy's (New Jersey)	24	1,440
6	Macy's (California)	25	1,335
7	Foley's (Houston)	37	1,107
8	Bloomingdale's (New York)	16	1,050
9	The Broadway (California)	43	1,045
10	Saks Fifth Avenue (New York)	44	1,005
11	Marshall Field (Chicago)	25	925
12	Lazarus (Cincinnati)	32	904
13	Lord & Taylor (New York)	45	865
14	Neiman-Marcus (Dallas)	22	850
15	May Co. (California)	34	814

Source: Reprinted from *Stores Magazine*, © 1987 National Retail Merchants Association.

Retail Advertising Characteristics

With a few exceptions retail advertising is less sophisticated and more utilitarian than national advertising. There are several reasons for this. First, retail advertising is more *short-term* than national advertising. Most retail ads deal with price and run for only a few days, whereas a national ad may be used for months or years.

In addition, retailers can't justify high production costs for advertising. National advertisers can easily justify spending $5,000 to produce a newspaper ad when they are paying $200,000 to run it in 100 large markets. A local retailer who places an ad in the local newspaper might have a media cost of only $400, making it difficult to justify spending $5,000 on production.

Most retailers have little formal training in advertising and therefore are often uncomfortable making professional advertising decisions. Consequently they rely on their media sales representatives to design and produce their ads. Most media advertising departments turn out several dozen ads a day, rather than working on one ad for 2 to 3 days as ad agencies do. Also, print media generally use *clip art* rather than custom art. The ads work, but they are generally less "creative" than national brand advertising.

Retail Advertising Strategy

Objectives   To build and maintain store traffic a retailer must continually work at building store *awareness,* creating consumer *understanding* of items or services offered, *convincing* consumers that the store's items and services are high-quality or economical, and creating *consumer desire* to shop at this particular store. In addition, most retailers use advertising to help attract new customers, build store loyalty, increase the amount of the average sale, maintain inventory balance by moving out overstocks and outdated merchandise, and help counter seasonal lows.

Targeting   In targeting, a retailer's first concern is geography: Where do my customers live? How far will they drive to come to my store? National advertising targeting, as discussed in Chapter 7, is more concerned with other factors such as age, income, education, and lifestyle.

Businesses that issue their own charge cards report that two-thirds of their sales come from their charge-card customers. Smart retailers send up to a dozen direct-mail pieces to these customers each year in addition to their regular advertising.

*C*OOPERATIVE ADVERTISING

cooperative advertising *A form of advertising in which the manufacturer reimburses the retailer for part or all of the advertising expenditures.*

Most manufacturers have some type of ongoing promotional program that provides retailers with advertising support in the form of money and advertising materials. Funds for **cooperative advertising** are available subject to certain guidelines and are generally based on a percentage of sales to the retailer.

Co-op funds, which are sometimes referred to as *ad allowances,* are no longer just "a little something extra" from the manufacturer. In 1987 such payments totaled nearly $11 billion.* Ad allowances have become so widespread that most retailers won't even consider taking on a new brand, especially one in a heavily advertised category, without receiving some support.

How Co-op Works

"Ad money," as it is also called, generally comes to retailers in one of three ways. An ad allowance is an amount that can change from month to month for each unit of purchase. The higher the amount, the more the retailer is expected to do. With an *accrual fund* the manufacturer automatically "accrues," or sets aside, a certain percentage of a retailer's purchases that the retailer may use for advertising at any time within a specified period.

Vendor support programs are developed by retailers themselves. Large drug and discount chains, for example, will periodically schedule a special advertising supplement. Their suppliers are offered an opportunity to "buy" space in this supplement. Suppliers are generally promised that no competing brands will be included.

tear sheet *The page from a newspaper on which an ad appears*

To receive co-op money retailers must send the manufacturer a **tear sheet,** which is proof that the ad ran, and an invoice showing the cost of the advertising. For broadcast ads, stations will provide the retailer with a letter, or *affadavit,* stating when the ad ran.

dealer tag *Time left at the end of a broadcast advertisement that permits identification of the local store.*

Manufacturers also make artwork available, which can be used for preparing catalogs and other print ads. Some manufacturers also provide a **dealer tag,** in which the store is mentioned at the end of a radio or television ad. Also available are window banners, bill inserts, and special direct-mail pieces, such as

*Kenn Hustel, Newspaper Advertising Bureau, Chicago, April 1988.

VOLKSWAGEN

- FOX • GOLF
- JETTA • GTI
- QUANTUM
- SCIROCCO
- CABRIOLET
- VANAGON
- VANAGON CAMPER

"WHERE TO BUY THEM"

AUTHORIZED DEALERS

MASSAPEQUA
LEGEND VOLKSWAGEN LTD
Merrick Rd & Clocks Blvd E Maspqa.......795-5790

NEW HYDE PARK
VOLKSWAGEN G C MOTORS
1 Jericho Trnpk Nw Hyd Pk 488-2420

OCEANSIDE
ISLAND VOLKSWAGEN INC
2555 Long Bch Rd Ocnsid....................536-0010

QUEENS VILLAGE
WEIS VOLKSWAGEN CORP
Authorized Body & Paint Shop
218-25 Hmpstd Av Qns Vlg
Call ....Lynbrook Tel No 599-6900

AD 22.7
This Volkswagen ad is an example of a co-op ad. What are the advantages of this type of advertising?
(Courtesy of Volkswagen, Ltd.)

supplements that are printed in four-color and carry the store's name and address.

The Robinson-Patman Act prohibits a manufacturer from offering one retailer a price or promotion incentive that will give that retailer an advantage over competitors in the same trading area. This restriction becomes especially delicate in food and pharmaceutical retailing, where almost all advertising is price advertising.

Advantages and Disadvantages of Co-op Programs

Co-op programs obviously have more advantages than disadvantages, or they wouldn't be so popular with retailers.

Advantages   Co-op funding allows both the retailer and the manufacturer to do more advertising because they are essentially pooling their money. If a retailer opens a single ad to several manufacturers, the combined ad allowances might pay for the ad, allowing the retailer to advertise free of cost. Unless the retailer is billing the manufacturer at the national rate, the manufacturer can stretch ad money even farther by spending at the local rate, which can be up to 50 percent less than the national rate. Even more important to the manufacturer than the media dollar savings is the increase in sales that results when its brand is advertised. Food, drug, and discount stores often feature ad items at reduced prices and give them more display space. All of this can increase sales of the featured item by as much as five to ten times.

Disadvantages   Some manufacturers require retailers to use the manufacturer's artwork and sometimes even a complete ad layout, only allowing the retailer to place its name at the bottom of the ad. If the retailer has established a certain look in its advertising, the ad can present a different store image and thus confuse the consumer.

Because the amount of co-op money available is so large, retailers sometimes fall into the trap of advertising the products with the largest ad allowances, even though these might not be the best items to attract consumers to their store.

Collecting co-op funds requires record keeping and paperwork. There are also deadlines for submitting reimbursement requests. Retailers, especially the smaller, single-store owners, are often lax in following the guidelines and meeting all the deadlines. Consequently they are sometimes refused reimbursement.

RETAIL ADVERTISING: CREATIVITY, MEDIA, AND RESEARCH

Creating the Retail Ad

The primary difference between national and retail ad copy is the emphasis in retail ads on *prices* and *store name.* Store image should be as important to a retailer as brand image is to a manufacturer. In order to build store traffic, ads are designed either to emphasize a reduced price on a popular item or to promote the store image by focusing on such things as unusual or varied merchandise, friendly clerks, or prestige brands.

Price or Image For retail operations that sell products and services where there is little product differentiation, such as gasoline, banking, and car rentals, a positive, distinctive image is a valuable asset. The retailer can only convey this image through advertising.

Price also can be a factor in a store image. Most discount stores signal their type of merchandise with large, bold prices. However, featuring prices doesn't have to mean ads that give the store a bargain or a discount image.

Executing Retail Ads Because the main objective of retail ads is to attract customers, store location (or telephone number, if a service) is essential. For merchandise that is infrequently purchased, such as cars, furniture, wallpaper, and hearing aids, the ad should have a map or mention a geographical reference point (for example, 3 blocks north of the state capitol building) in addition to the regular street address.

A creative mistake some retailers make is wanting to be the star or key spokesperson in their advertising. This is especially noticeable in broadcast commercials where a presenter needs acting talent or training.

Small- and medium-size retailers often save money by using stock artwork. All daily newspapers subscribe to clip art services that provide a wide range of photographs and line drawings. Larger retailers generally have their art custom-done, which gives all of their ads a similar look and helps give their stores a distinctive image. Retailers have also found ways to make their television production more efficient by using a "donut" format in which the opening and closing sections are the same.

The recent trend in shopping center advertising is to produce a slick, four-color "magazine" that carries editorial material such as recipes, a calendar of local events, and other topics of local interest, in addition to ads for the retail stores in the shopping center. Centers interested in projecting a status image to upscale consumers make the greatest use of this magazine concept.

Who Does the Creative Work? Most retail advertising is created and produced by one or a combination of the following: in-house staff, media, ad agency, free-lancer. The larger the retail operation, the more likely it is to have an in-house advertising staff. An in-house agency can guarantee a consistent look and can react on short notice. One disadvantage is a lack of creativity, as many good creative people prefer working for a multiclient agency where the work is more diversified and the pay is often higher.

All local media create and produce ads for retailers. With the exception of television, most provide this service free. The medium- and larger-sized newspapers and stations often have people whose only job is to write and produce ads.

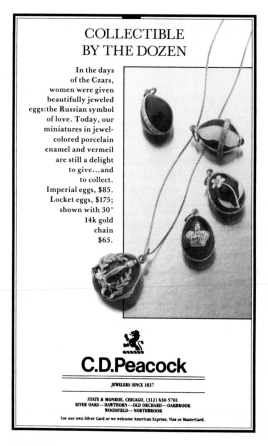

AD 22.8
The ad for Smith's Brokers, with its highlighted prices and busy layout, says "bargains." The Peacock ad, which also discusses savings, creates a more prestigious look by using more white space, emphasizing items over prices, and using photographs rather than drawings.

(Courtesy of Smith's Diamond Brokers and Shane Company, Inc. and Henry Birks Jewelers.)

Although most professional retail ads are created by agencies (with the exception of the major retail chains), this is the most costly way to have ads produced. Also, because agencies work for many different clients, they cannot always respond as quickly as an in-house agency can. Mary Joan Glynn, former marketing vice president at Bloomingdale's and now managing director of BBDO Merchants Group, claims that no agency is prepared to handle the large number of day-to-day copy changes that are characteristic of major retail adver-

This retail ad stresses two pieces of information that are important to consumers: prices have been reduced, and credit cards are accepted.

(Courtesy of Larry Mulvehill/Photo Researchers.)

tising. She says that what an agency can best do for a retailer is develop an image or position that can then "be set and implemented in house for newspapers with the agency handling the electronic media."*

Free-lancers are often a good compromise between an in-house staff and an ad agency. They generally charge a lower hourly rate than ad agencies because they work out of their home and therefore have minimal overhead.

Buying and Selling Local Media

Perhaps the most rapidly changing area in retail advertising is the buying and selling of local media time and space. On the buying side, retailers are becoming more sophisticated about media as they are being forced to work with tighter budgets, are getting more advertising help and advice from their suppliers, are being exposed to more media ideas at association workshops and seminars, and are being educated by a growing number of media salespeople.

At the same time local media competition has significantly increased. Nearly all major markets now have, in addition to network affiliates, at least one local independent plus a public television station (which now solicits underwriting, a type of soft-sell advertising). These stations, along with local advertising that is now being sold by the national cable networks, have created many more television opportunities for the retailer. Most of the top 50 markets have at least one local magazine offering retailers high-quality four-color ads to reach the upscale consumer.

The increase in competition for the retailers' ad dollar has resulted in a different type of selling. Salespeople increasingly emphasize advertising and promotion ideas rather than just rate cards and circulation figures.

Unfortunately many retailers still buy advertising strictly on price or number of spots. Some retailers don't realize that five spots during morning drive on the market's leading radio station can sometimes reach more people than 50 spots that run between 2:00 and 4:00 A.M.

Retail Media Strategy Unlike national advertisers, retailers generally prefer reach over frequency. A retailer with a "⅓ Off All Women's Casual Shoes" ad

*"Retail Report," *Television/Radio Age,* September 29, 1986, p. 59.

doesn't have to tell this more than once or twice to women interested in saving money on a pair of casual shoes. On the other hand, a national advertiser with an image campaign like Coke continually needs to remind soft drink users that "Coke is it."

Because retailers can choose from many local media, they must be careful not to buy a lot of wasted circulation (see Chapter 9). Take, for example, an ordinary bakery in an ADI like Des Moines, Iowa, that has approximately 380,000 households and 24 other bakeries. Over 80 percent of this bakery's business will come from within a 3-mile radius that contains only 6 percent of the ADI's households, as shown in Figure 22.2. If this bakery uses television advertising that covers the total ADI, the bakery will be wasting over 90 percent of its advertising dollars. Successful retailers use media that minimize waste. Direct mail, which is narrowly targeted, is now the second-largest advertising medium used by retailers. Also many newspapers can zone the delivery of advertising circulars and inserts, offering geographical targeting to neighborhoods, counties, or even zip codes.

Retail Market Research

Information about the local market is becoming more and more valuable to retailers. Although retail stores that belong to a national chain often receive research findings from their parent company, most independent retailers must depend on the media and their suppliers for local marketing research information. Many commercial research companies like Simmons and PRIZM provide information on the top markets.

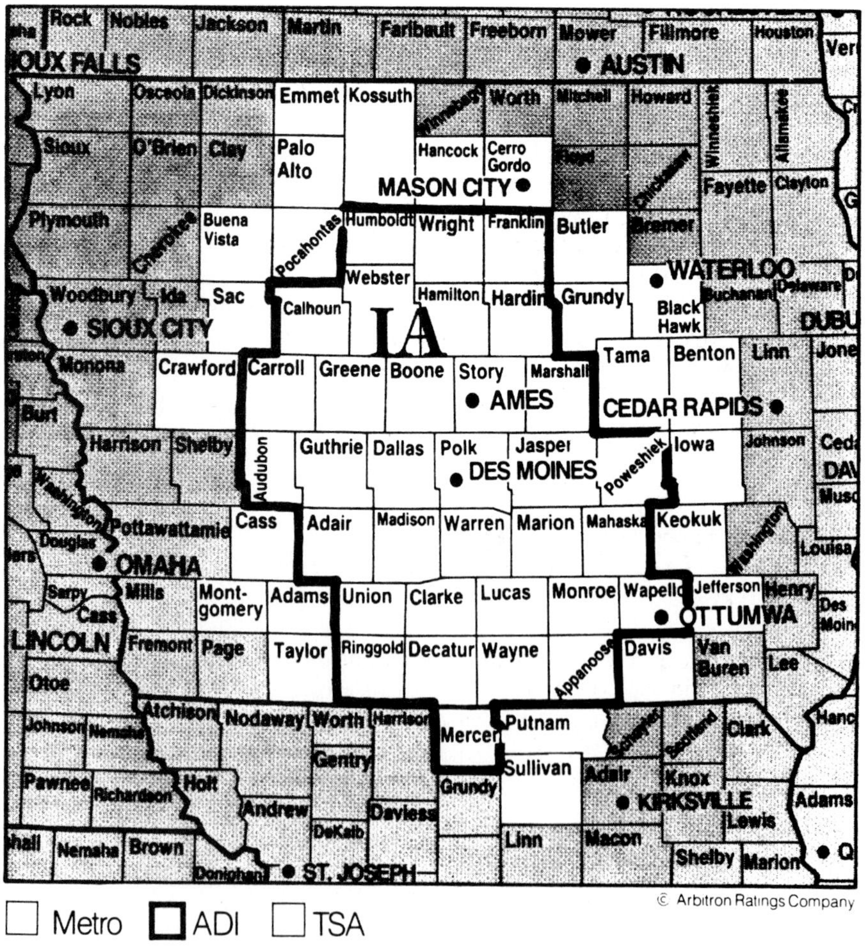

FIGURE 22.2
This ADI map illustrates how you might be buying more coverage than you need when you buy television. The Des Moines ADI, for example, includes 32 counties.
(Copyright 1988 Arbitron Ratings Company.)

One of the most valuable and yet inexpensive types of research a retailer can do is to identify its customers. This can be done by analyzing charge-card files or by sponsoring a contest or sweepstakes. The purpose of the sweepstakes is to use an entry form that asks for customer name, address, age, income, or whatever information is desired.

Retailers can also conduct focus groups to help determine their store's image. These are best if arranged and conducted by an outside trained research service. To help test ad copy one furniture retailer had a direct-mail piece made up for a mattress sale and sent it to a limited number of households. When he found it had a relatively good response, he then placed the same copy and artwork in a newspaper ad.

Just as most retailers can't justify spending large sums on ad production, neither can they for marketing research. Retailers have direct consumer contact and can quickly determine which ads work. That's one advantage they have over national advertisers.

■ SUMMARY

Corporate advertising is used to nurture positive attitudes toward the firm.

Business-to-business advertising is used to influence demand and is directed at people in the business arena who buy or specify products for business use. Its objectives include creating company awareness, increasing selling efficiency, and supporting channel members.

Compared to the consumer market, the market for business goods is relatively limited, decision making tends to be shared by a group of people, and purchasing decisions center around price, services, product quality, and assurance of supply.

Business-to-business media consist of general business and trade publications, directories, direct mail, catalogs, data sheets, and consumer media.

Compared to national advertising, retail advertising is less concerned with brand awareness and more concerned with attracting customers.

In cooperative advertising, the manufacturer and the retailer share the advertising costs.

■ QUESTIONS

1. What is the difference between corporate advertising and business-to-business advertising?

2. How do purchasing motives differ between the consumer market and the business market?

3. You are developing an ad to reach chemists in the oil industry. Would you place this ad in a general business magazine or in a trade publication? Why?

4. How does retail advertising differ from national advertising?

5. Explain the advantages and disadvantages of co-op advertising.

6. Explain how considerations of waste coverage affect a retailer's media buy.

7. Think of a restaurant in your community. What types of people does it target? Would you recommend that its advertising focus on price or image? What is (or should be) its image? Which media should it use?

■ FURTHER READINGS

BEISEL, JOHN L. *Contemporary Retailing.* New York: Macmillan, 1987.

BOLEN, WILLIAM H. *Contemporary Retailing.* 3rd ed. Englewood Cliffs, NJ: Prentice Hall, 1988.

DIAMOND, JAY, and GERALD PINTEL. *Retailing Today.* Englewood Cliffs, NJ: Prentice Hall, 1988.

FERN, EDWARD F., and JAMES R. BROWN. "The Industrial/Consumer Marketing Dichotomy: A Case of Insufficient Justification." *Journal of Marketing 48* (Spring 1984): 68–77.

"Firms That Use Corporate Ads Rate Better." *Industrial Marketing,* May 1978, p. 7.

HALL, S. ROLAND. *Retail Advertising and Selling.* New York: Garland Publications, 1985.

LOWRY, JAMES R. *Retail Management.* Cincinnati: South-Western Publishing, 1983.

23 *International Advertising*

DONT READ!

Chapter Outline

Evolution of International Marketing
Tools of International Management
Organization of International Advertising Agencies
The Scope of International Advertising
The Global Controversy
Creating and Planning International Advertising Campaigns
Special Problems in International Work

Chapter Objectives

When you have completed this chapter you should be able to:

- Distinguish between local, regional, international, and global brands
- Explain how international advertising is created and executed
- Understand how international agencies are organized
- List the special problems that international advertisers face

*E*VOLUTION OF INTERNATIONAL MARKETING

Since Wendell Willkie coined the phrase "One World" in his 1940 presidential campaign, the distance between the concept and the reality has narrowed. The top 25 worldwide marketers spent approximately 45 percent of their advertising dollars outside the United States in 1986—and only eight of those marketers were headquartered in the United States. The evolution of advertising from the home country to a foreign country to regional blocs to a worldwide audience is the subject of this chapter. Included in this discussion are the tools of international management, the means of organizing for international advertising, and special problems in the field.

In most countries markets are composed of local, regional, and international brands. A local brand is one marketed in a single country. A regional brand is one marketed throughout a region, for example, North America or Europe. An **international brand** is available virtually everywhere in the non-Communist world. This chapter deals with regional and international brands, products, and services, and with the advertising that supports them.

International advertising is a relatively recent development within international commerce. Ancient records in Egypt, Persia, Greece, and Rome refer to metals, spices, fabrics, gemstones, and other materials "of value" that were exchanged over extensive distances. This commercial intercourse was, except for tribute or taxes, based on the "trading" of goods from one region to another.

By the Middle Ages, tulip bulbs had become international exchange mechanism in Holland. Spices, tea, and silk were procured in the Orient for European consumers by English, French, and Dutch companies. Was this "marketing" as we define it? No. The old trading companies were not developing products for

international brand *A brand or product that is available in most parts of the world.*

international advertising *Advertising designed to promote the same product in different countries and cultures.*

Seventeenth-century Amsterdam. The Dutch were pioneers in the field of international commerce.

(Courtesy of Historical Pictures Service, Inc.)

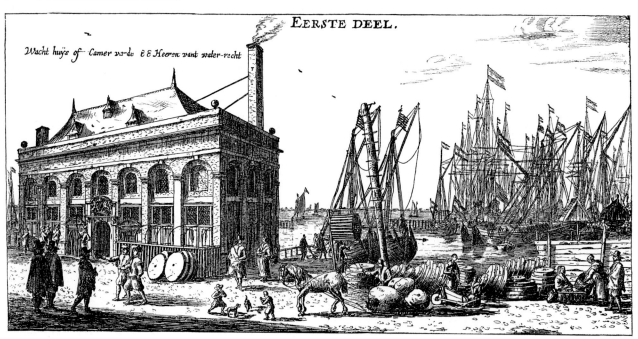

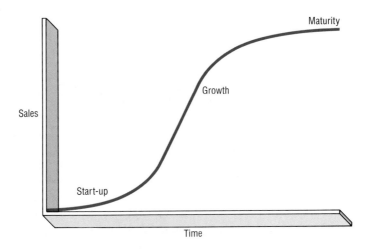

FIGURE 23.1
The typical S-curve life cycle of a product.

the European market, nor were producers in Turkey, China, and Indonesia seeking to stimulate demand for their goods in Europe.

Marketing emerged when the emphasis changed from importing products (tea, spices, silk) to exporting products. Advertising was used to introduce, explain, and sell the benefits of a product—especially a branded product—in markets outside the home country. The current patterns of international expansion emerged in the twentieth century. Understanding these patterns helps us to appreciate both how they operate and some of the restrictions that custom and history have imposed on them.

Home Country Production

Figure 23.1, although hypothetical, illustrates the development outside the home market of products from companies such as S. C. Johnson, Nestlé, and Stanley Tools. It starts with a product that begins to reach saturation in its home market and cannot grow faster than the population. At this point management seeks to recapture the sales gains of the growth period. How can this be done? New products are one answer. Expansion to foreign markets is another. This process involves the following steps:

- Production of goods in the home country
- Export of goods to another country and appointment of importer or local distributor
- Transfer of management from home-country export manager to on-site management
- Local manufacture of the imported products and then of new products for the product line; acquisition of local companies
- Coordinated regional manufacturing, marketing, and advertising

Export

The physical exportation of a product requires a means of inserting this product into the distribution system in a new country. The exporter typically appoints a distributor or an importer, who assumes responsibility for marketing and advertising.

As volume grows, the complexity of product sizes, product lines, pricing, and local adaption increases. The exporter might send one of his employees to work with the importer to handle details, to verify that promised activities are being carried out, and to solve communication problems. This employee is a

AD 23.1
A French ad for a popular German automobile.
(Courtesy of Volkswagen.)

facilitator between the exporter and the importer. Some companies prefer to appoint a local distributor who knows the language and the distribution system and can therefore handle customers and the government better than a foreigner could.

The Japanese, for example, followed this route in their export drive after World War II. Although they set up their own companies in some major countries, they relied heavily on local, especially U.S., ad agencies. The U.S. agencies built relationships with Japanese managements and learned Japanese business customs.

Transfer of Management

As the hypothetical product or product line grows in export markets, the exporter will devote greater attention to it. This process can involve sending someone from management to work in the importer's organization or to supervise the importer from an office in the importing country. At this point the company still sees itself as a domestic producer, exporting products to other markets. As long as this is true, the transferred employee still has to secure approval of plans, get funds for operations, and defend sales forecasts to a company management that is still primarily concerned with the domestic market.

Nationalization

As the local importer-distributor grows with the imported line, the exporter may want greater control over the product or a larger share of the profits. As a result, he or she may buy back the rights contracted to the importer or set up assembly (or even manufacturing) facilities in the importing country. The result is the transfer of management and manufacturing to what was the importing country. The resourceful transferee will seek means of increasing sales and profits. At this point the key marketing decisions focus on acquiring or introducing products especially for the local market.

Regionalization

As the exporter's operations become nationalized in a region, the company establishes a regional management center and transfers responsibilities for day-to-day management from the home country to the regional office. Numerous American companies followed this pattern after World War II: exporting, establishing local subsidiaries, and acquiring local companies. Corporations such as ITT, S. C. Johnson, Procter & Gamble, and IBM all had European management centers by the 1960s. At this point the company still focuses on the domestic market, but international considerations are becoming more important.

Development of a Global Perspective

global perspective *A corporate philosophy that directs products and advertising toward a worldwide, rather than a local or regional, market.*

After a company has regionalized its operations, it faces the ultimate decision: If the home office is in the United States, should it now create a North American division and separate its corporate management from identification with any one country or region? Once this separation occurs, it will take time, perhaps even a business generation, for a **global perspective** to emerge. This change has been made by such companies as Unilever, Shell (both of which have headquarters in the United Kingdom and the Netherlands), Arthur Andersen, IBM, Nestlé, and Interpublic. The achievement of a global perspective requires internationalizing the management group. As long as management is located exclusively in one country, a global perspective is difficult to achieve.

An IBM office in Singapore. How would international status affect a company's advertising strategies?
(Courtesy of IBM.)

As soon as a second country is added to a company's operations, management practices begin to change. Experience has shown that, regardless of the company's form or style of management, internationalization requires new management disciplines or tools. These tools include one language (usually English), one control mechanism (the budget), and one strategic plan.

Lingua Franca

That the language is English is not difficult to understand. Because the expansion of international marketing was accomplished chiefly by American companies within the Common Market, language was not an issue. To succeed within the company, and sometimes even to be hired, a person needed a working knowledge of English.

The American companies brought with them standardized forms of accounting, law, and banking. As a result, local lawyers, accountants, and bankers found it necessary to speak English in order to serve local clients and to have a hope of securing business from local companies owned or operated by Americans.

Budget Control

The budget became almost another language, in this instance one of control. Centralized companies spread budget responsibility to branch operations. Techniques of forecasting, currency fluctuation, hedging, and monitoring improved, especially with the development of computers. Companies refined budget steps, standardized budget philosophies, and tied performance to achievement. Local managements negotiated final budgets.

Strategic Plan

The strategic plan is prepared in conjunction with the budget. Basically the plan outlines the marketing strategy, while the budget allocates the funds.

Organizing for International Advertising

Most international advertisers can be analyzed according to the model presented in Figure 23.2. Most companies fall on the axis from similar products and centralized managements (quadrant 1) to different or localized products and decentralized managements (quadrant 3). However, McDonald's products are largely standardized, and its international management is decentralized. Nestlé allows substantial local autonomy but markets a large number of common products.

Henkel, a large German manufacturer of household products and cleaning agents, provides an example of how centralized management with similar products works. Their international strategy was designed to eliminate duplication of effort among their national companies, provide central direction for new products, and achieve efficiency in advertising production and impact. It included these steps:

- Identifying the need to be fulfilled or the function of a product
- Determining the commonality of that need or its benefit in Europe or a larger area
- Assigning that specific need or benefit to one product with one brand name

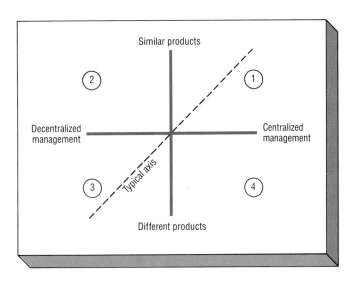

FIGURE 23.2
The product-management axis.

- Assigning that brand to one brand manager and one advertising agency to develop and market
- Not allowing the benefit, the name, or the creative campaign of that brand to be used by any other brand in the company.

Each company develops its own policy to guide its application of resources in regional or global marketing.

ORGANIZATION OF INTERNATIONAL ADVERTISING AGENCIES

Agencies have to develop techniques to service brands that are marketed around the world. Some agencies exercise tight central control, others allow more local autonomy. All of these techniques fall into three groups: tight central international control; centralized resources with moderate control; and matching the client.

Tight Central International Control

McCann-Erickson, a subsidiary of Interpublic Group, follows this pattern. McCann-Erickson handles Coca-Cola, the premier global brand. The Leo Burnett company approximates this system, especially for Marlboro cigarettes.

Centralized Resources with Moderate Control

Agencies such as BBDO Worldwide, Grey Advertising, NW Ayer, and DDB Needham centralize their resources for clients but allow their agencies local autonomy in executing centrally planned strategies.

Matching the Client

Matching the client has to be part of any international support for a client. Companies with few international clients can easily offer each one personalized services. Those with more clients must decide whether each client will get tailored service or some features will be standardized to establish a pattern of service.

The more centralized the client, the more likely the agency will have a headquarters group assigned to the client with a tactical team ready to fly anywhere a problem needs to be solved. In the future international agencies will increasingly base this team outside the United States and will have multiple centers of service.

In analyzing how clients work, the J. Walter Thompson agency saw three strata of support for international campaigns: exchange, encourage, and enforce. At the first level, the agency office at client headquarters (the lead agency) exchanges information, advertising campaigns, and material with their other international offices. At the next level, agency management more actively encourages local offices to follow the international direction. At the third level, agency management is asked to enforce international direction throughout the agency's network.

THE SCOPE OF INTERNATIONAL ADVERTISING

Starch INRA Hooper, in cooperation with the International Advertising Association, tabulates world advertising spending, converted to U.S. dollars. Table 23.1 lists the countries with over $1 billion in expenditures in 1986. Although the United States still dominates world advertising spending, advertising growth rates outside the United States, reinforced by a weaker dollar since 1985, have outstripped U.S. growth. Among the largest international marketers are Procter & Gamble, Philip Morris, General Motors, Nestlé, and Toyota.

THE GLOBAL CONTROVERSY

This chapter began with the statement that virtually every product category can be divided into local, regional, and international brands. *International* refers to brands that are marketed in two or more of the four major regional market blocs: North America, Latin America, Europe, and Asia-Pacific. (China is becoming a major part of the Asia-Pacific bloc.) The fifth bloc, Eastern Europe, accepts very few foreign brands. The sixth bloc, Africa–Middle East–Southern Asia, is so much smaller economically than the others that it is usually attached to Europe or even Asia-Pacific.

Global Brands

global brand *A brand that has the same name, same design, and same creative strategy everywhere in the world.*

Substitute the word *global* for *international* and the controversy starts. A **global brand** is one that has the same name, same design, and same creative strategy everywhere in the world. The product that is almost always used as an example

**TABLE 23.1
Advertising Expenditures
by Country, 1986**

Country	1986 Spending ($ billion)
USA	102.140
Japan	18.309
U.K.	8.222
Germany	8.094
Canada	4.797
France	4.475
Italy	3.075
Spain	3.002
Australia	2.380
Brazil	1.958
Netherland	1.721
Switzerland	1.377
Finland	1.195
Sweden	1.093
Denmark	1.036

Source: Starch INRA Hooper, in cooperation with the International Advertising Association, 1987.

of a global brand is Coca-Cola. Coke clearly is an international brand. But the global definition breaks down slightly because Classic Coke appears only in the United States and a few other markets. Elsewhere Coke is Coke, and it is marketed virtually the same way everywhere.

There is almost no second example of a global brand, though some are emerging: Revlon, Marlboro, Xerox (and Rank Xerox, Fuji Xerox), Avis, Chanel. Some international companies adjust their ads for local conditions: McDonald's, Kraft, PepsiCo Foods, Ford, Henkel. Some are confirmed localists, such as Nestlé and most Japanese brands. The controversy arises not so much over the concept of a global brand, as defined, but whether it will ever truly be realized.

The Global Debate This controversy was ignited by an article in the May/June 1983 issue of *Harvard Business Review* by Theodore Levitt, professor of business administration and marketing at Harvard Business School. The article argued that companies should operate as if there were only one global market, that differences among nations and cultures were not only diminishing but should be ignored because people throughout the world are motivated by the same desires and wants, and that businesses will be more efficient if they plan for a global rather than a multinational market.

Advertising Agencies and the Global Debate The London-based Saatchi & Saatchi company adopted this philosophy in a bid to become the first global advertising agency. In 1984 the agency ran a two-page ad in *The New York Times* and the *Times* of London with the headline, "The Opportunity for World Brands." This ad applied Levitt's proposition to advertising and the service to be expected of global agencies.

Under the subheading, "Impact on Agency Structure," Saatchi & Saatchi stated:

> What are the implications of these trends for the advertising industry? . . .
>
> Most observers believe that the trend to pan-regional or global marketing will have a marked impact on the structure of advertising agencies . . . because world brands require world agencies.
>
> A HANDFUL OF WORLDWIDE AGENCY NETWORKS WILL HANDLE THE BULK OF $140 BILLION IN WORLD ADVERTISING EXPENDITURE FOR MAJOR MULTINATIONALS.*

Other agencies tried to incorporate the global concept. A typical response was that of Grey Advertising, whose position was "Global Vision with Local Touch." As one of Grey's presentations states:

> Every idea needs a champion and Global Vision with Local Touch needs several at both the client company and its agencies. . . . The role of these Grey champions is to:
>
> * Provide the global vision
> * Look for the positive signals that point to global applications
> * Ward off the NIH (not invented here) factor and develop mutual trust and respect with local client managers
> * Employ all of Grey's tools, knowledge and considerable resources to achieve global application.†

Philip Kotler, marketing professor at Northwestern University, disagreed with Levitt. According to Kotler, Levitt misinterpreted the overseas success of Coca-Cola, PepsiCo, and McDonald's. "Their success," he argued, "is based on variation, not offering the same product everywhere."‡

---

*Courtesy of Saatchi & Saatchi.
†Courtesy of Grey Advertising.
‡"Colleague Says Levitt Wrong," *Advertising Age,* June 25, 1984, p. 50.

This controversy forced marketers to reexamine the entire question of how to advertise in foreign cultures. Two major lines of assessment developed, one market-oriented, the other culture-oriented.

The Market-Analysis Model

The market-analysis model was based on data and observation from several countries. It recognized the existence in almost every category of local, regional, and international brands. The two major variables are the share of market of brands within a category and the size of the category.

For example, the brand's percentage share of the category market might range like this in four countries:

	Country A	Country B	Country C	Country D
Global	25%	30%	50%	20%
Regional	60	30	10	55
Local	15	40	40	25

Figure 23.3 presents these markets as a bar chart.

This example would make Country C look very valuable for the global brand. But if the size of the market is factored in, the picture changes. Assume that category market in the four countries is as follows:

	Country A	Country B	Country C	Country D
Category Units	200,000	100,000	50,000	300,000
Global Brands	25%	30%	50%	20%
Global Market Size	50,000	30,000	25,000	60,000

When the market-analysis model is used, Country C is much less important. Half of this smaller market is already in global brands. Country D not only is a larger global brand market but also a much larger total market. A headquarters marketing manager must look not only at share but also at market size, growth rates, and assessment of opportunities for growth through new products or increased expenditures.

For example, in Germany cola-flavored soft drinks are not nearly as dominant as they are in the United States. To generate sales, a soft-drink company would have to develop orange and lemon-lime entries.

McDonald's serves beer in Germany, wine in France, a shake flavored with a local fruit in Singapore and Malaysia, and even a Portuguese sausage in Hawaii to cater to local tastes. These are in addition to Big Macs, fish-filet sandwiches, and French fries.

Such "adjustments" to the uniform global brand strategy vary by market, by season, and by company. Wise global companies have a flexible global strategy and allow management to test new local brands. They realize that every successful global or multinational brand started as a local brand somewhere.

The Culture-Oriented Model

The second line of analysis emphasizes the cultural differences among peoples and nations. This school recognizes that people worldwide share certain needs, but it stresses the fact that these needs are met differently in different cultures.*

*The following summary of this analysis is based on work by William Wells of DDB Needham Worldwide, Inc., and is used with the author's permission. It is fully contained in a paper published by the agency titled "What's Global; What's Not." The high-context/low-context distinction is adapted from Edward T. Hall, *The Silent Language* (New York: Doubleday, 1973); and *Beyond Culture* (New York: Doubleday, 1977).

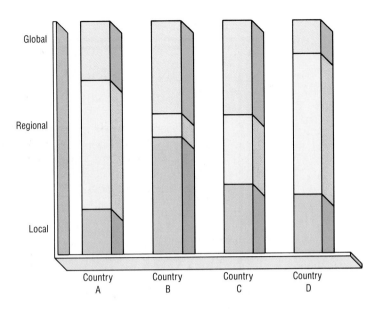

FIGURE 23.3
Typical market shares by country: global, regional, and local brands.

Although the same emotions are basic to all of humanity, the degree to which these emotions are expressed publicly varies from culture to culture. The camaraderie typical in an Australian business office would be unthinkable in Japan. The informal, first-name-basis relationships common in North America are frowned on in Germany, where co-workers often do not use one another's first names. Likewise the ways in which we categorize information and the values we attach to people, places, and things depend on the setting in which we were raised.

High-Context versus Low-Context Cultures How does this relate to advertising? According to this theory, although the *function* of advertising is the same throughout the world, the *expression* of its message varies in different cultural settings. The major distinction is between *high-context cultures,* in which the meaning of a message can be understood only within a specific context, and *low-context cultures,* in which the message can be understood as an independent entity. The following scale lists cultures from high to low context.

- High-context   Japanese
  Chinese
  Arab
  Greek
  Spanish
  Italian
  English
  French
  North American
  Scandinavian
- Low-context   German

The differences between Japanese and English are instructive. English is a low-context language. English words have very clearly defined meanings that are not highly dependent on the words surrounding them. In Japanese, however, a word can have multiple meanings. Listeners or readers will not understand the exact meaning of a word unless they clearly understand the preceding or following sentences; that is, the context in which the word is used.

What does this mean for advertising? Messages constructed by writers from high-context cultures might be difficult to understand in low-context cultures because they do not come to the point. Messages constructed by writers from

UN ATTERRISSAGE N'EST PARFAIT QUE S'IL EST PONCTUEL.

Chez American Airlines, nous sommes aussi fiers de la qualité de nos atterrissages que de notre ponctualité.

Sur une période récente de 5 mois, 97 % de nos passagers en provenance d'Europe ont effectué leurs correspondances sans le moindre problème aux USA où nous détenons le meilleur taux de ponctualité des 9 plus grandes compagnies aériennes.

Pour vous garantir heure après heure l'exactitude de nos horaires, que faisons-nous?

Nous n'hésitons pas à dépenser 760 millions de dollars chaque année pour la maintenance.

Nous n'hésitons pas à exiger le meilleur des 60000 professionnels qui composent nos équipes.

Ainsi le mécanicien qui accomplit sur le champ ce qui, selon le manuel d'entretien, est prévu pour le lendemain. Ainsi le commandant de bord qui arrive plus tôt pour inspecter son appareil. Ainsi l'agent d'escale qui fait tout pour permettre votre changement d'itinéraire au dernier moment.

Et si nous avons été élus parmi les 4 meilleures compagnies aériennes du monde, d'après l'étude menée par la Fédération Internationale des Associations de Passagers Aériens auprès des voyageurs internationaux, ce n'est pas seulement grâce à notre ponctualité.

Réservez votre place sur nos vols quotidiens sans escale au départ de Paris-Orly à destination de New York, Chicago, Dallas/Fort Worth et Raleigh/Durham. Nous vous assurons d'arriver à l'heure. Vous pourrez ainsi prendre votre correspondance vers l'une des 200 villes que nous desservons en Amérique du Nord (dont certaines en liaison avec notre partenaire régional American Eagle).

Pour tous renseignements, appelez votre agent de voyages ou contactez-nous au (1) 42.89.05.22.

AmericanAirlines

AD 23.2
An ad for American Airlines in English and in French.
(Courtesy of American Airlines.)

low-context cultures may be difficult to understand in high-context cultures because they omit essential contextural detail.

In discussing the Japanese way of advertising, Takashi Michioka, president of DYR, put it this way: "In Japan, differentiation among products does not consist of explaining with words the points of difference among competing products as in America. Differentiation is achieved by bringing out nuances and overall differences in tone, by dramatizing those differences in the people appearing in the commercial—the way they talk, the music, the scenery, etc.— rather than emphasizing the unique features and dissimilarities of the product itself."

The Problem of Global Media

Advertising practitioners can debate the applications of global theories to their profession, but one fact is inescapable: no global media currently exist. Televi-

AD 23.2 (Cont.)

sion can transmit the Olympics around the globe, but no one network controls this global transmission. Therefore an advertiser seeking global exposure would have to deal with different networks in different countries. Satellite transmission now places programs with advertising into many European homes, but its availability is not universal because of the "footprint" (coverage area of the satellite), technical limitations, and the regulations on transmission by the various European governments. Other satellites are planned that will beam signals to more than one country in Europe, the Asian subcontinent, North America, and the Pacific, but they will be regional, not global.

Gillette and its agency, BBDO, set a precedent with a "global" media buy in 1986. How this first buy was carried out is instructive. Each BBDO agency in Australia, London (for Europe), and New York negotiated a purchase with *local* elements of the Rupert Murdoch media empire. "Once that was completed, we came in and negotiated with Murdoch headquarters for a three-year deal, right of first refusal on new and up-coming programming and a 20% reduction in

AD 23.3
A Japanese commercial for a product familiar to most Americans.
(Courtesy of Adam's Company.)

rates," reported Arnie Semsky of BBDO. The buy covered the Murdoch properties on television in the United States (Fox Network), Europe (Sky Channel), and Australia (Channel 10). It did not, however, cover Latin America and the remainder of the Pacific Basin. "It was basically a three-continent buy," said Semsky. Because the products and packaging differed among the markets, the commercials were customized and localized. Thus, although the plan was global, the execution was local or regional.

The summary on the global controversy is that strategies are global, execution is not; ideas are global, brands are not—and will not be for at least the rest of the century.

CREATING AND PLANNING INTERNATIONAL ADVERTISING CAMPAIGNS

According to an old axiom, "All business is local." This generalization should be modified to state that "Almost all *transactions* are local." Although advertising campaigns can be created for worldwide exposure, the advertising is intended to persuade a reader or listener to do something (buy, vote, phone, order). That "something" is a transaction that is usually completed at home, near home, or at least in the same country. How are these campaigns, which can have near-global application, created? For international advertising campaigns, the two basic starting points are: (1) success in one country; or (2) a centrally conceived strategy, a need, a new product, or a directive.

Expanding a National Success

In the first case, a successful advertising campaign, conceived for *national* application, is modified for use in other countries. The acclaimed Avis campaign, "We try harder," began in the United States and was spread extensively. Wrigley, PepsiCo, McDonald's, Hasbro, and many other companies have taken successful campaigns from one country and transplanted them around the world. A strong musical theme, typical especially of McDonald's, makes the transfer work more smoothly because music is an international language.

Centrally Conceived Campaigns

The second form, a centrally conceived campaign, was pioneered by Coca-Cola and is now used increasingly in global strategies. Although the concept is simple, the application is difficult. A work team, task force, or action group (the names vary) is assembled from around the world. Usually a basic strategy is presented. The strategy is debated, modified if necessary, and accepted (or imposed) as the foundation for the campaign. Some circumstances require that a strategy be imposed even if a few countries object.

A variation on this procedure occurs when a promising new product is being developed. The team is assembled and might begin its work by developing a common global strategy.

Once the strategy is developed, the members of the team responsible for creative execution go to work. In the case of one recent Coke campaign, the multinational group was sequestered until a campaign emerged. In other cases the team may return to its home country, develop one or more approaches or prototype campaigns, reassemble in a matter of weeks, review all the work, and decide on one or two executions to develop into a full campaign. Such a campaign would include television, radio, newspaper, magazine, cinema, outdoor, and collateral extensions (brochures, mailings, counter cards, in-store posters, handouts, take-one folders, or whatever is appropriate). The team can stay together to finish the work, or it can ask the writer or developer of the campaign to do or supervise the completion of the entire project.

Variations on Central Campaigns

Variations on this process do exist. Rank Xerox handled its European creative development by asking the European offices of Young & Rubicam to develop a campaign for a specific product—typewriters, copiers, or whatever. The office that developed the approved campaign would be designated the "lead agency." That agency office would then develop all the necessary pattern elements of the campaign, shoot the photography or supervise the artwork, and prepare a standards manual for use in other countries. This manual would have examples of layouts, patterns for television (especially the treatment of the logo or the product), and design standards for all elements. Individual offices could either order the elements from the lead agency or produce them locally if this were less expensive. Because photography, artwork, television production, and color printing are very costly, performing all of these in one location and then overprinting or rerecording the voice track in the local language saves money.

McDonald's and others record basic music for campaigns and make available various sound tracks for local use. This work is not necessarily done in the home country. Superb sound stages and musicians are available, for example, in Spain, where costs are significantly lower than in the United States.

To review, the two usual starting points for international advertising are a success or a directive, and the two usual patterns are an extension of a successful campaign or a centralized developmental effort with many variations in execution. However, central approval at advertiser headquarters is necessary not only to launch the campaign but also to keep it on track. Changes, extensions, variations to meet local needs, and efforts in succeeding years to keep the campaign "fresh" may weaken the impact of a campaign. Uniform central approval is necessary to prevent this and to decide when a campaign is worn out.

Beyond central approval is local application and approval. Every ad in every country cannot come back to regional and world headquarters for approval. In cases in which common material originates from a central source, local application is simplified. Within a campaign framework, most companies allow a degree of local autonomy. Some companies want to approve only pattern ads (usually the two or three ads that introduce the campaign) and commercials and allow local approval of succeeding executions. Others want to approve only television commercials and allow local freedom for other media. Free-flowing communication is necessary. Senior officers travel, review work, and bring with them the best of what is being done in other countries. Seminars, workshops, and annual conventions all serve to disseminate campaign strategies, maintain the campaign's thrust, and stimulate development of new ideas.

Selecting Media for International Campaigns

Media planning for an international campaign follows the same principles for reaching a national target audience. The execution, however, is more complex.

International campaigns are not always centrally funded. The global corporation has operating companies locally registered in most major countries. Advertising might have to be funneled through these local entities for maximum tax benefits or to meet local laws of origination. Therefore the media planner might only be able to establish the media definition of the target audience, lay down a media strategy, and set the criteria for selecting media. Greater latitude is allowed in media application than in creative variation. For example, a media campaign in the southern hemisphere, especially for consumer goods and seasonal items, requires major changes from a northern hemisphere campaign. In the southern hemisphere summer, Christmas, and back-to-school campaigns are all compressed into the "summer" from November through January.

Media Choices   Once the basic global media strategy and plan have been created and approved, the central media planner will look for regional or multinational media. If magazines are part of the plan, *Time, Fortune, Newsweek, Reader's Digest,* and other magazines with international editions may be bought. Except for *Reader's Digest,* those publications are in English only. The *International Herald Tribune* and *The Wall Street Journal* are published simultaneously in a number of major cities using satellite technology. Magazines published by international airlines for their passengers may be used. Multinational satellites, such as Sky Channel in Europe, provide opportunities to place the same message before a target audience at the same time across national boundaries. Usually, however, such media reach only an international, English-speaking segment of the target audience. If the target audience being targeted is for a consumer product, local planning and purchase are required. This is accomplished in one of two ways: through an international advertising agency or an international media-buying service.

International Advertising Agencies   If the campaign is being handled by one of the international advertising agencies, the senior media officer in the office that works for client headquarters will supervise the efforts of that agency's offices in cities around the world in executing the media plan. Media orders will be placed locally, with copies sent to the coordinating agency office for review and compilation. Or the plan will be reviewed centrally and placement will be handled locally without reporting to headquarters.

A variation on this system occurs when the advertiser uses several agencies or has a mix of international and local agencies around the world. In this instance media will be placed by the national agencies according to a previously approved strategy and plan. Copies of insertion orders may or may not flow to client headquarters.

International Media-Buying Services   The other form of media placement is to use international media-buying services. These services usually work for smaller international companies that do not have well-developed agency relationships in each country in which they operate.

SPECIAL PROBLEMS IN INTERNATIONAL WORK

International advertising has a worldly glamor about it—extensive travel, cultural opportunities, exotic places and cuisines, and the delights of spending a weekend half a world away from home. It is also tough work, with long days, jet lag, insomnia, and dysentery.

The business itself has some peculiar problems:

- Language
- Laws
- Customs
- Time
- Inertia, resistance, rejection, and politics

Language

Language is the most obvious problem. English normally requires the least space in printed material or airtime. The range of words, estimated at over 900,000, and the ease with which English adopts words from other languages make it more exact and more economical than other languages. This creates a major problem when the space for copy is laid out for English and one-third more space is needed for French or Spanish.

Headlines in any language often involve a play on words, themes that are relevant to one country, or slang. The images called to mind in the originating language are distorted or poorly communicated in another. Unintentional meanings, slang, and national styles must be excised from the advertising unless the meaning or intent can be recreated in other languages. For this reason international campaigns are not translated, they are rewritten by a copywriter into a second language. Every international advertiser has an example of how a word translated into another language produced a disaster. A well-known example of the problem is the name of the Chevrolet Nova automobile. "Nova" in English is a star of sudden brightness. In Spanish-speaking countries the car did not sell well. But then, in Spanish "nova" means "no go."

Some languages simply do not have words equivalent to English expressions. Computer words and advertising terms are almost universally of English derivation. The French have a government agency to prevent English words from corrupting the French language. "Marketing" and "weekend," unacceptable to the French government agency, are translated literally as "study of the market" and "end of the week." Neither captures the essence of the English word.

Bilingual Copywriting   Experience has shown that the only reasonable solution to language problems is to employ bilingual (meaning English and the local language) copywriters who understand the full meaning of the English text and can capture the essence of the message in the second language. It takes a brave and trusting international creative director to approve copy he or she doesn't understand but is assured is right. A back translation into English is always a good idea, but it never conveys a cultural interpretation.

The language problem is intensified in bilingual countries such as Canada or Belgium, and even more in Switzerland with three main languages—or

AD 23.4
An example of translating humor into a foreign language. The caption translates: "Captain, we forgot the Colombian Coffee."
(Courtesy of Colombian Coffee.)

"Capitan...se nos olvidó el Café de Colombia."

Café de Colombia

A Kentucky Fried Chicken restaurant in Tokyo, Japan. American tourists with no knowledge of the Japanese language would have no problems recognizing the restaurant.

(Courtesy of B. Silverstein/FPG.)

China with more than 20 dialects. Multiple back translations can produce sharply different messages in English, even if they have the desired strategic focus in the language used.

Laws

International advertisers do not fear actual laws; they fear not knowing those laws. For example, a marketer may not advertise on television to children in Sweden or Germany, may not advertise a restaurant chain in France, and may not advertise at all on Sunday in Austria. Until recently a model wearing lingerie could not be shown on television in the United States, but nudity is acceptable in France. In Malaysia dogs cannot be shown on television, but cats are acceptable. In the same country jeans are Western, decadent, and prohibited. A commercial can be aired in Australia only if it is shot with an Australian crew. A contest or promotion might be successful in one country and illegal in another.

Customs

Customs can be even stronger than laws. When advertising to children 12 and over was approved in Germany, local custom was so strong that companies risked customer revolt by continuing to advertise. In many countries naming a competitor is considered bad form.

Customs are often more subtle, and therefore easier to violate, than laws. Quoting an obscure writer or poet would be risky in the United States, whose citizens would not respond to the unknown author. In Japan the audience would respect the advertiser for using the name or become embarrassed at not knowing a name they were expected to recognize. Thus the United States reaction might be a turn-off, whereas the Japanese reaction might be to search out the meaning. In one case, the communication might be terminated, and in the other case, reinforced.

Time

Time is the enemy in international advertising. Everything takes longer. The New York business day overlaps for 3 hours with the business day in London, for

2 hours with most of Europe, and for 1 hour with Greece. Normal business hours do not overlap at all with Japan, Hong Kong, the Middle East, or Australia. Overnight parcel service is dependable to most of Europe, if the planes can take off and land. For these reasons, telex and, increasingly, telecopy are used for international communication. No matter what the activity, it always seems to take longer in another country, even if that second country is the United States.

Time is an enemy in other ways. France and Spain virtually close down in August for vacation. National holidays are also a problem. U.S. corporations average 14 to 15 paid legal holidays. The number escalates to over 20 in Europe (and over 30 in Italy). Some countries have patron saints for industry sectors. Who would know to avoid Spain on St. Barbara's day? St. Barbara is the patron saint of advertising and artillery.

Inertia, Resistance, Rejection, and Politics

Inertia, resistance, rejection, and politics are sometimes lumped together as "not invented here." Advertising is an engine for change, and change can frighten people. Every new campaign is a change. A highly successful campaign from another country might or might not transplant. (Experience suggests the success rate in moving a winning campaign to another country is about 60 percent.) Creative directors resist advertising that arrives by mail rather than from within the local agency. This resistance is partially the result of a very real problem in international agency offices: an inability to develop a good creative team or a strong creative reputation when most of the advertising emanating from the office originates elsewhere. Government approval can be difficult to secure. Standards may seem to be applied more strictly to international than to national products.

"We do not do it that way here" or "You do not understand how different we are in this country" or "We tried that once and it did not work." Flat rejection or rejection by delay or lack of support must be anticipated with every global strategy and global campaign. The best solution is to test a locally produced version of the advertising.

Overcoming Inertia and Resistance At times the resistance and rejection are political, whether office politics or an extension of international politics. Trying to sell a U.S. campaign in a foreign country, for example, can be difficult if relations between the two nations are strained. Being politic in the diplomatic sense of the word is the only practical way to overcome local resistance. International advertising involves the forging of consensus. This cannot be accomplished by mail. Successful international companies have frequent regional and world conferences, maintain a constant flow of communication, transfer executives, and keep their executives well informed through travel, videotapes, teleconferences, and consultation. They have learned that few actions are as flattering as asking for advice. When local managements are asked to comment on a developing strategy or campaign, their involvement often turns into support.

Another proven axiom is always go to a problem, do not bring it to headquarters. Solutions worked out in the country that has the problem are seldom what either party anticipated and are frequently better than either could have hoped. The adrenalin that precedes an "international confrontation" can often be directed to very positive solutions.

Despite its complexities and difficulties, international advertising is growing and will continue to grow in an increasingly interconnected world economy. The growth of international agencies, and the fact that two of the largest agency groups are British-owned and the largest single agency is Japanese, are evidence that international advertising is no longer an American fiefdom and that U.S.

students need to understand how international advertising works if they wish to succeed in this ever-changing industry.

SUMMARY

The market structure in most countries consists of local brands, regional brands, and international brands. Regional brands operate in the market blocs of North America, Europe, Latin America, and Asia-Pacific.

International advertisers organize their operations on the basis of their attitude toward centralization and the similarity of their brands as marketed in various countries. The more central the management and the more similar the products, the more common will be their advertising around the world.

International advertising agencies have three options: tight international control, centralized resources but moderate control, or matching individual client needs.

The United States accounts for over half of all advertising in the world, but this percentage is dropping. Fewer than one-third of the 25 highest-spending world advertisers are headquartered in the United States.

The lack of global media forces advertisers to plan regionally or globally but to execute plans locally or regionally.

Market structures, based on the relative strength of local, regional, and international brands, and cultural differences shape international advertising strategy and execution.

International advertising campaigns evolve from a success in one country or a centrally conceived plan.

Placement of international advertising can be supervised centrally or delegated according to a centrally approved plan.

QUESTIONS

1. How does a local brand achieve international status? What are the main steps in this process?
2. How is international advertising created and supervised?
3. What special problems do international advertisers face? Give examples.
4. Think of a product that has international appeal. How would you market this product in South America? Germany? Japan? What factors would you have to consider within your strategic plan?
5. What is the difference between a global product and an international product? Why is this difference important to advertisers?

FURTHER READINGS

"Multinationals Tackle Global Marketing." *Advertising Age,* June 25, 1984, p. 50.

"The Opportunity for World Brands." *The New York Times,* June 3, 1984.

"Targeting the Globe." *Target Marketing,* January 1987, p. 12.

WELLS, WILLIAM D. "What's Global; What's Not." Published by DDB Needham Worldwide.

Xerox Corporation

For over 20 years, the name Xerox has been so closely associated with photocopying that many people use the word "xerox" instead of "copy." During the 1960s Xerox owned 90 percent of the world photocopier market. The 1970s likewise was a period of growth and expansion for the company. Sales, distribution, and manufacturing capabilities grew in the United States and around the world. Xerox entered into several key joint ventures with international companies during this time. One was with Rank Organisation for the purpose of distributing Xerox products in Europe, Africa, Australia, and parts of the Far East. Rank Xerox then became an equal partner with Fuji Photo Film of Japan. The new company, Fuji Xerox, became the distributor for the rest of Southeast Asia. Xerox began operations in Canada and formed partnerships in Central and South America. Xerox operations truly circled the earth.

However, by the mid-1970s the company's position had begun to decline. A major rise in inflation sparked by the worldwide energy crisis pushed manufacturing costs higher and higher. In addition Xerox lost its patent protection on the "xerographic" duplicating process that was the heart of its business, resulting in fierce competition. Japanese companies were especially threatening to Xerox in the part of the market that sold machines for low-copy volume.

These pressures forced Xerox to reevaluate its worldwide business strategies. Xerox wanted to develop one comprehensive plan to combat competition, to stop the sales decline, and to restore its international leadership position. Central to the plan was management's decision to design a new line of state-of-the-art copiers and duplicating products and to market them worldwide. Xerox wanted to formulate a common, affordable, global marketing strategy for the new

Exhibit A
An ad in Italian for the Marathon line of copiers.

Exhibit B
Examples of media ads for the Xerox Marathon.

line of products. To create a global strategy required the support of management in Xerox operating companies around the world.

The company's first step was to find out why customers around the world purchased Xerox equipment. Data from several countries revealed that the company's reputation for reliability and dependability was the key reason for purchasing Xerox equipment. This information convinced Xerox management to develop a new line of highly reliable products to cover each volume category.

Each of the major Xerox operations was given a part in developing this new line of products. Fuji Xerox was responsible for the low-volume segment. It produced plans for two new copiers, the Xerox 1020 and 1035. Rank Xerox was given the middle-volume part of the market. It came up with a new, internationally developed product, the Xerox 1045. The 1045 was designed in the United Kingdom and the Netherlands, manufactured in the Netherlands and Canada, and assembled in France. Xerox associates in the United States, responsible for the high-volume segment of the market, designed the Xerox 1075.

With a new line of products ready for global introduction, Xerox needed a comprehensive communication program. It wanted to promote the new products with a single, powerful message that would be instantly understood in any language. The international symbol that Xerox chose to represent the endurance of its products was the marathon. Marathon running was a booming sport at that time. Research conducted in the United States and Europe confirmed the company's belief that the marathon symbol would be appropriate for the new copiers, which it named the Xerox 10 Series Marathon Copiers.

Xerox set to work on a media program that would combine international with local media. It planned an umbrella campaign in English-language global media, which individual companies would reinforce with appropriate advertising in local languages. The global media chosen were the international editions of *Time, Newsweek, Business Week,* and *Fortune,* and the European and Far Eastern editions of *The Wall Street Journal* and the *Paris Herald Tribune.* Xerox also used two media aimed at business travelers: a high-visibility poster program in major international airports and a 2-minute, editorial-style commercial to be shown before the movie on international flights. Ads in the United States linked the Xerox brand name with marathons and reliability. Xerox companies in other countries produced a variety of local-language ads, all using the marathon theme in one way or another.

To reinforce the advertising program and maximize its impact, Xerox helped to stage major marathon races around the world. It also sponsored world-class runners Grete Waitz, Rob De Castella, and Bill Rodgers, who agreed to appear in six races a year wearing "Team Xerox" uniforms. In the United States, Xerox organized a series of corporate invitational marathons. Customers from the ten U.S. sales regions were invited to run in marathon team-relay races, in which each of ten contestants ran 2.6 miles. The winning team from each region was invited to a national run-off. Runners on the winning team were to be guests of Xerox at the 1984 Summer Olympic Games in Los Angeles.

Putting together an advertising program of any sort requires good planning; putting together a global advertising program on the scale that Xerox envisioned presented a number of special challenges. The company found that different operating companies perceived Xerox products in different ways. Xerox recognized that it had to allow a wide range of creative executions under the general marathon theme to make the global strategy effective. Xerox also recognized that different companies had strong national egos that needed to be recognized and dealt with sensitively. It further understood that the logistics of manufacturing and shipping copier products varied from country to country and would have to be dealt with on an individual basis. Most importantly, Xerox stressed that a full and complete commitment of Xerox management was necessary to achieve a single worldwide strategy, message, and look.

The marathon campaign seemed to fulfill all of those needs. The marathon framework conveyed a worldwide theme of quality and reliability while allowing individual operating companies wide flexibility. Companies could adjust their efforts to their own particular needs and schedules, such as heavy advertising in local media around the time of a local marathon. By creating a single global program Xerox was able to purchase advertising media and materials more efficiently and economically. Finally, the effort paid off in sales results. From 1983 to 1987 total sales increased by more than $2 million. Although many factors contributed to this increase, the marathon campaign played a key role. Xerox attributed sales results to the speedy awareness of its new line of products created by the global advertising strategy. Xerox put out a marathonlike effort from the planning stages of the Series 10 copiers to their introduction and global advertising strategy. It was an effort that paid off handsomely in a new line of champion products.

Questions for Discussion
1. Why do you think the Xerox marathon campaign was so successful?
2. What special problems would a company encounter on a global campaign like this that are not typical of a national campaign?
3. How much flexibility can an international advertiser like Xerox give to national companies? How much central control is necessary?

(Courtesy of Xerox Corporation.)

The new Xerox 1045.

A Marathon with many competitors but no competition.

Xerox has embarked on a Marathon effort. To create a complete line of copiers that can withstand the greatest tests of endurance and stamina.

Recently, the first of this new breed of running machines emerged. The Xerox 1075 and 1035 Marathon copiers. Now, the Xerox 1045 joins their ranks, ready to outrun every one of its competitors.

Amongst the crowd of compact copiers currently available, the Xerox 1045 Marathon stands out in a class by itself.

It has features so advanced and offers so many options that other "comparable" copiers simply can't compete with it.

For instance, the Xerox 1045 Marathon is so adaptable, you can custom design it to fit your needs, choosing from eight possible configurations. None of its competitors offers you such a choice.

And with options like a high-speed document handler and a finisher that automatically collates and staples reports, the Xerox 1045 is the only compact copier with such big copier capabilities.

But what makes the Xerox 1045 copier a Marathon that leaves the competition so far behind is how it's been designed to run.

Every one of its major components has had to pass an unprecedented array of stress tests.

And with the help of its sophisticated electronic technology, no other compact copier can come close to the 1045's ability to "think" for itself.

In fact, the Xerox 1045 is so intelligent, it can actually show you how to avoid minor interruptions and help you through complex copy jobs. It even has a message display panel, so in plain English the 1045 can walk you through what you need to do.

But when you see how the Xerox 1045 is as reliable as it is advanced, you'll also realize how this Marathon has been designed to run and run and run.

Hour after hour after hour.

The Xerox 1045 Marathon copier. Built to shatter the record for endurance.

Exhibit C
Ads in three different languages for the Xerox Marathon copiers.

Glossary

A

Account management. The function in an agency that serves as a liaison between the agency and the client.

Adese. Formula writing that uses clichés, generalities, stock phrases, and superlatives.

Advertiser. The individual or organization that initiates the advertising process.

Advertising. Paid communication from an identified sponsor using mass media to persuade or influence an audience.

Advertising campaign. A comprehensive advertising plan for a series of different but related ads that appear in different media across a specified time period.

Advertising objectives. Statements of the effect of the advertising message on the audience.

Advertising plan. A document that matches the right audience to the right message and presents it in the right media.

Advertising strategy. The development of a plan for persuasive communications in a competitive marketing situation.

Agent. Someone who acts on behalf of someone else, usually for a fee.

Agricultural advertising. Advertising directed at large and small farmers.

Allocations. Divisions or proportions of advertising dollars among the various media.

Animatic. A preliminary version of a commercial with the storyboard frames recorded on videotape along with a rough sound track.

Animation. A type of recording medium in which objects are sketched and then filmed one frame at a time.

Answer print. The final finished version of the commercial with the audio and video recorded together.

Appeal. Something that moves people.

Arranger. The person who orchestrates the music, arranging it for the various instruments, voices, and scenes.

Art. The visual elements in an ad, including illustrations, photos, type, logos and signatures, and the layout.

Art director. The person who is primarily responsible for the visual image of the advertisement.

Association. A link or connection between two ideas.

Attitude. A learned predisposition that we hold toward an object, person, or ideal.

Attitude-change test. A test that evaluates the effectiveness of an advertisement by measuring whether the ad affects consumers' intentions to buy a brand.

B

Benefits. Statements about what the product can do for the user.

Benefit segmentation. Segments identified by the appeal of the product to their personal interests.

Billboards. Large structures erected on highways and roads for the display of huge advertising posters.

Bleed. An ad in which the printed area runs to the trim edge of the page.

Body copy. The text of the message.

Brag-and-boast copy. Advertising text that is written from the company's point of view to extol its virtues and accomplishments.

Brainstorming. A creative-thinking technique using free association in a group environment to stimulate inspiration.

Brand Development Index (BDI). An index that identifies the demand for the brand within a region.

Branding. The process of creating an identity for a product using a distinctive name or symbol.

Brand loyalty. Existing positive opinions held by consumers about the product or service.

Broadsheet. A newspaper with a page size of 8 columns wide and 22 inches deep.

Broadsheets. Large brochures that unfold like a map.

Business-to-business advertising. Advertising directed at people who buy or specify products for business use.

Business units. Organizational units in a company that are focused around product lines, brands, or specific services.

C

Cable television. A form of subscription television in which the signals are carried to households by a cable.

Captions. Short descriptions of the content of a photograph or an illustration.

Car cards. Small advertisements that are mounted in racks inside a vehicle.

Carry-over effect. A measure of residual effect (awareness or recall) of the advertising message some time after the advertising period has ended.

Category Development Index (CDI). An index that identifies the demand for the category within a region.

Circulation. A measure of the number of copies sold.

Claim. A statement about the product's performance.

Classified advertising. Commercial messages arranged in the newspaper according to the interests of readers.

Claymation. A technique that uses figures sculpted from clay and filmed one frame at a time.

Cliché. A trite expression, an overused idea.

Color separation. The process of splitting a color image into four images recorded on negatives; each negative represents one of the four process colors.

Commission. A form of payment in which an agent or agency receives a certain percentage (often 15 percent) of media charges.

Competitive product advantage. The identification of a feature that is important to the consumer where your product is strong and the competition is vulnerable.

Composer. The person who writes the music.

Composition. The process of arranging the elements in a photograph or an illustration.

Comprehensive. A layout that looks as much like the final printed ad as possible.

Consumer research. Research that focuses on how consumers think, feel, decide, and behave.

Consumers. People who buy or use products.

Contests. Sales-promotion activities that require participants to compete for a prize on the basis of some skill or ability.

Continuity. The strategy and tactics used to schedule advertising over the time span of the advertising campaign.

Continuous pattern (scheduling). Advertising spending that remains relatively constant during the campaign period.

Convergent thinking. Thinking that uses logic to arrive at the "right" answer.

Cooperative advertising. A form of advertising in which the manufacturer reimburses the retailer for part or all of the advertising expenditures.

Copywriter. The person who writes the text for an ad.

Corporate advertising. Advertising used by businesses to influence consumer attitudes and public opinion.

Corporate identity advertising. Advertising used to enhance or maintain a company's reputation.

Corrective advertising. A remedy required by the FTC in which an advertiser who produced misleading messages is required to issue factual information to offset these messages.

Cost per Rating Point (CPRP). A method of comparing media vehicles by relating the cost of the message unit to the audience rating.

Cost per Thousand (CPM). The cost of exposing each 1,000 members of the target audience to the advertising message.

Coupons. Legal certificates offered by manufacturers and retailers that grant specified savings on selected products when presented for redemption at the point of purchase.

CPM trend analysis. Longitudinal (long-term) history of average cost-per-thousand tendencies of advertising media that is used to assist in forecasting future CPM levels.

Crawl. Computer-generated letters that move across the bottom of the screen.

Creative concept. A "Big Idea" that is original and dramatizes the selling point.

Creative platform. A document that summarizes the message strategy decisions behind an individual ad.

Culture. The complex whole of tangible items, intangible concepts, and social behaviors that define a group of people or a way of life.

Cut. An abrupt transition from one shot to another.

Cutouts. Irregularly shaped extensions added to the top or side of standard outdoor boards.

D

Data base. An extensive list of consumer information including names, addresses, telephone numbers, and psychographic and demographic data.

Data sheets. Advertising that provides detailed technical information.

Dealer loader. A premium given to a retailer by a manufacturer for buying a certain quantity of product.

Dealer tag. Time left at the end of a broadcast advertisement that permits identification of the local store.

Demand. The quantity of goods or services that consumers are willing and able to buy at various prices.

Demographics. The vital statistics about the human population, its distribution, and its characteristics.

Diagnostic research. Research used to identify the best approach from among a set of alternatives.

Direct competition. A product in the same category.

Directional. Advertising that channels the buyer to the store where the product or service is available.

Direct mail. A form of advertising that uses the mail to carry the message.

Direct marketing. A selling method that establishes a one-on-one relationship with customers; it can include direct-response advertising and other promotional techniques.

Director. The person in charge of the actual filming or taping of the commercial.

Direct-response advertising. Advertising that solicits a response from the prospect without the intervention of a third party.

Discretionary income. The money available to a household after taxes and spending on basic necessities are removed.

Dispersion. The use of as many different stations and programs as possible to avoid duplicating the message audience.

Display advertising. Sponsored messages that can be of any size and location within the newspaper, with the exception of the editorial page.

Display copy. Type set in larger sizes that is used to attract the reader's attention.

Divergent thinking. Thinking that uses free association to uncover all possible alternatives.

Drama. A story built around characters in a situation.

Dubbing. The process of making duplicate copies of a videotape.

Durable goods. A classification of products that are expected to last for an extended time period.

E

Economic concentration. The relative size and strength of firms within a given industry.

Economies of scale. A system in which firms are able to create a lower dollar cost per unit by producing larger quantities of goods.

Editor. The person who assembles the best shots to create scenes and who synchronizes the audio track with the images.

Effective frequency. A recent concept in planning that determines a range (minimum and maximum) of repeat exposure for a message.

Emotional. Messages built on psychological appeals such as fear and love.

Empathy. Understanding the feelings, thoughts, and emotions of someone else.

Evaluative research. Research intended to measure the effectiveness of finished or nearly finished advertisements.

Execution. The form of the complete advertisement; how the ideas are expressed and what the ad looks like.

Experiments. A research method that manipulates a set of variables to test hypotheses.

Exploratory research. Informal intelligence gathering, backgrounding.

Exterior transit advertising. Advertising posters that are mounted on the sides, rear, and top of vehicles.

F

Family. Two or more people who are related by blood, marriage, or adoption.

Feature analysis. A comparison of your product's features against the features of competing products.

Features. Attributes of a product such as size, color, and style.

Federal Communications Commission (FCC). A federal agency that regulates broadcast media and has the power to eliminate messages, including ads, that are deceptive or in poor taste.

Federal Trade Commission (FTC). A federal agency responsible for interpreting deceptive advertising and regulating unfair methods of competition.

Fee. A mode of payment in which an agency charges a client on the basis of the agency's hourly costs.

Film. A strip of celluloid with a series of still images, called frames.

Fixed pricing. A traditional method of media pricing where rates are published and are applied equally to all advertisers.

Flighting. An advertising pattern characterized by a period of intensified activity, called a flight, followed by periods of no advertising, called a hiatus.

Focal point. The first element in a layout that the eye sees.

Focus group. A group interview that tries to stimulate people to talk candidly about some topics or products.

Font. A complete set of letters in one size and face.

Food and Drug Administration (FDA). A federal regulatory agency that oversees package labeling and ingredient listings for food and drugs.

Forecasting. Estimating sales levels and the impact of various budget decisions on sales.

Frame-by-frame tests. Tests that evaluate consumers' reactions to the individual scenes that unfold in the course of a television commercial.

Franchising. Permission granted by a manufacturer, distributor, or supplier to a local merchant to sell the company's product.

Free association. An exercise in which you describe everything that comes into your mind when you think of a word or an image.

Free-lance artists. Independent artists who work on individual assignments for an agency or advertiser.

Free-standing insert advertisements. Preprinted advertisements that are placed loosely within the newspaper.

Frequency. (a) The number of times an audience has an opportunity to be exposed to a media vehicle or vehicles in a specified time span. (b) The number of radio waves produced by a transmitter in one second.

G

Generic products. Products that are marketed without any identifying brand; they are usually less expensive than branded products.

Global brand. A brand that has the same name, same design, and same creative strategy everywhere in the world.

Global perspective. A corporate philosophy that directs products and advertising toward a worldwide, rather than a local or regional, market.

Gravure. A type of printing that uses an image that is engraved, or recessed, into the surface of the printing plate.

Gross impressions. The sum of the audiences of all media vehicles used within a designated time span.

Gross Rating Points (GRP). The sum of the total exposure potential of a series of media vehicles expressed as a percentage of the audience population.

Guarantees. Agreements in which the medium promises to compensate the advertiser should the audience fall below a specified level.

Gutenberg diagonal. A visual path that flows from the upper left corner to the lower right.

H

Halftones. Images with a continuous range of shades from light to dark.

Hard-sell advertising. Messages that emphasize a strong argument and call for action.

Headline. The title of an ad; it is set in large type to get the reader's attention.

Hierarchy of effects. A set of consumer responses that moves from the least serious, involved, or complex up through the most serious, involved, or complex.

High-involvement products. Products that require an involved purchase process with information search and product comparison.

High-productivity agencies. Advertising agencies with a low staff-to-billings ratio.

Holography. A technique that produces a projected three-dimensional image.

Horizontal publications. Publications directed to people who hold similar jobs in different companies across different industries.

Household. All those people who occupy one living unit, whether or not they are related.

I

Idea. A mental representation; a concept created by combining thoughts.

Image. Messages built by associating or linking the product to symbols of life styles and desired values.

Impact. (a) A value of media influence on the audience that is expected to produce higher-than-normal awareness of the advertiser's message. (b) The effect that a message has on the audience.

Indicia. The postage label printed by a postage meter.

Indirect competition. A product that is in a different category but functions as an alternative purchase choice.

Industrial advertising. Advertising directed at businesses that buy products to incorporate into other products or to facilitate the operation of their businesses.

Informational. Messages built on facts and logic.

In-house agency. An advertising department on the advertiser's staff that handles most, if not all, of the functions of an outside agency.

In-market tests. Tests that measure the effectiveness of advertisements by measuring actual sales results in the marketplace.

In register. A precise matching of colors and images within an ad.

Institutional advertising. Advertising used to communicate with suppliers, dealers, or customers.

Integrated marketing communications. Promotional planning that focuses on integrated communication based on an analysis of consumer behavior.

Interactive. Advertising that uses personal interaction between the advertiser and the customer.

Interconnects. A special cable technology that allows local advertisers to run their commercials in small geographical areas through the interconnection of a number of cable systems.

Interior transit advertising. Advertising on posters that are mounted inside vehicles such as buses, subway cars, and taxis.

Interlock. A version of the commercial with the audio and video timed together, although the two are still recorded separately.

International advertising. Advertising designed to promote the same product in different countries and cultures.

International brand. A brand or product that is available in most parts of the world.

Intrusive. (a) A message that is not wanted by the audience; it uses techniques to force attention. (b) A message that forces itself on the audience in order to catch the audience's attention.

Italic. A type variation that uses letters that slant to the right.

J

Jingles. Commercials with a message that is presented musically.

Justified. A form of typeset copy in which the edges of the lines in a column of type are forced to align by adding space between words in the line.

K

Key frame. A single frame of a commercial that summarizes the heart of the message.

Key visual. A dominant image around which the commercial's message is planned.

Kinetic boards. Outdoor advertising that uses moving elements.

Kiosks. Multisided bulletin board structures designed for public posting of messages.

L

Layout. A drawing that shows where all the elements in the ad are to be positioned.

Lecture. Instruction delivered verbally to present knowledge and facts.

Letterpress. A type of printing that prints from an image onto a raised surface.

Lifestyle. The pattern of living that reflects how people allocate their time, energy, and money.

Line art. Art in which all elements are solid with no intermediate shades or tones.

Line extensions. New products introduced under existing brand names.

Logo. Logotype; a distinctive mark that identifies the product, company, or brand.

Loss leaders. Products advertised at or below cost in order to build store traffic.

Low-involvement products. Products that require limited deliberation; sometimes purchases are even made on impulse.

M

Mail order. A form of marketing that uses the mail to deliver the product.

Makegoods. Compensation given by the media to advertisers in the form of additional message units that are commonly used in situations involving production errors by the media and preemption of the advertiser's programming.

Margin. White space used to frame the ad content.

Market. An area of the country, a group of people, or the overall demand for a product.

Market competition school. The view of advertising as an information source that increases consumers' price sensitivity and stimulates competition among firms.

Marketing. Business activities that direct the exchange of goods and services between producers and consumers.

Marketing mix. A plan that identifies the most effective combination of promotional activities.

Marketing plan. A document that proposes strategies for employing the marketing elements to achieve a marketing goal.

Marketing public relations. An area of public relations activity involving the marketing of products and services.

Marketing research. Research that investigates all the elements of the marketing mix.

Market philosophy. The general attitude of the marketer toward the customer.

Market power school. The view of advertising as a persuasive communications tool that marketers use to distract the consumer's attention away from price.

Market research. Research that gathers information about specific markets.

Market segmentation. The process of identifying segments by demographic or psychographic characteristics.

Media. The channels of communication used by advertisers.

Media planning. A decision process leading to the use of advertising time and space to assist in the achievement of marketing objectives.

Media unit cost trends. A history of changes in the average unit (per message) prices for each medium that is used in cost forecasting.

Megamergers. Combinations of large international agencies under a central holding company.

Merging. The process of combining two or more lists of prospects.

Message fragment. A quick impression that gets filed away in the memory; highlights, but not details.

Mixing. Combining different tracks of music, voices, and sound effects to create the final ad.

Motive. An unobservable inner force that stimulates and compels a behavioral response.

N

Needs. Basic forces that motivate you to do or to want something.

Network radio. A group of local affiliates providing simultaneous programming via connection to one or more of the national networks through AT&T telephone wires.

Newsprint. An inexpensive but tough paper with a rough surface, used for printing newspapers.

Nondurable goods. A product category that includes items that are frequently purchased and consumed in a relatively short time period.

Nontraditional delivery. Delivery of magazines to readers through such methods as door hangers or newspapers.

O

Offset. A type of printing that prints from a flat surface on the printing plate. The image is transferred to a rubber blanket that carries the impression to the paper.

Open pricing. A method of media pricing in which prices are negotiated on a contract-by-contract basis for each unit of media space or time.

Optical center. A point slightly above the mathematical center of a page.

Original. One of a kind; unusual and unexpected.

Outcome evaluation. Measuring the effectiveness of public relations efforts in changing audience awareness, knowledge, attitudes, or behavior.

Overline. A subhead that leads into the headline.

P

Participations. An arrangement in which a television advertiser buys commercial time from a network.

Percent-of-sales method. A technique for computing the budget level that is based on the relationship between cost of advertising and total sales.

Perception. The process by which we receive information through our five senses and acknowledge and assign meaning to this information.

Perceptual map. A map that shows where consumers locate various products in the category in terms of several important features.

Personality. Relatively long-lasting personal qualities that allow us to cope with, and respond to, the world around us.

Personal selling. Face-to-face contact between a salesperson and a potential customer.

Photoboard. A type of rough commercial, similar to an animatic except that the frames are actual photos instead of sketches.

Physiological tests. Tests that measure emotional reactions to advertisements by monitoring reactions such as pupil dilation and heart rate.

Picas. A unit of type measurement used to measure width and depth of columns; there are 12 points in a pica and 6 picas in an inch.

Point-of-purchase display. A display designed by the manufacturer and distributed to retailers in order to promote a particular brand or line of products.

Points. A unit used to measure the height of type; there are 72 points in an inch.

Population. Everyone included in a designated group.

Positioning. The way in which a product is perceived in the marketplace by the consumers.

Preemptible rate. A form of open pricing in which spot television buyers purchase a spot position at a lower rate with the understanding that they might lose the position to an advertiser who is willing to pay a higher rate.

Preferred positions. Sections or pages of magazine and newspaper issues that are in high demand by advertisers because they have a special appeal to the target audience.

Premium. A tangible reward received for performing a particular act, such as purchasing a product or visiting the point of purchase.

Price deal. A temporary reduction in the price of a product.

Primary data. Information that is collected from original sources.

Problem definition. The use of research questions to identify a key problem that needs to be solved by the advertising.

Process colors. Four basic inks—magenta, cyan, yellow, and black—that are mixed to produce a full range of colors found in four-color printing.

Process evaluation. Measuring the effectiveness of media and nonmedia efforts to get the desired message out to the target audience.

Producer. The person in charge of all the arrangements for a commercial, including settings, casting, arranging for the music, and handling bids and budgets.

Product life cycle. The history of the product from its introduction to its eventual decline and withdrawal.

Professional advertising. Advertising directed at people such as lawyers, doctors, and accountants.

Profile. A personality sketch of a typical prospect in the targeted audience.

Program preemptions. Interruptions in local or network programming caused by special events.

Promise. A benefit statement that looks to the future.

Promotion. The element in the marketing mix that encourages the purchase of a product or service.

Prospects. (a) Consumers who are potential purchasers or users of a given product or service. (b) People who might buy the product or service.

Psychographics. All the psychological variables that combine to shape our inner selves, including activities, interests, opinions, needs, values, attitudes, personality traits, decision processes, and buying behavior.

Public relations. A management function enabling organizations to achieve effective relationships with their various audiences through an understanding of audience opinions, attitudes, and values.

Public relations advertising. Advertising used to bring about a change in audience attitudes or to express concern for environmental or social issues.

Puffery. Advertising or other sales representation that praises the item to be sold using subjective opinions, superlatives, and similar mechanisms that are not based on specific fact.

Pull strategy. A promotional strategy that is designed to encourage consumers to ask for the product.

Pulsing. An advertising pattern in which time and space are scheduled on a continuous but uneven pattern; lower levels are followed by bursts or peak periods of intensified activity.

Purging. The process of deleting repeated names when two or more lists are combined.

Push money (spiffs). A monetary bonus paid to a salesperson based on units sold over a period of time.

Push strategy. A promotional strategy that is directed to the trade in an attempt to move the product through the distribution channel.

Q

Qualitative studies. Research that seeks to understand how and why people think and behave as they do.

Quantitative studies. Research that uses statistics to describe consumers.

R

Reach. The percentage of different homes or persons exposed to a media vehicle or vehicles at least once during a specific period of time. It is the percentage of unduplicated audience.

Reason why. A statement that explains why the feature will benefit the user.

Recall test. A test that evaluates the memorability of an advertisement by contacting members of the advertisement's audience and asking them what they remember about it.

Recognition test. A test that evaluates the memorability of an advertisement by contacting members of the audience, showing them the ad, and asking them whether they remember having seen it.

Reference group. A group of people that an individual uses as a guide for behavior in specific situations.

Refund. An offer by the marketer to return a certain amount of money to the consumer who purchases the product.

Release prints. Duplicate copies of a commercial that are ready for distribution.

Relevance. That quality of an advertising message that makes it important to the audience.

Reliability. A characteristic that describes a test that yields essentially the same results when the same advertisement is tested time after time.

Reposition. Changing the consumer's perception of a product.

Research design. The structure of the research project.

Retail advertising. A type of advertising used by local merchants who sell directly to consumers.

Retailing. The selling of small quantities of goods directly to consumers.

Reverse type. A style of typesetting in which letters appear to be white against a darker background.

Rough cut. A preliminary rough edited version of the commercial.

Rushes. Rough versions of the commercial assembled from unedited footage.

S

Sales promotion. Those marketing activities that add value to the product for a limited period of time to stimulate consumer purchasing and dealer effectiveness.

Sample. A selection of people who are identified as representative of the larger population.

Sampling. An offer that allows the customer to use or experience the product or service free of charge or for a very small fee.

Sans serif. A typeface that does not have the serif detail.

Scripts. Written versions of radio or television commercials.

Secondary data. Information that has been compiled and published.

Segmentation. The process of identifying subgroups within a targeted population.

Selective perception. (a) The process of screening out information that does not interest us and retaining the information that does. (b) The tendency in most people to see or hear only information they agree with.

Selling premises. The sales logic behind an advertising message.

Semicomp. A layout drawn to size that depicts the art and display type; body copy is simply ruled in.

Serif. A typeface with a finishing stroke on the main strokes of the letters.

Services. Time or activities that are purchased from another person.

Set. A constructed setting where the action in a commercial takes place.

Share of market. The percentage of the total category sales owned by one brand.

Share of voice. The percentage of advertising messages in a medium or vehicle owned by one brand among all messages for that product or service.

Signals. A series of electrical impulses that compose radio and television broadcasting.

Signature. The name of the company or product written in a distinctive type style.

Silk screen. A form of printing where the non-image areas, represented by a "block-out" film or lacquer, are adhered to a porous fabric, while ink is forced through the image areas that aren't blocked out.

Simulated test market. Research procedure in which respondents are exposed to advertisements and then permitted to shop for the advertised products in an artificial environment where records are kept of their purchases.

Situation analysis. (a) The section of the marketing plan that analyzes the research findings. (b) A section of an advertising campaign plan that summarizes the relevant research findings about the company, the product, the competition, the marketplace, and the consumer.

Slice of life. A problem-solution message built around some common, everyday situation.

Slogans. Frequently repeated phrases that provide continuity to an advertising campaign.

Social class. A way to categorize people on the basis of their values, attitudes, lifestyles, and behavior.

Social influences. The forces that other people exert on your behavior.

Soft-sell advertising. Ads with indirect appeal that use mood, ambiguity, and suspense to create an intriguing message.

Sound effects (SFX). Lifelike imitations of sounds.

Spectaculars. Billboards with unusual lighting effects.

Sponsorship. An arrangement in which the advertiser produces both a television program and the accompanying commercials.

Spot radio advertising. A form of advertising in which an ad is placed with an individual station rather than through a network.

Stereotyping. Presenting a group of people in an unvarying pattern that lacks individuality and often reflects popular misconceptions.

Stop action. A technique in which inanimate objects are filmed one frame at a time, creating the illusion of movement.

Stopping power. The ability of an ad to capture and maintain audience interest.

Storyboard. A series of frames sketched to illustrate how the story line will develop.

Subheads. Sectional headlines used to break up masses of type.

Subliminal message. A message transmitted below the threshold of normal perception so that the receiver is not consciously aware of having viewed it.

Superimpose. A television technique where one image is added to another that is already on the screen.

Supplements. Syndicated or local full-color advertising inserts that appear in newspapers throughout the week.

Surprinting. Printing type over some other image.

Survey research. Research using structured interview forms that ask large numbers of people exactly the same questions.

Sweepstakes. Sales-promotion activities that require participants to submit their names to be included in a drawing or other type of chance selection.

Symbolism. The use of words and images that represent, or cue, something else.

Synchronize. Matching the audio to the video in a commercial.

Syndication. Television or radio shows that are reruns or original programs purchased by local stations to fill in during open hours.

T

Tabloid. A newspaper with a page size of 5 to 6 columns wide and 14 inches deep.

Taglines. Clever phrases used at the end of an advertisement to summarize the ad's message.

Talent. People who appear in television commercials.

Target audience. People who can be reached with a certain advertising medium and a particular message.

Target market. A section of the country or a group of consumers who are potential users of the product or service.

Task-objective method. A budgeting method that builds a budget by asking what it will cost to achieve the stated objectives.

Tear sheet. The page from a newspaper on which an ad appears.

Telemarketing. A type of marketing that uses the telephone to make a personal sales contact.

Television market. An unduplicated geographical area to which a county is assigned on the basis of the highest share of the viewing of television stations.

Testimonial. An advertising format in which a spokesperson describes a positive personal experience with the product.

Thumbnails. Small preliminary sketches of various layout ideas.

Tip-ins. Preprinted ads that are provided by the advertiser to be glued into the binding of a magazine.

Toll-free (800) number. A call that is free to the caller and paid for by the number being called.

Tracking study. An evaluation technique that tests the objectives of a campaign before and after it runs.

Trade advertising. Advertising used to influence resellers, wholesalers, and retailers.

Trade deals. An arrangement in which the retailer agrees to give the manufacturer's product a special promotional effort in return for product discounts, goods, or cash.

Trademark. Sign or design, often with distinctive lettering, that symbolizes the brand.

Trading stamps. A sales-promotion program that involves giving consumers stamps that can later be traded in for merchandise.

Traditional delivery. Delivery of magazines to readers through newsstands or home delivery.

Trailers. Advertisements that precede the feature film in a movie theater.

Transformation advertising. Image advertising that changes the experience of buying and using a product.

Trigger. Something that catches attention and sets off a complex set of consumer responses.

U

Underline. A subhead that leads from the headline into the body copy.

Unique selling proposition. A benefit statement about a feature that is both unique to the product and important to the user.

V

Validity. The ability of a test to measure what it is intended to measure.

Vampire creativity. An advertising problem in which an ad is so creative or entertaining that it overwhelms the product.

Verbatims. Spontaneous comments by people who are being surveyed.

Vernacular. Language that reflects the speech patterns of a particular group of people.

Vertical publications. Publications directed to people who hold different positions in the same industries.

Videotape. A type of recording medium that electronically records sound and images simultaneously.

Visualization. The ability to see images in the mind, to imagine how an ad or a concept will look when it is finished.

Visual path. The direction in which the reader's eye moves while scanning a layout.

Voice-over. A technique used in commercials in which an off-camera announcer talks about the on-camera scene.

W

Weighted audience values. Numerical values assigned to different audience characteristics that help advertisers assign priorities when devising media plans.

Wide Area Telephone Service (WATS). A system of mass telephone calling at discount rates.

Index